Collins
Primary
Dictionary

Published by Collins

An imprint of HarperCollins Publishers
Westerhill Road
Bishopbriggs
Glasgow G64 2QT

First Edition 2018

10 9 8 7 6 5 4 3 2

Text © HarperCollins Publishers 2018
Illustrations © Maria Herbert-Liew 2018

ISBN 978-0-00-820678-9

Collins® is a registered trademark of
HarperCollins Publishers Limited

www.collins.co.uk/dictionaries

Typeset by QBS Learning

Printed in Italy by GRAFICA VENETA S.p.A.

Acknowledgements

We would like to thank those authors and
publishers who kindly gave permission for
copyright material to be used in the Collins
Corpus. We would also like to thank Times
Newspapers Ltd for providing valuable data.

Managing Editors:

Maree Airlie
Mary O'Neill

Contributors:

Lucy Hollingworth
Lynne Tarvit

Artwork and Design:

Maria Herbert-Liew

For the Publisher:

Kerry Ferguson
Michelle Fullerton
Laura Waddell

MIX
Paper from
responsible sources

FSC
www.fsc.org
FSC™ C007454

Contents

Jan/2019

How to use this dictionary

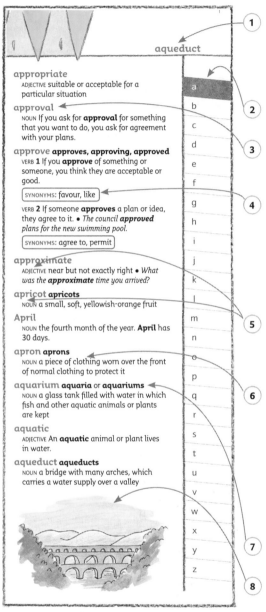

appropriate
ADJECTIVE suitable or acceptable for a particular situation

approval
NOUN If you ask for **approval** for something that you want to do, you ask for agreement with your plans.

approve **approves, approving, approved**
VERB **1** If you **approve** of something or someone, you think they are acceptable or good.

SYNONYMS: favour, like

VERB **2** If someone **approves** a plan or idea, they agree to it. • *The council approved plans for the new swimming pool.*

SYNONYMS: agree to, permit

approximate
ADJECTIVE near but not exactly right • *What was the approximate time you arrived?*

apricot apricots
NOUN a small, soft, yellowish-orange fruit

April
NOUN the fourth month of the year. **April** has 30 days.

apron aprons
NOUN a piece of clothing worn over the front of normal clothing to protect it

aquarium aquaria or **aquariums**
NOUN a glass tank filled with water in which fish and other aquatic animals or plants are kept

aquatic
ADJECTIVE An **aquatic** animal or plant lives in water.

aqueduct aqueducts
NOUN a bridge with many arches, which carries a water supply over a valley

aqueduct

a b c d e f g h i j k l m n o p q r s t u v w x y z

1 The **guide word** on a left-hand page tells you the first word you will find on the page. On a right-hand page, the guide word tells you the last word on the page.

2 The **alphabet line** shows you which letter you are in.

3 The **headword** is the word you are looking up. Headwords are in blue and in alphabetical order.

4 **Synonyms** are given for some words. These are words with a similar meaning that you can use instead. **Antonyms** are given for some words. These are words that have the opposite meaning.

5 The **word class** tells you if the headword is, for example, a noun, verb, adjective, adverb or pronoun.

6 The **definition** tells you what the word means. Sometimes definitions include a label, such *formal* or *informal*. *Formal* tells you that a word is used in serious writing and speech. *Informal* tells you that a word is used in a more relaxed way, between family and friends.

7 Some words or word forms can have more than one spelling.

8 Sometimes an **illustration** is included to give you more information.

9 Sometimes there is an **example** to show how the word is used.

10 If there is useful information about a word at an **illustration** elsewhere in the book, a note tells you where to find it.

11 A **pronunciation tip** shows you how to say a difficult word. A **language tip** helps you with the spelling of words or the way they are used.

12 There can be **other forms** of the word after the headword. These might be the plural of a noun, tenses of a verb, or comparative and superlative forms of an adjective.

13 A **word history** tells you where a word originally came from.

---

nuclear
ADJECTIVE relating to the energy produced when atoms are split • *We live near a **nuclear** power station.*

nucleus nuclei
NOUN **1** the central part of an atom or a cell
→ Have a look at the illustration for **atom**
NOUN **2** the important or central part of something • *We still have the **nucleus** of the team.*

PRONUNCIATION TIP
The singular is pronounced **nyoo**-clee-us. The plural is pronounced **nyoo**-clee-eye.

nude nudes
ADJECTIVE **1** If someone is **nude**, they are naked.
NOUN **2** A **nude** is a picture or statue of a naked person.

nudge nudges, nudging, nudged
VERB **1** If you **nudge** someone, you push them gently with your elbow to get their attention or to make them move.
NOUN **2** a gentle push with your elbow

nugget nuggets
NOUN a small rough lump of something, especially gold

nuisance nuisances
NOUN someone or something that is annoying or causing problems

numb
ADJECTIVE unable to feel anything • *I was so cold my hands and feet felt **numb**.*

WORD HISTORY
from Middle English *nomen* meaning paralysed

number numbers, numbering, numbered
NOUN **1** a word or symbol used for counting or calculating
NOUN **2** the series of numbers that you dial when you phone someone
VERB **3** If you **number** something, you give it a number, usually in a sequence. • *Please **number** each page you write on.*

number bond number bonds
NOUN any pair of numbers that add together to make up another number

numeracy
NOUN the ability to do arithmetic

Word classes

Each word in this dictionary belongs to a particular word class, for example, nouns, verbs or adjectives. To find out more about each of these word classes, look at pages 460–462 in the **Word Wizard**.

Nouns

A **noun** is a word that is used for talking about a person or thing. **Nouns** are sometimes called "naming words" because they are often the names of people, places, things and ideas. Examples of nouns are **book**, **child** and **smile**.

Adjectives

An **adjective** is a word that tells you more about a person or thing. **Adjectives** are often called "describing words" because they describe what something looks, feels or smells like. Examples of adjectives are **happy**, **green** and **cloudy**.

Verbs

A **verb** is a word that you use for saying what someone or something does. **Verbs** are often called "doing words" because they talk about an action that someone or something is doing. Examples of verbs are **walk**, **speak** and **look**.

Adverbs

An **adverb** is a word that tells you more about how someone does something. Examples of adverbs are **slowly**, **loudly** and **hungrily**.

Pronouns

A **pronoun** is a word you use instead of a noun, to refer to someone or something. Examples of pronouns are **he**, **it** and **their**.

Prepositions

A **preposition** is a word that links a noun, pronoun or noun phrase to some other word in the sentence. Examples of prepositions are **under**, **in** and **with**.

Conjunctions

A **conjunction** is a word that links two words or phrases or two parts of a sentence. Examples of conjunctions are **and**, **but** and **because**.

Determiners

A **determiner** is a specific word you use before a noun and/or an adjective. Examples of determiners are **a**, **the** and **some**.

a or an

ADJECTIVE **A** and **an** are used when you talk about one of something. **A** is used when the next sound is a consonant: *a car*, *a dog*. **An** is used when the next sound is a vowel (a, e, i, o or u): *an apple*, *an elephant*.

abacus abacuses

NOUN a frame with beads that slide along rods, used for counting

---

WORD HISTORY

from Greek *abax* meaning board covered with sand for doing sums on

---

abandon abandons, abandoning, abandoned

VERB If you **abandon** someone or something, you leave them or give them up for good. ● *He abandoned all hope of catching the train on time.*

abbey abbeys

NOUN a church with buildings attached to it in which monks or nuns live

abbreviation abbreviations

NOUN a short form of a word or phrase ● *N is an abbreviation for North.*

abdomen abdomens

NOUN **1** the front part of your body below your chest, containing your stomach and intestines

NOUN **2** the back part of the body of an insect or spider

→ Have a look at the illustrations for **insect** and **spider**

abdominal

ADJECTIVE **Abdominal** describes something that is in the front part of your body below your chest, where your stomach and intestines are. ● *abdominal pain*

ability abilities

NOUN If you have **ability**, you have the intelligence and skill to do things.

able

ADJECTIVE If you are **able** to do something, you can do it.

ANTONYM: unable

abnormal

ADJECTIVE not normal or usual

aboard

PREPOSITION **1** If you are **aboard** a plane or a ship you are on it. ● *The captain invited us aboard his boat.*

ADVERB **2** If you go **aboard** a plane or a ship, you go onto it. ● *It took two hours to bring all the passengers aboard.*

Aborigine Aborigines

NOUN someone descended from the people who were living in Australia before the European settlers arrived

about

PREPOSITION **1** If you talk or write **about** a particular thing, you say things that are to do with that subject. ● *a book about London*

ADVERB **2** You say **about** in front of a number to show it is not exact. ● *He arrived about two o'clock.*

PHRASE **3** If you are **about to** do something, you are just going to do it. ● *He was about to leave.*

above

PREPOSITION **1** If one thing is above another, it is higher up. ● *The plane was flying above the clouds.*

ANTONYM: below

PREPOSITION **2** If something is **above** a particular amount or level, it is more than it. ● *above average intelligence*

ANTONYM: below

abroad

ADVERB If you go **abroad**, you go to another country.

abscess abscesses

NOUN a painful swelling on the body, which contains pus

abseil abseils, abseiling, abseiled

VERB If you **abseil** down a rock face, you use ropes to go down it.

a
b
c
d
e
f
g
h
i
j
k
l
m
n
o
p
q
r
s
t
u
v
w
x
y
z

A
B
C
D
E
F
G
H
I
J
K
L
M
N
O
P
Q
R
S
T
U
V
W
X
Y
Z

absent

ADJECTIVE If you are **absent** from a place, you are not there.

ANTONYM: present

absolute

ADJECTIVE **1** total and complete ● *absolute darkness*
ADJECTIVE **2** having total power ● *an absolute ruler*

absolutely

ADVERB If you are **absolutely** sure about something, you are completely sure of it.

absorb absorbs, absorbing, absorbed

VERB If something **absorbs** liquid or gas, it soaks it up. ● *Plants absorb moisture from the soil.*

absorbent

ADJECTIVE If something is **absorbent**, it soaks up liquids easily.

abstract

ADJECTIVE **1** An **abstract** idea is based on thoughts and ideas rather than on real objects or happenings, for example *bravery* and *happiness*.
ADJECTIVE **2** **Abstract** art uses shapes rather than images of people or objects.
ADJECTIVE **3** In grammar, **abstract** nouns refer to qualities or ideas, rather than real objects, for example *happiness*.

absurd

ADJECTIVE Something that is **absurd** is stupid or ridiculous.

abundant

ADJECTIVE present in large amounts ● *There is abundant wildlife, including a pride of lions.*

abuse abuses, abusing, abused

NOUN **1** cruel treatment of someone
NOUN **2** rude and unkind remarks
VERB **3** To **abuse** someone is to treat them cruelly.
VERB **4** If you **abuse** someone, you speak to them in a rude and insulting way.

abysmal

ADJECTIVE very bad

academic academics

ADJECTIVE **1** **Academic** work is done in school, college and university.
NOUN **2** someone who teaches or does research in a college or university

academy academies

NOUN **1** a school or college, usually one that specialises in a particular subject
● *the Royal Academy of Arts*
NOUN **2** an organisation of scientists, writers, artists or musicians

accelerate accelerates, accelerating, accelerated

VERB To **accelerate** is to speed up.

ANTONYM: decelerate

acceleration

NOUN the rate at which the speed of something increases

accent accents

NOUN a way of pronouncing a language
● *She had an Australian accent.*

accept accepts, accepting, accepted

VERB **1** If you **accept** something, you say yes to it or you take it from someone.
● *She accepted our invitation to the party.*
VERB **2** If you **accept** a situation, you realise that it cannot be changed. ● *I accepted that I would have to work hard before my exams.*

acceptable

ADJECTIVE satisfactory ● *These are all acceptable answers.*

access

NOUN If you have **access** to a place, you may enter it. If you have **access** to a thing, you may use it.

accessible

ADJECTIVE **1** easy to reach or to see ● *The beach was accessible by a narrow path.*
ADJECTIVE **2** Books that are **accessible** are easy to understand.

accident accidents

NOUN **1** something that happens suddenly or unexpectedly, causing people to be hurt or killed
PHRASE **2** Something that happens **by accident** has not been planned. ● *We met by accident in the supermarket.*

accidental

ADJECTIVE Something that is **accidental** has not been planned.

accidentally

ADVERB If you do something **accidentally**, you do not plan to do it.

accommodate **accommodates, accommodating, accommodated**
VERB If you **accommodate** someone, you provide them with a place to sleep, live or work.

accommodation
NOUN a place where you can live, work or sleep

accompany **accompanies, accompanying, accompanied**
VERB 1 If you **accompany** someone, you go with them.
VERB 2 If you **accompany** a singer, you play an instrument while they sing.

accomplice **accomplices**
NOUN a person who helps someone else to commit a crime

accomplish **accomplishes, accomplishing, accomplished**
VERB If you **accomplish** something, you succeed in doing it.

according to
PREPOSITION If something is true **according to** a particular person, that person says that it is true. • *According to* my grandad, that castle is haunted.

account **accounts, accounting, accounted**
NOUN 1 a written or spoken report of something
NOUN 2 money that you keep at a bank
PHRASE 3 **On account of** means because of. • *He couldn't play football, on account of a sore throat.*
account for
VERB To **account for** something is to explain it.

accountant **accountants**
NOUN someone whose job is to look after the financial affairs of people and companies

accumulate **accumulates, accumulating, accumulated**
VERB If things **accumulate**, or if you **accumulate** things, they collect over a period of time. • *While they were away, a large pile of letters accumulated on the doormat.*

accuracy
NOUN the quality of being absolutely correct

accurate
ADJECTIVE absolutely correct

accusation **accusations**
NOUN An **accusation** is when you say that someone has done something wrong.

accuse **accuses, accusing, accused**
VERB If you **accuse** someone of doing something wrong, you say they have done it.

ace **aces**
NOUN 1 In a pack of cards, the **ace** is a card with a single symbol on it.
NOUN 2 In tennis, an **ace** is a serve that the other player is unable to return.
ADJECTIVE 3 (*informal*) good or skilful • *an ace squash player*

ache **aches, aching, ached**
NOUN 1 a continuous, dull pain
VERB 2 If a part of your body **aches**, you feel a continuous, dull pain there.

achieve **achieves, achieving, achieved**
VERB If you **achieve** something, you are successful at doing it or at making it happen.

LANGUAGE TIP
The *i* comes before the *e* in *achieve* and *achievement*.

---

achievement **achievements**
NOUN something which someone has been successful in doing or making happen, especially after a lot of effort

acid **acids**
NOUN 1 a chemical substance. Strong **acids** can damage skin, cloth and metal, for example sulphuric **acid**. Other **acids**, such as those found in citrus fruit and vinegar, are harmless.

ANTONYM: alkali

ADJECTIVE 2 If something has an **acid** taste, it tastes sharp or bitter.

ANTONYM: alkaline

WORD HISTORY
from Latin *acidus* meaning sour

---

acid rain
NOUN rain that has been polluted by the burning of fossil fuels, such as coal and oil

a
b
c
d
e
f
g
h
i
j
k
l
m
n
o
p
q
r
s
t
u
v
w
x
y
z

acknowledge **acknowledges, acknowledging, acknowledged**

VERB **1** If you **acknowledge** a fact or a situation, you admit that it is true.

VERB **2** If you **acknowledge** someone, you show that you have seen and recognised them, by waving or saying *hello*.

VERB **3** If you **acknowledge** a message or a letter, you tell the person who sent it that you have received it.

acne

NOUN a skin condition that causes spots on the face and neck. **Acne** is common among teenagers.

acorn **acorns**

NOUN a nut that grows on oak trees

acquaintance **acquaintances**

NOUN someone you know slightly but not well

acre **acres**

NOUN a unit for measuring land. One **acre** is equal to 4840 square yards or about 4047 square metres.

acrobat **acrobats**

NOUN an entertainer who performs difficult gymnastic acts

WORD HISTORY

from Greek *akrobates* meaning someone who walks on tiptoe

---

acrobatic

ADJECTIVE involving difficult gymnastic acts

acrobatics

PLURAL NOUN difficult gymnastic acts

acronym **acronyms**

NOUN a word made up of the initial letters of a phrase. NATO is an **acronym**, and stands for North Atlantic Treaty Organization.

across

PREPOSITION **1** If you go **across** a place, you go from one side of it to the other. ● *We walked across Hyde Park.*

PREPOSITION **2** Something that is situated **across** a road or river is on the other side of it.

act **acts, acting, acted**

VERB **1** If you **act**, you do something. ● *We have to act quickly in an emergency.*

VERB **2** If you **act** in a particular way, you behave in that way. ● *You're acting like a baby.*

VERB **3** If you **act** in a play or film, you play a role in it.

NOUN **4** a single thing someone does ● *The rescue was a brave act.*

NOUN **5** An **Act** of Parliament is a law passed by the government.

NOUN **6** Stage plays are divided into parts called **acts**.

action **actions**

NOUN **1** something you do for a particular purpose

NOUN **2** a physical movement, such as jumping

active

ADJECTIVE **1** Someone who is **active** moves around a lot or does a lot of things.

ADJECTIVE **2** In grammar the **active**, or the **active** voice, is the form of the verb in which the subject of the sentence is the person or thing doing the action, rather than having it done to them. For example, the sentence *The dog bit Ben* is in the **active** voice. In the passive voice the subject has the thing done to them: *Ben was bitten by the dog.*

ANTONYM: passive

activity **activities**

NOUN **1** a situation in which a lot of things are happening at the same time ● *There was a great deal of activity in the hall as we got ready for the school play.*

NOUN **2** something you do for pleasure, such as gymnastics or music

actor **actors**

NOUN a man or woman whose job is performing in plays or films

actress **actresses**

NOUN a woman whose profession is acting

actual

ADJECTIVE real, rather than imaginary or guessed at ● *You guessed I was eleven – my actual age is twelve.*

actually

ADVERB **1** You use **actually** to show that something is real or true. ● *Mum told me what actually happened.*

ADVERB **2** You use **actually** to politely tell someone that they are wrong. ● *No, I'm not eight. I'm nine, actually.*

acute

ADJECTIVE **1** severe or intense • *She had an* **acute** *pain in her arm.*

ADJECTIVE **2** In mathematics, an **acute** angle measures less than 90 degrees.

ADJECTIVE **3** Someone who is **acute** is intelligent.

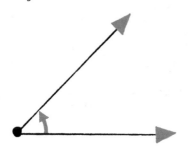

AD

ADJECTIVE You use **AD** in dates to show the number of years after the birth of Jesus Christ.

WORD HISTORY

an abbreviation of the Latin *Anno Domini* meaning the year of Our Lord

adapt adapts, adapting, adapted

VERB **1** If you **adapt** to something, you get used to it.

VERB **2** If you **adapt** something, you change it so that it can be used in a new way.

adaptable

ADJECTIVE If you are **adaptable**, you change easily in a new situation or to suit new circumstances.

adaptation

NOUN the act of changing something to make it suitable for a new purpose or situation • *Most living creatures are capable of adaptation when they need to be.*

add adds, adding, added

VERB **1** If you **add** something to a number of things, you put it with those things.
• *Each girl added more wood to the pile.*

VERB **2** If you **add** numbers together, or **add** them up, you work out the total. • *Two and three added together are five (2 + 3 = 5).*

adder adders

NOUN a small, poisonous snake

addicted

ADJECTIVE If you are **addicted** to something, you cannot stop doing it or wanting it.

addiction addictions

NOUN If you have an **addiction** to something, you cannot stop doing it or wanting it.

addition additions -

NOUN **1** the process of adding two or more numbers together

NOUN **2** something that is added to something else • *The addition of sugar would improve the taste of these plums.*

additional

ADJECTIVE extra or more

additive additives

NOUN something that is added to something else, such as food

address addresses, addressing, addressed

NOUN **1** Your **address** is the number of the house where you live, together with the name of the street and the town or village.

VERB **2** If someone **addresses** a letter to you, they write your name and address on it.

VERB **3** If you **address** a group of people, you speak to them formally.

LANGUAGE TIP

There are two *d*s and two *s*s in *address*.

adenoids

PLURAL NOUN small lumps of flesh at the back of the throat

adequate

ADJECTIVE just enough for what is needed

SYNONYMS: enough, satisfactory, sufficient

adhesive adhesives

NOUN **1** a substance used to stick things together, such as glue

ADJECTIVE **2** If something is **adhesive**, it sticks to other things.

adjacent

PREPOSITION If one thing is **adjacent** to another, the two things are next to each other.

adjective adjectives

NOUN a word that adds to the description of a noun. For example, *large* and *old* are both **adjectives**.

a
b
c
d
e
f
g
h
i
j
k
l
m
n
o
p
q
r
s
t
u
v
w
x
y
z

11

adjust adjusts, adjusting, adjusted
VERB **1** If you **adjust** something, you change its position or alter it in some other way.
• She **adjusted** her pillow to make herself more comfortable.
VERB **2** If you **adjust** to a new situation, you get used to it.

adjustment adjustments
NOUN **1** a small change that you make to something • By making **adjustments** to your diet, you can improve your health.
NOUN **2 Adjustment** is when you get used to a new situation.

administration administrations
NOUN the work of managing and supervising an organisation

admiral admirals
NOUN a senior officer in the navy

admire admires, admiring, admired
VERB If you **admire** someone or something, you respect and approve of them.

admirer admirers
NOUN someone who respects and approves of someone or something

admission admissions
NOUN **1** If you are allowed **admission** to a place, you may go into it.
NOUN **2** If you make an **admission**, you confess to something or agree that it is true.

admit admits, admitting, admitted
VERB **1** If you **admit** something, you agree that it is true.
VERB **2** If you **admit** to something, you agree that you did something you shouldn't have done.
VERB **3** To **admit** someone or something to a place is to allow them to enter it.

admittance
NOUN the right to enter somewhere
• There will be no **admittance** to the party after eight o'clock.

adolescent adolescents
NOUN a young person who is no longer a child, but is not yet an adult

WORD HISTORY
from Latin adolescere meaning to grow up

adopt adopts, adopting, adopted
VERB If someone **adopts** a child, they take them into their family as their son or daughter by a legal process.

WORD HISTORY
from Latin adoptare meaning to choose for oneself

adorable
ADJECTIVE loveable and attractive

adoration
NOUN a feeling of deep love and admiration for someone

adore adores, adoring, adored
VERB If you **adore** someone, you feel deep love and admiration for them.

adult adults
NOUN a mature and fully developed person or animal

advance advances, advancing, advanced
VERB **1** To **advance** is to move forward.
NOUN **2** An **advance** is progress in something. • There have been many scientific **advances** in the past century.
PHRASE **3** If you do something **in advance** of something, you do it beforehand.
• We booked our holiday well **in advance**.

advanced
ADJECTIVE If something is **advanced**, it is at a high level, or ahead in development or progress. • The children in the top group do **advanced** maths exercises.

advantage advantages
NOUN **1** a benefit, or something that puts you in a better position • The **advantage** of email is that it is quicker than the post.
PHRASE **2** If you **take advantage** of someone, you treat them unfairly for your own benefit.
PHRASE **3** If you **take advantage** of something, you make use of it.

adventure adventures
NOUN something that is exciting, and perhaps even dangerous

adverb adverbs
NOUN a word that tells you how, when, where or why something happens or something is done. For example, she walked slowly, he came yesterday, they live here.

WORD HISTORY
from Latin adverbium meaning added word

advert adverts
NOUN an abbreviation for advertisement

advertise advertises, advertising, advertised
VERB If you **advertise** something, you tell people about it online, in a newspaper, on a poster or on TV.

advertisement advertisements
NOUN a notice in a newspaper, on a poster, on TV or on the internet, about something such as a product, event or job

advice
NOUN a suggestion from someone about what you should do

LANGUAGE TIP
The noun *advice* ends in *ce*.
---

advisable
ADJECTIVE If it is **advisable** to do something, it is a sensible thing to do and will probably give the results that you want. • *It is advisable to wear a helmet when cycling.*

advise advises, advising, advised
VERB If you **advise** someone to do something, you tell them you think they should do it.

LANGUAGE TIP
The verb *advise* ends in *se*.
---

aerial aerials
NOUN **1** a piece of wire for receiving television or radio signals
ADJECTIVE **2** happening in the air • *We watched the aerial displays at the RAF airshow.*

aero-
PREFIX to do with the air, for example **aero**plane

WORD HISTORY
from Greek *aer* meaning air
---

aeroplane aeroplanes
NOUN a vehicle with wings and engines that enable it to fly
→ Have a look at the illustration

aerosol aerosols
NOUN a small, metal container in which liquid is kept under pressure so that it can be forced out as a spray

affair affairs
NOUN **1** an event or series of events
• *The wedding was a happy affair.*
NOUN **2** If something is your own **affair**, then it is your concern only.

affect affects, affecting, affected
VERB When something **affects** someone or something, it causes them to change.
• *Computers affect our lives in many ways.*

affection
NOUN a feeling of love and fondness for someone

affectionate
ADJECTIVE showing that you love or like someone • *He was a very affectionate child.*

affluent
ADJECTIVE People who are **affluent** have a lot of money and possessions.

a b c d e f g h i j k l m n o p q r s t u v w x y z

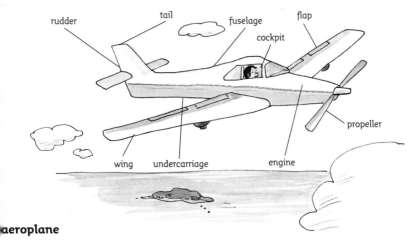

rudder tail fuselage flap cockpit propeller wing undercarriage engine

aeroplane

13

afford **affords, affording, afforded**
VERB **1** If you can **afford** something, you have enough money to pay for it.
VERB **2** If you can **afford** to relax, you feel you have done enough work for the moment, and have time to take things easy.

afloat
ADVERB If something or someone is **afloat**, they are floating.

afraid
ADJECTIVE **1** If you are **afraid**, you are frightened.

SYNONYM: scared

ADJECTIVE **2** If you are **afraid** something might happen, you worry that it might happen.

after
PREPOSITION **1** later than a particular time, date or event • *She left just **after** breakfast.*

ANTONYM: before

PREPOSITION **2** If you come **after** someone or something, you are behind them and following them. • *They ran **after** her.*
ADVERB **3** later • *Soon **after**, he went to work.*

afternoon **afternoons**
NOUN the part of the day between twelve noon and about six o'clock

afterwards
ADVERB after an event or time • *We went swimming, and **afterwards** we had an ice cream.*

again
ADVERB happening one more time • *The film was so good that we went to see it **again**.*

SYNONYM: once more

against
PREPOSITION **1** touching and resting on • *He leaned the ladder **against** the wall.*
PREPOSITION **2** in opposition to • *France played **against** England.*

ANTONYM: for

age **ages, ageing** or **aging, aged**
NOUN **1** The **age** of something or someone is the number of years they have lived or existed.
NOUN **2** a particular period in history • *the Iron **Age***

PLURAL NOUN **3** (*informal*) **Ages** means a very long time. • *He's been talking for **ages**.*
VERB **4** To **age** is to grow old or to appear older.

LANGUAGE TIP
Ageing and *aging* are both correct spellings.

agency **agencies**
NOUN an organisation or business that provides special services • *detective **agency*** • *advertising **agency***

agenda **agendas**
NOUN a list of items to be discussed at a meeting

agent **agents**
NOUN **1** someone who does business or arranges things for other people • *a travel **agent***
NOUN **2** someone who works for their country's secret service

aggravate **aggravates, aggravating, aggravated**
VERB **1** If you **aggravate** something, you make it worse.
VERB **2** (*informal*) If you **aggravate** someone, you annoy them.

aggressive
ADJECTIVE full of hostility and violence • *Some breeds of dog are more **aggressive** than others.*

SYNONYMS: belligerent, hostile

agile
ADJECTIVE able to move quickly and easily • *He is as **agile** as a cat.*

agility
NOUN the ability to move quickly and easily

agitated
ADJECTIVE worried and anxious

ago
ADVERB in the past • *She bought her flat three years **ago**.*

agony
NOUN very great physical or mental pain

SYNONYMS: suffering, torment

agree **agrees, agreeing, agreed**
VERB **1** If you **agree** with someone, you have the same opinion as they do.
VERB **2** If you **agree** to do something, you say you will do it.

A B C D E F G H I J K L M N O P Q R S T U V W X Y Z

agreeable
ADJECTIVE **1** pleasant or enjoyable
ADJECTIVE **2** If you are **agreeable** to something, you are willing to allow it or to do it.

agreement agreements
NOUN If you reach an **agreement** with one or more people, you make a decision with them or come to an arrangement with them.

agriculture
NOUN farming

ahead
ADVERB **1** in front ● *He looked **ahead** as he cycled down the road.*
ADVERB **2** more advanced than someone or something else ● *Some countries are **ahead** of others in space travel.*
ADVERB **3** in the future ● *I can't think that far **ahead**.*

aid aids
NOUN **1** money, equipment or services provided for people in need
NOUN **2** something that makes a job easier ● *The whiteboard is a useful teaching **aid**.*

ailment ailments
NOUN a minor illness

aim aims, aiming, aimed
VERB **1** If you **aim** at something, you point a weapon at it.
VERB **2** If you **aim** to do something, you are planning to do it.

SYNONYMS: intend, mean

NOUN **3** Your **aim** is what you intend to achieve. ● *The **aim** of the jumble sale is to raise money for charity.*

SYNONYMS: goal, objective

aimless
ADJECTIVE If you are **aimless**, you have no clear purpose or sense of direction.

air
NOUN **1** the mixture of oxygen and other gases that we breathe and that forms the Earth's atmosphere
NOUN **2** the space around things or above the ground ● *The balloons floated up into the **air**.*
NOUN **3** used to refer to travel in aircraft ● *My uncle often travels by **air**.*

air conditioning
NOUN a way of keeping cool, fresh air in a building or car

aircraft
NOUN any vehicle that can fly

air force air forces
NOUN the part of a country's armed services that fights using aircraft

airline airlines
NOUN a company that provides air travel

airmail
NOUN the system of sending letters and parcels by air ● *He sent letters from Hong Kong to Britain by **airmail**.*

airport airports
NOUN a place where people go to catch aeroplanes

airtight
ADJECTIVE If something is **airtight**, no air can get in or out.

aisle aisles
NOUN a long, narrow gap that people can walk along between rows of seats or shelves ● *The ticket collector was coming down the **aisle**.*

ajar
ADJECTIVE A door or window that is **ajar** is slightly open.

alarm alarms, alarming, alarmed
NOUN **1** a feeling of fear and worry ● *The cat sprang back in **alarm**.*
NOUN **2** an automatic device used to warn people of something ● *The burglar **alarm** went off accidentally.*
VERB **3** If something **alarms** you, it makes you worried and anxious.

album albums
NOUN **1** a recording with a collection of songs on it
NOUN **2** a book in which you keep a collection of things, such as photographs or stamps

alcohol
NOUN the name for drinks such as beer, wine and spirits

alert alerts, alerting, alerted
ADJECTIVE **1** If you are **alert**, you are paying full attention to what is happening.

SYNONYMS: vigilant, watchful

VERB **2** If you **alert** someone to a problem or danger, you warn them of it.

a b c d e f g h i j k l m n o p q r s t u v w x y z

15

algebra

NOUN a branch of mathematics in which symbols and letters are used to represent unknown numbers

WORD HISTORY
from Arabic *aljabr* meaning reunion

alias aliases

NOUN a false name

alibi alibis

NOUN If you have an **alibi**, you have evidence proving you were somewhere else when a crime was committed.

alien aliens

NOUN 1 In science fiction, an **alien** is a creature from outer space.
ADJECTIVE 2 Something that is **alien** to you seems strange because it is not part of your normal experience. • *The desert is an **alien** environment to many people.*

WORD HISTORY
from Latin *alienus* meaning foreign

alight alights, alighting, alighted

ADJECTIVE 1 Something that is **alight** is burning.
VERB 2 If something **alights** somewhere, it lands there.

alike

ADJECTIVE 1 Things that are **alike** are very similar in some way.
ADVERB 2 If people or things are treated **alike**, they are treated the same.

alive

ADJECTIVE If someone or something is **alive**, they are living.

alkali alkalis

NOUN a chemical substance sometimes used in cleaning materials. **Alkalis** can neutralise acids.

ANTONYM: acid

alkaline

ADJECTIVE If something is **alkaline**, it is made up of an alkali.

ANTONYM: acid

all

ADJECTIVE 1 used for talking about the whole of something • *He ate **all** the chocolate.*
ADVERB 2 completely • *I went away and left her **all** alone.*
ADVERB 3 used to show that both sides in a game or contest have the same score
• *The final score was three points **all**.*

Allah

PROPER NOUN **Allah** is the being worshipped by Muslims as the creator and ruler of the world

allege alleges, alleging, alleged

VERB If you **allege** that something is true, you say it's true, but you cannot prove it.

allergic

ADJECTIVE If you are **allergic** to something, it makes you ill to eat or touch it.
• *I'm **allergic** to peanuts.*

allergy allergies

NOUN If you have an **allergy** to something, it makes you ill to eat or touch it.

alley alleys

NOUN a narrow street or passageway between buildings

alliance alliances

NOUN a group of countries, organisations or people who have similar aims and who work together to achieve them

alligator alligators

NOUN a large, scaly reptile, similar to a crocodile

WORD HISTORY
from Spanish *el lagarto* meaning lizard

alliteration

NOUN the use of several words together that begin with the same letter or sound. For example, *the slithery snake slid silently across the sand.*

allotment allotments

NOUN a piece of land that people rent to grow fruit and vegetables on

allow allows, allowing, allowed

VERB If someone **allows** you to do something, they let you do it.

all right

ADJECTIVE 1 If something is **all right**, it is satisfactory, but not especially good.
• *Do you like mushrooms? They're **all right**.*
ADJECTIVE 2 If someone is **all right**, they are safe and not harmed.
ADJECTIVE 3 You say **all right** if you agree to something. • *Will you help? **All right**.*

ally allies
NOUN a person or a country that helps and supports another
SYNONYMS: friend, partner

almond almonds
NOUN an oval edible nut, cream in colour

almost
ADVERB very nearly ● *I have almost as many points as you.*
SYNONYMS: just about, practically

alone
ADJECTIVE not with other people or things

along
PREPOSITION **1** moving forward ● *We strolled along the road.*
PREPOSITION **2** from one end of something to the other ● *The cupboards stretched along the wall.*

alongside
PREPOSITION next to something ● *We tied our boat alongside the jetty.*

aloud
ADVERB When you read **aloud**, you read so that people can hear you.

alphabet alphabets
NOUN all the letters used to write words in a language. The letters of an **alphabet** are written in a special order.

alphabetical
ADJECTIVE If something is in **alphabetical** order, it is arranged according to the order of the letters of the alphabet.

alphabetically
ADVERB If something is arranged **alphabetically**, it is arranged according to the order of the letters of the alphabet.

already
ADVERB If you have done something **already**, you did it earlier. ● *Josh has already gone to bed.*

also
ADVERB in addition to something that has just been mentioned ● *I bought an ice cream, and I also bought a drink.*

altar altars
NOUN a holy table in a church or temple

alter alters, altering, altered
VERB If something **alters**, or if you **alter** it, it changes.

alternate alternates, alternating, alternated
ADJECTIVE **1** If something happens on **alternate** days, it happens on one in every two days.
VERB **2** If two things **alternate**, they regularly happen one after the other.

PRONUNCIATION TIP
The adjective is pronounced ol-**ter**-nut. The verb is pronounced **ol**-ter-nayt.

alternative alternatives
NOUN something you can do or have instead of something else ● *Is there an alternative to meat on the menu?*

although
CONJUNCTION in spite of the fact that ● *He wasn't well-known in America, although he had made a film there.*

altitude altitudes
NOUN height above sea level ● *The mountain range reaches an altitude of 1330 metres.*

altogether
ADVERB **1** completely or entirely ● *The car got slower, then stopped altogether.*
ADVERB **2** in total when used of amounts ● *I have two cats and two rabbits. That's four pets altogether.*

aluminium
NOUN a silvery-white, lightweight metal

always
ADVERB **1** all the time ● *He's always late.*
ADVERB **2** forever ● *I'll always remember this day.*

a.m.
a.m. is used to show times in the morning

WORD HISTORY
an abbreviation of the Latin *ante meridiem* meaning before noon

am
VERB a present tense of **be**

amateur amateurs
NOUN someone who does something without being paid for it ● *He began playing football as an amateur, but now he is a professional.*

amaze amazes, amazing, amazed
VERB If something **amazes** you, it surprises you very much.
SYNONYMS: astonish, astound

amazement
NOUN the feeling of being very surprised

a b c d e f g h i j k l m n o p q r s t u v w x y z

17

A
B
C
D
E
F
G
H
I
J
K
L
M
N
O
P
Q
R
S
T
U
V
W
X
Y
Z

amazing
ADJECTIVE If something is **amazing**, it is very surprising.

ambassador ambassadors
NOUN a person sent to a foreign country as the representative of their own government

amber
NOUN **1** a hard, yellowish-brown substance from trees, used in making jewellery
NOUN **2** an orange-brown colour
ADJECTIVE **3** having an orange-brown colour

ambiguous
ADJECTIVE If something is **ambiguous**, it can have more than one meaning.

ambition ambitions
NOUN If you have an **ambition** to do something, you want very much to do it.

amble ambles, ambling, ambled
VERB If you **amble**, you walk along in a slow, relaxed way.

ambulance ambulances
NOUN a vehicle for taking sick and injured people to hospital

ambush ambushes, ambushing, ambushed
NOUN **1** a surprise attack
VERB **2** If one group of people **ambushes** another, they hide and lie in wait, and then make a surprise attack.

ammonia
NOUN a strong-smelling, colourless liquid or gas, often used in cleaning substances

ammunition
NOUN anything that can be fired from a gun or other weapon, for example bullets and shells

amoeba amoebas or amoebae
NOUN a tiny living organism that has only one cell. An **amoeba** reproduces by dividing into two.

among or **amongst**
PREPOSITION **1** surrounded by
PREPOSITION **2** in the company of ● *He was* **among** *friends.*
PREPOSITION **3** between more than two ● *The money will be divided* **among** *seven charities.*

amount amounts
NOUN how much there is of something ● *You need a large* **amount** *of flour for this recipe.*

amphibian amphibians
NOUN an animal that lives partly on land and partly in water, for example a frog or a newt

amphibious
ADJECTIVE An **amphibious** animal lives partly on land and partly in water.

amphitheatre amphitheatres
NOUN a large open area, often in the shape of a semicircle, surrounded by rows of seats sloping upwards

amplifier amplifiers
NOUN a piece of equipment that makes sounds louder

amplify amplifies, amplifying, amplified
VERB If you **amplify** a sound, you make it louder.

amputate amputates, amputating, amputated
VERB If a surgeon **amputates** part of the body, such as an arm or a leg, they cut it off.

amputation amputations
NOUN **1 Amputation** is cutting off part of the body such as an arm or a leg.
NOUN **2** an operation to cut off part of the body, such as an arm or a leg ● *The surgeon had performed about 20* **amputations***.*

amuse amuses, amusing, amused
VERB **1** If something **amuses** you, you think it is funny.
VERB **2** If you **amuse** yourself, you find things to do that stop you from being bored.

amused
ADJECTIVE If you are **amused**, you think something is funny.

amusement amusements
NOUN **1** the feeling you have when you think that something is funny or when something gives you pleasure
NOUN **2** a mechanical device used for entertainment, at a fair for example

amusing
ADJECTIVE funny and making you smile or laugh ● *an* **amusing** *story*

an
ADJECTIVE **An** is used instead of *a* in front of words that begin with the vowels a, e, i, o, or u. ● *an apple* ● *an egg*

anaemia
NOUN a medical condition in which there are too few red cells in your blood. It makes you feel tired and look pale.

anaemic

ADJECTIVE If you are **anaemic**, you have a medical condition in which there are too few red cells in your blood. It makes you feel tired and look pale.

anaesthetic anaesthetics; also spelt **anesthetic**

NOUN a substance that stops you feeling pain. A general **anaesthetic** stops you from feeling pain in the whole of your body by putting you to sleep. A local **anaesthetic** makes just one part of your body go numb.

anagram anagrams

NOUN a word or phrase formed by changing the order of the letters of another word or phrase. For example, *draw* is an **anagram** of *ward* and *dear* is an **anagram** of *read*.

analogue

ADJECTIVE An **analogue** watch or clock shows the time with pointers that move round a dial.

ANTONYM: digital

analogy analogies

NOUN a comparison between two things that are similar in some ways

analyse analyses, analysing, analysed

VERB If you **analyse** something, you investigate it carefully to understand it or to find out what it consists of.

anatomical

ADJECTIVE **Anatomical** describes things that are to do with the structure of human and animal bodies.

anatomy anatomies

NOUN the study of the structure of human and animal bodies to find out how they work

ancestor ancestors

NOUN a member of your family who lived many years ago • *He could trace his ancestors back 700 years.*

WORD HISTORY
from Latin *antecessor* meaning one who goes before

anchor anchors, anchoring, anchored

NOUN **1** a heavy, hooked object at the end of a chain. It is dropped from a boat into the water to keep the boat from floating away.

→ Have a look at the illustration for **ship**

VERB **2** If you **anchor** something, you hold it down firmly.

ancient

ADJECTIVE Things that are **ancient** existed or happened a very long time ago.

ANTONYM: modern

and

CONJUNCTION You use **and** to link two or more parts of a sentence together. • *Let's go to the cinema and then have pizza*

anecdote anecdotes

NOUN a short, sometimes entertaining story about a person or an event

angel angels

NOUN a being who, some people believe, lives in heaven and acts as a messenger for God

WORD HISTORY
from Greek *angelos* meaning messenger

anger

NOUN the strong feeling you get about something unfair or cruel

SYNONYMS: fury, rage, wrath

angle angles

NOUN **1** the distance between two lines at the point where they join together. **Angles** are measured in degrees. • *an angle of 90 degrees*

NOUN **2** the direction from which you look at something • *He painted pictures of the garden from all angles.*

angry angrier, angriest

ADJECTIVE very annoyed

SYNONYMS: furious, cross

anguish

NOUN great suffering

animal animals

NOUN any living being that is not a plant

animated

ADJECTIVE **Animated** films are made with drawings that seem to move when you watch them.

a
b
c
d
e
f
g
h
i
j
k
l
m
n
o
p
q
r
s
t
u
v
w
x
y
z

19

animation animations

NOUN **1** a way of making films using drawings that seem to move when you watch them

NOUN **2** a film made using drawings that seem to move when you watch them

ankle ankles

NOUN the joint that connects your foot to your leg

annihilate annihilates, annihilating, annihilated

VERB If someone or something **annihilates** someone or something else, they destroy them completely.

anniversary anniversaries

NOUN a date that is remembered because something special happened on that date in a previous year • We celebrated Mum and Dad's twelfth wedding **anniversary**.

announce announces, announcing, announced

VERB If you **announce** something, you tell people about it publicly or officially. • They **announced** the team on Friday morning.

SYNONYM: make known

announcement announcements

NOUN something that you tell people in a speech or official statement • I have an **announcement** to make.

annoy annoys, annoying, annoyed

VERB If someone or something **annoys** you, they make you angry or impatient.

SYNONYMS: bother, irritate

annoyance annoyances

NOUN **1** something that makes you slightly angry or impatient

NOUN **2** the feeling of being slightly angry or impatient

annual annuals

ADJECTIVE **1** happening once a year • our **annual** sports day

NOUN **2** a book that is published once a year for children

anonymous

ADJECTIVE If something is **anonymous**, nobody knows who is responsible for it. • The charity received an **anonymous** donation.

anorak anoraks

NOUN a warm, waterproof jacket, usually with a hood

WORD HISTORY
an Inuit word

anorexia

NOUN a psychological illness in which the person refuses to eat

WORD HISTORY
from Greek an + orexis meaning no appetite

another

PRONOUN **1** one more person or thing • You've finished your cake – would you like **another**?

ADJECTIVE **2** used to talk about one more person or thing • I need **another** pencil.

answer answers, answering, answered

VERB **1** If you **answer** someone, you reply to them in speech or writing.

NOUN **2** the reply you give when you answer someone • I received an **answer** to my letter.

NOUN **3** a solution to a problem

ant ants

NOUN **Ants** are small insects that live in large groups.

antagonise antagonises, antagonising, antagonised; also spelt **antagonize**

VERB If you **antagonise** someone, you upset them and make them feel angry.

Antarctic

NOUN The **Antarctic** is the area around the South Pole.

➔ Have a look at the illustration for **equator**

antelope antelopes

NOUN a hoofed animal, similar to a deer

antenna antennae or antennas

NOUN **1** one of the two long, thin parts attached to the head of an insect or other animal, which it uses to feel with. The plural is **antennae**.

➔ Have a look at the illustration for **insect**

NOUN **2** In Australian, New Zealand and American English, an **antenna** is a radio or television aerial. The plural is **antennas**.

anthem anthems

NOUN usually a song of celebration, and sometimes a religious song

anther anthers
NOUN the part of the stamen in a flower where the pollen matures

anthology anthologies
NOUN a collection of writings by various authors, published in one book

---
WORD HISTORY
from Greek *anthologia* meaning flower gathering

---

anti-
PREFIX against or opposite ● *an **anti**malaria tablet*

ANTONYM: pro-

antibiotic antibiotics
NOUN a drug or chemical used in medicine to kill bacteria and cure infections

anticipate anticipates, anticipating, anticipated
VERB If you **anticipate** an event, you are expecting it and are getting prepared for it.

anticipation
NOUN 1 If you do something in **anticipation** of something else, you do it because you think that thing will happen. ● *Shops have taken on more staff in **anticipation** of the Christmas shopping rush.*
NOUN 2 a feeling of excitement about something that is going to happen

anticlimax anticlimaxes
NOUN If something is an **anticlimax**, it disappoints you because it is not as exciting as you expected, or because it occurs after something that was more exciting.

anticlockwise
ADVERB in the opposite direction to the hands of a clock

SYNONYM: vertex

antidote antidotes
NOUN a chemical substance that works against the effects of a poison

antique antiques
NOUN an object from the past that is collected because of its value or beauty

antiseptic
ADJECTIVE Something that is **antiseptic** can kill some germs.

antler antlers
NOUN **Antlers** are the branched horns on the top of a male deer's head.

antonym antonyms
NOUN a word that means the opposite of another word ● *Happy is the **antonym** of sad.*

anxiety anxieties
NOUN a feeling of nervousness or worry

anxious
ADJECTIVE 1 If you are **anxious**, you are nervous or worried.
ADJECTIVE 2 If you are **anxious** to do something, you very much want to do it.
● *She was **anxious** to pass her ballet exam.*

any
ADJECTIVE 1 one, some or several ● *Have you **any** sausages?*
ADJECTIVE 2 even the smallest amount or even one ● *She can't eat nuts of **any** kind.*
ADJECTIVE 3 no matter which or what ● *I'm so thirsty, **any** drink will do.*
PRONOUN 4 one, some or several ● *I need new clothes but I can't afford **any**.*

anybody
PRONOUN any person

anyhow
ADVERB 1 in any case ● *It's still early, but I'm going to bed **anyhow**.*
ADVERB 2 in a careless way ● *They were all shoved in **anyhow**.*

anyone
PRONOUN any person ● *I won't tell **anyone**.*

anything
PRONOUN any object, event, situation or action ● *Can you see **anything**?*

anyway
ADVERB in any case ● *It's raining, but I'm going out **anyway**.*

anywhere
ADVERB in, at or to any place ● *Can you see him **anywhere**? ● We haven't got **anywhere** to play.*

apart
ADVERB 1 When something is **apart** from something else, there is a space or a distance between them. ● *The gliders landed about seventy metres **apart**.*
ADVERB 2 If you take something **apart**, you separate it into pieces.

a
b
c
d
e
f
g
h
i
j
k
l
m
n
o
p
q
r
s
t
u
v
w
x
y
z

A
B
C
D
E
F
G
H
I
J
K
L
M
N
O
P
Q
R
S
T
U
V
W
X
Y
Z

apartment **apartments**
NOUN a set of rooms for living in, usually on one floor of a building

apatosaurus **apatosauruses**
NOUN a very large, plant-eating dinosaur

ape **apes, aping, aped**
NOUN **1** a large animal similar to a monkey, but without a tail. **Apes** include chimpanzees and gorillas.
VERB **2** If you **ape** someone's speech or behaviour, you imitate it.

apex **apexes** or **apices**
NOUN The **apex** of something is its pointed top. ● the **apex** of a cone

SYNONYM: vertex

apologise **apologises, apologising, apologised**; also spelt **apologize**
VERB When you **apologise** to someone, you say you are sorry for something you have said or done.

apology **apologies**
NOUN An **apology** is when you say sorry to someone, for something you have said or done.

apostrophe **apostrophes**
NOUN **1** a punctuation mark (') used to show that one or more letters have been missed out of a word, for example *he's* for *he is*
NOUN **2** **Apostrophes** are also used with -s at the end of a noun to show that what follows belongs to or relates to the noun. If the noun already has an -s at the end, for example because it is plural, the **apostrophe** comes after the -s. For example, *my brother's books* (one brother), *my brothers' books* (more than one brother).

app **apps**
NOUN a computer program with one main purpose, especially one that you use on your mobile phone

apparatus
NOUN the equipment used for a particular task ● The firefighters wore breathing **apparatus**.

apparent
ADJECTIVE **1** An **apparent** situation seems to exist, although you cannot be certain of it.
ADJECTIVE **2** clear and obvious ● It was **apparent** they would get on well together.

apparently
ADVERB You use **apparently** to say what seems to be true, although you cannot be certain of it. ● He was lying on the sofa, **apparently** asleep.

appeal **appeals, appealing, appealed**
VERB **1** If you **appeal** for something, you make an urgent request for it. ● The police **appealed** for witnesses to come forward.
VERB **2** If something or someone **appeals** to you, you find them attractive or interesting.
NOUN **3** a formal or serious request ● an **appeal** for funds to help people in need

appear **appears, appearing, appeared**
VERB **1** When something **appears**, it moves from somewhere you could not see to somewhere you can see it. ● The sun **appeared** from behind the clouds.
VERB **2** If something **appears** to be a certain way, it seems or looks that way.

appearance **appearances**
NOUN **1** Someone's or something's **appearance** is the way they look to other people.
NOUN **2** If a person makes an **appearance** in a film or a show, they take part in it.
NOUN **3** The **appearance** of something is the time it begins to exist.

appendicitis
NOUN a painful illness in which a person's appendix becomes infected

appendix **appendices** or **appendixes**
NOUN **1** Your **appendix** is a small, closed tube forming part of your digestive system.
NOUN **2** extra information that comes at the end of a book

LANGUAGE TIP
When *appendix* means the body part, the plural is *appendixes*. When it means the part of a book, the plural is *appendices*.

appetising; also spelt **appetizing**
ADJECTIVE When food is **appetising**, it looks or smells good and you want to eat it.

appetite **appetites**
NOUN a desire to eat

WORD HISTORY
from Latin *appetere* meaning to desire

applause
NOUN the sound of people clapping to show their enjoyment or approval of something

apple **apples**
NOUN a round fruit with smooth skin and firm white flesh

appliance **appliances**
NOUN any machine in your home that you use to do a job like cleaning or cooking. For example, a toaster is a kitchen **appliance**.

application **applications**
NOUN **1** If you make an **application** for something, you make a formal request, usually in writing.
NOUN **2** a piece of software designed to carry out a particular task on a computer

apply **applies, applying, applied**
VERB **1** If you **apply** for something, you ask for it formally, usually by writing a letter or an email. • *My brother is **applying** for jobs.*
VERB **2** If you **apply** something to a surface, you put it on or rub it into the surface. • *She **applied** sun cream to her face.*
VERB **3** If you **apply** yourself to a task, you give it all of your attention.

appoint **appoints, appointing, appointed**
VERB If a person **appoints** someone to a job or position, they formally choose them for it. • *The teacher **appointed** Sunita as team captain.*

appointment **appointments**
NOUN an arrangement you have with someone to meet them

appreciate **appreciates, appreciating, appreciated**
VERB If you **appreciate** something that someone has done for you, you are grateful to them for it.

apprehensive
ADJECTIVE If you are **apprehensive** about something, you feel worried and unsure about it.

apprentice **apprentices**
NOUN someone who works with another person for a length of time to learn that person's job or skill

approach **approaches, approaching, approached**
VERB If you **approach** something, you come near or nearer to it.

appropriate
ADJECTIVE suitable or acceptable for a particular situation

approval
NOUN If you ask for **approval** for something that you want to do, you ask for agreement with your plans.

approve **approves, approving, approved**
VERB **1** If you **approve** of something or someone, you think they are acceptable or good.

SYNONYMS: favour, like

VERB **2** If someone **approves** a plan or idea, they agree to it. • *The council **approved** plans for the new swimming pool.*

SYNONYMS: agree to, permit

approximate
ADJECTIVE near but not exactly right • *What was the **approximate** time you arrived?*

apricot **apricots**
NOUN a small, soft, yellowish-orange fruit

April
NOUN the fourth month of the year. **April** has 30 days.

apron **aprons**
NOUN a piece of clothing worn over the front of normal clothing to protect it

aquarium **aquaria** or **aquariums**
NOUN a glass tank filled with water in which fish and other aquatic animals or plants are kept

aquatic
ADJECTIVE An **aquatic** animal or plant lives in water.

aqueduct **aqueducts**
NOUN a bridge with many arches, which carries a water supply over a valley

a
b
c
d
e
f
g
h
i
j
k
l
m
n
o
p
q
r
s
t
u
v
w
x
y
z

arable
ADJECTIVE **Arable** land is used for growing crops.

arc arcs
NOUN **1** a smoothly curving line
NOUN **2** In geometry, an **arc** is a section of the circumference of a circle.

arcade arcades
NOUN a covered passageway where there are shops or market stalls

arch arches, arching, arched
NOUN **1** a structure that has a curved top, supported on either side by a pillar or wall
VERB **2** If something **arches**, or if you **arch** it, it forms a curved line or shape. ● *The cat **arched** its back.*

archaeology; also spelt **archeology**
NOUN the study of the past by digging up and examining the remains of things such as buildings, tools and pots

WORD HISTORY
from Greek *arkhaios* meaning ancient

archbishop archbishops
NOUN a bishop of the highest rank in a Christian Church ● *the **Archbishop** of Canterbury*

archery
NOUN a sport in which people shoot at a target with a bow and arrow

architect architects
NOUN a person who designs buildings

architecture
NOUN the art or practice of designing buildings

arctic
NOUN **1** The **Arctic** is the area around the North Pole.

➔ Have a look at the illustration for **equator**

ADJECTIVE **2** very cold indeed ● *You need specially warm clothes for **arctic** conditions.*

are
VERB a present tense of **be**

area areas
NOUN **1** a particular part of a place, country, or the world ● *a built-up **area** of the city*

SYNONYMS: district, region, zone

NOUN **2** the measurement of a flat surface ● *The **area** of the playground is 1500 square metres.*

arena arenas
NOUN a place where sports and other public events take place

WORD HISTORY
from Latin *harena* meaning sand, because of the sandy centre of an amphitheatre where gladiators fought

aren't
VERB a contraction of *are not*

argue argues, arguing, argued
VERB **1** If you **argue** with someone about something, you disagree with them about it, sometimes in an angry way.
VERB **2** If you **argue** that something is true, you give reasons why you think that it is.

argument arguments
NOUN a talk between people who do not agree

arid
ADJECTIVE **Arid** land is very dry because there has been very little rain.

ANTONYM: fertile

arise arises, arising, arose, arisen
VERB When something such as an opportunity or a problem **arises**, it begins to exist.

aristocracy
NOUN The **aristocracy** are people whose families have a high social rank, and who have a title such as Lord or Lady.

aristocrat aristocrats
NOUN someone whose family has a high social rank, and who has a title such as Lord or Lady

arithmetic
NOUN the part of mathematics that is to do with the addition, subtraction, multiplication and division of numbers

WORD HISTORY
from Greek *arithmos* meaning number

arm arms, arming, armed
NOUN **1** the part of your body between your shoulder and your wrist
PLURAL NOUN **2 Arms** are weapons used in a war.
VERB **3** If a country **arms** itself, it prepares for war.

armada armadas
NOUN a large fleet of warships ● *The Spanish **Armada** was the fleet sent to destroy the English in 1588.*

armchair armchairs

NOUN a large chair with a support on each side for your arms

armistice armistices

NOUN In war, an **armistice** is an agreement to stop fighting.

armour

NOUN **1** In the past, **armour** was metal clothing worn for protection in battle.
NOUN **2** In modern warfare, tanks are often referred to as **armour**.

army armies

NOUN a large group of soldiers who are trained to fight on land

aroma aromas

NOUN a strong, pleasant smell

WORD HISTORY
a Greek word meaning spice

around

PREPOSITION **1** situated at various points in a place or area • *There are several post boxes* **around** *the town.*
PREPOSITION **2** from place to place inside an area • *We walked* **around** *the stalls at the summer fair.*
PREPOSITION **3** surrounding or encircling a place or object • *We were sitting* **around** *the table.*
PREPOSITION **4** at approximately the time or place mentioned • *The jumble sale began* **around** *noon.*

arrange arranges, arranging, arranged

VERB **1** If you **arrange** to do something, or **arrange** something for someone, you make plans for it or make it possible. • *I* **arranged** *to meet him later.* • *Dad* **arranged** *a trip to the circus for us.*
VERB **2** If you **arrange** objects, you set them out in a particular way. • *We* **arranged** *the books in alphabetical order.*

array arrays

NOUN **1** a large number of different things displayed together
NOUN **2** a mathematical way of grouping

arrest arrests, arresting, arrested

VERB **1** If the police **arrest** someone, they take them to a police station because they believe they may have committed a crime.
NOUN **2** An **arrest** is the act of arresting someone.

arrival arrivals

NOUN **1 Arrival** is when you reach a place at the end of your journey. • *On their* **arrival** *in London, they went straight to the hotel.*
NOUN **2** someone or something that has just come to a place

arrive arrives, arriving, arrived

VERB **1** When you **arrive** at a place, you reach it at the end of your journey.
VERB **2** When you **arrive** at a decision you make up your mind.

arrogant

ADJECTIVE **Arrogant** people behave as if they are better than other people.

arrow arrows

NOUN a long, thin weapon with a sharp point at one end, shot from a bow

arsenal arsenals

NOUN a place where weapons and ammunition are stored or produced

arsenic

NOUN a strong, dangerous poison that can kill

arson

NOUN the crime of deliberately setting fire to something, especially a building

art arts

NOUN **1** the creation of objects, such as paintings and sculptures, that are thought to be beautiful or that express a particular idea • *He wanted to take* **art** *classes to learn how to draw and paint well.*
NOUN **2 Art** is also used to refer to the objects themselves. • *We saw lots of interesting paintings and sculptures at the* **art** *exhibition.*
NOUN **3** something that needs special skills or ability • *I would like to master the* **art** *of sewing.*

artery arteries

NOUN the tubes that carry blood from your heart to the rest of your body

arthritis

NOUN a condition in which the joints in someone's body become painful, and sometimes swollen

article articles

NOUN **1** a piece of writing in a newspaper or magazine
NOUN **2** a particular item • *an* **article** *of clothing*

a
b
c
d
e
f
g
h
i
j
k
l
m
n
o
p
q
r
s
t
u
v
w
x
y
z

25

artificial

ADJECTIVE Something **artificial** is created by people rather than occurring naturally.

ANTONYM: natural

artillery

NOUN **1 Artillery** consists of large, powerful guns and rockets.

NOUN **2** The **artillery** is the branch of an army that uses these weapons.

artist artists

NOUN a person who draws or paints or produces other works of art

as

CONJUNCTION **1** at the same time that • *We watched television **as** we ate our sandwiches.*

CONJUNCTION **2** because • ***As** I like school I get there early.*

PHRASE **3** You use **as if** or **as though** when you are giving an explanation for something. • *Shane walked past **as if** he didn't know me.*

ascend ascends, ascending, ascended

VERB *(formal)* If someone or something **ascends**, they move or lead upwards.

• *We **ascended** the stairs to the second floor.*

ANTONYM: descend

ash ashes

NOUN the grey or black powdery remains of anything that has been burnt • *We put the **ashes** from the bonfire on the compost heap.*

→ Have a look at the illustration for **volcano**

ashamed

ADJECTIVE **1** If you are **ashamed**, you feel embarrassed or guilty.

ADJECTIVE **2** If you are **ashamed** of someone, you feel embarrassed to be connected with them.

ashore

ADVERB If someone or something comes **ashore**, they come on to the land from the sea or a river.

aside

ADVERB If you move something **aside**, you move it to one side. • *She closed the book and laid it **aside**.*

ask asks, asking, asked

VERB **1** If you **ask** someone something, you put a question to them.

VERB **2** If you **ask** someone to do something, you tell them you want them to do it. • *We **asked** him to do his card trick.*

VERB **3** If you **ask** for something, you say you would like to have it. • *She **asked** for a drink of water.*

VERB **4** If you **ask** someone to come or go somewhere, you invite them there.

asleep

ADJECTIVE If you are **asleep**, your eyes are closed and your whole body is resting. • *The cat was **asleep** under the bed.*

aspect aspects

NOUN one of many ways of seeing or thinking about something

aspirin aspirins

NOUN a small white tablet of this drug

ass asses

NOUN another word for **donkey**

assassinate assassinates, assassinating, assassinated

VERB If someone **assassinates** an important person, they murder them.

assassination assassinations

NOUN An **assassination** is when someone murders an important person.

assault assaults

NOUN a violent attack on someone

WORD HISTORY
from Latin *assalire* meaning to leap upon

assemble assembles, assembling, assembled

VERB **1** If people **assemble**, they gather together. • *We **assembled** in the playground to watch the display.*

VERB **2** If you **assemble** something, you fit the parts of it together. • *It took us ages to **assemble** the model car.*

assembly assemblies

NOUN a group of people who have gathered together for a particular purpose • *The headteacher made the announcement during a school **assembly**.*

assess assesses, assessing, assessed

VERB If you **assess** something, you consider it carefully and make a judgement about it.

• *She tried to **assess** how much further they had to walk.*

SYNONYMS: judge, size up

asset assets

NOUN **1** If someone or something is an **asset**, they are useful or helpful. • *He's an **asset** to the school.*

NOUN **2** The **assets** of a person or a company are all the things they own that could be sold to raise money.

assignment assignments

NOUN a job you are given to do

assist assists, assisting, assisted

VERB If you **assist** someone, you help them to do something.

assistant assistants

NOUN someone who helps another person to do their job

associate associates, associating, associated

VERB **1** If you **associate** with someone, you spend time with them.

VERB **2** If you **associate** one thing with another, you make a connection between them.

association associations

NOUN **1** an organisation for people who have similar interests, jobs or aims

NOUN **2** An **association** between two things is a link you make in your mind between them.

assorted

ADJECTIVE **Assorted** things are a mixture of various sorts of something. They may be different colours, sizes and shapes.

assortment assortments

NOUN a group of similar things that are different sizes, shapes and colours • *There was an amazing **assortment** of toys in the shop.*

assume assumes, assuming, assumed

VERB **1** If you **assume** that something is true, you believe it, even if you have not thought carefully about it.

VERB **2** If you **assume** responsibility for something, you decide to do it. • *I **assumed** responsibility for feeding the hamster.*

assure assures, assuring, assured

VERB If you **assure** someone of something, you say something to make them less worried about it. • *I **assured** him that I wouldn't be late.*

asterisk asterisks

NOUN a symbol (*) used in writing and printing to draw attention to something that is explained somewhere else, usually at the bottom of the page

asteroid asteroids

NOUN one of the large number of rocks that move around the sun between the orbits of Jupiter and Mars in an area called the asteroid belt

asthma

NOUN a condition of the chest that causes wheezing and difficulty in breathing

---

WORD HISTORY

from Greek *azein* meaning to breathe hard

---

asthmatic

ADJECTIVE Someone who is **asthmatic** has a condition of the chest that causes wheezing and difficulty in breathing.

astonish astonishes, astonishing, astonished

VERB If something **astonishes** you, it surprises you very much.

astonished

ADJECTIVE very surprised

astonishing

ADJECTIVE very surprising

astonishingly

ADVERB in a way that is very surprising

astonishment

NOUN **Astonishment** is when you are very surprised.

astrology

NOUN the study of the sun, moon and stars in the belief that their movements can influence people's lives

astronaut astronauts

NOUN a person who operates a spacecraft

WORD HISTORY

from Greek *astron* meaning star and *nautes* meaning sailor

---

astronomer astronomers

NOUN someone who studies stars and planets

astronomy

NOUN the scientific study of stars and planets

at

PREPOSITION **1** where someone or something is • *John waited for me **at** the bus stop.*

PREPOSITION **2** the direction something is going in • *I threw the snowball **at** my brother.*

PREPOSITION **3** when something happens • *The party starts **at** six o'clock.*

ate

VERB the past tense of **eat**

a
b
c
d
e
f
g
h
i
j
k
l
m
n
o
p
q
r
s
t
u
v
w
x
y
z

A
B
C
D
E
F
G
H
I
J
K
L
M
N
O
P
Q
R
S
T
U
V
W
X
Y
Z

atheist atheists
NOUN someone who does not believe in any form of God

athlete athletes
NOUN a person who is very good at sport and who takes part in sporting competitions

athletic
ADJECTIVE physically fit and strong

athletics
NOUN sporting events such as running, long jump and discus

Atlantic
NOUN the ocean that separates North and South America from Europe and Africa

atlas atlases
NOUN a book of maps

WORD HISTORY
from the giant *Atlas* in Greek mythology, who supported the sky on his shoulders

atmosphere atmospheres
NOUN **1** gases that surround a planet
→ Have a look at the illustration for **greenhouse effect**
NOUN **2** the general mood of a place • *There was a friendly **atmosphere** at the party.*

atom atoms
NOUN the smallest part of an element that can take part in a chemical reaction

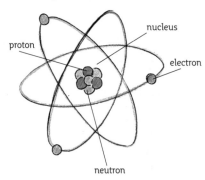

nucleus

proton

electron

neutron

atrocity atrocities
NOUN an extremely shocking and cruel act

attach attaches, attaching, attached
VERB If you **attach** something to something else, you join or fasten the two things together.

attached
ADJECTIVE If you are **attached** to someone, you are very fond of them.

attachment attachments
NOUN **1** a feeling of love and affection for someone
NOUN **2** a file attached to an email

attack attacks, attacking, attacked
VERB **1** If someone **attacks** another person or animal, they use violence in order to hurt or kill them. • *The lion **attacked** the zebra in order to kill it for food.*
VERB **2** In a game such as football or hockey, players **attack** to get the ball into a position from which a goal can be scored.
NOUN **3** violent, physical action against someone

attempt attempts, attempting, attempted
VERB **1** If you **attempt** to do something, you try to do it.
NOUN **2** the act of trying to do something
• *He made a brave **attempt** to help.*

attend attends, attending, attended
VERB **1** If you **attend** school, church or hospital, you go there regularly.
VERB **2** If you **attend** an event, you are present at it.
attend to
VERB If you **attend to** something, you deal with it. • *We should **attend to** our homework before going to the park.*

attendant attendants
NOUN someone whose job is to help people in a place such as a cloakroom or swimming pool

attention
NOUN the thought or care that you give to someone or something • *I paid a lot of **attention** to my homework.*

attentive
ADJECTIVE When you are **attentive**, you pay close attention.

attic attics
NOUN a room at the top of a house immediately below the roof

attitude attitudes
NOUN the way you think about someone or something and behave towards them
• *I'm not going in that shop again. I don't like their **attitude**.*

attract **attracts, attracting, attracted**
VERB **1** If something **attracts** people, it interests them and makes them want to go to it.
VERB **2** If someone **attracts** you, you like them and are interested in them.
VERB **3** When magnetic materials are **attracted** to a magnet, they are pulled towards it.

attraction **attractions**
NOUN **1** If you feel an **attraction** for someone, you like them very much.
NOUN **2** somewhere people like to visit for interest or pleasure, such as a fun fair or a stately home
NOUN **3** A force of **attraction** pulls magnetic materials towards a magnet.

attractive
ADJECTIVE **1** Someone who is **attractive** is good looking or has an exciting personality.
ADJECTIVE **2** If something is **attractive**, it is interesting.

aubergine **aubergines**
NOUN a dark purple, pear-shaped vegetable. It is also called an eggplant.

auburn
ADJECTIVE a red-brown hair colour

auction **auctions, auctioning, auctioned**
NOUN **1** a public sale in which goods are sold to the person who offers the highest price
VERB **2** to sell something in an auction

audible
ADJECTIVE If something is **audible**, you can hear it.

audience **audiences**
NOUN **1** the group of people who are watching or listening to a performance
NOUN **2** a private or formal meeting with an important person • The winners of the bravery awards had an **audience** with the Queen.

audition **auditions**
NOUN a short performance by an actor or musician, so that a director can decide whether they are suitable for a part in a play or a film, or for a place in an orchestra

auditorium **auditoriums** or **auditoria**
NOUN the part of a theatre or concert hall where the audience sits

August
NOUN the eighth month of the year. **August** has 31 days.

aunt **aunts**
NOUN Your **aunt** is the sister of your mother or father, or the wife of your uncle.

author **authors**
NOUN The **author** of a book is the person who wrote it.

authorisation; also spelt **authorization**
NOUN **Authorisation** is when someone gives official permission for something.

authorise **authorises, authorising, authorised**; also spelt **authorize**
VERB If someone **authorises** something, they give official permission for it.

authority **authorities**
NOUN **1** the power to tell other people what to do • The teacher had the **authority** to give me detention.
NOUN **2** an organisation that controls public interests • the local health **authority**
NOUN **3** Someone who is an **authority** on something, knows a lot about it.

autism
NOUN a condition that makes it difficult to communicate in the way most people expect

autistic
ADJECTIVE An **autistic** person has a condition that makes it difficult to communicate in the way most people expect.

auto-
PREFIX **1** self or same • **auto**biography
PREFIX **2** self-propelling • **auto**matic car

autobiography **autobiographies**
NOUN an account of someone's life that they have written themselves

autograph **autographs**
NOUN the signature of a famous person

WORD HISTORY
from Greek auto meaning self and graphos meaning written

---

automatic **automatics**
ADJECTIVE **1** An **automatic** machine is programmed to perform tasks without needing a person to operate it.
NOUN **2** a car in which the gears change automatically as the car's speed changes

autumn **autumns**
NOUN the season between summer and winter, when the leaves fall off the trees • I love the golden colours of the trees in **autumn**.

a
b
c
d
e
f
g
h
i
j
k
l
m
n
o
p
q
r
s
t
u
v
w
x
y
z

available

ADJECTIVE **1** If something is **available**, it is easy to get or to buy.

ADJECTIVE **2** A person who is **available** is ready for work or free to talk to.

avalanche avalanches

NOUN a huge mass of snow and ice that falls down a mountainside

avatar avatars

NOUN an image that represents you on the screen in an online game or chatroom

avenue avenues

NOUN a street, especially one with trees along it

average averages

NOUN **1** a result obtained by adding several amounts together and then dividing the total by the number of different amounts • *If I shared 36 sweets between four children, the **average** would be nine sweets per child.*

ADJECTIVE **2** standard or usual • *The **average** teenager is interested in pop music.*

SYNONYMS: normal, ordinary, typical

PHRASE **3** You say **on average** when mentioning what usually happens in a situation. • *Men are, **on average**, taller than women.*

aviary aviaries

NOUN a large cage or group of cages in which birds are kept

aviation

NOUN the science of flying aircraft

avocado avocados

NOUN a pear-shaped fruit with dark green skin, soft greenish-yellow flesh, and a large stone

avoid avoids, avoiding, avoided

VERB **1** If you **avoid** someone or something, you keep away from them. • *To **avoid** him, she went home the other way.*

VERB **2** If you **avoid** doing something, you make an effort not to do it.

SYNONYMS: dodge, shirk

awake

ADJECTIVE Someone who is **awake** is not sleeping.

award awards, awarding, awarded

NOUN **1** a prize or certificate for doing something well

VERB **2** If someone **awards** you something, they give it to you formally or officially. • *He was **awarded** the prize for fastest runner.*

aware

ADJECTIVE **1** If you are **aware** of something, you know about it. • *They are **aware** of the danger.*

ADJECTIVE **2** If you are **aware** of something, you can see, hear, smell or feel it.

away

ADVERB **1** moving from a place • *I saw them walk **away** from the house.*

ADVERB **2** at a distance from a place • *The nearest supermarket is 12 kilometres **away**.*

ADVERB **3** in its proper place • *He put his clothes **away**.*

ADVERB **4** not at home, school or work • *My friend's been **away** from school for a week.*

awe

NOUN (*formal*) a feeling of great respect mixed with amazement, and sometimes slight fear • *Looking up at the mountains, we felt a sense of **awe**.*

awful

ADJECTIVE very unpleasant or very bad • *Isn't the weather **awful**?*

SYNONYMS: dreadful, terrible

awkward

ADJECTIVE **1** difficult to deal with • *an **awkward** situation*

ADJECTIVE **2** clumsy and uncomfortable • *The large bag was **awkward** to carry.*

WORD HISTORY
from Old Norse *ofugr* meaning turned the wrong way

axe axes

NOUN a tool with a handle and a sharp blade, used for chopping wood

axis axes

NOUN **1** an imaginary line through the middle of something, around which it moves • *The Earth turns on its **axis**.*

NOUN **2** one of the two sides of a graph, the x-**axis** or the y-**axis**

axle axles

NOUN the long bar that connects a pair of wheels on a vehicle

Bb

babble **babbles, babbling, babbled**
VERB If someone **babbles**, they talk in a quick and confused way that is difficult to understand.

baboon **baboons**
NOUN an African monkey with a pointed face, large teeth and a long tail

baby **babies**
NOUN a child in the first year or two of its life

baby-sit **baby-sits, baby-sitting, baby-sat**
VERB If you **baby-sit** for someone, you look after their children while they are out.

bachelor **bachelors**
NOUN a man who has never been married

back **backs, backing, backed**
ADVERB **1** When people or things move **back**, they move in the opposite direction to the one they are facing.
ADVERB **2** When you go **back** to a place or situation, you return to it. • *She went **back** to sleep.*
NOUN **3** the rear part of your body
ADJECTIVE **4** The **back** parts of something are the ones at the rear. • *the dog's **back** legs*
VERB **5** If a building **backs** on to something, the back of it faces in that direction.

backbone **backbones**
NOUN the column of linked bones along the middle of the back of a human and other vertebrates

background **backgrounds**
NOUN **1** the things in a picture or scene that are less noticeable than the main things
NOUN **2** the kind of home you come from, and your education and experience

backstroke
NOUN a style of swimming movement on your back

backward
ADJECTIVE If you take a **backward** look, you look behind you.

backwards
ADVERB **1** If you move **backwards**, you move to a place behind you.
ADVERB **2** If you do something **backwards**, you do it opposite to the usual way. • *He told them to count **backwards** from 20 to 5.*

bacon
NOUN meat from the back or sides of a pig, which has been salted or smoked

bacteria
PLURAL NOUN very tiny organisms that can cause diseases

WORD HISTORY
from Greek *bakterion* meaning little rod; some bacteria are rod-shaped

---

bacterial
ADJECTIVE involving or caused by very tiny organisms that can cause diseases
• ***bacterial** infections*

bad **worse, worst**
ADJECTIVE **1** **Bad** things are harmful or upsetting. • *I have some **bad** news.*

SYNONYMS: distressing, grave, terrible

ADJECTIVE **2** not enough or of poor quality
• *The food was **worse** than usual.*
ADJECTIVE **3** **Bad** food is not fresh.

SYNONYMS: rotten, decayed

badge **badges**
NOUN a piece of plastic or metal with a design or message on it that you can pin to your clothes

badger **badgers, badgering, badgered**
NOUN **1** a nocturnal mammal that has a white head with two black stripes on it
VERB **2** If you **badger** someone, you keep asking them questions or pestering them to do something.

badly **worse, worst**
ADVERB **1** not well or poorly • *The script was **badly** written.*
ADVERB **2** seriously • *She was **badly** hurt in the accident.*

badminton
NOUN a game in which two or four players use rackets to hit a feathered object, called a shuttlecock, over a high net

a
b
c
d
e
f
g
h
i
j
k
l
m
n
o
p
q
r
s
t
u
v
w
x
y
z

bag **bags**
NOUN a container for carrying things in

WORD HISTORY
From Old Norse *baggi* meaning bundle

baggage
NOUN Your **baggage** is all the suitcases, holdalls and bags that you take with you when you travel.

bagpipes
PLURAL NOUN a musical instrument played by squeezing air out of a leather bag and through pipes

baguette **baguettes**
NOUN a long, thin French loaf of bread

bail **bails**
NOUN **1** a sum of money paid to a court to allow an accused person to go free until the time of the trial • *The accused man was released on **bail**.*
NOUN **2** In cricket, the **bails** are the two small pieces of wood placed on top of the stumps to form the wicket.

bait **baits, baiting, baited**
NOUN **1** a small amount of food placed on a hook, or in a trap, to attract and catch a fish or wild animal
VERB **2** If you **bait** a hook or a trap, you put some food on it to catch a fish or wild animal.

bake **bakes, baking, baked**
VERB **1** When you **bake** food, you cook it in an oven without using extra liquid or fat.
VERB **2** If you **bake** earth or clay, you heat it until it becomes hard.

baker **bakers**
NOUN a person who makes and sells bread and cakes

balance **balances, balancing, balanced**
VERB **1** When someone or something **balances**, they remain steady and do not fall over.
VERB **2** used in mathematics when weighing and comparing two weights. If two weights are equal, they **balance**.
NOUN **3** the state of being upright and steady • *She lost her **balance** and fell.*
NOUN **4** the amount of money in someone's bank account

balcony **balconies**
NOUN **1** a platform on the outside of a building, with a wall or railing round it
NOUN **2** an area of upstairs seats in a theatre or cinema

bald **balder, baldest**
ADJECTIVE A **bald** person has little or no hair on their head.

WORD HISTORY
from Middle English *ballede* meaning having a white patch

bale **bales, baling, baled**
NOUN **1** a large bundle of something, such as paper or hay, tied tightly
VERB **2** If you **bale** water from a boat, you remove it using a container.

LANGUAGE TIP
In meaning 2, the spelling *bail* can also be used.

ball **balls**
NOUN **1** a round object used in games such as tennis, football, and hockey
NOUN **2** The **ball** of your foot or thumb is the rounded part where your toes join your foot or your thumb joins your hand.

ballad **ballads**
NOUN **1** a long song or poem that tells a story
NOUN **2** a slow, romantic pop song

ballerina **ballerinas**
NOUN a female ballet dancer

ballet
NOUN a type of artistic dancing based on precise steps

WORD HISTORY
from Italian *balletto* meaning little dance

balloon **balloons**
NOUN **1** a small bag made of thin rubber that you blow into until it becomes larger. **Balloons** are often used as party decorations.
NOUN **2** a large, strong bag filled with gas or hot air, that travels through the air carrying passengers in a basket underneath it • *They went on a hot-air **balloon** flight over the city.*

ballpoint **ballpoints**
NOUN a pen with a small, metal ball at the writing point

bamboo
NOUN a tall tropical grass with hard, hollow stems used for making furniture

ban bans, banning, banned
VERB **1** If you **ban** something, you forbid it to be done.

SYNONYMS: forbid, prohibit

NOUN **2** If there is a **ban** on something, it is not allowed.

banana bananas
NOUN a long, curved fruit with a yellow skin

band bands
NOUN **1** a group of musicians who play jazz or pop music together
NOUN **2** a group of people who share a common purpose
NOUN **3** a narrow strip of something used to hold things together • *She tied her hair back with an elastic* ***band***.

bandage bandages
NOUN a strip of cloth wrapped round a wound to protect it

bang bangs, banging, banged
NOUN **1** a sudden, short, loud noise
NOUN **2** a hard, painful bump against something
VERB **3** If you **bang** something, you hit it or put it down violently so that it makes a loud noise.
VERB **4** If you **bang** a part of your body against something, you accidentally bump it.

banish banishes, banishing, banished
VERB **1** If someone is **banished**, they are sent away and never allowed to return.
VERB **2** If you **banish** something from your thoughts, you try not to think about it.

banishment
NOUN **Banishment** is when someone is sent away and never allowed to return.

banister banisters
NOUN a rail supported by posts up the side of a staircase

banjo banjos or banjoes
NOUN a musical instrument, like a small guitar with a round body

bank banks, banking, banked
NOUN **1** a business that looks after people's money
NOUN **2** the raised ground along the edge of a river or lake
bank on
VERB If you **bank on** something happening, you rely on it. • *I know we said we'd go swimming, but don't* ***bank on*** *it.*

banner banners
NOUN **1** a long strip of cloth with a message or slogan on it • *We saw* ***banners*** *advertising the fair.*
ADJECTIVE **2** A **banner** headline is a headline printed right across the page of a newspaper.

banquet banquets
NOUN a grand, formal dinner, often followed by speeches

WORD HISTORY
from Old French *banquet*, originally meaning little bench

baptise baptises, baptising, baptised; also spelt **baptize**
VERB When a church official **baptises** someone, they sprinkle water on them, or immerse them in water, as a sign that they have become a Christian.

baptism baptisms
NOUN the ceremony in which someone has water sprinkled on them, or they are immersed in water, as a sign that they have become a Christian

bar bars, barring, barred
NOUN **1** a long, straight piece of metal • *There were* ***bars*** *on the windows.*
VERB **2** If you **bar** a door or a window, you put a bar across it to fasten it.
VERB **3** If you **bar** someone's way, you stop them going somewhere by standing in front of them.
NOUN **4** a counter or room where alcoholic drinks are served
NOUN **5** a piece of something made in a rectangular shape • *a* ***bar*** *of soap* • *a chocolate* ***bar***

barbecue barbecues
NOUN **1** a grill with a charcoal fire on which you cook food, usually outdoors
NOUN **2** an outdoor party where you eat food cooked on a barbecue • *We were invited to their annual* ***barbecue***.

WORD HISTORY
from a Caribbean word meaning framework

a
b
c
d
e
f
g
h
i
j
k
l
m
n
o
p
q
r
s
t
u
v
w
x
y
z

barber barbers

NOUN a person who cuts men's hair

bar chart bar charts

NOUN a kind of graph where the information is shown in rows or bars

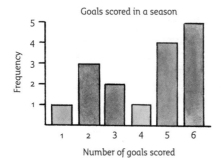

Goals scored in a season

bar code bar codes

NOUN a pattern of lines and numbers on something that is for sale, so that the price can be read by a machine

bare barer, barest

ADJECTIVE **1** If a part of your body is **bare**, it is not covered by any clothing. • *bare feet*

SYNONYMS: naked, uncovered

ADJECTIVE **2** If something is **bare**, it is not covered or decorated with anything.
• *bare wooden floors*

ADJECTIVE **3** The **bare** minimum, or the **bare** essentials, means the very least that is needed.

barely

ADVERB If you **barely** manage to do something, you only just succeed in doing it.

bargain bargains, bargaining, bargained

NOUN **1** an agreement in which two people or groups discuss and agree what each will do, pay or receive

NOUN **2** something that is sold at a low price and that is good value • *The apples are a **bargain** at this price.*

VERB **3** When people **bargain** with each other, they discuss and agree terms about what each will do, pay or receive.

barge barges, barging, barged

NOUN **1** a boat with a flat bottom used for carrying heavy loads, especially on canals

VERB **2** (*informal*) If you **barge** into a place, you push into it in a rough or rude way.

bark barks, barking, barked

VERB **1** When a dog **barks**, it makes a short, loud noise, once or several times.

NOUN **2** the tough material that covers the outside of a tree

barley

NOUN a cereal that is grown for food and is also used for making beer and whisky

bar mitzvah

NOUN A Jewish boy's **bar mitzvah** is a ceremony that takes place on his 13th birthday, after which he is regarded as an adult.

barn barns

NOUN a large farm building used for storing crops or animal food

WORD HISTORY
from Old English *beren* meaning barley room

barnacle barnacles

NOUN a small shellfish that fixes itself to rocks and to the bottom of boats

barometer barometers

NOUN an instrument that measures air pressure and shows when the weather is changing

barrel barrels

NOUN **1** a wooden container with rounded sides and flat ends

NOUN **2** The **barrel** of a gun is the long tube through which the bullet is fired.

barricade barricades, barricading, barricaded

NOUN **1** a temporary barrier put up to stop people getting past

VERB **2** If you **barricade** yourself inside a room or building, you put something heavy against the door to stop people getting in.

WORD HISTORY
from Old French *barriquer* meaning to block with barrels

barrier barriers

NOUN a fence or wall that prevents people or animals getting from one area to another

barrister barristers

NOUN a lawyer who is qualified to represent people in the higher courts

barrow barrows

NOUN **1** another word for **wheelbarrow**

NOUN **2** a large cart from which fruit or other goods are sold in the street

base bases, basing, based

NOUN **1** the lowest part of something • *The waves crashed at the base of the cliffs.*

NOUN **2** The **base** of a triangle or a square-shaped pyramid is the bottom.

NOUN **3** a place where part of an army, navy or air force works from

VERB **4** If you **base** one thing on another, you develop the first thing from it. • *She based the film on a true story.*

VERB **5** If you are **based** somewhere, you live there or work from there. • *My dad is based in Cardiff, but spends a lot of time abroad.*

baseball

NOUN a team game played with a bat and a ball. It is popular in the USA.

basement basements

NOUN a room or set of rooms below the level of the street • *My aunt lives in the basement of our house.*

basic

ADJECTIVE **1** The **basic** aspects of something are the most necessary ones. • *The basic ingredients of bread are flour, yeast and water.*

ADJECTIVE **2** having only the essentials, and no extras or luxuries

basically

ADVERB You use **basically** to give the most important facts or reasons, or to give a simple explanation. • *Basically, you have two choices.*

basin basins

NOUN **1** a round, wide container which is open at the top

NOUN **2** A river **basin** is a bowl of land from which water runs into the river.

basis bases

NOUN If something is the **basis** of something else, it is the main principle on which that thing is based, and from which other points and ideas can be developed.

bask basks, basking, basked

VERB If you **bask** in hot weather, you lie in the sun and enjoy the warmth.

basket baskets

NOUN a container made of thin strips of wood or metal woven together • *a shopping basket*

basketball

NOUN a game in which two teams try to score goals by throwing a large ball through one of two circular nets that are suspended high up at each end of the **basketball** court

bass basses

NOUN **1** a man with a very deep singing voice

ADJECTIVE **2** In music, a **bass** instrument produces a very deep sound. • *a bass guitar*

bassoon bassoons

NOUN a large woodwind instrument

bat bats, batting, batted

NOUN **1** a specially shaped piece of wood with a handle, used for hitting a ball in games such as table tennis or cricket

NOUN **2** a small mammal with leathery wings. **Bats** fly at night and sleep hanging upside down.

VERB **3** If you are **batting** in cricket, baseball or rounders, it is your turn to hit the ball.

batch batches

NOUN A **batch** of things is a group of things that are all the same or are being dealt with at the same time. • *They delivered the first batch of books at the start of term.*

bath baths

NOUN a long container that you fill with water and sit in to wash yourself

bathe bathes, bathing, bathed

VERB When you **bathe** in a sea, river or lake, you swim or play there.

bathroom bathrooms

NOUN a room with a bath or shower, a washbasin and often a toilet in it

bat mitzvah

NOUN A Jewish girls's **bat mitzvah** is a ceremony that usually takes place on her 12th birthday, after which she is regarded as an adult.

baton batons

NOUN **1** a light, thin stick that a conductor uses to direct an orchestra or choir

NOUN **2** a short stick passed from one runner to another at the changeover in a relay race

battalion battalions

NOUN an army unit consisting of three or more companies

a
b
c
d
e
f
g
h
i
j
k
l
m
n
o
p
q
r
s
t
u
v
w
x
y
z

35

batter batters, battering, battered
NOUN **1** a mixture of flour, eggs and milk, used to make pancakes, or to coat food before frying it
VERB **2** When someone or something **batters** someone or something, they hit them many times. ● *The waves **battered** the sides of the ship.*

battery batteries
NOUN a device for storing energy and producing electricity, for example in a torch or a car

battle battles
NOUN **1** a fight between armed forces
NOUN **2** a struggle between two people or groups with different aims

battlefield battlefields
NOUN a place where a battle has been fought or is being fought

battlements
PLURAL NOUN the top part of a castle where there are openings through which arrows or guns could be fired

→ Have a look at the illustration for **castle**

battleship battleships
NOUN a large fighting ship carrying powerful guns

bawl bawls, bawling, bawled
VERB If someone **bawls**, they shout or cry loudly.

bay bays, baying, bayed
NOUN **1** part of the coastline where the land curves
NOUN **2** a space or an area used for a particular purpose ● *a loading **bay***
NOUN **3** a tree with dark green leaves. The leaves are used for flavouring food.
VERB **4** When a dog or a wolf **bays**, it makes a deep, howling sound.
PHRASE **5** If you keep something **at bay**, you stop it hurting you. ● *Try eating an orange to keep a cold **at bay**.*

bayonet bayonets
NOUN a sharp blade that can be fixed to the end of a rifle

bazaar bazaars
NOUN **1** an area with many small shops and stalls, especially in Eastern countries
NOUN **2** a sale to raise money for charity
● *a Christmas **bazaar***

WORD HISTORY
from Persian *bazar* meaning market

BC
ADJECTIVE You use **BC** to show the dates before the birth of Jesus Christ. It is an abbreviation for *before Christ*.

BCE
ADJECTIVE You use **BCE** in dates to show the number of years or centuries before the year in which Jesus Christ is believed to have been born. **BCE** is an abbreviation for *before the Common Era*.

be am, is, are; being; was, were; been
VERB **1** You can use **be** with the present participle of other verbs. ● *Look! I **am** riding on my own!*
VERB **2** You can also use **be** to say that something will happen. ● *I will **be** nine in November.*
VERB **3** You use **be** to say more about something or somebody. ● *His name **is** Tom.*

beach beaches
NOUN an area of sand or pebbles beside the sea

beacon beacons
NOUN In the past, a **beacon** was a light or fire on a hill, which acted as a signal or warning.

bead beads
NOUN **1** a small, shaped piece of glass, stone or wood with a hole through the middle. **Beads** are strung together to make necklaces or bracelets.
NOUN **2** a drop of liquid ● ***beads** of perspiration*

beak beaks
NOUN the hard part of a bird's mouth that sticks out. It is used for pecking up food and for carrying things such as twigs.

→ Have a look at the illustration for **bird**

beam beams, beaming, beamed
NOUN **1** a long, thick bar of wood or metal, especially one that supports a roof
NOUN **2** a band of light that shines from something such as a torch or the sun
VERB **3** If you **beam**, you smile broadly.

bean beans
NOUN the seed or pod of a plant, eaten as a vegetable or used for other purposes
● *runner **beans*** ● *coffee **beans*** ● *soya **beans***

bear bears, bearing, bore, borne
NOUN **1** a large, strong, wild mammal with thick fur and sharp claws • *polar* **bear** • *grizzly* **bear**
VERB **2** If someone or something **bears** something, they carry it or support its weight. • *The ice wasn't thick enough to* **bear** *their weight.*
VERB **3** If something **bears** a mark or typical feature, it has it. • *The room* **bore** *all the signs of a violent struggle.*
VERB **4** If you **bear** something difficult, you accept it and are able to deal with it. • *The loneliness was hard to* **bear**.

beard beards
NOUN the hair that grows on the lower part of a man's face

bearing bearings
NOUN **Bearings** are used to work out the position of things or places by measuring the angle of the item, sometimes using a compass.

beast beasts
NOUN **1** an old-fashioned word for a large, wild animal
NOUN **2** (*informal*) If you call someone a **beast**, you mean that they are cruel or spiteful.

beat beats, beating, beat, beaten
VERB **1** If someone or something **beats** someone or something else, they hit them hard and repeatedly. • *The rain was* **beating** *against the window.*
VERB **2** If you **beat** someone in a race or game, you defeat them or do better than them.
VERB **3** When your heart **beats**, it pumps blood with a regular rhythm.
NOUN **4** the main pulse of a piece of music or poetry

beautiful
ADJECTIVE very attractive or pleasing
SYNONYM: lovely

beauty beauties
NOUN **1** the quality of being beautiful • *the* **beauty** *of the stars on a clear night*
NOUN **2** The **beauty** of an idea or a plan is what makes it attractive or worth doing. • *The* **beauty** *of going in September is that the sea will be warmer for swimming.*

beaver beavers
NOUN a mammal with a big, flat tail and webbed hind feet. **Beavers** build dams.

because
CONJUNCTION **1 Because** is used with other words to give the reason for something. • *I went home* **because** *I was tired.*
PHRASE **2 Because of** is used with a noun that gives the reason for something. • *I had to stay late* **because of** *detention.*

beckon beckons, beckoning, beckoned
VERB If you **beckon** to someone, you make a sign to them with your hand, asking them to come to you.

become becomes, becoming, became, become
VERB If someone or something **becomes** something else, they start feeling or being that thing. • *I* **became** *more and more angry.*

WORD HISTORY
from Old English *becuman* meaning to happen

bed beds
NOUN **1** a piece of furniture that you lie on when you sleep
NOUN **2** an area of ground in a garden which has been dug and prepared for planting
NOUN **3** The **bed** of the sea or a river is the bottom of it.

bedraggled
ADJECTIVE If a person or animal is **bedraggled**, they are wet, dirty and messy.

bedroom bedrooms
NOUN a room for sleeping in

bedtime bedtimes
NOUN the time when you go to bed

bee bees
NOUN a winged insect, some species of which make honey. Many types of **bee** live in large groups.

beech beeches
NOUN a tree with a smooth, grey trunk and shiny leaves

beef
NOUN the meat of a cow, bull or ox

beehive beehives
NOUN a specially designed structure in which bees are kept so that their honey can be collected

a
b
c
d
e
f
g
h
i
j
k
l
m
n
o
p
q
r
s
t
u
v
w
x
y
z

37

been
VERB the past participle of **be**

beer **beers**
NOUN an alcoholic drink made from malt and flavoured with hops

beetle **beetles**
NOUN a flying insect with hard wing cases that cover its body when it is not flying

---

WORD HISTORY
from Old English *bitan* meaning to bite

---

beetroot **beetroots**
NOUN a round, dark red root vegetable

before
PREPOSITION **1** If something happens **before** something else, it happens earlier than that. • *Annie was born a few minutes **before** midnight.*

ANTONYM: after

CONJUNCTION **2** used to show that something happens before something else • *Can I see you **before** you go?*

ANTONYM: after

ADVERB **3** If you have done something **before**, you have done it at an earlier time. • *I have been here **before**.*

beg **begs, begging, begged**
VERB **1** When people **beg**, they ask for food or money, because they are very poor.
VERB **2** If you **beg** someone to do something, you ask them very anxiously to do it. • *David **begged** his dad to take him to the cinema.*

began
VERB the past tense of **begin**

begin **begins, beginning, began, begun**
VERB If you **begin** something, you start it.

beginner **beginners**
NOUN someone who has just started to learn something

SYNONYM: learner

beginning **beginnings**
NOUN The **beginning** of something is when or where it starts.

begun
VERB the past participle of **begin**

behalf
PHRASE If you do something **on behalf of** someone or something, you do it for them or in their name. • *We did the sponsored swim **on behalf of** various charities.*

behave **behaves, behaving, behaved**
VERB **1** If you **behave** in a particular way, you act in that way. • *He knew that he'd **behaved** badly.*
VERB **2** If you **behave** yourself, you act correctly or properly.

behind
PREPOSITION **1** at the back of • *The moon disappeared **behind** a cloud.*
PREPOSITION **2** supporting someone • *The whole school was **behind** him in the competition.*
ADVERB **3** If you stay **behind**, you remain after other people have gone.
ADVERB **4** If you leave something **behind**, you do not take it with you.

beige
ADJECTIVE having a cream-brown colour

being
VERB the present participle of **be**

belch **belches, belching, belched**
VERB **1** If you **belch**, you make a sudden noise in your throat because air has risen up from your stomach.
VERB **2** If something **belches** smoke or fire, it sends it out in large amounts. • *Smoke **belched** from the factory chimneys.*
NOUN **3** the noise you make when you belch

belief **beliefs**
NOUN If you have a **belief** in something, you are certain that it is right or true.

believe **believes, believing, believed**
VERB **1** If you **believe** that something is true, you think that it is true.
VERB **2** If you **believe** someone, you accept that they are telling the truth.

bell **bells**
NOUN **1** a cup-shaped metal object with a piece inside it called a clapper that hits the side and makes a ringing sound
NOUN **2** an electrical device that you can ring or buzz to get attention

bellow **bellows, bellowing, bellowed**
VERB If a human or other animal **bellows**, they shout very loudly or make a very loud, deep noise like a roar.

belly **bellies**
NOUN the part of a human or other animal's body, especially the stomach, that holds and digests food

→ Have a look at the illustration for **bird**

belong **belongs, belonging, belonged**

VERB **1** If something **belongs** to you, it is yours and you own it.

VERB **2** If you **belong** to a group, you are a member of it.

VERB **3** If something **belongs** in a particular place, that is where it should be. • *That book belongs on the top shelf.*

belongings

PLURAL NOUN Your **belongings** are all the things that you own.

below

PREPOSITION **1** If something is **below** something else, it is in a lower position.
• *We could hear music coming up from the flat two floors below ours.*

ANTONYM: above

PREPOSITION **2** If something is **below** a particular amount or level, it is less than it.
• *below average rainfall*

ANTONYM: above

belt **belts**

NOUN a strip of leather or cloth that you fasten round your waist to hold your trousers or skirt up

bench **benches**

NOUN a long seat that two or more people can sit on

bend **bends, bending, bent**

VERB **1** When you **bend** something, you use force to make it curved or angular.

VERB **2** When you **bend**, you move your head and shoulders forwards and downwards.
• *I bent over to pick up my glasses.*

NOUN **3** a curved part of something • *a bend in the road*

beneath

PREPOSITION (*formal*) underneath • *There is a car park beneath the shopping centre.*

benefit **benefits, benefiting, benefited**

NOUN **1** the advantage that something brings to people • *the benefit of a good education*

VERB **2** If you **benefit** from something, it helps you. • *He'll benefit from some extra tuition.*

WORD HISTORY
from Latin *benefactum* meaning good deed

bent

ADJECTIVE curved or twisted out of shape

bereaved

ADJECTIVE (*formal*) You say that someone is **bereaved** when a close relative of theirs has recently died.

bereavement **bereavements**

NOUN (*formal*) **Bereavement** is when a close relative has recently died.

berry **berries**

NOUN a small, round fruit that grows on bushes or trees

berserk

ADVERB If somebody goes **berserk**, they lose control of themselves and become extremely violent.

WORD HISTORY
from Icelandic *berserkr* meaning a Viking who wore a shirt made from the skin of a bear and who worked himself into a mad frenzy before going into battle

berth **berths**

NOUN **1** a space in a harbour where a ship stays when it is being loaded or unloaded

NOUN **2** In a boat or caravan, a **berth** is a bed.

PHRASE **3** If you give someone or something **a wide berth**, you avoid them because they are unpleasant or dangerous.

beside

PREPOSITION If one thing is **beside** another thing, it is next to it.

besides

ADVERB also or in addition to • *The trip is far too expensive. Besides, I don't want to go away for two days.*

best

ADJECTIVE **1** the superlative of *good* • *That was one of the best films I've ever seen.*

ANTONYM: worst

ADVERB **2** the superlative of *good* or *well*
• *I did best in maths in my class.*

ANTONYM: worst

ADVERB **3** The thing that you like **best** is the thing that you prefer to everything else.

a
b
c
d
e
f
g
h
i
j
k
l
m
n
o
p
q
r
s
t
u
v
w
x
y
z

bet bets, betting, bet
VERB **1** If you **bet** on the result of an event, you will win money if what you bet on happens, and lose money if it does not.
VERB **2** If you say that you **bet** something happens or is the case, you mean you are sure of it • *I bet you were good at sports when you were at school.*

betray betrays, betraying, betrayed
VERB If you **betray** someone who trusts you, you tell people something secret about them.

better
ADJECTIVE **1** the comparative of *good* • *This book is **better** than her last one.*

ANTONYM: worse

ADJECTIVE **2** If you are **better** after an illness, you are no longer ill.

SYNONYM: cured

ADVERB **3** the comparative of *well* • *I am feeling **better** today.*

ANTONYM: worse

between
PREPOSITION **1** If something is **between** two other things, it is situated or happens in the space or time that separates them. • *He was head teacher **between** 1989 and 2000.*
PREPOSITION **2** A relationship or a difference **between** two people or two things is one that involves them both. • *the difference **between** frogs and toads*

beware
VERB If you tell someone to **beware** of something, you are warning them that it might be dangerous or harmful.

bewilder bewilders, bewildering, bewildered
VERB If something **bewilders** you, it confuses and muddles you so that you can't understand.

bewilderment
NOUN a feeling of being confused, muddled and not able to understand something

beyond
PREPOSITION **1** If something is **beyond** a certain place, it is on the other side of it. • ***Beyond** the mountains was the secret valley.*
PREPOSITION **2** If something is **beyond** you, you cannot do it or understand it.

bi-
PREFIX added to a word to mean two or twice. For example, someone who is **bi**lingual can speak two languages.

bib bibs
NOUN a piece of cloth or plastic put under a baby's chin to protect its clothes from stains

Bible Bibles
NOUN the sacred book of the Christian religion • *I read about Noah and the Ark in the **Bible**.*

bibliography bibliographies
NOUN a list of books or articles

bicycle bicycles
NOUN a two-wheeled vehicle that you ride by pushing two pedals with your feet

→ Have a look at the illustration

bid bids, bidding, bid
VERB If you **bid** for something, you offer to buy it for a certain sum of money. • *He **bid** for an old bike at the auction.*

big bigger, biggest
ADJECTIVE large or important

ANTONYMS: small, tiny, little

bike bikes
NOUN an abbreviation for *bicycle*

bikini bikinis
NOUN a small, two-piece swimming costume worn by women

bilingual
ADJECTIVE involving or using two languages • ***bilingual** street signs*

WORD HISTORY
from Latin *bis* meaning two and *lingua* meaning tongue

bill bills
NOUN **1** a written statement of how much is owed for goods or services • *a phone **bill***
NOUN **2** a formal statement of a proposed new law that is discussed and then voted on in Parliament
NOUN **3** A **bill** can be a piece of paper money. • *a dollar **bill***
NOUN **4** A bird's **bill** is its beak.

billiards
NOUN a game in which a long stick called a cue is used to move balls on a table

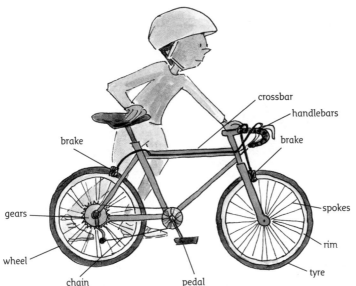

crossbar
handlebars
brake
brake
spokes
gears
rim
wheel
tyre
chain
pedal

bicycle

billion **billions**

NOUN a thousand million. You can write one **billion** like this: 1,000,000,000.

billow **billows, billowing, billowed**

VERB **1** When things made of cloth **billow**, they swell out and flap slowly in the wind.
• *The sails **billowed** in the light breeze.*
VERB **2** When smoke or cloud **billows**, it spreads upwards and outwards.

billy goat **billy goats**

NOUN a male goat

bin **bins**

NOUN a container, especially one that you put rubbish in

binary

ADJECTIVE The **binary** system is a number system used when working with computers. It uses only two digits, 0 and 1.

bind **binds, binding, bound**

VERB **1** If you **bind** something, you tie rope or string round it so that it is held firmly.
VERB **2** If you **bind** a wound, you wrap bandages round it.
VERB **3** When a book is **bound**, the pages are joined together and a cover is put on.

bingo

NOUN a game in which players aim to match the numbers that someone calls out with the numbers on the card they have been given

binoculars

PLURAL NOUN an instrument with lenses for both eyes, which you look through in order to see objects far away • *They used **binoculars** for bird watching.*

biodegradable

ADJECTIVE **Biodegradable** materials can be broken down naturally, and so they are not dangerous to the environment.

biography **biographies**

NOUN the history of someone's life, written by someone else • *a **biography** of the late prime minister*

biology

NOUN the study of living things

WORD HISTORY
from Greek *bios* + *logos* meaning life study

birch **birches**

NOUN a tall, deciduous tree with thin branches and thin bark

41

bird birds

NOUN an egg-laying animal with feathers, two wings, two legs and a beak

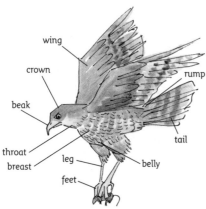

wing

crown

rump

beak

throat

breast

leg

feet

belly

tail

birth births

NOUN Your **birth** was when you were born.

birthday birthdays

NOUN Your **birthday** is the anniversary of the date on which you were born.

birthmark birthmarks

NOUN a mark on your skin that has been there since you were born

biscuit biscuits

NOUN a small, flat cake that is crisp and usually sweet

bisect bisects, bisecting, bisected

VERB to divide a line or an area in half

bishop bishops

NOUN a high-ranking clergyman in some Christian Churches

bison

NOUN a large, hairy animal, related to cattle, with a large head and shoulders. **Bison** used to be very common on the prairies in North America, but they are now almost extinct.

bit bits

VERB **1** the past tense of **bite** • She **bit** into the toast.

NOUN **2** A **bit** of something is a small amount of it.

PHRASE **3** (informal) A **bit** means slightly or to a small extent. • That's **a bit** difficult.

bitch bitches

NOUN a female dog

bite bites, biting, bit, bitten

VERB If you **bite** something, you cut into it with your teeth.

bitter bitterest

ADJECTIVE **1** A **bitter** taste is sharp and unpleasant.

ADJECTIVE **2** A **bitter** wind is extremely cold.

ADJECTIVE **3** If you are **bitter** about something, you feel angry and resentful.

bizarre

ADJECTIVE very strange and weird

SYNONYMS: odd, peculiar

black blacker, blackest

NOUN **1** the darkest possible colour, like the sky at night when there is no light

ADJECTIVE **2** having the darkest possible colour

blackberry blackberries

NOUN a small, soft black fruit that grows on brambles

blackbird blackbirds

NOUN a common European bird, the male of which has black feathers and a yellow beak

blackboard blackboards

NOUN a dark-coloured board which people can write on using chalk

blackcurrant blackcurrants

NOUN **Blackcurrants** are very small, dark, purple fruits that grow in bunches on bushes.

black hole black holes

NOUN the empty space made by the collapse of a star

blacksmith blacksmiths

NOUN a person whose job is making things out of metal, and making and fitting horseshoes

bladder bladders

NOUN the part of your body where urine is held until it leaves your body

blade blades

NOUN **1** the sharp part of a knife, axe or saw

NOUN **2** a single piece of grass

NOUN **3** the long, flat parts that turn round on a windmill, fan or propeller

→ Have a look at the illustration for **turbine**

A B C D E F G H I J K L M N O P Q R S T U V W X Y Z

blame blames, blaming, blamed
VERB If someone **blames** a person for something bad that has happened, they believe that person caused it.

SYNONYM: accuse

blank blanker, blankest
ADJECTIVE **1** Something that is **blank** has nothing on it. • *a blank sheet of paper*
ADJECTIVE **2** If you look **blank**, your face shows no feeling or interest.

blanket blankets
NOUN a large rectangle of thick cloth that is put on a bed to keep people warm

WORD HISTORY
from Old French *blancquete* meaning little white thing

blare blares, blaring, blared
VERB to make a loud, unpleasant noise
• *The radio blared from the flat below.*

blast blasts, blasting, blasted
VERB **1** When people **blast** a hole in something, they make a hole with an explosion. • *They're using dynamite to blast away rocks.*
NOUN **2** a big explosion, especially one caused by a bomb

blaze blazes, blazing, blazed
NOUN **1** a large, hot fire
VERB **2** If something **blazes**, it burns or shines brightly. • *The fire blazed in the fireplace.*

blazer blazers
NOUN a kind of jacket, often in the colours of a school or sports team

bleach bleaches, bleaching, bleached
NOUN **1** a chemical that is used to make material white or to clean thoroughly and kill germs
VERB **2** If you **bleach** material or hair, you make it white, usually by using a chemical.

bleak bleaker, bleakest
ADJECTIVE **1** If a place is **bleak**, it is cold, bare and exposed to the wind. • *a bleak mountain top*
ADJECTIVE **2** If a situation is **bleak**, it is bad and seems unlikely to improve.

bleat bleats, bleating, bleated
VERB When sheep or goats **bleat**, they make a high-pitched cry.

bleed bleeds, bleeding, bled
VERB When you **bleed**, you lose blood as a result of an injury. • *My hand bled a lot after I cut it.*

blend blends, blending, blended
VERB **1** When you **blend** substances, you mix them together to form a single substance.
• *Blend the butter with the sugar.*
VERB **2** When colours or sounds **blend**, they combine in a pleasing way.

bless blesses, blessing, blessed or **blest**
VERB When a priest or vicar **blesses** people or things, they ask God to give his protection to them.

WORD HISTORY
from Old English *bloedsian* meaning to sprinkle with sacrificial blood

blew
VERB the past tense of **blow**

blind blinds, blinding, blinded
ADJECTIVE **1** Someone who is **blind** cannot see.
VERB **2** If something **blinds** you, it stops you seeing, either for a short time or permanently.
NOUN **3** a roll of cloth or paper that you pull down over a window to keep out the light

blindfold blindfolds
NOUN a strip of cloth tied over someone's eyes to stop them seeing

blink blinks, blinking, blinked
VERB When you **blink**, you close your eyes quickly for a moment.

bliss
NOUN a state of complete happiness

blister blisters
NOUN a small bubble on your skin containing watery liquid, caused by a burn or rubbing

blizzard blizzards
NOUN a heavy snowstorm with strong winds

bloated
ADJECTIVE Something that is **bloated** is much larger than normal, often because there is a lot of liquid or gas inside it.

a
b
c
d
e
f
g
h
i
j
k
l
m
n
o
p
q
r
s
t
u
v
w
x
y
z

A
B
C
D
E
F
G
H
I
J
K
L
M
N
O
P
Q
R
S
T
U
V
W
X
Y
Z

44

block blocks, blocking, blocked
> NOUN **1** a large building containing flats or offices
> NOUN **2** In a town, a **block** is an area of land with streets on all its sides.
> NOUN **3** a large, rectangular, three-dimensional piece of something • *Elizabeth carves animals from* **blocks** *of wood.*
> VERB **4** If someone or something **blocks** a road or channel, they put something across it so that nothing can get through.
>
> SYNONYM: obstruct

block capitals
> PLURAL NOUN large upper-case letters. THESE ARE BLOCK CAPITALS.

block graph block graphs
> NOUN another name for **bar chart**

blog blogs, blogging, blogged
> NOUN **1** a person's online diary that they put on the internet so that other people can read it
> VERB **2** If you **blog** about something, you write about it in a blog. • *He* **blogs** *about cooking and restaurants.*

blogger bloggers
> NOUN a person who writes an online diary that they put on the internet so that other people can read it

blonde blondes
> ADJECTIVE **1 Blonde** hair is pale yellow in colour. The spelling **blond** is used when referring to men.
> NOUN **2** A **blonde** or **blond** is a person with pale yellow hair.

blood
> NOUN the red liquid that is pumped by the heart round the bodies of human beings and other vertebrates

bloodstream
> NOUN the flow of blood through your body

bloodthirsty
> ADJECTIVE Someone who is **bloodthirsty** enjoys using or watching violence.

bloom blooms, blooming, bloomed
> NOUN **1** a flower on a plant
> VERB **2** When a plant **blooms**, it produces flowers.

blossom blossoms, blossoming, blossomed
> NOUN **1** all the flowers that appear on a tree before the fruit

> VERB **2** When a tree **blossoms**, it produces flowers.

blot blots
> NOUN a mark made by a drop of liquid, especially ink

blouse blouses
> NOUN a light shirt, worn by a girl or a woman

blow blows, blowing, blew, blown
> VERB **1** When the wind **blows**, the air moves.
> VERB **2** If you **blow**, you send a stream of air from your mouth.
> VERB **3** If you **blow** your nose, you force air out of it through your nostrils in order to clear it.
> NOUN **4** If you receive a **blow**, someone or something hits you.

blow up
> > VERB **1** If something **blows up**, it is destroyed by an explosion.
> > VERB **2** If you **blow up** a balloon or a tyre, you fill it with air.

blubber
> NOUN the layer of fat beneath the skin of animals such as whales and seals that protects them from the cold

blue bluer, bluest
> NOUN **1** the colour of the sky on a clear, sunny day
> ADJECTIVE **2** having the colour of the sky on a clear, sunny day

bluebell bluebells
> NOUN a woodland plant with blue, bell-shaped flowers

bluff bluffs, bluffing, bluffed
> NOUN **1** an attempt to make someone believe that you will do something when you do not really intend to do it
> VERB **2** If you are **bluffing**, you are trying to make someone believe that you are in a strong position when you are not.
> NOUN **3** a steep cliff or river bank

WORD HISTORY
from Dutch *bluffen* meaning to boast

blunder blunders, blundering, blundered
> NOUN **1** a silly mistake
> VERB **2** If you **blunder**, you make a silly mistake.

blunt blunter, bluntest
ADJECTIVE **1** A **blunt** object has a rounded point or edge, rather than a sharp one.
● *My pencil was **blunt** so I could not write with it.*
ADJECTIVE **2** If you are **blunt**, you say exactly what you think, without trying to be polite.

SYNONYMS: outspoken, straightforward

blur
NOUN If something is a **blur**, you can't see it clearly. ● *The mountain was a **blur** through the mist.*

blurb blurbs
NOUN the description of a book printed on the back cover

blurt out blurts out, blurting out, blurted out
VERB If you **blurt out** something, you say it suddenly, after trying to keep it a secret.

blush blushes, blushing, blushed
VERB If you **blush**, your face becomes red, because you are embarrassed or ashamed.

WORD HISTORY
from Old English *blyscan* meaning to glow

boa boas
NOUN a large snake that kills its prey by coiling round it and crushing it

boar boars
NOUN **1** a male wild pig
NOUN **2** a male domestic pig used for breeding

board boards, boarding, boarded
NOUN **1** a long, flat piece of wood
NOUN **2** a flat piece of wood, plastic or cardboard, which is used for a particular purpose ● *a chess**board*** ● *a surf**board***
NOUN **3** the group of people who control a company or organisation ● *My mum is on the **board** of governors.*
NOUN **4** the meals provided when you stay in a hotel or guesthouse ● *The price includes full **board**.*
VERB **5** If you **board** a ship or aircraft, you get on it or in it.
PHRASE **6** If you are **on board** a ship or aircraft, you are on it or in it.

LANGUAGE TIP
Do not confuse *board* with *bored*.

boarder boarders
NOUN **1** a pupil who lives at school during term
NOUN **2** a lodger

boast boasts, boasting, boasted
VERB If you **boast**, you talk proudly about what you have or what you can do.

SYNONYM: brag

boat boats
NOUN a small vehicle for travelling across water

body bodies
NOUN **1** Your **body** is all of you, from your head to your feet.
NOUN **2** You can say **body** when you mean just the main part of a human or other animal, not counting head, arms and legs.

bodyguard bodyguards
NOUN a person employed to protect someone

bog bogs
NOUN an area of wet, spongy ground

boil boils, boiling, boiled
VERB **1** When a hot liquid **boils**, or when you **boil** it, it starts to bubble and to give off steam.
VERB **2** When you **boil** food, you cook it in boiling water.

boiler boilers
NOUN a piece of equipment that burns fuel to provide hot water

boiling point
NOUN the temperature at which a liquid starts to change into steam or vapour

boisterous
ADJECTIVE Someone who is **boisterous** is noisy and lively.

SYNONYMS: loud, rowdy

bold bolder, boldest
ADJECTIVE **1** brave or confident ● *He was **bold** enough to ask for her autograph.*
ADJECTIVE **2** clear and noticeable ● *The sign was painted in **bold** colours.*

WORD HISTORY
from Old Norse *ballr* meaning dangerous or terrible

bollard bollards
NOUN a short, thick post used to stop vehicles from entering a road

a
b
c
d
e
f
g
h
i
j
k
l
m
n
o
p
q
r
s
t
u
v
w
x
y
z

bolt bolts, bolting, bolted

NOUN **1** a metal object that screws into a nut and is used to fasten things together

VERB **2** If you **bolt** one thing to another, you fasten them together using a bolt.

• *They **bolted** the chair to the floor.*

VERB **3** If you **bolt** a door or window, you slide a metal bar across in order to fasten it.

bomb bombs, bombing, bombed

NOUN **1** a container filled with material that explodes when it hits something or when it is set off by a timer

VERB **2** If you **bomb** something, you attack it with a bomb.

WORD HISTORY

from Greek *bombos* meaning a booming sound

---

bond bonds

NOUN a close relationship between people

• *the **bond** between mothers and babies*

bone bones

NOUN the hard parts that form the internal framework of a person's or animal's body

bonfire bonfires

NOUN a large fire made outdoors, to burn rubbish or to celebrate something

---

WORD HISTORY

from *bone* + *fire* – bones were used as fuel in the Middle Ages

---

bonnet bonnets

NOUN **1** the metal cover over a car's engine

→ Have a look at the illustration for **car**

NOUN **2** a baby's or woman's hat tied under the chin

bonus bonuses

NOUN **1** an amount of money added to a person's usual pay

NOUN **2** a good thing that you get in addition to something else

bony bonier, boniest

ADJECTIVE **Bony** people or animals are very thin, with not much flesh covering their bones.

book books, booking, booked

NOUN **1** a number of pages held together inside a cover

VERB **2** When you **book** something, you arrange to have it or use it at a particular time. • *Mum **booked** two rooms at the hotel.*

bookcase bookcases

NOUN a piece of furniture where you keep books

booklet booklets

NOUN a thin book with a paper cover

boom booms, booming, boomed

NOUN **1** a deep, echoing sound

NOUN **2** a fast increase in something

• *There has been a **boom** in the sale of sun cream this summer.*

VERB **3** If something **booms**, it makes a loud booming sound. • *We heard the foghorn **boom** in the distance.*

boomerang boomerangs

NOUN a curved, wooden missile that can be thrown so that it returns to the thrower. **Boomerangs** were traditionally used as weapons by Australian Aborigines.

boost boosts, boosting, boosted

VERB If someone **boosts** something, they improve or increase it. • *The teacher **boosted** Juliet's confidence when she praised her story.*

boot boots

NOUN **1** strong shoes that come up over your ankle, and sometimes your calf

NOUN **2** the covered space in a car, usually at the back, for carrying things in

→ Have a look at the illustration for **car**

booth booths

NOUN **1** a small, partly-enclosed area

• *a phone **booth***

NOUN **2** a stall where you can buy things, for example at a market or a fair

border borders

NOUN **1** the dividing line between two countries

NOUN **2** a strip or band round the edge of something

NOUN **3** flower beds round the edges of a garden

borderline borderlines

NOUN If someone or something is on the **borderline**, they are on the division between two different categories.

bore bores, boring, bored

VERB **1** If something **bores** you, you find it dull and uninteresting.

VERB **2** If you **bore** a hole in something, you make it using a tool such as a drill.

VERB **3** the past tense of **bear**

NOUN **4** someone or something that bores you

bored

ADJECTIVE If you are **bored**, you are miserable because you have nothing interesting to do.

LANGUAGE TIP
Do not confuse *bored* with *board*.

boring

ADJECTIVE dull and uninteresting

ANTONYM: interesting

born

VERB When an animal such as a human baby is **born**, it comes out of its mother's body and starts to live.

borrow borrows, borrowing, borrowed
VERB If you **borrow** something that belongs to someone else, they let you have it for a period of time. • *I borrowed a book from my friend.*

boss bosses, bossing, bossed
NOUN **1** Someone's **boss** is the person in charge of the place where they work.
VERB **2** If someone **bosses** you, they keep telling you what to do.

bossy bossier, bossiest
ADJECTIVE If you are **bossy**, you like to order other people around.

botany
NOUN the study and classification of plants

both
ADJECTIVE **1 Both** is used to refer to two things or two people. • *Stand up straight with both arms at your sides.*
PRONOUN **2 Both** is used when saying something about two things or two people. • *You can both come to my party.*

bother bothers, bothering, bothered
VERB **1** If you don't **bother** to do something, you don't do it because it takes too much effort or it's not important.
VERB **2** If something **bothers** you, you are worried about it.
VERB **3** If you are not **bothered** about something, you don't care about it.
VERB **4** If you **bother** someone, you interrupt them when they are busy.
NOUN **5** trouble, fuss or difficulty • *Mum's having a bit of bother with the car.*

bottle bottles, bottling, bottled
NOUN **1** a glass or plastic container for keeping liquids in
VERB **2** If you **bottle** something, you put it in a bottle to store it.

bottom bottoms
NOUN **1** the lowest part of something • *It sank to the bottom of the pond.*
NOUN **2** Your **bottom** is the part of your body that you sit on.

bottomless
ADJECTIVE If something is **bottomless**, it has no bottom or it is very deep.

bough boughs
NOUN a large branch of a tree

PRONUNCIATION TIP
This word rhymes with "cow".

bought
VERB the past tense and past participle of **buy**

LANGUAGE TIP
Do not confuse *bought* with *brought*.

boulder boulders
NOUN a large, rounded rock

bounce bounces, bouncing, bounced
VERB When an object **bounces**, it springs back from something after hitting it. • *The ball bounced high off the ground.*

bound bounds, bounding, bounded
ADJECTIVE **1** If you say that something is **bound** to happen, you mean that it is certain to happen. • *He's bound to find out.*
NOUN **2** a large leap
VERB **3** When humans or other animals **bound**, they move quickly with large leaps.

boundary boundaries
NOUN the limit of an area

bouquet bouquets
NOUN an attractively arranged bunch of flowers

bout bouts
NOUN **1** something that lasts for a short period of time • *I had a bout of flu.*
NOUN **2** a boxing or wrestling match

boutique boutiques
NOUN a small shop that sells fashionable clothes

A
B
C
D
E
F
G
H
I
J
K
L
M
N
O
P
Q
R
S
T
U
V
W
X
Y
Z

bow **bows, bowing, bowed**

VERB **1** When you **bow**, you bend your body or lower your head as a sign of respect or greeting.

NOUN **2** the movement you make when you bow

NOUN **3** the front part of a ship

→ Have a look at the illustration for **ship**

NOUN **4** a knot with two loops and two loose ends • *The ribbon was tied in a **bow**.*

NOUN **5** a long, thin piece of wood with horsehair strings stretched along it, used to play some stringed instruments, such as the violin and the cello

NOUN **6** a long, flexible piece of wood used for shooting arrows

PRONUNCIATION TIP

Meanings 1, 2 and 3 rhyme with "now".
Meanings 4, 5 and 6 rhyme with "low".

bowel **bowels**

NOUN the tubes leading from your stomach, through which waste passes before it leaves your body

WORD HISTORY

from Latin *botellus* meaning little sausage

bowl **bowls, bowling, bowled**

NOUN **1** a round container with a wide, uncovered top, used for holding liquid or for serving food • *a **bowl** of soup*

NOUN **2** the hollow, rounded part of something • *a toilet **bowl***

VERB **3** When you **bowl** in cricket and rounders, you throw the ball towards the batsman.

bowling

NOUN a game in which you roll a heavy ball down a narrow track towards a set of wooden objects called pins, and try to knock them down

bowls

NOUN a game in which the players try to roll large wooden balls as near as possible to a small ball

box **boxes, boxing, boxed**

NOUN **1** a container with a firm base and sides, and usually a lid

VERB **2** If someone **boxes**, they fight according to special rules.

boxer **boxers**

NOUN **1** a person who boxes

NOUN **2** a medium-sized, smooth-haired dog with a flat face

Boxing Day

NOUN the day after Christmas Day

boy **boys**

NOUN a male child

boyfriend **boyfriends**

NOUN Someone's **boyfriend** is the man or boy with whom they are having a romantic relationship.

bra **bras**

NOUN a piece of underwear worn by a woman to support her breasts

brace **braces, bracing, braced**

NOUN **1** an object fixed to something to straighten or support it • *I wore a **brace** on my teeth for two years.*

PLURAL NOUN **2 Braces** are elastic straps worn over the shoulders to hold trousers up.

VERB **3** If you **brace** yourself, you stiffen your body to steady yourself. • *We **braced** ourselves as the bus went round the corner.*

VERB **4** If you **brace** yourself for something unpleasant, you prepare yourself to deal with it.

bracelet **bracelets**

NOUN a chain or band worn around someone's wrist as an ornament

WORD HISTORY

from Old French *bracel* meaning little arm

bracken

NOUN a plant like a large fern that grows on hills and in woods

bracket **brackets**

NOUN a pair of written marks, ( ), { } or [ ], placed round a word or sentence that is not part of the main text, or to show that the items inside the **brackets** belong together

brag **brags, bragging, bragged**

VERB If you **brag**, you boast about something.

Braille

NOUN a system of printing for blind people in which letters are represented by raised dots that can be felt with the fingers

brain brains
NOUN the organ inside your head that controls your body and enables you to think and feel
→ Have a look at the illustration for **organ**

brainstorm brainstorms
NOUN **1** a clever idea that you think of suddenly
NOUN **2** If you have a **brainstorm**, you become confused and cannot think clearly.

brainy brainier, brainiest
ADJECTIVE clever and good at learning things

brake brakes, braking, braked
NOUN **1** a device for making a vehicle stop or slow down
→ Have a look at the illustration for **bicycle**
VERB **2** When drivers **brake**, they make a vehicle stop or slow down by using its brakes.

bramble brambles
NOUN a wild, trailing bush with thorns, which produces blackberries

branch branches, branching, branched
NOUN **1** part of a tree that grows out from the trunk
NOUN **2** A **branch** of a business or organisation is one of its offices or shops.
VERB **3** A road that **branches** off from another road splits off from it to lead in a different direction.

brand brands
NOUN a particular kind or make of something

brandy
NOUN a strong, alcoholic drink, often drunk after a meal

WORD HISTORY
from Dutch *brandewijn* meaning burnt wine

brass
NOUN **1** a yellow-coloured metal made from copper and zinc
ADJECTIVE **2 Brass** instruments are musical instruments such as trumpets and trombones, made of metal.

brave braver, bravest; braves, braving, braved
ADJECTIVE **1** A **brave** person is willing to do dangerous things and does not show any fear.

SYNONYMS: courageous, daring

VERB **2** If you **brave** an unpleasant or dangerous situation, you face up to it in order to do something. ● *We **braved** the snow to go to the party.*

WORD HISTORY
from Italian *bravo* meaning courageous or wild

brawl brawls, brawling, brawled
NOUN **1** a rough fight
VERB **2** When people **brawl**, they take part in a rough fight.

bread
NOUN a very common food made from flour, and baked in an oven

breadth breadths
NOUN the distance between two sides of something ● *I can swim the **breadth** of the pool.*

break breaks, breaking, broke, broken
VERB **1** When an object **breaks**, or when you **break** it, it becomes damaged or separates into pieces.
VERB **2** If you **break** a rule or promise, you fail to keep it.
VERB **3** To **break** a record means to do better than the previous recorded best. ● *She **broke** the record for the long jump.*
NOUN **4** a short period during which you rest or do something different
break down
VERB When a machine or a vehicle **breaks down**, it stops working.
break up
VERB When schools **break up**, the term ends. ● *We **break up** on Thursday.*

breakable
ADJECTIVE easy to break

breakdown breakdowns
NOUN If there is a **breakdown** in a system, it stops working.

breakfast breakfasts
NOUN the first meal of the day

breast breasts
NOUN A woman's **breasts** are the two soft, fleshy parts on her chest, which produce milk after she has had a baby.

49

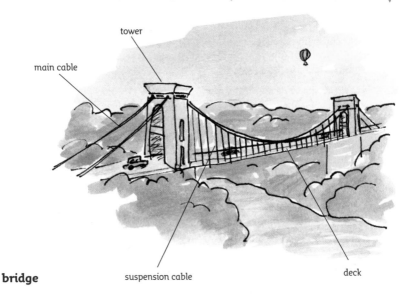

tower

main cable

suspension cable

deck

bridge

breast-feed breast-feeds, breast-feeding, breast-fed
VERB If a woman **breast-feeds** her baby, she feeds it with milk from her breasts.

breath breaths
NOUN **1** the air you take into your lungs and let out again when you breathe ● *He took a deep breath before jumping into the pool.*
PHRASE **2** If you are **out of breath**, you are breathing with difficulty after doing something energetic.

breathe breathes, breathing, breathed
VERB When you **breathe**, you take air into your lungs and let it out again.

breathless
ADJECTIVE If you are **breathless**, you are breathing very fast or with difficulty.

breed breeds, breeding, bred
NOUN **1** a particular type of animal. For example, an Alsatian is a **breed** of dog.
VERB **2** Someone who **breeds** animals or plants keeps them in order to produce more animals or plants with particular qualities.
VERB **3** When animals **breed**, they produce young.

SYNONYM: reproduce

breeze breezes
NOUN a gentle wind

breezy breezier, breeziest
ADJECTIVE If the weather is **breezy**, there is a gentle wind.

brewery breweries
NOUN a place where beer is made, or a company that makes beer

bribe bribes, bribing, bribed
NOUN **1** a gift or money given to someone to persuade them to allow you to do something
VERB **2** If someone **bribes** someone else, they give them a bribe.

brick bricks
NOUN a rectangular block of baked clay used in building

bride brides
NOUN a woman who is getting married or who has just got married

bridegroom bridegrooms
NOUN a man who is getting married or who has just got married

bridesmaid bridesmaids
NOUN a woman or girl who helps a bride on her wedding day

bridge bridges
NOUN **1** a structure built over a river, road or railway so that vehicles and people can cross
NOUN **2** a card game for four players

bridle bridles
NOUN a set of straps round a horse's head and mouth, which the rider uses to control the horse

brief briefer, briefest; briefs, briefing, briefed
ADJECTIVE **1** Something that is **brief** lasts only a short time. • We only had time for a **brief** visit.
VERB **2** When you **brief** someone on a task, you give them all the necessary instructions or information about it.

briefcase briefcases
NOUN a small, flat case for carrying papers

bright brighter, brightest
ADJECTIVE **1** strong and startling • a **bright** light

SYNONYMS: brilliant, dazzling

ADJECTIVE **2** clever • That's a **bright** idea.

SYNONYMS: intelligent, quick

brighten brightens, brightening, brightened
VERB If something **brightens**, it becomes brighter.
brighten up
VERB If you **brighten up** something, you make it look brighter and more attractive.

brilliant
ADJECTIVE **1** A **brilliant** person is extremely clever.
ADJECTIVE **2** (informal) Something that is **brilliant** is extremely good or enjoyable.
ADJECTIVE **3** A **brilliant** colour or light is extremely bright.

brim brims
NOUN **1** the wide part of a hat that sticks outwards from the head
NOUN **2** If a container is filled to the **brim**, it is filled right to the top.

bring brings, bringing, brought
VERB If you **bring** something or someone with you when you go to a place, you take them with you.
bring up
VERB When someone **brings up** children, they look after them while they grow up.

brink
NOUN **1** the edge of a deep hole, cliff or ravine
PHRASE **2** If you are **on the brink** of something, you are about to do it. • They were **on the brink** of discovering a cure for the common cold.

brisk brisker, briskest
ADJECTIVE **1** quick and energetic • a **brisk** walk
ADJECTIVE **2** If someone's manner is **brisk**, it shows that they want to get things done quickly and efficiently.

bristle bristles, bristling, bristled
NOUN **1** **Bristles** are strong animal hairs used to make brushes.
VERB **2** If the hairs on an animal's body **bristle**, they rise up because it is frightened.

bristly bristlier, bristliest
ADJECTIVE Something that is **bristly** is covered with or has short, stiff hairs. • a **bristly** moustache

brittle
ADJECTIVE An object that is **brittle** is hard but breaks easily.

broad broader, broadest
ADJECTIVE **1** A **broad** river is wide.
ADJECTIVE **2** The **broad** outline of a story gives the main points, but no details.

broadband
NOUN **Broadband** is a type of very fast internet connection that allows many messages to be sent at the same time. • What is the **broadband** speed like here?

broadcast broadcasts, broadcasting, broadcast
NOUN **1** a programme or announcement on radio or television
VERB **2** When someone **broadcasts** something, they send it out by radio waves, so that it can be seen on television or heard on radio.

broadsheet broadsheets
NOUN a newspaper that is usually printed on large sheets of paper, and which is considered to be more serious than some other newspapers

A
B
C
D
E
F
G
H
I
J
K
L
M
N
O
P
Q
R
S
T
U
V
W
X
Y
Z

broccoli
NOUN a vegetable with green stalks and green or purple flower buds

brochure brochures
NOUN a booklet that gives information about a product or a service • holiday **brochure**

broke
VERB **1** the past tense of **break**
ADJECTIVE **2** (informal) If you are **broke**, you have no money.

broken
ADJECTIVE A **broken** object is damaged in some way.

bronchitis
NOUN an illness in which the tubes connecting your windpipe to your lungs become infected, making you cough

bronze
NOUN a yellowish-brown metal that is a mixture of copper and tin

brooch brooches
NOUN a piece of jewellery with a pin at the back for attaching to clothes

---
PRONUNCIATION TIP
This word rhymes with "coach".

---

brood broods, brooding, brooded
NOUN **1** a family of baby birds
VERB **2** If you **brood** about something, you are worried about it and can't stop thinking about it.

brook brooks
NOUN a stream

broom brooms
NOUN a long-handled brush

brother brothers
NOUN Your **brother** is a boy or man who has the same parents as you.

brother-in-law brothers-in-law
NOUN Someone's **brother-in-law** is the brother of their husband or wife, or the husband of one of their siblings.

brought
VERB the past tense and past participle of **bring**

LANGUAGE TIP
Do not confuse brought with bought.

---

brown browner, brownest
NOUN **1** the colour of earth or wood
ADJECTIVE **2** having the colour of earth or wood

Brownie Brownies
NOUN a junior member of the Girl Guides

bruise bruises, bruising, bruised
NOUN **1** a purple mark that appears on your skin after something has hit it
VERB **2** If something **bruises** you, it hits you so that a bruise appears on your skin.

brunette brunettes
NOUN a girl or a woman with dark brown hair

brush brushes, brushing, brushed
NOUN **1** an object with bristles. There are **brushes** for cleaning things, painting or tidying your hair.
VERB **2** If you **brush** something, you clean it or tidy it with a brush.

Brussels sprout Brussels sprouts
NOUN a vegetable that looks like a tiny cabbage

brutal
ADJECTIVE **Brutal** behaviour is violent and cruel

brutality
NOUN violent and cruel behaviour

bubble bubbles, bubbling, bubbled
NOUN **1** a ball of air in a liquid
VERB **2** When a liquid **bubbles**, bubbles form in it.

buck bucks, bucking, bucked
NOUN **1** the male of various animals, including deer and rabbits
VERB **2** If a horse **bucks**, it jumps into the air with all four feet off the ground.

bucket buckets
NOUN a deep, round container with an open top and a handle

buckle buckles, buckling, buckled
NOUN **1** a fastening on the end of a belt or strap
VERB **2** If you **buckle** a belt or strap, you fasten it.
VERB **3** If metal **buckles**, it crumples up.

bud buds
NOUN a small, tight swelling on a tree or plant, which develops into a flower or leaf

Buddhism
NOUN a religion based on the teachings of Buddha, who taught in India in the fifth century. In **Buddhism**, people believe that the way to end suffering is by overcoming our desires.

Buddhist Buddhists
NOUN a person whose religion is Buddhism

budgerigar budgerigars
NOUN a small, brightly-coloured pet bird. **Budgerigars** originated in Australia.

WORD HISTORY
an Australian Aboriginal name, from *budgeri* + *gar* meaning good cockatoo

budget budgets, budgeting, budgeted
NOUN 1 a plan showing how much money will be available and how it will be spent
VERB 2 If you **budget** for something, you plan how you use your money carefully, so as to be able to afford what you want.

buffalo buffaloes
NOUN 1 a wild animal like a large cow with long curved horns
NOUN 2 another word for **bison**

buffet buffets
NOUN 1 a café at a station or on a train
NOUN 2 a meal at which people serve themselves

bug bugs, bugging, bugged
NOUN 1 a small insect, especially one that causes damage
NOUN 2 an infection or virus that makes you ill
NOUN 3 a small error in a computer programme that stops it working properly
VERB 4 If a place is **bugged**, tiny microphones are hidden there to pick up what people are saying.

bugle bugles
NOUN a simple brass musical instrument that looks like a small trumpet

build builds, building, built
VERB If you **build** something, you make it from all its parts.

builder builders
NOUN a person whose job is to build buildings

building buildings
NOUN a structure with walls and a roof

bulb bulbs
NOUN 1 the glass part of an electric lamp
NOUN 2 an onion-shaped root from which a flower or plant grows. Tulips and daffodils are grown from **bulbs**.

WORD HISTORY
from Greek *bolbos* meaning onion

bulge bulges, bulging, bulged
VERB 1 If something **bulges**, it swells out.
NOUN 2 a lump on a normally flat surface

bulk bulks
NOUN 1 a large mass of something
PHRASE 2 If you buy something **in bulk**, you buy it in large quantities.

bulky bulkier, bulkiest
ADJECTIVE Something that is **bulky** is large and heavy and sometimes difficult to move.

bull bulls
NOUN the male of some animal species including cattle, elephants and whales

bulldozer bulldozers
NOUN a powerful tractor with a broad blade in front, which is used for moving earth or knocking things down

bullet bullets
NOUN a small piece of metal fired from a gun

bulletin bulletins
NOUN a short news report on radio or television

bullion
NOUN gold or silver bars

bullock bullocks
NOUN a young male bull that is reared for meat

bully bullies, bullying, bullied
NOUN 1 someone who tries to hurt or frighten other people, often repeatedly
VERB 2 If someone **bullies** you into doing something, they make you do it by using force or threats.

WORD HISTORY
a sixteenth-century word meaning fine fellow or hired ruffian

bump bumps, bumping, bumped
VERB 1 If you **bump** into something, you knock into it accidentally.
NOUN 2 a soft noise made by something knocking into something else
NOUN 3 a raised, uneven part of a surface

SYNONYMS: bulge, lump

bumper bumpers
NOUN a bar on the front or back of a vehicle that protects it if it bumps into something

a
b
c
d
e
f
g
h
i
j
k
l
m
n
o
p
q
r
s
t
u
v
w
x
y
z

bumpy bumpier, bumpiest
ADJECTIVE Something that is **bumpy** has a rough, uneven surface. • a **bumpy** road

bun buns
NOUN a small, round bread roll or cake

bunch bunches
NOUN a group of things together • a **bunch** of flowers

bundle bundles, bundling, bundled
NOUN 1 a number of things tied together or wrapped up in a cloth
VERB 2 If you **bundle** someone or something somewhere, you push them there quickly and roughly.

bungalow bungalows
NOUN a one-storey house

WORD HISTORY
from Hindi *bangla* meaning house

bunk bunks
NOUN a bed fixed to a wall in a ship or caravan

bunk beds
PLURAL NOUN two beds fixed together, one above the other

buoy buoys
NOUN a floating object anchored to the bottom of the sea, marking a channel or warning of danger

buoyancy
NOUN Something that has **buoyancy** is able to float in liquid or in the air.

buoyant
ADJECTIVE 1 Something that is **buoyant** is able to float.
ADJECTIVE 2 Someone who is **buoyant** is lively and cheerful.

burden burdens
NOUN a heavy load

burger burgers
NOUN a flat fried cake of meat, vegetables or cheese, served in a bread roll

burglar burglars
NOUN someone who breaks into buildings and steals things

burglary burglaries
NOUN the crime of breaking into buildings and stealing things

burgle burgles, burgling, burgled
VERB If a building is **burgled**, someone breaks into it and steals things.

burn burns, burning, burned or **burnt**
VERB 1 If something is **burning**, it is on fire.
VERB 2 To **burn** something means to damage or destroy it with fire.
VERB 3 People often **burn** fuel, such as coal, to keep warm.
NOUN 4 A **burn** is an injury caused by fire or by something hot.

LANGUAGE TIP
You can write either *burned* or *burnt* as the past form of *burn*.

burqa burqas; also spelt **burka**
NOUN a long garment worn by some Muslim women in public, covering everything except the eyes

PRONUNCIATION TIP
This word is pronounced **bur**-ka.

burrow burrows, burrowing, burrowed
NOUN 1 a tunnel or hole in the ground dug by a small animal
VERB 2 When an animal **burrows**, it digs a burrow.

burst bursts, bursting, burst
VERB 1 When something **bursts**, or when you **burst** it, it splits open suddenly.
VERB 2 When you **burst** into a room, you enter suddenly and with force.
NOUN 3 A **burst** of something is a sudden short period of it. • a **burst** of applause

bury buries, burying, buried
VERB 1 If you **bury** something, you put it in a hole in the ground and cover it with earth.
VERB 2 If something is **buried** under something, it is covered by it. • My trainers were **buried** under a pile of clothes.

bus buses
NOUN a large motor vehicle that carries passengers

WORD HISTORY
from Latin *omnibus* meaning for all

bush bushes
NOUN 1 a large plant, smaller than a tree and with a lot of woody branches
NOUN 2 In Australia and South Africa, an uncultivated area outside a town or city is called the **bush**.
NOUN 3 In New Zealand, the **bush** is land covered by rainforest.

bushy bushier, bushiest
ADJECTIVE **Bushy** hair or fur grows very thickly.
• *My dad has **bushy** eyebrows.*

business businesses
NOUN **1** work relating to the buying and selling of goods and services
NOUN **2** an organisation that produces or sells goods, or provides a service

SYNONYMS: company, firm, organization

busker buskers
NOUN someone who sings or plays music in public places for money

bus stop bus stops
NOUN a place where the bus stops regularly for passengers to get on or off, usually marked with a sign

busy busier, busiest
ADJECTIVE **1** If you are **busy**, you are doing something and are not free to do anything else. • *She was too **busy** to come to the cinema with us.*
ADJECTIVE **2** A **busy** place is full of people doing things or moving about.

but
CONJUNCTION **1** used to introduce an idea that is opposite to what has gone before • *I love cooking, **but** I hate washing up afterwards.*
CONJUNCTION **2** used when you apologise for something • *Sorry, **but** I can't come to play tomorrow.*
PREPOSITION **3** except • *There was nothing to eat **but** potatoes.*

butcher butchers
NOUN a shopkeeper who prepares and sells meat

butter
NOUN a soft, fatty food made from cream, which is spread on bread and used in cooking

buttercup buttercups
NOUN a wild plant with bright yellow flowers

butterfly butterflies
NOUN a type of insect with large, colourful wings. **Butterflies** develop from caterpillars.
→ Have a look at the illustration for **life cycle**

buttocks
PLURAL NOUN Your **buttocks** are the part of your body that you sit on.

WORD HISTORY
from Old English *buttuc* meaning rounded slope

button buttons, buttoning, buttoned
NOUN **1** a small, hard round object sewn on to clothing such as shirts • *My new jeans fasten with **buttons** instead of a zip.*
NOUN **2** a small object on a piece of equipment that you press to make it work • *You must push the **button** down to switch the video on.*
VERB **3** If you **button** a garment, you fasten it using its buttons.

buy buys, buying, bought
VERB If you **buy** something, you get it by paying money for it.

buzz buzzes, buzzing, buzzed
VERB If something **buzzes**, it makes a humming sound, like a bee.

buzzer buzzers
NOUN a device that makes a buzzing sound. **Buzzers** are used to attract attention.
• *I pressed the door **buzzer** but nobody was home.*

by
PREPOSITION **1** used to show who or what has done something • *The announcement was made **by** the head teacher.*
PREPOSITION **2** used to show how something is done • *He cheered us up **by** taking us to the cinema.*
PREPOSITION **3** next to or near to • *They live **by** the park.*
PREPOSITION **4** before a particular time • *We should finish **by** tea time.*
PREPOSITION **5** going past • *We drove **by** her house.*
ADVERB **6** past • *They would always say hello as they walked **by**.*

bypass bypasses
NOUN a road that takes traffic around the edge of a town instead of through the middle • *The centre of town is much quieter since they built the **bypass**.*

byte bytes
NOUN a unit of storage in a computer

A
B
C
D
E
F
G
H
I
J
K
L
M
N
O
P
Q
R
S
T
U
V
W
X
Y
Z

cab cabs
NOUN **1** a taxi
NOUN **2** The **cab** is where the driver sits in a lorry, bus or train.

cabbage cabbages
NOUN a large, green, leafy vegetable

cabin cabins
NOUN **1** a room in a ship where a passenger sleeps
NOUN **2** a small wooden house, usually in the country

cabinet cabinets
NOUN **1** a small cupboard • *a medicine* ***cabinet***
NOUN **2** The **cabinet** in a government is a group of ministers who advise the leader and decide policies.

cable cables
NOUN **1** a strong, thick rope or chain

→ Have a look at the illustration for **bridge**

NOUN **2** a bundle of wires with a rubber covering, which carries electricity

cable television
NOUN a television service that comes through underground wires

cactus cacti or cactuses
NOUN a thick, fleshy plant that grows in deserts. **Cactuses** are usually covered in spikes.

cadet cadets
NOUN a young person being trained in the armed forces or police

café cafés
NOUN a place where you can buy light meals and drinks

WORD HISTORY
from the French *café* meaning coffee or coffee house

caffeine; also spelt **caffein**
NOUN a chemical in coffee and tea that makes you more active

cage cages
NOUN a box or room made with bars, in which birds or animals are kept

cake cakes, caking, caked
NOUN **1** a sweet food made from eggs, flour, butter and sugar
NOUN **2** a block of a hard substance such as soap
VERB **3** If something is **caked**, it becomes covered with a solid layer of something else.
• *My shoes were **caked** in mud.*

calamity calamities
NOUN something terrible that happens, causing destruction and misery
• *The earthquake was a terrible **calamity**.*

SYNONYMS: disaster, catastrophe

calcium
NOUN a soft white mineral found in bones and teeth and in some foods. Milk and cheese are good sources of **calcium**.

calculate calculates, calculating, calculated
VERB If you **calculate** something, you work it out, usually by doing some arithmetic.
• *We **calculated** how much money we had raised from the sponsored walk.*

WORD HISTORY
from Latin *calculus* meaning stone or pebble, which the Romans used for counting

calculation calculations
NOUN something that you think about carefully and work out mathematically, or that you do on a machine such as a calculator

calculator calculators
NOUN a small electronic machine used for doing mathematical calculations

calendar calendars
NOUN a chart, usually organised month by month, showing the date of each day in a particular year • *We marked the end of term on the **calendar** in red.*

calf calves
NOUN **1** a young cow
NOUN **2** Your **calves** are the backs of your legs between your knees and ankles.

call calls, calling, called
VERB **1** If you **call** someone or something a particular name, that is their name. ● *I will call my cat Pip.* ● *That type of machine is called a combine harvester.*
VERB **2** If you **call** someone, you phone them.
VERB **3** If you **call** someone, you shout their name loudly.
NOUN **4** A **call** is a shout or a cry. ● *We heard a call for help.*

call off
VERB If something is **called off** it is cancelled. ● *The party was called off.*

call on
VERB If you **call on** someone, you pay them a short visit.

calm calmer, calmest
ADJECTIVE **1** Someone who is **calm** is quiet and does not show any worry or excitement.
ADJECTIVE **2** If the sea is **calm**, the water is not moving very much.

calorie calories
NOUN The amount of energy that food gives you is measured in **calories**.

came
VERB the past tense of **come**

camel camels
NOUN a large mammal with either one or two humps on its back. **Camels** live in hot desert areas and are used for carrying people and things.

camera cameras
NOUN a piece of equipment used for taking photographs or for filming

camouflage camouflages, camouflaging, camouflaged
NOUN **1** a way of avoiding being seen by having the same colour or appearance as the surroundings
VERB **2** To **camouflage** something is to hide it by giving it the same colour or appearance as its surroundings.

camp camps, camping, camped
NOUN **1** a place where people live in tents or stay in tents for a holiday
VERB **2** If you **camp**, you stay in a tent.
NOUN **3** a collection of buildings for soldiers or prisoners

campaign campaigns, campaigning, campaigned
VERB **1** When people **campaign**, they take action in order to achieve something. ● *She campaigned against the export of live animals.*

NOUN **2** a series of actions that a group of people does in order to achieve something ● *Parents began a campaign to save the school from closure.*

camper campers
NOUN someone who is staying in a tent for a holiday

can could; cans
VERB **1** If someone says you **can** do something, you are allowed to do it.
VERB **2** If you **can** do something, you are able to do it. ● *I can say "hello" in French.*
NOUN **3** a metal container, often sealed, with food or drink inside

canal canals
NOUN a long, narrow, man-made stretch of water

canary canaries
NOUN a yellow songbird

cancel cancels, cancelling, cancelled
VERB If you **cancel** something that has been arranged, you stop it from happening. ● *They cancelled the school trip.*

cancer cancers
NOUN a serious disease in which abnormal cells in a part of the body increase rapidly, causing growths

candidate candidates
NOUN a person who is being considered for a job

candle candles
NOUN a stick of hard wax with a piece of string called a wick through the middle. You light the wick to produce a flame.

cane canes
NOUN **1** the long, hollow stem of a plant such as bamboo
NOUN **2** strips of cane used for weaving baskets and other containers
NOUN **3** a long, narrow stick used to support plants

canine canines
ADJECTIVE **1** relating to dogs
NOUN **2** A **canine** is one of the pointed teeth near the front of the mouth in humans and some animals.

→ Have a look at the illustration for **teeth**

cannibal cannibals
NOUN a person who eats human flesh

cannon cannons or cannon

NOUN a large gun, usually on wheels, which fires heavy iron balls

cannot

VERB the same as can not

canoe canoes

NOUN a small, narrow boat that you row using a paddle

can't

VERB a contraction of cannot

canteen canteens

NOUN a place to eat in a school or workplace

canvas canvases

NOUN 1 strong, heavy cloth used for making things such as sails and tents
NOUN 2 a piece of canvas on which an artist does a painting

canyon canyons

NOUN a narrow river valley with steep sides

cap caps

NOUN 1 a soft, flat hat, often with a peak at the front
NOUN 2 a bottle top
NOUN 3 a small explosive used in toy guns

capable

ADJECTIVE 1 If you are **capable** of doing something, you are able to do it.
ADJECTIVE 2 Someone who is **capable** is able to do something well.

capacity capacities

NOUN the maximum amount that something can hold or produce ● The arena has a seating **capacity** of two thousand.

capital capitals

NOUN 1 The **capital** of a country is the city where the government meets. ● Paris is the **capital** of France.

NOUN 2 A **capital**, or a **capital** letter, is a larger, upper-case letter used at the beginning of a sentence or a name: **C**arol, **T**im.

capsize capsizes, capsizing, capsized

VERB If a boat **capsizes**, it turns upside down.

capsule capsules

NOUN 1 a small container with medicine inside, which you swallow
NOUN 2 the part of a spacecraft in which astronauts travel

WORD HISTORY
from Latin capsula meaning little box

captain captains

NOUN 1 the officer in charge of a ship or aeroplane
NOUN 2 the leader of a sports team

caption captions

NOUN a title printed underneath a picture or a photograph

captive captives

NOUN someone who is locked up and kept prisoner

capture captures, capturing, captured

VERB If someone **captures** someone or something, they take them prisoner.

car cars

NOUN 1 a four-wheeled road vehicle with an engine and room to carry a few passengers

→ Have a look at the illustration

NOUN 2 a railway carriage used for a particular purpose ● the buffet **car**

caravan caravans

NOUN 1 a vehicle pulled by a car in which people live or spend their holidays
NOUN 2 a group of people and animals travelling together, usually across a desert

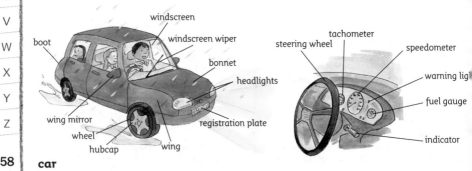

windscreen, windscreen wiper, bonnet, headlights, registration plate, wing, hubcap, wheel, wing mirror, boot, steering wheel, tachometer, speedometer, warning light, fuel gauge, indicator

car

carbohydrate **carbohydrates**
NOUN a substance that gives you energy. It is found in foods like sugar and bread.

carbon
NOUN a chemical found in coal, diamonds and graphite. All living things contain **carbon**.

carbon dioxide
NOUN the gas that human beings and other animals breathe out

carbon footprint **carbon footprints**
NOUN the amount of carbon monoxide produced by a person, company or country

carbon monoxide
NOUN a poisonous gas that is produced especially by the engines of vehicles

card **cards**
NOUN **1** a piece of stiff paper or plastic with a message or information on it ● *birthday* **card** ● *credit* **card**
NOUN **2** When you play **cards**, you play a game using special playing cards.
NOUN **3** strong, stiff paper

cardboard
NOUN thick, stiff paper, which is stronger than card

cardigan **cardigans**
NOUN a knitted jacket that fastens up the front

cardinal
ADJECTIVE A **cardinal** number is a number such as 1, 3, or 10 that tells you how many things there are in a group but not what order they are in.

care **cares, caring, cared**
VERB **1** If you **care** about something or someone, you are concerned about them and interested in them.
VERB **2** If you **care** for a person or an animal, you look after them.
NOUN **3** worry or trouble ● *She didn't have a* **care** *in the world.*
NOUN **4** If you do something with **care**, you concentrate very hard on it so that you don't make mistakes. ● *He wrote the phone number down with great* **care**.
PHRASE **5** If you **take care of** a person or an animal, you look after them. ● *Shakira said she would* **take care of** *the hamsters while we were on holiday.*

career **careers**
NOUN Your **career** is the series of jobs you have in life, often in the same occupation. ● *a teaching* **career**

careful
ADJECTIVE behaving sensibly and with care
> ANTONYM: careless

carefully
ADVERB behaving in a sensible way and with care
> ANTONYM: carelessly

careless
ADJECTIVE not paying attention to what you are doing
> SYNONYMS: slapdash, sloppy
> ANTONYM: careful

carelessly
ADJECTIVE without paying attention to what you are doing
> ANTONYM: carefully

carelessness
NOUN **Carelessness** is when you do not pay attention to what you are doing.
> ANTONYM: carefulness

caretaker **caretakers**
NOUN a person who looks after a large building such as a school

cargo **cargoes**
NOUN goods carried on a ship or plane

Caribbean
NOUN **1** short for the **Caribbean** Sea, which lies between the West Indies and South America
ADJECTIVE **2** to do with the **Caribbean** Sea or the islands in it ● *I love* **Caribbean** *food.*

carnation **carnations**
NOUN a plant with thin leaves and scented white, pink or red flowers

carnival **carnivals**
NOUN a public festival with music, processions and dancing

carnivore **carnivores**
NOUN an animal that eats meat

carnivorous
ADJECTIVE A **carnivorous** animal eats meat.

carol **carols**
NOUN a religious song usually sung at Christmas time

a
b
c
d
e
f
g
h
i
j
k
l
m
n
o
p
q
r
s
t
u
v
w
x
y
z

59

carpenter **carpenters**
NOUN a person who makes and repairs wooden things

carpentry
NOUN the work of making and repairing wooden things

carpet **carpets**
NOUN a thick floor covering usually made of material like wool

carriage **carriages**
NOUN **1** one of the separate sections of a passenger train
NOUN **2** an old-fashioned vehicle for carrying passengers, usually pulled by horses

Carroll diagram **Carroll diagrams**
NOUN a way of sorting and displaying information in the form of a grid

Girls and boys that have black hair

carrot **carrots**
NOUN a long, thin, orange-coloured root vegetable

carry **carries, carrying, carried**
VERB **1** If you **carry** something, you hold it and take it somewhere.
VERB **2** When a vehicle **carries** people, they travel in it.
VERB **3** If people or animals **carry** a germ or a disease, they can pass it on to others.
VERB **4** If a sound **carries** it can be heard a long way off. • *Their voices **carried** across the valley.*

cart **carts**
NOUN a vehicle with wheels, used for carrying things and usually pulled by horses or cattle

carton **cartons**
NOUN a cardboard or plastic container

cartoon **cartoons**
NOUN **1** a humorous drawing in a newspaper comic or magazine
NOUN **2** a film in which all the characters and scenes are drawn

cartridge **cartridges**
NOUN **1** a tube containing a bullet and an explosive substance, used in guns
NOUN **2** a small plastic container filled with ink that you put in a pen or a printer

cartwheel **cartwheels**
NOUN an acrobatic movement in which you lift both arms in the air then throw yourself sideways on to one hand, swinging your body around in a circle with your legs straight until you land on your feet again

carve **carves, carving, carved**
VERB If you **carve** something, you shape it or slice it with a knife.

cascade **cascades, cascading, cascaded**
NOUN **1** a small waterfall or group of waterfalls flowing down a rocky hillside
VERB **2** When water **cascades**, it flows very fast down a hillside or over rocks.

case **cases**
NOUN **1** a box for keeping or carrying things in
NOUN **2** a particular situation or event
• *a bad **case** of measles*
NOUN **3** A crime that the police are investigating is called a **case**.
NOUN **4** If something is written in lower **case** it is written in small letters. If it is written in upper **case**, it is written in capital letters.

cash
NOUN money in notes and coins

cashier **cashiers**
NOUN the person who deals with money in a place such as a shop or a bank

casserole **casseroles**
NOUN **1** a stew made with meat, vegetables or fish that is baked in the oven
NOUN **2** a dish with a lid, which is used for cooking

cast **casts, casting, cast**
NOUN **1** all the people who act in a play or film
NOUN **2** an object made by pouring a liquid such as plaster into a container and leaving it to harden
VERB **3** If an object **casts** a shadow on to a place, it makes a shadow fall there.

castaway castaways

NOUN someone who has been shipwrecked but manages to survive on a lonely shore or an island

castle castles

NOUN a large building with walls or ditches round it to protect it from attack

→ Have a look at the illustration

WORD HISTORY
from Latin *castellum* meaning small fort

casual

ADJECTIVE **1** happening by chance and without planning • *I made a casual remark.*
ADJECTIVE **2** **Casual** clothes are suitable for informal occasions.

casualty casualties

NOUN a person killed or injured in an accident or a war • *There were many **casualties** after the motorway crash.*

cat cats

NOUN a small, furry mammal with whiskers, a tail and sharp claws, often kept as a pet

catalogue catalogues

NOUN a list of things, such as the goods you can buy from a company, the objects in a museum, or the books in a library • *All the products are shown in their new **catalogue**.*

catalyst catalysts

NOUN a substance that causes a chemical reaction to take place more quickly

catastrophe catastrophes

NOUN a terrible disaster

catastrophic

ADJECTIVE Something that is **catastrophic** is extremely bad and causes a lot of damage, suffering or problems. • *catastrophic floods*

catch catches, catching, caught

VERB **1** If you **catch** an object that is moving through the air, you grasp it with your hands.
VERB **2** If you **catch** a person or animal, you capture them. • *The police **caught** the thief.*
VERB **3** If you **catch** a bus, train or plane, you get on it and travel somewhere.
VERB **4** If you **catch** a cold or a disease, you become ill with it.
NOUN **5** a hook that fastens or locks a door or window

catching

ADJECTIVE If a disease or illness is **catching**, it spreads very quickly. • *Measles is **catching**.*

catchy catchier, catchiest

ADJECTIVE Something that is **catchy**, such as a tune, is pleasant and easy to remember.

category categories

NOUN a group of things that have something in common

caterpillar caterpillars

NOUN the larva of a butterfly or moth. **Caterpillars** look like small, coloured worms and feed on plants.

→ Have a look at the illustration for **life cycle**

cathedral cathedrals

NOUN an important church with a bishop in charge of it • *Canterbury **Cathedral***

a
b
c
d
e
f
g
h
i
j
k
l
m
n
o
p
q
r
s
t
u
v
w
x
y
z

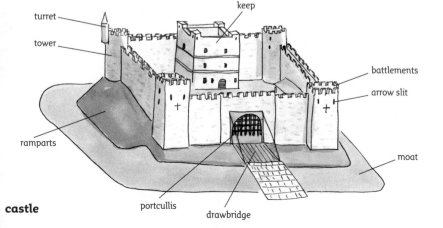

turret
tower
ramparts
keep
battlements
arrow slit
moat
portcullis
drawbridge

castle

Catholic Catholics
NOUN **1** a Roman **Catholic**
ADJECTIVE **2** belonging to the Roman **Catholic** religion

cattle
PLURAL NOUN cows and bulls kept by farmers

caught
VERB the past tense of **catch**

cauldron cauldrons
NOUN a large, round metal cooking pot, especially one that sits over a fire

WORD HISTORY
from Latin *caldarium* meaning hot bath

cauliflower cauliflowers
NOUN a large, round, white vegetable surrounded by green leaves

cause causes, causing, caused
VERB **1** To **cause** something means to make it happen.
NOUN **2** The **cause** of something is the thing that makes it happen. • *The cause of the explosion was a gas leak.*

cautious
ADJECTIVE Someone who is **cautious** acts carefully in order to avoid danger or disappointment.

cavalry
NOUN The **cavalry** is the part of an army that fights on horseback or in armoured vehicles such as tanks.

cave caves, caving, caved
NOUN a large hole in the side of a cliff or under the ground
cave in
VERB If a roof **caves in**, it collapses inwards.

caveman cavemen
NOUN **Cavemen** were men who lived in caves in prehistoric times.

cavewoman cavewomen
NOUN **Cavewomen** were women who lived in caves in prehistoric times.

cavity cavities
NOUN a small hole in something solid
• *There were cavities in his back teeth.*

CD
NOUN an abbreviation for *compact disc*

CD-ROM
NOUN a way of storing video, sound or text on a compact disc that can be played on a computer. **CD-ROM** is an abbreviation for *compact disc read-only memory*.

CE
ADJECTIVE You use **CE** in dates to show the number of years or centuries after the year in which Jesus Christ is believed to have been born. **CE** is an abbreviation for *Common Era*.

cease ceases, ceasing, ceased
VERB **1** If something **ceases**, it stops.
VERB **2** If you **cease** doing something, you stop doing it.

ceiling ceilings
NOUN the roof inside a room

celebrate celebrates, celebrating, celebrated
VERB If you **celebrate** something, you do something special and enjoyable because of it. • *We felt like celebrating the end of exams.*

celebration celebrations
NOUN a party or special event that you have because something good has happened
• *All the family were there for my grandma's 60th birthday celebration.*

celebrity celebrities
NOUN a famous person

celery
NOUN a vegetable with long, pale green stalks

celestial
ADJECTIVE relating to the sky • *She was fascinated by stars and other celestial objects.*

cell cells
NOUN **1** In biology, a **cell** is the smallest part of an animal or plant that can exist by itself. Humans, animals and plants are made up of millions of **cells**.
NOUN **2** a small room in a prison or police station where a prisoner is locked up
NOUN **3** In physics, a **cell** is a device that produces electrical energy by chemical reaction.

cellar cellars
NOUN a room underneath a building

cellist cellists
NOUN someone who plays a cello

PRONUNCIATION TIP
This word is pronounced **chell**-ist.

cello cellos
NOUN a large, stringed musical instrument that you play sitting down

PRONUNCIATION TIP
This word is pronounced **chell**-oh.

Celsius
NOUN a scale for measuring temperature in which water freezes at 0 degrees (0 °C) and boils at 100 degrees (100 °C)

WORD HISTORY
named after Anders *Celsius* (1701–1744) who invented it

cement
NOUN a grey powder that is mixed with sand and water to make concrete

cemetery cemeteries
NOUN an area of land where dead people are buried

census censuses
NOUN an official survey of the population of a country

cent cents
NOUN In some countries a **cent** is a unit of currency.

centenary centenaries
NOUN the hundredth anniversary of something

centigrade
NOUN another word for **Celsius**

centilitre centilitres
NOUN a unit of volume (cl). One **centilitre** is equal to ten millilitres (ml) and is the same as a cubic centimetre (cc).

centimetre centimetres
NOUN a unit of length (cm). One **centimetre** is equal to ten millimetres (mm).

centipede centipedes
NOUN a long, thin creature with many pairs of legs

WORD HISTORY
from Latin *centum* + *pedes* meaning a hundred feet

central
ADJECTIVE **1** Something **central** is in the middle.
ADJECTIVE **2** An idea that is **central** is the main idea.

central heating
NOUN a heating system in which water or air is heated and passed round a building through pipes and radiators

centre centres
NOUN **1** the middle of an object or area
NOUN **2** a building where people go for activities, meetings or help • *We played badminton at the sports centre.*

century centuries
NOUN a period of one hundred years

ceramic ceramics
NOUN **1** a hard material made by baking clay at very high temperatures
PLURAL NOUN **2 Ceramics** are objects made out of clay.

cereal cereals
NOUN **1** a food made from grain, often eaten with milk for breakfast
NOUN **2** a plant that produces edible grain, such as wheat, oats, barley and rye

ceremony ceremonies
NOUN a formal event such as a wedding or prizegiving

certain
ADJECTIVE **1** If you are **certain** about something, you are sure it is true. • *She is certain she wants to be a vet.*
ADJECTIVE **2** You use **certain** to refer to a particular person, place or thing. • *I like certain animals, for example cats and dogs.*

certainly
ADVERB without any doubt • *"Will you be at the party?" "I certainly will."*

certificate certificates
NOUN an official piece of paper that proves that something took place • *a birth certificate*

chaffinch chaffinches
NOUN a small European bird with black and white wings

chain chains
NOUN **1** a number of metal rings linked together in a line
→ Have a look at the illustration for **bicycle**
NOUN **2** a number of things in a series or connected to each other • *a chain of shops* • *a chain of events*

chair chairs
NOUN a seat for one person to sit on, with a back and four legs

A
B
C
D
E
F
G
H
I
J
K
L
M
N
O
P
Q
R
S
T
U
V
W
X
Y
Z

chalet chalets
NOUN a small wooden house with a sloping roof, especially found in mountain areas or holiday camps

chalk
NOUN a soft, white rock. Small sticks of **chalk** are used for writing or drawing with.

chalky chalkier, chalkiest
ADJECTIVE looking, feeling or tasting like chalk

challenge challenges, challenging, challenged
NOUN 1 something new and exciting that needs a lot of effort ● *Learning how to cook is a new **challenge** for me.*
VERB 2 If someone **challenges** you, they suggest that you compete with them. ● *She **challenged** me to a game of table tennis.*

challenging
ADJECTIVE If you find something **challenging**, you find it quite difficult.

chameleon chameleons
NOUN a lizard that is able to change the colour of its skin to match the colour of its surroundings

WORD HISTORY
from Greek *khamai* + *leon* meaning ground lion

champagne champagnes
NOUN a sparkling white wine made in France

champion champions
NOUN a person who wins a competition

championship championships
NOUN a competition to find the best player or players of a particular sport

chance chances
NOUN 1 how possible or likely something is ● *I think we've got a good **chance** of winning.*
NOUN 2 an opportunity to do something ● *This is your **chance** to be a TV star!*
NOUN 3 a possibility that something dangerous or unpleasant may happen
PHRASE 4 Something that happens **by chance** happens unexpectedly, without being planned.

chancellor chancellors
NOUN the head of government in some European countries

Chancellor of the Exchequer
NOUN the government minister in charge of finance and taxes in the UK

change changes, changing, changed
NOUN 1 money you get back when you pay for something with more money than it costs
VERB 2 When something **changes**, or you **change** it, it becomes different. ● *The wind changed direction.*

channel channels
NOUN 1 a wavelength on which television programmes are broadcast. **Channel** can also mean the television station itself.
NOUN 2 a passage for water or other liquid
NOUN 3 The **Channel**, or the English **Channel**, is the stretch of sea between England and France.

chaos
NOUN a state of complete disorder ● *The demonstration ended in **chaos**.*

chaotic
ADJECTIVE A **chaotic** situation is one that is completely disorganised and confusing. ● *There were **chaotic** scenes at the airport when hundreds of flights were cancelled.*

chapel chapels
NOUN 1 a section of a church or cathedral with its own altar
NOUN 2 a type of small church

chapter chapters
NOUN one of the parts into which a book is divided

character characters
NOUN 1 all the qualities that make a person or a place special ● *She has a gentle character.*
NOUN 2 The **characters** in a film, play or book are the people in it.

characteristic characteristics
NOUN 1 a special quality about a person, place or thing
ADJECTIVE 2 typical of a place or person ● *Nois and traffic fumes are **characteristic** of cities.*

charades
NOUN a party game where one team guesses what the other team is acting out

charcoal
NOUN burnt wood used as a fuel. **Charcoal** is also used for drawing.

charge charges, charging, charged
VERB **1** If someone **charges** you money, they ask you to pay for something you have bought or received.
VERB **2** If someone **charges** an electronic device, they put electricity into its battery.
• *Alex forgot to* **charge** *his mobile phone.*
VERB **3** If someone **charges** somewhere, they rush in that direction. • *She* **charged** *into the room.*
PHRASE **4** If you are **in charge of** someone or something, you are responsible for them.
• *I left him* **in charge of** *the shop while I went out.*

chariot chariots
NOUN a two-wheeled open vehicle pulled by horses in ancient times

charity charities
NOUN **1** an organisation that raises money to help people in need
NOUN **2** money or other help given to people in need

charm charms, charming, charmed
NOUN **1** something you wear for good luck
NOUN **2** the quality of being attractive and pleasant
VERB **3** If you **charm** someone, you use your charm to please them.

chart charts
NOUN a diagram or table showing information

chase chases, chasing, chased
VERB If you **chase** someone, you run after them or follow them in order to catch them or make them leave a place.

chat chats, chatting, chatted
NOUN **1** a friendly talk with someone
VERB **2** When people **chat**, they talk to each other in a friendly way about things that are not very important.
VERB **3** When people **chat**, they send each other short messages on the internet or on their phones.

chatroom chatrooms
NOUN an internet site where users have discussions with each other

chatter chatters, chattering, chattered
VERB **1** When people **chatter**, they talk about unimportant things.
VERB **2** If your teeth **chatter**, they knock together and make a clicking noise because you are cold.

chatty chattier, chattiest
ADJECTIVE Someone who is **chatty** likes to talk to people.

chauffeur chauffeurs
NOUN a person whose job is to drive another person's car • *He had a* **chauffeur** *to drive him everywhere.*

cheap cheaper, cheapest
ADJECTIVE **1** Something that is **cheap** costs very little money.
ADJECTIVE **2** **Cheap** sometimes means of poor quality.

cheat cheats, cheating, cheated
VERB If someone **cheats** in a game or exam, they break the rules in order to do better.

check checks, checking, checked
VERB **1** If you **check** something, you examine it to make sure that everything is all right.
• **Check** *your work carefully when you finish.*
NOUN **2** an inspection to make sure that everything is all right
NOUN **3** **Checks** are different coloured squares that form a pattern.

checkout checkouts
NOUN the place in a supermarket where you pay for your goods

cheek cheeks
NOUN **1** Your **cheeks** are the sides of your face below your eyes.
NOUN **2** speech or behaviour that is rude and disrespectful • *Their grandparents won't stand any* **cheek** *from them.*

cheekily
ADVERB in a way that is rude and disrespectful, but can be slightly amusing

cheeky cheekier, cheekiest
ADJECTIVE speaking or behaving in a way that is rude and disrespectful, but can be slightly amusing

cheer cheers, cheering, cheered
VERB When people **cheer**, they shout loudly and happily. • *We* **cheered** *our team when they won.*

cheerful
ADJECTIVE A **cheerful** person is happy.

cheerfully
ADVERB in a happy way

cheese cheeses
NOUN a solid savoury food made from milk

a
b
c
d
e
f
g
h
i
j
k
l
m
n
o
p
q
r
s
t
u
v
w
x
y
z

65

A
B
C
D
E
F
G
H
I
J
K
L
M
N
O
P
Q
R
S
T
U
V
W
X
Y
Z

cheetah cheetahs
NOUN a wild mammal like a large cat with black spots, mainly found in Africa

---

WORD HISTORY
from Sanskrit *citra* + *kaya* meaning speckled body

---

chef chefs
NOUN a head cook in a restaurant or hotel

WORD HISTORY
from French *chef* meaning head

---

chemical chemicals
NOUN **1** a substance made by the use of chemistry • *Dangerous* **chemicals** *should be handled carefully.*
ADJECTIVE **2** involved in chemistry or using chemicals • *a* **chemical** *reaction*

chemist chemists
NOUN a shop that sells medicines and cosmetics

chemistry
NOUN the scientific study of substances and the ways in which they change when they are combined

cheque cheques
NOUN a personalised printed piece of paper that people can use to pay for things

cherry cherries
NOUN a small, juicy fruit with a red, yellow or black skin and a hard stone in the centre

chess
NOUN a game played on a board with 64 squares. Each player has 16 pieces.

chest chests
NOUN **1** the front part of your body between your shoulders and your waist
NOUN **2** a large wooden box used for storing things

chestnut chestnuts
NOUN **1** a reddish-brown nut that grows inside a prickly, green outer covering
NOUN **2** the tree that produces these nuts
ADJECTIVE **3** Something that is **chestnut** is reddish-brown in colour.

chew chews, chewing, chewed
VERB When you **chew** something, you use your teeth to break it up in your mouth before swallowing it.

chewing gum
NOUN a kind of sweet that you chew for a long time, but which you do not swallow

chick chicks
NOUN a young bird

chicken chickens
NOUN a bird kept on a farm for its eggs and meat; also the meat of this bird

chickenpox
NOUN an illness that causes a fever and blister-like spots to appear on the skin

chief chiefs
NOUN **1** the leader of a group or organisation
ADJECTIVE **2** main or most important

chilblain chilblains
NOUN a sore, itchy swelling on a finger or toe, which causes discomfort in cold weather

child children
NOUN **1** a young person who is not yet an adult

SYNONYMS: kid, youngster

NOUN **2** Someone's **child** is their son or daughter.

childhood childhoods
NOUN Your **childhood** is the time when you are a child.

childish
ADJECTIVE If someone is **childish**, they are not acting in an adult way.

ANTONYM: adult

childminder childminders
NOUN a person who is paid to look after children while their parents are at work

children
PLURAL NOUN the plural of **child**

chill chills, chilling, chilled
VERB **1** When you **chill** something, you make it cold. • *Chill the orange juice before you drink it.*
NOUN **2** a feverish cold
NOUN **3** a feeling of cold • *the* **chill** *of early morning*

chilli chillies
NOUN the red or green seed pod of a type of pepper that has a very hot, spicy taste

chilly chillier, chilliest
ADJECTIVE **1** **Chilly** weather is rather cold.
ADJECTIVE **2** If people behave in a **chilly** way, they are not very friendly.

chime chimes, chiming, chimed
VERB **1** When a bell **chimes**, it makes a clear ringing sound.
NOUN **2 Chimes** are a set of bells or other objects that make ringing sounds.

chimney chimneys
NOUN a pipe above a fireplace or furnace through which smoke from the fire can escape

chimpanzee chimpanzees
NOUN a small ape with dark fur that lives in forests in Africa

chin chins
NOUN the part of your face below your mouth

china
NOUN plates, cups, saucers and other dishes that are made from fine clay

chink chinks
NOUN **1** a small, narrow opening • *a chink in the fence*
NOUN **2** a small ringing sound, like glasses touching each other

chip chips, chipping, chipped
NOUN **1 Chips** are thin strips of fried potato.
NOUN **2** a tiny piece of silicon inside a computer, which is used to form electronic circuits • *computer chips*
VERB **3** If you **chip** an object, you break a small piece off it.

chirp chirps, chirping, chirped
VERB When a bird **chirps**, it makes a short, high-pitched sound.

chisel chisels, chiselling, chiselled
NOUN **1** a tool with a long metal blade and a sharp edge at the end. **Chisels** are used for cutting and shaping wood, stone or metal.
VERB **2** If you **chisel** wood, stone or metal, you cut or shape it using a chisel.

chlorine
NOUN a poisonous greenish-yellow gas with a strong, unpleasant smell. It is used to disinfect water and to make bleach.

chocolate chocolates
NOUN a sweet food made from cocoa beans

WORD HISTORY
from Aztec *xococ* + *atl* meaning bitter water

choice choices
NOUN **1** a range of different things that are available to choose from

SYNONYMS: range, variety

NOUN **2** something that you choose • *You made a good choice when you bought this book.*

choir choirs
NOUN a group of singers, for example in a church

choke chokes, choking, choked
VERB If you **choke** on something, it prevents you from breathing properly. • *He choked on a fish bone.*

cholesterol
NOUN a substance found in all animal fats, tissues and blood

choose chooses, choosing, chose, chosen
VERB If you **choose** something, you decide to have it or do it.

SYNONYMS: pick, select

chop chops, chopping, chopped
VERB **1** If you **chop** something, you cut it with quick, heavy strokes using an axe or a knife. • *Mum chopped the logs for firewood.*
NOUN **2** a small piece of pork or lamb that contains a bone • *We had chops and broccoli for dinner.*

choppy
ADJECTIVE When the sea or a stretch of water is **choppy**, there are a lot of waves on it because it is windy.

chopstick chopsticks
NOUN **Chopsticks** are a pair of thin sticks used for eating Chinese and Japanese food.

choral
ADJECTIVE for a choir

chord chords
NOUN a group of three or more musical notes played together

chore chores
NOUN an uninteresting job that has to be done

chorus choruses
NOUN **1** a part of a song that is repeated after each verse
NOUN **2** a large group of singers

a
b
c
d
e
f
g
h
i
j
k
l
m
n
o
p
q
r
s
t
u
v
w
x
y
z

67

A
B
C
D
E
F
G
H
I
J
K
L
M
N
O
P
Q
R
S
T
U
V
W
X
Y
Z

chose
VERB the past tense of **choose**

chosen
VERB **1** the past participle of **choose**
VERB **2** When you are **chosen**, you are picked to do something. • *I was **chosen** for the volleyball team.*

christen christens, christening, christened
VERB When a priest **christens** someone, they name them in a ceremony where water is poured over their head as a sign that they are a member of the Christian church.

christening christenings
NOUN a ceremony in which a person becomes a member of the Christian church

Christian Christians
NOUN a person who believes in Jesus Christ and his teachings

Christianity
NOUN a religion based on Jesus Christ and his teachings

Christmas Christmases
NOUN a Christian festival held on December 25th to celebrate the birth of Jesus Christ

chrome
NOUN metal plated with chromium, a hard, silver-grey metal

chromosome chromosomes
NOUN the part of a cell in living things that contains the genes that determine what characteristics the animal or plant will have

chronic
ADJECTIVE lasting a very long time or never stopping • *He suffers from **chronic** hay fever.*

chronological
ADJECTIVE arranged in the order in which things happened • *Tell me the whole story in **chronological** order.*

chrysalis chrysalises
NOUN a butterfly or moth when it is developing from being a caterpillar to being a fully grown adult

→ Have a look at the illustration for **life cycle**

chrysanthemum chrysanthemums
NOUN a plant with large, brightly-coloured flowers

chuckle chuckles, chuckling, chuckled
VERB When you **chuckle**, you laugh quietly. • *They were **chuckling** quietly to themselves.*

chunk chunks
NOUN a thick piece of something

SYNONYMS: hunk, lump, piece

chunky chunkier, chunkiest
ADJECTIVE large and thick • *a **chunky** silver necklace*

church churches
NOUN a building where Christians go for religious services and worship

churchyard churchyards
NOUN an area of land around a church, often used as a graveyard

churn churns, churning, churned
NOUN **1** a container used for making milk or cream into butter
VERB **2** When you **churn** something, you stir it vigorously, for example when making milk into butter.

churn out
VERB If you **churn out** something, you produce it quickly in large numbers.
• *They **churned out** hundreds of leaflets advertising the dance.*

chutney
NOUN a strong-tasting, thick sauce made from fruit, vinegar and spices

cider
NOUN an alcoholic drink made from apples

cigar cigars
NOUN a roll of dried tobacco leaves, which people smoke

cigarette cigarettes
NOUN a thin tube of paper containing tobacco, which people smoke

cinder cinders
NOUN **Cinders** are small pieces of burnt material left after something such as wood or coal has burned.

cinema cinemas
NOUN a place where people go to watch films • *Every Saturday night they used to go to the **cinema**.*

circle circles, circling, circled

NOUN **1** a regular, two-dimensional round shape. Every point on the edge is the same distance from the centre.

VERB **2** to move around in a circle

• We stood and watched as the gulls **circled** overhead.

circuit circuits

NOUN **1** the path of an electric current

NOUN **2** a racecourse

NOUN **3** A training **circuit** is a course of physical activities.

circular

ADJECTIVE having the shape of a circle

circulation circulations

NOUN **1** the movement of blood around a body

NOUN **2** the number of copies of a newspaper or magazine that are sold each time it is issued

circulatory system

NOUN Your **circulatory system** is the system that moves blood around your body.

circumference circumferences

NOUN the outer line or edge of a circle. The length of this line is also called the **circumference**.

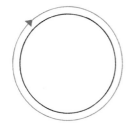

circumstance circumstances

NOUN The **circumstances** of a situation or event are the conditions that affect what happens. • He did well under difficult **circumstances**.

circus circuses

NOUN a travelling show performed in a large tent, with performers such as clowns and acrobats

cistern cisterns

NOUN a tank in which water is stored, such as in the roof of a house, or above a toilet

citizen citizens

NOUN The **citizens** of a country or city are the people who live in it or belong to it.

citrus fruit citrus fruits

NOUN **Citrus fruits** are juicy, sharp-tasting fruits such as oranges, lemons and grapefruit.

city cities

NOUN a large town where many people live and work

civil

ADJECTIVE **1** relating to the citizens of a place

ADJECTIVE **2** Someone who is **civil** is polite.

civilian civilians

NOUN a person who is not in the armed forces

civilisation civilisations; also spelt **civilization**

NOUN **1** a large group of people with a high level of organisation and culture • We're learning about the ancient **civilisations** of Greece, Rome and Egypt.

NOUN **2** a highly developed and organised way of life

civilised; also spelt **civilized**

ADJECTIVE **1** A **civilised** society is one with a highly developed social organisation and a comfortable way of life.

ADJECTIVE **2** A **civilised** person is polite and reasonable.

civil war civil wars

NOUN a war between groups of people who live in the same country

cl

an abbreviation for centilitre

claim claims, claiming, claimed

VERB **1** If you **claim** that something is the case, you say that it is so.

VERB **2** If you **claim** something, you ask for it because you believe you have a right to it.

clamber clambers, clambering, clambered

VERB If you **clamber** somewhere, you climb there with difficulty. • We **clambered** over the rocks to get to the beach.

clammy clammier, clammiest
  ADJECTIVE unpleasantly damp and sticky
  • The weather was very **clammy**.

clamp clamps, clamping, clamped
  NOUN **1** a device that holds something firmly in place
  VERB **2** When you **clamp** one thing to another, you fasten them together with a clamp.

clan clans
  NOUN a group of families related to each other by being descended from the same ancestor

clang clangs, clanging, clanged
  VERB When something made of metal **clangs**, or when you **clang** it, it makes a loud, ringing sound.

clank clanks, clanking, clanked
  VERB When something **clanks**, it makes a loud, metallic sound.

clap claps, clapping, clapped
  VERB **1** When you **clap**, you hit your hands together loudly to show that you have enjoyed something or that you approve of something.
  NOUN **2** a sudden loud noise of thunder

clarify clarifies, clarifying, clarified
  VERB If you **clarify** something, you make it clear and easier to understand.

clarinet clarinets
  NOUN a woodwind instrument with a straight tube and a single reed in its mouthpiece

clarity
  NOUN The **clarity** of something is its clearness. • The **clarity** of the water made me think it was very clean.

clash clashes, clashing, clashed
  VERB **1** Colours or ideas that **clash** are so different that they do not go together.
  • Debbie's red shirt **clashed** with her green shorts.
  VERB **2** If one event **clashes** with another, they happen at the same time, so you cannot go to both.
  VERB **3** If people **clash** with each other, they fight or argue.

clasp clasps, clasping, clasped
  VERB **1** If you **clasp** something, you hold it tightly.
  NOUN **2** a fastening such as a hook or a catch

class classes
  NOUN **1** a group of pupils or students taught together, or a lesson that they have together

NOUN **2** A **class** of people or things is a group of them of a particular type. • Beetles and ants belong to different **classes** of insect.

SYNONYMS: group, kind, type

classic
  ADJECTIVE Something described as **classic** is considered a high quality example of something. • He has a **classic** car.

classical
  ADJECTIVE **1** traditional in style and content
  • **classical** ballet
  ADJECTIVE **2 Classical** music is serious music thought to be of lasting value.

classification classifications
  NOUN the process of arranging things into groups with something in common

classify classifies, classifying, classified
  VERB to arrange things into groups with something in common • We **classified** the foods into three groups: fruits, vegetables and meats.

classroom classrooms
  NOUN a room in a school where lessons take place

clatter clatters, clattering, clattered
  VERB **1** When things **clatter**, they hit each other with a loud, rattling noise.
  NOUN **2** a loud noise made by hard things hitting against each other • There was a great **clatter** when the waitress dropped the tray.

clause clauses
  NOUN In grammar, a **clause** is a group of words with a subject and a verb, which may be a complete sentence or part of a sentence.

claw claws, clawing, clawed
  NOUN **1** An animal's **claws** are the hard, curved nails at the end of its feet.
  NOUN **2** The **claws** of a crab or a lobster are the two jointed parts at the end of the leg, used for holding things.
  VERB **3** If an animal **claws** something, it digs its claws into it.

clay
  NOUN a type of earth that is soft and sticky when wet and hard when baked dry. It is used to make pottery and bricks.

clean cleaner, cleanest; cleans, cleaning, cleaned
  ADJECTIVE **1** free from dirt or unwanted marks
  VERB **2** to remove dirt from something

A B C D E F G H I J K L M N O P Q R S T U V W X Y Z

clear **clearer, clearest; clears, clearing, cleared**

ADJECTIVE **1** easy to understand, see or hear • *The instructions on the packet were very **clear**.*

ADJECTIVE **2** easy to see through • *a **clear** liquid*

ANTONYM: opaque

VERB **3** To **clear** unwanted things from a place is to remove them. • *We **cleared** the dirty dishes from the table.*

VERB **4** If you **clear** a fence or other obstacle, you jump over it without touching it.

clear up
VERB When you **clear up** a place, you tidy it and put things away.

clearly

ADVERB **1** in a way that people can easily understand, see or hear • *He spoke loudly and **clearly**.*

ADVERB **2** obviously and without any doubt • ***Clearly**, the answer has to be no.*

clef **clefs**
NOUN a symbol at the beginning of a line of music that shows the pitch of the notes

clench **clenches, clenching, clenched**
VERB **1** When you **clench** your fist, you curl your fingers up tightly.
VERB **2** When you **clench** your teeth, you squeeze them together tightly, either in pain or in anger.

clerk **clerks**
NOUN a person who keeps records or accounts in an office, bank or law court

clever **cleverer, cleverest**
ADJECTIVE **1** intelligent and quick to understand things

SYNONYMS: bright, intelligent, smart

ADJECTIVE **2** very effective or skilful • *We came up with a **clever** plan.*

cliché **clichés**
NOUN an idea or phrase that is no longer effective because it has been used so much. For example, *in this day and age* and *over the moon*.

click **clicks, clicking, clicked**
VERB **1** When something **clicks** or when you **click** it, it makes a short snapping sound.
VERB **2** If you **click** on an area of a computer screen, you point the cursor at that area and press one of the buttons on the mouse in order to make something happen. If you

double-**click**, you press it quickly twice.
• ***Click** on the link at the top of the page.*
NOUN **3** a sound of something clicking

client **clients**
NOUN someone who pays a professional person or company for a service

cliff **cliffs**
NOUN a high area of land with a very steep side, usually next to the sea

cliffhanger **cliffhangers**
NOUN a very exciting or frightening situation, usually in a television or radio serial, where you are left not knowing what is going to happen next

climate **climates**
NOUN the general weather conditions that are typical of a place

climate change
NOUN changes in the Earth's climate, especially the rise in temperature caused by high levels of pollution

climax **climaxes**
NOUN the most exciting moment of something, usually near the end

climb **climbs, climbing, climbed**
VERB **1** If you **climb** something, such as a tree, mountain or ladder, you move towards the top of it.
VERB **2** If you **climb** somewhere, you move there with difficulty. • *We **climbed** over the high wall.*
NOUN **3** a movement upwards • *I was tired after the long **climb** to the top of the hill.*

climber **climbers**
NOUN someone who climbs rocks or mountains

cling **clings, clinging, clung**
VERB If you **cling** to something, you hold on to it tightly.

clinic **clinics**
NOUN a place where people go for medical advice or treatment

clip **clips, clipping, clipped**
NOUN **1** a small metal or plastic object used for holding things together
NOUN **2** a short piece of a film shown by itself
VERB **3** If you **clip** something, you cut bits from it to shape it.

clipboard **clipboards**
NOUN a stiff piece of board or plastic, with a clip at the top to keep papers in place

clippers

PLURAL NOUN a tool used for cutting
● hedge **clippers**

cloak cloaks, cloaking, cloaked

NOUN **1** a wide, loose coat without sleeves
VERB **2** If something **cloaks** something else, it covers or hides it. ● *The mist cloaked the land.*

cloakroom cloakrooms

NOUN **1** a room where you can leave coats and luggage for a while
NOUN **2** a room with toilets and washbasins in a public building

clock clocks

NOUN an instrument that measures and shows the time

clockwise

ADVERB in the same direction as the hands on a clock

ANTONYM: anticlockwise

clockwork

NOUN **1** Toys that move by **clockwork** are wound up with a key.
PHRASE **2** If something goes **like clockwork**, it happens with no problems or delays.

clog clogs, clogging, clogged

VERB **1** When something is **clogged**, or when you **clog** something up, it becomes blocked and doesn't work properly or doesn't allow things to move freely. ● *The traffic was clogging the roads.*
NOUN **2** a shoe made entirely of wood, originally from the Netherlands

clone clones

NOUN an animal or plant that is an identical copy of another animal or plant

close closes, closing, closed; closer, closest

VERB **1** If you **close** something, you move it so that it is no longer open. ● *He closed the door behind him.*
VERB **2** If a shop or other building **closes** at a certain time, it does not do business after that time.
ADJECTIVE **3** Something that is **close** to something else is near to it.

SYNONYMS: near, nearby

ADJECTIVE **4** People who are **close** are very friendly with each other and know each other well.

ADJECTIVE **5** If the weather is **close**, it is uncomfortably warm and stuffy.
NOUN **6** a street that is closed at one end
● *We live in Park Close.*

PRONUNCIATION TIP
Meanings 1 and 2 are pronounced **klohz**. Meanings 3, 4, 5 and 6 are pronounced **klohss**.

closely

ADVERB **1** very carefully ● *She was watching him closely.*
ADVERB **2** to a very large degree ● *We work closely with other schools.*
ADVERB **3** without much time or distance between two people or things ● *She came into the room, closely followed by a young boy.*

PRONUNCIATION TIP
This word is pronounced **klohss**-li.

close-up close-ups

NOUN A **close-up** in a film or a photograph is taken at very close range and shows things in great detail.

PRONUNCIATION TIP
This word is pronounced **klohss**-up.

clot clots

NOUN a sticky lump that forms when a liquid such as blood dries up or becomes thick

cloth cloths

NOUN **1** fabric made by a process such as weaving
NOUN **2** a piece of material used for wiping or protecting things

clothes

PLURAL NOUN things people wear on their bodies

cloud clouds

NOUN **1** a mass of water vapour that is seen as a white or grey patch in the sky ● *The sun went behind a cloud.*
NOUN **2** A **cloud** of smoke or dust is a mass of it floating in the air.
NOUN **3** **Cloud** computing is when data and programs are stored and accessed over the internet instead of through your computer's hard drive.

cloudy cloudier, cloudiest

ADJECTIVE **1** full of clouds • *The sky was **cloudy**.*

SYNONYMS: dull, overcast

ADJECTIVE **2** difficult to see through • *a **cloudy** liquid*

SYNONYM: murky

clover

NOUN a small plant with leaves made up of three similar parts

clown clowns

NOUN a circus performer who wears funny clothes and make-up and does silly things to make people laugh

club clubs

NOUN **1** a group of people with similar interests, who meet regularly. The place where they meet is also called a **club**. • *a youth **club***
NOUN **2** a team that competes in sports competitions

clue clues

NOUN something that helps solve a problem or mystery • *Police have found **clues** to the robbery.*

clueless

ADJECTIVE (*informal*) If you say that someone is **clueless**, you think they are stupid and not able to do things properly.

clump clumps

NOUN a small group of things growing or standing close together • *a **clump** of trees*

clumsily

ADVERB in and awkward and careless way

clumsy clumsier, clumsiest

ADJECTIVE moving awkwardly and carelessly

SYNONYMS: awkward, ungainly

clung

VERB the past tense and past participle of **cling**

cluster clusters, clustering, clustered

NOUN **1** a group of things together • *There is a **cluster** of houses by the lake.*
VERB **2** If people **cluster** together, they stay together in a close group.

WORD HISTORY
from Old English *clyster* meaning bunch of grapes

clutch clutches, clutching, clutched

VERB If you **clutch** something, you hold it tightly or seize it.

clutter clutters, cluttering, cluttered

NOUN **1** an untidy mess
VERB **2** Things that **clutter** a place fill it and make it untidy.

cm

an abbreviation for *centimetre*

coach coaches, coaching, coached

NOUN **1** a large bus that takes passengers on long journeys
NOUN **2** a section of a train that carries passengers
VERB **3** If someone **coaches** you, they help you to get better at a sport or a subject.

SYNONYMS: instruct, train

NOUN **4** someone who coaches a person or sports team

coal

NOUN a hard, black rock taken from under the ground and burned as a fuel

coarse coarser, coarsest

ADJECTIVE **1** Something that is **coarse** is rough in texture.
ADJECTIVE **2** Someone who is **coarse** talks or behaves in a rude, offensive way.

coarseness

NOUN **1** the quality that something has when it feels rough
NOUN **2 Coarseness** is when someone talks or behaves in a rude, offensive way.

coast coasts, coasting, coasted

NOUN **1** the edge of the land where it meets the sea
VERB **2** If a vehicle **coasts** somewhere, it moves there with the engine switched off.
• *The car **coasted** quietly down the hill.*

coastal

ADJECTIVE on the edge of the land where it meets the sea • ***coastal** villages*

coastguard coastguards

NOUN an official who watches the sea near a coast to get help for sailors when they need it

coat coats, coating, coated

NOUN **1** a piece of outdoor clothing with sleeves, which you wear over other clothes
NOUN **2** An animal's **coat** is the fur or hair on its body.
NOUN **3** A **coat** of paint or varnish is a layer of it.
VERB **4** If you **coat** something, you cover it with a thin layer of something. • *We **coated** the biscuits with chocolate.*

a
b
c
d
e
f
g
h
i
j
k
l
m
n
o
p
q
r
s
t
u
v
w
x
y
z

A
B
C
D
E
F
G
H
I
J
K
L
M
N
O
P
Q
R
S
T
U
V
W
X
Y
Z

coating coatings
NOUN a thin layer of something spread over a surface

coax coaxes, coaxing, coaxed
VERB If you **coax** someone to do something, you persuade them gently to do it.

cobble cobbles
NOUN **Cobbles** or cobblestones are stones with a rounded surface that were used in the past for making roads.

cobra cobras
NOUN a type of large poisonous snake from Africa and Asia

cobweb cobwebs
NOUN the very thin net that a spider spins to catch insects

cock cocks
NOUN an adult male chicken, or any other male bird

cockerel cockerels
NOUN a young cock

cockle cockles
NOUN a type of small, edible shellfish

Cockney Cockneys
NOUN someone who was born in the East End of London

cockpit cockpits
NOUN **1** the area in a plane where the pilot sits in control

→ Have a look at the illustration for **aeroplane**

NOUN **2** the driver's compartment in a racing car

cockroach cockroaches
NOUN a large, dark-coloured insect often found in dirty rooms

WORD HISTORY
from Spanish *cucaracha*

cocky cockier, cockiest
ADJECTIVE (*informal*) If you are **cocky**, you are sure of yourself and sometimes rather cheeky.

cocoa
NOUN **1** a brown powder made from the seeds of a tropical tree and used for making chocolate
NOUN **2** a hot drink made from this powder

coconut coconuts
NOUN a very large nut with white flesh, milky juice, and a hard hairy shell

cocoon cocoons
NOUN a silky covering over the larvae of moths and some other insects

cod
NOUN a large, edible fish

LANGUAGE TIP
The plural of *cod* is *cod*.

code codes
NOUN **1** a system of replacing the letters or words in a message with other letters or words, so that nobody can understand the message unless they know the system
• *They wrote messages in **code**.*
NOUN **2** a group of numbers and letters used to identify something • *the area **code** for Falmouth*
NOUN **3** the set of instructions in a computer program
VERB **4** When you **code**, you write the instructions in a computer program.

coeducation
NOUN **Coeducation** is a system where girls and boys are taught together at the same school.

coffee
NOUN **1** a powder made by roasting and grinding the beans of the coffee plant
NOUN **2** a hot drink made from coffee

coffin coffins
NOUN a box in which a dead body is buried or cremated

cog cogs
NOUN a wheel with teeth, which turns another wheel or part of a machine

coil coils, coiling, coiled
NOUN **1** a length of rope or wire wound into a series of loops
NOUN **2** A single loop is also called a **coil**.
VERB **3** If something **coils**, or if you **coil** it, it winds into a series of loops. • *The snake **coiled** around the branch.*

coin coins, coining, coined
NOUN **1** a small metal disc used as money
VERB **2** If you **coin** a word or a phrase, you invent it.

coinage
NOUN the coins that are used in a particular country

coincide coincides, coinciding, coincided
VERB When two things **coincide**, they happen at the same time. • *Auntie's visit **coincided** with my birthday.*

coincidence coincidences
NOUN what happens when two or more things occur at the same time by chance

coke
NOUN a grey fuel produced from coal

cola colas
NOUN a sweet, brown fizzy drink

colander colanders
NOUN a bowl-shaped container with holes in it, used for washing or draining food

cold colder, coldest; colds
ADJECTIVE 1 If something is **cold**, it has a very low temperature.
ADJECTIVE 2 If the weather is **cold**, the air temperature is very low.
NOUN 3 a minor illness that makes you sneeze and cough, and sometimes gives you a sore throat

cold-blooded
ADJECTIVE 1 A **cold-blooded** animal has a body temperature that changes according to the surrounding temperature.
ADJECTIVE 2 Someone who is **cold-blooded** does not show any pity.

coleslaw
NOUN a salad of chopped cabbage and other vegetables in mayonnaise

collaborate collaborates, collaborating, collaborated
VERB When people **collaborate**, they work together to produce something. • *The two schools **collaborated** to produce a play.*

collaboration
NOUN **Collaboration** is when people work together to produce something.

collaborator collaborators
NOUN someone who works together with someone else to produce something.

collage collages
NOUN a picture made by sticking pieces of paper or cloth on to a surface

collapse collapses, collapsing, collapsed
VERB 1 If something such as a building **collapses**, it falls down suddenly.
VERB 2 If a person **collapses**, they fall down suddenly because they are ill.

collapsible
ADJECTIVE A **collapsible** object can be folded flat when it is not in use. • *collapsible chairs*

collar collars
NOUN 1 the part around the neck of something, such as a coat or shirt
NOUN 2 a leather band round the neck of a dog or cat

colleague colleagues
NOUN A person's **colleagues** are the people they work with.

collect collects, collecting, collected
VERB 1 If you **collect** things, you gather them together for a special purpose or as a hobby.
VERB 2 If you **collect** someone or something from a place, you call there and take them away. • *We **collected** Ali from school.*
VERB 3 When things **collect** in a place, they gather there over a period of time. • *Dust **collects** in corners.*

collection collections
NOUN 1 a group of things you have gathered over a period of time • *a stamp **collection***
NOUN 2 the organised collecting of money, for example for charity, or the money collected

collective noun collective nouns
NOUN a noun that refers to a group of people or things. For example, a flock, a herd and a shoal are all **collective nouns**.

college colleges
NOUN a place where students study after they have left school

collide collides, colliding, collided
VERB If a moving object **collides** with something, it hits it. • *They **collided** with each other as they rushed through the door.*

collision collisions
NOUN A **collision** is when a moving object hits something.

SYNONYM: crash

colon colons
NOUN 1 the punctuation mark (:). It is used to introduce a list, a quotation or an explanation of a statement. • *We need to buy several things: bread, milk, fruit and toothpaste.*
NOUN 2 part of your intestine

→ Have a look at the illustration for **stomach**

colonel colonels
NOUN an army officer with a fairly high rank

a
b
c
d
e
f
g
h
i
j
k
l
m
n
o
p
q
r
s
t
u
v
w
x
y
z

colony colonies

NOUN **1** a country that is controlled by another country

NOUN **2** a group of people or animals living together

colossal

ADJECTIVE very large indeed

WORD HISTORY
from Greek *kolossos* meaning huge statue

colour colours

NOUN the appearance something has as a result of reflecting light • *Red, blue and yellow are the primary* **colours**.

colour blind

ADJECTIVE Someone who is **colour blind** is not able to see the difference between certain colours.

colourful

ADJECTIVE **1** Something that is **colourful** has a lot of different colours or bright colours.

ANTONYMS: dull, colourless

ADJECTIVE **2** A **colourful** story is very exciting and interesting.

ANTONYMS: dull, boring

colourless

ADJECTIVE **1** without colour

ANTONYM: colourful

ADJECTIVE **2** dull and uninteresting

colt colts

NOUN a young male horse

column columns

NOUN **1** a tall, solid, upright cylinder, especially one supporting part of a building

NOUN **2** In a newspaper or magazine, a **column** is a vertical section of writing.

NOUN **3** a group of people or vehicles moving in a long line

coma comas

NOUN a state of deep unconsciousness

comb combs, combing, combed

NOUN **1** a flat object with long, thin, pointed parts, which you use for tidying your hair

VERB **2** When you **comb** your hair, you tidy it with a comb.

combat combats, combating, combated

NOUN **1** fighting • *In the Falklands War many soldiers had to take part in armed* **combat**.

VERB **2** If someone **combats** something, they try to stop it happening. • *We need new ways to* **combat** *crime.*

combination combinations

NOUN **1** a mixture of things • *Fatima won the competition through a* **combination** *of skill and determination.*

NOUN **2** a series of numbers or letters used to open a special lock

combine combines, combining, combined

VERB If you **combine** things, you mix them together. • **Combine** *the butter and sugar, then add the eggs.* • *The book* **combines** *adventure and mystery.*

combine harvester combine harvesters

NOUN a large machine used on farms to cut, sort and clean grain

combustion

NOUN the process of burning

come comes, coming, came

VERB **1** If you **come** to a place, you move or arrive there.

VERB **2** If something **comes** to a particular point, it reaches that point. • *The water* **came** *up to her waist.*

VERB **3** When a particular time **comes**, it happens. • *Spring* **came** *early this year.*

comedian comedians

NOUN an entertainer whose job is to make people laugh

comedy comedies

NOUN a play, film, or television programme that is intended to make people laugh

comet comets

NOUN an object that travels around the sun leaving a bright trail behind it

WORD HISTORY
from Greek *kometes* meaning long-haired

comfort comforts, comforting, comforted

NOUN **1** the state of being pleasantly relaxed

NOUN **2** a feeling of relief from worry or unhappiness • *It's a* **comfort** *to me to know that they are safe.*

VERB **3** If you **comfort** someone, you make them less worried or unhappy.

comfortable
ADJECTIVE **1** If you are **comfortable**, you are at ease and relaxed.
ADJECTIVE **2** Something that is **comfortable** makes you feel relaxed. ● *a comfortable chair*

comfortably
ADVERB in a way that makes someone feel relaxed and without pain ● *He was sitting comfortably in a chair.*

comic comics
NOUN **1** a magazine that contains stories told in pictures
ADJECTIVE **2** funny ● *a comic song*

comma commas
NOUN the punctuation mark (,). It can show a short pause, or it can separate items in a list or words in speech marks from the rest of the sentence.

command commands, commanding, commanded
NOUN **1** an order to do something
VERB **2** If you **command** someone to do something, you order them to do it.

commandment commandments
NOUN one of the ten rules of behaviour that, according to the Bible, people should obey

commemorate commemorates, commemorating, commemorated
VERB If you **commemorate** something, you do something special to show that you remember it. ● *On Remembrance Day we commemorate all the people who died in the two World Wars.*

comment comments, commenting, commented
NOUN **1** a remark about something
VERB **2** If you **comment** on something, you make a remark about it.

commentary commentaries
NOUN a description of an event that is broadcast on radio or television while the event is happening ● *The commentary on the match was on the radio.*

commentator commentators
NOUN someone who gives a radio or television commentary

commerce
NOUN the buying and selling of goods

commercial commercials
NOUN **1** an advertisement on television or radio
ADJECTIVE **2 Commercial** activities involve producing large amounts of goods to sell and make money.

commit commits, committing, committed
VERB When someone **commits** a crime or sin, they do it. ● *The police know who committed the burglary.*

committee committees
NOUN a group of people who make decisions on behalf of a larger group

common commoner, commonest; commons
ADJECTIVE **1** Something that is **common** exists in large numbers or happens often.
NOUN **2** an area of grassy land where everyone can go
ADJECTIVE **3** If something is **common** to two or more people, they all have it or use it. ● *We had a common interest in butterflies.*
PHRASE **4** If two things or people have something **in common**, they both have it. ● *Sarah and I have a lot in common.*

common noun common nouns
NOUN **Common nouns** name things in general. They begin with lower-case letters: *girl, boy, animal, picture.*

common sense
NOUN knowing how to behave sensibly in any situation

Commonwealth
NOUN The **Commonwealth** is a group of countries that used to be ruled by Britain.

commotion
NOUN a lot of noise and excitement

communal
ADJECTIVE shared by a group of people ● *The shop had communal changing rooms.*

communicate communicates, communicating, communicated
VERB When people **communicate**, they exchange information, usually by talking or writing to each other.

communication communications
NOUN **1** the act of exchanging information, usually by talking, writing or, in the case of animals, making sounds ● *the communication of ideas*
PLURAL NOUN **2 Communications** are electrical or radio systems that allow people to broadcast or communicate information.

a
b
c
d
e
f
g
h
i
j
k
l
m
n
o
p
q
r
s
t
u
v
w
x
y
z

77

A
B
C
D
E
F
G
H
I
J
K
L
M
N
O
P
Q
R
S
T
U
V
W
X
Y
Z

communion
NOUN **1** a Christian religious service in which people share holy bread and wine
NOUN **2** the sharing of thoughts and feelings

community communities
NOUN all the people living in a particular area

commuter commuters
NOUN a person who travels to work every day

compact
ADJECTIVE Something that is **compact** takes up very little space, or no more space than is necessary.

compact disc compact discs
NOUN a small plastic disc on which sound, especially music, is recorded. **Compact discs** can also be used to store information which can be read by a computer.

companion companions
NOUN someone you travel or spend time with

company companies
NOUN **1** a business that sells goods or provides a service
NOUN **2** If you have **company**, you have a friend or visitor with you.
PHRASE **3** If you **keep someone company**, you spend time with them.

comparative comparatives
ADJECTIVE **1** You use **comparative** to show that something is true only when compared with something else. • *The group of tourists watched the lions from the comparative safety of their truck.*
NOUN **2** In grammar, the **comparative** is the form of an adjective or adverb that shows an increase in size, quality or amount. It is usually formed by adding *-er* to a word, for example, *bigger, faster*, or by putting *more* before the word, for example, *more difficult.*

comparatively
ADVERB You use **comparatively** to show that something is true only when compared with something else. • *Some children find it hard to make friends, while others find it* **comparatively** *easy.*

compare compares, comparing, compared
VERB When you **compare** things, you see in what ways they are different or similar.
• *We* **compared** *our hair to see whose was longest.*

comparison comparisons
NOUN When you make a **comparison**, you consider two things together and decide in what ways they are different or imilar.

compartment compartments
NOUN **1** a section of a railway carriage
NOUN **2** one of the separate sections of something such as a bag or a box

compass compasses
NOUN **1** an instrument with a magnetic needle that always points north. You use a **compass** to find your way.

→ Have a look at the illustration for **compass point**

PLURAL NOUN **2** **Compasses** are a hinged instrument for drawing circles.

compassion
NOUN pity and sympathy for someone who is suffering

compassionate
ADJECTIVE showing pity and sympathy for someone who is suffering

compass point compass points
NOUN one of the 32 marks on the dial of a compass that show direction • *North, south, east and west are* **compass points***.*

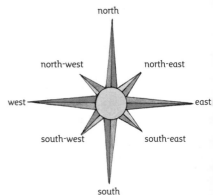

compatible
ADJECTIVE **1** If people or things are **compatible**, they can live or work together uccessfully.
ADJECTIVE **2** If two or more devices are **compatible**, they can be used together.

compel compels, compelling, compelled
VERB **1** If you **compel** someone to do something, you force them to do it.
ADJECTIVE **2** A **compelling** story or event is extremely interesting.
ADJECTIVE **3** A **compelling** argument or reason makes you believe that something is true.

compensate compensates, compensating, compensated
VERB **1** To **compensate** someone means to give them money to replace something that has been lost or damaged.
VERB **2** If one thing **compensates** for another, it cancels out the bad effects of it. • *The trip to Blackpool **compensated** for her missing the school outing.*

compete competes, competing, competed
VERB **1** If you **compete** in a contest or game, you take part in it.
VERB **2** If you **compete**, you try to do better than others.

competent
ADJECTIVE Someone who is **competent** at something can do it satisfactorily. • *He is a **competent** nurse.*

competition competitions
NOUN an event in which people take part to find out who is the best at something

compile compiles, compiling, compiled
VERB When you **compile** information, you collect it and put it together.

complain complains, complaining, complained
VERB **1** If you **complain**, you say that you are not happy about something. • *The neighbours **complained** about the noise.*
VERB **2** If you **complain** of pain or illness, you say that you have it.

complaint complaints
NOUN **1** If you make a **complaint**, you say that you are not happy about something. • *The magazine received several **complaints** from readers about the picture.*
NOUN **2** an illness that affects a particular part of your body • *a skin **complaint***

complement complements, complementing, complemented
VERB **1** If one thing **complements** another, the two things go well together. • *Her piano music **complements** the poem.*

NOUN **2** In grammar, a **complement** is a word or phrase that gives information about the subject or object of a sentence. For example, in the sentence *Rover is a dog*, *is a dog* is the **complement**.

LANGUAGE TIP
Do not confuse *complement* with *compliment*.

---

complete completes, completing, completed
VERB **1** If you **complete** something, you finish it. • *She has just **completed** her third short story.*
ADJECTIVE **2** If something is **complete**, none of it is missing.

completely
ADVERB totally

SYNONYM: utterly

complex complexes
ADJECTIVE **1** **Complex** things have many different parts and are hard to understand.
NOUN **2** a group of buildings used for a particular purpose, such a sports **complex**

complexion complexions
NOUN the quality of the skin on your face

complicated
ADJECTIVE Something that is **complicated** is hard to understand.

complication complications
NOUN something that makes a situation more difficult to deal with

compliment compliments
NOUN If you pay someone a **compliment**, you tell them you admire or like something about them.

LANGUAGE TIP
Do not confuse *compliment* with *complement*.

---

component components
NOUN The **components** of something are the parts it is made of.

compose composes, composing, composed
VERB **1** If you **compose** a piece of music, a letter or a speech, you write it.
VERB **2** If something is **composed** of particular things or people, it is made up of them.

composer composers
NOUN someone who writes music

a
b
c
d
e
f
g
h
i
j
k
l
m
n
o
p
q
r
s
t
u
v
w
x
y
z

79

composition compositions

NOUN **1** a piece of music or writing

NOUN **2** the things that something is made up of • *The **composition** of the two liquids is very different.*

compost

NOUN a mixture of rotted plants and manure that gardeners add to the soil to help plants grow

compound compounds

NOUN a substance that consists of two or more chemical elements • *Water is a **compound** made up of hydrogen and oxygen.*

compound word compound words

NOUN a word with a single meaning, but made up of two or more words. For example, *gingerbread*, *housework* and *teapot* are all **compound words**.

comprehend comprehends, comprehending, comprehended

VERB If you **comprehend** something, you understand it.

comprehensive comprehensives

ADJECTIVE **1** Something that is **comprehensive** includes everything that you need to know.

NOUN **2** a school where children of all abilities are taught together • *She goes to the local **comprehensive**.*

compress compresses, compressing, compressed

VERB If you **compress** something, you squeeze it or shorten it. • *She **compressed** her story into one page.*

compromise compromises, compromising, compromised

NOUN **1** an agreement in which people accept less than they really wanted • *We will need to reach a **compromise** between what we both want.*

VERB **2** When people **compromise**, they settle for less than they really wanted.

compulsory

ADJECTIVE If something is **compulsory**, you have to do it.

ANTONYM: optional

computer computers

NOUN an electronic machine that stores information and makes calculations

screen

keyboard

trackpad

USB port

mouse

computerise computerises, computerising, computerised; also spelt **computerize**

VERB When a system or process is **computerised**, such as train timetables or bank accounts, the work is done by computers.

comrade comrades

NOUN a companion, especially in battle

con cons, conning, conned

VERB **1** If someone **cons** you, or you are **conned**, you are tricked into doing something. • *He **conned** me into buying the tickets.*

NOUN **2** a trick that makes you believe or do something that you would not normally believe or do

concave

ADJECTIVE A **concave** surface curves inwards, rather than being level or bulging outwards.

ANTONYM: convex

conceal conceals, concealing, concealed

VERB If you **conceal** something, you hide it.

conceited

ADJECTIVE Someone who is **conceited** is too proud of their appearance or abilities.

SYNONYMS: bigheaded, self-important

conceive conceives, conceiving, conceived

VERB **1** If you can't **conceive** of something, you can't imagine it or believe it.
• *He couldn't **conceive** of anything more fun than surfing.*

VERB **2** If you **conceive** something such as a plan, you think of it and work out how it could be done. • *Alex **conceived** the idea while eating his lunch.*

VERB **3** When a woman **conceives**, she becomes pregnant.

concentrate concentrates, concentrating, concentrated

VERB **1** If you **concentrate** on something, you give it all your attention. • *I need to **concentrate** on my homework.*

VERB **2** When something is **concentrated** in one place, it is all there rather than in several places. • *The shops were **concentrated** in the town centre.*

concentrated

ADJECTIVE A **concentrated** liquid has been made stronger by having water removed from it. • *concentrated orange juice*

concentration concentrations

NOUN **1** the ability to give your full attention to something you do or hear

NOUN **2** A **concentration** of something is a large amount of it in one place.

concentric

ADJECTIVE **Concentric** circles have the same centre.

concept concepts

NOUN an abstract or general idea

conception conceptions

NOUN the idea you have of something

concern concerns, concerning, concerned

NOUN **1** worry about something or someone

NOUN **2** If something is your **concern**, it is your duty or responsibility.

VERB **3** If something **concerns** you or if you are **concerned** about it, it worries you.

concerned

ADJECTIVE worried about something or someone

concerning

PREPOSITION You use **concerning** to show what something is about. • *an article **concerning** fox hunting*

concert concerts

NOUN a public performance by musicians

concession concessions

NOUN If you make a **concession**, you agree to let someone have or do something.

concise

ADJECTIVE giving all the necessary information using as few words as possible • *a **concise** explanation*

SYNONYMS: brief, short

conclude concludes, concluding, concluded

VERB **1** If you **conclude** something, you examine the facts and decide what your opinion is. • *We **concluded** that the letter was a fake.*

VERB **2** When you **conclude** something, you finish it.

conclusion conclusions

NOUN **1** the end of something

NOUN **2** a final decision about something
• *We wanted to go for a swim in the sea, but we came to the **conclusion** that it was too cold.*

concrete

NOUN **1** a building material made by mixing cement, sand and water

ADJECTIVE **2** real and physical, rather than abstract • *He had no **concrete** evidence.*

concussed

ADJECTIVE If you are **concussed**, you are unconscious or feel confused and sick because something has hit your head.

concussion

NOUN damage to the brain caused by something hitting your head, which makes you unconscious, confused or sick for a short time

condemn condemns, condemning, condemned

VERB **1** If you **condemn** something, you say it is bad and unacceptable.

VERB **2** If someone is **condemned** to a punishment, they are given it. • *The burglar was **condemned** to five years in prison.*

condensation

NOUN a coating of tiny drops of liquid formed on a cold surface by steam or vapour

→ Have a look at the illustration for **water cycle**

a
b
c
d
e
f
g
h
i
j
k
l
m
n
o
p
q
r
s
t
u
v
w
x
y
z

condense **condenses, condensing, condensed**

VERB **1** If you **condense** a piece of writing or a speech, you shorten it.

VERB **2** When a gas or vapour **condenses**, it changes into a liquid.

condition **conditions**

NOUN **1** the state someone or something is in • *The antique clock was still in good* ***condition***.

NOUN **2** something that must happen in order for something else to be possible • *I can go swimming on Saturday on the* ***condition*** *that I do my homework first.*

conduct **conducts, conducting, conducted**

NOUN **1** behaviour • *He won a prize for good* ***conduct*** *in school.*

VERB **2** When you **conduct** an activity, you carry it out. • *I decided to* ***conduct*** *an experiment.*

VERB **3** When someone **conducts** an orchestra, a band or a choir, they direct it in a piece of music.

VERB **4** If something **conducts** heat or electricity, heat or electricity can pass along it. • *Copper* ***conducts*** *electricity well.*

PRONUNCIATION TIP

The noun is pronounced **kon**-duct. The verb is pronounced kon-**duct**.

conductivity

NOUN the ability of a substance to conduct heat or electricity

conductor **conductors**

NOUN **1** someone who conducts an orchestra or choir

NOUN **2** someone who moves round a bus or train selling and checking tickets

NOUN **3** a substance that conducts heat or electricity

cone **cones**

NOUN **1** a regular three-dimensional shape with a circular base and a point at the top

NOUN **2** the fruit of a fir or pine tree

conference **conferences**

NOUN a meeting at which formal discussions take place

confess **confesses, confessing, confessed**

VERB If you **confess** to something, you admit that you did it.

confession **confessions**

NOUN **1** If you make a **confession**, you admit that you have done something wrong.

SYNONYM: admission

NOUN **2** the act of confessing something, especially as a religious act, where people confess their sins to a priest

confetti

NOUN small pieces of coloured paper thrown over the newly married couple at a wedding

WORD HISTORY

from Italian *confetto* meaning a sweet

confide **confides, confiding, confided**

VERB If you **confide** in or to someone, you tell them a secret.

confidence

NOUN **1** If you have **confidence** in someone, you feel you can trust them.

NOUN **2** Someone who has **confidence** is sure of their own abilities or qualities.

confident

ADJECTIVE **1** If you are **confident** about something, you are sure it will happen the way you want it to.

ADJECTIVE **2** Someone who is **confident** is very sure of themselves and their own abilities.

confidential

ADJECTIVE **Confidential** information is meant to be kept secret.

confine confines, confining, confined
VERB **1** If someone **confines** you to a place, you can't leave it. • *The doctor confined Debbie to bed for two weeks as she had pneumonia.*
VERB **2** If you **confine** yourself to doing something, you do only that thing. • *On their trip abroad, they confined themselves to drinking bottled water.*

confirm confirms, confirming, confirmed
VERB **1** If you **confirm** something, you say or show that it is true. • *The teacher confirmed that we had all passed our spelling test.*
VERB **2** If you **confirm** an arrangement or appointment, you say it is definite. • *Dad confirmed our holiday booking.*

confirmation confirmations
NOUN **1 Confirmation** is when something is said to be definite or shown to be true.
NOUN **2** a ceremony that confirms a baptised person as a Christian and allows them to belong fully to the church

confiscate confiscates, confiscating, confiscated
VERB If someone **confiscates** something, they take it away from someone as a punishment.

WORD HISTORY
from Latin *confiscare* meaning to seize for the public treasury

confiscation
NOUN **Confiscation** is when someone takes something away from someone else as a punishment.

conflict conflicts, conflicting, conflicted
NOUN **1** disagreement and argument
NOUN **2** a war or battle
VERB **3** When two ideas or interests **conflict**, they are different and it seems impossible for them both to be true.

conform conforms, conforming, conformed
VERB **1** If you **conform**, you behave the way people expect you to.
VERB **2** If something **conforms** to a law or to someone's wishes, it does what is required or wanted.

confront confronts, confronting, confronted
VERB **1** If you are **confronted** with a problem or task, you have to deal with it.
VERB **2** If you **confront** someone, you meet them face to face, especially when you are going to fight or argue with them.

confrontation confrontations
NOUN a serious dispute between two people or groups of people who come face to face

confuse confuses, confusing, confused
VERB **1** If you **confuse** two people or things, you mix them up and are not sure which is which.
VERB **2** If you **confuse** someone, you make them uncertain about what is happening or what to do.

confusion
NOUN **1 Confusion** is when you mix up people or things and are not sure which is which. • *The teacher calls me "Sam" to avoid confusion with the other Samuel in the class.*
NOUN **2** the feeling of being uncertain about what is happening or what to do

congested
ADJECTIVE **1** When a road is **congested**, it is so full of traffic that normal movement is impossible.
ADJECTIVE **2** If your nose is **congested**, it is blocked and you cannot breathe properly.

congestion
NOUN **1** There is **congestion** when a road is so full of traffic that normal movement is impossible.
NOUN **2 Congestion** is when your nose is blocked and you cannot breathe properly.

congratulate congratulates, congratulating, congratulated
VERB If you **congratulate** someone, you say that you're pleased about something good that has happened to them, or praise them for something they have done.
• *He congratulated us on winning the competition.*

congratulations
INTERJECTION You say **congratulations** to someone when you are pleased about something good that has happened to them or to praise them for something they have done.

congregation congregations
NOUN the people attending a service in a church.

a
b
c
d
e
f
g
h
i
j
k
l
m
n
o
p
q
r
s
t
u
v
w
x
y
z

83

A
B
C
D
E
F
G
H
I
J
K
L
M
N
O
P
Q
R
S
T
U
V
W
X
Y
Z

congruent
ADJECTIVE In mathematics, things that are **congruent** are exactly the same size and shape, and would fit exactly on top of each other. • *congruent* triangles

conifer **conifers**
NOUN any type of evergreen tree that produces cones

coniferous
ADJECTIVE A **coniferous** tree is any type of evergreen tree that produces cones.

conjunction **conjunctions**
NOUN In grammar, a **conjunction** is a word that links two other words or two clauses, such as *and*, *but*, *or*, *while* and *that*. For example: "I love bacon *and* eggs." "I'm happy, *but* my brother is not".

conjurer **conjurers**
NOUN someone who entertains people by doing magic tricks

conker **conkers**
NOUN a brown nut from a horse chestnut tree

connect **connects, connecting, connected**
VERB 1 If you **connect** two things, you join them together.
VERB 2 If one thing or person is **connected** with another, there is a link between them.

connection **connections**
NOUN 1 the point where two things are joined together
NOUN 2 a relationship between two people, groups or things
NOUN 3 If you make a **connection** at a station or airport, you continue your journey by catching another train, bus or plane. • *Our train was late, so we missed our **connection**.*

connective **connectives**
NOUN a word that connects phrases, clauses or words together

conquer **conquers, conquering, conquered**
VERB 1 If you **conquer** something difficult or dangerous, you succeed in controlling it. • *She **conquered** her fear of spiders.*
VERB 2 to take control of a country by force

conqueror **conquerors**
NOUN someone who takes control of a country by force

conscience
NOUN Your **conscience** is the part of your mind that tells you what is right or wrong.

conscientious
ADJECTIVE Someone who is **conscientious** takes great care over their work.

conscious
ADJECTIVE 1 Someone who is **conscious** is awake, rather than asleep or unconscious.
ADJECTIVE 2 If you are **conscious** of something, you are aware of it.
ADJECTIVE 3 A **conscious** action or effort is done deliberately.

consecutive
ADJECTIVE 1 **Consecutive** events or periods of time happen one after the other. • *We had eight **consecutive** days of rain.*
ADJECTIVE 2 **Consecutive** numbers follow each other in order. For example, 1, 2, 3, 4 are **consecutive** numbers.

consent **consents, consenting, consented**
NOUN 1 permission to do something
NOUN 2 agreement between two or more people • *By common **consent** we went to France for the holiday.*
VERB 3 If you **consent** to something, you agree to do it or allow it to happen.

consequence **consequences**
NOUN result or effect

conservation
NOUN work done to protect the environment or things such as old buildings, and prevent them from being damaged or destroyed

conservationist **conservationists**
NOUN someone whose job is to protect the environment or things such as old buildings

conservative **conservatives**
NOUN 1 a member or supporter of the **Conservative** Party in Britain
ADJECTIVE 2 Someone who is **conservative** does not like change or new ideas.
ADJECTIVE 3 A **conservative** estimate or guess is a cautious or moderate one.

conservatory **conservatories**
NOUN a room with glass walls and a glass roof in which plants are kept

conserve **conserves, conserving, conserved**
VERB 1 If you **conserve** a supply of something, you make it last as long as possible. • *I switched off my torch to **conserve** the battery.*
VERB 2 If you **conserve** something, you keep it as it is and do not change it. • *We should **conserve** this old building.*

consider considers, considering, considered
VERB If you **consider** something, you think about it carefully.

considerable
ADJECTIVE A **considerable** amount of something is a lot of it.

considerate
ADJECTIVE Someone who is **considerate** thinks of other people's needs and feelings.

consideration considerations
NOUN **1** careful thought about something
NOUN **2** something that should be thought about when you are planning or deciding something
NOUN **3** Someone who shows **consideration** pays attention to the needs and feelings of other people.

consist consists, consisting, consisted
VERB Something that **consists** of certain things is made up of them. • *This bread* **consists** *of flour, yeast and water.*

consistent
ADJECTIVE Something that is **consistent** does not change.

console consoles, consoling, consoled
VERB **1** If you **console** someone who is unhappy, you comfort them and cheer them up.
NOUN **2** a panel with switches or knobs for operating a machine

PRONUNCIATION TIP
The verb is pronounced kon-**sole**. The noun is pronounced **kon**-sole.

consonant consonants
NOUN all the letters of the alphabet that are not vowels

conspicuous
ADJECTIVE If something is **conspicuous**, you can see or notice it very easily.

conspiracy conspiracies
NOUN an illegal plan made in secret by a group of people

constable constables
NOUN a police officer of the lowest rank

constant
ADJECTIVE **1** Something that is **constant** happens all the time or is always there. • *We could hear the* **constant** *sound of the waves pounding the shore.*

ADJECTIVE **2** If an amount or level is **constant**, it stays the same.

constellation constellations
NOUN a group of stars

constipated
ADJECTIVE Someone who is **constipated** is suffering from constipation.

constipation
NOUN a condition that affects your bowels so that you find it difficult to go to the lavatory

constitution constitutions
NOUN **1** The **constitution** of a country is the system of laws and principles by which it is governed.
NOUN **2** Your **constitution** is your health.

construct constructs, constructing, constructed
VERB If you **construct** something, you build or make it.

construction constructions
NOUN **1** the process of building or making something
NOUN **2** something built or made

constructive
ADJECTIVE helpful • *The tennis coach made some* **constructive** *comments about my backhand.*

consult consults, consulting, consulted
VERB **1** If you **consult** someone, you ask for their opinion or advice.
VERB **2** If you **consult** a book or map, you look at it for information.

consultant consultants
NOUN an experienced doctor who specialises in one type of medicine • *a* **consultant** *heart surgeon*

consume consumes, consuming, consumed
VERB **1** If you **consume** something, you eat or drink it.
VERB **2** To **consume** fuel or energy is to use it up.

consumer consumers
NOUN someone who buys things or uses services • *magazines aimed at teenage* **consumers**

consumption
NOUN The **consumption** of fuel or food is the using of it, or the amount used. • *The* **consumption** *of ice cream rises in hot weather.*

contact contacts, contacting, contacted

NOUN **1** If you are in **contact** with someone, you talk or write to them regularly. ● *I am in* **contact** *with a pen pal in France.*

NOUN **2** When things are in **contact**, they are touching each other.

VERB **3** If you **contact** someone, you phone them or write to them.

contact lens contact lenses

NOUN small plastic lenses that you put in your eyes instead of wearing glasses, to help you see better

contagious

ADJECTIVE A **contagious** disease can be caught by touching people or things infected with it. ● *Measles is* **contagious**.

contain contains, containing, contained

VERB **1** If a substance **contains** something, that thing is a part of it.

VERB **2** The things a box or room **contains** are the things inside it.

container containers

NOUN something that you keep things in, such as a box or a jar

contaminate contaminates, contaminating, contaminated

VERB If dirt, chemicals or radiation **contaminate** something, they make it impure and harmful.

contamination

NOUN **Contamination** is dirt, chemicals or radiation that make something impure and harmful.

contemplate contemplates, contemplating, contemplated

VERB **1** If you **contemplate**, you think very carefully about something. ● *She* **contemplated** *what she would do at the weekend.*

VERB **2** If you **contemplate** something, you look at it for a long time.

contemporary

ADJECTIVE **1** produced or happening now

ADJECTIVE **2** A **contemporary** work is one that was written at the time of the events it describes.

contempt

NOUN If you treat someone with **contempt**, you show no respect for them at all.

content

ADJECTIVE **1** If you are **content**, you are happy and satisfied with your life.

ADJECTIVE **2** If you are **content** to do something, you are willing to do it.

PRONUNCIATION TIP
This word is pronounced kon-**tent**.

contents

PLURAL NOUN **1** The **contents** of something like a box or a book are the things in it.

PLURAL NOUN **2** The **contents** page of a book tells you what is in it.

PRONUNCIATION TIP
This word is pronounced **kon**-tents.

contest contests

NOUN a competition or game

contestant contestants

NOUN someone who takes part in a competition

SYNONYMS: competitor, player

context contexts

NOUN The **context** of a word or sentence is the words or sentences that come before and after it, which help to make the meaning clear.

continent continents

NOUN **1** a very large area of land, such as Africa or Asia

NOUN **2** In Britain, the mainland of Europe is sometimes called the **Continent**.

→ Have a look at the illustration

WORD HISTORY
from Latin *terra continens* meaning continuous land

continental

ADJECTIVE In Britain, **continental** means on, belonging to or typical of the mainland of Europe. ● **continental** *breakfast*

continual

ADJECTIVE happening again and again ● *Mum had a* **continual** *stream of phone calls.*

continue continues, continuing, continued

VERB **1** If you **continue** to do something, you keep doing it.

VERB **2** If something **continues**, it does not stop.

VERB **3** You say something **continues** when it starts again after stopping. ● *She paused for a moment, then* **continued**.

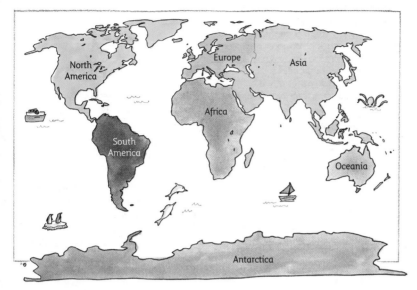

continents

continuous

ADJECTIVE happening all the time without stopping • *The television made a continuous buzzing noise.*

contour contours

NOUN **1** The **contour** of something is its general shape or outline.

NOUN **2** On a map, a **contour** is a line joining points of equal height.

→ Have a look at the illustrations for **map** and **weather**

contract contracts, contracting, contracted

NOUN **1** a legal agreement about the sale of something or work done for money • *He was given a two-year contract.*

VERB **2** When something **contracts**, it gets smaller or shorter. • *Metals contract with cold and expand with heat.*

ANTONYM: expand

PRONUNCIATION TIP
The noun is pronounced **kon**-tract. The verb is pronounced kon-**tract**.

---

contraction contractions

NOUN a shortened form of a word or words, often marked by an apostrophe • *"I've" is a contraction of "I have".*

contradict contradicts, contradicting, contradicted

VERB If you **contradict** someone, you say that what they have just said is wrong.

contradiction contradictions

NOUN a difference between two statements that means they cannot both be true

contrary

ADJECTIVE **1 Contrary** ideas, opinions or attitudes are completely different from each other.

PHRASE **2 On the contrary** is used to contradict something that has just been said.

contrast contrasts, contrasting, contrasted

NOUN **1** a great difference between things • *the contrast between town and country*

VERB **2** If you **contrast** things, you describe or emphasise the differences between them.

PRONUNCIATION TIP
The noun is pronounced **kon**-trast. The verb is pronounced kon-**trast**.

---

a
b
c
d
e
f
g
h
i
j
k
l
m
n
o
p
q
r
s
t
u
v
w
x
y
z

contribute contributes, contributing, contributed

VERB **1** If you **contribute** to something, you do something to make it successful.
● Everyone **contributed** to the class project.
VERB **2** If you **contribute** money to something, you help to pay for it. ● We **contributed** some money to the appeal for the homeless.

SYNONYMS: donate, give

contribution contributions

NOUN **1** If you make a **contribution** to something, you do something to make it successful.
NOUN **2** an amount of money that you give to help pay for something

control controls, controlling, controlled

NOUN **1** If you have **control** over something, you are able to make it work the way you want it to.
NOUN **2** The **controls** on a machine are the knobs or other devices used to work it.
VERB **3** If someone **controls** a country or an organisation, they make the decisions about how it is run.
VERB **4** If someone **controls** something such as a machine, they make it work the way they want it to.
PHRASE **5** If something is **out of control**, nobody has any power over it. ● The fire was **out of control**.

controversial

ADJECTIVE Something that is **controversial** causes a lot of discussion and argument, because many people disapprove of it.
● The film was **controversial**.

controversy controversies

NOUN discussion and argument because many people disapprove of something

convalescent convalescents

NOUN someone who is resting while recovering from an illness

convenience

NOUN The **convenience** of something is how easy it is to use or do.

convenient

ADJECTIVE If something is **convenient**, it is easy to use or it makes something easy to do.
● It's **convenient** living close to the bus stop.

convent convents

NOUN **1** a building where nuns live
NOUN **2** a school run by nuns

conventional

ADJECTIVE Someone who is **conventional** thinks or behaves in an ordinary and accepted way.

converge converges, converging, converged

VERB When things meet or join at a particular place, they **converge**. ● The roads **converge** after three kilometres.

conversation conversations

NOUN When people have a **conversation**, they talk to each other.

convert converts, converting, converted

VERB **1** If you **convert** something, it changes from one thing to another. ● Dad **converted** the loft into a workshop.
VERB **2** If someone **converts** you, they persuade you to change your religious or political beliefs.
VERB **3** In mathematics, **convert** means to change a number from one form to another. These are equal to each other. For example, you can **convert** a fraction to a decimal ($\frac{1}{2}$ = 0.5).

convex

ADJECTIVE A **convex** surface bulges outwards, rather than being level or curving inwards.

ANTONYM: concave

convey conveys, conveying, conveyed

VERB **1** If someone **conveys** people or things to a place, they take them there.
VERB **2** If you **convey** information, ideas or feelings, you tell people about them.

conveyor belt conveyor belts

NOUN a moving strip used in factories for moving objects along

convict convicts, convicting, convicted

VERB **1** If a law court **convicts** someone of a crime, it says they are guilty of it.
NOUN **2** someone serving a prison sentence

PRONUNCIATION TIP

The verb is pronounced kon-**vict**. The noun is pronounced **kon**-vict.

convince convinces, convincing, convinced

VERB If you **convince** someone of something, you persuade them to do it or that it is true. • I **convinced** mum and dad to let me go on the school trip.

convoy convoys

NOUN a group of ships or vehicles travelling together

cook cooks, cooking, cooked

VERB 1 When you **cook**, you prepare food for eating by boiling, baking or frying it.
NOUN 2 a person whose job is to prepare food

cooker cookers

NOUN an apparatus for cooking food

cookery

NOUN the art of preparing and cooking food

cookie cookies

NOUN 1 a sweet biscuit • a chocolate **cookie**
NOUN 2 a small file placed on a user's computer by a website • This website uses **cookies**.

cool cooler, coolest; cools, cooling, cooled

ADJECTIVE 1 Something **cool** has a low temperature but is not cold.
ADJECTIVE 2 If you are **cool** in a difficult situation, you stay calm.
VERB 3 When something **cools**, it becomes less warm.

cooperate cooperates, cooperating, cooperated

VERB 1 When people **cooperate**, they work or act together.
VERB 2 If you **cooperate**, you do what someone asks you to do.

cooperative cooperatives

ADJECTIVE 1 A **cooperative** person does what they are asked to do willingly and cheerfully.
NOUN 2 a business or organisation run by the people who work for it, and who share its profits

coordinates

PLURAL NOUN a pair of numbers or letters that tell you exactly where a point is on a grid, map or graph

cop cops

NOUN (informal) a police officer

cope copes, coping, coped

VERB If you **cope**, you are able to do something even if the circumstances are difficult. • I managed to **cope** with my homework and with looking after my little brother at the same time.

copper

NOUN a soft, reddish-brown metal

copy copies, copying, copied

NOUN 1 something made to look like something else • a **copy** of a famous painting
NOUN 2 A **copy** of a book, newspaper or record is one of many identical ones produced at the same time. • a **copy** of today's newspaper
VERB 3 If you **copy** what someone does, you do the same thing.
VERB 4 If you **copy** something, you make a copy of it.

copyright copyrights

NOUN If someone has the **copyright** on a piece of writing or music, it cannot be copied or performed without their permission.

coral corals

NOUN a hard substance that forms in the sea from the skeletons of tiny animals called **corals**

cord cords

NOUN 1 strong, thick string
NOUN 2 electrical wire covered in rubber or plastic

corduroy

NOUN heavy, ribbed cloth made of cotton

core cores

NOUN the most central part of an object or place • an apple **core** • the Earth's **core**

→ Have a look at the illustration for **earth**

cork corks

NOUN 1 a soft, light substance that forms the bark of a Mediterranean tree
NOUN 2 a piece of **cork** pushed into the end of a bottle to close it

corkscrew corkscrews

NOUN a device for pulling corks out of bottles

corn

NOUN 1 crops such as wheat and barley
NOUN 2 the seeds of these crops

corner corners, cornering, cornered

NOUN 1 the point where two sides or edges of something meet • The TV was in the **corner** of the room.
VERB 2 If someone **corners** a person or animal, they get them into a place they can't escape from. • The police **cornered** the thief.

a
b
c
d
e
f
g
h
i
j
k
l
m
n
o
p
q
r
s
t
u
v
w
x
y
z

A
B
C
D
E
F
G
H
I
J
K
L
M
N
O
P
Q
R
S
T
U
V
W
X
Y
Z

cornet **cornets**
NOUN a small, brass instrument used in brass and military bands

coronation **coronations**
NOUN the ceremony at which a king or queen is crowned

coroner **coroners**
NOUN an official who investigates the deaths of people who have died in a violent or unusual way

corporal **corporals**
NOUN an officer of low rank in the army or air force

corporal punishment
NOUN punishing of people by beating them

corps
NOUN part of an army with special duties
• the Medical **Corps**

PRONUNCIATION TIP
This word is pronounced **kor**.

corpse **corpses**
NOUN a dead body

correct **corrects, correcting, corrected**
ADJECTIVE **1** If something is **correct**, there are no mistakes in it.
VERB **2** If you **correct** something that is wrong, you make it right. • She **corrected** my maths homework.

correction **corrections**
NOUN a change that you make in order to make something right

correspond **corresponds, corresponding, corresponded**
VERB **1** If one thing **corresponds** with another, it is similar to it or it matches it in some way.
VERB **2** If numbers or amounts **correspond**, they are the same.
VERB **3** When people **correspond**, they write to each other.

correspondence
NOUN **1** letters or the writing of letters
NOUN **2** If there is a **correspondence** between two things, there is a similarity between them.

correspondent **correspondents**
NOUN **1** a newspaper, radio or television reporter
NOUN **2** someone who writes letters

corridor **corridors**
NOUN a long passage in a building, with doors and rooms on one or both sides

WORD HISTORY
from Old Italian **corridore** meaning place for running

corrode **corrodes, corroding, corroded**
VERB When something **corrodes**, it is eaten away. When iron and steel are **corroded**, rust is formed.

corrosion
NOUN a process in which metal becomes rusty or damaged by water or chemicals

corrosive
ADJECTIVE A **corrosive** substance can damage or destroy solid materials such as metal or plastic.

corrugated
ADJECTIVE **Corrugated** metal or cardboard has parallel folds to make it stronger.

corrupt **corrupts, corrupting, corrupted**
ADJECTIVE **1** People who are **corrupt** act dishonestly or illegally in return for money or power.

SYNONYM: dishonest

VERB **2** If you **corrupt** someone, you make them dishonest.
VERB **3** If a bug in a computer spoils files, it **corrupts** them.

cosmetics
PLURAL NOUN lipstick, face powder and other make-up

cosmic
ADJECTIVE belonging to or relating to the whole universe

cosmos
NOUN the universe

cost **costs, costing, cost**
NOUN **1** the amount of money needed to buy, do or make something
VERB **2** You use **cost** to talk about the amount of money you have to pay for things. • You can't have that – it **costs** too much.

costume **costumes**
NOUN **1** a set of clothes worn by an actor
NOUN **2** the clothing worn in a particular place or during a particular period

cosy **cosier, cosiest**
ADJECTIVE warm and comfortable

cot **cots**
NOUN a small bed for a baby, with bars or panels round it to stop the baby falling out

cottage **cottages**
NOUN a small house, especially in the country

cotton
NOUN 1 cloth made from the soft fibres of the **cotton** plant • a **cotton** shirt
NOUN 2 thread used for sewing • a needle and **cotton**

couch **couches**
NOUN a long, soft piece of furniture for sitting or lying on

cough **coughs, coughing, coughed**
VERB When you **cough**, you force air out of your throat with a sudden harsh noise.

could
VERB 1 the past tense of **can**
VERB 2 You use **could** to say that something might happen or might be true. • It **could** rain later.
VERB 3 You use **could** when you are asking for something politely. • **Could** you tell me the way to the station, please?

couldn't
VERB a contraction of could not

council **councils**
NOUN a group of people elected to look after something, especially the affairs of a town, district or county

counsel **counsels, counselling, counselled**
NOUN 1 advice
VERB 2 If someone **counsels** people, they give them advice about their problems.

count **counts, counting, counted**
VERB 1 When you **count**, you say all the numbers in order up to a particular number.
VERB 2 If you **count**, or **count** up, all the things in a group, you add them up to see how many there are.
PHRASE 3 If you **keep count** of something, you keep a record of how often it happens. • Who's **keeping count** of the score?
PHRASE 4 If you **lose count** of something, you cannot remember how often it has happened.
count on
VERB If you can **count** on someone or something, you can rely on them. • You can **count** on me to help.

counter **counters**
NOUN 1 a long, flat surface in a shop, over which goods are sold
NOUN 2 a small, flat, round object used in board games

counterfeit **counterfeits, counterfeiting, counterfeited**
ADJECTIVE 1 **Counterfeit** things are not genuine, but have been made to look genuine in order to deceive people. • **counterfeit** money
VERB 2 If someone **counterfeits** something, they make an exact copy of it in order to trick people.

PRONUNCIATION TIP
This word is pronounced **kown**-ter-fit.

countless
ADJECTIVE too many to count

country **countries**
NOUN 1 one of the political areas the world is divided into
NOUN 2 land away from towns and cities • It is peaceful living in the **country**.

countryside
NOUN land away from towns and cities

county **counties**
NOUN a region with its own local government • The **county** of Lincolnshire is in the east of England.

coup **coups**
NOUN a group of people taking power in a country

PRONUNCIATION TIP
This word is pronounced **koo**.

couple **couples**
NOUN 1 two people who are married or having a romantic relationship
NOUN 2 A **couple** of things or people means two of them, or not very many.

couplet **couplets**
NOUN two lines of poetry together that usually rhyme

coupon **coupons**
NOUN 1 a piece of printed paper that entitles you to pay less than usual for something
NOUN 2 a form you fill in to ask for information or to enter a competition

91

courage

NOUN the quality shown by people who do things that they know are dangerous or difficult ● *She showed great courage in her efforts to save them from the burning house.*

courageous

ADJECTIVE Someone who is **courageous** is willing to do things that they know are dangerous or difficult.

courageously

ADVERB in a way that shows you are willing to do things that you know are dangerous or difficult

courgette courgettes

NOUN a long vegetable with dark green or yellow skin

courier couriers

NOUN **1** someone employed by a travel company to look after people on holiday
NOUN **2** someone employed to deliver letters and parcels quickly

course courses

NOUN **1** a series of lessons or lectures
NOUN **2** a piece of land where races take place or golf is played
NOUN **3** the route something such as a ship or a river takes ● *The captain changed course to avoid the storm.*
NOUN **4** one of the parts of a meal ● *The first course was soup.*
PHRASE **5** If you say *of course*, you are showing that you are absolutely sure about something. ● *Of course she wouldn't do a thing like that.*

court courts

NOUN **1** a place where legal matters are decided by a judge and jury or a magistrate. The judge and jury or magistrate can also be referred to as the **court**. ● *He is due to appear in court next week.* ● *The court awarded him ten thousand pounds in compensation.*
NOUN **2** a place where a game such as tennis or badminton is played
NOUN **3** the place where a king or queen lives and works

courteous

ADJECTIVE **Courteous** behaviour is polite and considerate.

courtyard courtyards

NOUN a flat area of ground surrounded by buildings or walls

cousin cousins

NOUN Your **cousin** is the child of your uncle or aunt.

cove coves

NOUN a small bay on the coast

cover covers, covering, covered

VERB **1** If you **cover** something, you put something else over it to protect it or hide it.
VERB **2** If something **covers** something else, it forms a layer over it.
VERB **3** If you **cover** a particular distance, you travel that distance.
VERB **4** If you **cover** a subject, you discuss it in a lesson, course or book. ● *We covered the Vikings in today's lesson.*
NOUN **5** something put over an object to protect it or keep it warm
NOUN **6** The **cover** of a book or magazine is its outside.
NOUN **7** **Cover** is trees, rocks or other places where you can shelter or hide. ● *When it started raining they ran for cover.*

coverage

NOUN The **coverage** of something in the news is the reporting of it. ● *There was complete coverage of the Wimbledon finals on television.*

cow cows

NOUN a large female mammal kept on farms for its milk and meat

coward cowards

NOUN a person who is easily frightened and avoids dangerous situations

cowardice

NOUN the quality shown by someone who is easily frightened and avoids dangerous situations

cowboy cowboys

NOUN a man employed to look after cattle in America

coy coyer, coyest

ADJECTIVE If someone behaves in a **coy** way, they pretend to be shy and modest.

crab crabs

NOUN a crustacean with four pairs of legs, two claws, and a flat, round body covered by a shell

crack cracks, cracking, cracked
VERB **1** If something **cracks**, or if something **cracks** it, it becomes damaged, with lines appearing on its surface.
VERB **2** If you **crack** a joke, you tell it.
VERB **3** If you **crack** a problem or code, you solve it.
NOUN **4** one of the lines appearing on something when it cracks
NOUN **5** a narrow gap • *My ring fell into a* **crack** *in the pavement.*

cracker crackers
NOUN **1** a thin, crisp biscuit that is often eaten with cheese
NOUN **2** a paper-covered tube that pulls apart with a bang, and usually has a toy and paper hat inside

crackle crackles, crackling, crackled
VERB **1** If something **crackles**, it makes a series of short sharp sounds. • *The bonfire started to* **crackle** *as the flames grew higher.*
NOUN **2** a short sharp sound

cradle cradles, cradling, cradled
NOUN **1** a box-shaped bed for a baby
VERB **2** If you **cradle** something in your arms or hands, you hold it there carefully.

craft crafts
NOUN **1** an activity that needs skill with the hands, such as weaving, carving or pottery
NOUN **2** a boat, plane or spacecraft

craftsman craftsmen
NOUN a man who makes things skilfully with his hands

craftswoman craftswomen
NOUN a woman who makes things skilfully with her hands

crafty craftier, craftiest
ADJECTIVE **Crafty** people get what they want by tricking other people in a clever way.

SYNONYMS: cunning, wily

crag crags
NOUN a steep, rugged rock or peak

cram crams, cramming, crammed
VERB If you **cram** people or things into a place, you put more in than there is room for. • *I* **crammed** *my dirty washing into the washing machine.*

cramp cramps
NOUN pain caused when muscles contract

cramped
ADJECTIVE If a room or a building is **cramped**, it is not big enough for the people or things in it.

crane cranes, craning, craned
NOUN **1** a machine that moves heavy things by lifting them in the air
NOUN **2** a large bird with a long neck and long legs
VERB **3** If you **crane** your neck, you extend your head in a particular direction to see or hear something better.

crash crashes, crashing, crashed
NOUN **1** an accident in which a moving vehicle hits something and is damaged
NOUN **2** a sudden, loud noise
VERB **3** If a vehicle **crashes**, it hits something and is badly damaged.

crate crates
NOUN a large box used for transporting or storing things

crater craters
NOUN a wide hole in the ground caused by something hitting it or by an explosion • *The surface of the moon has many* **craters**.

WORD HISTORY
from Greek *krater* meaning mixing-bowl

crave craves, craving, craved
VERB If you **crave** something, you want it very much. • *I* **craved** *a bar of chocolate.*

craving cravings
NOUN a feeling of wanting something very much

crawl crawls, crawling, crawled
VERB **1** When you **crawl**, you move forward on your hands and knees.
VERB **2** When an insect or vehicle **crawls** somewhere, it moves there very slowly.

crayon crayons
NOUN a coloured pencil or a stick of coloured wax

craze crazes
NOUN something that is very popular for a short time

crazy crazier, craziest
ADJECTIVE **1** (*informal*) very strange or foolish
ADJECTIVE **2** (*informal*) If you are **crazy** about something or someone, you like them very much.

a
b
c
d
e
f
g
h
i
j
k
l
m
n
o
p
q
r
s
t
u
v
w
x
y
z

93

creak creaks, creaking, creaked
VERB **1** If something **creaks**, it makes a harsh sound when it moves or when you stand on it.
NOUN **2** a harsh, squeaking noise

creaky creakier, creakiest
ADJECTIVE Something that is **creaky** makes a harsh sound when it moves or when you stand on it. • *creaky* floorboards

cream creams
NOUN **1** a thick, yellowish-white liquid taken from the top of milk
NOUN **2** a substance that you can rub into your skin to make it soft or protect it
ADJECTIVE **3** a yellowish-white colour

crease creases, creasing, creased
NOUN **1** an irregular line that appears on cloth or paper when it is crumpled
NOUN **2** a straight line on something that has been pressed or folded neatly • *Dad ironed a sharp* **crease** *in his best trousers.*
VERB **3** If you **crease** something, you make lines appear on it.

create creates, creating, created
VERB If someone **creates** something, they cause it to happen or exist.

creation creations
NOUN **1 Creation** is when someone makes something happen or exist.
NOUN **2** something that has been made

creative
ADJECTIVE **Creative** people are good at inventing and developing new ideas.

creature creatures
NOUN any living thing that can make itself move

crèche crèches
NOUN a place where small children are looked after while their parents are working

---

WORD HISTORY
from old French *crèche* meaning crib or manger

---

credit credits
NOUN **1** a system where you pay for something in small amounts, regularly over a period of time
NOUN **2** praise given to you for good work
PLURAL NOUN **3 Credits** are the list of people who helped make a film, record or television programme.
PHRASE **4** If your bank account is **in credit**, you have money in it.

credit card credit cards
NOUN a plastic card that allows someone to buy goods on credit rather than paying with cash

creek creeks
NOUN a narrow inlet where the sea comes a long way into the land

creep creeps, creeping, crept
VERB If you **creep** somewhere, you move there quietly and slowly.

creepy creepier, creepiest
ADJECTIVE strange and frightening • *The film was* **creepy**.

SYNONYMS: eerie, spooky

cremate cremates, cremating, cremated
VERB If someone is **cremated** when they die, their body is burned instead of buried.

crematorium crematoriums or crematoria
NOUN a building in which people are cremated

crescent crescents
NOUN a curved shape that is wider in the middle than at the ends, like a new moon

cress
NOUN a plant with small, strong-tasting leaves, used in salads

crest crests
NOUN **1** the highest part of a hill or wave
NOUN **2** a tuft of feathers on top of a bird's head
NOUN **3** a special sign of something, such as a school or other organisation

crevice crevices
NOUN a narrow crack or gap in rock

crew crews
NOUN The **crew** of a ship, aeroplane or spacecraft are the people who operate it.

cricket crickets
NOUN **1** an outdoor game played by two teams, who take turns at scoring runs by hitting a ball with a bat
NOUN **2** a small, jumping insect that produces sounds by rubbing its wings together

cried
VERB the past tense and past participle of **cry**

crime crimes
NOUN an action for which you can be punished by law

criminal criminals
NOUN 1 someone who has committed a crime
ADJECTIVE 2 involving or relating to crime

crimson
NOUN 1 a dark, purplish-red colour
ADJECTIVE 2 having a dark, purplish-red colour

crinkle crinkles, crinkling, crinkled
VERB 1 If something **crinkles**, it becomes slightly creased or folded.
NOUN 2 a small crease or fold

cripple cripples, crippling, crippled
VERB If someone is **crippled** by something, they are injured so severely that they can never move properly again.

crippling
ADJECTIVE causing so much pain that someone is not able to move properly

crisis crises
NOUN a serious or dangerous situation
• The food **crisis** was caused by drought.

crisp crisper, crispest; crisps
ADJECTIVE 1 pleasantly fresh and firm
• **crisp** lettuce leaves
NOUN 2 a thin slice of potato that has been fried until it is hard and crunchy

critic critics
NOUN 1 someone who writes reviews of books, films, plays or musical performances for newspapers or magazines
NOUN 2 a person who criticises someone or something publicly

critical
ADJECTIVE 1 A **critical** time or situation is a very important and serious one when things must be done correctly.
ADJECTIVE 2 If the state of a sick or injured person is **critical**, they are in danger of dying.
ADJECTIVE 3 Someone who is **critical** judges people and things very severely.

criticise criticises, criticising, criticised;
also spelt **criticize**
VERB If you **criticise** someone or something, you say what you think is wrong with them.

criticism criticisms
NOUN 1 spoken or written disapproval of someone or something

NOUN 2 A **criticism** of a book, film or play is an examination of its good and bad points.

croak croaks, croaking, croaked
VERB 1 When animals and birds **croak**, they make harsh, low sounds.
NOUN 2 a harsh, low sound

croaky croakier, croakiest
ADJECTIVE If your voice is **croaky**, it sounds low and harsh as if you have a sore throat.

crochet crochets, crocheting, crocheted
NOUN 1 a kind of knitting done with a hooked needle and cotton or wool
VERB 2 If you **crochet**, you use a hooked needle and wool or cotton to make lacy material for things such as clothes and shawls.

PRONUNCIATION TIP
This word is pronounced **kroh**-shay.

---

crockery
NOUN things you use for eating and drinking, such as plates, cups, bowls and saucers

crocodile crocodiles
NOUN a large, scaly, meat-eating reptile that lives in tropical rivers

---

WORD HISTORY
from Greek *krokodeilos* meaning lizard

---

crocodile clip crocodile clips
NOUN a small clip used for making electrical connections

crocus crocuses
NOUN **Crocuses** are yellow, purple or white flowers that grow in early spring.

crook crooks
NOUN 1 a criminal
NOUN 2 The **crook** of your arm or leg is the soft, inside part of your elbow or your knee.
NOUN 3 a long stick with a hooked end used by shepherds

crooked
ADJECTIVE 1 bent or twisted
ADJECTIVE 2 dishonest

crop crops, cropping, cropped
NOUN 1 plants such as wheat and potatoes that are grown for food
NOUN 2 the plants collected at harvest time
• They gather two **crops** of rice a year.
VERB 3 If you **crop** something such as your hair, you cut it very short.

a
b
c
d
e
f
g
h
i
j
k
l
m
n
o
p
q
r
s
t
u
v
w
x
y
z

95

cross crosses, crossing, crossed; **crosser, crossest**

VERB **1** If you **cross** something, such as a room or a road, you go to the other side of it.

VERB **2** Lines or roads that **cross** meet and go across each other.

VERB **3** If you **cross** your arms, legs or fingers, you put one on top of the other.

NOUN **4** a mark or a shape like + or ×

ADJECTIVE **5** Someone who is **cross** is rather angry.

cross out

VERB If you **cross out** words on a page, you draw a line through them.

cross-country

NOUN the sport of running across open countryside, rather than on roads or a track

crossing crossings

NOUN **1** a place where you can cross the road, a railway or a river

NOUN **2** a journey by ship to a place across the sea

crossroads

NOUN a place where two roads meet and cross each other

cross-section cross-sections

NOUN **1** the flat part of something that you see when you cut straight through it to see inside • We looked at **cross-sections** of kiwi fruit and oranges.

NOUN **2** a typical sample of people or things • We interviewed a **cross-section** of teenagers.

crossword crosswords

NOUN a word puzzle in which you work out answers to clues and write them in a grid

crouch crouches, crouching, crouched

VERB If you **crouch**, you lower your body with your knees bent.

crow crows, crowing, crowed

NOUN **1** a large black bird that makes a loud, harsh sound

VERB **2** When a cock **crows**, it makes a series of loud sounds, usually early in the morning.

crowbar crowbars

NOUN a heavy, iron bar used as a lever or for forcing things open

crowd crowds, crowding, crowded

NOUN **1** a large group of people gathered together

VERB **2** When people **crowd** around someone or something, they gather closely together around them.

crown crowns, crowning, crowned

NOUN **1** a circular ornament made of gold or jewels, which a king or queen wears on their head

VERB **2** When a king or queen is **crowned**, a crown is put on their head and they are officially made king or queen.

crucial

ADJECTIVE Something that is **crucial** is very important.

crucifixion crucifixions

NOUN **Crucifixion** is when a person is tied or nailed to a cross and left there to die.

crucify crucifies, crucifying, crucified

VERB When a person is **crucified** they are tied or nailed to a cross and left there to die.

crude cruder, crudest

ADJECTIVE **1** rough and simple • a **crude** shelter made of old boxes

ADJECTIVE **2** rude and vulgar

cruel crueller, cruellest

ADJECTIVE **Cruel** people deliberately cause pain or distress to other people or to animals.

SYNONYMS: brutal, unkind

cruelly

ADVERB in a way that deliberately causes pain or distress to other people or to animals

cruelty

NOUN behaviour in which someone deliberately causes pain or distress to other people or to animals

cruise cruises, cruising, cruised

NOUN **1** a holiday in which you travel on a ship and visit places

VERB **2** When a vehicle **cruises**, it moves at a constant, moderate speed.

crumb crumbs

NOUN a very small piece of bread or cake

crumble crumbles, crumbling, crumbled

VERB When something **crumbles**, or when you **crumble** it, it breaks into small pieces.

crumple crumples, crumpling, crumpled

VERB If you **crumple** paper or cloth, you squash it so that it is full of creases and folds.

crunch crunches, crunching, crunched
VERB If you **crunch** something, you crush it noisily, for example between your teeth or under your feet.

crusade crusades
NOUN **1** In the Middle Ages, the **Crusades** were a number of expeditions to Palestine by Christians who were attempting to recapture the Holy Land from Muslims.
NOUN **2** a long and determined attempt to achieve something

WORD HISTORY
from Spanish *cruzar* meaning to take up the cross

crusader crusaders
NOUN **1** In the Middle Ages, the **Crusaders** were Christians who made expeditions to Palestine to try to recapture the Holy Land from Muslims.
NOUN **2** someone who makes a long and determined attempt to achieve something

crush crushes, crushing, crushed
VERB **1** If you **crush** something, you squeeze it hard until its shape is destroyed. • *He* **crushed** *the empty can.*
VERB **2** If you **crush** against someone or something, you press hard against them. • *We* **crushed** *against each other in the crowded bus.*

crust crusts
NOUN **1** the hard outside part of a loaf
NOUN **2** a hard layer on top of something • *the Earth's* **crust**
→ Have a look at the illustration for **earth**

crustacean crustaceans
NOUN an animal with a hard outer shell and several pairs of legs, which usually lives in water • *Crabs, lobsters and shrimps are* **crustaceans***.*

PRONUNCIATION TIP
This word is pronounced krus-**tay**-shun.

crutch crutches
NOUN a support like a long stick that you lean on if you have injured your leg or foot • *I was on* **crutches** *while my ankle healed.*

cry cries, crying, cried
VERB **1** When you **cry**, tears come from your eyes because you are unhappy or hurt.
VERB **2** If you **cry** something, you shout it or say it loudly.

NOUN **3** a shout or other loud sound made with your voice

crypt crypts
NOUN an underground room beneath a church, usually used as a burial place

crystal crystals
NOUN **1** a piece of a mineral that has formed naturally into a regular shape
NOUN **2** a type of transparent rock, used in jewellery
NOUN **3** a type of very high-quality glass

cub cubs
NOUN **1** the young of some wild animals • *a fox* **cub** • *a lion* **cub**
NOUN **2** The **Cubs** is an organisation for young boys before they join the Scouts.

cube cubes
NOUN a solid shape with six square faces that are all the same size

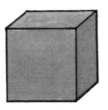

cubic
ADJECTIVE **1** shaped like a cube
ADJECTIVE **2** used to describe volume when you measure height, width and depth • *a* **cubic** *metre*

cubicle cubicles
NOUN a small enclosed area in a place such as a sports centre or a shop, where you can dress and undress

cuboid cuboids
NOUN a rectangular, three-dimensional box shape. A **cuboid** has six faces, all of which are rectangles.

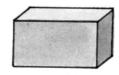

cuckoo cuckoos
NOUN a grey bird with a two-note call. **Cuckoos** lay their eggs in other birds' nests.

a
b
c
d
e
f
g
h
i
j
k
l
m
n
o
p
q
r
s
t
u
v
w
x
y
z

cucumber cucumbers
NOUN a long, thin, green vegetable that is eaten raw

cud
NOUN food that has been chewed and digested more than once by cows, sheep or other animals that have more than one stomach

cuddle cuddles, cuddling, cuddled
VERB 1 If you **cuddle** someone, you hold them closely in your arms as a way of showing your affection.
NOUN 2 If you give someone a **cuddle**, you cuddle them.

cuddly cuddlier, cuddliest
ADJECTIVE 1 If a person or animal is **cuddly**, you want to cuddle them.
ADJECTIVE 2 A **cuddly** toy is soft and is intended for children to cuddle.

cuff cuffs
NOUN the end part of a sleeve, especially a shirt sleeve

cul-de-sac cul-de-sacs
NOUN a road that does not lead to any other roads because one end is blocked off

WORD HISTORY
from French *cul* + *de* + *sac* meaning bottom of the bag

culprit culprits
NOUN someone who has done something harmful or wrong

cult cults
NOUN 1 a small religious group, especially one that is considered strange
ADJECTIVE 2 very popular or fashionable among a particular group of people • *It became a **cult** film.*

cultivate cultivates, cultivating, cultivated
VERB When someone **cultivates** land, they grow crops on it.

cultivation
NOUN **Cultivation** is when someone grows crops on land.

culture cultures
NOUN the ideas, customs and art of a particular society

cunning
ADJECTIVE A **cunning** person or plan achieves things in a clever way, often by deceiving people.

SYNONYMS: crafty, sly, wily

cup cups, cupping, cupped
NOUN 1 a small, round container with a handle, which you drink from
NOUN 2 a large metal container with two handles, which is given as a prize
VERB 3 If you **cup** your hands, you put them together to make a shape like a cup.

cupboard cupboards
NOUN 1 a piece of furniture with doors and shelves
NOUN 2 a very small room for storing things in • *The broom is in the **cupboard** under the stairs.*

curator curators
NOUN the person in a museum or art gallery in charge of its contents

curb curbs, curbing, curbed
VERB If you **curb** something, you keep it within limits. • *You must **curb** your spending on comics.*

curdle curdles, curdling, curdled
VERB When milk **curdles**, it turns sour.

cure cures, curing, cured
VERB 1 If a doctor **cures** someone of an illness, they help them get better.
NOUN 2 something that heals or helps someone to get better • *There is still no **cure** for a cold.*
VERB 3 If someone **cures** meat or fish, they smoke it to give it flavour and preserve it.

curfew curfews
NOUN a rule or a law stating that people must stay indoors between particular times at night

curiosity curiosities
NOUN 1 the desire to know something or about many things
NOUN 2 something unusual and interesting

curious

ADJECTIVE **1** Someone who is **curious** wants to know more about something.

SYNONYMS: inquisitive, nosy

ADJECTIVE **2** Something that is **curious** is unusual or difficult to understand.

SYNONYMS: strange, peculiar

curl **curls, curling, curled**

NOUN **1 Curls** are lengths of hair shaped in tight curves and circles.

NOUN **2** a curved or spiral shape • *A **curl** of smoke rose from the chimney.*

VERB **3** If something **curls**, it moves in a curve or spiral. • *Smoke **curled** up the chimney.*

curly **curlier, curliest**

ADJECTIVE **1 Curly** hair has tight curves and circles in it.

ADJECTIVE **2** curved in shape

currant **currants**

NOUN a small, dried grape. **Currants** are often used in cakes and puddings.

currency **currencies**

NOUN A country's **currency** is its coins and banknotes.

current **currents**

NOUN **1** a steady continuous flowing movement of water or air

NOUN **2** An electric **current** is a flow of electricity through a wire or circuit.

ADJECTIVE **3** Something that is **current** is happening now. • ***current** fashion trends*

curriculum **curriculums** or **curricula**

NOUN the different courses taught at a school or university

curry **curries**

NOUN an Indian dish made with hot spices

curse **curses, cursing, cursed**

NOUN **1** an evil spell • *She said the old house had a **curse** on it.*

VERB **2** If you **curse**, you swear because you are angry.

cursor **cursors**

NOUN a sign on a computer monitor that shows where the next letter or symbol is

curtain **curtains**

NOUN a hanging piece of material that can be pulled across a window

curtsy **curtsies, curtsying, curtsied**

NOUN **1** a little bobbing bow to show respect

• *I made a little **curtsy** to the Queen.*

VERB **2** the action of making a curtsy

curve **curves, curving, curved**

NOUN **1** a smooth, gradually bending line

VERB **2** When something **curves**, it moves in a curve or has the shape of a curve.

• *The lane **curved** to the right.*

curved

ADJECTIVE moving in a curve or having the shape of a curve

cushion **cushions, cushioning, cushioned**

NOUN **1** a soft object that you put on a seat to make it more comfortable

VERB **2** When something **cushions** something else, it reduces its effect. • *The pile of leaves **cushioned** his fall.*

custard

NOUN a sweet, yellow sauce made from milk and eggs

custody

NOUN **1** If someone has **custody** of a child, they have the legal right to keep it and look after it.

PHRASE **2** Someone who is **in custody** is being kept in prison until they can be tried in a court.

WORD HISTORY
from Latin *custos* meaning a guard

custom **customs**

NOUN something that people usually do

• *the **custom** of decorating the house for Christmas*

customary

ADJECTIVE usual

customer **customers**

NOUN a person who buys things from a shop or company

customs

NOUN the place at a border, airport or harbour where you declare any goods that you are bringing into the country

cut **cuts, cutting, cut**

VERB **1** If you **cut** something, you use a pair of scissors, a knife or another sharp tool to mark it or remove parts of it.

VERB **2** If you **cut** yourself, you injure yourself with a sharp object.

NOUN **3** a mark made with a knife or a sharp tool

NOUN **4** a reduction in something • *There were lots of price **cuts** during the sales.*

A
B
C
D
E
F
G
H
I
J
K
L
M
N
O
P
Q
R
S
T
U
V
W
X
Y
Z

cutlery
NOUN knives, forks and spoons

cyberattack cyberattacks
NOUN an attempt to damage or break into a computer system, usually to get the information stored there • *The company claimed its website had been hit by a* **cyberattack**.

cyberbullying
NOUN sending nasty or threatening messages to someone on an electronic device like a phone, tablet or computer • *The girl was a victim of* **cyberbullying**.

cycle cycles, cycling, cycled
NOUN **1** a bicycle
NOUN **2** a series of events that is repeated again and again • *the* **cycle** *of the seasons*
VERB **3** When you **cycle**, you ride a bicycle.

cyclist cyclists
NOUN someone who rides a bicycle

cyclone cyclones
NOUN a violent wind that blows in a spiral like a corkscrew

cygnet cygnets
NOUN a young swan

cylinder cylinders
NOUN **1** a hollow or solid shape with straight sides and equal circular faces at each end
NOUN **2** the part of an engine that the piston moves in

cylindrical
ADJECTIVE Something that is **cylindrical** has a hollow or solid shape with straight sides and equal circular faces at each end.

cymbal cymbals
NOUN a circular brass plate used as a percussion instrument. **Cymbals** are clashed together or hit with a stick.

dab dabs, dabbing, dabbed
VERB **1** f you **dab** something, you touch it several times using quick light movements. • *He* **dabbed** *the stain with a tissue.*
VERB **2** If you **dab**, you do a dance move where you put one arm in front of your face and the other out to the side.

dabble dabbles, dabbling, dabbled
VERB If you **dabble** in something, you work or play at it without being seriously involved in it.

dad or **daddy dads** or **daddies**
NOUN (*informal*) Your **dad** or your **daddy** is your father.

daffodil daffodils
NOUN a plant with yellow, trumpet-shaped flowers that blooms in spring

daft dafter, daftest
ADJECTIVE silly and not very sensible

dagger daggers
NOUN a weapon like a short knife

daily
ADJECTIVE occurring every day

dainty daintier, daintiest
ADJECTIVE very delicate and pretty

dairy dairies
NOUN **1** a shop or company that supplies milk and milk products
NOUN **2** In New Zealand, a **dairy** is a small shop selling groceries.
ADJECTIVE **3** **Dairy** products are foods made from milk, such as butter, cheese, cream and yogurt.

daisy daisies
NOUN a small, wild flower with a yellow centre and small, white petals

WORD HISTORY
from Old English *deagesege* meaning day's eye, because the daisy opens in the daytime and closes at night

Dalmatian Dalmatians
NOUN a large, smooth-haired white dog with black or brown spots

dam dams
NOUN a barrier built across a river to hold back water

damage damages, damaging, damaged
VERB If you **damage** something, you harm or spoil it.

damp damper, dampest
ADJECTIVE slightly wet

damson damsons
NOUN **1** a small, blue-black plum
NOUN **2** the tree that damsons grow on

dance dances, dancing, danced
VERB **1** When you **dance**, you move around in time to music.
NOUN **2** a series of rhythmic movements that you do in time to music
NOUN **3** a social event where people dance with each other

dandelion dandelions
NOUN a wild plant with yellow flowers that form a ball of fluffy seeds

WORD HISTORY
from Old French *dent de lion* meaning lion's tooth, referring to the shape of the leaves

dandruff
NOUN small, loose scales of dead skin in someone's hair

danger dangers
NOUN the possibility that someone may be harmed or killed

SYNONYMS: peril, risk

dangerous
ADJECTIVE If something is **dangerous**, it is likely to harm or kill someone. • *It is dangerous to walk close to the edge of the cliff.*

SYNONYMS: unsafe, hazardous

dangerously
ADVERB in a way that is likely to harm or kill someone • *He was dangerously overweight.*

dangle dangles, dangling, dangled
VERB When something **dangles**, or when you **dangle** it, it swings or hangs loosely. • *We sat by the pool and dangled our legs in the water.*

dappled
ADJECTIVE marked with patches of a different or darker shade • *The lawn was dappled with the shadows of the leafy trees.*

dare dares, daring, dared
VERB **1** If you **dare** to do something, you have the courage to do it. • *She doesn't dare to tell them how she really feels.*
VERB **2** If you **dare** someone to do something, you challenge them to do it. • *I dare you to ask him his name.*

WORD HISTORY
from Old English *durran* meaning to venture or to be bold

daredevil daredevils
NOUN a person who enjoys doing dangerous things

daring
ADJECTIVE **1** bold and willing to take risks • *Ben was probably more daring than I was.*
NOUN **2** the courage required to do things that are dangerous

dark darker, darkest
ADJECTIVE **1** If it is **dark**, there is not enough light to see properly.

ANTONYM: light

ADJECTIVE **2 Dark** colours have a lot of black, grey or brown tones in them.

ANTONYM: light

NOUN **3** The **dark** is when there is no light. • *Many children are scared of the dark.*

darken darkens, darkening, darkened
VERB If something **darkens**, it becomes darker than it was before. • *The sky darkened as the storm approached.*

darkness
NOUN the state of being dark • *The house was in complete darkness.*

darling darlings
NOUN You call someone **darling** if you love them or like them very much.

darn darns, darning, darned
VERB When you **darn** a hole in a garment, you mend it with crossing stitches.

A
B
C
D
E
F
G
H
I
J
K
L
M
N
O
P
Q
R
S
T
U
V
W
X
Y
Z

dart **darts, darting, darted**
NOUN **1** a small, pointed arrow
NOUN **2 Darts** is a game in which the players throw **darts** at a round board divided into numbered sections.
VERB **3** If you **dart** somewhere, you move there quickly and suddenly.

dash **dashes, dashing, dashed**
VERB **1** If you **dash** somewhere, you rush there.
NOUN **2** the punctuation mark (–) which may be used to show a break in a sentence, or instead of brackets to separate extra information from the main text

dashboard **dashboards**
NOUN the instrument panel in a car

data
NOUN information, usually in the form of facts or statistics

LANGUAGE TIP
Data is really a plural word, but is usually used as a singular word: *Customer data is stored here.*

---

database **databases**
NOUN a collection of information stored in a computer

date **dates**
NOUN **1** a particular day or year that can be named • *What is your **date** of birth?*
NOUN **2** If you have a **date**, you have an appointment to meet someone.
NOUN **3** a small, brown, sticky fruit with a stone inside. **Dates** grow on palm trees.

daughter **daughters**
NOUN Someone's **daughter** is their female child.

dawdle **dawdles, dawdling, dawdled**
VERB If you **dawdle**, you are slow about doing something or going somewhere.
• *Don't **dawdle**, we have to be there in ten minutes.*

dawn **dawns**
NOUN the time in the morning when light first appears in the sky

day **days**
NOUN **1** the time taken between one midnight and the next. There are 24 hours in one **day**.
NOUN **2** the period of light between sunrise and sunset

daydream **daydreams, daydreaming, daydreamed**
NOUN **1** pleasant thoughts about things that you would like to happen
VERB **2** When you **daydream**, you drift off into a daydream.

daylight
NOUN the part of the day when it is light

daytime
NOUN the part of the day when it is light

daze
PHRASE If you are **in a daze**, you are confused and bewildered.

dazzle **dazzles, dazzling, dazzled**
VERB If a bright light **dazzles** you, it blinds you for a moment.

dazzling
ADJECTIVE A **dazzling** light is so bright that it blinds you for a moment.

de-
PREFIX added to some words to mean removal or reversal of something • *She **de**bugged the computer program.* • *We had to **de**frost the windscreen before leaving.*

dead
ADJECTIVE **1** no longer living
ADJECTIVE **2** no longer functioning • *The phone went **dead**.*
ADVERB **3** precisely or exactly • *We arrived **dead** on eight o'clock.*

deadly **deadlier, deadliest**
ADJECTIVE **1** likely or able to cause death • *a **deadly** disease*
ADVERB **2** used to emphasise how serious or unpleasant something is • ***deadly** dangerous* • ***deadly** serious*

deaf **deafer, deafest**
ADJECTIVE **Deaf** people are unable to hear anything or unable to hear well.

deafening
ADJECTIVE A **deafening** sound is so loud that you cannot hear anything else.

deal **deals, dealing, dealt**
NOUN **1** an agreement or arrangement, especially in business
VERB **2** When you **deal** cards, you give them out to the players.
PHRASE **3 A good deal** or **a great deal** of something is a lot of it.

deal with
VERB If you **deal with** something, you do what is necessary to sort it out.

dear dearer, dearest
NOUN **1** You call someone **dear** as a sign of affection.
ADJECTIVE **2** Something that is **dear** is very expensive.
ADJECTIVE **3** You use **dear** at the beginning of a letter, with the name of the person you are writing to. • *Dear Sunita.*

death deaths
NOUN the end of the life of a human being or other animal or plant

debate debates, debating, debated
NOUN **1** argument or discussion
NOUN **2** a formal discussion in which opposing views are expressed
VERB **3** When people **debate** something, they discuss it in a formal way.

debit card debit cards
NOUN a plastic card that allows someone to buy goods using the money in their bank account

debris
NOUN fragments or rubble left after something has been destroyed • *After the eruption, volcanic **debris** was found scattered for miles.*

debt debts
NOUN a sum of money that someone owes

debut debuts
NOUN a performer's first public appearance

decade decades
NOUN a period of ten years

decaffeinated
ADJECTIVE **Decaffeinated** coffee or tea has had most of the caffeine removed.

decagon decagons
NOUN a flat shape with ten straight sides

decathlon decathlons
NOUN an athletic competition in which competitors take part in ten different events

decay decays, decaying, decayed
VERB When things **decay**, they rot or go bad.

deceased
ADJECTIVE (*formal*) A **deceased** person is someone who has recently died.

deceit
NOUN behaviour that makes people believe something to be true that is not true

deceive deceives, deceiving, deceived
VERB If you **deceive** someone, you make them believe something that is not true.

decelerate decelerates, decelerating, decelerated
VERB To **decelerate** is to slow down.

ANTONYM: accelerate

December
NOUN the twelfth month of the year. **December** has 31 days.

decent
ADJECTIVE honest and respectable

deception deceptions
NOUN **1** something that is intended to trick or deceive someone
NOUN **2** the act of deceiving someone

deceptive
ADJECTIVE likely to make people believe that something is true when it is not

decibel decibels
NOUN the unit used to measure how loud a sound is

decide decides, deciding, decided
VERB If you **decide** to do something, you choose to do it, usually after thinking about it carefully.

SYNONYM: make up one's mind

deciduous
ADJECTIVE **Deciduous** trees lose their leaves in the autumn every year.

decimal decimals
ADJECTIVE **1** A **decimal** system involves counting in units of ten.
NOUN **2** A **decimal**, or **decimal** fraction, is a fraction in which a dot, called a **decimal** point, separates the whole numbers on the left from tenths, hundredths and thousandths on the right. For example, 0.5 represents $\frac{5}{10}$ (or $\frac{1}{2}$); 0.05 represents $\frac{5}{100}$ (or $\frac{1}{20}$). The number of digits to the right of the decimal point are **decimal** places. • *3.142 is pi given to three **decimal** places.*

decision decisions
NOUN a choice or judgement that you make about something

decisive
ADJECTIVE **1** A **decisive** person is able to make decisions quickly.
ADJECTIVE **2** having an important influence on the result of something • *The first goal was a **decisive** moment in the match.*

a
b
c
d
e
f
g
h
i
j
k
l
m
n
o
p
q
r
s
t
u
v
w
x
y
z

103

deck decks

NOUN a downstairs or upstairs area on a bus or ship

→ Have a look at the illustration for **ship**

declare declares, declaring, declared

VERB **1** If you **declare** something, you say it firmly and forcefully.

SYNONYMS: announce, proclaim, state

VERB **2** (*formal*) If something is **declared**, it is announced publicly. • *War was declared in 1939.*

decline declines, declining, declined

VERB **1** If something **declines**, it becomes smaller or weaker. • *The number of students has declined this year.*

VERB **2** If you **decline** something, you politely refuse to accept it or do it.

decode decodes, decoding, decoded

VERB If you **decode** a coded message, you convert it into ordinary language.

decompose decomposes, decomposing, decomposed

VERB If something **decomposes**, it rots after it dies.

decorate decorates, decorating, decorated

VERB **1** If you **decorate** something, you make it more attractive by adding things to it.

VERB **2** If you **decorate** a room or building, you paint or wallpaper it.

decoy decoys

NOUN something used to lead a person or animal into a trap

decrease decreases, decreasing, decreased

VERB If something **decreases**, or if you **decrease** it, it becomes less. • *The number of children in the class decreased rapidly.*

ANTONYM: increase

decree decrees, decreeing, decreed

NOUN **1** an official order by the government, church or the rulers of a country

VERB **2** If someone **decrees** something, they announce formally that it will happen.

dedicate dedicates, dedicating, dedicated

VERB **1** If you **dedicate** yourself to something, you give your time and energy to it.

VERB **2** If you **dedicate** a book or piece of music to someone, you say that it is written for them.

deduct deducts, deducting, deducted

VERB If you **deduct** an amount from a total, you take it away.

deed deeds

NOUN **1** something that is done • *a good deed*

NOUN **2** an important piece of paper or document that an agreement is written on

deep deeper, deepest

ADJECTIVE **1** going a long way down from the surface • *a deep hole*

ADJECTIVE **2** great or intense • *deep affection*

ADJECTIVE **3** a low sound • *a deep voice*

deer

NOUN a large, fast-running, graceful mammal with hooves, that lives wild in parts of Britain and other countries. Male **deer** have antlers.

LANGUAGE TIP
The plural of *deer* is *deer* or *deers*.

deface defaces, defacing, defaced

VERB If you **deface** something, you damage its appearance in some way. • *The gang defaced the walls with spray paint.*

defeat defeats, defeating, defeated

VERB **1** If you **defeat** someone or something, you win a victory over them, or cause them to fail.

NOUN **2** the state of being beaten or of failing • *The team was downhearted after its defeat.*

defect defects, defecting, defected

NOUN **1** a fault or flaw in something

VERB **2** If someone **defects**, they leave their own country or organisation and join an opposing one.

defective

ADJECTIVE Something that is **defective** is not perfect or has something wrong with it.

defence defences

NOUN **1** something that protects you against attack • *The walls around the castle were a good defence against invaders.*

NOUN **2** A country's **defences** are its armed forces and its weapons.

defend defends, defending, defended
VERB **1** If you **defend** someone or something, you protect them from harm or danger.
VERB **2** If you **defend** a person or their ideas, you argue in support of them.

defendant defendants
NOUN a person in a court of law who is accused of a crime

defer defers, deferring, deferred
VERB If you **defer** something, you put off doing it until later.

defiance
NOUN behaviour that shows you are not willing to obey someone

defiant
ADJECTIVE If you are **defiant**, you behave in a way that shows you are not willing to obey someone.

deficiency deficiencies
NOUN A **deficiency** is when there is not enough of something.

deficient
ADJECTIVE lacking in something

define defines, defining, defined
VERB If you **define** something, you say what it is or what it means.

definite
ADJECTIVE **1** clear and unlikely to be changed • We must arrange a **definite** date for the party.
ADJECTIVE **2** true rather than being someone's guess or opinion

---

LANGUAGE TIP
There is no a in definite.

---

definitely
ADVERB certainly; without doubt • I am **definitely** going on holiday next week.

definition definitions
NOUN a statement explaining the meaning of a word or an idea

deflate deflates, deflating, deflated
VERB If you **deflate** something, such as a tyre or balloon, you let all the air or gas out of it.

ANTONYMS: inflate, blow up

deforestation
NOUN the cutting down or the destruction of all the trees in an area

deformed
ADJECTIVE disfigured or abnormally shaped

defrost defrosts, defrosting, defrosted
VERB **1** If you **defrost** frozen food, you let it thaw out.
VERB **2** If you **defrost** a freezer or refrigerator, you remove the ice from it.

defuse defuses, defusing, defused
VERB **1** If someone **defuses** a bomb, they remove its fuse or detonator so that it cannot explode.
VERB **2** If you **defuse** a dangerous or tense situation, you make it less dangerous or tense.

defy defies, defying, defied
VERB If you **defy** a person or a law, you openly refuse to obey.

degree degrees
NOUN **1** a unit of measurement for temperatures, angles, and longitude and latitude, written as ° after a number • The temperature was 20 °C. • A right angle is a ninety-**degree** angle.
NOUN **2** an amount of a feeling or quality • As captain you have a high **degree** of responsibility.
NOUN **3** a university qualification gained after completing a course of study there

dehydrated
ADJECTIVE If someone is **dehydrated**, they are weak or ill because they have lost too much water from their body.

deity deities
NOUN a god or goddess

PRONUNCIATION TIP
This word is pronounced **day**-i-ti.

---

dejected
ADJECTIVE If you are **dejected**, you are sad and gloomy.

dejection
NOUN a sad and gloomy feeling

delay delays, delaying, delayed
VERB **1** If you **delay** doing something, you put it off until later.

SYNONYM: postpone

VERB **2** If something **delays** you, it makes you late or slows you down.
NOUN **3** If there is a **delay**, something does not happen until later than planned or expected.

a
b
c
d
e
f
g
h
i
j
k
l
m
n
o
p
q
r
s
t
u
v
w
x
y
z

A
B
C
D
E
F
G
H
I
J
K
L
M
N
O
P
Q
R
S
T
U
V
W
X
Y
Z

delete deletes, deleting, deleted
VERB If you **delete** something written, you cross it out or remove it.

deliberate
ADJECTIVE **1** done on purpose or planned in advance
ADJECTIVE **2** slow and careful in speech and action • **deliberate** movements

deliberately
ADVERB **1** on purpose or planned in advance • Police believe the fire was started **deliberately**.
ADVERB **2** in a slow and careful way • He spoke slowly and **deliberately**.

delicate
ADJECTIVE **1** light and attractive • a **delicate** perfume
ADJECTIVE **2** fragile and needing to be handled carefully • a **delicate** china cup
ADJECTIVE **3** precise or sensitive • **delicate** instruments

delicatessen delicatessens
NOUN a shop selling unusual or imported foods

delicious
ADJECTIVE **Delicious** food or drink has an extremely pleasant taste.

SYNONYMS: delectable, scrumptious

delight delights, delighting, delighted
NOUN **1** great pleasure or joy
VERB **2** If something **delights** you, or if you are **delighted** by it, it gives you a lot of pleasure.

delighted
ADJECTIVE very pleased and happy

delinquent delinquents
NOUN a young person who commits minor crimes

delirious
ADJECTIVE **1** unable to speak or act in a rational way because of illness or fever
ADJECTIVE **2** wildly excited and happy

deliver delivers, delivering, delivered
VERB **1** If you **deliver** something to someone, you take it and give it to them.
VERB **2** If someone **delivers** a baby, they help the woman who is giving birth.

delta deltas
NOUN a triangular piece of land at the mouth of a river where it divides into separate streams

deluge deluges
NOUN a sudden, heavy downpour of rain

demand demands, demanding, demanded
VERB **1** If you **demand** something, you ask for it forcefully.
NOUN **2** If there is **demand** for something, a lot of people want to buy it or have it.

democracy democracies
NOUN a system of government in which the people choose their leaders by voting for them in elections

democratic
ADJECTIVE using a system of government in which the people choose their leaders by voting for them in elections

demolish demolishes, demolishing, demolished
VERB If someone **demolishes** a building, they knock it down.

demolition
NOUN **Demolition** is when a building is knocked down.

demon demons
NOUN a devil or an evil spirit

demonstrate demonstrates, demonstrating, demonstrated
VERB **1** If you **demonstrate** something to somebody, you show them how to do it or how it works.
VERB **2** If people **demonstrate**, they march or gather together to show that they oppose or support something.

demonstration demonstrations
NOUN **1** If someone gives a **demonstration**, they show how to do something or how something works.
NOUN **2** a march or a gathering of people to show publicly what they think about something

den dens
NOUN **1** a home or hiding place of a wild animal
NOUN **2** a special place where you can do what you want without being disturbed

denial denials
NOUN **1** A **denial** of something is a statement that it is untrue.
NOUN **2** The **denial** of a request is the refuse to grant it.

denim denims
NOUN strong, cotton cloth used for making clothes, especially jeans

---

WORD HISTORY
from French *serge de Nîmes*, meaning serge (a type of cloth) from Nîmes

---

denominator denominators
NOUN In mathematics, the **denominator** is the bottom number of a fraction.

dense denser, densest
ADJECTIVE 1 Something that is **dense** contains a lot of things or people in a small area. • We cut our way through the **dense** forest.
ADJECTIVE 2 difficult to see through • The **dense** fog prevented us from enjoying the view over the hills.

density densities
NOUN 1 **Density** is how many people or things are contained in an area.
NOUN 2 In science, **density** is the amount of much space something occupies (its volume) in relation to the amount of matter in it (its mass).

dent dents, denting, dented
VERB 1 If you **dent** something, you damage its surface by hitting it.
NOUN 2 a hollow in the surface of something

dental
ADJECTIVE to do with teeth

dentist dentists
NOUN a person who is qualified to treat people's teeth

dentures
PLURAL NOUN false teeth

deny denies, denying, denied
VERB 1 If you **deny** something, you say that it is not true.
VERB 2 If you are **denied** something, you are refused it.

deodorant deodorants
NOUN a substance used to hide or prevent the smell of sweat on your body

depart departs, departing, departed
VERB When you **depart**, you leave.

department departments
NOUN one of the sections into which a large shop or an organisation is divided

department store department stores
NOUN a very large shop divided into departments, each selling different types of goods

departure departures
NOUN **Departure** is when you leave a place.

depend depends, depending, depended
VERB 1 If one thing **depends** on another, it is influenced by it. • The cooking time **depends** on the size of the potato.
VERB 2 If you **depend** on someone or something, you trust them and rely on them.

dependable
ADJECTIVE If someone is **dependable**, you can trust them to be helpful, sensible and reliable.

depict depicts, depicting, depicted
VERB If you **depict** someone or something, you paint, draw or describe them.

deport deports, deporting, deported
VERB If someone is **deported** from a country they are sent out of it, either because they have no right to be there, because they have done something wrong or because they did not ask permission to be there.

deposit deposits, depositing, deposited
VERB 1 If you **deposit** something, you put it down or leave it somewhere.
NOUN 2 a sum of money given in part payment for goods or services

depot depots
NOUN 1 a place where supplies of food or equipment are stored until they are needed
NOUN 2 a large building or yard where buses or railway engines are kept when they are not being used

depressed
ADJECTIVE sad and gloomy

depression depressions
NOUN 1 a state of mind in which someone feels unhappy and has no energy or enthusiasm for anything
NOUN 2 a hollow in the ground or on any other surface
NOUN 3 a time when there is a lot of unemployment and poverty

deprive deprives, depriving, deprived
VERB If you **deprive** someone of something, you take it away from them or prevent them from having it.

107

depth **depths**

NOUN **1** the measurement or distance between the top and bottom of something, or the back and front of something • The **depth** of the swimming pool at the deep end is 1.5 m.

PHRASE **2 In depth** means thoroughly. • We studied the poem **in depth**.

deputy **deputies**

NOUN a person who helps someone in their job and acts on their behalf when they are away

derail **derails, derailed, derailing**

VERB If a train is **derailed**, it comes off the railway tracks.

derivation **derivations**

NOUN The **derivation** of something is where it has come from.

derive **derives, deriving, derived**

VERB **1** (formal) If you **derive** something from someone or something, you get it from them. • He **derives** great pleasure from music.

VERB **2** If something is **derived** from something else, it comes from that thing. • His name is **derived** from a Greek word.

descant **descants**

NOUN **1** The **descant** to a tune is another tune played at the same time but at a higher pitch.

ADJECTIVE **2** A **descant** musical instrument plays the highest notes in a range of instruments. • a **descant** recorder

descend **descends, descending, descended**

VERB If someone or something **descends**, they move downwards. • We **descended** to the basement in the lift.

ANTONYM: ascend

descendant **descendants**

NOUN A person's **descendants** are all the people in later generations who are related to them.

describe **describes, describing, described**

VERB If you **describe** someone or something, you say what they are like.

desert **deserts, deserting, deserted**

NOUN **1** an area of land, usually in a hot region, that has almost no water, rain, trees or plants • the Sahara **Desert**

VERB **2** If someone **deserts** you, they leave you and no longer help or support you.

PRONUNCIATION TIP
The noun is pronounced **dez**-ert. The verb is pronounced de-**zert**.

deserted

ADJECTIVE A **deserted** building or place is one that people have left and never come back to.

deserve **deserves, deserving, deserved**

VERB If you **deserve** something, you earn it or have a right to it.

design **designs, designing, designed**

VERB **1** If you **design** something new, you plan what it should be like.

NOUN **2** a drawing from which something can be built or made

NOUN **3** a decorative pattern of lines or shapes

desire **desires, desiring, desired**

VERB **1** If you **desire** something, you want it.

NOUN **2** a strong feeling of wanting something

SYNONYMS: longing, want, wish

desk **desks**

NOUN a piece of furniture with a flat or sloping top, which you sit at to write, read or work

desktop

ADJECTIVE small enough to be used at a desk • a **desktop** computer

desolate

ADJECTIVE **1** deserted and bleak • a **desolate** mountain top

ADJECTIVE **2** lonely, very sad, and without hope

desolation

NOUN **1 Desolation** is when a place is deserted and bleak.

NOUN **2** the feeling of being lonely, very sad, and without hope

despair **despairs, despairing, despaired**

NOUN **1** a total loss of hope

VERB **2** If you **despair**, you lose hope completely.

desperate

ADJECTIVE **1** If you are **desperate**, you are in such a bad situation that you will try anything to change it.

ADJECTIVE **2** A **desperate** situation is extremely dangerous or serious.

despicable

ADJECTIVE Something that is **despicable** is nasty, cruel or evil.

despise despises, despising, despised

VERB If you **despise** someone or something, you have a very low opinion of them.

despite

PREPOSITION If you do something **despite** some difficulty, you manage to do it anyway.

dessert desserts

NOUN a sweet food that you eat at the end of a meal

PRONUNCIATION TIP
This word is pronounced de-**zert**.

destination destinations

NOUN the place you are going to

destined

ADJECTIVE meant to happen • *They were destined to meet.*

destiny destinies

NOUN Your **destiny** is your fate: the things that will happen to you in the future.

destitute

ADJECTIVE without money or possessions, and therefore in great need

destroy destroys, destroying, destroyed

VERB If you **destroy** something, you damage it so much that it is completely ruined.

SYNONYMS: demolish, ruin, wreck

destruction

NOUN the process of damaging something so much that it is completely ruined.

destructive

ADJECTIVE Something that is **destructive** can cause great damage, harm or injury.

SYNONYM: damaging

detach detaches, detaching, detached

VERB If you **detach** something, you remove or unfasten it.

detachable

ADJECTIVE able to be removed or unfastened from something • *a coat with a detachable hood*

detached

ADJECTIVE separate or standing apart • *It was a detached house, standing alone at the top of the hill.*

detail details

NOUN **1** an individual fact or feature of something • *I remember every detail of that film.*

PLURAL NOUN **2 Details** about something are information about it. For example, your **details** might be your name and address.

detain detains, detaining, detained

VERB If you **detain** someone, you keep them from going somewhere or doing something.

detect detects, detecting, detected

VERB If you **detect** something, you notice or find it. • *X-rays can detect broken bones.*

detective detectives

NOUN a person, usually a police officer, whose job is to investigate crimes

detector detectors

NOUN an instrument used to detect the presence of something • *a metal detector*

detention

NOUN **1** a form of punishment in which a pupil is made to stay in school for extra time when other children do not have to

NOUN **2** arrest or imprisonment

deter deters, deterring, deterred

VERB If you **deter** someone from doing something, you persuade them not to do it or try to stop them in some way.

detergent detergents

NOUN a chemical substance used for washing or cleaning things

deteriorate deteriorates, deteriorating, deteriorated

VERB If something **deteriorates**, it gets worse.

determination

NOUN great strength and will to do something

determined

ADJECTIVE having your mind firmly made up • *She was determined to pass her exams.*

a b c d e f g h i j k l m n o p q r s t u v w x y z

A
B
C
D
E
F
G
H
I
J
K
L
M
N
O
P
Q
R
S
T
U
V
W
X
Y
Z

110

deterrent **deterrents**
> NOUN something that prevents people from doing something, usually by making them afraid to do it • *We have a car alarm as a **deterrent** to thieves.*

detest **detests, detesting, detested**
> VERB If you **detest** someone or something, you dislike them intensely.

WORD HISTORY
from Latin *detestari* meaning to curse

detonate **detonates, detonating, detonated**
> VERB If someone **detonates** a bomb or mine, they cause it to explode.

detour **detours**
> NOUN If you make a **detour** on a journey, you go by a longer or less direct route.

devastate **devastates, devastating, devastated**
> VERB A place that has been **devastated** has been severely damaged or destroyed.

devastation
> NOUN extreme damage or destruction that affects a large area or a lot of people • *The storm caused **devastation** across three states.*

develop **develops, developing, developed**
> VERB 1 When something **develops**, it grows or becomes more advanced.
> VERB 2 If you **develop** photographs or film, you produce a visible image from them.

development **developments**
> NOUN gradual growth or progress • *There have been great **developments** in technology over the past fifty years.*

device **devices**
> NOUN a machine or tool that is used for a particular purpose

devil **devils**
> NOUN an evil spirit

devious
> ADJECTIVE **Devious** people behave in an underhand, nasty and secretive way.

devise **devises, devising, devised**
> VERB If you **devise** something, you invent it or design it.

devoted
> ADJECTIVE very loving and loyal

devour **devours, devouring, devoured**
> VERB 1 If you **devour** food, you eat it quickly and greedily.
> VERB 2 If one creature **devours** another, it eats it.
> VERB 3 If you **devour** a book, you read it very quickly.

devout
> ADJECTIVE very deeply religious

dew
> NOUN drops of moisture that form on the ground and other cool surfaces at night

diabetes
> NOUN a condition in which a person has too much sugar in their blood

diabetic
> ADJECTIVE suffering from a condition in which you have too much sugar in your blood

diagnose **diagnoses, diagnosing, diagnosed**
> VERB If someone **diagnoses** an illness or problem, they identify what is wrong.

diagonal **diagonals**
> NOUN 1 a straight line that slopes from one corner of a shape to another
> ADJECTIVE 2 in a slanting direction
> • *a **diagonal** line*

WORD HISTORY
from Greek *diagonios* meaning from angle to angle

diagram **diagrams**
> NOUN a drawing that shows or explains something, for example a Carroll diagram or a Venn diagram

dial **dials, dialling, dialled**
> NOUN 1 the part of a clock or meter where the time or a measurement is shown
> VERB 2 If you **dial** a phone number, you press the buttons to select the number you want.

dialect **dialects**
> NOUN the form of a language spoken in a particular area

dialogue **dialogues**
> NOUN In a novel, play or film, **dialogue** is conversation.

diameter diameters

NOUN the length of a straight line drawn across a circle through its centre

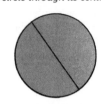

diamond diamonds

NOUN **1** a precious stone made of pure carbon
NOUN **2** a shape with four straight sides of equal length that are not at right angles to each other

diaphragm diaphragms

NOUN a muscle between your lungs and your stomach that is used when you breathe

→ Have a look at the illustration for **respiratory system**

diarrhoea

NOUN a condition that affects your bowels so that you can't stop going to the lavatory

diary diaries

NOUN a notebook with a separate space or page for each day of the year

dice dices, dicing, diced

NOUN **1** a small cube with dots on each of its six faces
VERB **2** If you **dice** food, you cut it into small cubes.

LANGUAGE TIP
Dice is really a plural word, but is usually used as a singular word: *The dice is on the table.*

dictate dictates, dictating, dictated

VERB **1** If you **dictate** something, you say it or read it aloud for someone else to write down.
VERB **2** If you **dictate** to someone, you give them orders in a bossy way.

dictation dictations

NOUN **Dictation** is when you say something or read something aloud for someone else to write down.

dictionary dictionaries

NOUN a book in which words are listed alphabetically and their meanings explained

did

VERB the past tense of **do**

didgeridoo didgeridoos

NOUN an Australian wind instrument made from a long, hollowed-out piece of wood

didn't

VERB a contraction of *did not*

die dies, dying, died

VERB **1** When humans, other animals or plants **die**, they stop living.
VERB **2** When something **dies**, **dies away** or **dies down**, it becomes less intense and disappears. • *The wind **died down**.*

diesel diesels

NOUN **1** a heavy fuel used in trains, buses and lorries
NOUN **2** a vehicle with a diesel engine

diet diets

NOUN **1** the food you usually eat
NOUN **2** If you are on a **diet**, you eat only certain foods for health reasons or to lose weight.

difference differences

NOUN **1** the way in which things are unlike each other
NOUN **2** the amount by which one number is less than another
NOUN **3** a change in someone or something

different

ADJECTIVE If one thing is **different** from another, it is not like it.

LANGUAGE TIP
There are two *es* in *different*.

difficult

ADJECTIVE **1** **Difficult** things are not easy to do, understand or solve.
ADJECTIVE **2** Someone who is **difficult** behaves in an unreasonable way.

difficulty difficulties

NOUN a problem

dig digs, digging, dug

VERB **1** If you **dig**, you make a hole in earth or sand, especially with a spade.
VERB **2** If you **dig** something, you poke it.

A
B
C
D
E
F
G
H
I
J
K
L
M
N
O
P
Q
R
S
T
U
V
W
X
Y
Z

digest **digests, digesting, digested**
VERB To **digest** food means to break it down in the gut so that it can be easily absorbed and used by the body.

digestible
ADJECTIVE Food that is **digestible** is easily digested.

digestive system
NOUN Your **digestive system** is the system in your body that digests the food you eat.

digit **digits**
NOUN **1** a written symbol for any of the numbers from zero (0) to nine (9). The number 46, for example, has two **digits**.
NOUN **2** a finger or toe

digital
ADJECTIVE **1 Digital** computers and devices record or send information in the form of thousands of very small signals.
ADJECTIVE **2 Digital** instruments, such as clocks or watches, have changing numbers instead of a dial with hands.

ANTONYM: analogue

dignified
ADJECTIVE **Dignified** people are calm, and behave in a way that other people admire and respect.

dilemma **dilemmas**
NOUN a situation where you have to choose between two alternatives that are equally difficult or unpleasant

diligence
NOUN **Diligence** is when you work hard and carefully.

diligent
ADJECTIVE hard-working and showing care

dilute **dilutes, diluting, diluted**
VERB If you **dilute** a liquid, you add water or another liquid to it to make it weaker.

dim **dimmer, dimmest; dims, dimming, dimmed**
ADJECTIVE **1** lacking in brightness and badly lit
VERB **2** If lights **dim**, or are **dimmed**, they become less bright.

dimension **dimensions**
NOUN The **dimensions** of something are its measurements or its size.

diminish **diminishes, diminishing, diminished**
VERB If something **diminishes**, or you **diminish** it, it reduces in size or importance.

diminutive **diminutives**
ADJECTIVE **1** very small
NOUN **2 Diminutives** are suffixes that you add to words to show affection or that something is small. For example, -*let* or -*ette* are **diminutives**. • *notelet* • *statuette*

dimple **dimples**
NOUN a small hollow in someone's cheek or chin

din
NOUN a very loud and unpleasant noise

dine **dines, dining, dined**
VERB (*formal*) When you **dine**, you eat dinner in the evening.

dinghy **dinghies**
NOUN a small boat that is rowed, sailed or powered by an outboard motor

dingo **dingoes**
NOUN an Australian wild dog

dingy **dingier, dingiest**
ADJECTIVE shabby and dirty to look at

PRONUNCIATION TIP
This word is pronounced **din**-ji.

dinner **dinners**
NOUN the main meal of the day, eaten either in the evening or in the middle of the day

dinosaur **dinosaurs**
NOUN a large reptile that lived in prehistoric times

WORD HISTORY
from Greek *deinos* + *sauros* meaning fearful lizard

dip **dips, dipping, dipped**
VERB **1** If you **dip** something into a liquid, you lower it in and take it out again quickly.

VERB **2** If something **dips**, it slopes downwards or goes below a certain level.
• *The road **dipped** suddenly.*
NOUN **3** a downward slope or hollow
• *There was a **dip** in the road.*
NOUN **4** a quick swim
NOUN **5** a savoury mixture for eating, in which you dip crisps, crackers or vegetables

diploma diplomas
NOUN a certificate that is awarded to a student who has successfully completed a course of study

diplomat diplomats
NOUN an official who negotiates with another country on behalf of his or her own country

diplomatic
ADJECTIVE If you are **diplomatic**, you are tactful and say and do things without offending people.

direct directs, directing, directed
ADVERB **1** If you go **direct** to a place, you go straight there. • *This train goes **direct** to Paris.*
ADJECTIVE **2** If someone's speech or behaviour is **direct**, they are honest and say what they mean.

SYNONYMS: frank, open, straightforward

VERB **3** If you **direct** someone to a place, you show them how to get there.
VERB **4** Someone who **directs** a film or play decides the way it is made and performed.

direction directions
NOUN **1** the way that someone or something is moving or pointing
PLURAL NOUN **2** instructions that tell you how to do something or how to get somewhere

direct message direct messages
NOUN a message sent to someone privately on a social media website

director directors
NOUN **1** a senior manager of a company
NOUN **2** the person who decides how a film or play is made and performed

directory directories
NOUN **1** a book that gives lists of information, such as people's names, addresses and telephone numbers

NOUN **2** an area of a computer disk which contains one or more files or other directories

dirt
NOUN **1** any unclean substance such as mud, dust or stains
NOUN **2** earth or soil

dirty dirtier, dirtiest
ADJECTIVE **1** marked or covered with dirt

SYNONYMS: filthy, grubby, mucky

ADJECTIVE **2** unfair or dishonest

dis-
PREFIX added to some words to make them mean the opposite. For example, **dis**contented means not content.

disability disabilities
NOUN a condition or illness that limits the way in which someone can use their body or part of their body

disabled
ADJECTIVE A **disabled** person has a disability.

disadvantage disadvantages
NOUN something that makes things difficult

disagree disagrees, disagreeing, disagreed
VERB **1** If you **disagree** with someone, you have a different opinion or view from them.
VERB **2** If you **disagree** with an action or proposal, you believe it is wrong.

disagreeable
ADJECTIVE unpleasant or unhelpful and unfriendly • *The woman was very **disagreeable** and did not even offer to help.*

disappear disappears, disappearing, disappeared
VERB **1** If someone or something **disappears**, they go where they cannot be seen or found.
VERB **2** If something **disappears**, it stops existing or happening.

disappoint disappoints, disappointing, disappointed
VERB If someone or something **disappoints** you, they fail to live up to what you expected.

disapproval
NOUN **Disapproval** is thinking that something or someone is bad or wrong.

a
b
c
d
e
f
g
h
i
j
k
l
m
n
o
p
q
r
s
t
u
v
w
x
y
z

113

A
B
C
D
E
F
G
H
I
J
K
L
M
N
O
P
Q
R
S
T
U
V
W
X
Y
Z

disapprove disapproves, disapproving, disapproved
VERB If you **disapprove** of something or someone, you think they are bad or wrong.

disapproving
ADJECTIVE showing that you think something or someone is bad or wrong
• a **disapproving** look

disaster disasters
NOUN **1** a very damaging event or accident, such as an earthquake or a plane crash

SYNONYMS: calamity, catastrophe

NOUN **2** a complete failure • The party was a **disaster**.

disastrous
ADJECTIVE Something that is **disastrous** is a complete failure.

disc discs; also spelt **disk**
NOUN **1** anything with a flat, circular shape, such as a DVD
NOUN **2** a disc-shaped storage device used in computers • All my music is stored on the hard **disc**.

discard discards, discarding, discarded
VERB If you **discard** something, you throw it away because it is of no use to you anymore.

discharge discharges, discharging, discharged
VERB **1** If a doctor **discharges** someone from hospital, they allow them to leave.
VERB **2** If something **discharges** or is **discharged**, it is given or sent out. • Cars **discharge** exhaust fumes into the atmosphere.

disciple disciples
NOUN a follower of someone or something

WORD HISTORY
from Latin *discipulus* meaning pupil

discipline disciplines, disciplining, disciplined
NOUN **1** making people obey rules, by training them and by punishing them when they break the rules
NOUN **2** the ability to behave and work in a controlled way
VERB **3** If an parent or teacher **disciplines** a child, they punish them.

disco discos
NOUN a party or a club where people go to dance to pop music

discomfort
NOUN slight pain or worry

disconnect disconnects, disconnecting, disconnected
VERB If you **disconnect** something, you detach it from something else or break its connection.

discontinue discontinues, discontinuing, discontinued
VERB If you **discontinue** something, you stop doing it.

discount discounts
NOUN a reduction in the price of something

discourage discourages, discouraging, discouraged
VERB **1** If you **discourage** someone, you take away their enthusiasm for doing something.
VERB **2** If you **discourage** someone from doing something, you try to persuade them not to do it.

discouragement
NOUN a feeling of being less enthusiastic about something and less determined to continue doing it

discouraging
ADJECTIVE making you feel less enthusiastic and less determined to continue doing something

discover discovers, discovering, discovered
VERB If you **discover** something, you find it or learn about it for the first time.
• She **discovered** that they'd escaped.

discreet
ADJECTIVE If you are **discreet**, you keep private things to yourself and can be trusted with a secret.

discretion
NOUN the quality that you have if you are able to keep private things to yourself and can be trusted with a secret

discriminate discriminates, discriminating, discriminated
VERB **1** If you **discriminate** between people, you treat them differently, and often unfairly, because of their race, religion or gender.
VERB **2** If you are **discriminating**, you can recognise differences between things and use your judgement to make choices.

discrimination
NOUN **1 Discrimination** is when people are treated differently, and often unfairly, because of their race, religion or gender.
NOUN **2 Discrimination** is when you can recognise differences between things and use your judgement to make choices.

discus discuses
NOUN a flat, circular weight that athletes throw in a competition

discuss discusses, discussing, discussed
VERB When people **discuss** something, they talk about it in detail.

discussion discussions
NOUN **1** A **discussion** is a detailed conversation about something, especially something important. • *We had a discussion about what we were going to do.*
NOUN **2 Discussion** is when people talk about something in detail. • *There was a lot of discussion about the new school uniform.*

disease diseases
NOUN an illness that affects human beings, other animals or plants

disgrace disgraces, disgracing, disgraced
NOUN **1** something unacceptable • *Tidy your room – it's a disgrace.*
VERB **2** If you **disgrace** yourself, you do something that others disapprove of.

disgruntled
ADJECTIVE If you are **disgruntled**, you are cross and discontented about something.

disguise disguises, disguising, disguised
VERB **1** If you **disguise** yourself, you change your appearance so that people will not recognise you.
NOUN **2** something you wear or a change you make to your appearance so that people will not recognise you

disgust disgusts, disgusting, disgusted
NOUN **1** a very strong feeling of dislike and loathing
VERB **2** If you **disgust** someone, you make them feel a strong sense of dislike and disapproval.

disgusting
ADJECTIVE **1** extremely unpleasant • *The bin smells disgusting.*
ADJECTIVE **2** shocking or very wrong • *It's disgusting that people still have to sleep on the streets.*

dish dishes
NOUN **1** a shallow container for cooking or serving food
NOUN **2** a particular kind of food, or food cooked in a particular way • *a vegetarian dish*

disheartened
ADJECTIVE If you are **disheartened**, you feel disappointed.

dishonest
ADJECTIVE not truthful or fit to be trusted

dishwasher dishwashers
NOUN a machine that washes crockery, cutlery, pots and pans

disinfectant disinfectants
NOUN a chemical substance that kills germs

disintegrate disintegrates, disintegrating, disintegrated
VERB If an object **disintegrates**, it breaks into many pieces and so is destroyed.

disintegration
NOUN **Disintegration** is when something breaks apart into many small pieces.

disk
NOUN another spelling of **disc**

dislike dislikes, disliking, disliked
VERB If you **dislike** something or someone, you think they are unpleasant.

dislocate dislocates, dislocating, dislocated
VERB If you **dislocate** a bone in your body, you put it out of its usual position by accident.

disloyal
ADJECTIVE Someone who is **disloyal** to their friends or family does not support them or does things that could harm them.

dismal
ADJECTIVE depressing and bleak • *It was a dismal day, with rain pouring down and cold winds blowing.*

WORD HISTORY
from Latin *dies mali* meaning evil days

dismantle dismantles, dismantling, dismantled
VERB If you **dismantle** something, you take it apart.

dismay dismays, dismaying, dismayed
VERB **1** If something **dismays** you, it worries and alarms you.
NOUN **2** a feeling of fear and worry

dismiss dismisses, dismissing, dismissed
VERB 1 If you **dismiss** something, you decide that it is not important enough for you to think about.
VERB 2 If someone is **dismissed**, they are told to leave a place or leave their job.
• She **dismissed** the class.

dismount dismounts, dismounting, dismounted
VERB to get off a horse or a bicycle

disobedience
NOUN **Disobedience** is when a person breaks the rules or does not do what someone tells them to do.

disobedient
ADJECTIVE breaking the rules or not doing what someone tells you to do

disobey disobeys, disobeying, disobeyed
VERB If you **disobey** the rules, you break them. If you **disobey** a person, you refuse to do as they say.

disorder disorders
NOUN 1 a state of untidiness
NOUN 2 lack of organisation
NOUN 3 an illness • a stomach **disorder**

disorganised; also spelt **disorganized**
ADJECTIVE Someone or something that is **disorganised** is muddled, confused or badly prepared.

dispatch dispatches, dispatching, dispatched
VERB 1 If you **dispatch** someone or something to a particular place, you send them there for a particular reason.
NOUN 2 an official message

dispensary dispensaries
NOUN a place where medicines are prepared and given out

dispersal
NOUN The **dispersal** of something is its spreading or scattering out in many directions.

disperse disperses, dispersing, dispersed
VERB If a group of people **disperses**, the people in it go away in different directions.

display displays, displaying, displayed
NOUN 1 an arrangement of things designed to attract people's attention • a firework **display**

VERB 2 If you **display** something, you put it on show.
VERB 3 If you **display** an emotion, you behave in a way that shows how you feel.

disposable
ADJECTIVE **Disposable** things are designed to be thrown away after they have been used.

dispose disposes, disposing, disposed
VERB If you **dispose** of something, you get rid of it. • We **disposed** of our litter carefully.

disprove disproves, disproving, disproved
VERB If you **disprove** something, you show that it is not true.

dispute disputes, disputing, disputed
NOUN 1 an argument
VERB 2 If you **dispute** a fact or theory, you say that it is incorrect or untrue.

disqualify disqualifies, disqualifying, disqualified
VERB If someone **disqualifies** someone from a competition or activity, they officially stop them from taking part in it. • The team was **disqualified** from the competition for cheating.

disregard disregards, disregarding, disregarded
VERB 1 If you **disregard** someone or something, you take no notice of them.
NOUN 2 If you show **disregard** for something, you show that you do not care for it.

disrespect
NOUN contempt or lack of respect

disrespectful
ADJECTIVE showing that you do not respect someone

disrupt disrupts, disrupting, disrupted
VERB to cause problems and stop something continuing in its usual way • Rain **disrupted** the school's sports day.

WORD HISTORY
from Latin dirumpere meaning to smash to pieces

---

disruptive
ADJECTIVE causing problems and stopping something from continuing in its usual way

dissatisfied
ADJECTIVE not pleased or contented

dissect dissects, dissecting, dissected
VERB When you **dissect** a plant or part of the body of an animal, you cut it up carefully so that you can examine it closely.

dissolve dissolves, dissolving, dissolved
VERB If you **dissolve** something, or if something **dissolves** in a liquid, it mixes with the liquid and becomes part of it.

distance distances
NOUN 1 The **distance** between two points is the amount of space between them.
NOUN 2 the fact of being far away • *My friend's house is a great **distance** from mine.*

distant
ADJECTIVE far away in space or time • *a **distant** planet*

distil distils, distilling, distilled
VERB When you **distil** a liquid, you purify it by boiling it and condensing the vapour.

distinct
ADJECTIVE 1 If one thing is **distinct** from another, there is an important difference between them. • *The word "chest" has two **distinct** meanings.*
ADJECTIVE 2 If something is **distinct**, you can hear, smell, see or sense it clearly.

distinction distinctions
NOUN 1 a difference between two things
NOUN 2 a quality of excellence and superiority • *a woman of **distinction***
NOUN 3 the highest level of achievement in an examination

distinctive
ADJECTIVE If something is **distinctive**, it has a special quality that makes it recognisable. • *Peppermint has a **distinctive** smell.*

distinguish distinguishes, distinguishing, distinguished
VERB 1 If you can **distinguish** one thing from another, you can see or understand the difference between them.
VERB 2 If you can **distinguish** something, you can see, hear or taste it. • *I heard shouting but couldn't **distinguish** the words.*

distort distorts, distorting, distorted
VERB 1 If you **distort** something, you twist it out of shape.
VERB 2 If you **distort** an argument or the truth, you alter the facts to suit yourself.

distract distracts, distracting, distracted
VERB If you **distract** someone, you take their attention away from what they are doing.

distraction distractions
NOUN someone or something that takes your attention away from what you are doing

distress distresses, distressing, distressed
NOUN 1 **Distress** is suffering caused by pain or sorrow.
VERB 2 If something **distresses** you, it causes you to be upset or worried.
PHRASE 3 If someone or something is **in distress**, they are in danger and need help.

distribute distributes, distributing, distributed
VERB 1 If you **distribute** things, you hand them out or deliver them.
VERB 2 If you **distribute** something, you share it among a number of people.

district districts
NOUN an area of a town or country

distrust distrusts, distrusting, distrusted
VERB 1 If you **distrust** someone, you are suspicious of them because you are not sure whether they are honest.
NOUN 2 suspicion

disturb disturbs, disturbing, disturbed
VERB If you **disturb** someone, you interrupt their peace or privacy.

disturbance disturbances
NOUN 1 something that interrupts someone's peace or privacy
NOUN 2 a situation in which people behave in a noisy or violent way in the street or another public place

disused
ADJECTIVE If something is **disused**, it is neglected or no longer used.

ditch ditches
NOUN a channel cut into the ground at the side of a road or field

dive dives, diving, dived
VERB 1 If you **dive**, you plunge head first into deep water.
VERB 2 If something or someone **dives**, they move suddenly and quickly. • *The birds **dived** to catch the insects.*

diver divers

NOUN **1** a person who uses breathing apparatus to swim or work under water

NOUN **2** a person who takes part in diving competitions

NOUN **3** a bird that catches its food by diving into water

diverse

ADJECTIVE If things are **diverse**, they show a wide range of differences. • *There was a **diverse** collection of paintings in the gallery.*

diversion diversions

NOUN **1** an alternative road you can use if the main one is blocked

NOUN **2** something that takes your attention away from what you are doing

divert diverts, diverting, diverted

VERB **1** to make traffic use a different road because the main one is blocked

VERB **2** to take someone's attention away from something

divide divides, dividing, divided

VERB **1** When you **divide** something, or when it divides, it separates into two or more parts. • *We **divided** the cake into six equal slices.*

ANTONYM: multiply

VERB **2** If something **divides** two areas, it forms a barrier between them. • *A tall hedge **divided** the two gardens.*

ANTONYM: multiply

VERB **3** If you **divide** a larger number by a smaller number, or into a smaller number, you calculate how many times the larger number contains the smaller number. • *Thirty-five **divided** by five is seven (35 ÷ 5 = 7). Six **divided** into three is two.*

divine

ADJECTIVE having the qualities of a god or goddess

divisible

ADJECTIVE A number that is **divisible** can be divided by another number. • *8, 20, 46 and 166 are all **divisible** exactly by two.*

division

NOUN the process of dividing numbers or things

divorce divorces, divorcing, divorced

VERB When married couples **divorce**, they end their marriage legally.

Diwali

NOUN a Hindu festival of light, celebrated in the autumn

DIY

NOUN the activity of making or repairing things yourself. **DIY** is an abbreviation for *do-it-yourself*.

dizzy dizzier, dizziest

ADJECTIVE If you feel **dizzy**, you feel that you are losing your balance and are about to fall.

DJ DJs

NOUN someone who introduces and plays pop records on the radio or at a night club. **DJ** is an abbreviation for *disc jockey*.

DM DMs

NOUN an abbreviation for *direct message*

DNA

NOUN an acid in the chromosomes in the centre of the cells of living things. It is an abbreviation for *deoxyribonucleic acid*.

do does, doing, did, done

VERB **1** If you **do** something, you get on and finish it. • *I've **done** my homework.*

VERB **2** You can use **do** with other verbs. • ***Do** you like ice cream?*

VERB **3** If you ask people what they **do**, you want to know what their job is.

docile

ADJECTIVE A **docile** person or other animal is calm and unlikely to cause any trouble.

dock docks

NOUN an enclosed space in a harbour where ships go to be loaded, unloaded or repaired

doctor doctors

NOUN a person who is qualified in medicine and treats people who are ill

document documents, documenting, documented

NOUN **1** a piece of paper that provides an official record of something

NOUN **2** a piece of text or graphics that is stored as a file on a computer and can be edited

VERB **3** If you **document** something, you make a detailed record of it.

documentary documentaries

NOUN a radio or television programme, or a film, that gives information about real events

dodecagon dodecagons
NOUN a flat shape with twelve straight sides

dodge dodges, dodging, dodged
VERB If you **dodge** something, you move suddenly to avoid being seen, hit or caught.

dodgy
ADJECTIVE (*informal*) dangerous, risky or unreliable

dodo dodos
NOUN an extinct very large bird that was unable to fly

doe does
NOUN a female deer, rabbit or hare

does
VERB a present tense of **do**

doesn't
VERB a contraction of *does not*

dog dogs
NOUN a mammal that is often kept as a pet or used to guard or hunt things

dole doles, doling, doled
VERB If you **dole** something out, you give a certain amount of it to each individual in a group.

doll dolls
NOUN a toy that looks like a baby or a person

dollar dollars
NOUN a unit of money in the USA, Australia, Canada, New Zealand and some other countries. A **dollar** is worth 100 cents.

dolphin dolphins
NOUN a mammal that lives in the sea

dome domes
NOUN a rounded roof

domestic
ADJECTIVE involving or concerned with the home and family • *Dogs and cats are often kept as domestic pets.*

dominant
ADJECTIVE most powerful or important

dominate dominates, dominating, dominated
VERB 1 If someone or something **dominates** a situation or an event, they are the most powerful or important thing in it.
VERB 2 If one person **dominates** another, they have power and control over them.

WORD HISTORY
from Latin *dominari* meaning to be lord over

domino dominoes
NOUN a small, rectangular block marked with two groups of spots on one side, used for playing the game called **dominoes**

donate donates, donating, donated
VERB If you **donate** something, you give it, especially to a charity.

done
VERB the past participle of **do**

donkey donkeys
NOUN an animal like a horse, but smaller and with longer ears

donor donors
NOUN someone who donates something, such as a blood **donor** or someone who gives to charity

don't
VERB a contraction of *do not*

doodle doodles, doodling, doodled
NOUN 1 a drawing done when you are thinking about something else or when you are bored
VERB 2 When you **doodle**, you draw doodles.

doomed
ADJECTIVE If someone or something is **doomed** to an unhappy or unpleasant experience, they are certain to suffer it.

door doors
NOUN a swinging or sliding panel for opening or closing the entrance to something

dormitory dormitories
NOUN a large bedroom where several people sleep

dormouse dormice
NOUN a mammal, like a large mouse, with a furry tail

dose doses
NOUN a measured amount of a medicine or drug

dot dots, dotting, dotted
NOUN 1 a very small, round mark, such as a full stop or a decimal point
VERB 2 When things **dot** a place or an area they are scattered all over it. • *The hillside was dotted with trees.*
PHRASE 3 If you arrive somewhere **on the dot**, you arrive at exactly the right time.

119

A
B
C
D
E
F
G
H
I
J
K
L
M
N
O
P
Q
R
S
T
U
V
W
X
Y
Z

double doubles, doubling, doubled
  ADJECTIVE **1** twice the usual size
  ADJECTIVE **2** consisting of two parts
  VERB **3** If something **doubles**, or if you **double** it, it becomes twice as large.
  • *The number of pupils has **doubled** over the last year.*
  NOUN **4** Your **double** is someone who looks exactly like you.

double bass double basses
  NOUN a very large stringed instrument • *My brother plays the **double bass** in a jazz band.*

doubt doubts, doubting, doubted
  VERB If you **doubt** something, you think that it is probably not true or possible. • *I **doubt** if I'll be allowed to go to the party.*

doubtful
  ADJECTIVE uncertain or unlikely

doubtless
  ADVERB certainly; without any doubt

dough
  NOUN a mixture of flour and water used to make bread, pastry or biscuits

doughnut doughnuts
  NOUN a ring of sweet dough cooked in hot fat

dove doves
  NOUN a bird of the pigeon family that makes a soft, cooing sound

down
  PREPOSITION **1** towards the ground, towards a lower level, or in a lower place • *A man came **down** the stairs to meet them.*
  ADVERB **2** towards the ground, towards a lower level, or in a lower place • *Mum came **down** to the sitting room.*
  ADVERB **3** If you put something **down**, you place it on a surface.
  ADVERB **4** If an amount of something goes **down**, it decreases. • *The water level in the river has gone **down**.*
  NOUN **5** the tiny, soft feathers on baby birds

downcast
  ADJECTIVE If you are **downcast**, you feel sad and without hope.

downhill
  ADVERB down a slope

download downloads, downloading, downloaded
  VERB When you **download** a program from a disk or from the internet, you move it into a file on your own computer.

downpour downpours
  NOUN a very heavy shower of rain

downstairs
  ADVERB **1** If you go **downstairs**, you go towards the ground floor.
  ADJECTIVE **2** on a lower floor

doze dozes, dozing, dozed
  VERB When you **doze**, you sleep lightly for a short period.

dozen dozens
  NOUN **1** A **dozen** is twelve.
  ADJECTIVE **2** A **dozen** things are twelve of them.

Dr
  NOUN an abbreviation for *Doctor*

drab
  ADJECTIVE plain, dull and unattractive

draft drafts
  NOUN an early plan for a story, a book, a letter or a speech that you are going to write

drag drags, dragging, dragged
  VERB If you **drag** a heavy object somewhere, you pull it there slowly and with difficulty.

dragon dragons
  NOUN In stories and legends, **dragons** are large, fire-breathing, lizard-like creatures with claws and leathery wings.

dragonfly dragonflies
  NOUN a colourful insect that is often found near water

drain drains, draining, drained
  NOUN **1** a pipe that carries water or sewage away from a place, or an opening in a surface that leads to the pipe
  VERB **2** If you **drain** something, or if it **drains**, liquid flows out of it or off it.

drake drakes
  NOUN a male duck

drama dramas
  NOUN **1** a serious play for the theatre, television or radio
  NOUN **2** You can refer to the exciting aspects of a situation as **drama**.

dramatic
  ADJECTIVE Something **dramatic** is very exciting, interesting and impressive.

drank
  VERB the past tense of **drink**

drape drapes, draping, draped
VERB If you **drape** a piece of material over something, you hang it loosely.

drastic
ADJECTIVE A **drastic** course of action is very severe and is usually taken urgently.

draught draughts
NOUN **1** a current of cold air
PLURAL NOUN **2 Draughts** is a game for two people, played on a chessboard with round pieces.

PRONUNCIATION TIP
This word is pronounced **draft**.

---

draughty draughtier, draughtiest
ADJECTIVE If a building or room is **draughty**, you can feel a current of cold air in it.

PRONUNCIATION TIP
This word is pronounced **drafty**.

---

draw draws, drawing, drew, drawn
VERB **1** When you **draw** something, you use a pen or pencil to make a picture of it.
VERB **2** If you **draw** the curtains, you pull them so that they cover or uncover the window.
NOUN **3** the result of a game or competition in which both sides have the same score, so nobody wins
PHRASE **4** If you **draw lots**, you decide who will do something by a method that depends on chance, such as taking names out of a hat.

drawback drawbacks
NOUN a problem that upsets a plan • One **drawback** of eating too much chocolate is that you feel sick.

drawbridge drawbridges
NOUN a bridge at the entrance to a castle that could be pulled up to prevent people from getting in
→ Have a look at the illustration for **castle**

drawer drawers
NOUN part of a desk or other piece of furniture that is shaped like a box and slides in and out

drawing drawings
NOUN a picture made with a pencil, pen or crayon

drawing pin drawing pins
NOUN a short nail with a broad flat top. You pin papers to a board by pressing a **drawing pin** through them with your thumb.

dread dreads, dreading, dreaded
VERB If you **dread** something, you feel very worried and frightened about it.

dreadful
ADJECTIVE very bad or unpleasant • The weather has been **dreadful** this week.

SYNONYMS: atrocious, awful, terrible

dreadlocks
PLURAL NOUN a hairstyle where the hair is grown long and twisted into tightly curled strands

dream dreams, dreaming, dreamed or dreamt
NOUN **1** a series of events that you experience in your mind while asleep
NOUN **2** a hope or ambition that you often think about because you would very much like it to happen
VERB **3** When you **dream**, you see events in your mind while you are asleep.

LANGUAGE TIP
You can write either *dreamed* or *dreamt* as the past form of *dream*.

---

dreary drearier, dreariest
ADJECTIVE extremely dull and boring

drenched
ADJECTIVE soaking wet

dress dresses, dressing, dressed
NOUN **1** a piece of clothing worn by women and girls, made up of a top and skirt joined together
NOUN **2 Dress** is used to describe clothing or costumes in general, such as national **dress** or fancy **dress**.
VERB **3** When you **dress**, you put on your clothes.
VERB **4** When you **dress** a wound, you clean it and treat it.

dress up
VERB When you **dress up**, you put on clothes that make you look like something else. • Let's **dress up** as witches for the party.

dressing dressings
NOUN **1** a bandage or plaster to put on a wound
NOUN **2** a mixture of oils and spices that can be added to salads and other dishes to heighten the flavour

a
b
c
d
e
f
g
h
i
j
k
l
m
n
o
p
q
r
s
t
u
v
w
x
y
z

dressing gown **dressing gowns**
NOUN a long, warm garment, usually worn over night clothes

drew
VERB the past tense of **draw**

dribble **dribbles, dribbling, dribbled**
VERB **1** If a person or animal **dribbles**, saliva trickles from their mouth.
VERB **2** In sport, when you **dribble** a ball, you move it along by repeatedly tapping it with your foot, your hand or a stick.

drift **drifts, drifting, drifted**
VERB **1** When something **drifts**, it is carried along by the wind or by water.
VERB **2** When people **drift**, they move aimlessly from one place or one activity to another.
NOUN **3** snow or sand piled up by the wind
NOUN **4** (informal) the general meaning of something

drill **drills, drilling, drilled**
NOUN **1** a tool for making holes
NOUN **2** a routine exercise or routine training
VERB **3** If you **drill** a hole, you make a hole using a drill.

drink **drinks, drinking, drank, drunk**
VERB **1** When you **drink** a liquid, you take it into your mouth and swallow it.
NOUN **2** A **drink** is an amount of liquid for drinking.

drip **drips, dripping, dripped**
VERB **1** When liquid **drips**, it falls in small drops.
VERB **2** When an object **drips**, drops of liquid fall from it. • Stop that tap **dripping**.
NOUN **3** a drop of liquid that is falling

drive **drives, driving, drove, driven**
VERB **1** When someone **drives** a car, bus or other vehicle, they make it move, and control where it goes.
VERB **2** If something **drives** a machine, it supplies the power that makes it work.
NOUN **3** a journey in a vehicle
NOUN **4** a private road that leads from a public road to a person's house

driver **drivers**
NOUN the person who makes a car, bus or other vehicle move, and who controls where it goes

drizzle
NOUN light rain

drone **drones, droning, droned**
VERB **1** If something **drones**, it makes a low, continuous humming noise.
NOUN **2** a continuous, low, dull sound
NOUN **3** a male bee

drool **drools, drooling, drooled**
VERB If someone **drools**, saliva drips from their mouth continuously.

droop **droops, drooping, drooped**
VERB If something **droops**, it hangs or sags downwards with no strength or firmness.

drop **drops, dropping, dropped**
VERB **1** If you **drop** something, you let it fall.
VERB **2** If something **drops**, it falls straight down.
VERB **3** If the level or the amount of something **drops**, it becomes less.
NOUN **4** a very small, round quantity of liquid
NOUN **5** the distance between the top and the bottom of something • There was a fifty-metre **drop** to the river below.

drought **droughts**
NOUN a long period during which there is no rain

drove
VERB the past tense of **drive**

drown **drowns, drowning, drowned**
VERB When someone **drowns**, or when they are **drowned**, they die because they have gone under water and cannot breathe.

drowsy **drowsier, drowsiest**
ADJECTIVE feeling sleepy

drug **drugs**
NOUN **1** a chemical used by the medical profession to treat people with illnesses or diseases
NOUN **2** a substance that some people smell, smoke, inject or swallow because of its stimulating or calming effects. **Drugs** can be harmful to health and may be illegal.

drum **drums**
NOUN **1** a musical instrument consisting of a skin stretched tightly over a round frame
NOUN **2** an object or container shaped like a **drum** • an oil **drum**

drunk drunker, drunkest
VERB **1** the past participle of **drink**
ADJECTIVE **2** If someone is **drunk**, they have consumed too much alcohol.

dry drier or **dryer, driest; dries, drying, dried**
ADJECTIVE **1** Something that is **dry** is not wet, and contains no water or liquid.
VERB **2** When you **dry** something, or when it **dries**, liquid is removed from it.

dual
ADJECTIVE having two parts, functions or aspects ● *This is a **dual**-purpose room – it is both the office and the spare bedroom.*

dual carriageway dual carriageways
NOUN a road with several lanes in each direction

dubious
ADJECTIVE **1** not entirely honest, safe or reliable
ADJECTIVE **2** doubtful ● *I felt **dubious** about the idea.*

duchess duchesses
NOUN a woman who has the same rank as a duke, or who is a duke's wife or widow

duck ducks, ducking, ducked
NOUN **1** a bird that lives in water and has webbed feet and a large flat bill
VERB **2** If you **duck**, you move your head quickly downwards in order to avoid being hit by something.
VERB **3** If you **duck** someone, you push them under water for a very short time.

duckling ducklings
NOUN a young duck

due
ADJECTIVE expected to happen or arrive
● *The train is **due** at eight o'clock.*

duel duels
NOUN a fight arranged between two people

duet duets
NOUN a piece of music sung or played by two people

dug
VERB the past tense of **dig**

duke dukes
NOUN a nobleman with a rank just below that of a prince

dull duller, dullest
ADJECTIVE **1** not interesting ● *I thought the story was rather **dull**.*
ADJECTIVE **2** not bright, sharp or clear ● *a **dull** day*

dumb dumber, dumbest
ADJECTIVE **1** unable to speak ● *She was so shocked that she was momentarily struck **dumb**.*
ADJECTIVE **2** (*informal*) stupid

dumbfounded
ADJECTIVE If you are **dumbfounded**, you are so shocked or surprised about something that you cannot speak.

dummy dummies
NOUN **1** a rubber or plastic teat given to a baby to suck to keep it happy
NOUN **2** an imitation or model of something that is used for display ● *I first saw the jacket on a **dummy** in a shop window.*

dump dumps, dumping, dumped
VERB **1** If you **dump** something somewhere, you put it there in a careless way.
NOUN **2** a place where rubbish is left
NOUN **3** (*informal*) You refer to a place as a **dump** when it is unattractive and unpleasant to live in.

dune dunes
NOUN a hill of sand near the sea or in the desert

dung
NOUN body waste excreted by large animals

dungarees
PLURAL NOUN trousers that have a bib covering the chest and straps over the shoulders

WORD HISTORY
named after *Dungri* in India, where dungaree material was first made

dungeon dungeons
NOUN an underground prison

dunk dunks, dunking, dunked
VERB If you **dunk** something, you dip it into water or some other liquid for a short time.

duo duos
NOUN any two people who do something together, especially a pair of musical performers

A
B
C
D
E
F
G
H
I
J
K
L
M
N
O
P
Q
R
S
T
U
V
W
X
Y
Z

duplicate duplicates, duplicating, duplicated
VERB **1** If someone **duplicates** something, they make an exact copy of it.
NOUN **2** something that is identical to something else, or an exact copy

PRONUNCIATION TIP
The verb is pronounced **dyoo**-pli-kayt. The noun is pronounced **dyoo**-pli-kut.

duplication
NOUN **Duplication** is when you make an exact copy of something.

durable
ADJECTIVE Things that are **durable** are very strong and last a long time.

duration
NOUN the length of time during which something happens or exists

during
PREPOSITION happening throughout a particular time or while something else is going on ● We had an ice cream **during** the interval.

dusk
NOUN the time just before nightfall when it is not completely dark

dust dusts, dusting, dusted
NOUN **1** dry, fine, powdery material such as particles of earth, dirt or pollen
VERB **2** When you **dust** furniture or other objects, you remove dust from them using a duster.
VERB **3** If you **dust** a surface with something powdery, you cover it lightly with that substance. ● **Dust** the top of the cake with icing sugar.

dustbin dustbins
NOUN a large container for rubbish

duster dusters
NOUN a cloth for dusting things

dusty dustier, dustiest
ADJECTIVE covered with dust

duty duties
NOUN **1** Your **duty** is what you should do because it is part of your job or because it is expected of you.
PHRASE **2** When workers are **on duty**, they are at work.

duvet duvets
NOUN a large bed cover filled with feathers or similar material, which you use instead of sheets and blankets

DVD DVDs
NOUN a type of compact disc that can store large amounts of video and sound information. **DVD** is an abbreviation for *digital video* or *versatile disc*.

dwarf dwarfs, dwarfing, dwarfed
NOUN **1** a person or thing that is smaller than average
VERB **2** If one thing **dwarfs** another, it is so much bigger that it makes it look very small. ● The mountains **dwarfed** the village.

dwindle dwindles, dwindling, dwindled
VERB If something **dwindles**, it becomes smaller or weaker. ● Their supplies of firewood **dwindled**. ● As it got later the light **dwindled**.

dye dyes, dyeing, dyed
VERB **1** If you **dye** something, you change its colour by soaking it in a special liquid.
NOUN **2** a substance used to change the colour of something such as cloth or hair

dying
VERB the present participle of **die**

dyke dykes; also spelt **dike**
NOUN a thick wall or barrier that prevents a river or the sea from flooding the land

dynamic
ADJECTIVE A **dynamic** person is full of energy, ambition and new ideas.

dynamite
NOUN a powerful explosive

dynamo dynamos
NOUN a device that uses movement to produce electricity. A **dynamo** can be used for lighting bicycle lamps.

dynasty dynasties
NOUN a series of rulers of a country, all belonging to the same family

dyslexia
NOUN a certain type of difficulty with reading and spelling

dyslexic
ADJECTIVE having a condition that makes it difficult to read and spell

each
ADJECTIVE **1** every one of a group • **Each** book is beautifully illustrated.
PRONOUN **2** every one of a group • We **each** have different needs and interests.

eager
ADJECTIVE If you are **eager**, you are keen to do something. • She was **eager** to hear all about my trip.

SYNONYM: enthusiastic

eagle eagles
NOUN a large bird of prey

ear ears
NOUN Your **ears** are the parts of your body on either side of your head, with which you hear sounds.

earache
NOUN a pain in your ear • I had really bad **earache**.

eardrum eardrums
NOUN the thin skin inside your ear, which vibrates when sound waves reach it

earlobe earlobes
NOUN Your **earlobes** are the soft parts at the bottom of your ears.

early earlier, earliest
ADVERB **1** before the arranged or expected time • She arrived **early** to get a place at the front.
ADJECTIVE **2** near the beginning of something • I like to go for a walk in the **early** morning.

earn earns, earning, earned
VERB **1** If you **earn** money, you receive it in return for work that you do. • He **earned** some money washing the car.
VERB **2** If you **earn** something such as praise, you receive it because you deserve it.

earnest
ADJECTIVE If you are **earnest** about something, you are very serious about it.

earnings
PLURAL NOUN the money or payment that you receive for working

earphone earphones
NOUN a very small speaker worn in your ear so you can listen to your phone, a radio or an MP3 player

earring earrings
NOUN a piece of jewellery that you wear on your ear

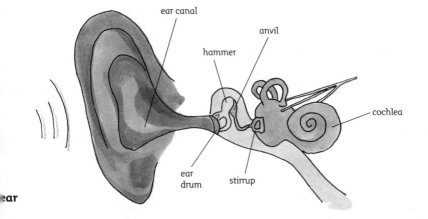

ear canal, anvil, hammer, cochlea, ear drum, stirrup

ear

A
B
C
D
E
F
G
H
I
J
K
L
M
N
O
P
Q
R
S
T
U
V
W
X
Y
Z

earth

NOUN **1** The **Earth** is the planet we live on.

→ Have a look at the illustrations for **greenhouse effect** and **solar system**

NOUN **2** another word for **soil**

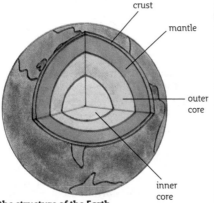

the structure of the Earth

earthquake earthquakes

NOUN a violent shaking of the ground caused by movement of the Earth's crust

earthworm earthworms

NOUN a worm that lives in the soil

earwig earwigs

NOUN a small, brown insect with pincers at the tail end of its body

WORD HISTORY
from Old English *earwicga* meaning ear insect, because it was once believed that earwigs would creep into people's ears

ease eases, easing, eased

VERB **1** When something **eases**, it becomes less difficult or intense. • *The rain **eased** as the dark clouds were blown away.*
NOUN **2** a lack of difficulty or trouble • *She finished her homework with **ease**.*
VERB **3** If you **ease** something, you move it gently and slowly. • *He **eased** himself into the chair.*

easel easels

NOUN an upright frame that supports a picture that someone is painting

easily

ADVERB If you do something **easily**, you do it without difficulty.

east

NOUN one of the four main points of the compass. The sun rises in the **east**. The abbreviation for **east** is E.

→ Have a look at the illustration for **compass point**

Easter

NOUN a Christian religious festival in spring, celebrating Christ's return to life after his death

WORD HISTORY
from Old English *Eostre*, a goddess whose festival was at the spring equinox

eastern

ADJECTIVE in or from the east

easy easier, easiest

ADJECTIVE If something is **easy**, you can do it without difficulty.

eat eats, eating, ate, eaten

VERB When you **eat** food, you chew it and swallow it.

ebb ebbs, ebbing, ebbed

VERB When the sea or the tide **ebbs**, it goes out.

ebony

NOUN a hard, dark-coloured wood

e-book e-books

NOUN a book for reading on an electronic device

e-card e-cards

NOUN a digital card that you send over the internet • *I sent her an **e-card** on her birthday.*

eccentric

ADJECTIVE Someone who is **eccentric** has habits or opinions that other people think are odd or peculiar.

echo echoes, echoing, echoed

NOUN **1** the repeat of a sound caused by the sound being reflected off a surface
VERB **2** When a sound **echoes**, it is reflected off a surface so that it can be heard again. • *Their cries **echoed** back from the mountain.*

eclipse eclipses

NOUN A solar **eclipse** happens when the moon passes between the sun and the Earth and part or all of the sun is hidden from view. A lunar **eclipse** happens when the Earth is between the sun and the moon, so that for a short time the shadow of the Earth makes the moon look red.

solar eclipse

lunar eclipse

ecological

ADJECTIVE involving the relationship between living things and their environment

ecologically

ADVERB in a way that involves the relationship between living things and their environment

ecologist ecologists

NOUN someone who studies the relationship between living things and their environment

ecology

NOUN the relationship between living things and their environment, or the study of this relationship

economical

ADJECTIVE If you are **economical**, you are not wasteful with money or things.

economically

ADVERB in a way that is not wasteful with money or things

economics

NOUN the system of organising the money, production and trade of a country, region or group

economist economists

NOUN someone who studies the way in which industries, banks and businesses are organised to make money

economy economies

NOUN The **economy** of a country or region is the way in which its industries, banks and businesses are organised to make money.

ecosystem ecosystems

NOUN the relationship between plants and animals and their environment

ecstasy

NOUN a feeling of extreme happiness

ecstatic

ADJECTIVE feeling extremely happy

eczema

NOUN a skin condition that makes the skin rough and itchy

edge edges

NOUN the part along the side or end of something

edible

ADJECTIVE Things that are **edible** are safe to eat.

edit edits, editing, edited

VERB 1 If you **edit** a piece of writing, you correct it.
VERB 2 If you **edit** a film or a television programme, you select different parts of it and arrange them in a particular order.

edition editions

NOUN An **edition** of a book or newspaper is one or all of the copies printed at one time.

editor editors

NOUN 1 someone who is responsible for the contents of a newspaper or magazine
NOUN 2 someone who edits a piece of writing, a film or a television programme

editorial editorials

NOUN an article in a newspaper or magazine which expresses the opinion of the editor

educate educates, educating, educated

VERB If you **educate** someone about something, you teach them so that they learn about it.

education

NOUN When you receive an **education**, you get knowledge and understanding through learning.

a
b
c
d
e
f
g
h
i
j
k
l
m
n
o
p
q
r
s
t
u
v
w
x
y
z

127

A
B
C
D
E
F
G
H
I
J
K
L
M
N
O
P
Q
R
S
T
U
V
W
X
Y
Z

educational

ADJECTIVE **1** relating to teaching and learning • the English **educational** system

ADJECTIVE **2** Something that is **educational** teaches you something that you did not know before. • Some programmes can be very **educational**.

eel eels

NOUN a long, thin fish shaped like a snake

eerie eerier, eeriest

ADJECTIVE strange and frightening • There was an **eerie** silence after the thunderstorm.

effect effects

NOUN **1** something that happens as a result of something else • The **effects** of global warming are now becoming clear.

NOUN **2** the impression something makes • The **effect** of the moonlight in the mist was eerie.

effective

ADJECTIVE If something is **effective**, it works well and gives the results that were intended.

efficient

ADJECTIVE capable of doing something well, without wasting time or energy

effort efforts

NOUN the physical or mental energy needed to do something

effortless

ADJECTIVE done easily and without much effort

eg; also spelt e.g.

eg means for example.

egg eggs

NOUN **1** a rounded object produced by female birds, reptiles, fish and insects. The young animal develops in the **egg** until it is ready to hatch.

→ Have a look at the illustration for **life cycle**

NOUN **2** a hen's **egg** used as food

Eid

NOUN a religious Muslim festival

PRONUNCIATION TIP
This word is pronounced **eed**.

---

eight

NOUN **Eight** is the number 8.

eighteen

NOUN **Eighteen** is the number 18.

eighteenth eighteenths

NOUN **1** one of eighteen equal parts of something

ADJECTIVE **2** The **eighteenth** item in a series is the one that you count as number eighteen

eighth eighths

NOUN **1** one of eight equal parts of something. It can be written as ⅛.

ADJECTIVE **2** The **eighth** item in a series is the one that you count as number eight. It can be written as 8th.

eightieth

NOUN **1** one of eighty equal parts of something

ADJECTIVE **2** The **eightieth** item in a series is the one that you count as number eighty.

eighty

NOUN **Eighty** is the number 80.

either

PRONOUN **1** You use **either** to refer to one of two things or people. • She has two brothers and I don't like **either**.

ADJECTIVE **2** You use **either** to refer to one of two things or people. • You can choose **either** date to come.

ADJECTIVE **3** You also use **either** to refer to both of two things. • There were fields on **either** side of the road.

CONJUNCTION **4** You use **either** to refer to each of two possible alternatives. • You can **either** come with me or stay here.

eject ejects, ejecting, ejected

VERB If you **eject** someone or something, you push or send them out of something. • There is a small button to **eject** DVDs.

elaborate

ADJECTIVE having many different parts, often very detailed or complicated

elastic

NOUN rubber material that stretches when you pull it, and returns to its original shape when you let it go

elated

ADJECTIVE very happy or excited

elbow elbows

NOUN the joint where your arm bends in the middle

elder

ADJECTIVE Your **elder** brother or sister is older than you.

elderly

ADJECTIVE Someone who is **elderly** is old.

eldest

ADJECTIVE If you are the **eldest** person in a family, you are the oldest.

elect elects, electing, elected

VERB If you **elect** someone, you choose them as your representative by voting for them.

election elections

NOUN When there is an **election**, people choose someone to represent them by voting for them.

WORD HISTORY
from Latin *eligere* meaning to select

electric

ADJECTIVE powered or produced by electricity

electrical

ADJECTIVE powered by or involving electricity
• *The fire was caused by an **electrical** fault.*
• *electrical* goods

electrician electricians

NOUN a person whose job it is to install and repair electrical equipment

electricity

NOUN a form of energy that provides power for heating, lighting and machines

WORD HISTORY
from Greek *elektron* meaning amber. In early experiments, scientists rubbed amber in order to get an electrical charge.

electrocute electrocutes, electrocuting, electrocuted

VERB If someone **electrocutes** themselves, they accidentally kill themselves or injure themselves badly by touching a strong electric current.

electrocution

NOUN **Electrocution** is when someone is killed or injured because a strong electric current passes through their body.

electron electrons

NOUN a particle with a negative electrical charge

→ Have a look at the illustration for **atom**

electronic

ADJECTIVE An **electronic** device contains transistors or silicon chips that control an electric current. Computers and televisions are examples of **electronic** devices. • *They sell laptops and other **electronic** devices.*

electronically

ADVERB in a way that involves electronic equipment • *electronically* controlled gates

elegance

NOUN the quality someone or something has when they are attractive and graceful

elegant

ADJECTIVE attractive and graceful

element elements

NOUN 1 a part of something that combines with others to make a whole
NOUN 2 In chemistry, an **element** is a substance that is made up of only one atom.
NOUN 3 The **elements** are the weather, especially when it is bad.

elephant elephants

NOUN a very large mammal with a long trunk, large ears, thick skin and ivory tusks

eleven

NOUN **Eleven** is the number 11.

eleventh elevenths

NOUN 1 one of eleven equal parts of something. It can be written as $\frac{1}{11}$.
ADJECTIVE 2 The **eleventh** item in a series is the one that you count as number eleven. It can be written as 11th.

elf elves

NOUN a small, mischievous creature in fairy stories

eligible

ADJECTIVE If you are **eligible** for something, you are suitable or have the right qualifications for it. • *You are **eligible** to enter the under-twelves competition.*

eliminate eliminates, eliminating, eliminated

VERB If you **eliminate** something or someone, you get rid of them.

ellipse ellipses

NOUN a regular oval shape

129

ellipsis
NOUN a sequence of three dots (...) which shows that some text has been missed out in a piece of writing, or suggests that it is not finished • *Two red eyes appeared in the cave ...*

elm elms
NOUN a tall tree with broad leaves

else
ADJECTIVE **1** besides or as well as • *What **else** do you see?*
PHRASE **2 Or else** means otherwise. • *You'd better hurry, **or else** you'll miss the bus.*

elsewhere
ADVERB If you do something **elsewhere**, you do it in another place.

email emails, emailing, emailed; also spelt **e-mail**
NOUN **1 Email** is a system of sending messages from one computer to another. It is short for *electronic mail*.
NOUN **2** When you send an **email**, you send a message from one computer to another.
VERB **3** If you **email** someone, you send an email to them.

embark embarks, embarking, embarked
VERB **1** When you **embark**, you go on to a ship at the start of your journey.
VERB **2** When you **embark** on a project, you start it.

embarrass embarrasses, embarrassing, embarrassed
VERB If you **embarrass** someone, you make them feel ashamed or awkward.

LANGUAGE TIP
There are two rs and two ss in *embarrass*, *embarrassed*, *embarrassing* and *embarrassment*.

---

embarrassed
ADJECTIVE feeling ashamed or awkward

embarrassing
ADJECTIVE making you feel ashamed or awkward

embarrassment
NOUN the feeling you have when you feel ashamed or awkward

embassy embassies
NOUN the building in which an ambassador and his or her staff work

emblem emblems
NOUN an object or a design representing an organisation or a country

embrace embraces, embracing, embraced
VERB If you **embrace** someone, you put your arms round them to show your affection for them.

embroider embroiders, embroidering, embroidered
VERB If you **embroider** fabric, you sew a decorative design on to it.

embroidery
NOUN **Embroidery** is when you sew a decorative design on to fabric, or the design that you sew.

embryo embryos
NOUN an unborn animal, such as a human being, in the very early stages of development

emerald emeralds
NOUN **1** a bright-green precious stone
NOUN **2** a bright green colour
ADJECTIVE **3** having a bright-green colour

emerge emerges, emerging, emerged
VERB If you **emerge** from somewhere, you come out from it.

emergence
NOUN **Emergence** is when something starts to be known about or noticed.

emergency emergencies
NOUN an unexpected and serious situation that must be dealt with quickly

emigrate emigrates, emigrating, emigrated
VERB If you **emigrate**, you leave your native country and go to live permanently in another one.

ANTONYM: immigrate

emigration
NOUN **Emigration** is when you leave your native country and go to live permanently in another one.

ANTONYM: immigrate

eminent
ADJECTIVE If someone is **eminent**, they are well known and respected for what they do.

emission emissions
NOUN 1 **Emission** is when something lets out light, sound, heat or smell.
NOUN 2 **Emissions** are gases or other substances that a vehicle or factory lets out into the air.

emit emits, emitting, emitted
VERB If something **emits** light, sound, heat or smell, it produces it or lets it out.

emoji emojis
NOUN a digital image that you use to express a feeling or an idea in a text or a post on a social media website • *He added a "wink" **emoji** to his message to show that he was joking.*

emotion emotions
NOUN a strong feeling, such as love or fear

emotional
ADJECTIVE 1 having strong feelings that you show to other people, especially by crying • *He got very **emotional** when it was time to say goodbye.*
ADJECTIVE 2 involving your feelings and how you control them • ***emotional** problems*

emperor emperors
NOUN a male ruler of an empire

emphasis emphases
NOUN the special importance or stress put on something • *When you read out the poem, you must put **emphasis** on the important words.*

emphasise emphasises, emphasising, emphasised; also spelt **emphasize**
VERB If you **emphasise** something, you make it look or sound more important than the things around it. • *He **emphasised** the word by underlining it.*

empire empires
NOUN a group of countries controlled by one ruler • *The Roman **Empire** covered many lands.*

WORD HISTORY
from Latin *imperium* meaning rule

employ employs, employing, employed
VERB If you **employ** someone, you pay them to work for you.

employee employees
NOUN someone who works for someone else

employer employers
NOUN the person or company that someone works for

employment
NOUN the state of having a paid job

empress empresses
NOUN 1 a female ruler of an empire
NOUN 2 the wife or widow of an emperor

emptiness
NOUN **Emptiness** is when there is nothing or nobody in a place.

empty emptier, emptiest; empties, emptying, emptied
ADJECTIVE 1 having nothing or nobody inside
ANTONYM: full
VERB 2 If you **empty** something, you remove the contents.

emu emus
NOUN a large Australian bird that can run fast but cannot fly

enable enables, enabling, enabled
VERB If you **enable** something to happen, you make it possible. • *The ramp **enables** people in wheelchairs to access the library.*

enchanted
ADJECTIVE If you are **enchanted** by something or someone, you are fascinated or charmed by them. • *The audience were **enchanted** by her dancing.*

encircle encircles, encircling, encircled
VERB If you **encircle** someone or something, you surround them completely.

enclose encloses, enclosing, enclosed
VERB 1 If you **enclose** something with a letter, you put it in the same envelope.
VERB 2 If you **enclose** an object or area, you surround it with something solid. • *They **enclosed** the garden with a strong fence.*

encore encores
NOUN an extra item at the end of a performance, when the audience asks for more

WORD HISTORY
from French *encore* meaning again

encounter encounters, encountering, encountered
VERB 1 If you **encounter** someone or something, you meet them or are faced with them. • *Did you **encounter** any problems?*
NOUN 2 a meeting, especially when it is difficult or unexpected

a
b
c
d
e
f
g
h
i
j
k
l
m
n
o
p
q
r
s
t
u
v
w
x
y
z

131

A
B
C
D
E
F
G
H
I
J
K
L
M
N
O
P
Q
R
S
T
U
V
W
X
Y
Z

encourage encourages, encouraging, encouraged
VERB If you **encourage** someone, you give them the confidence to do something.

encouragement
NOUN support and praise that you give to someone so that they have the confidence to do something

encouraging
ADJECTIVE giving someone the confidence to do something

encyclopedia encyclopedias; also spelt **encyclopaedia**
NOUN a book or set of books that gives information about a number of different subjects

end ends, ending, ended
NOUN 1 The **end** of something is the furthest point of it.
NOUN 2 The **end** of an event is the last part of it.
VERB 3 When something **ends**, it finishes.

endanger endangers, endangering, endangered
VERB If someone **endangers** something, they cause it to be in a dangerous or harmful situation.

endangered
ADJECTIVE An **endangered** animal or plant may soon not exist because there are not many of them.

endeavour endeavours, endeavouring, endeavoured
VERB If you **endeavour** to do something, you try very hard to do it.

ending endings
NOUN The **ending** of something is when it finishes.

endless
ADJECTIVE Something that is **endless** has, or seems to have, no end. • His **endless** chatter was very boring.

endure endures, enduring, endured
VERB 1 If you **endure** someone or something unpleasant, you put up with them.
VERB 2 If something **endures**, it continues or lasts.

enduring
ADJECTIVE continuing for a very long time

enemy enemies
NOUN Your **enemy** is someone who is very much against you and may wish to harm you.

energetic
ADJECTIVE full of energy

SYNONYMS: active, lively

energy energies
NOUN 1 the physical strength needed to do active things • He is saving his **energy** for next week's race.
NOUN 2 the power that makes things move, light up, make a sound or get hotter
• electrical **energy** • nuclear **energy**

engage engages, engaging, engaged
VERB 1 If you **engage** in an activity, you take part in it.
VERB 2 If you **engage** someone to do something, you pay them to do it.

engaged
ADJECTIVE 1 If two people are **engaged**, they have agreed to marry each other.
ADJECTIVE 2 If a phone number is **engaged**, it is busy. • Every time I tried to phone you, your number was **engaged**.

engine engines
NOUN 1 the part of a vehicle that produces the power to make it move

→ Have a look at the illustration for **aeroplane**

NOUN 2 the large vehicle that pulls a railway train

engineer engineers
NOUN a person trained in designing and building machinery and electrical devices, or roads and bridges

engineering
NOUN the job of designing and building machinery and electrical devices

engrave engraves, engraving, engraved
VERB If you **engrave** a hard surface, you cut letters or designs into it with a tool.
• He **engraved** the stone with an unusual design.

engraving engravings
NOUN 1 the work or skill of cutting letters or designs into a hard surface with a tool
NOUN 2 a design that has been cut into a hard surface with a tool

enjoy enjoys, enjoying, enjoyed
VERB **1** If you **enjoy** something, it gives you pleasure.
VERB **2** If you **enjoy** yourself, you are happy and have fun.

enjoyable
ADJECTIVE Something that is **enjoyable** gives you pleasure.

enjoyment
NOUN a feeling of pleasure that you get from having or doing something

enlarge enlarges, enlarging, enlarged
VERB When you **enlarge** something, you make it bigger.

enormous
ADJECTIVE very large in size or amount

SYNONYMS: vast, huge, massive

enough
ADJECTIVE **1** as much or as many as is necessary • Do you have **enough** money to buy that?
ADVERB **2** as much or as many as is necessary • John is old **enough** to work and earn money.

enquire enquires, enquiring, enquired
VERB If you **enquire** about something or someone, you ask for information about them.

enrol enrols, enrolling, enrolled
VERB If you **enrol** for something, such as a course or a society, you register to join or become a member of it.

ensure ensures, ensuring, ensured
VERB If you **ensure** that something happens, you make certain that it happens. • I will **ensure** that I arrive on time.

enter enters, entering, entered
VERB **1** To **enter** a place means to go into it.
VERB **2** If you **enter** a competition, you take part in it.
VERB **3** If you **enter** something in a diary or a list, you write it down.

enterprise enterprises
NOUN **1** something new and exciting that you try to do
NOUN **2** a large business or company

enterprising
ADJECTIVE able to think of new ideas and ways of doing things

entertain entertains, entertaining, entertained
VERB If you **entertain** someone, you do something to amuse them.

enthusiasm
NOUN If you show **enthusiasm** for something, you show much interest and excitement about it.

enthusiastic
ADJECTIVE If you are **enthusiastic** about something, you are very keen on it and talk or behave in a way that shows how much you like it.

enthusiastically
ADVERB in a way that shows you are very keen on something

entire
ADJECTIVE whole or complete • The **entire** class went on the trip.

entirely
ADVERB wholly and completely • My sister and I are **entirely** different.

entrance entrances
NOUN the doorway or gate to a building or area

ANTONYM: exit

entry entries
NOUN **1** the act of entering a place • No **entry** after 11 p.m.
NOUN **2** something you write in order to take part in a competition • Send your **entry** to the address below.
NOUN **3** something written in a diary or list • the **entry** for March 23 in her diary

envelope envelopes
NOUN the paper cover in which you put a letter

envious
ADJECTIVE If you are **envious**, you wish you could have what someone else has.

environment environments
NOUN **1** Your **environment** is your surroundings, especially the conditions in which you live or work.
NOUN **2** the natural world around us • Many people are keen to preserve the **environment**.

LANGUAGE TIP
There is an n before the m in environment.

envy envies, envying, envied
VERB If you **envy** someone, you wish that you had what they have.

a b c d e f g h i j k l m n o p q r s t u v w x y z

133

A
B
C
D
E
F
G
H
I
J
K
L
M
N
O
P
Q
R
S
T
U
V
W
X
Y
Z

epicentre epicentres
NOUN The **epicentre** of an earthquake is the place where it is felt most strongly as it is where the earthquake started.

epidemic epidemics
NOUN an outbreak of a disease that takes place in one area, spreading quickly and affecting many people

epilepsy
NOUN a condition of the brain that causes seizures and periods of unconsciousness

epileptic
ADJECTIVE caused by a brain condition that makes someone have seizures and periods of unconsciousness • *an **epileptic** seizure*

epilogue epilogues
NOUN a passage or speech which is added to the end of a book or play as a conclusion

episode episodes
NOUN **1** one of the programmes in a serial on television or radio
NOUN **2** an event or period of time, especially one that is important or unusual

epitaph epitaphs
NOUN words about a person who has died, usually found on their gravestone

equal equals, equalling, equalled
ADJECTIVE **1** being the same in size, number or amount
VERB **2** If something **equals** another thing, it is the same in quality, amount or value.
VERB **3** In mathematics, the symbol (=) stands for **equals**. The numbers before it equal the numbers after it. For example, $3 + 3 = 6$.

equally
ADVERB to the same extent or in the same amounts • *We shared the sweets **equally** between the three of us.*

equation equations
NOUN a mathematical number sentence stating that two amounts or values are the same. $3 + 6 = 9$ is an **equation** because what is on the left equals what is on the right.

equator
NOUN an imaginary line drawn round the middle of the Earth, lying halfway between the North and South Poles

→ Have a look at the illustration

equatorial
ADJECTIVE at or near the equator

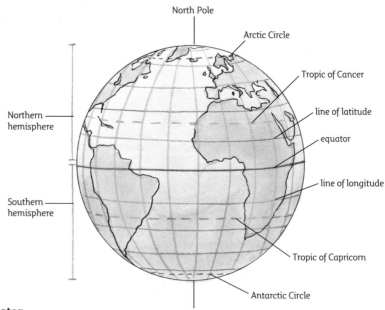

North Pole

Arctic Circle

Tropic of Cancer

line of latitude

equator

line of longitude

Northern hemisphere

Southern hemisphere

Tropic of Capricorn

Antarctic Circle

South Pole

equilateral

ADJECTIVE An **equilateral** triangle has sides that are all the same length, and angles that are all the same size.

equinox equinoxes

NOUN one of the two days in the year when the day and night are of equal length. The spring **equinox** occurs in March and the autumn **equinox** in September.

WORD HISTORY
from Latin *aequinoctium* meaning equal night

equip equips, equipping, equipped

VERB If you **equip** yourself, you collect together everything that you need to do a particular thing.

equipment

NOUN all the things that are needed or used for a particular job or activity ● *camping equipment*

equivalent equivalents

ADJECTIVE **1** equal in use, size, value or effect
ADJECTIVE **2** In mathematics, **equivalent** means of equal value. Fractions can be **equivalent** if they are of equal value, for example ¾ = ½. Different forms can be **equivalent**, for example 0.5 = ½ = 50%.
NOUN **3** something that has the same use, size, value or effect as something else ● *One mile is the equivalent of 1.6 kilometres.*

erase erases, erasing, erased

VERB If you **erase** writing, you rub it out.

erect erects, erecting, erected

VERB If you **erect** something, you put it up or construct it. ● *They erected the tent in the garden.*

erosion

NOUN the gradual wearing away of rock or soil by the weather, the sea or a river ● *soil erosion*

errand errands

NOUN If you run an **errand** for someone, you go a short distance to do a job for them, such as taking a message or fetching something.

erratic

ADJECTIVE not following a regular pattern ● *His attendance at school was erratic.*

erratically

ADVERB in a way that does not follow a regular pattern

error errors

NOUN a mistake, or something that is wrong

erupt erupts, erupting, erupted

VERB **1** When a volcano **erupts**, it throws out a lot of hot lava and ash.
VERB **2** When a situation **erupts**, it begins suddenly and violently. ● *A family row erupted.*

escalator escalators

NOUN a mechanical moving staircase

escape escapes, escaping, escaped

VERB **1** If you **escape** from someone or something, you succeed in getting away from them.
VERB **2** If you **escape** something unpleasant or difficult, you succeed in avoiding it. ● *She was lucky to escape serious injury.*
NOUN **3** If you make an **escape** from somewhere, you manage to get away.

escort escorts, escorting, escorted

NOUN **1** a person or vehicle that travels with another in order to protect or guide them
VERB **2** If you **escort** someone, you go with them somewhere, especially in order to protect or guide them. ● *I will escort you round the new buildings.*

Eskimo Eskimos

NOUN a name that used to be used for a member of a group of people who live in North America, Greenland and eastern Siberia. This name is not used now because it is rude. Those people in this group who come from North America and Greenland are called Inuits.

especially

ADVERB You say **especially** to show that something applies more to one thing, person or situation than to others. ● *It is always cold at the top of the mountain, especially when the wind is blowing.*

a
b
c
d
e
f
g
h
i
j
k
l
m
n
o
p
q
r
s
t
u
v
w
x
y
z

135

espionage

NOUN the act of spying to get secret information, especially to find out military or political secrets

WORD HISTORY
from French *espionner* meaning to spy

essay **essays**

NOUN a short piece of writing on a particular subject, especially one written as an exercise by a student

essential **essentials**

ADJECTIVE **1** Something that is **essential** is absolutely necessary.
NOUN **2** something that is very important or necessary

establish **establishes, establishing, established**

VERB **1** If you **establish** something, you set it up and keep it going.
VERB **2** If you **establish** a fact, you confirm that it is definitely correct.

estate **estates**

NOUN **1** a large area of land in the country, owned by one person or organisation
NOUN **2** an area of land that has been developed for housing or industry
• *a housing* **estate**

estate agent **estate agents**

NOUN a person who works for a company that sells houses and land

estimate **estimates, estimating, estimated**

VERB **1** If you **estimate** an amount or quantity, you calculate it approximately.
• *They* **estimated** *that the trip would take around three hours.*
NOUN **2** an approximate calculation of an amount or quantity • *The final cost was twice the original* **estimate***.*

PRONUNCIATION TIP
The verb is pronounced **ess**-ti-mayt. The noun is pronounced **ess**-ti-mit.

estuary **estuaries**

NOUN the wide part of a river near where it joins the sea, and where fresh water mixes with salt water

etc.

a written abbreviation for *et cetera*

et cetera

Et cetera means *and so on* or *and similar things.*

WORD HISTORY
from a Latin phrase that means the other things

eternal

ADJECTIVE lasting forever, or seeming to last forever

SYNONYMS: endless, everlasting, perpetual

ethnic

ADJECTIVE connected with a particular racial group of people • *There were many different* **ethnic** *groups in the school.*

WORD HISTORY
from Greek *ethnos* meaning race

etymology **etymologies**

NOUN the study of the history and origin of words

EU

NOUN an abbreviation for *European Union*

euro **euros**

NOUN the unit of currency used in many countries in Europe, including Germany, France, Italy, Ireland, Spain and the Netherlands

euthanasia

NOUN the act of helping someone to die painlessly, so that they do not suffer during an incurable illness

WORD HISTORY
from Greek *eu* meaning well and *thanatos* meaning death

evacuate **evacuates, evacuating, evacuated**

VERB If people **evacuate**, or are **evacuated**, they move from somewhere dangerous to a place of safety. • *The police* **evacuated** *shoppers from a store after a bomb scare.*

evacuee **evacuees**

NOUN someone who is sent away from a dangerous place, for example because there is a war there

evaluate **evaluates, evaluating, evaluated**

VERB If you **evaluate** something, you assess how good and useful it is.

evaluation evaluations
NOUN a judgement of how good or useful something is

evaporate evaporates, evaporating, evaporated
VERB When a liquid **evaporates**, it gradually changes from a liquid into a gas or vapour.

WORD HISTORY
from Latin *vapor* meaning steam

---

evaporation
NOUN the process of a liquid gradually changing into a gas or vapour ● *This slowed the **evaporation** of water from the soil.*

→ Have a look at the illustration for **water cycle**

even
ADJECTIVE **1** An **even** number is one that can be divided by two , such as 2, 4 and 6.

ANTONYM: odd

ADJECTIVE **2** An **even** surface is level, smooth and flat.
ADJECTIVE **3** An **even** measurement or rate stays at about the same level. ● *Keep the cooker at an **even** temperature.*
ADVERB **4 Even** is used to say that something is greater in degree than something else. ● *He was speaking **even** more slowly than usual.*
PHRASE **5 Even if** or **even though** are used to introduce something that is surprising in relation to the rest of the sentence. ● *She did not say anything, **even though** she had been left out again.*

evening evenings
NOUN the part of the day between the end of the afternoon and the time you go to bed

event events
NOUN **1** something that happens, especially when it is unusual or important

SYNONYMS: happening, incident, occurrence

NOUN **2** an organised activity, such as a sports match or a concert

eventually
ADVERB in the end ● *It was a long way, but we got there **eventually**.*

ever
ADVERB at any time in the past or future ● *That's the biggest dog I've **ever** seen.*

evergreen evergreens
NOUN An **evergreen** is a plant that does not lose its leaves in the winter.

every
ADJECTIVE **1 Every** is used to refer to all the members of a group or all the parts of something. ● *Every shop in the town was closed.*
ADJECTIVE **2 Every** is also used to indicate that something happens at regular intervals. ● *The clock strikes **every** hour.*
PHRASE **3** If something happens **every other** day or week, it happens on alternate days or weeks. ● *Practice sessions are held **every other** week.*

everybody
PRONOUN every person

everyone
PRONOUN all the people in a group

everything
PRONOUN all or the whole of something

everywhere
ADVERB in many or most places

evict evicts, evicting, evicted
VERB To **evict** someone means to officially force them to leave a place they are occupying.

evidence
NOUN **1** anything that causes you to believe that something is true or exists
NOUN **2** the information used in a court of law to try to prove something

evident
ADJECTIVE If something is **evident**, it is clear and obvious.

evil
NOUN **1 Evil** is used to refer to all the wicked or bad things that happen in the world.
ADJECTIVE **2** Someone or something **evil** is very bad and causes harm to people.

evolution
NOUN a process that takes place over many generations. During this time, living things slowly change as they adapt to different environments.

evolutionary
ADJECTIVE to do with or involving the process of evolution

a
b
c
d
e
f
g
h
i
j
k
l
m
n
o
p
q
r
s
t
u
v
w
x
y
z

137

evolve evolves, evolving, evolved
VERB When living things **evolve**, they slowly change as they adapt to different environments. • *Many people believe that man **evolved** from apes.*

ewe ewes
NOUN a female sheep

ex-
PREFIX former • *the **ex**-prime minister*

exact
ADJECTIVE If something is **exact**, it is accurately measured or made.

exactly
ADVERB **1** You use **exactly** to say that something is accurate. • *These predictions are not always **exactly** right.*
ADVERB **2** You use **exactly** to show that you agree with someone. • *"You think he stole your bike?" "**Exactly**."*

exaggerate exaggerates, exaggerating, exaggerated
VERB If you **exaggerate**, you make something seem better, worse, bigger or more important than it really is.

LANGUAGE TIP
There are two *g*s but only one *r* in *exaggerate* and *exaggeration*.

---

exaggeration exaggerations
NOUN **1 Exaggeration** is when you make something seem better, worse, bigger or more important than it really is.
NOUN **2** a statement that makes something seem better, worse, bigger or more important than it really is • *He said he had fifty followers, but that's an **exaggeration**.*

exam exams
NOUN an official test that aims to find out your knowledge in a subject • *a science **exam***

examination examinations
NOUN **1** the full word for **exam**
NOUN **2** If someone makes an **examination** of something, they look at it very carefully.

examine examines, examining, examined
VERB **1** If you **examine** something, you inspect it carefully.
VERB **2** If a doctor **examines** you, he or she checks your body to find out how healthy you are.

example examples
NOUN **1** something that is typical of a particular group of things

SYNONYMS: sample, specimen

NOUN **2** Someone who is an **example** to others is worth imitating.
PHRASE **3** You use **for example** to give an example of something you are talking about. • *large mammals, **for example** whales*

WORD HISTORY
from Latin *exemplum* meaning pattern

exasperate exasperates, exasperating, exasperated
VERB If someone or something **exasperates** you, they annoy and frustrate you.

exasperating
ADJECTIVE annoying and frustrating

exasperation
NOUN the feeling you have when you are annoyed and frustrated

excavate excavates, excavating, excavated
VERB **1** When someone **excavates**, they remove earth from the ground by digging.
VERB **2** When archaeologists **excavate** objects, they carefully uncover remains in the ground to discover information about the past. • *They found some interesting Roman artefacts while they were **excavating**.*

excavation excavations
NOUN **1** the process of digging a large hole in the ground
NOUN **2** the process of digging in the ground to find very old objects in order to discover information about the past

excavator excavators
NOUN **1** a machine that digs holes in the ground and moves earth
NOUN **2** a person who digs in the ground to find very old objects in order to discover information about the past

exceed exceeds, exceeding, exceeded
VERB If something **exceeds** a particular amount, it is greater than that amount.

excel excels, excelling, excelled
VERB If someone **excels** in or at something, they are very good at doing it.

excellence
NOUN the quality that something has when it is extremely good

excellent

ADJECTIVE very good indeed

SYNONYMS: first-rate, outstanding, superb

except

PREPOSITION apart from or not including someone or something • *Everyone laughed* **except** *Ben.*

exception exceptions

NOUN somebody or something that is not included in a general rule • *All my family are musicians, with the* **exception** *of my father.*

exceptional

ADJECTIVE If someone or something is **exceptional**, they are unusual or remarkable in some way. For example, they may be very clever or have special talents.

excerpt excerpts

NOUN a short piece of writing, music or film that is taken from a longer piece

excess excesses

NOUN too much of something

excessive

ADJECTIVE more than is needed or allowed

exchange exchanges, exchanging, exchanged

VERB If you **exchange** something for something else, you replace it with that thing. • *I took the shoes back to the shop and* **exchanged** *them for another pair.*

exchange rate exchange rates

NOUN The **exchange rate** of a country's unit of currency is the amount of a different currency that you get when you change from one currency into the other.

excite excites, exciting, excited

VERB If something **excites** you, it makes you feel very happy and enthusiastic.

excited

ADJECTIVE feeling very happy because something good has happened or will happen • *I'm really* **excited** *about the party.*

excitedly

ADVERB in a happy way because something good has happened or will happen

excitement

NOUN a very happy feeling because something good has happened or will happen

exciting

ADJECTIVE making you feel excited

exclaim exclaims, exclaiming, exclaimed

VERB When you **exclaim**, you cry out suddenly or loudly because you are excited or shocked.

exclamation exclamations

NOUN something that you say suddenly or loudly because you are excited or shocked

exclamation mark exclamation marks

NOUN a punctuation mark (!) used in writing to show a strong feeling

exclude excludes, excluding, excluded

VERB If you **exclude** someone from a place or activity, you prevent them from entering or taking part.

ANTONYM: include

exclusion

NOUN **Exclusion** is when you prevent someone from entering a place or taking part in an activity.

ANTONYM: inclusion

exclusive

ADJECTIVE **1** available to a small group of rich or privileged people
ADJECTIVE **2** belonging to a particular person or group only • *Our group will have* **exclusive** *use of the pool.*

excruciating

ADJECTIVE extremely painful

excursion excursions

NOUN a short journey or outing

excuse excuses, excusing, excused

NOUN **1** a reason you give to explain why something has been done, has not been done or will not be done
VERB **2** If you **excuse** someone's behaviour, you give reasons for why they behaved in that way.
PHRASE **3** You say **excuse me** to try to catch somebody's attention or to apologise for an interruption.

PRONUNCIATION TIP
The noun is pronounced ex-**kyooss**. The verb is pronounced ex-**kyooz**.

---

execute executes, executing, executed

VERB To **execute** somebody means to kill them as a punishment for a crime.

A
B
C
D
E
F
G
H
I
J
K
L
M
N
O
P
Q
R
S
T
U
V
W
X
Y
Z

execution executions
NOUN An **execution** is when somebody is killed as a punishment for a crime.

executive executives
NOUN a person who works at a senior level in a company

exercise exercises, exercising, exercised
NOUN 1 any activity that you do in order to get fit or stay healthy
NOUN 2 a piece of work that you do for practice
VERB 3 When you **exercise**, you do activities that help you to get fit and stay healthy.

exert exerts, exerting, exerted
VERB If you **exert** yourself, you make a great deal of effort to do something.

exhale exhales, exhaling, exhaled
VERB When you **exhale**, you breathe out.

ANTONYM: inhale

exhaust exhausts, exhausting, exhausted
VERB 1 If something **exhausts** you, it makes you very tired.
VERB 2 If something has been **exhausted**, it has been used up. • *Logging companies have largely **exhausted** the country's forests.*
NOUN 3 the pipe that carries the gas or steam out of the engine of a vehicle

exhausted
ADJECTIVE If you are **exhausted**, you are very tired.

exhibit exhibits, exhibiting, exhibited
VERB 1 If someone **exhibits** something, they put it on show for others to see, especially in a gallery or museum.
NOUN 2 something that is put on show for others to see, especially in a gallery or museum

exhibition exhibitions
NOUN a public display of works of art, products or skills

exile exiles, exiling, exiled
NOUN 1 a person who is not allowed to live in their own country
VERB 2 If someone is **exiled**, they are sent away from their own country, usually as a punishment.

exist exists, existing, existed
VERB If something **exists**, it is in the world as a real thing.

existence
NOUN the fact that something is a real thing or situation • *We can understand the **existence** of stars and planets.*

exit exits, exiting, exited
NOUN 1 a doorway through which you can leave a public place

ANTONYM: entrance

NOUN 2 If you make an **exit**, you leave a place.

ANTONYM: entrance

VERB 3 If you **exit** a place, you leave it.

exotic
ADJECTIVE If something is **exotic**, it is unusual and interesting, usually because it comes from another country.

expand expands, expanding, expanded
VERB If something **expands**, or if you **expand** it, it becomes larger.

ANTONYM: contract

expanse expanses
NOUN a large area of something such as the sky or land

expansion
NOUN **Expansion** is when something becomes larger.

ANTONYM: contraction

expect expects, expecting, expected
VERB 1 If you **expect** something to happen, you believe that it will happen.
VERB 2 If you are **expecting** someone, you are waiting for them to arrive.
VERB 3 If you **expect** something, you believe that you ought to get it or have it.
• *I'm **expecting** you to help me.*

expectation expectations
NOUN 1 An **expectation** is what you believe will happen.
NOUN 2 Your **expectations** are how you think a situation should be or how you think somebody should behave.

expedition expeditions
NOUN 1 an organised journey made for a special purpose, often to explore
NOUN 2 the party of people who go on an expedition • *The **expedition** set out through the rainforest.*

expel **expels, expelling, expelled**
VERB **1** If someone **expels** a person from a school or club, they tell them officially to leave because they have behaved badly.
VERB **2** If a gas or liquid is **expelled** from a place, it is forced out of it.

expense **expenses**
NOUN the amount of money it costs to do something or buy something • *They could not afford the **expense** of the school trip.*

expensive
ADJECTIVE If something is **expensive**, it costs a lot of money.

experience **experiences, experiencing, experienced**
NOUN **1** all the things that you have done or that have happened to you • *No previous **experience** is necessary for this job.*
NOUN **2** something that you do or something that happens to you, especially something new or unusual • *What has been your most enjoyable **experience**?*
VERB **3** If you **experience** something, it happens to you or you are affected by it. • *We had never **experienced** this kind of holiday before.*

experiment **experiments, experimenting, experimented**
NOUN **1** a scientific test that aims to prove or discover something
VERB **2** If you **experiment** with something or on something, you do a scientific test to prove or discover something about it.

experimental
ADJECTIVE done to prove or discover something

expert **experts**
NOUN a person who is very skilled at something or who knows a lot about a particular subject

SYNONYMS: authority, specialist

expire **expires, expiring, expired**
VERB If something **expires**, it comes to an end and you can no longer use it.

explain **explains, explaining, explained**
VERB If you **explain** something, you give information about it or reasons for it so that it can be understood.

SYNONYMS: clarify, make clear

explanation **explanations**
NOUN An **explanation** explains something.

explanatory
ADJECTIVE Something that is **explanatory** gives information about something or reasons for it so that you can understand it.

explode **explodes, exploding, exploded**
VERB If something such as a bomb **explodes**, it bursts with great force.

exploit **exploits, exploiting, exploited**
VERB **1** If somebody **exploits** a person or a situation, they take advantage of them for their own ends.
NOUN **2** something daring or interesting that somebody has done

PRONUNCIATION TIP
The verb is pronounced ex-**ploit**. The noun is pronounced **ex**-ploit.

exploration
NOUN **Exploration** is when you travel around a place to discover what it is like.

explore **explores, exploring, explored**
VERB If you **explore** a place, you travel around it to discover what it is like.

explorer **explorers**
NOUN someone who travels to a place that people do not know much about, in order to discover what it is like • *space **explorers***

explosion **explosions**
NOUN An **explosion** is when something such as a bomb bursts with great force.

explosive **explosives**
ADJECTIVE **1** If something is **explosive**, it is likely to explode.
NOUN **2** something that can cause an explosion

export **exports, exporting, exported**
VERB **1** If someone **exports** goods, they sell them to another country.

ANTONYM: import

NOUN **2** **Exports** are goods that are sold to another country.

PRONUNCIATION TIP
The verb is pronounced ex-**port**. The noun is pronounced **ex**-port.

a
b
c
d
e
f
g
h
i
j
k
l
m
n
o
p
q
r
s
t
u
v
w
x
y
z

A
B
C
D
E
F
G
H
I
J
K
L
M
N
O
P
Q
R
S
T
U
V
W
X
Y
Z

expose exposes, exposing, exposed
VERB **1** If you **expose** something, you uncover it so that it can be seen.
VERB **2** If a person is **exposed** to something dangerous, they are put in a situation in which that thing might harm them. • *The patients were isolated so that no one else would be* **exposed** *to the disease.*

exposure
NOUN the harmful effect of the weather on the body if a person is outside too long without any protection

express expresses, expressing, expressed
VERB **1** When you **express** an idea or feeling, you show what you think or feel by saying or doing something. • *She* **expressed** *her gratitude by giving me a hug.*
ADJECTIVE **2** very fast • *an* **express** *train*

expression expressions
NOUN **1** Your **expression** is the look on your face that shows what you are thinking or feeling.
NOUN **2** The **expression** of ideas or feelings is the act of showing them through words, actions or art.
NOUN **3** An **expression** is a phrase with a special meaning, such as *nosy parker*.

expressive
ADJECTIVE showing what someone thinks or feels • *He has a very* **expressive** *face.*

expulsion
NOUN **1** **Expulsion** is when someone is officially told to leave a school or club because they have behaved badly.
NOUN **2** **Expulsion** is when a gas or liquid is forced out of a place.

exquisite
ADJECTIVE Something that is **exquisite** is extremely beautiful and pleasing.

extend extends, extending, extended
VERB If you **extend** something, you make it longer or bigger.

extension extensions
NOUN **1** a room or building that is added on to an existing building
NOUN **2** an additional telephone connected to the same landline as another telephone

extensive
ADJECTIVE **1** covering a large area • *The gardens are* **extensive**.
ADJECTIVE **2** very great in effect • *After the storm the house required* **extensive** *repairs.*

extent extents
NOUN The **extent** of something is its length or the area it covers.

exterior exteriors
NOUN the outside of something

exterminate exterminates, exterminating, exterminated
VERB To **exterminate** people or animals means to kill a lot of them deliberately.

extermination
NOUN **Extermination** is when a lot of people or animals are deliberately killed.

external
ADJECTIVE existing or happening on the outside of something • *The* **external** *walls of the house need painting.*

extinct
ADJECTIVE **1** An **extinct** species of animal or plant does not exist anymore.
ADJECTIVE **2** An **extinct** volcano is no longer likely to erupt.

extinction
NOUN **Extinction** is when a species of animal or plant does not exist anymore.

extinguish extinguishes, extinguishing, extinguished
VERB If you **extinguish** a light or fire, you put it out.

extra
ADJECTIVE more than is usual, necessary or expected • *He used the* **extra** *time to check his work.*

SYNONYMS: added, additional, further

extract extracts, extracting, extracted
VERB **1** If you **extract** something from a place you get it out, often by force. • *The dentist had to* **extract** *my wisdom tooth.*
NOUN **2** a small section taken from a book or a piece of music

PRONUNCIATION TIP
The verb is pronounced ex-**trakt**. The noun is pronounced **ex**-trakt.

extraordinary
ADJECTIVE very unusual or surprising

SYNONYMS: exceptional, remarkable

extraterrestrial

ADJECTIVE If something is **extraterrestrial**, it happens or exists beyond the Earth's atmosphere.

extravagance

NOUN **Extravagance** is when you spend a lot of money, especially more than you should do.

extravagant

ADJECTIVE spending or costing more money than is reasonable or affordable

extreme extremes

ADJECTIVE **1** very great in degree or intensity • **extreme** cold
NOUN **2** the furthest point or edge of something
NOUN **3** the highest or furthest degree of something • *You experience extremes of temperature in the desert, where it is very cold at night and very hot during the day.*

extremely

ADVERB very • *The illness is extremely rare.*

eye eyes, eyeing or **eying, eyed**

NOUN **1** the parts of a human or other animal's body with which they see

→ Have a look at the illustrations for **insect**, **spider** and **whale**

VERB **2** To **eye** something means to look at it. • *They eyed each other's new shoes with interest.*

eyebrow eyebrows

NOUN Your **eyebrows** are the lines of hair that grow on the ridges of bone above your eyes. • *She raised her eyebrows in surprise when she saw her dad's new hat.*

eyelash eyelashes

NOUN Your **eyelashes** are the hairs that grow on the edges of your eyelids.

eyelid eyelids

NOUN Your **eyelids** are the folds of skin that cover your eyes when they are closed. • *I was so tired that my eyelids started to droop.*

eyesight

NOUN the ability to see • *His eyesight is not very good, so he wears glasses.*

eyewitness eyewitnesses

NOUN someone who has seen something happen and can describe it, especially an accident or a crime • *The police appealed for any eyewitnesses to the crash to come forward.*

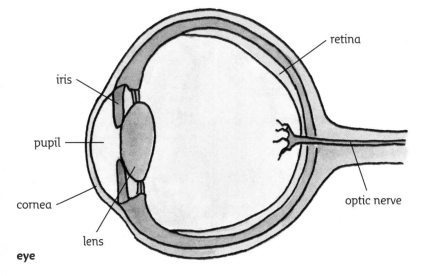

iris

pupil

cornea

lens

retina

optic nerve

eye

Ff

fable fables

NOUN a story intended to teach a moral lesson • *the well-known **fable** of the tortoise and the hare*

fabric fabrics

NOUN cloth • *Silk is a delicate **fabric**.*

fabulous

ADJECTIVE **1** wonderful or very impressive
ADJECTIVE **2 Fabulous** creatures are only found in legends or fairytales.

face faces, facing, faced

NOUN **1** the front part of your head, from your chin to your forehead
NOUN **2** a surface or side of something • *We could see the north **face** of the mountain.*
VERB **3** If you **face** something or someone, you are opposite them and look in their direction.
VERB **4** If you **face** in a certain direction, you look there.

Facetime Facetimes, Facetiming, Facetimed

VERB (trademark) If you **Facetime** someone, you call them using a video connection.

facility facilities

NOUN a piece of equipment or a service that is provided for a particular purpose • *The school has excellent sports **facilities**.*

fact facts

NOUN **1** a piece of information that is true, or something that has actually happened
PHRASE **2 In fact** and **as a matter of fact** mean *actually* or *really* and are used for emphasis. • *As a matter of fact, I do like the idea.*

factor factors

NOUN **1** something that affects an event or situation • *One of the main **factors** in our success was our strong team.*

SYNONYMS: element, part

NOUN **2** The **factors** of a number are the whole numbers that will divide exactly into it. • *Two and five are **factors** of 10: $2 \times 5 = 10$, $10 \div 5 = 2$, $10 \div 2 = 5$.*

factory factories

NOUN a building or group of buildings where goods are made in large quantities

factual

ADJECTIVE If something is **factual**, it has actually happened.

fade fades, fading, faded

VERB When something **fades**, it slowly becomes less bright or less loud. • *The colour has **faded** from my favourite T-shirt.*

Fahrenheit

NOUN the temperature scale that has the freezing point for water at 32 °F and the boiling point at 212 °F

PRONUNCIATION TIP
This word is pronounced **fa**-ren-hite.

fail fails, failing, failed

VERB **1** If you **fail** to do something, you do not succeed in doing it.

ANTONYM: succeed

VERB **2** If you **fail** an exam, your marks are too low and you do not pass.
VERB **3** If someone or something **fails** to do something that they should have done, they do not do it. • *The bomb **failed** to explode.*
PHRASE **4 Without fail** means definitely or regularly. • *He plays football every Sunday **without fail**.*

failure failures

NOUN **1** a lack of success in doing something • *Her attempt to win the race ended in **failure**.*
NOUN **2** an unsuccessful person, thing or action

faint fainter, faintest; faints, fainting, fainted

ADJECTIVE **1** A sound, colour or feeling that is **faint** is not strong or intense. • *Their voices grew **fainter** as they moved away.*
ADJECTIVE **2** If you feel **faint**, you feel dizzy and unsteady. • *I was feeling **faint**, so I sat down.*
VERB **3** If you **faint**, you lose consciousness for a short time.

fair fairer, fairest; fairs

ADJECTIVE **1** Something that is **fair** seems reasonable to most people.

ADJECTIVE **2** If the weather is **fair** it is fine.

ADJECTIVE **3** quite good or moderate • *I think I have a **fair** chance of passing my exams.*

ADJECTIVE **4** People who are **fair** have light-coloured hair.

NOUN **5** a form of entertainment that takes place outside, with stalls, games and rides

fairground fairgrounds

NOUN an open piece of ground where fairs are held

fairly

ADVERB **1** quite or rather • *My room's **fairly** small.*

ADVERB **2** in a way that seems reasonable to most people • *Everyone should be treated **fairly**.*

fairness

NOUN **Fairness** is when something seems reasonable to most people.

fairy fairies

NOUN In stories, **fairies** are small, supernatural creatures with magical powers.

fairy tale fairy tales

NOUN a story of magical events

faith faiths

NOUN **1** If you have **faith** in someone, you trust them.

NOUN **2** a religious belief

faithful

ADJECTIVE If you are **faithful** to someone or something, you are loyal and continue to support them. • *He is one of my most **faithful** friends.*

fake fakes, faking, faked

NOUN **1** an imitation of something, made to trick people into thinking that it is genuine

ADJECTIVE **2** imitation and not genuine • *The coat was made of **fake** fur.*

VERB **3** If you **fake** a feeling, you pretend that you are experiencing it. • *I **faked** illness to avoid the games lesson.*

fall falls, falling, fell, fallen

VERB **1** If someone or something **falls**, or **falls** over, or **falls** down, they drop towards the ground. • *The snow **fell** all day, covering the fields and trees.*

VERB **2** to become lower or less • *The temperature usually **falls** at night.*

VERB **3** If you **fall ill**, you become ill.

VERB **4** If you **fall asleep**, you begin to sleep.

VERB **5** If you **fall in love**, you begin to love someone.

NOUN **6** If you have a **fall**, you fall over.

fall out

VERB If you **fall out** with someone, you disagree and quarrel with them.

false

ADJECTIVE **1** untrue or incorrect

ADJECTIVE **2** not real or genuine, but intended to seem real • *Grandad has **false** teeth.*

fame

NOUN the state of being very well known

familiar

ADJECTIVE **1** well-known or easy to recognise • *The room was full of **familiar** faces.*

ANTONYM: unfamiliar

ADJECTIVE **2** If you are **familiar with** something, you know it or understand it well. • *He was very **familiar with** the local area.*

ANTONYM: unfamiliar

family families

NOUN a group of people who are related to each other, especially parents and their children

family tree family trees

NOUN a diagram that shows how different members of a family are related to each other

famine famines

NOUN a serious shortage of food that may cause many deaths

WORD HISTORY
from Latin *fames* meaning hunger

famished

ADJECTIVE very hungry

famous

ADJECTIVE very well-known

fan fans, fanning, fanned

NOUN **1** If you are a **fan** of something or someone famous, you like them very much.

NOUN **2** a hand-held or mechanical device that moves air to make it cooler

VERB **3** If you **fan** yourself, you cool the air around you with a fan.

a
b
c
d
e
f
g
h
i
j
k
l
m
n
o
p
q
r
s
t
u
v
w
x
y
z

fancy fancies, fancying, fancied; fancier, fanciest

VERB **1** If you **fancy** something, you want to have it.
ADJECTIVE **2** highly decorated and special

fancy dress

NOUN clothing worn for a party at which people dress up to look like a particular character or animal

fang fangs

NOUN a long, sharp tooth

fantastic

ADJECTIVE **1** wonderful and very pleasing

SYNONYM: marvellous

ADJECTIVE **2** strange or unusual, like a fantasy

WORD HISTORY
from Greek *phantasia* meaning imagination

fantasy fantasies

NOUN an imaginative story that is unlikely to happen in real life

far farther or further, farthest or furthest

ADVERB **1** a long distance away

ANTONYMS: near, close

ADJECTIVE **2** You can use **far** to ask questions about distance. • How **far** is the nearest supermarket?

ANTONYMS: near, close

fare fares

NOUN the amount that you pay to travel on a bus, train or plane

farewell

INTERJECTION goodbye

far-fetched

ADJECTIVE unlikely to be true

farm farms, farming, farmed

NOUN **1** an area of land and buildings, used for growing crops or raising animals
VERB **2** If someone **farms** land, they plant crops or keep animals there.

farmer farmers

NOUN someone who looks after a farm

farming

NOUN the work of planting crops or keeping animals on a farm

fascinate fascinates, fascinating, fascinated

VERB If something **fascinates** you, it interests and attracts you.

fascinating

ADJECTIVE very interesting

fashion fashions

NOUN a style of dress or way of behaving that is popular at a particular time

fashionable

ADJECTIVE popular at a particular time
• **fashionable** clothes

fashionably

ADVERB in a way that is popular at a particular time

fast faster, fastest; fasts, fasting, fasted

ADJECTIVE **1** If something is **fast**, it moves quickly. • Our car is very **fast**.
ADJECTIVE **2** If a clock is **fast**, it shows a time that is ahead of the real time.
ADVERB **3** If something happens **fast**, it happens quickly or with great speed.
• Can you run **fast**?
ADVERB **4** If a clock goes **fast**, it keeps showing a time that is ahead of the real time.
PHRASE **5** If you are **fast asleep**, you are in a deep sleep.
VERB **6** If you **fast**, you eat no food for a period of time, usually for religious reasons

fasten fastens, fastening, fastened

VERB If you **fasten** something, you close it or attach it firmly to something else.

fastener fasteners

NOUN something that is used to join two parts of something together, especially on a piece of clothing, for example a button on a coat

fastening fastenings

NOUN something that is used to join two parts of something together

fat fatter, fattest

ADJECTIVE **1** having a lot of flesh on the body
NOUN **2** the greasy, white substance that animals and humans have under their skin. It is used to store energy and helps to keep them warm.
NOUN **3** the greasy or oily substance from animals and plants that is used in cooking

fatal

ADJECTIVE A **fatal** accident or illness causes someone's death.

fatally
ADVERB in a way that causes someone's death • *He was **fatally** injured.*

fate fates
NOUN 1 a power that some people believe controls events
NOUN 2 Someone's **fate** is what becomes of them.

father fathers
NOUN a male parent

father-in-law fathers-in-law
NOUN the father of someone's husband or wife

fatigue
NOUN extreme tiredness

fault faults, faulting, faulted
NOUN 1 a mistake or something wrong with the way something is made
NOUN 2 If something bad is your **fault**, you are to blame for it.
VERB 3 If you **fault** someone or something, you find something wrong with them. • *You can't **fault** his piano playing.*

faultless
ADJECTIVE without any mistakes or anything wrong

faulty
ADJECTIVE If something is **faulty**, there is something wrong with it.

fauna
NOUN animals, especially those that are found in a particular area • *the flora and **fauna** of the African jungle*

favour favours, favouring, favoured
NOUN 1 If you do someone a **favour**, you do something to help them.
VERB 2 If you **favour** someone or something, you prefer them to others.

favourite favourites
ADJECTIVE 1 Your **favourite** person or thing is the one you like best. • *Peaches are my **favourite** fruit.*
NOUN 2 Someone's **favourite** is the person or thing they like best. • *I like all sports, but soccer is my **favourite**.*

fawn fawns
NOUN 1 a young deer
NOUN 2 a light-brown colour
ADJECTIVE 3 having a light-brown colour

fax faxes
NOUN an exact copy of a document sent electronically along a phone line using a special machine

fear fears, fearing, feared
NOUN 1 the feeling of worry you have when you think that you are in danger or that something bad might happen
VERB 2 If you **fear** someone or something, you are afraid of them.

fearful
ADJECTIVE If you are **fearful** of someone or something, you are afraid of them.

fearless
ADJECTIVE If you are **fearless**, you are brave and have no fear.

fearsome
ADJECTIVE frightening or terrible

feast feasts
NOUN a large and special meal for many people

feat feats
NOUN a difficult and impressive achievement

feather feathers
NOUN A bird's **feathers** are the light, soft growths covering its body.

feature features
NOUN 1 a particular part or characteristic of something that is interesting or important
PLURAL NOUN 2 Your **features** are your eyes, nose, mouth and other parts of your face.
• *Your **features** are similar to your mother's.*

February
NOUN the second month of the year. **February** usually has 28 days, but has 29 days in a leap year.

LANGUAGE TIP
There is an *r* after the *b* in *February*.

fed
VERB the past participle of **feed**

fed up
ADJECTIVE (*informal*) unhappy or bored
• *I'm **fed up** with this rainy weather.*

fee fees
NOUN a charge or payment for a job, service or activity

feeble feebler, feeblest
ADJECTIVE weak, with no strength or power

a
b
c
d
e
f
g
h
i
j
k
l
m
n
o
p
q
r
s
t
u
v
w
x
y
z

147

A
B
C
D
E
F
G
H
I
J
K
L
M
N
O
P
Q
R
S
T
U
V
W
X
Y
Z

feed **feeds, feeding, fed**
VERB **1** If you **feed** a person or animal, you give them food. • *She **feeds** the pigeons every day.*
VERB **2** When an animal or baby **feeds**, it eats. • *These insects **feed** on wood.*
VERB **3** If you **feed** something into a machine, you put it in there. • *They **fed** the information into a computer.*

feel **feels, feeling, felt**
VERB **1** If you **feel** an emotion or sensation, you experience it. • *I **felt** very happy on my birthday.*
VERB **2** If you **feel** something, you touch it. • *The doctor **felt** my forehead.*
PHRASE **3** If you **feel like** doing something, you want to do it.

feeler **feelers**
NOUN **Feelers** are long, thin antennae on the heads of some insects, used to sense things around them.

feeling **feelings**
NOUN **1** an emotion • *Finishing my homework gave me a **feeling** of satisfaction.*
NOUN **2** a physical sensation • *I had a **feeling** of pins and needles in my foot.*
NOUN **3** Your **feelings** about something are your general attitudes or thoughts about it.

feet
PLURAL NOUN the plural of **foot**

feline
ADJECTIVE relating to the cat family, or like a cat • *The dancer moved with **feline** grace.*

felt
VERB **1** the past tense and past participle of **feel**
NOUN **2** a thick cloth made by pressing short threads together

female **females**
NOUN **1** a person or animal that belongs to the gender that can have babies or young

ANTONYM: male

ADJECTIVE **2** concerning or relating to females

ANTONYM: male

feminine
ADJECTIVE relating to women or considered to be typical of women

ANTONYM: masculine

WORD HISTORY
from Latin *femina* meaning woman

fence **fences**
NOUN a wooden or wire barrier between two areas of land

ferment **ferments, fermenting, fermented**
VERB When beer, wine or fruit **ferments**, a chemical change takes place and alcohol is often produced.

fern **ferns**
NOUN a plant with long, feathery leaves and no flowers

ferocious
ADJECTIVE violent and fierce

ferret **ferrets**
NOUN a small mammal that can be trained to hunt rabbits or rats

---

WORD HISTORY
from Old French *furet* meaning little thief

ferry **ferries, ferrying, ferried**
NOUN **1** a boat that carries people and vehicles across short stretches of water • *We took the **ferry** across to France.*
VERB **2** If someone **ferries** people or goods somewhere, they transport them there, usually on a short, regular journey. • *A fleet of buses **ferried** people to the concert.*

fertile
ADJECTIVE **1** If soil is **fertile** it can produce strong, healthy plants.
ADJECTIVE **2** If a human or other animal is **fertile**, they are able to have babies or young.

fertilise **fertilises, fertilising, fertilised**; also spelt **fertilize**
VERB **1** When an egg is **fertilised**, the process of reproduction has begun. • *Pollen **fertilises** the female part of a plant.*
VERB **2** When you **fertilise** land, you put manure or chemicals on to it to help the growth of plants.

fertiliser; also spelt **fertilizer**
NOUN a substance such as manure or chemicals added to the soil to improve plant growth

festival festivals
NOUN **1** an organised series of events and performances • *The film **festival** at Cannes in France is very famous.*
NOUN **2** a time when something special is celebrated • *Harvest **festival** is in the autumn.*

fetch fetches, fetching, fetched
VERB If you **fetch** something, you go to where it is and bring it back. • *She **fetched** a towel from the bathroom.*

fête fêtes; also spelt fete
NOUN an outdoor event with games, displays and goods for sale • *The school **fête** was a big success.*

PRONUNCIATION TIP
This word is pronounced **fayt**.

WORD HISTORY
from the French *feste* meaning feast

feud feuds, feuding, feuded
NOUN **1** a long-running and bitter quarrel, especially between families
VERB **2** When people **feud**, they quarrel over a long period of time.

PRONUNCIATION TIP
This word is pronounced **fyood**.

fever fevers
NOUN If you have a **fever**, your temperature is higher than usual because you are ill.

feverish
ADJECTIVE If you are **feverish**, you have a higher body temperature than usual.

few fewer, fewest
ADJECTIVE **1** not many • *I saw him a **few** moments ago.*
PRONOUN **2** a small number of things or people • ***Few** of the houses still had lights on.*

LANGUAGE TIP
Use *fewer* to talk about things that can be counted and *less* for things that can't be counted: *fewer apples; less time.*

fiancé fiancés
NOUN Someone's **fiancé** is the man to whom they are engaged to be married.

PRONUNCIATION TIP
This word is pronounced fee-**on**-say.

WORD HISTORY
the words *fiancé* and *fiancée* are from Old French *fiancer* meaning to promise or betroth

fiancée fiancées
NOUN Someone's **fiancée** is the woman to whom they are engaged to be married.

PRONUNCIATION TIP
This word is pronounced fee-**on**-say.

fiasco fiascos
NOUN When something is a **fiasco**, it fails completely, especially in a ridiculous or disorganised way.

PRONUNCIATION TIP
This word is pronounced fee-**ass**-koh.

fib fibs, fibbing, fibbed
VERB **1** If you **fib** about something, you tell a small lie about it.
NOUN **2** a small lie

fibber fibbers
NOUN someone who tells fibs

fibre fibres
NOUN **1** a thin thread of a substance used to make cloth • *Many fabrics today are made from artificial **fibres**.*
NOUN **2** a part of plants that can be eaten but not digested by your body • ***Fibre** is good for your digestive system.*

fickle
ADJECTIVE If you are **fickle**, you keep changing your mind about what you want.

fiction
NOUN stories about imaginary people and events

ANTONYM: non-fiction

fictional
ADJECTIVE from a book or story about imaginary people and events • *Harry Potter is a **fictional** character.*

fiddle fiddles, fiddling, fiddled
VERB **1** If you **fiddle** with something, you keep touching it and playing with it in a restless way.
NOUN **2** another word for **violin**

a
b
c
d
e
f
g
h
i
j
k
l
m
n
o
p
q
r
s
t
u
v
w
x
y
z

149

A
B
C
D
E
F
G
H
I
J
K
L
M
N
O
P
Q
R
S
T
U
V
W
X
Y
Z

fidget fidgets, fidgeting, fidgeted
VERB If you **fidget**, you keep changing your position or making small restless movements because you are nervous or bored.

field fields
NOUN **1** an area of land where crops are grown or animals are kept
NOUN **2** an area of land where sports are played • *a football field*
NOUN **3** a particular subject or area of interest

fiend fiends
NOUN **1** a devil or evil spirit
NOUN **2** a very wicked or cruel person

PRONUNCIATION TIP
This word is pronounced **feend**.

fierce fiercer, fiercest
ADJECTIVE very aggressive or intense • *a fierce dog* • *fierce competition*

fiery fierier, fieriest
ADJECTIVE If you are **fiery**, you show great anger, energy or passion in what you do.

fifteen
NOUN **Fifteen** is the number 15.

fifteenth fifteenths
NOUN **1** one of fifteen equal parts of something
ADJECTIVE **2** The **fifteenth** item in a series is the one that you count as number fifteen.

fifth
NOUN **1** one of five equal parts of something. It can be written as ⅕.
ADJECTIVE **2** The **fifth** item in a series is the one that you count as number five. It can be written as 5th.

fiftieth fiftieths
NOUN **1** one of fifty equal parts of something
ADJECTIVE **2** The **fiftieth** item in a series is the one that you count as number fifty.

fifty
NOUN **Fifty** is the number 50.

fig figs
NOUN a very sweet fruit that is full of seeds and can be eaten dried

fight fights, fighting, fought
VERB **1** When people **fight**, they take part in a battle, a boxing match, or in some other attempt to hurt or kill someone.
VERB **2** If you **fight** something, or if you fight against it, you try in a determined way to

stop it happening. • *I've fought all my life against cruelty to animals.*
NOUN **3** a situation in which people hit or try to hurt each other

SYNONYMS: battle, conflict

figurative
ADJECTIVE If you use a word or expression in a **figurative** sense, you use it for effect, with a more abstract or imaginative meaning than its usual one. For example, you could write about a person as if he or she was a bird. • *He flew down the stairs.* • *She perched on a chair.*

figure figures
NOUN **1** a written number • *He wrote the figures down and then added them up.*
NOUN **2** Your **figure** is the shape of your body.
NOUN **3** a diagram or table in a book or a magazine

figure of speech figures of speech
NOUN an expression, such as a metaphor or a simile, where the words should not be taken literally. *She was as cold as ice* (simile). *The road was a ribbon of moonlight* (metaphor).

file files, filing, filed
NOUN **1** a box or folder in which papers are kept
NOUN **2** In computing, a **file** is a set of related data with its own name. • *He copied the file onto his memory stick.*
NOUN **3** a tool with rough surfaces, used for smoothing and shaping hard materials
VERB **4** When someone **files** something, they put it in its correct place with others that are similar. • *They filed the students' papers alphabetically.*
VERB **5** When a group of people **file** somewhere, they walk one behind the other in a line. • *The children filed out of the school.*
PHRASE **6** If people walk **in single file**, they walk one behind the other.

fill fills, filling, filled
VERB **1** If you **fill** something, or if it **fills** up, it becomes full. • *The arena soon began to fill up.*
VERB **2** If something **fills** a space, there is very little room left. • *The water filled the jug.*
fill in
VERB If you **fill in** a form, you write information in the spaces on it.

illing fillings
NOUN **1** the mixture inside a sandwich, cake or pie
NOUN **2** a small amount of metal or plastic that a dentist puts into a hole in a tooth

ilm films, filming, filmed
NOUN **1** a series of moving pictures that can be shown in a cinema or on television
NOUN **2** a strip of thin plastic that is used in some types of camera to take photographs
NOUN **3** a very thin layer of powder or liquid • A *film* of dust covered every surface.
VERB **4** If you *film* someone or something, you use a camera to take moving pictures of them.

ilter filters, filtering, filtered
NOUN **1** a device that allows some substances, lights or sounds to pass through it, but not others • The suntan cream acted as a *filter* against the harmful rays of the sun.
NOUN **2** something you can choose on some apps that allows you to change your photographs in some way
VERB **3** If you *filter* something, you pass it through a filter to remove tiny particles from it.

ilthy filthier, filthiest
ADJECTIVE very dirty

iltration
NOUN the process of passing a liquid through a filter to remove tiny particles from it

in fins
NOUN a flat object on the body of a fish that helps it to swim and keep its balance
→ Have a look at the illustrations for **fish** and **whale**

inal finals
ADJECTIVE **1** The **final** thing in a series is the last one, or the one that happens at the end. • the **final** chapter of a book
ADJECTIVE **2** A decision that is **final** cannot be changed or questioned. • The judges' decision is **final**.
NOUN **3** The **final** is the last game or contest in a series, that decides the overall winner.

inalist finalists
NOUN someone who takes part in the final of a competition

finally
ADVERB **1** If something **finally** happens, it happens after a long delay. • **Finally**, he answered the phone.

SYNONYMS: at last, eventually

ADVERB **2** You use **finally** to introduce the last point or topic. • **Finally**, I would like to thank everyone for coming.

SYNONYMS: in conclusion, lastly

finance finances, financing, financed
NOUN **1** **Finance** describes affairs to do with money.
VERB **2** If someone **finances** something, they provide the money for it.

find finds, finding, found
VERB **1** If you **find** someone or something, you see them or discover where they are. • He eventually **found** the book under his bed.
VERB **2** If you **find** something, you know it from experience. • I **find** that air travel tires me.

find out
VERB If you **find out** something, you learn or discover something. • He wants to **find out** what really happened.

fine finer, finest; fines
ADJECTIVE **1** Something that is **fine** is very good or very beautiful.
ADJECTIVE **2** If something is **fine** it is satisfactory or suitable. • That outfit is **fine** for the party.
ADJECTIVE **3** If you are **fine**, you are well and happy.
ADJECTIVE **4** **Fine** sand or powder is made up of very small particles.
ADJECTIVE **5** When the weather is **fine**, it is bright and sunny.
NOUN **6** a sum of money that must be paid as a punishment

finger fingers
NOUN one of the four long structures at the end of your hands that you use to feel and hold things

fingernail fingernails
NOUN the hard coverings at the ends of your fingers

fingerprint fingerprints
NOUN the unique marks made by the tip of your fingers when you touch something

a
b
c
d
e
f
g
h
i
j
k
l
m
n
o
p
q
r
s
t
u
v
w
x
y
z

151

A
B
C
D
E
F
G
H
I
J
K
L
M
N
O
P
Q
R
S
T
U
V
W
X
Y
Z

finish finishes, finishing, finished

VERB **1** When you **finish** something, you do the last part of it and complete it.

VERB **2** When something **finishes**, it ends. • The film **finished** at eight o'clock.

NOUN **3** The **finish** of something is the last part of it. • There was a very exciting **finish** to the match.

SYNONYMS: close, conclusion, end

fir firs

NOUN an evergreen tree with thin, needle-like leaves and cones

fire fires, firing, fired

NOUN **1** the flames produced when something burns

NOUN **2** a mass of burning material • We lit a **fire** on the beach.

NOUN **3** a device that uses electricity, coal, gas or wood to heat a room

VERB **4** If someone **fires** a gun, they shoot a bullet. • He **fired** the gun into the air.

VERB **5** (informal) If an employer **fires** someone, that person loses their job.

PHRASE **6** If something is **on fire**, it is burning.

fire brigade fire brigades

NOUN the organisation that has the job of putting out fires

fire engine fire engines

NOUN a vehicle used by firefighters to help them put out fires

fire escape fire escapes

NOUN an emergency exit or staircase for use if there is a fire

fire extinguisher fire extinguishers

NOUN a device that contains water or foam that is sprayed on to fires to put them out

firefighter firefighters

NOUN a person whose job is to put out fires

fireplace fireplaces

NOUN the opening beneath a chimney where a fire can be lit

fireproof

ADJECTIVE If something is **fireproof**, it is resistant to fire.

firework fireworks

NOUN a small object that produces coloured sparks or smoke when lit

firm firmer, firmest; firms

ADJECTIVE **1** Something that is **firm** is fairly hard and does not change shape very much when it is pressed. • I like sleeping on a **firm** mattress.

ADJECTIVE **2** A **firm** grasp or push is strong or controlled. • His handshake was **firm** and confident.

ADJECTIVE **3** Someone who is **firm** behaves in a fairly strict way and will not change their mind.

NOUN **4** a business that sells or produces something • an engineering **firm**

first firsts

ADJECTIVE **1** happening, coming or done before all the others • January is the **first** month of the year.

ADJECTIVE **2** the most important • Her painting won **first** prize.

NOUN **3** the person or thing that happens or comes before all the others • I was the **first** to arrive.

ADVERB **4** happening, coming or done before all the others • Andrea came **first** in the 100 metres race.

ADVERB **5** the time before any others • They **first** met in 1995.

PHRASE **6** You use **at first** to refer to what happens to start with, or what happens at the beginning of something.

first aid

NOUN simple treatment given as soon as possible to a person who is injured or who suddenly becomes ill

first class

ADJECTIVE Something that is **first class** is of the highest quality or standard.

first person

NOUN In grammar, the **first person** refers to yourself when you are speaking or writing. It is expressed as I or me. • William wrote his story in the **first person**.

fish fishes, fishing, fished

NOUN **1** an animal with a tail and fins that lives in water

VERB **2** If you **fish**, you try to catch fish.

→ Have a look at the illustration

LANGUAGE TIP

The plural of the noun fish can be either fish or fishes, but fish is more common.

fisherman fishermen

NOUN someone who catches fish for a living or as a sport

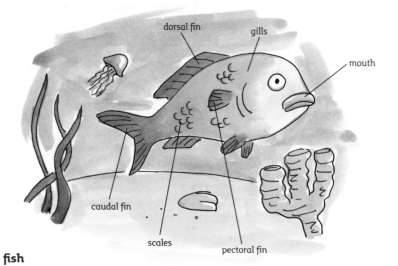

dorsal fin

gills

mouth

caudal fin

scales

pectoral fin

fish

fishing
NOUN the activity or job of trying to catch fish

fist fists
NOUN a hand with the fingers curled tightly towards the palm

fit fits, fitting, fitted; fitter, fittest
VERB **1** If something **fits**, it is the right shape or size for a particular person or position. • *a computer that **fits** into your pocket*
VERB **2** If you **fit** something, you put it securely in place. • *We need to **fit** a new pane of glass in the broken window.*
VERB **3** If something **fits** a particular situation, person or thing, it is suitable or appropriate.
NOUN **4** A **fit** of laughter, coughing, rage or panic is a sudden, uncontrolled outburst of it. • *They collapsed in a **fit** of laughter.*
NOUN **5** If someone has a **fit**, they lose consciousness and their body makes uncontrollable movements.
ADJECTIVE **6** Someone who is **fit** is healthy and physically strong.

fitness
NOUN Someone's **fitness** is how healthy and physically strong they are. • *exercises to improve **fitness***

five
NOUN **Five** is the number 5.

fix fixes, fixing, fixed
VERB **1** If you **fix** something somewhere, you attach it there securely. • *He **fixed** the clock to the wall.*
VERB **2** If you **fix** something that is broken, you repair it.
SYNONYM: mend

fixture fixtures
NOUN **1** a sports event that takes place on a particular date
NOUN **2** an object such as a cupboard or a bath that is fixed in position in a building

fizz fizzes, fizzing, fizzed
VERB When something **fizzes** it makes a hissing or bubbling sound.

fizzy fizzier, fizziest
ADJECTIVE A **fizzy** drink has a gas called carbon dioxide in it to make it bubbly.

flag flags
NOUN a piece of cloth that has a particular colour or design, and is used as the symbol of a country or as a signal

flake flakes, flaking, flaked
NOUN **1** a small, thin piece of something • *Flakes of rust came off the old bicycle.*
VERB **2** When something such as paint **flakes**, small, thin pieces of it come off.

flaky flakier, flakiest
ADJECTIVE breaking easily into small, thin pieces

153

A
B
C
D
E
F
G
H
I
J
K
L
M
N
O
P
Q
R
S
T
U
V
W
X
Y
Z

flame flames
NOUN a hot, bright stream of burning gas
• The **flames** of the fire flickered.

flamingo flamingos or flamingoes
NOUN a long-legged wading bird with pink feathers and a long neck

flammable
ADJECTIVE likely to catch fire and burn easily

flan flans
NOUN a flat, open tart that can be sweet or savoury

flannel flannels
NOUN **1** a small square of towelling, used for washing yourself
NOUN **2** a lightweight woollen fabric

flap flaps, flapping, flapped
VERB **1** If something **flaps**, or if you **flap** it, it moves quickly up and down or from side to side. • The flag was **flapping** in the wind.
NOUN **2** a loose piece of something, such as cloth or plastic, that is attached at one edge • a cat **flap**

flare flares, flaring, flared
NOUN **1** a device that produces a brightly coloured flame, used especially as an emergency signal
VERB **2** If a fire **flares**, it suddenly burns much more vigorously.

flash flashes, flashing, flashed
NOUN **1** a sudden, short burst of light • There was a **flash** of lightning in the middle of the storm.
VERB **2** If a light **flashes**, or if you **flash** it, it shines suddenly and briefly. • The light from the lighthouse **flashed** in the night.
VERB **3** If something **flashes**, it moves or happens very quickly. • A car **flashed** past the window.

flask flasks
NOUN a special bottle used for keeping drinks hot or cold, and for carrying around with you. It is an abbreviation for vacuum flask or Thermos flask.

flat flats; flatter, flattest
NOUN **1** a set of rooms for living in. A **flat** is part of a larger building. • We live in a block of **flats**.
ADJECTIVE **2** Something that is **flat** is level and smooth.
ADJECTIVE **3** A **flat** tyre or ball has not got enough air in it.
ADJECTIVE **4** A **flat** battery has lost its electrical charge.

flatten flattens, flattening, flattened
VERB If you **flatten** something, you make it flat or flatter.

flatter flatters, flattering, flattered
VERB If you **flatter** someone, you praise them in an exaggerated way, either to please them or to persuade them to do something.
• When she **flatters** me I know she wants me to do something for her.

flaunt flaunts, flaunting, flaunted
VERB If you **flaunt** something, you show it off to others.

flavour flavours, flavouring, flavoured
NOUN **1** the taste of food and drink • This cheese has a very strong **flavour**.
VERB **2** If you **flavour** food, you add something to it to give it a particular taste.
• You can **flavour** the pasta sauce with herbs.

flaw flaws
NOUN a fault or weakness in something

flax
NOUN a plant that is used for making rope and cloth

flea fleas
NOUN a small, wingless, jumping insect that feeds on blood

fleece fleeces
NOUN A sheep's **fleece** is its coat of wool.

fleet fleets
NOUN a group of ships or vehicles owned by the same organisation, or travelling together

flesh
NOUN the soft part of your body between the bones and the skin

flew
VERB the past tense of **fly**

flex flexes, flexing, flexed
NOUN **1** a length of wire covered in plastic, that carries electricity to an appliance
VERB **2** If you **flex** your muscles, you bend and stretch them.

flexibility
NOUN **Flexibility** is the quality that something has when it can be bent easily without breaking.

flexible
ADJECTIVE Something that is **flexible** can be bent easily without breaking.

lick flicks, flicking, flicked
VERB **1** If you **flick** something, you move it sharply with your finger. • *He **flicked** through the pages of the book to find where he was up to.*
NOUN **2** a sudden, quick movement or sharp touch with the finger • *The cat gave a sudden **flick** of its tail.*

licker flickers, flickering, flickered
VERB If a light or a flame **flickers**, its brightness comes and goes.

lies
PLURAL NOUN the plural of **fly**

light flights
NOUN **1** a journey made by aeroplane
NOUN **2** the action of flying or the ability to fly
NOUN **3** A **flight** of stairs or steps is a row of them.
NOUN **4** the action of running away • *The girl took **flight** when she saw the big dog.*

light attendant flight attendants
NOUN a person who looks after the passengers on an aeroplane

limsy flimsier, flimsiest
ADJECTIVE made of something very thin and easily damaged • *The shelter they made in the garden was very **flimsy**.*

linch flinches, flinching, flinched
VERB If you **flinch**, you make a sudden, small movement in fear or pain. • *She **flinched** when the dentist's drill started.*

SYNONYMS: cringe, wince

ling flings, flinging, flung
VERB If you **fling** something somewhere, you throw it there using a lot of force. • *He **flung** his shoes into the corner.*

lint flints
NOUN a very hard, grey-black stone used for building

lip flips, flipping, flipped
VERB If you **flip** something, you turn it over quickly. • *He **flipped** open the book to start his homework.*

lipper flippers
NOUN one of the flat limbs of an animal like a penguin or seal that they use for swimming

loat floats, floating, floated
VERB **1** Something that **floats** is supported by liquid. • *A branch **floated** down the river.*
VERB **2** If something **floats** in the air, it hangs in the air or moves slowly through it. • *A leaf **floated** on the breeze.*

NOUN **3** an object attached to a fishing line to keep the hook floating in the water
NOUN **4** an amount of money that a shop or stall keeps for change

flock flocks, flocking, flocked
NOUN **1** a group of birds, sheep or goats
VERB **2** If people **flock** somewhere, they go there in large numbers.

flood floods, flooding, flooded
NOUN **1** If there is a **flood**, a large amount of water covers an area that is usually dry.
NOUN **2** A **flood** of something is a large amount of it occurring suddenly. • *There was a **flood** of emails after the programme.*
VERB **3** If water **floods** an area that is usually dry, or if the area **floods**, it becomes covered with water. • *He left the tap running and **flooded** the kitchen.*

floodlight floodlights
NOUN a very powerful outdoor light that is used to illuminate buildings and sports fields

floor floors
NOUN **1** the part of a room that you walk on
NOUN **2** one of the levels in a building • *Our flat is on the fifth **floor** of the building.*

flop flops, flopping, flopped
VERB **1** If someone or something **flops**, they fall loosely and heavily. • *He **flopped** down on to the sofa when he got home.*
VERB **2** (*informal*) If something **flops**, it fails. • *The play **flopped** after some bad reviews.*

flora
NOUN plants, especially those that grow in a particular area • *the **flora** and fauna of the African jungle*

florist florists
NOUN a person or shop selling flowers

flour
NOUN a white or brown powder made by grinding grain. It is used for making bread, cakes and pastry.

flourish flourishes, flourishing, flourished
VERB Something that **flourishes** develops or grows successfully or healthily.

WORD HISTORY
from Latin *florere* meaning to flower

A
B
C
D
E
F
G
H
I
J
K
L
M
N
O
P
Q
R
S
T
U
V
W
X
Y
Z

flow flows, flowing, flowed

VERB **1** If something **flows** somewhere, it moves there in a steady and continuous manner. ● *The river **flows** south from the town.*
NOUN **2** A **flow** of something is a steady, continuous movement of it. ● *There is a constant **flow** of traffic down the main road.*

flow chart flow charts

NOUN a diagram that shows the sequence of steps and choices that lead to various results and courses of action

flower flowers, flowering, flowered

NOUN **1** the part of a plant that grows at the end of a stem. It carries the reproductive parts of the plant from which the fruit and seeds develop.

→ Have a look at the illustration for **plant**

VERB **2** When a plant **flowers**, its flowers open.

flown

VERB the past participle of **fly**

flu

NOUN an abbreviation of *influenza*. **Flu** is an illness similar to a bad cold, but more serious.

fluent

ADJECTIVE Someone who is **fluent** in a foreign language can speak it correctly and without hesitation.

fluently

ADVERB Someone who speaks a foreign language **fluently** can speak it correctly and without hesitation.

fluff

NOUN soft, light, woolly threads or fibres bunched together

fluffy fluffier, fluffiest

ADJECTIVE soft and woolly ● *The kitten was small, grey and very **fluffy**.*

fluid fluids

NOUN a liquid ● *Drink plenty of **fluids** in hot weather.*

fluke flukes

NOUN an accidental success ● *It must be a **fluke** that I did so well in my exams.*

fluorescent

ADJECTIVE **1** When something is **fluorescent**, it gives out its own light when another light is shone on it.
ADJECTIVE **2** A **fluorescent** light is in the form of a tube that shines with a harsh, bright light.

fluoride

NOUN a chemical mixture that is often added to drinking water and to toothpaste because it is thought to prevent tooth decay

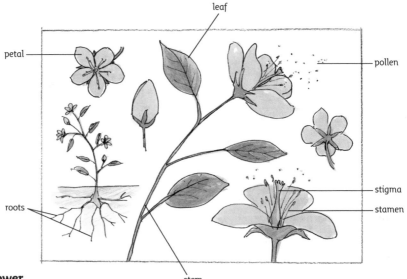

leaf

petal

pollen

roots

stigma

stamen

stem

flower

flush flushes, flushing, flushed
VERB **1** If you **flush**, your face goes red.
VERB **2** If you **flush** a toilet or something such as a pipe, you force water through it to clean it.

flute flutes
NOUN a musical wind instrument in the shape of a long tube with holes along it. You play it by blowing over a hole near one end while holding it sideways to your mouth.

flutter flutters, fluttering, fluttered
VERB If something **flutters**, it flaps or waves with small, quick movements. • *I felt the bird* ***flutter*** *in my hands.*

fly flies, flying, flew, flown
NOUN **1** an insect with two pairs of wings
VERB **2** When a bird, insect or aircraft **flies**, it moves through the air. • *The bird* ***flew*** *away.*
VERB **3** If you **fly** somewhere, you travel there in an aircraft.

flyer flyers
NOUN a piece of paper that advertises something

flying
NOUN **1** the activity of travelling in a plane
ADJECTIVE **2** moving through the air

flyover flyovers
NOUN a bridge that takes one road over the top of another one

foal foals
NOUN a young horse

foam foams, foaming, foamed
NOUN **1** a mass of tiny bubbles • *The bubble bath produced a lot of* ***foam***.
VERB **2** When something **foams**, it forms a mass of small bubbles. • *The powder* ***foamed*** *in the washing machine.*

focus focuses, focusing, focused or focusses, focussing, focussed
VERB **1** If you **focus** your eyes or a camera on something, you adjust your eyes or the camera so that the image is clear. • *She* ***focused*** *her eyes on the ball.*
VERB **2** If you **focus** on a particular topic, you concentrate on it.
PHRASE **3** If an image is **in focus**, the edges of the image are clear and sharp. If it is **out of focus**, the edges are blurred.

WORD HISTORY
from Latin *focus* meaning hearth, which was seen as the centre of a Roman home

---

LANGUAGE TIP
You can spell the inflections of *focus* with one *s* or two *ss* in the middle but the spellings with one *s* are much more common: *focuses, focusing, focused.*

---

fodder
NOUN food given to horses and cattle

foe foes
NOUN If someone is your **foe**, they are your enemy.

foetus foetuses; also spelt **fetus**
NOUN A **foetus** is an unborn child or other animal in the womb.

fog
NOUN a thick mist caused by tiny drops of water in the air

foil foils, foiling, foiled
VERB **1** If you **foil** someone's attempt at something, you prevent it from succeeding. • *The police officer* ***foiled*** *the robbery.*
NOUN **2** thin, paper-like sheets of metal used to wrap food

fold folds, folding, folded
VERB **1** If you **fold** something, you bend it so that one part lies over another. • *He* ***folded*** *the letter and put it back in the envelope.*
NOUN **2** a crease or bend in paper or cloth

folder folders
NOUN **1** a thin piece of folded cardboard used for keeping papers together
NOUN **2** a group of files that are stored together on a computer

foliage
NOUN the leaves of plants

folk
PLURAL NOUN **1** people • *These are the* ***folk*** *I was telling you about.*
ADJECTIVE **2** **Folk** music and art are traditional or typical of the people of a particular area. • *My dad likes Irish* ***folk*** *music.*

folklore
NOUN the traditional stories and beliefs of a community

a
b
c
d
e
f
g
h
i
j
k
l
m
n
o
p
q
r
s
t
u
v
w
x
y
z

157

A
B
C
D
E
F
G
H
I
J
K
L
M
N
O
P
Q
R
S
T
U
V
W
X
Y
Z

follow follows, following, followed
VERB **1** If you **follow** someone or something, you move along behind them. ● *We* **followed** *him up the steps.*
VERB **2** If you **follow** a path or a sign, you go somewhere using the path or sign to direct you. ● *I* **followed** *the signs to the dining room.*
VERB **3** If you **follow** instructions or advice, you do what you are told.
VERB **4** If you **follow** an explanation or the plot of a story, you understand each stage of it.
VERB **5** If you **follow** someone on a social media website, you choose to look at the messages and pictures that they post.

follower followers
NOUN someone who chooses to look at the messages and pictures that someone else posts on a social media website

fond fonder, fondest
ADJECTIVE If you are **fond** of someone or something, you like them.

font fonts
NOUN **1** a large, stone bowl in a church that holds the water for baptisms
NOUN **2** a style of printed writing. There are many **fonts** to choose from, for example, Helvetica, Times, Courier or Frutiger.

food foods
NOUN what people and other animals eat

food chain food chains
NOUN a series of living things that are linked together because each one feeds on another in the chain

→ Have a look at the illustration

fool fools, fooling, fooled
NOUN **1** someone who is silly and is not sensible
VERB **2** If you **fool** someone, you deceive or trick them. ● *Don't be* **fooled** *by his appearance.*

foolish
ADJECTIVE stupid or silly

foolproof
ADJECTIVE If something is **foolproof**, it cannot fail.

foot feet
NOUN **1** the part of a human or other animal's body at the end of their leg

→ Have a look at the illustration for **bird**

NOUN **2** the part of something that is farthest from the top ● *The hotel was at the* **foot** *of the mountain.*
NOUN **3** a unit of length equal to 12 inches or about 30.5 centimetres

football footballs
NOUN **1** a game such as soccer and American **football**, in which the ball can be kicked and two teams try to score goals
NOUN **2** a ball used in these games

footballer footballers
NOUN someone who plays soccer or American football, especially as their job

foothold footholds
NOUN a place where you can put your foot when climbing

footpath footpaths
NOUN a path for people to walk on, especially in the countryside

footprint footprints
NOUN **1** the mark made by a foot on the ground
NOUN **2** You can call the impact that something has on the environment its **footprint**. ● *Many countries are working hard to reduce their carbon* **footprint**.

footstep footsteps
NOUN the sound made by someone's feet when they are walking ● *They heard* **footsteps** *in the corridor.*

for
PREPOSITION **1** to be used by or given to a particular person ● *I bought a present* **for** *my brother.*
PREPOSITION **2** **For** is used when explaining the reason, cause or purpose of something. ● *I'm going shopping* **for** *a pair of shoes.*
PREPOSITION **3** You use **for** to show a distance, time or quantity. ● *I have been waiting here* **for** *ages.*
PREPOSITION **4** If you are **for** something, you support it. ● *My parents are all* **for** *the new school.*

ANTONYM: against

forbid forbids, forbidding, forbade, forbidden
VERB If someone **forbids** you to do something, they order you not to do it.

forbidden
ADJECTIVE not allowed

FOOD CHAIN

force forces, forcing, forced
VERB **1** If you **force** someone to do something, you make them do it.
NOUN **2** violence or great strength • *He used a lot of force to pull the wall down.*
NOUN **3** an organised group of people, especially soldiers or police • *The police force helped to maintain order at the football match.*
NOUN **4** a push or pull. **Forces** are measured in newtons.

forceful
ADJECTIVE **1** giving your opinions very strongly, and good at persuading people • *He has a very forceful personality.*
ADJECTIVE **2** A **forceful** argument or reason is clear and likely to persuade people
ADJECTIVE **3** using a lot of physical force

forcefully
ADVERB **1** in a way that is likely to persuade people
ADVERB **2** with a lot of physical force

forecast forecasts, forecasting, forecast or **forecasted**
NOUN **1** A **forecast** says what is likely to happen. • *the weather forecast*
VERB **2** If you **forecast** an event, you say what is likely to happen. • *We forecast that we would win the game.*

foreground foregrounds
NOUN In a picture, the **foreground** is the part that seems nearest to you.

forehead foreheads
NOUN the area at the front of your head, above your eyebrows and below your hair

foreign
ADJECTIVE belonging to or involving a country that is not your own • *It is useful to learn a foreign language.*

foreigner
NOUN someone who comes from a country that is not your own

forest forests
NOUN a large area of trees growing close together

forever
ADVERB permanently or continually

forfeit forfeits, forfeiting, forfeited
VERB If you **forfeit** something, you have to give it up as a penalty.

forgave
VERB the past tense of **forgive**

forge forges, forging, forged
NOUN **1** a place where a blacksmith works making metal goods by hand
VERB **2** If someone **forges** metal, they hammer and bend it into shape while it is hot.
VERB **3** Someone who **forges** money, documents or paintings makes illegal copies of them.

forgery forgeries
NOUN **1** the crime of making false copies of something
NOUN **2** an illegal false copy of something

forget forgets, forgetting, forgot, forgotten
VERB If you **forget** something, you do not remember it.

forgetful
ADJECTIVE Someone who is **forgetful** often forgets things.

forgive forgives, forgiving, forgave, forgiven
VERB If you **forgive** someone who has done something wrong, you stop being angry with them.

fork forks
NOUN **1** an instrument with prongs on the end of a handle, used for eating food or for digging earth
NOUN **2** If there is a **fork** in a road or river, it divides into two or more parts.

forlorn
ADJECTIVE If you are **forlorn**, you are unhappy and lonely.

form forms, forming, formed
NOUN **1** a particular type or kind of something • *Running is a form of exercise.*
NOUN **2** the shape or pattern of something • *Cut out your paper in the form of a star.*
NOUN **3** a class in school
NOUN **4** a piece of paper with questions and spaces where you fill in your answers
VERB **5** If you **form** something, you make it or give it a particular shape. • *Please all stand up and form a circle.*
VERB **6** If something **forms**, it develops or comes into existence. • *The puddles formed on the pavement after the rain.*

formal
ADJECTIVE **1 Formal** speech, writing or behaviour is correct and serious, rather than relaxed and friendly. • *At the prizegiving everyone wore **formal** clothes.*

ANTONYM: informal

ADJECTIVE **2** A **formal** action or event is an official one that follows accepted rules.

ANTONYM: informal

format formats
NOUN the way something is arranged and presented • *The **format** of the book is easy to follow.*

formation formations
NOUN **1** the start or creation of something
NOUN **2** the pattern or shape of something

former
ADJECTIVE **1** happening or existing before now, or in the past • *The **former** tennis champion presented the trophy to the new champion.*
NOUN **2 Former** refers to the first of two things mentioned. • *Exams and coursework are both important, but the **former** must take priority this term.*

formerly
ADVERB before now, or in the past • *The hotel was **formerly** a farmhouse.*

formula formulae or **formulas**
NOUN a group of letters, numbers or symbols that stand for a mathematical or scientific rule

fort forts
NOUN a strong, fortified building built for defence

fortieth fortieths
NOUN **1** one of forty equal parts of something
ADJECTIVE **2** The **fortieth** item in a series is the one that you count as number forty.

fortify fortifies, fortifying, fortified
VERB If someone **fortifies** a building, they make it stronger against attack.

fortnight fortnights
NOUN a period of two weeks

fortress fortresses
NOUN a very strong and well-protected castle or town

fortunate
ADJECTIVE lucky

fortunately
ADVERB You use **fortunately** to say that it is lucky that something has happened. • ***Fortunately**, no one was hurt in the accident.*

fortune fortunes
NOUN **1** luck
NOUN **2** a lot of money

forty
NOUN **Forty** is the number 40.

forward forwards
ADVERB **1** If you move something **forward** or **forwards**, you move it towards the front.
NOUN **2** In a game like hockey or football, a **forward** is someone in an attacking position.

fossil fossils
NOUN the remains or impression of an animal or plant from a previous age, which has been preserved in rock

fossil fuel fossil fuels
NOUN fuel such as coal or oil that is formed from the rotting of plants or animals from millions of years ago

fossilise fossilises, fossilising, fossilised; also spelt **fossilize**
VERB to become a fossil by being preserved in rock

foster fosters, fostering, fostered
VERB If someone **fosters** a child, they look after the child for a period in their home, but do not become his or her legal parent.

foster child foster children
NOUN a child who lives with you for a period of time because their own parents cannot look after them

a
b
c
d
e
f
g
h
i
j
k
l
m
n
o
p
q
r
s
t
u
v
w
x
y
z

161

foster home foster homes
NOUN a home where a child goes to live for a period of time when their own parents cannot look after them

foster parent foster parents
NOUN someone who looks after a child for a period of time, but who does not become the child's legal parent

fought
VERB the past tense of **fight**

foul fouler, foulest; fouls
ADJECTIVE **1** dirty and very unpleasant • *There was a **foul** smell coming from the drains.*
NOUN **2** In sport, a **foul** is an action that breaks the rules.

found founds, founding, founded
VERB **1** the past tense and past participle of **find**
VERB **2** If someone **founds** an organisation or company, they create it. • *He **founded** the charity ten years ago.*

foundation foundations
NOUN **1** the basic ideas on which something is based • *A good education is the **foundation** for a successful life.*
PLURAL NOUN **2** The **foundations** of a building are the layer of concrete or bricks below the ground on which it is built.
NOUN **3** the founding of something

fountain fountains
NOUN an ornamental structure in which a jet of water is forced into the air by a pump

fountain pen fountain pens
NOUN a pen that has a nib which is supplied with ink from a container inside the pen

four
NOUN **Four** is the number 4.

fourteen
NOUN **Fourteen** is the number 14.

fourteenth fourteenths
NOUN **1** one of fourteen equal parts of something
ADJECTIVE **2** The **fourteenth** item in a series is the one that you count as number fourteen.

fourth
ADJECTIVE The **fourth** item in a series is the one that you count as number four. It can be written as 4th.

fowl fowls
NOUN a bird, such as chicken or duck, that is kept or hunted for its meat or eggs

fox foxes
NOUN a wild mammal that looks like a dog and has reddish-brown fur and a thick tail

foyer foyers
NOUN a large entrance hall just inside the main doors of a cinema, hotel or public building

PRONUNCIATION TIP
This word is pronounced **foy**-ay.

fracking
NOUN a method of getting oil or gas from rock by forcing liquid and sand into the rock

fraction fractions
NOUN **1** In mathematics, a **fraction** is a part of a whole number.
NOUN **2** a tiny proportion or amount of something

fracture fractures, fracturing, fractured
NOUN **1** a crack or break in something, especially a bone
VERB **2** If something **fractures**, or if you **fracture** it, it breaks. • *She **fractured** her arm while playing netball.*

fragile
ADJECTIVE easily broken or damaged

fragility
NOUN the quality that something has when it is easily broken or damaged.

fragment fragments
NOUN a small piece or part of something • *There were **fragments** of glass on the floor after I dropped the vase.*

fragrant
ADJECTIVE Something that is **fragrant** smells sweet or pleasant.

frail frailer, frailest
ADJECTIVE weak or fragile

frame frames, framing, framed
NOUN **1** the structure surrounding a door, window or picture
VERB **2** If you **frame** a picture, you make a frame for it.

framework frameworks
NOUN a structure that forms a support or frame for something • *wooden shelves on a steel **framework***

frantic
ADJECTIVE If you are **frantic**, you behave in a wild, desperate way because you are anxious or frightened.

frantically
ADVERB in a wild and desperate way

fraud frauds
NOUN the crime of getting money by deceit

fraught
ADJECTIVE 1 If a situation is **fraught**, it is full of potential problems or difficulties.
ADJECTIVE 2 If someone is **fraught**, they are tense and upset.

frayed
ADJECTIVE If material is **frayed**, the edges are worn and ragged.

freak freaks
NOUN 1 A **freak** is someone whose appearance or behaviour is very unusual.
ADJECTIVE 2 A **freak** event is very unusual. • We had a **freak** storm in the middle of the summer.

freckle freckles
NOUN a small, light-brown spot on someone's skin, especially their face

freckled
ADJECTIVE having small, light-brown spots on your skin, especially your face

free freer, freest; frees, freeing, freed
ADJECTIVE 1 If something is **free**, you can have it without paying for it.
ADJECTIVE 2 Someone who is **free** is no longer a prisoner.
ADJECTIVE 3 If someone is **free**, they are not busy. • Are you **free** on Saturday afternoon?
VERB 4 If you **free** someone or something that is trapped, you release them.

freedom
NOUN If you have the **freedom** to do something, you are free to do it.

free verse
NOUN poetry that does not use patterns of rhyme or rhythm

freeway freeways
NOUN In Australia, South Africa and the USA, a **freeway** is a road for fast-moving traffic.

freeze freezes, freezing, froze, frozen
VERB 1 When a liquid **freezes**, or when something **freezes** it, it becomes solid because it is very cold.
VERB 2 If you **freeze** food, you make it very cold to preserve it.
VERB 3 If you **freeze**, you suddenly stop moving because there is danger.
ADJECTIVE 4 You say you are **freezing** when you are very cold.

freezer freezers
NOUN a refrigerator in which you can store food for a long time at very low temperatures

freezing
ADJECTIVE You say you are **freezing** when you are very cold.

freezing point
NOUN the temperature at which a liquid starts to change into a solid

freight
NOUN goods moved by lorries, ships or other transport

frenzied
ADJECTIVE done by someone who is behaving in a wild and uncontrolled way • a **frenzied** attack

frenzy frenzies
NOUN If someone is in a **frenzy**, their behaviour is wild and uncontrolled.

frequency frequencies
NOUN 1 The **frequency** of an event is how often it happens.
NOUN 2 The **frequency** of a sound or radio wave is the rate at which it vibrates.

frequency table frequency tables
NOUN a chart where you write down how often something happens

frequent
ADJECTIVE If something happens at **frequent** intervals, it happens often.

frequently
ADVERB happening often or a lot of the time • He was **frequently** unhappy.

fresh fresher, freshest
ADJECTIVE 1 not old or used • We put **fresh** towels out for the guests.
ADJECTIVE 2 **Fresh** food has been made or picked recently, and is not tinned or frozen.
ADJECTIVE 3 **Fresh** water is water that is not salty. • The water in a river or lake is **fresh** water.

freshwater
ADJECTIVE A **freshwater** animal lives in a river, lake or pool and not in the sea.

fret frets, fretting, fretted
VERB 1 If you **fret** about something, you worry about it.
NOUN 2 The **frets** on a stringed instrument, such as a guitar, are the metal ridges across its neck.

163

friction

NOUN **1** the force that slows things down and can stop them from moving

NOUN **2 Friction** between people is disagreement and quarrels. • *There was a lot of friction between the two families.*

Friday Fridays

NOUN the sixth day of the week, coming between Thursday and Saturday

WORD HISTORY

from Old English *Frigedæg* meaning Freya's day. Freya was the Norse goddess of love.

fridge fridges

NOUN a short form of *refrigerator*

friend friends, friending, friended

NOUN **1** someone you know well and like, but who is not related to you

VERB **2** If you **friend** someone, you ask them to be your friend on a social media website.

friendly friendlier, friendliest

ADJECTIVE A **friendly** person is kind and pleasant to others.

friendship friendships

NOUN the state of being friends with someone • *Her friendship means a lot to me.*

frieze friezes

NOUN a decorative band, often around the top of a wall. It can be a carving, or a long strip of paper with a picture or pattern on it.

fright

NOUN a sudden feeling of fear

frighten frightens, frightening, frightened

VERB If something or someone **frightens** you, they make you afraid.

frightened

ADJECTIVE afraid or scared

frightening

ADJECTIVE making you feel afraid or scared

frill frills

NOUN a strip of material with a lot of folds in it, attached to something as decoration

fringe fringes

NOUN **1** the hair that hangs over a person's forehead • *She had a long fringe that almost covered her eyes.*

NOUN **2** a decoration on clothes and other objects, consisting of a row of hanging threads • *There is a fringe along the bottom of the curtains.*

frivolous

ADJECTIVE Someone who is **frivolous** behaves in a silly or light-hearted way, especially when they should be serious or sensible.

frizzy frizzier, frizziest

ADJECTIVE **Frizzy** hair has tight, wiry curls.

frog frogs

NOUN a small, amphibious animal with long back legs

→ Have a look at the illustration

frogspawn

NOUN a jelly-like substance containing the eggs of frogs

→ Have a look at the illustration for **frog**

frolic frolics, frolicking, frolicked

VERB When children and other young animals **frolic**, they run around and play in a lively way. • *In the spring, the lambs frolic in the fields.*

from

PREPOSITION **1 From** tells you where someone or something started. • *The river flows from the north.*

PREPOSITION **2** If you take something **from** an amount, you reduce the amount by that much. • *If you take 5 from 20 you are left with 15.*

PREPOSITION **3** You use **from** to state the range of something. • *Lunchtime is from 12 o'clock to 1 o'clock.*

front fronts

NOUN **1** the part of something that faces forward • *a jacket with buttons down the front*

ADJECTIVE **2** The **front** part of something is the part that is furthest forward. • *I like to sit in the front seats of the cinema.*

NOUN **3** In a war, the **front** is the place where two armies are fighting.

NOUN **4** At the seaside, the **front** is the road or promenade that runs alongside the beach.

NOUN **5** When talking about the weather, a **front** is a line where cold air meets warm air.

→ Have a look at the illustration for **weather**

frontier frontiers

NOUN a border between two countries • *Their passports were checked at the frontier.*

A
B
C
D
E
F
G
H
I
J
K
L
M
N
O
P
Q
R
S
T
U
V
W
X
Y
Z

frost frosts

NOUN powdery, white ice that forms on the ground when the temperature outside falls below freezing

frosty frostier, frostiest

ADJECTIVE When it is **frosty**, the temperature outside falls below freezing and powdery, white ice forms on the ground.

froth froths, frothing, frothed

NOUN **1** a mass of small bubbles on the surface of a liquid

VERB **2** If a liquid **froths**, small bubbles appear on its surface.

frothy frothier, frothiest

ADJECTIVE If a liquid is **frothy**, there are a lot of small bubbles on its surface.

frown frowns, frowning, frowned

VERB **1** If you **frown**, you move your eyebrows closer together and wrinkle your forehead, usually because you are annoyed, worried or puzzled.

NOUN **2** an expression on the face of someone who is frowning

froze

VERB the past tense of **freeze**

frozen

VERB **1** the past participle of **freeze**

ADJECTIVE **2** If you say you are **frozen**, you mean you have become very cold. ● *My fingers were absolutely **frozen**.*

fruit fruits

NOUN the part of a plant that develops after the flower has been fertilised, that contains the seeds. Apples, oranges and bananas are all **fruit**.

→ Have a look at the illustration for **plant**

WORD HISTORY

from Latin *fructus* meaning produce or benefit

---

frustrate frustrates, frustrating, frustrated

VERB **1** If something **frustrates** you, it prevents you doing what you want and makes you upset.

VERB **2** If you **frustrate** something, such as a plan, you prevent it. ● *They deliberately **frustrated** my attempts to do my homework.*

a
b
c
d
e
f
g
h
i
j
k
l
m
n
o
p
q
r
s
t
u
v
w
x
y
z

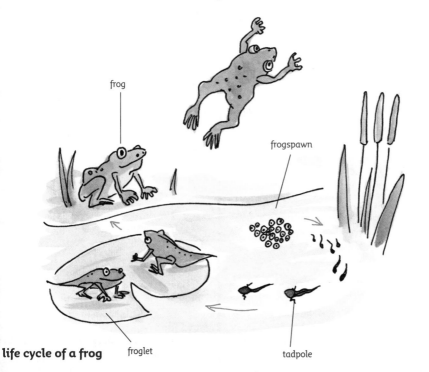

frog

frogspawn

life cycle of a frog froglet

tadpole

frustrated
ADJECTIVE upset or annoyed because you cannot do or achieve what you want

frustrating
VERB making you feel frustrated

frustration
NOUN the feeling of being frustrated

fry fries, frying, fried
VERB When you **fry** food, you cook it in a pan containing hot fat.

fudge
NOUN a soft, brown sweet made from butter, milk and sugar

fuel fuels
NOUN a substance such as coal, gas, oil or wood that is burned to provide heat or power

fugitive fugitives
NOUN someone who is running away or hiding, especially from the police

fulcrum fulcrums or fulcra
NOUN the point at which something is balancing or turning

fulfil fulfils, fulfilling, fulfilled
VERB 1 If you **fulfil** a promise, you keep it.
VERB 2 If something **fulfils** you, it gives you satisfaction.

fulfilling
ADJECTIVE making you feel satisifed because you are doing something good ● a **fulfilling** life

fulfilment
NOUN the feeling you have when you are satisifed because you are doing something good

full fuller, fullest
ADJECTIVE 1 Something that is **full** contains as much as it is possible to hold. ● The bus was **full** so we had to wait for the next one.

ANTONYM: empty

ADJECTIVE 2 to the greatest possible extent ● The radio was playing at **full** volume.
ADJECTIVE 3 complete or whole ● I will tell you the **full** story later.
ADVERB 4 completely or wholly ● Turn the taps **full** on.

fullness
NOUN **Fullness** is when something contains as much as it is possible to hold.

ANTONYM: emptiness

full stop full stops
NOUN the punctuation mark (.) used at the end of a sentence and after an abbreviation or initial

full-time
ADJECTIVE If you have a **full-time** job, you work for the whole of each normal working week.

fully
ADVERB completely ● Are you **fully** recovered from your illness?

fumble fumbles, fumbling, fumbled
VERB If you **fumble**, you feel or handle something clumsily. ● I **fumbled** with the door handle because it was so dark.

fume fumes, fuming, fumed
PLURAL NOUN 1 **Fumes** are unpleasant-smelling gases and smoke that are sometimes poisonous, and are produced by burning and by some chemicals.
VERB 2 If something **fumes**, it produces smoke or gas.
VERB 3 If you **fume**, you are very angry.

fun
NOUN 1 pleasant, enjoyable and light-hearted activity ● Let's have some **fun**!
ADJECTIVE 2 If someone or something is **fun**, you enjoy being with them or you enjoy doing it. ● She is always **fun** to be with.
PHRASE 3 If you **make fun** of someone or something, you tease them or make jokes about them.

function functions, functioning, functioned
VERB 1 If a thing **functions**, it works as it should.
NOUN 2 The **function** of someone or something is their purpose or the work they are supposed to do.

functional
ADJECTIVE 1 If a thing **functional**, it works as it should.
ADJECTIVE 2 designed to be useful, not just to look attractive

fund funds
NOUN an amount of money that is collected for a particular purpose

fundamental
ADJECTIVE If something is **fundamental**, it is basic and necessary. • *You must understand the **fundamental** rules of the game before you can progress.*

funeral funerals
NOUN a ceremony for the burial or cremation of someone who has died

fungal
ADJECTIVE involving or caused by a fungus • *a **fungal** infection*

fungus fungi or **funguses**
NOUN an organism, such as a mushroom or mould, that does not have flowers or leaves

funnel funnels
NOUN **1** an open cone that narrows to a tube, and is used to pour substances into containers
NOUN **2** a metal chimney on a ship or steam engine
→ Have a look at the illustration for **ship**

funny funnier, funniest
ADJECTIVE **1** causing amusement or laughter • *He told us a **funny** story.*

SYNONYMS: amusing, comical, humorous

ADJECTIVE **2** strange or puzzling • *We could hear a **funny** noise.*

SYNONYMS: odd, peculiar

fur
NOUN the thick hair that grows on the bodies of many animals • *Polar bears have thick **fur**.*

furious
ADJECTIVE extremely angry

furnace furnaces
NOUN a very large, hot oven used for heating glass and melting metal

furnish furnishes, furnishing, furnished
VERB If you **furnish** a house or a room, you put furniture into it.

furniture
NOUN movable objects such as tables, chairs and wardrobes that you need inside a building • *bedroom **furniture***

furrow furrows
NOUN a shallow, straight channel dug into the earth by a plough

furry furrier, furriest
ADJECTIVE covered with fur • *furry animals*

further furthest
ADVERB or ADJECTIVE another word for *farther*

furtive
ADJECTIVE secretive, sly and cautious

fury
NOUN violent or extreme anger

WORD HISTORY
from Latin *furia* meaning madness

fuse fuses, fusing, fused
NOUN **1** a safety device in an electrical plug or appliance, consisting of a piece of wire that melts to stop the electric current if a fault occurs
VERB **2** When an electrical appliance **fuses**, it stops working because the fuse has melted to protect it.

fuss fusses, fussing, fussed
NOUN **1** unnecessarily anxious or excited behaviour
VERB **2** If someone **fusses**, they behave with unnecessary anxiety and concern for unimportant things.

fussy fussier, fussiest
ADJECTIVE If you are **fussy**, you worry too much about unnecessary details.

future futures
NOUN **1** the period of time after the present • *He is already making plans for his **future**.*
ADJECTIVE **2** relating to or occurring at a time after the present
PHRASE **3 In future** means from now on. • *Be more careful **in future**.*

fuzzy fuzzier, fuzziest
ADJECTIVE **1** soft and fluffy
ADJECTIVE **2** If a picture is **fuzzy**, it is not clear.

a b c d e f g h i j k l m n o p q r s t u v w x y z

167

Gg

g
an abbreviation for *gram*

gadget gadgets
NOUN a small mechanical device or tool

gain gains, gaining, gained
VERB **1** If you **gain** something, you get more of it or get something you didn't have before. • *She was pleased when she began to gain better marks.*
VERB **2** If a clock or watch **gains** time, it starts telling a later time than it is. • *I think my watch has gained five minutes. It says five past one and the clock says one o'clock.*

gala galas
NOUN a special, public celebration or performance • *a swimming gala*

galaxy galaxies
NOUN a huge group of stars that extends over millions of kilometres

gale gales
NOUN an extremely strong wind

gallant
ADJECTIVE brave and honourable

gall bladder gall bladders
NOUN the part of your body beside your liver that helps to break down fat cells

→ Have a look at the illustration for **stomach**

galleon galleons
NOUN a large Spanish sailing ship in the sixteenth and seventeenth centuries

gallery galleries
NOUN a building where paintings and other works of art are shown

gallon gallons
NOUN a measure of liquid that is equal to eight pints or 4.55 litres

gallop gallops, galloping, galloped
VERB When a horse **gallops**, it runs very fast, so that during each stride all four feet are off the ground at the same time.

gallows
NOUN a framework on which criminals used to be hanged

gamble gambles, gambling, gambled
VERB When someone **gambles**, they bet money on the result of a contest or race.

game games, gaming, gamed
NOUN **1** an activity with a set of rules that is played by individuals or teams against each other
NOUN **2** a term for wild birds and animals that are hunted for food or sport, such as pheasant or boar
VERB **3** If you **game**, you play video games.

gamer gamers
NOUN someone who plays video games

gaming
NOUN **Gaming** is playing video games.

gammon
NOUN cured meat from a pig, similar to bacon but usually in thicker and larger slices

gander ganders
NOUN a male goose

gang gangs, ganging, ganged
NOUN **1** a group of people who join together for some purpose, for example to commit a crime
VERB **2** (*informal*) If people **gang up** on you, they join together to oppose you. • *Sometimes male chimps gang up on another group member.*

gangster gangsters
NOUN a violent criminal who is a member of a gang

gangway gangways
NOUN **1** a space left between rows of seats, for example in a train or cinema, for people to walk through
NOUN **2** a movable passenger bridge between a ship and the shore

gaol

NOUN or VERB another spelling of **jail**

gap gaps

NOUN a space between two things or a hole in something solid • He was just able to squeeze through the **gap** in the hedge.

gape gapes, gaping, gaped

VERB **1** If you **gape**, you stare with your mouth wide open.

VERB **2** If something **gapes**, it is wide open.

garage garages

NOUN **1** a building in which you can keep a car

NOUN **2** a place where cars are repaired or where petrol is sold

garbage

NOUN In American English, **garbage** is rubbish, especially waste from a kitchen.

garden gardens

NOUN an area of land next to a house, with plants, trees and grass

gardener gardeners

NOUN a person who looks after a garden as a job or as a hobby

gargle gargles, gargling, gargled

VERB When you **gargle**, you rinse the back of your throat by putting some liquid in your mouth and making a bubbling sound without swallowing the liquid.

gargoyle gargoyles

NOUN a stone carving below the roof of an old building, in the shape of an ugly person or animal

garlic

NOUN the small, white bulb of an onion-like plant that has a strong taste and smell and is used in cooking

garment garments

NOUN an item of clothing

gas gases

NOUN a substance that is not a liquid or a solid. The particles in a **gas** are far apart and can move around quickly. Air is a mixture of **gases**. The bubbles in fizzy lemonade contain a **gas** called carbon dioxide.

→ Have a look at the illustration for **state of matter**

gasp gasps, gasping, gasped

VERB If you **gasp**, you quickly draw in your breath through your mouth because you are surprised or in pain.

gate gates

NOUN a barrier that can be opened or shut and is used to close off the entrance to a field, garden or path

gateau gateaux

NOUN a rich, layered cake with cream in it

WORD HISTORY
from French *gâteau* meaning cake

gather gathers, gathering, gathered

VERB **1** If you **gather** things, you collect or pick them. • I **gathered** some flowers from the garden.

VERB **2** When people **gather**, they come together in a group. • We **gathered** at my house before we went to the party.

VERB **3** If you **gather** information, you learn it, often from hearing or reading about it. • I **gather** you passed your exams.

gathering gatherings

NOUN a meeting of people who gather together for a particular purpose

gauge gauges, gauging, gauged

VERB **1** If you **gauge** something, you estimate or work out how much of it there is or how much is required.

NOUN **2** an instrument used for measuring • The fuel **gauge** shows that we need more petrol.

→ Have a look at the illustration for **car**

gauze

NOUN a thin, cotton cloth, often used for bandages

gave

VERB the past tense of **give**

gaze gazes, gazing, gazed

VERB If you **gaze** at something, you look steadily at it for a long time. • We **gazed** up at the stars.

gazelle gazelles

NOUN a small antelope found in Africa and Asia

a b c d e f g h i j k l m n o p q r s t u v w x y z

169

gear gears

NOUN **1** The **gears** in a car or on a bicycle are a set of cogs that work together to send power to the wheels.

→ Have a look at the illustration for **bicycle**

NOUN **2** the clothes or equipment that you need for an activity • climbing **gear**

geese

PLURAL NOUN the plural of **goose**

gel gels

NOUN a smooth, soft, jelly-like substance • hair **gel**

gem gems

NOUN a jewel or precious stone

gender genders

NOUN The **gender** of a person or animal is whether they are male or female.

gene genes

NOUN one of the parts of the chromosomes found inside the cells of an organism. Offspring inherit **genes** from their parents.

PRONUNCIATION TIP
This word is pronounced **jeen**.

general generals

ADJECTIVE **1** relating to the whole of something or to most things in a group • There has been a **general** improvement in your work.
ADJECTIVE **2** including or involving a range of different things • There was a **general** knowledge quiz at the end of term.
NOUN **3** an army officer of very high rank
PHRASE **4 In general** is used to indicate that a statement is true in most cases, or that it applies to most people or things.
• **In general**, people take their holidays over the summer.

general election general elections

NOUN an election in which people vote for who they want to represent them in the national parliament

generally

ADVERB You use **generally** to say what usually happens or what is usually true. • I **generally** get home from school about 4 o'clock.

generate generates, generating, generated

VERB If someone or something **generates** something else, they produce or create it.
• They built a new power station to **generate** more electricity.

generation generations

NOUN **1** all the people of a similar age
• the younger **generation**
NOUN **2** the length of time that it takes for children to grow up and have children of their own • The next **generation** will see a lo more changes.

generator generators

NOUN a machine that produces electricity from another form of energy, such as wind or water power

generous

ADJECTIVE A **generous** person gives or shares what they have, especially time or money.

genetic

ADJECTIVE involving or caused by a gene
• **genetic** diseases

genetically

ADVERB in a way that involves a gene or gene

genetically modified

ADJECTIVE **Genetically modified** plants and animals have had one or more genes changed, for example so that they resist pests and diseases better.

genie genies

NOUN a magical being that obeys the wishes of the person who controls it • Aladdin rubbed his magic lamp and the **genie** appeared

WORD HISTORY
from Arabic jinni meaning demon

genitals

PLURAL NOUN The **genitals** are the reproductive organs. The technical name is **genitalia**.

genius geniuses

NOUN a highly intelligent, creative or talente person • a mathematical **genius**

genre genres

NOUN a particular type of literature, painting music or film

gentle gentler, gentlest

ADJECTIVE Someone or something that is **gentle** is mild and calm. • A **gentle** breeze blew across the field.

ANTONYMS: violent, rough

gentleman gentlemen

NOUN **1** a man who is polite and well-educated
NOUN **2** a polite way of referring to any man

genuine

ADJECTIVE real and exactly what it appears to be ● *It's a **genuine** diamond.*

geographical

ADJECTIVE relating to the study of the physical features of the Earth, its countries, climate and people

geography

NOUN the study of the physical features of the Earth, its countries, climate and people

geologist geologists

NOUN someone who studies the Earth's structure, especially the layers of rock and soil that make up the surface of the Earth

geology

NOUN the study of the Earth's structure, especially the layers of rock and soil that make up the surface of the Earth

geometry

NOUN that part of mathematics that deals with lines, angles, curves and shapes

geranium geraniums

NOUN a plant with bright red, pink or white flowers

gerbil gerbils

NOUN a small rodent with long back legs that is often kept as a pet

germ germs

NOUN a very small organism that can cause disease

germinate germinates, germinating, germinated

VERB When a seed **germinates**, it starts to grow.

germination

NOUN the process of a seed starting to grow ● *Dry weather in May affected the **germination** of our carrots this year.*

→ Have a look at the illustration for **plant**

gestation

NOUN the period during which babies grow inside their mother's body before they are born

gesture gestures, gesturing, gestured

NOUN **1** a movement of your hands or head that suggests a message or feeling ● *She made an angry **gesture** with her fist.*

VERB **2** If you **gesture**, you move your hands or head in order to communicate a message or feeling. ● *She **gestured** to me to come over.*

get gets, getting, got

VERB **1** If you **get** something, you fetch it or receive it. ● *He **got** his report on the last day of term.*

VERB **2** If you **get** a bus, you travel on it.

VERB **3** If you **get** a meal ready, you prepare it.

VERB **4** If you **get** someone to do something for you, you persuade them to do it.

VERB **5** If you **get** a joke, you understand it.

VERB **6** If you **get** ill, you become ill.

VERB **7** If you **get** to a place, you arrive there.

geyser geysers

NOUN a natural spring out of which hot water and steam gush in spurts. There are many geysers in Iceland and New Zealand.

WORD HISTORY
from Old Norse *geysa* meaning to gush

ghastly ghastlier, ghastliest

ADJECTIVE extremely horrible and unpleasant

ghost ghosts

NOUN the spirit of a dead person that appears to someone who is still alive ● *She believes she saw a **ghost** in the old house.*

giant giants

NOUN **1** a huge person in a myth or legend

ADJECTIVE **2** much larger than other similar things ● *There was a **giant** Christmas tree in the town centre.*

a
b
c
d
e
f
g
h
i
j
k
l
m
n
o
p
q
r
s
t
u
v
w
x
y
z

giddiness

NOUN the feeling you have if you feel unsteady and unable to balance properly, usually because you are ill

giddy giddier, giddiest

ADJECTIVE If you feel **giddy**, you feel unsteady on your feet, usually because you are ill.

gift gifts

NOUN **1** something that you give someone as a present

NOUN **2** a natural skill or ability • *He has a **gift** for acting.*

gifted

ADJECTIVE If you are **gifted**, you have special talents. • *She is a **gifted** musician.*

gigabyte gigabytes

NOUN a unit of storage in a computer, equal to 1024 megabytes

gigantic

ADJECTIVE extremely large • *She was keen to ride on the **gigantic** big wheel.*

SYNONYMS: huge, massive, enormous

giggle giggles, giggling, giggled

VERB If you **giggle**, you laugh in a nervous, quiet way.

gill gills

NOUN the organs on the sides of a fish that it uses for breathing

→ Have a look at the illustration for **fish**

gimmick gimmicks

NOUN something that is not really necessary, but is unusual and used to attract interest • *The new shop needed a **gimmick** to attract customers.*

gin

NOUN a strong, colourless alcoholic drink made from grain and juniper berries

ginger

NOUN **1** a plant root with a hot, spicy flavour, used in cooking

ADJECTIVE **2** bright orangey-brown

Gipsy

NOUN another spelling of **Gypsy**

giraffe giraffes

NOUN a large African mammal with a very long neck, long legs and yellowish skin with dark patches

girder girders

NOUN a strong metal or concrete beam used in building

girl girls

NOUN a female child

girlfriend girlfriends

NOUN Someone's **girlfriend** is the woman or girl with whom they are having a romantic relationship.

give gives, giving, gave, given

VERB **1** If you **give** something to someone, you hand it to them or provide it for them. • *Please would you **give** me back the book I lent to you?*

VERB **2** If you **give** a party, you host it.

VERB **3 Give** can be used to express an action. • *give a speech* • *give the door a push*

PHRASE **4** If something **gives way**, it collapses.

glacier glaciers

NOUN a huge, frozen river of slow-moving ice

→ Have a look at the illustration

glad gladder, gladdest

ADJECTIVE happy or pleased

gladiator gladiators

NOUN In ancient Rome, **gladiators** were slaves trained to fight in arenas to provide entertainment.

glance glances, glancing, glanced

VERB **1** If you **glance** at something, you look at it quickly. • *He **glanced** at his watch.*

NOUN **2** a quick look

gland glands

NOUN an organ in your body which produces and releases special chemicals. Some **glands** help to get rid of waste products from your body. Sweat **glands** are small **glands** in your skin that produce sweat.

glare glares, glaring, glared

VERB **1** If you **glare** at someone, you look at them angrily.

NOUN **2** a hard, angry look

glass glasses

NOUN **1** the hard, transparent substance that windows and bottles are made of

NOUN **2** a container made of glass, from which you can drink • *a **glass** of water*

glasses

PLURAL NOUN two lenses in a frame, that some people wear over their eyes to improve their eyesight

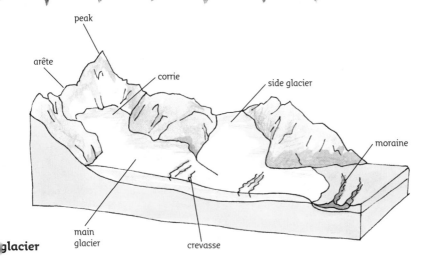

peak

arête

corrie

side glacier

moraine

main glacier

crevasse

glacier

glaze glazes, glazing, glazed
NOUN **1** a smooth, shiny surface on pottery or food
VERB **2** If you **glaze** pottery or food, you cover it with a glaze.
VERB **3** If someone **glazes** a window, they fit a sheet of glass into the window frame.

gleam gleams, gleaming, gleamed
VERB **1** If something **gleams**, it shines and reflects light. ● *He polished the silver teapot until it gleamed.*
NOUN **2** a pale, shining light ● *There was a gleam of light at the end of the dark tunnel.*

glide glides, gliding, glided
VERB **1** If you **glide**, you move smoothly.
● *The skater glided across the ice.*
VERB **2** When birds or aeroplanes **glide**, they float on air currents.

glider gliders
NOUN an aeroplane without an engine, that flies by floating on air currents

glimmer glimmers, glimmering, glimmered
NOUN **1** a faint, unsteady light ● *There was a glimmer of light ahead.*
VERB **2** If something **glimmers**, it produces a faint, unsteady light.

glimpse glimpses, glimpsing, glimpsed
NOUN **1** a brief sight of something
VERB **2** If you **glimpse** something, you see it briefly. ● *They glimpsed a rare bird through the trees.*

glisten glistens, glistening, glistened
VERB If something **glistens**, it shines or sparkles. ● *The frost glistened in the moonlight.*

glitter glitters, glittering, glittered
VERB **1** If something **glitters**, it shines in a sparkling way. ● *The diamond glittered in the sunlight.*
NOUN **2** sparkling light

gloat gloats, gloating, gloated
VERB If you **gloat**, you cruelly show how pleased you are about your own success or someone else's failure.

global
ADJECTIVE to do with the whole world
● *Pollution of the atmosphere is a global concern.*

global warming
NOUN an increase in the world's overall temperature, believed to be caused by a thinning of the ozone layer

globe globes
NOUN **1** the Earth, the planet you live on
NOUN **2** a sphere fixed to a stand, with a map of the world on it

gloom
NOUN **1** darkness or dimness ● *I could not see in the gloom of the forest.*
NOUN **2** a feeling of unhappiness or despair

gloomily
ADVERB **1** in a way that shows you are unhappy
ADVERB **2** in a way that is depressing

a
b
c
d
e
f
g
h
i
j
k
l
m
n
o
p
q
r
s
t
u
v
w
x
y
z

173

A
B
C
D
E
F
G
H
I
J
K
L
M
N
O
P
Q
R
S
T
U
V
W
X
Y
Z

gloomy gloomier, gloomiest
ADJECTIVE **1** Something that is **gloomy** is dull and dark, and sometimes depressing.
• *It was a gloomy winter day.*
ADJECTIVE **2** If you are **gloomy**, you are unhappy.

glorious
ADJECTIVE beautiful and splendid • *We were lucky to have glorious weather while we were on holiday.*

glory glories
NOUN something considered splendid or admirable • *They enjoyed the glory of their son's success.*

gloss
NOUN a bright shine on a smooth surface

glossary glossaries
NOUN a list of explanations of specialist words, usually found at the back of a book

glossy glossier, glossiest
ADJECTIVE smooth and shiny • *This new shampoo makes my hair glossy.*

glove gloves
NOUN **Gloves** cover your hands and keep them warm or give them protection.

glow glows, glowing, glowed
VERB **1** If something **glows**, it shines with a dull, steady light.
NOUN **2** a dull, steady light
NOUN **3** a strong feeling of pleasure or happiness

glucose
NOUN a natural sugar found in plants and produced in the bodies of animals, including humans, to give them energy

glue glues, gluing or glueing, glued
NOUN **1** a substance used for sticking things together
VERB **2** If you **glue** one object to another, you stick them together using glue.

glutton gluttons
NOUN a person who eats too much

GMT
NOUN an abbreviation for *Greenwich Mean Time*

gnarled
ADJECTIVE If something is **gnarled** it is old, twisted and rough. • *There is a big, gnarled tree in the churchyard.*

gnash gnashes, gnashing, gnashed
VERB If you **gnash** your teeth, you make a noise with them by grinding them together because you are angry or upset.

gnat gnats
NOUN a tiny flying insect that bites

gnaw gnaws, gnawing, gnawed
VERB If someone or something **gnaws** at something, they chew and bite at it repeatedly. • *The hamster gnawed at the bars of its cage.*

gnome gnomes
NOUN a tiny old man in fairy stories, who usually lives underground

go goes, going, went, gone
VERB **1** If you **go** somewhere, you walk, move or travel there.
VERB **2** If something **goes** well, it is a success.
VERB **3** If you **go**, you start to move. • *When you hear the whistle, go as fast as you can.*
VERB **4** If something **goes** somewhere, it leads there. • *This road goes to the centre of town.*
VERB **5** If something **goes**, it works properly.
• *My watch doesn't go any more.*
VERB **6** become • *This fruit has gone bad.*
NOUN **7** an attempt or a turn at doing something
VERB **8** disappear • *The mist has gone.*
VERB **9** If you are **going** to do something, you will do it.

go down
VERB **1** If you **go down** with an illness, you catch it.
VERB **2** If something **goes down** well, people like it. If it **goes down** badly, they do not like it.

go off
VERB **1** If you **go off** someone or something, you stop liking them.
VERB **2** If a bomb **goes off**, it explodes.

go on
VERB **1** If you **go on** doing something, you continue to do it.
VERB **2** If you **go on** about something, you keep talking about it in a rather boring way.
VERB **3** If something is **going on**, it is happening.

go through
VERB If you **go through** an unpleasant event, you experience it.

goal goals
NOUN **1** In games like football and hockey, the **goal** is the space into which the players try to get the ball to score a point.
NOUN **2** In games like football and hockey, if a player scores a **goal**, they get the ball into the **goal**.
NOUN **3** something that you hope to achieve • *Our **goal** is to raise as much money as possible for charity.*

goat goats
NOUN an animal similar to a sheep, with shaggy hair, a beard and horns

gobble gobbles, gobbling, gobbled
VERB **1** If you **gobble** food, you eat it very quickly.
VERB **2** When a turkey **gobbles**, it makes a loud gurgling sound.

goblet goblets
NOUN a kind of drinking cup or glass

goblin goblins
NOUN a small, ugly and mischievous creature found in fairy stories

god gods
PROPER NOUN **1 God** is the being worshipped by Christians and Jews as the creator and ruler of the world.
NOUN **2** any of the beings that are believed in many religions to have power over an aspect of the world • *Mars was the Roman **god** of war.*

goddess goddesses
NOUN a female god

godparent godparents
NOUN someone who agrees, at a child's christening, to be responsible for their religious upbringing

goggles
PLURAL NOUN special glasses that fit closely round your eyes to protect them • *I usually wear **goggles** when I go swimming.*

go-kart go-karts
NOUN a small motorised vehicle that can be raced

gold
NOUN **1** a valuable, yellow-coloured metal, used for making jewellery and as an international currency
ADJECTIVE **2** made of gold • *a solid **gold** necklace*

golden
ADJECTIVE gold in colour or made of gold • *a beach of **golden** sand*

goldfish
NOUN a small, orange fish, often kept as a pet in a bowl or pond

---

LANGUAGE TIP
The plural of *goldfish* can be either *goldfish* or *goldfishes*, but *goldfish* is more common.

golf
NOUN a game in which players use special clubs to hit a ball into holes that are spread out over a large area of grassy land

gondola gondolas
NOUN a long, narrow boat used on the canals in Venice. **Gondolas** are propelled by using a long pole.

gone
VERB the past participle of **go**

gong gongs
NOUN a flat, circular piece of metal that is hit with a hammer to make a loud sound, often as a signal for something • *They sounded the **gong** for dinner.*

good better, best
ADJECTIVE **1** pleasant or enjoyable • *The weather turned out to be **good**.*
ADJECTIVE **2** of a high quality • *The food was very **good**.*
ADJECTIVE **3** sensible or valid • *The rain gives me a **good** reason for staying at home.*
ADJECTIVE **4** well-behaved • *Have the children been **good**?*
PHRASE **5 For good** means forever. • *He decided to leave **for good**.*

goodbye
GREETING You say **goodbye** when you are leaving someone or ending a phone conversation.

goodness
NOUN the quality of being good and kind

good night
GREETING You say **good night** to someone when you are leaving them at night.

goods
PLURAL NOUN things that are bought and sold in a shop or warehouse • *The shop sold household **goods**.*

google googles, googling, googled
VERB If you **google** a person or thing, you search the internet for information about them.

a
b
c
d
e
f
g
h
i
j
k
l
m
n
o
p
q
r
s
t
u
v
w
x
y
z

goose geese
NOUN a fairly large bird, with webbed feet and a long neck

gooseberry gooseberries
NOUN a round, green berry that grows on a bush and has a sharp taste

gore gores, goring, gored
NOUN **1** the blood from a wound
VERB **2** If an animal **gores** someone, it wounds them by sticking a horn or tusk into them.

gorge gorges, gorging, gorged
NOUN **1** a deep, narrow valley
VERB **2** If you **gorge** yourself, you eat a lot of food greedily.

gorgeous
ADJECTIVE extremely pleasant or attractive
• a **gorgeous** dress

gorilla gorillas
NOUN a very strong, large ape, that lives in family groups

gory gorier, goriest
ADJECTIVE involving a lot of blood and violence
• a **gory** film

gosling goslings
NOUN a young goose

gospel gospels
NOUN one of the four books in the New Testament that describe the life and teachings of Jesus Christ

gossip gossips, gossiping, gossiped
NOUN **1** informal conversation, often about people's private affairs
VERB **2** If you **gossip**, you talk informally with someone, especially about other people.

got
VERB the past tense of **get**

gouge gouges, gouging, gouged
VERB If you **gouge** something out, you scoop it out forcefully with a pointed object. • She **gouged** a hole in the apple with a knife.

govern governs, governing, governed
VERB When someone **governs** something, they rule or control it, especially a country or state.

government governments
NOUN The **government** is the group of people who officially control a country.

LANGUAGE TIP
There is an *n* before the *m* in *government*.

governor governors
NOUN **1** someone who controls or helps to run a state or organisation
NOUN **2** In Australia, New Zealand and other commonwealth countries the **Governor** represents the British King or Queen.

GP GPs
NOUN an abbreviation of *general practitioner*. A **GP** is a doctor who treats all kinds of illnesses, and sends people to a specialist if necessary.

grab grabs, grabbing, grabbed
VERB If you **grab** something, you take it or pick it up quickly and roughly.
• He **grabbed** a sandwich before running for the bus.

grace graces
NOUN **1** an elegant and attractive way of moving
NOUN **2** a short prayer before or after a meal
NOUN **3** a pleasant and kind way of behaving

graceful
ADJECTIVE If you are **graceful**, you move in a smooth and elegant way.

gracious
ADJECTIVE kind, polite and pleasant
• He always acts in a **gracious** and thoughtful manner.

grade grades, grading, graded
VERB **1** If someone **grades** things, they judge them according to their quality.
NOUN **2** the mark that you get in an exam

gradient gradients
NOUN a slope or the steepness of a slope
• The **gradient** of this hill means it will be difficult to climb.

gradual
ADJECTIVE happening or changing slowly over a long period of time • Her spelling showed **gradual** improvement.

gradually
ADVERB slowly over a long period of time
• Prices have **gradually** increased.

graduate graduates
NOUN someone who has a degree from a university or college

graffiti
NOUN slogans or drawings scribbled on walls

grain grains

NOUN **1** a cereal plant, such as wheat, that is grown and harvested for food

NOUN **2** a seed from a cereal plant such as wheat or rice

NOUN **3** a tiny, hard particle of something • I have got **grains** of sand in my shoes from walking on the beach.

NOUN **4** the natural pattern of lines in a piece of wood, made by the fibres in it

gram grams

NOUN a unit of mass and weight (g). There are one thousand **grams** in a kilogram (kg).

grammar

NOUN the rules of a language that state how words can be combined to form sentences

grand grander, grandest

ADJECTIVE splendid or impressive

grandad grandads

NOUN (informal) grandfather

grandchild grandchildren

NOUN Someone's **grandchildren** are the children of their son or daughter.

granddaughter granddaughters

NOUN Someone's **granddaughter** is the daughter of their son or daughter.

grandfather grandfathers

NOUN Your **grandfather** is your father's father or your mother's father.

grandmother grandmothers

NOUN Your **grandmother** is your father's mother or your mother's mother.

grandparent grandparents

NOUN Your **grandparents** are the parents of your father or mother.

grandson grandsons

NOUN Someone's **grandson** is the son of their son or daughter.

granite

NOUN a very strong, hard rock often used in building

granny grannies

NOUN (informal) grandmother

grant grants, granting, granted

NOUN **1** an amount of money that an official body gives to someone for a particular purpose • He was given a **grant** to go to university.

VERB **2** If you **grant** something to someone, you allow them to have it. • I will **grant** you a wish.

grape grapes

NOUN a small, green or purple fruit that grows in bunches on vines. **Grapes** are eaten raw or used to make wine.

grapefruit grapefruits

NOUN a large, round, yellow citrus fruit

graph graphs

NOUN a diagram that gives information about how two sets of numbers and measurements are related

graphic graphics

ADJECTIVE **1** A **graphic** description is very detailed and clear.

PLURAL NOUN **2 Graphics** are drawings, designs and diagrams. • computer **graphics**

graphics

NOUN the activity of drawing or making pictures, especially in publishing or computing

grasp grasps, grasping, grasped

VERB **1** If you **grasp** something, you hold it firmly. • He **grasped** both my hands.

VERB **2** If you **grasp** an idea, you understand it. • She finally **grasped** the answer.

grass grasses

NOUN the common green plant that grows on lawns and in parks

grasshopper grasshoppers

NOUN an insect with long back legs that it uses for jumping and making a high-pitched sound

grate grates, grating, grated

VERB **1** If you **grate** food, you shred it into small pieces by rubbing it against a tool called a grater.

NOUN **2** a framework of metal bars in a fireplace for holding coal or wood • A wood fire burned in the **grate**.

grateful

ADJECTIVE If you are **grateful** for something, you feel thankful for it. • I'm **grateful** to you for your help.

SYNONYM: appreciative

gratitude

NOUN If you show **gratitude** to someone for something, you are thankful.

SYNONYMS: thankfulness, appreciation

177

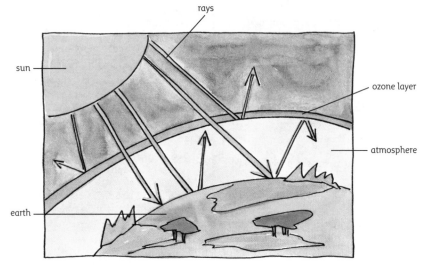

rays

sun

ozone layer

atmosphere

earth

greenhouse effect

grave graves; graver, gravest
NOUN **1** a place where a dead person is buried
ADJECTIVE **2** (*formal*) very serious • *We are in* **grave** *danger.*

gravel
NOUN small stones used for making roads and paths

graveyard graveyards
NOUN a place where people are buried, usually in a churchyard

gravity
NOUN the force that pulls things down towards the Earth

gravy
NOUN a brown sauce made from meat juices

graze grazes, grazing, grazed
VERB **1** When animals **graze**, they eat grass that is growing. • *The cows* **grazed** *in the field.*
VERB **2** If something **grazes** a part of your body, it scrapes against it, injuring you slightly.
NOUN **3** a slight injury caused by something scraping against your skin

grease greases, greasing, greased
NOUN **1** a substance used for oiling machines
NOUN **2** animal fat used in cooking
VERB **3** If you **grease** something, you put grease on it. • *Lightly* **grease** *a baking tray.*

great greater, greatest
ADJECTIVE **1** very large in size, amount or degree • *She had* **great** *difficulty in staying awake.*
ADJECTIVE **2** very important • *a* **great** *artist*
ADJECTIVE **3** very good • *That's a* **great** *idea.*

greedily
ADVERB in a greedy way

greedy greedier, greediest
ADJECTIVE Someone who is **greedy** wants more of something than is necessary or fair.

green greener, greenest; greens
NOUN **1** a colour between yellow and blue on the spectrum. Grass and leaves are usually **green**.
NOUN **2** a smooth, flat area of grass • *We played cricket on the village* **green**.
ADJECTIVE **3** having a colour between yellow and blue

green belt green belts
NOUN an area of land with fields or parks around a town or city, where people are not allowed to build houses or factories by law

greengrocer greengrocers
NOUN a shopkeeper who sells fruit and vegetables

greenhouse greenhouses
NOUN a glass building in which people grow plants that need to be kept warm

greenhouse effect

NOUN the gradual increase in the temperature of the Earth's atmosphere because the heat absorbed from the sun is not able to escape

→ Have a look at the illustration

Greenwich Mean Time

NOUN **Greenwich Mean Time** is the standard time in Great Britain which is used to work out the time in the rest of the world.

greet greets, greeting, greeted

VERB If you **greet** someone, you say something friendly and welcoming to them when you meet them.

greeting greetings

NOUN the words or actions that you use when you meet someone

grenade grenades

NOUN a small bomb that can be thrown by hand

WORD HISTORY

from Spanish *granada* meaning pomegranate, which is a similar shape to a grenade

---

grew

VERB the past tense of **grow**

grey greyer, greyest

NOUN **1** the colour of ashes or of clouds on a rainy day

ADJECTIVE **2** having the colour of ashes or of clouds on a rainy day

grid grids

NOUN a pattern of lines crossing each other to form squares

→ Have a look at the illustration for **map**

grief

NOUN extreme sadness

grieve grieves, grieving, grieved

VERB If you **grieve** you are very sad, especially because someone has died.

grill grills, grilling, grilled

NOUN **1** the part of a cooker where food is cooked by heat from above ● *Place the fish under a hot grill.*

VERB **2** If you **grill** food, you cook it under or over direct heat. ● *We grilled the chicken on the barbecue.*

grim grimmer, grimmest

ADJECTIVE If a situation or piece of news is **grim**, it is very unpleasant and worrying.

grimace grimaces

NOUN a twisted facial expression that shows disgust or pain

grime

NOUN thick dirt that gathers on the surface of something

grimy

ADJECTIVE covered in dirt ● *grimy windows*

grin grins, grinning, grinned

VERB **1** If you **grin**, you have a broad smile.

NOUN **2** a broad smile

grind grinds, grinding, ground

VERB **1** If you **grind** something, you crush it into a fine powder. ● *He ground the mud into the carpet.*

VERB **2** If you **grind** your teeth, you rub your upper and lower teeth together.

PHRASE **3** If something **grinds to a halt**, it slows down and stops.

grip grips, gripping, gripped

VERB **1** If you **grip** something, you hold it firmly. ● *He gripped his mother's hand tightly.*

NOUN **2** a handle on a bat or racket ● *The grip on his tennis racket needed repairing.*

gristle

NOUN the tough, rubbery part of meat that is difficult to eat

groan groans, groaning, groaned

VERB **1** If you **groan**, you make a long, low sound of pain, unhappiness or disapproval.

NOUN **2** the sound you make when you groan

grocer grocers

NOUN a person who runs a shop that sells all kinds of food and household supplies

groceries

PLURAL NOUN the goods that you buy in a grocer's shop

groove grooves

NOUN a deep line cut into a surface

grope gropes, groping, groped

VERB If you **grope** for something, you feel for it with your hands because you cannot see it.

gross grosser, grossest
ADJECTIVE **1** extremely bad • *I made a **gross** error on my exam paper.*
ADJECTIVE **2 Gross** language or behaviour is very rude.
ADJECTIVE **3** The **gross** amount of something is its total, without anything taken away. For example, the **gross** weight of something is its total weight, including the weight of its container.
ADJECTIVE **4** unpleasantly fat or ugly

grotesque
ADJECTIVE **1** exaggerated and absurd
ADJECTIVE **2** very strange and ugly

grotto grottoes or **grottos**
NOUN a small cave that people visit because it is attractive

ground grounds
NOUN **1** the surface of the land • *They sat on the **ground**.*
NOUN **2** an area of land, especially land that is used for a particular purpose • *a football **ground***
PLURAL NOUN **3** The **grounds** of a large building are the garden or area of land that surrounds it. • *We camped in the **grounds** of the stately home.*
PLURAL NOUN **4** (*formal*) The **grounds** for something are the reason for it. • *I had **grounds** to believe that he was telling the truth.*
VERB **5** the past tense and past participle of grind

group groups, grouping, grouped
NOUN **1** a number of things or people that are linked in some way • *a small **group** of friends*
VERB **2** When things or people **group** together, they are linked in some way. • *We **grouped** together for the school photograph.*

group chat group chats
NOUN a chat on a social media website involving a number of people

grovel grovels, grovelling, grovelled
VERB If you **grovel**, you behave in an unpleasantly humble way towards someone you think is important.

WORD HISTORY
from Middle English *on grufe* meaning lying on your belly

grow grows, growing, grew, grown
VERB **1** When someone or something **grows**, it gets bigger or increases. • *Children **grow** at different rates.*
VERB **2** When people **grow** plants, they plant them and look after them.
VERB **3** You use **grow** to say that someone or something gradually changes into a different state. • *He's **growing** old.*
grow up
VERB When a child **grows up**, they become an adult.

growl growls, growling, growled
VERB **1** When an animal **growls**, it makes a low rumbling sound, usually because it is angry.
NOUN **2** the sound an animal makes when it growls

grown-up grown-ups
NOUN an adult

growth
NOUN The process by which something develops to its full size.

grub grubs
NOUN **1** a worm-like creature that is the young of some insects, after it has hatched but before it becomes an adult
NOUN **2** (*informal*) food

grubby grubbier, grubbiest
ADJECTIVE rather dirty • *That shirt looks a bit **grubby**.*

grudge grudges
NOUN If you have a **grudge** against someone, you resent them because they have harmed or upset you in the past.

gruelling
ADJECTIVE difficult and exhausting • *It was a long and **gruelling** race.*

gruesome
ADJECTIVE shocking and horrible • *The film was unsuitable for the children because it was so **gruesome**.*

gruff gruffer, gruffest
ADJECTIVE If someone's voice is **gruff**, it sounds rough and unfriendly.

grumble grumbles, grumbling, grumbled
VERB **1** If you **grumble**, you complain in a bad-tempered way.
NOUN **2** a bad-tempered complaint

grumpily
ADVERB in a bad-tempered way

grumpy grumpier, grumpiest
ADJECTIVE bad-tempered and fed-up ● *She is often **grumpy** in the morning.*

grunt grunts, grunting, grunted
VERB **1** If a person or a pig **grunts**, they make a short, low, gruff sound.
NOUN **2** the sound a person or a pig makes when they grunt

guarantee guarantees, guaranteeing, guaranteed
NOUN **1** a promise by a company to do something, especially to replace or repair a product free of charge within a given time period if it develops a fault ● *This television has a five-year **guarantee**.*
VERB **2** If something or someone **guarantees** something, they promise that it will happen. ● *I **guarantee** that after all your hard work the day will be a success.*

guard guards, guarding, guarded
VERB **1** If you **guard** a person or object, you watch them carefully, either to protect them or to stop them from escaping.
NOUN **2** a person whose job is to guard a person, object or place

guardian guardians
NOUN someone who has been legally appointed to look after a child, but is not the child's parent

guerrilla guerrillas; also spelt
guerilla
NOUN a member of a small, unofficial army fighting an official army

guess guesses, guessing, guessed
VERB **1** If you **guess** something, you form an opinion about it without knowing all the relevant facts. ● *She **guessed** that he was probably older than her.*
NOUN **2** an attempt to give an answer or opinion about something without knowing all the relevant facts ● *If you don't know the answer, have a **guess**.*

guest guests
NOUN someone who has been invited to stay at your home or attend an event

guide guides, guiding, guided
NOUN **1** someone who shows you round places, or leads the way through difficult country
VERB **2** If you **guide** someone somewhere, you lead them there.

guidebook guidebooks
NOUN a book that gives information about a place

guillotine guillotines
NOUN a piece of equipment with a long, sharp blade, used for cutting paper

WORD HISTORY
named after Joseph-Ignace *Guillotin*, who first recommended the guillotine as a way of executing people

guilt
NOUN **1** the unhappy feeling of having done something wrong
NOUN **2** Someone's **guilt** is the fact that they have done something wrong. ● *After hearing the evidence, the jury felt that his **guilt** was clear.*

guiltily
ADVERB in a way that shows you know you have done something wrong

guilty guiltier, guiltiest
ADJECTIVE **1** If you are **guilty** of doing something wrong, you did it.

ANTONYM: innocent

ADJECTIVE **2** feeling unhappy and ashamed because you think you have done something wrong or not done something that you should have done ● *I felt **guilty** about lying to my mum.*

guinea pig guinea pigs
NOUN **1** a small, furry mammal without a tail, often kept as a pet
NOUN **2** a person used to try something out ● *You will be a **guinea pig** in this experiment.*

guitar guitars
NOUN a musical instrument with six strings and a long neck

gulf gulfs
NOUN a very large bay

gull gulls
NOUN a sea bird with long wings, white and grey or black feathers, and webbed feet

gullible
ADJECTIVE If someone is **gullible**, they are easily tricked.

gulp gulps, gulping, gulped
VERB **1** If you **gulp** food or drink, you swallow large quantities of it quickly and noisily.
NOUN **2** a large quantity of food or drink swallowed quickly and noisily

181

gum **gums**

NOUN **1** Your **gums** are the firm flesh in which your teeth are set.
NOUN **2** a soft, flavoured substance that people chew but do not swallow
NOUN **3** glue

gumboot **gumboots**

NOUN a wellington boot

gumtree **gumtrees**

NOUN a eucalyptus or other tree that produces gum

gun **guns**

NOUN a weapon that fires bullets or shells

gunpowder

NOUN a powder that explodes when it is lit. It is used for making things such as fireworks.

gurdwara **gurdwaras**

NOUN a Sikh place of worship

gust **gusts**

NOUN a sudden rush of wind • A **gust** of wind blew his hat off.

gutter **gutters**

NOUN the edge of a road next to the pavement, where rain collects and flows away

gym **gyms**

NOUN a hall or room for sports and exercise. It is short for *gymnasium*.

gymkhana **gymkhanas**

NOUN a competition in which people take part in horse-riding contests

gymnasium **gymnasiums**

NOUN a room with special equipment for physical exercises

gymnastics

NOUN physical exercises, especially ones using equipment such as bars and ropes

Gypsy **Gypsies**; also spelt **Gipsy**

NOUN a member of an ethnic group scattered across most countries of Europe, the Middle East and the Americas. They migrated from north-west India in the 9th century and still have a nomadic lifestyle, although some are settled on sites and in houses. The **Gypsy** language is Romani.

WORD HISTORY
from *Egyptian* because in the 16th century they were thought to have come from Egypt

habit **habits**

NOUN something that you do often or regularly

habitat **habitats**

NOUN the natural home of a plant or animal

hack **hacks, hacking, hacked**

VERB **1** If you **hack** at something, you cut it using rough strokes.
VERB **2** If someone **hacks** into a computer system, they break into the system, usually to get the information stored there. • *He is charged with **hacking** into the firm's computer system.*

had

VERB the past participle of **have**

haddock

NOUN an edible sea fish

LANGUAGE TIP
The plural of *haddock* can be either *haddock* or *haddocks*, but *haddock* is more common.

hadn't

VERB a contraction of *had not*

haggard

ADJECTIVE A person who is **haggard** looks very tired and ill.

haggis **haggises**

NOUN a Scottish dish made of the minced internal organs of a sheep, boiled together with oatmeal and spices in a skin

haggle **haggles, haggling, haggled**

VERB If you **haggle** with someone, you argue with them about the price of something.

haiku **haiku**

NOUN a short, Japanese verse form in 17 syllables

hail **hails, hailing, hailed**

NOUN **1** frozen rain
VERB **2** When it is **hailing**, frozen rain is falling.

hailstone hailstones
NOUN a drop of frozen rain

hair hairs
NOUN one of the large number of fine threads that grow on your head and body. **Hair** grows on the bodies of some other animals.

haircut haircuts
NOUN the cutting of someone's hair and the style into which it is cut

hairdresser hairdressers
NOUN a person who is trained to cut and style hair

hairstyle hairstyles
NOUN the way in which your hair is arranged or cut

hairy hairier, hairiest
ADJECTIVE covered in a lot of hair

hajj
NOUN the pilgrimage to Mecca that every Muslim must make at least once in their life, if they are healthy and wealthy enough to do so

WORD HISTORY
from Arabic *hajj* meaning pilgrimage

halal; also spelt **hallal**
NOUN meat from animals that have been killed according to Muslim law

half halves
NOUN **1** one of two equal parts that make up a whole. It can be written as ½. ● *the second **half** of the match*
ADJECTIVE **2** with one of two equal parts that make up a whole ● *My cup is only **half** full.*
ADVERB **3** You can use **half** to say that something is only partly true. ● *I **half** expected to see the teacher walk in.*
PHRASE **4 Half past** refers to a time that is thirty minutes after a particular hour. ● *half past twelve*

halfway
ADVERB If something is **halfway** between two points or two times, it is at the middle point between them.

hall halls
NOUN **1** the room just inside the front entrance of a house that leads into the other rooms
NOUN **2** a large room or building for public events ● *a school **hall***

hallo
GREETING another spelling of **hello**

Halloween
NOUN **Halloween** is October 31st. In the past people thought that ghosts and witches would be about on this night, and it is now celebrated by children dressing up, often as ghosts and witches.

hallucinate hallucinates, hallucinating, hallucinated
VERB If someone **hallucinates**, they imagine that they see strange things, for example because they are ill.

halo haloes or **halos**
NOUN a circle of light around something, especially the head of a holy person in a picture

halt halts, halting, halted
VERB **1** When someone or something **halts**, they stop. ● *They **halted** a short distance from the house.*
PHRASE **2** When something **comes to a halt**, it stops.

halter halters
NOUN a strap fastened round a horse's head so that it can be led easily

halve halves, halving, halved
VERB If you **halve** something, you divide it into two equal parts.

ham
NOUN meat from the hind leg of a pig

hamburger hamburgers
NOUN a flat disc of minced meat, fried and eaten in a bread roll

WORD HISTORY
named after *Hamburg* in Germany, the city where they were first made

hammer hammers, hammering, hammered
NOUN **1** a tool consisting of a heavy piece of metal at the end of a handle, used for hitting nails into things
VERB **2** If you **hammer** something, you hit it repeatedly with a hammer.

hammock hammocks
NOUN a piece of net or canvas hung between two supports and used as a bed

a
b
c
d
e
f
g
h
i
j
k
l
m
n
o
p
q
r
s
t
u
v
w
x
y
z

183

hamper hampers, hampering, hampered

NOUN **1** a large basket with a lid, used for carrying food

VERB **2** If something **hampers** you, it makes it difficult for you to do what you are trying to do. ● *The bad weather **hampered** their expedition.*

hamster hamsters

NOUN a small, furry rodent, often kept as a pet

hand hands, handing, handed

NOUN **1** the part of your body at the end of your arm, below the wrist

NOUN **2** The **hands** of a clock or watch are the pointers that indicate what time it is.

NOUN **3** In a game of cards, a **hand** is the set of cards dealt to each player.

VERB **4** If you **hand** something to someone, you pass it to them.

PHRASE **5** If you **give a hand**, you help someone to do something.

PHRASE **6** If you do something **by hand**, you do it using your hands rather than a machine.

PHRASE **7** If something gets **out of hand**, it becomes beyond your control.

handbag handbags

NOUN a small bag, usually carried by a woman

handcuffs

PLURAL NOUN two strong metal rings joined by chains that are locked round a prisoner's wrists

handful handfuls

NOUN **1** A **handful** of something is the amount of it you can hold in your hand.

NOUN **2** a small number or quantity of something ● *Only a **handful** of people were invited to the party.*

handicap handicaps

NOUN a disadvantage, or anything that makes it more difficult to do something

handicraft handicrafts

NOUN an activity that involves making things with your hands, such as pottery or knitting

handkerchief handkerchiefs

NOUN a small square of fabric used for blowing your nose

handle handles, handling, handled

NOUN **1** the part of a tool, bag, cup or other object that you hold in order to pick it up or use it ● *door **handle***

VERB **2** If you **handle** an object, you hold it or touch it with your hands.

VERB **3** If you **handle** something, you deal with it successfully. ● *She **handled** the stress of the examination very well.*

handlebars

PLURAL NOUN the bars with handles that are used to steer a bicycle

→ Have a look at the illustration for **bicycle**

handset handsets

NOUN The **handset** of a telephone connected to a landline is the part that you speak into and listen with.

handsome

ADJECTIVE very attractive in appearance

handstand handstands

NOUN the act of balancing upside down on your hands, with your feet in the air

handwriting

NOUN Someone's **handwriting** is their style of writing with a pen or pencil.

handy handier, handiest

ADJECTIVE If something is **handy**, it is useful or conveniently near.

hang hangs, hanging, hung or hanged

VERB **1** If you **hang** something on a hook, nail or line, or if it **hangs** there, it is attached so that it does not touch the ground. ● *His jacket **hung** from a hook on the door.*

VERB **2** To **hang** someone means to kill them by suspending them by a rope around the neck.

LANGUAGE TIP

When *hang* means to kill someone by suspending them by a rope, the past tense and past participle are *hanged*.

hang about or **hang around**

VERB (*informal*) If you **hang about** or **hang around** somewhere, you stay or wait there. ● *Although he had left, he still **hung around** outside his old school.*

hang on

VERB **1** If you **hang on** to something, you hold it tightly or keep it.

VERB **2** (*informal*) If you **hang on**, you wait.

hang up
VERB If you **hang up** when you are speaking on the phone, you press a key or put down the receiver and end the call.

hangar **hangars**
NOUN a large building where aircraft are kept

hanger **hangers**
NOUN a piece of shaped wood, plastic or wire for hanging up clothes

hang-glider **hang-gliders**
NOUN a glider that is made for one or two people who hang below the frame in a harness

Hanukkah or **Chanukah**
NOUN an eight-day Jewish festival of lights

haphazard
ADJECTIVE not organised or planned • *He piled the books up in a **haphazard** way.*

happen **happens, happening, happened**
VERB **1** When something **happens**, it occurs or takes place.
VERB **2** If you **happen** to do something, you do it by chance. • *I **happened** to notice he'd dropped his glove.*

happily
ADVERB **1** in a happy way • *The children were playing **happily**.*

ANTONYM: miserably

ADVERB **2** You say **happily** to show that you are willing to do something. • *I would **happily** share a room with my brother.*

ANTONYM: reluctantly

happiness
NOUN a feeling of great contentment or pleasure

happy **happier, happiest**
ADJECTIVE **1** full of contentment or joy

ANTONYMS: miserable, sad

ADJECTIVE **2** If you are **happy** with something, you are satisfied with it.

ANTONYM: dissatisfied

ADJECTIVE **3** If you are **happy** to do something, you are willing to do it.

ANTONYM: reluctant

harass **harasses, harassing, harassed**
VERB If someone **harasses** you, they annoy or trouble you continually.

harbour **harbours**
NOUN a protected area of deep water where boats can be moored

hard **harder, hardest**
ADVERB **1** with a lot of effort • *If I work **hard**, I'll pass my tests.*
ADVERB **2** with a lot of force • *I kicked the ball very **hard**.*
ADJECTIVE **3** requiring a lot of effort • *The sponsored walk was **hard** work.*
ADJECTIVE **4** difficult • ***hard** sums*
ADJECTIVE **5** not easy to bend or break

hard disk **hard disks**
NOUN a part of a computer that holds a large amount of information

harden **hardens, hardening, hardened**
VERB If something **hardens** it becomes hard or gets harder. • *The glue took a long time to **harden**.*

hardly
ADVERB only just • *I could **hardly** believe it.*

hardship
NOUN a time or situation of suffering and difficulty

hardware
NOUN **1** tools and equipment for use in the home and garden
NOUN **2** computer machinery rather than computer programs

hardy **hardier, hardiest**
ADJECTIVE tough and able to bear cold and difficult conditions

hare **hares**
NOUN an animal like a large rabbit, but with longer ears and legs

harm **harms, harming, harmed**
VERB **1** If someone **harms** someone or something, they injure or damage them.

SYNONYM: hurt

NOUN **2** injury or damage

SYNONYM: hurt

harmful
ADJECTIVE having a bad effect on something • *Too much sun can be **harmful** to your skin.*

harmless
ADJECTIVE safe to use or be near

a
b
c
d
e
f
g
h
i
j
k
l
m
n
o
p
q
r
s
t
u
v
w
x
y
z

harmonica harmonicas
NOUN a small musical instrument played by moving it across the lips and blowing and sucking air through it. Also called a mouth organ.

harmony harmonies
NOUN **1** a state of peaceful agreement and cooperation • *The neighbours lived in* **harmony**.
NOUN **2** In music, **harmony** is the pleasant combination of two or more notes played at the same time.

harness harnesses, harnessing, harnessed
NOUN **1** a set of straps fastened round an animal to control it or attach it to something, such as a horse to a cart
VERB **2** If you **harness** an animal, you put a harness on it.
VERB **3** If someone **harnesses** something, they control it so that they can use it.
• *The windmills* **harnessed** *the power of the wind.*

harp harps
NOUN a musical instrument consisting of a triangular frame with vertical strings that you pluck with your fingers

harpist harpists
NOUN someone who plays a harp

harpoon harpoons
NOUN a barbed spear attached to a rope, thrown or fired from a gun and used for catching whales or large fish

harsh harsher, harshest
ADJECTIVE **1 Harsh** living conditions or climates are rough and unpleasant.

SYNONYMS: hard, severe, tough

ADJECTIVE **2 Harsh** actions or remarks are unkind and show no sympathy.

harshly
ADVERB in a way that is unkind and shows no sympathy

harshness
NOUN **1 Harshness** is when living conditions or climates are rough and unpleasant.
NOUN **2 Harshness** is when someone's actions or remarks are unkind and show no sympathy.

harvest harvests
NOUN the act of gathering a crop, or the time when this is done

WORD HISTORY
from Old German *herbist* meaning autumn

has
VERB part of the verb *have*

hashtag hashtags
NOUN a word or phrase with a hash sign (#) in front of it, to show that it is the topic of a message on a social media website
• *All my friends posted tweets using the* **hashtag** *#silent.*

hasn't
VERB a contraction of *has not*

hassle hassles, hassling, hassled
NOUN **1** (*informal*) Something that is a **hassle** is difficult or causes trouble. • *Organising the school trip is always a* **hassle**.
VERB **2** If you **hassle** someone, you annoy them by repeatedly asking them to do something.

hasty hastier, hastiest
ADJECTIVE done quickly and without preparation • *Do not give a* **hasty** *answer.*

hat hats
NOUN a covering for the head

hatch hatches, hatching, hatched
VERB **1** When an egg **hatches**, or when a bird or a reptile **hatches** from an egg, the shell breaks open and the young bird or reptile comes out.
NOUN **2** an opening in a wall where food can be passed through

hatchback hatchbacks
NOUN a car with a door at the back that opens upwards

hatchet hatchets
NOUN a small axe

hate hates, hating, hated
VERB If you **hate** someone or something, you dislike them very much.

hateful
ADJECTIVE very nasty and unpleasant

hatred
NOUN an extremely strong feeling of dislike

haul hauls, hauling, hauled
VERB If you **haul** something somewhere, you pull it with great effort.

haunt haunts, haunting, haunted
VERB If a ghost **haunts** a place, it is seen or heard there regularly.

A B C D E F G H I J K L M N O P Q R S T U V W X Y Z

haunted

ADJECTIVE Somewhere that is **haunted** is visited often by a ghost. • *People believe that the house on the hill is* ***haunted***.

have has, having, had

VERB **1** If you **have** something, it belongs to you or you possess it.

VERB **2** If you **have** something such as a cold or an accident, you feel or experience it.

VERB **3** If you **have** something such as lunch or a letter, you take or get it.

VERB **4** If you **have** something such as a haircut, you cause it to be done.

PHRASE **5** If you **have to** do something, you must do it. • *I* ***have to*** *clean my room before I go out.*

VERB **6 Have** can be used with other verbs to form the past tense. • *I* ***have*** *already read that book.*

haven't

VERB a contraction of *have not*

havoc

NOUN disorder and confusion • *The bad weather played* ***havoc*** *with our plans.*

hawk hawks

NOUN a bird of prey with short, rounded wings and a long tail

hay

NOUN grass that has been cut and dried and is used to feed animals

hay fever

NOUN an allergy to pollen and grass, causing sneezing and watering eyes

haystack haystacks

NOUN a large, firmly-built pile of hay, usually covered and left out in the open

hazard hazards

NOUN something that could be dangerous to you • *The pollution in the city centre is a health* ***hazard***.

WORD HISTORY
from the Arabic *al zahr* meaning the dice, because games using dice involved risk

haze

NOUN If there is a **haze**, it is difficult to see clearly because there is moisture or smoke in the air.

hazel hazels

NOUN **1** a small tree with edible nuts
ADJECTIVE **2** a green-brown colour • *He has* ***hazel*** *eyes.*

hazelnut hazelnuts

NOUN the nut of the hazel tree. It has a hard, smooth, light-brown shell.

hazy hazier, haziest

ADJECTIVE dim or vague • ***hazy*** *sunshine* • *a* ***hazy*** *memory*

he

PRONOUN **He** is used to refer to a man, boy or male animal that has already been mentioned.

head heads, heading, headed

NOUN **1** the part of a human or other animal's body that has their eyes, brain and mouth in it

→ Have a look at the illustration for **insect**

NOUN **2** the top or front of something, or the most important end of it • *We went to the* ***head*** *of the queue.*

NOUN **3** When you toss a coin, the side called **heads** is the one with the **head** on it.

NOUN **4** In an organisation or group of people, the **head** is the main person in charge.

VERB **5** If you **head** something, you lead it. • *She* ***headed*** *the expedition to the North Pole.*

VERB **6** If you **head** somewhere, you go in that direction or towards something. • *We* ***headed*** *to the canteen for lunch.*

VERB **7** If you **head** a ball, you hit it with your head. • *He* ***headed*** *the ball into the goal.*

headache headaches

NOUN a pain in your head

heading headings

NOUN a piece of writing that is written or printed at the top of a page

headlight headlights

NOUN the large, powerful lights on the front of a motor vehicle

→ Have a look at the illustration for **car**

headline headlines

NOUN The **headline** of a newspaper is the heading printed in big, bold letters on the front page at the top of an article.

headphones

NOUN a pair of small speakers that you wear over your ears to listen to a radio, a television or a stereo without other people hearing

headquarters

NOUN the main place from which an organisation is run

a
b
c
d
e
f
g
h
i
j
k
l
m
n
o
p
q
r
s
t
u
v
w
x
y
z

187

A
B
C
D
E
F
G
H
I
J
K
L
M
N
O
P
Q
R
S
T
U
V
W
X
Y
Z

head teacher **head teachers**
NOUN the teacher who is in charge of a school

heal **heals, healing, healed**
VERB If a cut or a wound **heals**, it gets better.
• *The cut on my leg **healed** quickly.*

health
NOUN the condition of someone's body and mind • *I felt in very good **health** after our holiday.*

healthy **healthier, healthiest**
ADJECTIVE **1** Someone who is **healthy** is fit and well, and is not suffering from any illness. • *She goes to the gym to stay **healthy**.*
ADJECTIVE **2** Something that is **healthy** is good for you. • *You should try and eat a **healthy** diet.*

heap **heaps, heaping, heaped**
NOUN **1** an untidy pile of things
VERB **2** If you **heap** things, you pile them up.

hear **hears, hearing, heard**
VERB **1** When you **hear** sounds, you are aware of them because they reach your ears.
• *We could **hear** the waves crashing on the beach.*
VERB **2** When you **hear** from someone, they write to you or phone you.

heard
VERB the past tense and past participle of **hear**

hearing
NOUN **1** the ability to hear
NOUN **2** If someone gives you a **hearing**, they let you give your point of view and listen to you.

hearse **hearses**
NOUN a large car that carries the coffin at a funeral

heart **hearts**
NOUN **1** the organ in your chest that pumps the blood around your body

→ Have a look at the illustration for **organ**

NOUN **2** Your **heart** is also thought of as the centre of your emotions and feelings.
• *When his hamster died it broke his **heart**.*
NOUN **3** the most central or important part of something • *It is always busy in the **heart** of the city.*
NOUN **4** courage
NOUN **5** a curved shape like this ♥, or a playing card with this shape on it

PHRASE **6** If you learn something **by heart**, you learn it so that you know it from memory.

aorta
right atrium
left atrium
left ventricle
right ventricle

heart attack **heart attacks**
NOUN a serious medical condition in which someone's heart suddenly beats irregularly or stops completely

hearth **hearths**
NOUN the floor of a fireplace

PRONUNCIATION TIP
This word is pronounced **harth**.

heat **heats, heating, heated**
NOUN **1** warmth or the quality of being hot
• *the fierce **heat** of the sun*
NOUN **2** a contest or race in a competition that decides who will compete in the final
VERB **3** When you **heat** something, you warm it.

heater **heaters**
NOUN a device used to produce heat in order to warm a place, such as a room or a car

heath
NOUN a large open area of land covered in rough grass or heather, with very few trees

heather
NOUN a plant with small purple or white flowers that grows wild on hills and moorland

heave **heaves, heaving, heaved**
VERB If you **heave** something, you lift, push or throw it with a lot of effort.

heaven
NOUN In some religions, **heaven** is the place where God lives and where good people go when they die.

heavy heavier, heaviest
ADJECTIVE **1** Something that is **heavy**
weighs a lot.

ANTONYM: light

ADJECTIVE **2** You use **heavy** to talk about how
much something weighs. ● *How **heavy** is
the baby?*

Hebrew
NOUN an ancient language that is now
spoken in Israel by the Jewish people

hectare hectares
NOUN a unit for measuring an area of land,
equal to 10,000 square metres or about
2.471 acres

hectic
ADJECTIVE involving a lot of rushed activity
● *She leads a very **hectic** life.*

he'd
a contraction of *he had* or *he would*

hedge hedges
NOUN a row of bushes along the edge of a
garden, field or road

hedgehog hedgehogs
NOUN a small, brown mammal with sharp
spikes covering its back

heel heels
NOUN **1** the back part of your foot, below your
ankle
NOUN **2** the part on the bottom at the back of
a shoe or sock

heifer heifers
NOUN a young cow that has not yet had
calves

height heights
NOUN **1** a measurement from the bottom to
the top of someone or something
NOUN **2** a high position or place ● *He's afraid
of **heights**.*
NOUN **3** the highest or most important part of
something ● *He's at the **height** of his success.*

heir heirs
NOUN the person who is entitled to inherit
someone's property or title ● *the **heir** to the
throne*

PRONUNCIATION TIP
This word is pronounced **air**.

held
VERB the past tense of **hold**

helicopter helicopters
NOUN an aircraft with rotating blades
instead of wings, that enable it to take off
vertically

helium
NOUN a gas that is lighter than air. It is
sometimes used to fill party balloons.

he'll
a contraction of *he will* or *he shall*

hell
NOUN **1** In some religions, **hell** is the place
where the Devil lives and where wicked
people are sent to be punished when
they die.
NOUN **2** (*informal*) If you say that something is
hell, you mean that it is very unpleasant.

hello
GREETING You say **hello** when you meet
someone or answer the phone.

helmet helmets
NOUN a hard hat that you wear to protect
your head

help helps, helping, helped
VERB **1** If you **help** someone, you make
something easier or better for them.
NOUN **2** assistance ● *Thanks for your **help**.*

helpful
ADJECTIVE If you are **helpful**, you cooperate
with others and support them.

helping helpings
NOUN a portion of food at a meal

helpless
ADJECTIVE If you are **helpless**, you are
unable to protect yourself or do anything
useful.

hem hems, hemming, hemmed
NOUN **1** The **hem** of a garment is the edge
of it that has been folded up and stitched
in place.
VERB **2** If you **hem** a garment, you make a
hem on it.

hemisphere hemispheres
NOUN one half of the Earth or
a sphere

→ Have a look at the
illustration for **equator**

189

A
B
C
D
E
F
G
H
I
J
K
L
M
N
O
P
Q
R
S
T
U
V
W
X
Y
Z

hen hens
NOUN **1** a female chicken
NOUN **2** any female bird

heptagon heptagons
NOUN a flat shape with seven flat sides

her
PRONOUN **1** refers to a woman, girl or female animal that has already been mentioned • *I like Amy. I often play with **her***.
ADJECTIVE **2** shows that something belongs to a woman, girl or female animal that has already been mentioned • *Mum is going to wear **her** blue jumper*.

heraldry
NOUN the study of coats of arms

herb herbs
NOUN a plant whose leaves are used as a medicine or to flavour food

herbivore herbivores
NOUN an animal that eats only plants

herbivorous
ADJECTIVE eating only plants

herd herds, herding, herded
NOUN **1** a large group of animals grazing together • *a **herd** of cattle*
VERB **2** If you **herd** animals or people, you make them move together as a group. • *The teachers **herded** the children on to the bus.*

here
ADVERB at, to or in the place where you are

hereditary
ADJECTIVE passed on to a child from a parent

heritage
NOUN The **heritage** of a country is all its traditions, customs and art that have been passed from one generation to another.

hermit hermits
NOUN someone who prefers to live a simple life alone and far from other people, often for religious reasons

hero heroes
NOUN **1** the main male character in a book, film or play
NOUN **2** a person who is admired because they have done something brave or good

heroine heroines
NOUN the main female character in a book, play or film

heron herons
NOUN a wading bird with very long legs and a long beak and neck

herring herrings
NOUN a silvery fish that lives in large shoals in northern seas

hers
PRONOUN refers to something that belongs or relates to a woman, girl or other female animal

herself
PRONOUN refers to the same woman, girl or female animal who does an action and is affected by it • *She pulled **herself** up.*

he's
a contraction of *he is* or *he has*

hesitate hesitates, hesitating, hesitated
VERB If you **hesitate**, you pause or show uncertainty.

hexagon hexagons
NOUN a flat shape with six straight sides

hexagonal
ADJECTIVE having six straight sides

hibernate hibernates, hibernating, hibernated
VERB Animals that **hibernate** spend the winter in a state like a deep sleep.

hibernation
NOUN **Hibernation** is when an animal spends the winter in a state like a deep sleep.

hiccup hiccups, hiccupping, hiccupped; also spelt **hiccough**
NOUN **1** a short, uncontrolled sound in your throat
VERB **2** When you **hiccup**, you make short, uncontrolled sounds in your throat.

hide hides, hiding, hid, hidden
VERB **1** If you **hide** something, you put it where it cannot be seen, or prevent it from being discovered. • *He **hid** his disappointment.*
VERB **2** If you **hide**, you go somewhere where you cannot be seen or found easily.

hideous
ADJECTIVE extremely ugly or unpleasant

hieroglyphics
PLURAL NOUN ancient Egyptian writing that uses pictures instead of words. It involves over 700 picture signs.

PRONUNCIATION TIP
This word is pronounced hy-ro-**gliff**-iks.

---

high **higher, highest**
ADJECTIVE **1 High** refers to how much something measures from the bottom to the top. • *The statue was three metres **high**.*
ADJECTIVE **2** great in degree, quantity or intensity • *My aunt bought a house, despite the **high** price.*

ANTONYM: low

ADVERB **3** a long way above the ground • *He jumped **high** into the air.*

ANTONYM: low

highlight **highlights, highlighting, highlighted**
NOUN **1** the most interesting part of something • *The **highlight** of the week was our trip to the cinema.*
VERB **2** If you **highlight** a point or a problem, you emphasise it.

high-rise
ADJECTIVE **High-rise** buildings are very tall.

highway **highways**
NOUN a main road

hijab **hijabs**; also spelt **hejab**
NOUN a veil worn by some Muslim women in public, covering the hair and the chest

---

PRONUNCIATION TIP
This word is pronounced hi-**jab**.

---

hijack **hijacks, hijacking, hijacked**
VERB If someone **hijacks** a vehicle, they take control of it unlawfully and by force.

hike **hikes, hiking, hiked**
VERB **1** If you **hike**, you go for a long walk across country.
NOUN **2** a long and demanding walk

hilarious
ADJECTIVE very funny

hill **hills**
NOUN a high, rounded piece of ground

hilt **hilts**
NOUN the handle of a knife or sword

him
PRONOUN refers to a man, boy or male animal that has already been mentioned • *Let's invite Ben. I really like **him**.*

himself
PRONOUN refers to the same man, boy or male animal that does an action and is affected by it • *He pushed **himself** to the front of the crowd.*

hind **hinds**
NOUN **1** a female deer
ADJECTIVE **2** The **hind** legs of an animal are its back legs.

hieroglyphics

a
b
c
d
e
f
g
h
i
j
k
l
m
n
o
p
q
r
s
t
u
v
w
x
y
z

hinder hinders, hindering, hindered
VERB If you **hinder** someone or something, you get in their way and make it difficult for them to do what they want to do.

hindrance
NOUN someone or something that causes difficulties or is an obstruction

Hindu Hindus
NOUN a person who believes in Hinduism, an Indian religion that has many gods and involves the belief that people have another life on Earth after death

hinge hinges
NOUN the movable joint that attaches a door or window to its frame

hint hints, hinting, hinted
NOUN 1 an indirect suggestion • He dropped **hints** about his birthday present.
NOUN 2 a helpful piece of advice
VERB 3 If you **hint** that something is true, you suggest it indirectly. • The teacher **hinted** that they had all done well in the tests.

hip hips
NOUN Your **hips** are the joints and the bony parts at the top of your thigh and below your waist.

hippopotamus hippopotamuses or hippopotami
NOUN a large, African mammal with thick, wrinkled skin and short legs, that lives near rivers

WORD HISTORY
from Greek hippos + potamos meaning river horse

hire hires, hiring, hired
VERB 1 If you **hire** something, you pay money to use it for a period of time.
PHRASE 2 Something that is **for hire** is available for people to hire. • There are bicycles **for hire** down by the beach.

his
ADJECTIVE shows that something belongs to a man, boy or other male animal that has already been mentioned • He took off **his** coat.

hiss hisses, hissing, hissed
VERB If someone or something **hisses**, they make a long s sound.

historic
ADJECTIVE important in the past, or likely to be seen as important in the future

historical
ADJECTIVE occurring in the past, or relating to the study of the past

history histories
NOUN 1 the study of the past
NOUN 2 the set of facts that are known about a place or subject • There was a leaflet on the **history** of the stately home.

WORD HISTORY
from Greek historein meaning to narrate a story

hit hits, hitting, hit
VERB 1 If you **hit** someone or something, you strike or knock them with force.
VERB 2 If something **hits** you, it affects you suddenly and forcefully. • The answer suddenly **hit** me.
NOUN 3 If someone or something is a big **hit**, they are a great success.
NOUN 4 the action of hitting something

hitch hitches, hitching, hitched
VERB 1 If you **hitch** something, you tie it up using a loop.
VERB 2 (informal) If you **hitch** somewhere, you travel by getting lifts from passing vehicles.
NOUN 3 a slight problem of difficulty • Their plans went ahead without a **hitch**.

hitchhike hitchhikes, hitchhiking, hitchhiked
VERB to travel by getting lifts from passing vehicles

hitchhiker hitchhikers
NOUN a person who travels by hitchhiking

hive hives
NOUN 1 a beehive
NOUN 2 A place that is a **hive** of activity is very busy.

hoard hoards, hoarding, hoarded
VERB 1 If you **hoard** things, you save them even though they may no longer be useful.
NOUN 2 a store of things that has been saved or hidden

hoarse hoarser, hoarsest
ADJECTIVE A **hoarse** voice sounds rough and unclear.

hoax hoaxes
NOUN a trick or an attempt to deceive someone ● *It turned out to be a **hoax**.*

hobby hobbies
NOUN something that you do for enjoyment in your spare time

hockey
NOUN a game in which two teams use long sticks with curved ends to try to hit a small ball into the other team's goal

hoe hoes
NOUN a long-handled gardening tool with a small, square blade, used to remove weeds and break up the soil

Hogmanay
NOUN New Year's Eve and its celebrations in Scotland

hoist hoists, hoisting, hoisted
VERB If someone **hoists** something, they lift it, especially using ropes and pulleys, a crane or other machinery.

hold holds, holding, held
VERB **1** If you **hold** something, you carry it or keep it in place, usually with your hands or arms.
VERB **2** If you **hold** a meeting or a party, you arrange it and cause it to happen.
VERB **3** If you **hold** someone responsible for something, you decide that they did it.
VERB **4** If something **holds** a certain amount, it can contain that amount. ● *This jug **holds** a litre of water.*
VERB **5** If you **hold** something, you possess it. ● *She **holds** the world long jump record.*
NOUN **6** the part of a ship or aircraft where cargo or luggage is stored
NOUN **7** If someone has a **hold** over you, they have power over you.
NOUN **8** If you keep a **hold** on something, you hold it securely.

hole holes
NOUN an opening or hollow space in something

Holi
NOUN a Hindu festival celebrated in spring

holiday holidays
NOUN **1** a period of time spent away from home for enjoyment
NOUN **2** a day when people do not go to work or school because of a national festival ● *In Britain, Christmas Day is always a **holiday**.*

hollow hollows, hollowing, hollowed
ADJECTIVE **1** Something that is **hollow** has a hole or space inside it.

ANTONYM: solid

NOUN **2** a small valley or sunken place
VERB **3** If you **hollow** something out, you make it hollow. ● *We **hollowed** out the pumpkin to make a lantern for Halloween.*

holly
NOUN an evergreen tree or shrub with spiky leaves. It often has red berries in winter.

hologram holograms
NOUN a three-dimensional picture made by laser beams

holster holsters
NOUN a holder for a hand gun, worn at the side of the body or under the arm

holy holier, holiest
ADJECTIVE Something that is **holy** relates to God or to a particular religion.

home homes
NOUN **1** the building or place in which you live
NOUN **2** A nursing **home** is a building in which elderly or ill people live and are looked after.
NOUN **3** the place where you feel you belong

homeless
ADJECTIVE Someone who is **homeless** has nowhere to live.

homelessness
NOUN the situation when someone has nowhere to live

home page home pages
NOUN the first page you see on a website, which tells you about the site and has links to the information or services provided

homesick
ADJECTIVE If you are **homesick**, you are unhappy because you are away from your home and family. ● *I enjoyed my exchange trip to Germany, but I did feel **homesick** sometimes.*

homework
NOUN school work given to pupils to be done at home

homograph homographs
NOUN one of a group of words spelt in the same way but with different meanings, such as *saw* (meaning a tool for cutting) and *saw* (the past tense of *see*)

a
b
c
d
e
f
g
h
i
j
k
l
m
n
o
p
q
r
s
t
u
v
w
x
y
z

homonym homonyms
NOUN one of a group of words that are pronounced or spelt in the same way but have different meanings; for example *eight* and *ate*, or *bank* (meaning a slope) and *bank* (meaning a place where you keep your money)

homophone homophones
NOUN one of a group of words with different meanings that are pronounced in the same way but spelt differently. *Write* and *right* are **homophones**.

honest
NOUN If you are **honest**, you can be trusted to tell the truth.

SYNONYMS: trustworthy, truthful

honestly
ADVERB You use **honestly** to emphasise that what you are saying is true. ● *I didn't do it.* ***Honestly!*** ● *I can* ***honestly*** *say that she is the best teacher I've ever had.*

honey
NOUN a sweet, edible, sticky substance made by bees

honeycomb honeycombs
NOUN a wax structure made with six-sided cells by bees for storing honey

honeymoon honeymoons
NOUN a holiday for a newly married couple after their wedding

honour honours, honouring, honoured
NOUN 1 An **honour** is an award given to someone for something they have done.
NOUN 2 If you feel that it is an **honour** to do something, you feel proud or privileged to do it.
VERB 3 If you **honour** someone, you give them special praise or attention, or an award.

hood hoods
NOUN 1 a loose covering for the head, usually part of a coat or jacket
NOUN 2 In American English, the **hood** of a car is the cover over the engine at the front.

hoodie hoodies
NOUN a piece of clothing made of thick cotton with a hood, which covers your upper body ● *She wore jeans and a red* ***hoodie***.

hoof hooves or **hoofs**
NOUN the hard, bony part of the feet of horses, cattle and deer

hook hooks, hooking, hooked
NOUN 1 a curved piece of metal or plastic that is used for catching things or for holding things up
VERB 2 If you **hook** one thing on to another, you attach it there using a hook. ● *He* ***hooked*** *the caravan to the car.*

hooligan hooligans
NOUN a destructive and violent person

hooliganism
NOUN noisy and violent behaviour

hoop hoops
NOUN a large wooden, metal or plastic ring

hoot hoots, hooting, hooted
VERB 1 If a car horn **hoots**, it makes a loud, honking noise.
VERB 2 If someone **hoots**, they make a long *oo* sound like an owl or a car horn. ● *We all* ***hooted*** *with laughter at his joke.*

hop hops, hopping, hopped
VERB 1 If you **hop**, you jump on one foot.
VERB 2 When animals such as kangaroos, birds or insects **hop**, they jump with two or more feet together.

hope hopes, hoping, hoped
VERB 1 If you **hope** that something will happen, you want or expect it to happen.
NOUN 2 the wish or expectation that things will go well in the future

hopeful
ADJECTIVE If you are **hopeful** about something, you hope it will turn out well.

hopefully
ADVERB 1 You use **hopefully** to say what you hope will happen. ● ***Hopefully***, *your mum will let you come to the park with us.*
ADVERB 2 in a way that shows you are hopeful ● *She looked at him* ***hopefully***.

hopeless
ADJECTIVE 1 You say something is **hopeless** when it is very bad and you do not feel it can get any better.
ADJECTIVE 2 unable to do something well ● *I'm* ***hopeless*** *at art.*

hopelessly
ADVERB 1 You use **hopelessly** to emphasise that a situation is very bad and you do not feel it can get any better. ● *Everything was* ***hopelessly*** *disorganised.*
ADVERB 2 in a way that shows you have no hope ● *He stared* ***hopelessly*** *out of the window.*

A B C D E F G H I J K L M N O P Q R S T U V W X Y Z

horde *hordes*
NOUN a large group or number of people or other animals

horizon *horizons*
NOUN the distant line where the sky seems to touch the land or sea

horizontal
ADJECTIVE flat and level with, or parallel to the ground

horn *horns*
NOUN 1 a warning device on a vehicle that makes a loud noise
NOUN 2 one of the hard, pointed things that grow from the head of a cow or goat

hornet *hornets*
NOUN 1 a type of very large wasp
PHRASE 2 A situation described as **a hornet's nest** is very difficult to deal with and likely to cause trouble.

horoscope *horoscopes*
NOUN a prediction about what is going to happen to someone, based on the position of the stars when they were born

horrible
ADJECTIVE disagreeable and unpleasant

horrific
ADJECTIVE If something is **horrific**, it horrifies people.

horrify *horrifies, horrifying, horrified*
VERB If someone or something **horrifies** you, they make you feel disgusted and shocked.

horror
NOUN a strong feeling of alarm caused by something very unpleasant

horse *horses*
NOUN a large mammal with a mane and tail, that people can ride

horse chestnut *horse chestnuts*
NOUN a large tree with flowers and shiny, brown nuts known as conkers

horsepower
NOUN a unit used for measuring how powerful an engine is

horseshoe *horseshoes*
NOUN a U-shaped piece of iron that is nailed to the bottom of a horse's hoof to protect it

hose *hoses*
NOUN a long, flexible tube through which liquid or gas can be passed • *a garden hose*

hospitable
ADJECTIVE If you are **hospitable**, you are friendly, welcoming and generous to others.

hospital *hospitals*
NOUN a place where sick people are looked after by doctors and nurses

host *hosts, hosting, hosted*
NOUN 1 the person who gives a party or organises an event, and who welcomes and looks after the guests
NOUN 2 a large number of things • *There was a host of things to do at the fair.*
VERB 3 If you **host** an event, you organise it and act as the host.

hostage *hostages*
NOUN a person who is illegally held prisoner and threatened with injury or death unless certain demands are met by other people

hostel *hostels*
NOUN a large house where people can stay cheaply for a short time • *a youth hostel*

hostile
ADJECTIVE If someone is **hostile** to you, they behave in an unfriendly aggressive way towards you.

hot *hotter, hottest*
ADJECTIVE 1 having a high temperature
ADJECTIVE 2 having a burning taste caused by spices

hotel *hotels*
NOUN a building where people stay, paying for their room and meals

hound *hounds*
NOUN a dog, especially one used for hunting or racing

hour *hours*
NOUN a period of 60 minutes

WORD HISTORY
from Greek *hora* meaning season or time of day

house *houses*
NOUN a building where people live

household *households*
NOUN 1 all the people who live as a group in a house or flat
PHRASE 2 Someone who is **a household name** is very well known.

A B C D E F G **H** I J K L M N O P Q R S T U V W X Y Z

housewife **housewives**
NOUN a married woman who does not have a paid job, but instead looks after her home and children

housework
NOUN all the work done in the home, like the cleaning and cooking

hover **hovers, hovering, hovered**
VERB When a bird, insect or aircraft **hovers**, it stays in the same place in the air.

hovercraft **hovercraft** or **hovercrafts**
NOUN a vehicle that can travel over water or land supported by a cushion of air

how
ADVERB used to ask about, explain or refer to the way something is done ● *How did you get so dirty?*

however
ADVERB **1** You use **however** when you are adding a comment that contrasts with what has just been said. ● *He is very chatty and seems confident. However, he is quite shy.*
ADVERB **2** You use **however** to say that something makes no difference to a situation. ● *However hard she tried, nothing seemed to work.*

howl **howls, howling, howled**
VERB **1** If someone or something **howls**, they make a long, loud wailing noise such as that made by a dog or a baby when it is upset.
NOUN **2** a long, loud wailing noise

hub **hubs**
NOUN **1** the centre part of a wheel

→ Have a look at the illustration for **turbine**

NOUN **2** the most important or active part of a place or organisation

huddle **huddles, huddling, huddled**
VERB **1** If you **huddle** up, or are **huddled**, you are curled up with your arms and legs close to your body.
VERB **2** When people or animals **huddle** together, they sit or stand close to each other, often for warmth.

hug **hugs, hugging, hugged**
VERB If you **hug** someone, you put your arms round them and hold them close to you, usually to comfort them or to show affection.

huge
ADJECTIVE extremely large in amount, size or degree ● *The party was a **huge** success.*

SYNONYMS: enormous, gigantic, vast

hull **hulls**
NOUN The **hull** of a ship is the main part of its body that sits in the water.

hum **hums, humming, hummed**
VERB **1** If something **hums**, it makes a continuous, low noise.
VERB **2** If you **hum**, you sing with your lips closed.
NOUN **3** a continuous, low noise

human **humans**
ADJECTIVE **1** relating to or concerning people ● *We are all part of the **human** race.*
NOUN **2** a person

WORD HISTORY
from Latin *homo* meaning man

human being **human beings**
NOUN a person

humane
ADJECTIVE showing kindness and sympathy towards others

humanity
NOUN **1** the human race
NOUN **2** Someone who shows **humanity** is kind and sympathetic.

humble **humbler, humblest**
ADJECTIVE A **humble** person is modest and thinks that they are not very important.

humbly
ADVERB in a modest way that shows you think you are not very important

humid
ADJECTIVE If the weather is **humid**, the air feels damp, heavy and warm.

humidity
NOUN **1** **Humidity** is when the air feels damp, heavy and warm.
NOUN **2** **Humidity** is the amount of moisture in the air.

humiliate **humiliates, humiliating, humiliated**
VERB If you **humiliate** someone, you make them feel ashamed or appear stupid to other people.

humiliation
NOUN the feeling of being ashamed or embarrassed because you have been made to look stupid

humour humours, humouring, humoured
NOUN 1 the quality of being funny
NOUN 2 the ability to be amused by certain things • *She's got a peculiar sense of humour*.
VERB 3 If you **humour** someone, you try to please them, so that they will not become upset.

hump humps
NOUN a small, rounded lump or mound • *a camel's hump*

hunch hunches, hunching, hunched
VERB 1 If you **hunch** your shoulders, you raise them and push them forward, bending forward slightly.
VERB 2 If you have a **hunch** about something, you have an idea that something will happen.

hundred hundreds
NOUN A **hundred** is the number 100.

hundredth hundredths
NOUN 1 one of a hundred equal parts of something. It can be written as ¹⁄₁₀₀.
ADJECTIVE 2 The **hundredth** item in a series is the one that you count as number one hundred. It can be written as 100th.

hung
VERB a past tense and past participle of **hang**

hunger
NOUN the need or desire to eat

hungrily
ADVERB in a way that shows you are hungry

hungry hungrier, hungriest
ADJECTIVE If you are **hungry**, you need or want food.

hunt hunts, hunting, hunted
VERB 1 If you **hunt** for something, you search for it.
VERB 2 When people **hunt**, they chase and kill wild animals for food or sport.
NOUN 3 the act of searching for something • *The neighbours joined in the hunt for the missing cat.*

hurdle hurdles
NOUN 1 one of the frames or barriers that you jump over in an athletics race called

hurdles • *She knocked over the last hurdle, but still managed to win the race.*
NOUN 2 a problem or difficulty • *Several hurdles had to be overcome before the school play could go ahead.*

hurl hurls, hurling, hurled
VERB If you **hurl** something, you throw it with great force.

hurricane hurricanes
NOUN a very violent storm with strong winds

hurry hurries, hurrying, hurried
VERB 1 If you **hurry** somewhere, you go there quickly.
VERB 2 If you **hurry** someone or something, you try to make something happen more quickly.
PHRASE 3 If you are **in a hurry** to do something, you want to do it quickly. If you do something **in a hurry**, you do it quickly.
hurry up
VERB If you tell someone to **hurry up**, you try to get them to do something more quickly.

hurt hurts, hurting, hurt
VERB 1 If you **hurt** yourself or someone else, you injure or cause physical pain to yourself or someone else.
VERB 2 If a part of your body **hurts**, you feel pain there.
VERB 3 If you **hurt** someone, or **hurt** their feelings, you upset them by being unkind towards them.
ADJECTIVE 4 If you are **hurt**, you are injured.
ADJECTIVE 5 If you feel **hurt**, you are upset because of someone's unkindness towards you. • *She was hurt that they did not invite her to the party.*

WORD HISTORY
from Old French *hurter* meaning to knock against

hurtle hurtles, hurtling, hurtled
VERB If someone or something **hurtles**, they move along very fast in an uncontrolled way. • *The car hurtled along the bumpy road.*

husband husbands
NOUN Someone's **husband** is the man they are married to.

hustle hustles, hustling, hustled
VERB 1 If you **hustle** someone, you make them move by pushing and jostling them.
VERB 2 If you **hustle**, you go somewhere or do something in a hurry.

a
b
c
d
e
f
g
h
i
j
k
l
m
n
o
p
q
r
s
t
u
v
w
x
y
z

A
B
C
D
E
F
G
H
I
J
K
L
M
N
O
P
Q
R
S
T
U
V
W
X
Y
Z

hut **huts**
NOUN a small house or shelter

hutch **hutches**
NOUN a wooden box with wire mesh at one side, in which small pets can be kept

hydrant **hydrants**
NOUN a pipe connected to the main water supply of a town and used for emergencies

hydraulic
ADJECTIVE operated by water or other fluid that is under pressure

hydroelectric
ADJECTIVE **Hydroelectric** power is electricity produced from the energy of moving water.

hydrogen
NOUN a colourless gas that is the lightest and most common element in the world. **Hydrogen**-filled balloons may explode because this gas is very flammable.

hyena **hyenas**; also spelt **hyaena**
NOUN a wild, dog-like animal found in Africa and Asia, that hunts in packs

---

WORD HISTORY
from Greek *huaina* meaning hog

---

hygiene
NOUN the state of being clean and free of germs

hymn **hymns**
NOUN a Christian song in praise of God

hyphen **hyphens**
NOUN a punctuation mark (-) used to join together words or parts of words, as in *left-handed*

hypocrisy
NOUN behaviour that shows that someone does not really believe what they say they do

hypocrite **hypocrites**
NOUN someone who pretends to have certain views and beliefs that are different from their actual views and beliefs

hypocritical
ADJECTIVE behaving in a way that shows you do not really have the beliefs that you say you do

hypothermia
NOUN a condition in which a person is very ill because their body has been extremely cold for a long time ● *After spending the night stuck on the mountain, the climbers had **hypothermia**.*

I
PRONOUN A speaker or writer uses **I** to refer to themselves.

ice
NOUN water that has frozen solid

iceberg **icebergs**
NOUN a large mass of ice floating in the sea

WORD HISTORY
from Dutch *ijsberg* meaning ice mountain

---

ice cream **ice creams**
NOUN a very cold, sweet, creamy food

ice skate **ice skates, ice skating, ice skated**; also spelt **ice-skate**
NOUN **1** a boot with a metal blade on the bottom, that you wear to move around on ice
VERB **2** When you **ice-skate**, you move about on the ice wearing ice skates.

icicle **icicles**
NOUN a piece of ice shaped like a pointed stick, that hangs down from a surface

icing
NOUN a sweet covering for a cake or biscuits

icon icons

NOUN **1** a picture on a computer screen representing a program that can be activated by moving the cursor over it

NOUN **2** a holy picture of Christ, the Virgin Mary or a saint

ICT

NOUN an abbreviation of *Information and Communication Technology*. **ICT** is the use of computers, telephones, television and radio to store, organise and give out information.

icy icier, iciest

ADJECTIVE **1** Something that is **icy** is very cold. • *We tried to shelter from the **icy** wind.*

ADJECTIVE **2** An **icy** road has ice on it.

I'd

a contraction of *I had* or *I would*

idea ideas

NOUN **1** a plan or possible course of action

NOUN **2** an opinion or belief

NOUN **3** If you have an **idea** of something, you have a general but not a detailed knowledge of it. • *Could you give me an **idea** of the cost?*

ideal

ADJECTIVE The **ideal** person or thing for a particular purpose is the best possible one.

identical

ADJECTIVE exactly the same • *They are **identical** twins.*

identifiable

ADJECTIVE possible to recognise and name

identification

NOUN a document, such as a driving licence or passport, that states who you are

identify identifies, identifying, identified

VERB If you **identify** someone or something, you recognise and name them.

identity identities

NOUN the things that make you who you are

idiom idioms

NOUN a group of words that, when used together, mean something different from when the words are used individually. For example, *it rained cats and dogs.*

idiot idiots

NOUN someone who is stupid or foolish

idiotic

ADJECTIVE very stupid

idle idler, idlest

ADJECTIVE **1** If you are **idle**, you are doing nothing.

ADJECTIVE **2** Machines or factories that are **idle** are not being used.

ADJECTIVE **3** lazy

idleness

NOUN **1** **Idleness** is when a person or machine is doing nothing.

NOUN **2** laziness

idly

ADVERB **1** without any particular purpose • *He was playing **idly** with his pen.*

ADVERB **2** without doing anything

idol idols

NOUN a famous person who is loved and admired by fans

i.e.

i.e. means *that is.* • *Please meet me in three days' time, **i.e.** on Sunday.*

WORD HISTORY
from Latin *id est* meaning that is

---

if

CONJUNCTION **1** on condition that • *You can watch TV **if** you do your homework first.*

CONJUNCTION **2** whether • *I asked him **if** he could come to the party.*

igloo igloos

NOUN a dome-shaped house built out of blocks of snow by Inuit people

---

WORD HISTORY
from *igdlu*, an Inuit word meaning house

---

ignite ignites, igniting, ignited

VERB If you **ignite** something, or it **ignites**, you set it on fire or it catches fire.

WORD HISTORY
from Latin *ignis* meaning fire

---

ignorant

ADJECTIVE If you are **ignorant** of something, you do not know about it.

ignore ignores, ignoring, ignored

VERB If you **ignore** someone or something, you do not take any notice of them.

iguana iguanas

NOUN a large, tropical lizard

a
b
c
d
e
f
g
h
i
j
k
l
m
n
o
p
q
r
s
t
u
v
w
x
y
z

199

il-

PREFIX You add **il-** to the beginning of a word to mean that it is not something. For example, **il**legal means not legal, and **il**legible means not legible.

I'll

a contraction of *I will* or *I shall*

ill

ADJECTIVE unhealthy or sick

SYNONYM: unwell

WORD HISTORY
from Norse *illr* meaning bad

illegal

ADJECTIVE If something is **illegal** it is forbidden by the law.

SYNONYMS: criminal, unlawful

illegible

ADJECTIVE Writing that is **illegible** is unclear and very difficult to read.

ANTONYM: legible

illegibly

ADVERB in a way that is unclear and very difficult to read

ANTONYM: legibly

illegitimate

ADJECTIVE If something is **illegitimate** it is not allowed by law, or is not accepted as fair by most people.

illiterate

ADJECTIVE unable to read or write

ANTONYM: literate

illness illnesses

NOUN **1** the state or experience of being ill
NOUN **2** a particular disease • *Flu is a common **illness** during the winter months.*

illogical

ADJECTIVE An **illogical** feeling or action is not reasonable or sensible.

ANTONYM: logical

illuminate illuminates, illuminating, illuminated

VERB If you **illuminate** something, you shine light on to it so that it is easier to see, or you decorate it with lights.

illumination illuminations

NOUN one of the coloured lights put up to decorate a town, especially at Christmas

illusion illusions

NOUN **1** an idea that you think is true, but is not • *We were under the **illusion** that this was going to be an easy project.*
NOUN **2** something that seems to be there but does not really exist

illustrate illustrates, illustrating, illustrated

VERB **1** If you **illustrate** a book, you help to explain its meaning by putting in pictures and diagrams.
VERB **2** If you **illustrate** a point when you are speaking, you make its meaning clearer, often by giving examples.

illustration illustrations

NOUN a picture or a diagram that helps to explain something

illustrator illustrators

NOUN someone who creates the pictures that go into books

I'm

a contraction of *I am*

im-

PREFIX You add **im-** to the beginning of a word to mean not something. For example, something that is **im**movable cannot be moved, and something that is **im**perfect is not perfect.

image images

NOUN a picture or photograph • *There are some beautiful **images** in the book.*

imagery

NOUN The **imagery** of a poem or book is the words that are used to produce a picture in the mind of the reader.

imaginary

ADJECTIVE Something that is **imaginary** exists only in your mind, not in real life.

ANTONYM: real

imagination imaginations

NOUN If you show **imagination**, you have the ability to form ideas and pictures in your mind.

imaginative

ADJECTIVE If you are **imaginative**, you find it easy to create new and exciting ideas in your mind.

ANTONYM: unimaginative

imagine imagines, imagining, imagined

VERB If you **imagine** something or someone, you create a picture of them in your mind.

imam

NOUN a person who leads a group in prayer in a mosque

imitate imitates, imitating, imitated

VERB If you **imitate** someone or something, you copy them.

SYNONYM: mimic

imitation imitations

NOUN a copy of something else

immature

ADJECTIVE **1** Something that is **immature** is not fully grown or developed.

ANTONYM: mature

ADJECTIVE **2** An **immature** person does not behave in a sensible way.

ANTONYM: mature

immediate

ADJECTIVE Something that is **immediate** happens or is done without delay.

immediately

ADVERB If something happens **immediately**, it happens at once.

immense

ADJECTIVE very large

SYNONYMS: huge, vast

immerse immerses, immersing, immersed

VERB **1** If you **immerse** something, you cover it completely with liquid.
VERB **2** If you **immerse** yourself in an activity, you become completely occupied with it.

immersion

NOUN **1 Immersion** is when you cover something completely with liquid.
NOUN **2 Immersion** is when you become completely involved in an activity.

immigrant immigrants

NOUN someone who has come to live in a country from another country

immigrate immigrates, immigrating, immigrated

VERB If someone **immigrates**, they come to live permanently in a country that is not their own.

ANTONYM: emigrate

immobile

ADJECTIVE If something or someone is **immobile**, they are not moving.

immoral

ADJECTIVE If someone is **immoral**, they do not follow most people's standards of acceptable behaviour.

immortal

ADJECTIVE **1** Someone or something that is **immortal** is famous and will be remembered for a long time.
ADJECTIVE **2** Something that is **immortal** will last forever.

immune

ADJECTIVE If you are **immune** to a particular disease, you cannot catch it.

immunisation; also spelt immunization

NOUN **Immunisation** is when a doctor or nurse gives you an injection so that you are protected from catching a disease.

immunise immunises, immunising, immunised; also spelt immunize

VERB If a doctor or nurse **immunises** you against a disease, they give you an injection so that you are protected from the disease.

immunity

NOUN If you have **immunity** to a particular disease, you cannot catch it.

impact impacts

NOUN **1** The **impact** of one object on another is the force with which it hits it.
NOUN **2** If something has an **impact** on a situation or person, it has a strong effect on them.

WORD HISTORY
from Latin *impactus* meaning pushed against

a
b
c
d
e
f
g
h
i
j
k
l
m
n
o
p
q
r
s
t
u
v
w
x
y
z

impartial
ADJECTIVE If you are **impartial** about something, you are fair and unbiased.

ANTONYM: partial

impatience
NOUN a feeling of being annoyed because you do not want to wait for someone or something

ANTONYM: patience

impatient
ADJECTIVE If you are **impatient**, you become annoyed easily because you do not want to wait for someone or something.

ANTONYM: patient

impatiently
ADVERB in a way that shows you are annoyed because you do not want to wait for someone or something

ANTONYM: patiently

imperfect
ADJECTIVE Something that is **imperfect** has faults.

imperial
ADJECTIVE **1** relating to an empire, emperor or empress
ADJECTIVE **2** The **imperial** system of measurement is a system that uses inches, feet and yards, ounces and pounds, and pints and gallons.

impersonal
ADJECTIVE Something that is **impersonal** makes you feel that individuals and their feelings do not matter.

impersonate **impersonates, impersonating, impersonated**
VERB If you **impersonate** someone, you pretend to be that person.

impertinent
ADJECTIVE If you are **impertinent**, you are disrespectful and rude to someone.

imply **implies, implying, implied**
VERB If you **imply** that something is the case, you suggest it but do not say it directly.
● Are you **implying** that I lied?

import **imports, importing, imported**
VERB **1** If someone **imports** something, they buy it or bring it in from another country.

ANTONYM: export

NOUN **2 Imports** are goods brought into one country from another country.

ANTONYM: export

PRONUNCIATION TIP
The verb is pronounced im-**port**. The noun is pronounced **im**-port.

important
ADJECTIVE **1** Something that is **important** is very valuable, necessary or significant. ● It is **important** not to tell lies.
ADJECTIVE **2** An **important** person has a lot of influence or power.

impose **imposes, imposing, imposed**
VERB If someone **imposes** something on someone, they force it on them.

imposing
ADJECTIVE If someone or something is **imposing**, they look impressive and important.

impossibility **impossibilities**
NOUN something that cannot happen or cannot be done

impossible
ADJECTIVE Something that is **impossible** cannot happen or cannot be done. ● It is **impossible** to see in the dark.

impossibly
ADVERB in a way that does not seem possible

imposter **imposters**
NOUN An **imposter** is someone who pretends to be someone else, usually as part of a trick or a crime.

impractical
ADJECTIVE If someone or something is **impractical**, they are not sensible or realistic. ● It is **impractical** to camp in this wet weather.

ANTONYM: practical

impress impresses, impressing, impressed

VERB **1** If you **impress** someone, you cause them to admire or respect you.
VERB **2** If you **impress** something on someone, you make sure that they understand it and remember it.

impression impressions

NOUN **1** An **impression** of someone or something is a vague idea or feeling that you have about them. • *I have the impression that I've met you before.*
NOUN **2** a mark made by pressing • *You leave an impression when you press a coin into putty then take it away.*
NOUN **3** an imitation of a person, animal or thing

impressive

ADJECTIVE If someone or something is **impressive**, it causes you to admire or respect it.

imprison imprisons, imprisoning, imprisoned

VERB If someone **imprisons** another person, they put them in prison or lock them up somewhere.

imprisonment

NOUN **Imprisonment** is when someone is kept in prison or is locked up somewhere.

improbable

ADJECTIVE not probable or likely to happen

ANTONYM: probable

improper fraction improper fractions

NOUN In mathematics, an **improper fraction** is a fraction where the numerator is bigger than the denominator.

improve improves, improving, improved

VERB If something **improves**, or if you **improve** it, it gets better.

improvement improvements

NOUN a change that shows something or someone is getting better

improvise improvises, improvising, improvised

VERB **1** If you **improvise** something, you make or do something without planning it in advance, and with whatever materials are available. • *In order to save money the children improvised their costumes for the school play.*

VERB **2** When musicians or actors **improvise**, they make up the music or words as they go along.

impudent

ADJECTIVE If you are **impudent**, you are rude and disrespectful.

impulse impulses

NOUN If you have an **impulse** to do something, you have a strong urge to do it immediately.

impulsive

ADJECTIVE Someone who is **impulsive** does things immediately without thinking about the possible risks or problems.

in

PREPOSITION **1** at or inside • *The cow was in the field.*
PREPOSITION **2** during • *It snows in winter.*
ADVERB **3** towards the inside of a place or thing • *I knocked on the door, and went in.*
ADVERB **4** at home • *Is Jake in?*

in-

PREFIX You add **in-** to the beginning of a word to mean not something. For example, **in**accurate means not accurate, and **in**accessible means not accessible.

inability inabilities

NOUN If you have an **inability** to do something, you cannot do it.

ANTONYM: ability

inaccessible

ADJECTIVE If something is **inaccessible**, it is very difficult or impossible to reach.

ANTONYM: accessible

inaccurate

ADJECTIVE If something is **inaccurate**, it is incorrect.

ANTONYM: accurate

inadequate

ADJECTIVE If something is **inadequate**, there is not enough of it, or it is not good enough for a particular purpose.

ANTONYM: adequate

inanimate

ADJECTIVE not alive. For example, rocks and furniture are **inanimate**.

a
b
c
d
e
f
g
h
i
j
k
l
m
n
o
p
q
r
s
t
u
v
w
x
y
z

A
B
C
D
E
F
G
H
I
J
K
L
M
N
O
P
Q
R
S
T
U
V
W
X
Y
Z

inaudible

ADJECTIVE If something is **inaudible**, it cannot be heard.

ANTONYM: audible

incapable

ADJECTIVE Someone who is **incapable** of doing something is not able to do it.

ANTONYM: capable

incendiary

ADJECTIVE An **incendiary** device is designed to set fire to things.

incense

NOUN a spicy substance that gives off a sweet smell when it is burned

incessant

ADJECTIVE If something is **incessant**, it continues without stopping. • *The sound of the rain on the windows was **incessant**.*

inch **inches**

NOUN a unit of length equal to about 2.54 centimetres

WORD HISTORY
from Latin *uncia* meaning twelfth part; there are twelve inches in a foot

incident **incidents**

NOUN an event or occurrence, especially an unusual one

incidentally

ADVERB If something happens **incidentally**, it happens along with something else, as a minor part of it.

incinerate **incinerates, incinerating, incinerated**

VERB If you **incinerate** something, you burn it until only ashes are left.

incineration

NOUN the process of burning something until only ashes are left

incisor **incisors**

NOUN Your **incisors** are the sharp teeth at the front of your mouth, used for biting and cutting food.

→ Have a look at the illustration for **teeth**

inclination **inclinations**

NOUN If you have an **inclination** to do something, you want to do it.

incline **inclines, inclining, inclined**

VERB **1** If you are **inclined** to do something, you often do it or you would like to do it.
NOUN **2** a slope

PRONUNCIATION TIP
The verb is pronounced in-**klyn**. The noun is pronounced **in**-klyn.

include **includes, including, included**

VERB If one thing **includes** another, the second thing is part of the first thing.
• *Meals are **included** in the price at this hotel.*

ANTONYM: exclude

inclusive

ADJECTIVE When something is **inclusive**, it includes everything and nothing is left out. • *The price for the meal was **inclusive**, so Gran had nothing extra to pay for our milkshakes.*

incognito

ADVERB If someone is **incognito**, they are in disguise.

WORD HISTORY
from Latin *in* + *cognitus* meaning not known

income **incomes**

NOUN the money a person earns

incomplete

ADJECTIVE Something that is **incomplete** is not complete or finished.

ANTONYM: complete

incongruous

ADJECTIVE If something is **incongruous** in a particular place or situation, it seems unsuitable and out of place.

inconsiderate

ADJECTIVE If you are **inconsiderate**, you do not consider the needs or feelings of others. • *What an **inconsiderate** thing to do!*

ANTONYM: considerate

conspicuous

ADJECTIVE If someone or something is **inconspicuous**, they are not noticeable or obvious, and cannot easily be seen.

ANTONYM: conspicuous

convenient

ADJECTIVE If something is **inconvenient**, it is awkward and causes difficulties.
● an **inconvenient** time to call

ANTONYM: convenient

corporate incorporates, incorporating, incorporated

VERB If someone **incorporates** one thing into another thing, they include the first thing so that it becomes part of the second.

correct

ADJECTIVE Something that is **incorrect** is wrong or untrue.

ANTONYM: correct

crease increases, increasing, increased

VERB 1 If something **increases**, or if you **increase** it, it becomes larger in number, level or amount. ● Her dad **increased** her pocket money.

ANTONYM: decrease

NOUN 2 a rise in the number, level or amount of something ● There has been an **increase** in the number of children walking to school.

ANTONYM: decrease

credible

ADJECTIVE totally amazing or impossible to believe

SYNONYM: unbelievable

cubate incubates, incubating, incubated

VERB When eggs **incubate**, or a bird **incubates** them, they are kept warm until they hatch.

cubator incubators

NOUN a piece of hospital equipment in which sick or weak newborn babies are kept warm and safe

incurable

ADJECTIVE If someone has an **incurable** disease, they cannot be cured.

ANTONYM: curable

indebted

ADJECTIVE If you are **indebted** to someone, you are very grateful to them.

indecent

ADJECTIVE Something that is **indecent** is shocking or rude.

ANTONYM: decent

indecisive

ADJECTIVE If someone is **indecisive**, they find it difficult to make up their mind.

ANTONYM: decisive

indeed

ADVERB 1 You use **indeed** to emphasise a point that you are making. ● The cake was very good **indeed**.

ADVERB 2 You use **indeed** to show that you agree with something. ● "Are you going to the party?" "**Indeed** I am."

indefinite

ADJECTIVE If something is **indefinite**, it is vague and unclear.

ANTONYM: definite

indefinitely

ADVERB If something goes on **indefinitely**, there is no clear time when it will finish and it can go on for an unlimited time.

indent indents, indenting, indented

VERB If you **indent** a paragraph when you write, you start the first line further to the right, away from the margin.

independence

NOUN 1 the ability to do things yourself without help from other people
NOUN 2 the freedom to make your own decisions and not be controlled by anyone else

independent

ADJECTIVE 1 If you are **independent**, you are able to do things yourself and do not need help from other people.
ADJECTIVE 2 free and not controlled by anyone

independently

ADVERB without help from other people

a
b
c
d
e
f
g
h
i
j
k
l
m
n
o
p
q
r
s
t
u
v
w
x
y
z

indestructible
ADJECTIVE If something is **indestructible**, it cannot be destroyed.

index indexes
NOUN an alphabetical list at the back of a book which tells you where to find information in the book

indicate indicates, indicating, indicated
VERB 1 If you **indicate** something to someone, you point it out or show it to them.
VERB 2 If the driver of a vehicle **indicates**, they give a signal to show which way they are going to move or turn. ● *The cyclist **indicated** that he was turning right.*

indicator indicators
NOUN 1 something that tells you what something is like or what is happening
NOUN 2 A car's **indicators** are the lights at the front and back that are used to show when it is turning left or right.

→ Have a look at the illustration for **car**

indifferent
ADJECTIVE If you are **indifferent** to something, you have no interest in it.

indigestion
NOUN a pain you get when you have difficulty digesting food

indignant
ADJECTIVE If you are **indignant** about something, you are angry about it because you think it is unfair.

indigo
ADJECTIVE deep blue or violet

indirect
ADJECTIVE If something happens in an **indirect** way, it does not happen in a straightforward way.

ANTONYM: direct

indispensable
ADJECTIVE absolutely necessary; essential

indistinct
ADJECTIVE not clear

ANTONYM: distinct

individual individuals
ADJECTIVE 1 relating to one particular person or thing ● *Each child in the class gets **individual** attention.*
ADJECTIVE 2 single or separate ● *Each sweet i. the packet comes in an **individual** wrapper.*
NOUN 3 a person, different from any other person ● *We should treat people as **individuals**.*

indoor
ADJECTIVE happening inside a building ● *The hotel has an **indoor** swimming pool.*

indoors
ADVERB If something happens **indoors**, it takes place inside a building.

indulge indulges, indulging, indulged
VERB 1 If you **indulge** in something, you allow yourself to do it because you enjoy i
VERB 2 If you **indulge** someone, you allow them to have or do what they want.

indulgence indulgences
NOUN 1 something that you allow yourself have or do because you like it
NOUN 2 **Indulgence** is when you allow someone to have or do what they want.

industrial
ADJECTIVE to do with the work and processes involved in making things in factories

industrious
ADJECTIVE If you are **industrious**, you work hard.

industry industries
NOUN 1 the work involved in making things in factories
NOUN 2 all the people and processes involv in manufacturing a particular thing ● *My dad works in the computer **industry**.*

WORD HISTORY
from Latin *industria* meaning diligence or hard work

inedible
ADJECTIVE If something is **inedible**, it is too unpleasant or poisonous to eat.

inefficient
ADJECTIVE badly organised, wasteful and slo

inevitable
ADJECTIVE certain to happen

inexpensive
ADJECTIVE not costing much

inexplicable
ADJECTIVE If something is **inexplicable**, you cannot explain it.

inexplicably

ADVERB in a way that cannot be explained

infamous

ADJECTIVE Someone or something that is **infamous** is well known for their bad qualities.

SYNONYM: notorious

PRONUNCIATION TIP
This word is pronounced **in**-fum-uss.

infant infants

NOUN a baby or very young child

WORD HISTORY
from Latin *infans* meaning unable to speak

infantry

NOUN In an army, the **infantry** are soldiers who fight on foot rather than in tanks or on horses.

infatuated

ADJECTIVE If you are **infatuated** with someone, you are so much in love with them that you cannot think reasonably about them.

infect infects, infecting, infected

VERB If someone or something **infects** another person or animal, they pass a disease on to them.

infection infections

NOUN an illness caused by germs

infectious

ADJECTIVE Something that is **infectious** spreads from one person to another.
● *Measles is an infectious disease.*

infer infers, inferring, inferred

VERB If you **infer** that something is happening or is correct, you work it out from the details you already have.

inference inferences

NOUN something that you think must be true, based on the details that you already have

inferior

ADJECTIVE Something that is **inferior** is not as good as something else of a similar kind.
● *The trainers were of inferior quality.*

inferiority

NOUN **Inferiority** is a lower quality or level of importance than something else.

inferno infernos

NOUN a huge and fierce fire

infertile

ADJECTIVE **1 Infertile** soil is of poor quality and plants cannot grow well in it.
ADJECTIVE **2** A person, animal or plant that is **infertile** is unable to reproduce.

infested

ADJECTIVE If something is **infested**, it is full of pests, like insects, rats or fleas.

infinite

ADJECTIVE If something is **infinite**, it is endless and without limits.

infinitely

ADVERB very much ● *I think good health is infinitely more important than having lots of money.*

infinitive infinitives

NOUN the base form of a verb. An **infinitive** often has "to" in front of it, for example *to be* or *to see*.

infinity

NOUN a number that is larger than any other number and cannot be given an exact value

infirm

ADJECTIVE If someone is **infirm**, they are weak because they are ill or old.

infirmary infirmaries

NOUN a hospital

inflammable

ADJECTIVE An **inflammable** material burns easily.

inflammation

NOUN painful redness or swelling of a part of the body

inflatable

ADJECTIVE An **inflatable** object must be filled with air before you use it.

inflate inflates, inflating, inflated

VERB If you **inflate** something, you put air or a gas such as helium into it to make it swell.

ANTONYM: deflate

inflation

NOUN a general increase in the price of goods and services in a country

inflexible

ADJECTIVE If someone or something is **inflexible**, they cannot be bent or altered.

a
b
c
d
e
f
g
h
i
j
k
l
m
n
o
p
q
r
s
t
u
v
w
x
y
z

207

inflict inflicts, inflicting, inflicted
VERB If you **inflict** something unpleasant on someone, you make them suffer it.

influence influences, influencing, influenced
VERB If you **influence** someone or something, you have an effect on what they do or what happens.

influential
ADJECTIVE Someone who is **influential** is important and can influence people or events.

WORD HISTORY
from Latin *influentia* meaning power flowing from the stars

---

influenza
NOUN (*formal*) flu

inform informs, informing, informed
VERB If you **inform** somebody about something, you let them know about it.

informal
ADJECTIVE relaxed and casual

informally
ADVERB in a relaxed and casual way • *She was informally dressed in jeans and a T-shirt.*

information
NOUN knowledge about something • *He used the encyclopedia to find more information.*

information technology
NOUN the storage and communication of information using computers

informative
ADJECTIVE Something that is **informative** gives you information.

infrastructure infrastructures
NOUN the basic facilities such as transport, communications, power supplies and buildings, which enable a country to function properly

infuriate infuriates, infuriating, infuriated
VERB If someone or something **infuriates** you, they make you very angry.

infuriating
ADJECTIVE making you very angry

ingenious
ADJECTIVE Something that is **ingenious** is clever and involves new ideas.

ingratitude
NOUN If you show **ingratitude**, you show lack of care or thanks for something that has been done for you.

ANTONYM: gratitude

ingredient ingredients
NOUN **Ingredients** are the things that something is made from, especially in cookery.

inhabit inhabits, inhabiting, inhabite
VERB If you **inhabit** a place, you live there.

inhabitant inhabitants
NOUN If you are an **inhabitant** of a place, you live there.

inhalation
NOUN **Inhalation** is breathing in.

inhale inhales, inhaling, inhaled
VERB When you **inhale** something, you breathe it in.

ANTONYM: exhale

inherit inherits, inheriting, inherited
VERB 1 If you **inherit** money or property, yo receive it from someone who has died.
VERB 2 If you **inherit** a feature or quality fro a parent or ancestor, you are born with it.
• *Her children have inherited her love of spo*

inheritance
NOUN 1 Your **inheritance** is the money or property you get from someone who has died.
NOUN 2 the physical or mental qualities tha you get from your parents

inhospitable
ADJECTIVE 1 If you are **inhospitable**, you ar unwelcoming to people who visit you.
ADJECTIVE 2 An **inhospitable** place is an unpleasant and difficult place to live in.

inhuman
ADJECTIVE 1 not human or not behaving like human
ADJECTIVE 2 extremely cruel

initial initials
NOUN 1 one of the capital letters that begin each word of a name
ADJECTIVE 2 first or at the beginning

initiative
NOUN If you show **initiative**, you have the ability to see what needs to be done and d it, without relying on others.

inject injects, injecting, injected
VERB If a doctor or nurse **injects** you, they use a needle and syringe to put medicine into your body.

WORD HISTORY
from Latin *in* + *jacere* meaning to throw into

injure injures, injuring, injured
VERB If you **injure** someone, you hurt or harm them in some way.

injury injuries
NOUN damage to part of a person's or animal's body

injustice
NOUN If someone suffers **injustice**, they are treated unfairly.

ink
NOUN the coloured liquid used for writing or printing

inland
ADJECTIVE **1** If a place is **inland**, it is away from the coast. ● **inland** lakes
ADVERB **2** away from the coast ● *Most of the population lives* **inland**.

inlet inlets
NOUN a narrow bay or channel of water that goes inland from the sea, a lake or a river

inmate inmates
NOUN someone who lives in an institution, such as a prison

inn inns
NOUN a small, old country pub or hotel

inner
ADJECTIVE contained inside a place or object ● *The* **inner** *tube of my front tyre has a puncture.*

innings
NOUN In cricket, an **innings** is a period of time when a particular team is batting.

innocence
NOUN **Innocence** is when someone is not guilty of a crime or of doing something wrong.

ANTONYM: guilt

innocent
ADJECTIVE not guilty of a crime or of doing something wrong

ANTONYM: guilty

innocently
ADVERB **1** without intending to harm or offend anyone ● *The argument began* **innocently** *enough.*
ADVERB **2** in a way that shows you do not have much experience of bad things that can happen ● *"What's the problem?" Carl asked* **innocently**.

innovation innovations
NOUN a completely new idea, product or way of doing things

inoculate inoculates, inoculating, inoculated
VERB If a doctor or nurse **inoculates** you, they give you an injection to protect you from catching a particular disease.

inoculation
NOUN **Inoculation** is the process of giving people injections to protect them from catching particular diseases.

input inputs, inputting, input
NOUN **1** Your **input** is your contribution and what you put into something. ● *The class project requires* **input** *from everyone.*
NOUN **2** In computing, **input** is information that is fed into a computer.
VERB **3** To **input** information into a computer means to feed it in.

inquest inquests
NOUN an official inquiry to find out what caused a person's death

inquire inquires, inquired, inquiring; also spelt **enquire**
VERB If you **inquire** about something, you ask for information about it.

inquiry inquiries
NOUN **1** an official investigation
NOUN **2** a question or a request for information

inquisitive
ADJECTIVE Someone who is **inquisitive** is keen to find out about things.

insane
ADJECTIVE Someone or something **insane** is mad.

inscription inscriptions
NOUN the words that are carved or engraved on something such as a monument, gravestone or coin, or written in the front of a book

a
b
c
d
e
f
g
h
i
j
k
l
m
n
o
p
q
r
s
t
u
v
w
x
y
z

209

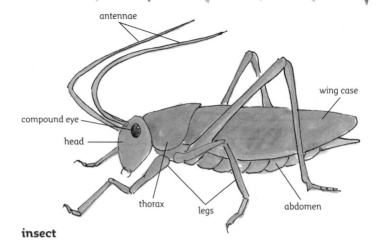

antennae

wing case

compound eye

head

thorax

legs

abdomen

insect

insect insects

NOUN a small animal with six legs and no backbone, with its skeleton on the outside. **Insects** often have wings, for example beetles, butterflies and grasshoppers.

WORD HISTORY
from Latin *insectum* meaning animal that has been cut into, because the bodies of many insects are divided into parts

insecticide insecticides

NOUN a poisonous chemical used to kill insects

insecure

ADJECTIVE **1** If you feel **insecure**, you lack confidence and feel worried.
ADJECTIVE **2** If something is **insecure**, it is not fixed properly.

insecurity insecurities

NOUN the feeling you have when you are not confident about yourself because you think that you are not good enough

inseparable

ADJECTIVE **1** If people are **inseparable**, they are always together. ● *The three of them are such good friends, they're **inseparable**.*
ADJECTIVE **2** If things are **inseparable**, they cannot be parted.

insert inserts, inserting, inserted

VERB If you **insert** an object into something, you put it inside. ● *He **inserted** the key into the lock.*

inside insides

PREPOSITION **1 Inside** means in something. ● *I waited **inside** the house.*

ANTONYM: outside

ADJECTIVE **2** describes something that is in something else ● *an **inside** pocket*

ANTONYM: outside

ADVERB **3** into a building ● *We chatted for a while before going **inside**.*

ANTONYM: outside

NOUN **4** The **inside** of something is the part that is surrounded by the main part, and is often hidden. ● *I painted the **inside** of the she*

ANTONYM: outside

PHRASE **5 Inside out** means with the inside part facing outwards. ● *Her umbrella blew **inside out**.*

PLURAL NOUN **6** Your **insides** are the parts within your body that cannot be seen.

LANGUAGE TIP
Do not use *of* after *inside* when it is a preposition. It is correct to say *I waited insi* *the shop*, not *I waited inside of the shop*.

insight insights

NOUN If you show **insight** into a problem, you show a deep and accurate understanding of it.

insignificance

NOUN the quality that something has when is small and unimportant

insignificant
ADJECTIVE small and unimportant

insist insists, insisting, insisted
VERB If you **insist** on something, you demand it forcefully. • *As it was already dark, she insisted on giving us a lift home.*

insistent
ADJECTIVE If you are **insistent**, you insist on having or doing something.

insolence
NOUN very rude behaviour that shows no respect

insolent
ADJECTIVE very rude and showing no respect

insolently
ADVERB in a very rude way that shows no respect

insoluble
ADJECTIVE 1 impossible to solve
ADJECTIVE 2 unable to dissolve

insomnia
NOUN difficulty in sleeping

inspect inspects, inspecting, inspected
VERB If you **inspect** something, you examine or check it carefully.

inspector inspectors
NOUN 1 someone in authority whose job it is to inspect things
NOUN 2 a rank of police officer

inspiration
NOUN someone or something that gives you new ideas for something • *Her experiences in China were the inspiration for this book.*

inspire inspires, inspiring, inspired
VERB If someone or something **inspires** you, they give you new ideas, confidence and enthusiasm.

install installs, installing, installed
VERB If you **install** something, you put it in place so that it is ready to be used.

installation
NOUN the process of putting something in place so that it is ready to be used

instalment instalments
NOUN 1 If you pay for something in **instalments**, you pay small amounts of money regularly over a period of time.
NOUN 2 one of the parts of a story or television series

instance instances
NOUN 1 a particular example or occurrence of something
PHRASE 2 You use **for instance** to give an example of something you are talking about. • *In some countries, for instance in Spain, many shops are closed at lunchtime.*

instant instants
NOUN 1 a moment or short period of time
ADJECTIVE 2 immediate and without delay • *The book was an instant success.*

instantly
ADVERB immediately • *His booming voice was instantly recognizable.*

instead
ADVERB If you do one thing **instead** of another, you do the first thing and not the second thing. • *They took the stairs instead of the lift.*

instinct instincts
NOUN a natural tendency to do something in a particular way • *Her instincts told her to run away as quickly as possible.*

institute institutes
NOUN an organisation set up for a purpose, such as teaching or research

institution institutions
NOUN a large, important organisation, such as a university or bank

instruct instructs, instructing, instructed
VERB 1 If you **instruct** someone to do something, you tell them to do it.
VERB 2 If someone **instructs** you in a subject or skill, they teach you about it.

instruction instructions
NOUN If you follow an **instruction**, you do what someone tells you to do.

instructor instructors
NOUN someone who teaches you how to do something • *a ski instructor*

instrument instruments
NOUN 1 a tool that is used to do a particular job
NOUN 2 an object, such as a piano or guitar, that you play to make music

instrumental
ADJECTIVE **Instrumental** music is performed by instruments and not by voices.

211

A
B
C
D
E
F
G
H
I
J
K
L
M
N
O
P
Q
R
S
T
U
V
W
X
Y
Z

212

insufficient
ADJECTIVE not enough for a particular purpose
• There is **insufficient** flour to make two cakes.

insulate insulates, insulating, insulated
VERB If you **insulate** something, you cover it with materials such as foam or plastic to stop heat or electricity passing out of it.

insulation
NOUN a thick layer of a substance that keeps something warm, especially a building

insulator insulators
NOUN a material that insulates something

insulin
NOUN a substance that controls the level of sugar in your blood

insult insults, insulting, insulted
VERB 1 If you **insult** someone, you offend them by being rude to them.
NOUN 2 a rude remark that offends someone

PRONUNCIATION TIP
The verb is pronounced in-**sult**. The noun is pronounced **in**-sult.

insurance
NOUN an amount of money paid on a regular basis to a company that, in return, will pay you money if you have an accident or need medical treatment

intact
ADJECTIVE If something is **intact**, it is complete and undamaged.

integer integers
NOUN a whole number. For example, 2 is an **integer** but 2½ is not.

integrate integrates, integrating, integrated
VERB If a person **integrates** into a group, they become a part of it.

integrity
NOUN the quality of being honest and trustworthy

intellectual
ADJECTIVE involving thought, ideas and understanding • an **intellectual** exercise, like learning French

intelligence
NOUN Your **intelligence** is your ability to understand and learn things.

intelligent
ADJECTIVE clever and able to understand things easily

intend intends, intending, intended
VERB If you **intend** to do something, you decide or plan to do it.

intense
ADJECTIVE very great in strength or amount
• **intense** heat

intensity
NOUN the strength of something such as a feeling, colour or temperature

intensive
ADJECTIVE If something is **intensive**, it involves a lot of energy or effort over a short time.

intention intentions
NOUN an idea or a plan of what you mean to do • He had every **intention** of working hard that day.

intentional
ADJECTIVE If something is **intentional**, it is done on purpose.

intentionally
ADVERB deliberately • I would never **intentionally** hurt anyone.

inter-
PREFIX You add **inter-** to a word to mean between or among two or more people or things. • **inter**-school competitions • **inter**national travel

interactive
ADJECTIVE If a computer is **interactive**, it allows two-way communication between itself and the person using it, so that information can pass in both directions.

intercept intercepts, intercepting, intercepted
VERB If you **intercept** someone or something as they move from one place to another, you stop them reaching their destination.

intercom intercoms
NOUN a device that people use to communicate with each other if they are in different rooms

interest interests, interesting, interested

NOUN **1** a thing you enjoy doing

NOUN **2 Interest** is an extra payment that you receive if you have invested money, or an extra payment that you make if you have borrowed money.

VERB **3** If something **interests** you, you want to know more about it.

interface interfaces

NOUN The **interface** of a particular piece of computing software is how it looks on screen and how easy it is to use.

interfere interferes, interfering, interfered

VERB **1** If you **interfere** in a situation, you try to influence it, although it does not concern you.

VERB **2** If you **interfere** with a plan, you get in the way of it.

interior interiors

NOUN **1** the inside part of something
• the **interior** of the building

ADJECTIVE **2** inside • the **interior** walls

interjection interjections

NOUN a word or phrase spoken suddenly to expresses an emotion, such as surprise, excitement or anger. For example, *Help!* is an **interjection**.

intermediate

ADJECTIVE An **intermediate** stage occurs in the middle, between two others. • *This dance class is for beginners. The next one is at **intermediate** level.*

internal

ADJECTIVE happening on, or part of, the inside of something • *Your lungs are **internal** organs.*

international

ADJECTIVE involving different countries • *This is an important **international** match.*

internet; also spelt **Internet**

NOUN a worldwide system where people communicate using computers

interpret interprets, interpreting, interpreted

VERB **1** If you **interpret** something, you decide what it means. • *I tried to **interpret** his painting.*

VERB **2** If you **interpret** what someone is saying, you immediately translate it into another language.

interpretation interpretations

NOUN Your **interpretation** of something is what you think it means.

interpreter interpreters

NOUN someone who translates what another person is saying into a different language

interrogate interrogates, interrogating, interrogated

VERB If you **interrogate** someone, you ask them a lot of questions in order to get information from them.

interrogation interrogations

NOUN the process of asking someone a lot of questions in order to get information from them

interrogator interrogators

NOUN someone who asks another person a lot of questions in order to get information from them

interrupt interrupts, interrupting, interrupted

VERB If you **interrupt** someone, you start talking while they are talking.

intersect intersects, intersecting, intersected

VERB When two roads **intersect**, they cross each other.

intersection intersections

NOUN **1** a point where two roads cross over each other

NOUN **2** the point where lines, arcs or sets cross each other

interval intervals

NOUN a short break during a play, concert or performance

intervene intervenes, intervening, intervened

VERB If you **intervene** in a situation, you step in, usually to sort out an argument or fight.

intervention

NOUN **Intervention** is when you do something to help stop an argument or fight.

interview interviews, interviewing, interviewed

NOUN **1** a formal meeting where someone is asked questions

VERB **2** When someone **interviews** you, they ask you questions, usually in order to find out if you are suitable for something in particular.

a
b
c
d
e
f
g
h
i
j
k
l
m
n
o
p
q
r
s
t
u
v
w
x
y
z

213

intestinal

ADJECTIVE involving the long tube in your body that carries food from your stomach

intestine intestines

NOUN the part of your digestive system that carries food from your stomach. Your **intestines** are long tubes folded up inside your abdomen.

→ Have a look at the illustrations for **organ** and **stomach**

intimate

ADJECTIVE **1** If you are **intimate** with someone, you are very friendly with them.
ADJECTIVE **2 Intimate** details or thoughts are personal or private.

intimidate intimidates, intimidating, intimidated

VERB If you **intimidate** someone, you frighten them in a threatening way.

WORD HISTORY
from Latin *timidus* meaning fearful

intimidating

ADJECTIVE making you feel frightened

into

PREPOSITION **1** If you go **into** something, you go inside it. ● *Come into the house.*
PREPOSITION **2** If you bump or crash **into** something, you bump or crash against it.

intrepid

ADJECTIVE brave and fearless

intricate

ADJECTIVE detailed and complicated

intrigue intrigues, intriguing, intrigued

VERB If something **intrigues** you, you are fascinated by it and curious about it.

introduce introduces, introducing, introduced

VERB **1** If you **introduce** one person to another, you tell them each other's name so that they can get to know each other.
VERB **2** If you **introduce** someone to something, they learn about it for the first time from you. ● *My friend **introduced** me to water-skiing on holiday.*

introduction introductions

NOUN a piece of writing at the beginning of a book, that tells you what the book is about

introductory

ADJECTIVE giving information that tells you what a book or speech is about

intrude intrudes, intruding, intruded

VERB If you **intrude** on someone or something, you disturb them.

intruder intruders

NOUN a person who forces their way into someone else's property without their consent ● *The security guard caught an **intruder** last night.*

intrusion intrusions

NOUN someone or something that disturbs yo

intrusive

ADJECTIVE disturbing someone

intuition intuitions

NOUN the ability to know about something without thinking about it or being able to explain it

intuitive

ADJECTIVE based on a feeling rather than on facts or knowledge ● *She has an **intuitive** understanding of human nature.*

intuitively

ADVERB in a way that is based on a feeling rather than on facts or knowledge

Inuit Inuits

NOUN a member of a group of people who live in North America or Greenland, and who lived there before European settlers arrived

invade invades, invading, invaded

VERB If an army **invades** a country, it enter it by force.

invalid invalids

NOUN **1** someone who is so ill that they nee to be looked after by someone else
ADJECTIVE **2** If something is **invalid**, it canno be accepted because there is something wrong with it. ● *Your ticket is **invalid** for th train service.*

PRONUNCIATION TIP
The noun is pronounced **in**-va-lid. The adjective is pronounced in-**val**-id.

invaluable

ADJECTIVE extremely useful

invasion invasions

NOUN the forceful entering or attacking of a place ● *At the end of the match, there was an **invasion** of the pitch by fans.*

invent invents, inventing, invented
VERB 1 If you **invent** something, you are the first person to think of it or make it.
VERB 2 If you **invent** a story or an excuse, you make it up.

invention inventions
NOUN 1 something that has been designed and made for the first time
NOUN 2 **Invention** the process of designing and making something for the first time.
NOUN 3 an excuse or explanation that is not true

inventive
ADJECTIVE good at thinking of new and interesting ideas

inventiveness
NOUN **Inventiveness** is the ability to think of new and different ideas.

inventor inventors
NOUN someone who is the first person to think of or make something

inverse
NOUN (*formal*) In mathematics, if you turn something upside down or back to front, you have its **inverse**. • The **inverse** of 23 is 32.

invert inverts, inverting, inverted
VERB 1 If you **invert** something, you turn it upside down.
VERB 2 If you **invert** a fraction, the top number changes places with the bottom number.

invertebrate invertebrates
NOUN an animal without a backbone

inverted commas
NOUN punctuation marks (" ") are used to show where speech begins and ends
• "Good morning!" she cried.

invest invests, investing, invested
VERB If you **invest** money in something, you try to increase its value, for example by putting it into a bank or building society so that it will gain interest.

investigate investigates, investigating, investigated
VERB If someone **investigates** something, they try to find out all the facts about it.
• Police are still **investigating** the accident.

SYNONYMS: examine, look into, study

investigation investigations
NOUN If you conduct an **investigation** into something, you examine it carefully and try to find out the facts about it.
• The police have begun an **investigation** into the accident.

investigator investigators
NOUN someone who tries to find out all the facts about something

investment investments
NOUN 1 **Investment** is the process of putting money into a bank or business in order to make some money.
NOUN 2 an amount of money that you put into a bank or business in order to make some money
NOUN 3 something you buy that will be very useful • The city travel card is a good **investment**.

investor investors
NOUN someone who puts money into a bank or business in order to make some money

invincible
ADJECTIVE If something is **invincible**, it cannot be defeated.

invisibility
NOUN the quality that something has when you cannot see it

invisible
ADJECTIVE If something is **invisible**, you cannot see it.

invitation invitations
NOUN a request for someone to come to something, such as a party

invite invites, inviting, invited
VERB If you **invite** someone to an event, you ask them to come to it.

involve involves, involving, involved
VERB 1 If a situation or activity **involves** something, that thing is a necessary part of it. • Being president **involves** a lot of responsibility.
VERB 2 If you **involve** yourself in something, you take part in it. • I'm **involved** in the production of the school play.

ir-
PREFIX a variation of in-, meaning not. For example, **ir**relevant means not relevant, and **ir**replaceable means not replaceable.

irate
ADJECTIVE very angry

215

iris irises
NOUN the coloured part of your eye
→ Have a look at the illustration for **eye**

WORD HISTORY
from Greek *iris* meaning rainbow or coloured circle

iron irons, ironing, ironed
NOUN **1** a hard, dark metal used to make steel
NOUN **2** an appliance you heat up and press on clothes to remove creases
VERB **3** If you **iron** clothes, you use a hot iron to remove creases from them.

ironic
ADJECTIVE using words, often in a humorous way, to say the opposite of what you really mean

ironing
NOUN the work of using a hot iron to remove creases from clothes

irony
NOUN When you use **irony**, you use words, often in a humorous way, to say the opposite of what you really mean.

irrational
ADJECTIVE If you act in an **irrational** way, you show no reason or logic in what you do.

irregular
ADJECTIVE **1** Something that is **irregular** is not smooth or straight, or does not make a regular pattern.
ADJECTIVE **2 Irregular** verbs do not follow the usual rules.

irrelevance
NOUN something that has nothing to do with what is being said or discussed

irrelevant
ADJECTIVE If something is **irrelevant**, it has nothing to do with what is being said or discussed.

irresistible
ADJECTIVE **1** If something is **irresistible**, it cannot be controlled. • *I had an irresistible urge to laugh.*
ADJECTIVE **2** If someone is **irresistible**, they are very attractive.

irresponsible
ADJECTIVE If you do something in an **irresponsible** way, you act thoughtlessly and carelessly.

SYNONYMS: careless, thoughtless

irreversible
ADJECTIVE If something is **irreversible**, it cannot be reversed or changed back to the way it was before.

irrigate irrigates, irrigating, irrigated
VERB To **irrigate** land is to supply it with water brought through pipes or ditches.
• *In hot, dry countries the land is irrigated.*

WORD HISTORY
from Latin *rigare* meaning to moisten

irrigation
NOUN the process of supplying land with water through pipes or ditches

irritable
ADJECTIVE If you are **irritable**, you are easily annoyed.

irritate irritates, irritating, irritated
VERB If something **irritates** you, it annoys you.

irritation
NOUN the feeling of being annoyed

is
VERB a present tense of **be**

Islam
NOUN the Muslim religion, which teaches that there is only one God, Allah, and Mohammed is his prophet

island islands
NOUN a piece of land surrounded by water

isle isles
NOUN a literary word for an island

isn't
VERB a contraction of *is not*

isolate isolates, isolating, isolated
VERB **1** If you **isolate** yourself, you separate yourself from other people. • *I isolated myself in my room.*
VERB **2** To **isolate** a sick person or animal means to keep them away from others so that the disease does not spread.

isosceles

ADJECTIVE An **isosceles** triangle has two sides of the same length and two equal angles.

ISP **ISPs**

NOUN a business that provides access to the internet. **ISP** is an abbreviation for *internet service provider*.

issue **issues**

NOUN **1** an important subject that people are talking about • The **issue** of homeless people is important to many people.
NOUN **2** a particular newspaper or magazine • this week's **issue** of the local paper

it

PRONOUN **1** used to refer to something that has already been mentioned. **It** can also refer to babies or other animals whose gender is not known. • I like that dog. **It** is very friendly.
PRONOUN **2** You use **it** to talk about the weather, time or date. • **It**'s been raining all day.

IT

NOUN an abbreviation of *Information Technology*

italics

PLURAL NOUN letters printed in a particular sloping way. They are often used for emphasis. • This writing is in **italics**.

itch **itches, itching, itched**

VERB **1** When a part of your body **itches**, you have an unpleasant feeling that makes you want to scratch it.
NOUN **2** an unpleasant feeling on your skin that makes you want to scratch it

item **items**

NOUN one of a collection or list of objects • Milk is the most important **item** on my shopping list.

itinerary **itineraries**

NOUN The **itinerary** of a journey is a detailed plan of where to go and what to see along the route.

it's

a contraction of *it is* or *it has*

LANGUAGE TIP
Do not confuse *it's* with *its*.

---

its

ADJECTIVE **Its** is used to refer to something belonging to things, children or animals that have already been mentioned. • The cat won't eat. **Its** bowl needs cleaning.

LANGUAGE TIP
Do not confuse *its* with *it's*.

I've

a contraction of *I have*

ivory

NOUN **1** the valuable, creamy-white bone that forms the tusk of an elephant. It is used to make ornaments.
NOUN **2** a creamy-white colour
ADJECTIVE **3** having a creamy-white colour

ivy

NOUN an evergreen plant that creeps along the ground and up walls

a
b
c
d
e
f
g
h
i
j
k
l
m
n
o
p
q
r
s
t
u
v
w
x
y
z

jab jabs, jabbing, jabbed

VERB **1** If you **jab** something, you poke at it roughly.

NOUN **2** a sharp, sudden poke • *a jab in the ribs*

NOUN **3** (*informal*) an injection • *a measles jab*

jack jacks

NOUN **1** a piece of equipment for lifting heavy objects, especially for lifting a car when changing a wheel

NOUN **2** In a pack of cards, a **jack** is a card whose value is between a ten and a queen.

jackal jackals

NOUN a wild animal related to the dog

jacket jackets

NOUN **1** a short coat

NOUN **2** the paper cover of a book

jackpot jackpots

NOUN the top prize in a gambling game • *He was excited to hear he had won the jackpot in the lottery.*

jagged

ADJECTIVE A **jagged** rock has a rough, uneven shape with sharp edges.

jail jails, jailing, jailed; also spelt gaol

NOUN **1** a building where people convicted of a crime are locked up

VERB **2** To **jail** someone means to lock them up in a jail.

jam jams, jamming, jammed

NOUN **1** a food made by boiling fruit with sugar

NOUN **2** a situation where there are so many people or things that it is difficult to move • *There is often a traffic jam at that junction.*

VERB **3** If you **jam** something into a place, you squeeze it in. • *He jammed his clothes into the suitcase.*

VERB **4** If you **jam** something, or if it **jams**, it becomes stuck. • *The coin was jammed in the slot.*

January

NOUN the first month of the year. **January** has 31 days.

jar jars, jarring, jarred

NOUN **1** a glass container used for storing food

VERB **2** If something **jars**, you find it unpleasant or annoying.

jargon

NOUN language containing lots of technical words, used by particular groups of people • *Our doctor often uses jargon.*

jaundice

NOUN an illness of the liver, where the skin and the whites of the eyes become yellow

javelin javelins

NOUN a long spear that is thrown in sports competitions

jaw jaws

NOUN **1** the bone in which teeth are set

NOUN **2** the mouth and teeth of a person or animal

jazz

NOUN a style of popular music with a strong rhythm

jealous

ADJECTIVE If you are **jealous**, you feel envious of others, wanting to have what they have or wanting to be like them.

jealously

ADVERB in a way that shows you feel envious of someone else and want to have what they have or want to be like them

jealousy

NOUN the feeling of being unhappy because you want to have what someone else has or because you want to be like them

jeans

PLURAL NOUN cotton trousers, often made of denim

Jeep Jeeps

NOUN (trademark) a four-wheeled motor vehicle designed for driving over rough ground

jeer jeers, jeering, jeered

VERB **1** If you **jeer** at someone, you insult them in a loud, unpleasant way.

NOUN **2** **Jeers** are rude and insulting remarks.

jelly jellies
NOUN **1** a clear, sweet food eaten as a dessert
NOUN **2** a type of clear, set jam ● *I like mint jelly with lamb.*

jellyfish jellyfishes
NOUN a sea animal with a clear, soft body and tentacles that may sting

jerk jerks, jerking, jerked
VERB **1** If you **jerk** something, you give it a sudden, sharp pull.
VERB **2** If something **jerks**, it moves suddenly and sharply.

jersey jerseys
NOUN a knitted garment for the upper half of the body

jet jets
NOUN **1** an aeroplane that can fly very fast
NOUN **2** a rush of air, steam or liquid that is forced out under pressure

jetty jetties
NOUN a wide stone wall or wooden platform at the edge of the sea or a river, where boats can be moored

Jew Jews
NOUN a person who practises the religion of Judaism or who is of Hebrew descent

jewel jewels
NOUN a precious stone, often used to decorate valuable items such as rings or necklaces

jewelled
ADJECTIVE decorated with precious stones

jeweller jewellers
NOUN a person who makes or sells jewellery

jewellery
NOUN the ornaments that people wear, like rings and necklaces

Jewish
ADJECTIVE to do with the religion of Judaism or Hebrew people ● *the Jewish festival of Hanukah*

jigsaw jigsaws
NOUN a puzzle that is made up of odd-shaped pieces that must be fitted together to make a picture

jingle jingles
NOUN **1** a short, catchy phrase or rhyme with music, used to advertise something on radio or television
NOUN **2** a gentle ringing sound

job jobs
NOUN **1** the work that someone does to earn money
NOUN **2** anything that has to be done

jockey jockeys
NOUN someone who rides a horse in a race

joey joeys
NOUN a young kangaroo

jog jogs, jogging, jogged
VERB **1** If you **jog**, you run slowly, often for exercise.
VERB **2** If you **jog** something, you knock it slightly so that it shakes or moves. ● *My pen slipped when he jogged my arm.*

jogger joggers
NOUN someone who runs slowly for exercise

jogging
NOUN the activity of running slowly

join joins, joining, joined
VERB **1** If you **join** a club, you become a member of it.
VERB **2** When two things **join**, or when one thing **joins** another, they come together. ● *The two streams join and form a river.*

SYNONYMS: connect, link

join in
VERB If you **join in** an activity, you take part in it.

joiner joiners
NOUN a person who makes wooden window frames, doors and furniture

joint joints
ADJECTIVE **1** shared by or belonging to two or more people ● *The project was a joint effort.*
NOUN **2** a part of your body, such as your elbow or knee, where two bones meet and are able to move together

joke jokes, joking, joked
NOUN **1** something that you say to make people laugh
VERB **2** If you **joke**, you say something amusing or tell a funny story.

jolly jollier, jolliest
ADJECTIVE If you are **jolly**, you are happy and cheerful.

jolt jolts, jolting, jolted

VERB **1** If something **jolts**, it moves or shakes roughly and violently. • *The bus **jolted** along the bumpy road.*

VERB **2** If something or someone **jolts** you, they bump into you clumsily.

NOUN **3** a sudden, jerky movement

NOUN **4** an unpleasant shock or surprise

jostle jostles, jostling, jostled

VERB If people or animals **jostle**, they push and bump into each other roughly, usually because they are in a crowd.

jot jots, jotting, jotted

VERB If you **jot** something down, you write a quick, brief note.

journal journals

NOUN **1** a magazine that deals with a particular interest

NOUN **2** a diary where you write what happens each day

journalist journalists

NOUN a person whose job is to gather news and write about it for a newspaper or magazine, or present it on television or radio

journey journeys

NOUN the act of travelling from one place to another

joy joys

NOUN **1** a feeling of great happiness or pleasure

NOUN **2** something that makes you happy or gives you pleasure • *It was a **joy** to see my friend again.*

joystick joysticks

NOUN **1** a lever in a plane that the pilot uses to control height and direction

NOUN **2** a lever that controls the cursor on a computer screen, especially in computer games

jubilee jubilees

NOUN a special anniversary of an event such as a coronation • *Queen Elizabeth's Golden **Jubilee** was in 2002.*

WORD HISTORY

from Hebrew *yobhel* meaning ram's horn, blown during festivals and celebrations to mark the freedom of Hebrew slaves each 50th year, known as the jubilee

Judaic

ADJECTIVE to do with the religion of the Jewish people

Judaism

NOUN the religion of the Jewish people. It is based on a belief in one God, and draws its laws from the Old Testament.

judge judges, judging, judged

NOUN **1** the person in a law court who decides how criminals should be punished according to the law

NOUN **2** the person who chooses the winner of a competition

VERB **3** If a person **judges** someone or something, they act as a judge.

VERB **4** If you **judge** someone or something, you decide what they are like.

judgment judgments; also spelt **judgement**

NOUN an opinion that you have after thinking carefully about something

judo

NOUN a sport in which two people try to force each other to the ground using special throwing techniques. It originated in Japan as a form of self-defence.

WORD HISTORY

from Japanese *ju do* meaning gentleness art

jug jugs

NOUN a container with a handle and a lip, used for holding and pouring liquids

juggernaut juggernauts

NOUN a large, heavy lorry

WORD HISTORY

from Hindi *Jagannath*, the name of a huge idol of the god Krishna, which is wheeled through the streets of Puri in India every year

juggle juggles, juggling, juggled

VERB When someone **juggles** they throw different objects into the air, keeping more than one object in the air at the same time without dropping them.

juice juices

NOUN the liquid that can be obtained from fruit, vegetables and other food

• *orange **juice***

juicy juicier, juiciest
ADJECTIVE having a great deal of juice • *The orange was very **juicy***.

July
NOUN the seventh month of the year. **July** has 31 days.

jumble jumbles, jumbling, jumbled
NOUN **1** an untidy muddle of things
NOUN **2** articles for a **jumble** sale
VERB **3** If you **jumble** things, you mix them up untidily.

jumble sale jumble sales
NOUN an event where second-hand items are sold to raise money cheaply, often for charity

jump jumps, jumping, jumped
VERB **1** When you **jump**, you spring off the ground using the muscles in your legs.
VERB **2** If someone **jumps**, they make a sudden, sharp movement because they are surprised.

jumper jumpers
NOUN a warm piece of clothing that covers the top part of your body

junction junctions
NOUN a place where roads or railway lines meet or cross

June
NOUN the sixth month of the year. **June** has 30 days.

jungle jungles
NOUN a dense, tropical forest where many trees and other plants grow close together

WORD HISTORY
from Hindi *jangal* meaning wasteland

junior
ADJECTIVE **1** A **junior** official or employee holds a lower position in an organisation. • *She will be a **junior** doctor after finishing her training.*
ADJECTIVE **2** younger • *He is the **junior** of the two brothers.*

junk junks
NOUN **1** old, unwanted or worthless things that are sold cheaply or thrown away
NOUN **2** a Chinese sailing boat that has a flat bottom and wide sails

junk food
NOUN food that is easy and quick to prepare, or bought ready to eat, but is not always very good for you

jury juries
NOUN a group of people in a court of law who are chosen to listen to the facts about a crime and then decide whether the accused person is guilty or not

just
ADJECTIVE **1** Someone who is **just** is fair.
ADVERB **2** If something has **just** happened, it happened a very short time ago.
ADVERB **3** If you **just** do something, you almost don't do it. • *He **just** managed to climb the fence.*
ADVERB **4** If something is **just** what you want, it is exactly what you want.

justice
NOUN **1** fairness in the way that people are treated
NOUN **2** the system of laws created by a community

justifiable
ADJECTIVE acceptable and done for good reasons

justification justifications
NOUN a good reason for doing something • *There can be no **justification** for this level of violence.*

justify justifies, justifying, justified
VERB **1** If you **justify** what you are doing or saying, you prove or explain why it is reasonable or necessary.
VERB **2** If you **justify** a piece of text, you change the spaces between the words so that each line of text is exactly the same length.

jut juts, jutting, jutted
VERB If something **juts** out, it sticks out beyond a surface or an edge. • *The pier **jutted** out into the sea.*

juvenile juveniles
ADJECTIVE **1** suitable for or to do with young people
ADJECTIVE **2** childish and rather silly
NOUN **3** a young person not old enough to be considered an adult

a
b
c
d
e
f
g
h
i
j
k
l
m
n
o
p
q
r
s
t
u
v
w
x
y
z

K k

A
B
C
D
E
F
G
H
I
J
K
L
M
N
O
P
Q
R
S
T
U
V
W
X
Y
Z

222

kaleidoscope kaleidoscopes

NOUN a toy made of a tube with a hole at one end. When you look through the hole and twist the other end of the tube, you can see a changing pattern of colours.

kangaroo kangaroos

NOUN a large, Australian marsupial with very strong back legs that it uses for jumping

karate

NOUN a sport in which people fight each other using only their hands, elbows, feet and legs

---
WORD HISTORY
from Japanese *kara* + *te* meaning empty hand
---

kayak kayaks

NOUN a covered canoe with a small opening for the person sitting in it, originally used by Inuit people

kebab kebabs

NOUN pieces of meat or vegetable grilled on a stick

WORD HISTORY
from Arabic *kabab* meaning roast meat
---

keel keels

NOUN a long piece of wood or steel along the bottom of a boat

→ Have a look at the illustration for **ship**

keen keener, keenest

ADJECTIVE **1** If you are **keen** to do something, or for something to happen, you want very much to do it or for it to happen. • *I was **keen** to meet my cousins from Australia.*
ADJECTIVE **2** If you are **keen** on something or someone, you are fond of them or attracted to them.
ADJECTIVE **3** If your senses are **keen**, you are able to see, hear, taste and smell things very clearly or strongly.

keep keeps, keeping, kept

VERB **1** If you **keep** something, you have it and don't give it away. • *I will **keep** this book forever.*
VERB **2** If you **keep** an animal, you look after it. • *He **keeps** rabbits.*
VERB **3** If you **keep** something somewhere, you store it there. • *I **keep** my bicycle in the garage.*
VERB **4** If you **keep** doing something, you do it again and again.
VERB **5** If something **keeps** you a certain way, you stay that way because of it. • *The duvet **keeps** me warm.*
VERB **6** If you **keep** a promise, you do what you have said you will do.
VERB **7** If you **keep** a secret, you do not tell it to anyone else.
NOUN **8** the main tower inside the walls of a castle

→ Have a look at the illustration for **castle**

keeper keepers

NOUN **1** a person whose job is to look after the animals in a zoo
NOUN **2** a goalkeeper in soccer or hockey
• *The **keeper** managed to stop the ball and save the penalty.*

kennel kennels

NOUN **1** a small hut for a dog to sleep in
NOUN **2** A **kennels** is a place where dogs are bred, trained or looked after .

kept

VERB the past tense and past participle of **keep**

kerb kerbs

NOUN the raised edge of a pavement, that separates it from the road • *You must look both ways for traffic before stepping off the **kerb**.*

kernel kernels

NOUN the part of a nut that is inside the shell

kestrel kestrels

NOUN a type of small hawk

ketchup

NOUN a cold sauce, usually made from tomatoes

kettle kettles

NOUN a covered container with a spout, in which you boil water

key **keys**

NOUN **1** a specially shaped piece of metal that fits in a lock, and is turned in order to open the lock

NOUN **2** The **keys** on a piano or a computer are the buttons that you press in order to operate it.

ADJECTIVE **3 Key** words or sentences are the important ones in a piece of text.

NOUN **4** information arranged in a way that can be used to identify animals, plants and materials. You can use a **key** to help you name an unknown animal, plant or material.

keyboard **keyboards**

NOUN a set of keys on a phone, computer or piano

→ Have a look at the illustration for **computer**

keyhole **keyholes**

NOUN the hole in a lock where you put a key

kg

an abbreviation for *kilogram*

khaki

NOUN **1** a yellowish-brown colour

ADJECTIVE **2** having a yellowish-brown colour. Soldiers' uniforms are often made of **khaki** material.

WORD HISTORY
from Urdu *kaki* meaning dusty

kick **kicks, kicking, kicked**

VERB **1** If you **kick** someone or something, you hit them with your foot.

NOUN **2** If you give something a **kick**, you hit it with your foot.

NOUN **3** (*informal*) If you get a **kick** out of something, you enjoy it very much.

kick off

VERB When a soccer or rugby team **kicks off**, they begin playing.

kid **kids, kidding, kidded**

NOUN **1** (*informal*) a child

NOUN **2** a young goat

VERB **3** If you **kid** someone, you tease them and try to make them believe something that isn't true.

SYNONYM: tease

kidnap **kidnaps, kidnapping, kidnapped**

VERB If someone **kidnaps** someone else, they take them away by force and demand something in exchange for returning them.

WORD HISTORY
from *kid* + *nap* meaning child stealing; in the 17th century children were kidnapped to work on American plantations

kidney **kidneys**

NOUN one of the two organs in your body that remove waste products from your blood

→ Have a look at the illustration for **organ**

kill **kills, killing, killed**

VERB If someone **kills** a person, animal or plant, they make them die.

kiln **kilns**

NOUN an oven for baking china or pottery until it becomes hard and dry

kilo **kilos**

NOUN a kilogram

kilogram **kilograms**

NOUN a unit of mass and weight (kg) equal to 1000 grams

kilohertz

NOUN a unit of measurement of radio waves (kHz) equal to 1000 hertz

kilometre **kilometres**

NOUN a unit of distance (km) equal to 1000 metres

kilowatt **kilowatts**

NOUN a unit of power (kW) equal to 1000 watts

kilt **kilts**

NOUN a tartan skirt worn by men as part of Scottish Highland dress

kimono **kimonos**

NOUN a long, loose garment with wide sleeves and a sash, worn in Japan

kin

PLURAL NOUN Your **kin** are your relatives.

kind **kinder, kindest; kinds**

ADJECTIVE **1** Someone who is **kind** behaves in a caring and helpful way towards other people.

SYNONYM: considerate

NOUN **2** a particular thing of the same type as other things • *I do not like this **kind** of bread.*

SYNONYMS: sort, class

a b c d e f g h i j k l m n o p q r s t u v w x y z

223

kindly

ADVERB **1** in a way that shows you are kind
• Danny has **kindly** offered to help.
ADJECTIVE **2** a word that means **kind**, used in stories • *a **kindly** old lady*

kindness

NOUN the quality that someone has when they are kind

king kings

NOUN a man who is the head of state in a country, and who inherited his position from his parents

kingdom kingdoms

NOUN a country that is governed by a king or queen

kingfisher kingfishers

NOUN a brightly-coloured bird that lives near water and feeds on fish

kiosk kiosks

NOUN a small shop or hut where you can buy newspapers, snacks, and sweets

kipper kippers

NOUN a herring that has been dried in smoke to preserve it and give it a special taste

kiss kisses, kissing, kissed

VERB **1** When you **kiss** someone, you touch them with your lips in order to show your affection.
NOUN **2** When you give someone a **kiss**, you kiss them.

kit kits

NOUN **1** a collection of equipment and clothing that you use for a sport or other activity • *football **kit***
NOUN **2** a set of parts that you fit together to make something • *I got a model aeroplane **kit** for my birthday.*

kitchen kitchens

NOUN a room used for cooking and preparing food

kite kites

NOUN **1** a light frame covered with paper or cloth, that you fly in the air at the end of a long string

NOUN **2** a plane shape like a diamond, with two pairs of equal sides and no right angles

kitten kittens

NOUN a very young cat

kiwi kiwi or kiwis

NOUN **1** a type of bird found in New Zealand. **Kiwis** cannot fly.
NOUN **2** (*informal*) Someone who comes from New Zealand is called a **kiwi**.

WORD HISTORY
A Maori word

kiwi fruit kiwi fruits

NOUN a fruit with a brown, hairy skin and green flesh

km

an abbreviation for *kilometre*

knack

NOUN an ability to do something easily

knead kneads, kneading, kneaded

VERB If you **knead** dough, you press it and squeeze it with your hands before baking it.

knee knees

NOUN the joint in your leg between your ankle and your hip

kneel kneels, kneeling, knelt

VERB When you **kneel**, or **kneel down**, you bend your legs and lower your body so that one or both knees are touching the ground.

knew

VERB the past tense of **know**

knickers

PLURAL NOUN underpants worn by women and girls

knife knives
NOUN a sharp, metal tool used for cutting things

knight knights, knighting, knighted
NOUN **1** In medieval times, a **knight** was a nobleman who served his king or lord in battle. • *King Arthur and the **Knights** of the Round Table*
VERB **2** If a king or queen **knights** a man, they give him the title *Sir* before his name.

WORD HISTORY
from Old English *cniht* meaning servant

knit knits, knitting, knitted
VERB If you **knit** a piece of clothing, you make it from wool, using knitting needles or a knitting machine.

knob knobs
NOUN a round handle or switch on doors, furniture and machinery

knock knocks, knocking, knocked
VERB **1** If you **knock** on something, you hit it hard with your hand to make a noise. • *I **knocked** on the door when I arrived.*
VERB **2** If you **knock** against something, you bump into it.

knocker knockers
NOUN a metal lever attached to a door, that you use to knock on the door

knot knots, knotting, knotted
NOUN **1** a fastening made by passing one end of a piece of string or fabric through a loop and pulling it tight • *The **knot** in my laces was so tight that I could not undo it.*
NOUN **2** a hard, round spot on a piece of wood, where a branch grew on the tree
NOUN **3** a unit for measuring the speed of ships and aircraft
VERB **4** If you **knot** a piece of string, you tie a knot in it.

know knows, knowing, knew, known
VERB **1** If you **know** something, you have it clearly in your mind and you do not need to learn it. • *I **know** how to swim.*
VERB **2** If you **know** a person, place or thing, you are familiar with them. • *I've **known** him for five years.*

knowledge
NOUN all the information and facts that you know • *general **knowledge***

knuckle knuckles
NOUN one of the joints in your fingers

koala koalas
NOUN an Australian marsupial with grey fur and small, tufted ears. **Koalas** live in trees and eat eucalyptus leaves.

Koran or **Qur'an**
NOUN the holy book of Islam

WORD HISTORY
from Arabic *kara'a* meaning to read

kosher
ADJECTIVE **Kosher** food has been specially prepared to be eaten according to Jewish law.

a
b
c
d
e
f
g
h
i
j
k
l
m
n
o
p
q
r
s
t
u
v
w
x
y
z

l

an abbreviation for *litre*

label labels, labelling, labelled

NOUN **1** a piece of paper or plastic attached to something and giving information about it ● *The **label** on the bottle told him when to have his medicine.*

VERB **2** If you **label** something, you put a label on it.

laboratory laboratories

NOUN a place where scientific experiments are carried out

labour

NOUN **1** hard work

NOUN **2** In Britain, **Labour,** or the **Labour** Party, is one of the main political parties.

Labrador Labradors

NOUN a large dog with short black, golden or chocolate brown hair

labyrinth labyrinths

NOUN a complicated series of paths or passages that are difficult to find your way around

lace laces, lacing, laced

NOUN **1** a fine, decorated cloth, with a pattern of many holes in it

NOUN **2** one of the thin pieces of material that are used to fasten shoes

VERB **3** When you **lace** up your shoes, you fasten them by tying their laces.

lack lacks, lacking, lacked

NOUN **1** If there is a **lack** of something, there is not enough of it or there is none of it. ● *Despite his **lack** of training, he won the race.*

VERB **2** If someone or something **lacks** something, they do not have it.

lacquer lacquers

NOUN thin, clear paint that you put on wood to protect it and make it shiny

lactic acid

NOUN a type of acid that is found in sour milk and is also produced by your muscles when you have been exercising a lot

lactose

NOUN a type of sugar which is found in milk and which is sometimes added to food

ladder ladders

NOUN a wooden or metal frame consisting of two long poles with short bars in between. **Ladders** are used for climbing up and down things.

ladle ladles

NOUN a long-handled spoon with a deep, round bowl, which you use to serve soup

lady ladies

NOUN **1** a polite word for woman

NOUN **2** In Britain, **Lady** is the title of the wife of a knight or a lord.

ladybird ladybirds

NOUN a small, flying beetle with a round body, usually red, patterned with black spots

lag lags, lagging, lagged

VERB **1** If a person or a thing **lags** behind, they make slower progress than other people or other things and do not keep up. ● *Don't **lag** behind, or you'll get lost!*

VERB **2** If you **lag** pipes or water tanks, you cover them with insulating material to stop heat escaping and prevent freezing.

lager lagers

NOUN a kind of light beer

lagoon lagoons

NOUN an area of water separated from the sea by reefs or sand

laid

VERB the past tense of **lay**

lain

VERB the past participle of some meanings of *lie* ● *It must have **lain** there for days.*

lair lairs

NOUN a place where a wild animal lives

lake lakes

NOUN a large area of fresh water surrounded by land

lamb lambs

NOUN **1** a young sheep

NOUN **2** the meat from a lamb

lame
ADJECTIVE **1** Someone who is **lame** has an injured leg and cannot walk easily.
ADJECTIVE **2** A **lame** excuse is unconvincing.

lamely
ADVERB in a way that does not seem enthusiastic or convincing

lameness
NOUN **Lameness** is when a person or animal has an injured leg and cannot walk easily.

lamp lamps
NOUN a device that produces light • *Please turn on the table **lamp** now that it is getting dark.*

lamppost lampposts
NOUN a tall column in a street, with a lamp at the top

lance lances
NOUN a long spear that was used in the past by soldiers on horseback

land lands, landing, landed
NOUN **1** an area of ground • *We camped on the **land** surrounding the castle.*
NOUN **2** the parts of the Earth's surface that are not covered by water
VERB **3** When someone or something **lands** somewhere, they reach the ground after moving through the air.
VERB **4** When you **land** somewhere on a plane or a ship, you arrive there.

landing landings
NOUN the flat area at the top of a flight of stairs in a building

landlady landladies
NOUN a woman who owns a house or small hotel and who lets rooms to people

landline landlines
NOUN A **landline** is the telephone connection that comes into a building using cables, rather than a mobile phone connection.

landlord landlords
NOUN **1** a man who owns a house or small hotel and who lets rooms to people
NOUN **2** a person who looks after a public house
NOUN **3** someone who owns a large amount of land or houses and lets some of it out in return for rent

landmark landmarks
NOUN a noticeable feature in a landscape, that you can use to check your position
• *The tower on the hill is a local **landmark**.*

landscape landscapes
NOUN everything you can see when you look across an area of land

lane lanes
NOUN **1** a narrow road, especially in the country
NOUN **2** one of the parallel strips into which a road, a race track or a swimming pool is divided

language languages
NOUN a system of words used by a particular group of people to communicate with each other

lantern lanterns
NOUN a lamp in a metal frame with glass sides

lap laps, lapping, lapped
NOUN **1** the flat area formed by your thighs when you are sitting down
NOUN **2** one circuit of a running track or racecourse
VERB **3** When water **laps** against something, it gently moves against it in little waves.
VERB **4** When an animal **laps** a drink, it uses its tongue to flick the liquid into its mouth.

lapel lapels
NOUN the part of a collar that folds back over the front of a jacket or coat

lapse lapses, lapsing, lapsed
NOUN **1** a moment of bad behaviour by someone who usually behaves well
NOUN **2** a period of time that has passed
VERB **3** If you **lapse** into a different way of behaving, you start behaving that way.
• *The class **lapsed** into silence.*
VERB **4** If something such as a promise or an agreement **lapses**, it is no longer valid.

laptop laptops
NOUN a portable computer small enough to fit on your lap, which is especially useful if you are travelling

lard
NOUN fat from a pig, used in cooking

larder larders
NOUN a room for storing food, often next to a kitchen

large larger, largest
ADJECTIVE bigger than usual

largely
ADVERB to a great extent • *It was **largely** a party for his birthday, but we celebrated his sister's exam results too.*

a
b
c
d
e
f
g
h
i
j
k
l
m
n
o
p
q
r
s
t
u
v
w
x
y
z

lark larks, larking, larked

NOUN **1** a small, brown bird with a very pleasant song

NOUN **2** If you do something for a **lark**, you do it in a high-spirited or mischievous way for fun.

VERB **3** If you **lark** about, you enjoy yourself in a high-spirited way.

larva larvae

NOUN an insect after it has hatched from its egg, and before it becomes an adult. A caterpillar is the **larva** of a butterfly.

lasagne

NOUN an Italian dish made with wide, flat sheets of pasta, meat or vegetables and cheese sauce

---

WORD HISTORY
from Latin *lasanum* meaning cooking pot

---

laser lasers

NOUN **1** a narrow beam of concentrated light produced by a special machine. It is used to cut very hard materials and in some kinds of surgery.

NOUN **2** the machine that produces the beam of light

WORD HISTORY
from the first letters of *Light Amplification by Stimulated Emission of Radiation*

---

lash lashes, lashing, lashed

NOUN **1** Your **lashes** are the hairs growing on the edge of your eyelids.

VERB **2** If rain **lashes** down, it beats down strongly.

VERB **3** If you **lash** things together, you tie them together firmly.

lash out
  VERB If you **lash out** at someone you speak to them or strike them harshly.

lasso lassoes or lassos, lassoing, lassoed

NOUN **1** a length of rope looped at one end with a slip-knot, used by cowboys to catch cattle and horses

VERB **2** If you **lasso** an animal, you catch it by throwing the loop of a lasso around its neck.

last lasts, lasting, lasted

ADJECTIVE **1** The **last** person or thing is the one that comes after all the others of the same kind. • *I was the last person to arrive.*

ADJECTIVE **2** The **last** one of a group of things is the only one that remains after all the others have gone. • *No one wanted the last piece of pizza.*

ADJECTIVE **3** The **last** thing or event is the most recent one. • *The last time we went to the beach it rained.*

VERB **4** If something **lasts**, it continues to exist or happen. • *The sunny weather seems to have lasted for ages.*

VERB **5** If something **lasts** for a particular time, it remains in good condition for that time.

PHRASE **6** At last means after a long time. • *The bus arrived at last.*

late later, latest

ADJECTIVE **1** If something or someone is **late**, they arrive after the time that was arranged or expected.

ADJECTIVE **2** If something is **late**, it happens near the end of something. • *The visiting team scored a late goal.*

ADVERB **3** If something happens **late**, it happens after the time that was arranged or expected. • *She always arrives late at school.*

ADVERB **4** If something happens **late**, it happens near the end of something. • *In the summer it doesn't get dark until late in the evening.*

lately

ADVERB If something happened **lately**, it happened recently. • *We've had a lot of homework lately.*

lather

NOUN the frothy foam that you get when you rub soap in water

Latin

NOUN **1** the language of ancient Rome

ADJECTIVE **2** **Latin** peoples and cultures are those of countries such as France, Italy, Spain and Portugal, whose languages developed from Latin.

latitude latitudes

NOUN The **latitude** of a place is its distance north or south of the equator measured in degrees.

→ Have a look at the illustration for **equator**

latter

NOUN **1** You use **latter** to refer to the second of two things you have just mentioned. • *They were eating sandwiches and cakes (the latter bought from Mrs Paul's bakery).*

ADJECTIVE **2** The **latter** part of something is the second or later part of it. • *the latter stages of the race*

laugh laughs, laughing, laughed
VERB **1** When you **laugh**, you make a noise that shows that you are amused or happy.
NOUN **2** the sound you make when you laugh

laughter
NOUN laughing or the sound of people laughing

launch launches, launching, launched
VERB **1** When someone **launches** a ship, they put it into water for the first time.
VERB **2** When someone **launches** a rocket, they send it into space.

laundry laundries
NOUN **1** dirty clothes and sheets that are being washed or waiting to be washed
NOUN **2** a business that washes and irons clothes and sheets

lava
NOUN the very hot, liquid rock that shoots out of a volcano when it erupts, and becomes solid as it cools
→ Have a look at the illustration for **volcano**

lavatory lavatories
NOUN a toilet

lavender
NOUN a small bush with blue flowers that have a strong, pleasant scent

lavish
ADJECTIVE If you are **lavish**, you are very generous with your time, money or gifts.

law laws
NOUN **1** the system of rules developed by the government of a country, that tells people what they are allowed to do
NOUN **2** one of the rules established by a government, that tells people what they are allowed to do

lawn lawns
NOUN a piece of well-kept grass, usually in a park or garden

lawnmower lawnmowers
NOUN a machine for cutting grass

lawyer lawyers
NOUN someone who is trained in the law and who speaks for people in court

lay lays, laying, laid
VERB **1** When you **lay** something somewhere, you place it there.
VERB **2** If you **lay** the table, you put things such as knives and forks on the table ready for a meal.

VERB **3** When a bird **lays** an egg, an egg comes out of its body.

layer layers
NOUN a single thickness of something underneath or above something else ● *There was a thin **layer** of snow on the ground.*

layout layouts
NOUN the pattern in which something is arranged ● *The clear **layout** of this book makes it a lot easier to use.*

laziness
NOUN **Laziness** is the habit of being idle and unwilling to work.

lazy lazier, laziest
ADJECTIVE If you are **lazy**, you are idle and are unwilling to work.

lb
an abbreviation for *pound*

lead leads, leading, led
VERB **1** If you **lead** someone somewhere, you go in front of them in order to show them the way.
VERB **2** If a road or door **leads** somewhere, you can get to that place by following the road or going through the door.
VERB **3** If you **lead** in a race or competition, you are at the front.
VERB **4** Someone who **leads** a group of people is in charge of them.
NOUN **5** If you take the **lead** in a race or competition, or if you are in the **lead**, you are winning.
NOUN **6** a length of leather or chain attached to an animal's collar, used for controlling the animal
NOUN **7** an electric cable for connecting an electrical appliance to a battery or the mains
NOUN **8** a soft, grey, heavy metal
NOUN **9** The **lead** in a pencil is the part that makes marks on paper.

PRONUNCIATION TIP
Meanings 1-7 are pronounced **leed**.
Meanings 8 and 9 are pronounced **led**.

leader leaders
NOUN **1** If you are the **leader** of a group, you are in charge of it.
NOUN **2** If you are the **leader** in a race or a competition, you are winning.

A
B
C
D
E
F
G
H
I
J
K
L
M
N
O
P
Q
R
S
T
U
V
W
X
Y
Z

leaf leaves
NOUN **1** a flat structure growing from the stem of a plant. Most plants have green **leaves**.

→ Have a look at the illustrations for **flower** and **photosynthesis**

NOUN **2** one of the sheets of paper in a book

leaflet leaflets
NOUN a piece of paper or thin booklet with information or advertisements

leafy leafier, leafiest
ADJECTIVE **1** having a lot of leaves • green **leafy** vegetables
ADJECTIVE **2** A place that is **leafy** has a lot of trees. • He grew up in a **leafy** suburb of London.

league leagues
NOUN a group of people, clubs or countries that have joined together for a particular purpose or because they share a common interest

leak leaks, leaking, leaked
VERB **1** If a container or other object **leaks**, it has a hole through which gas or liquid escapes.
NOUN **2** If a container or other object has a **leak**, it has a hole through which gas or liquid escapes.

lean leans, leaning, leant or leaned; leaner, leanest
VERB **1** When you **lean** in a particular direction, you bend your body in that direction. • She **leant** out of the window.
VERB **2** When you **lean** on something, you rest your body against it for support. • He was **leaning** on the railing.
VERB **3** If you **lean** something somewhere, you place it there so that its weight is supported. • He **leaned** his bike against the wall.
ADJECTIVE **4** If meat is **lean**, it does not have much fat.

LANGUAGE TIP
You can write either leant or leaned as the past form of lean.

leap leaps, leaping, leapt or leaped
VERB **1** If you **leap** somewhere, you jump a long distance or high in the air.
NOUN **2** a jump over a long distance or high in the air

leap year leap years
NOUN A **leap year** has 366 days instead of 365, with an extra day in February. It occur every four years.

learn learns, learning, learnt or learned
VERB When you **learn** something, you gain knowledge or a skill by practice or by being taught. • He's **learning** to play the piano.

LANGUAGE TIP
You can write either learnt or learned as the past form of learn.

lease leases
NOUN A **lease** is an agreement that lets someone use a house or a flat in return for rent.

least
ADJECTIVE **1** a smaller amount than anyone or anything else • He ate the **least** amount of food because he felt ill.
ADVERB **2** a smaller amount than anyone or anything else • He is one of the **least** friendly people I have ever met.
NOUN **3** the smallest possible amount of something
PHRASE **4** You use **at least** to show that you are referring to the minimum amount of something, and that the true amount may be greater. • There were **at least** 500 people at the concert.

leather
NOUN animal skin that has been specially treated so that it can be used to make shoes, clothes, bags and other things

leave leaves, leaving, left
VERB **1** When you **leave** a place or person, you go away from them.
VERB **2** If you **leave** something somewhere, you let it stay there, or put it there before you go away. • I **left** my bags in the car.
VERB **3** If you **leave** a job or a school, you stop being a part of it.
VERB **4** In arithmetic, when you take one number from another, it **leaves** a third number. For example, if you take 2 from 12 it **leaves** 10.
NOUN **5** holiday time • I'm going to use my **leave** to go abroad this year.

lecture lectures
NOUN a formal talk intended to teach people about a particular subject

led
VERB the past tense of **lead**

edge ledges
NOUN a narrow shelf on the side of a cliff or rock face, or on the outside of a building, directly under a window

eek leeks
NOUN a long vegetable of the onion family, that is white at one end and has green leaves at the other

eft
VERB **1** the past tense of **leave**
NOUN **2** one of the two opposite directions, sides or positions. The **left** is the side of a page that you begin reading on in English.

ANTONYM: right

ADJECTIVE **3** on the **left** of something • *a cut over his **left** eye*

ANTONYM: right

ADJECTIVE **4** If a certain amount of something is **left** or **left over**, it remains when the rest has gone. • *They have two games **left** to play.*
ADVERB **5** on or towards the **left** of something • *Turn **left** at the corner.*

ANTONYM: right

eftovers
PLURAL NOUN the bits of uneaten food that are left at the end of a meal

eg legs
NOUN **1** one of the long parts of a human or other animal's body that they stand on and walk with

→ Have a look at the illustrations for **bird**, **insect** and **spider**

NOUN **2** The **legs** of a pair of trousers are the parts that cover your legs.
NOUN **3** The **legs** of a table or chair are the parts that rest on the floor and support it.
NOUN **4** A **leg** of a journey or a sports match is one part of it. • *The first **leg** of the race was very hard work.*

egacy legacies
NOUN property or money that is given to someone in the will of a person who has died

egal
ADJECTIVE relating to the law

egend legends
NOUN a very old and popular story

legible
ADJECTIVE Writing that is **legible** is clear enough to be read.

ANTONYM: illegible

legislation
NOUN a law or group of laws made by a government

legitimate
ADJECTIVE If something is **legitimate** it is allowed by law, or is accepted as fair by most people.

leisure
NOUN time when you do not have to work and can do things that you enjoy

lemon lemons
NOUN a yellow citrus fruit with a sour taste

lemonade
NOUN a sweet drink made from lemons, water and sugar. **Lemonade** is often fizzy.

lend lends, lending, lent
VERB **1** If you **lend** something to someone, you let them have it for a period of time.
VERB **2** If a person or bank **lends** you money, they give you money and you agree to pay it back later, usually with interest.

length lengths
NOUN **1** The **length** of something is the distance from one end to the other.
• *We walked the **length** of the street.*
NOUN **2** The **length** of an event or activity is the amount of time it continues. • *The film is over two hours in **length**.*

lengthen lengthens, lengthening, lengthened
VERB If you **lengthen** something, you make it longer.

ANTONYM: shorten

lengthy lengthier, lengthiest
ADJECTIVE Something that is **lengthy** lasts for a long time. • *The speech was rather **lengthy**.*

lens lenses
NOUN **1** a thin, curved piece of glass, plastic or other transparent material that makes things appear larger or clearer • *a camera **lens***
NOUN **2** the part of the eye behind the pupil that focuses light and helps you to see clearly

→ Have a look at the illustration for **eye**

lent
VERB the past tense and past participle of **lend**

A
B
C
D
E
F
G
H
I
J
K
L
M
N
O
P
Q
R
S
T
U
V
W
X
Y
Z

Lent

NOUN the forty-day period before Easter when some Christians fast or give up something that they enjoy

lentil lentils

NOUN **Lentils** are small, dried, red or brown seeds that are cooked and eaten in soups, stews and curries.

leopard leopards

NOUN a large wild cat, with yellow fur and black or brown spots, found in Africa and Asia

leotard leotards

NOUN a tight-fitting garment that covers the body rather like a swimming costume, which is worn for dancing or exercise

less

ADJECTIVE **1** a smaller amount of something • It is **less** than three weeks until we go back to school.

ANTONYM: more

PRONOUN **2** a smaller amount • Dad says I should spend **less**.

ANTONYM: more

ADVERB **3** You use **less** in front of some adjectives and adverbs to form comparatives. • I am **less** worried about the test than I was last time.

ANTONYM: more

PREPOSITION **4** You use **less** to show that one number or amount is to be subtracted from another. • You can have your pocket money, **less** the money you borrowed last week.

LANGUAGE TIP
Use less to talk about things that can't be counted and fewer for things that can be counted: less time; fewer apples.

lesson lessons

NOUN **1** a fixed period of time during which people are taught something by a teacher
NOUN **2** an experience that makes you understand something important

let lets, letting, let

VERB **1** If you **let** someone do something, you allow them to do it.
VERB **2** If someone **lets** a house or flat that they own, they allow others to use it in return for payment.

lethal

ADJECTIVE Something that is **lethal** can kill you. • A gun is a **lethal** weapon.

WORD HISTORY
from Latin letum meaning death

let's

VERB a contraction of let us

letter letters

NOUN **1** a message written on paper and sent to someone, usually through the post
NOUN **2** one of the written symbols that go together to make words

letter box letter boxes; also spelt letterbox

NOUN **1** an oblong gap in a front door, through which letters are delivered
NOUN **2** a large, metal container in the street or at a post office, for posting letters

lettering

NOUN You use **lettering** to describe writing that is done in a certain way. • The poster had large black **lettering**.

lettuce lettuces

NOUN a vegetable with large, green leaves that you eat in salads

leukaemia; also spelt leukemia

NOUN a serious illness that affects the blood

WORD HISTORY
from Greek leukos meaning white and haima meaning blood

level levels, levelling, levelled

NOUN **1** the height, position or amount of something • This is the lowest **level** of rainfall for years.
NOUN **2** a standard or grade of achievement • Now that I have passed this piano exam, I will move on to the next **level**.

SYNONYMS: grade, stage

ADJECTIVE **3** A surface that is **level** is completely flat.
ADJECTIVE **4** If one thing is **level** with another it is at the same height or position.
VERB **5** If you **level** something, you make it flat.

level crossing level crossings

NOUN a place where traffic is allowed to drive across a railway track

ever levers

NOUN **1** a handle on a machine that you pull in order to make the machine work

NOUN **2** a bar that you wedge underneath a heavy object and press down on to make the object move

iability liabilities

NOUN If you say that someone is a **liability**, you mean that they cause problems or embarrassment.

iable

ADJECTIVE **1** Something that is **liable** to happen will probably happen. ● *Britain is* **liable** *to be cold in January.*

ADJECTIVE **2** If someone is **liable** for something such as a crime or a debt, they are legally responsible for it.

iar liars

NOUN a person who tells lies

iberal

ADJECTIVE **1** If someone is **liberal**, they are tolerant of other people's behaviour and opinions.

ADJECTIVE **2** If you are **liberal** with something, you are generous with it.

iberty

NOUN the freedom to do what you want to do and go where you want to go

ibrarian librarians

NOUN a person who works in, or is in charge of, a library

ibrary libraries

NOUN a building in which books are kept, especially a public building from which people can borrow books

---

LANGUAGE TIP

There is an *r* after the *b* in *library*.

---

icence licences

NOUN an official document that gives you permission to do, use or own something ● *You have to pass a test before you receive a full driving* **licence***.*

LANGUAGE TIP

The noun *licence* ends in *ce*.

---

icense licenses, licensing, licensed

VERB If someone **licenses** an activity, they give official permission for it to be carried out.

LANGUAGE TIP

The verb *license* ends in *se*.

---

lichen lichens

NOUN a green or greeny-grey mossy growth, found on rocks, trees and walls

---

PRONUNCIATION TIP

This word is pronounced **lie**-kun.

---

lick licks, licking, licked

VERB If you **lick** something, you move your tongue over it. ● *I* **licked** *the stamp and stuck it to the envelope.*

lid lids

NOUN a cover for a box, jar or other container

lie lies, lying, lay, lain

VERB **1** If someone or something **lies** somewhere, they rest there in a flat position.

VERB **2** You use **lie** to say where something is or what its position is. ● *The village* **lies** *to the east of the river.*

LANGUAGE TIP

The past tense of this verb *lie* is *lay*. Do not confuse it with the verb *lay* meaning 'put'.

---

lie lies, lying, lied

VERB **1** If you **lie**, you say something that you know is not true. ● *He* **lied** *about his age.*

NOUN **2** something you say that you know is not true

lieutenant lieutenants

NOUN a junior officer in the army or navy

PRONUNCIATION TIP

This word is pronounced lef-**ten**-ant.

---

life lives

NOUN **1** the state of being alive that makes people, animals and plants different from objects ● *A baby's first few minutes of* **life** *are important.*

NOUN **2** your existence from the time you are born until the time you die ● *For the first time in his* **life** *he was sorry.*

lifeboat lifeboats

NOUN a boat used for rescuing people who are in danger at sea

a
b
c
d
e
f
g
h
i
j
k
l
m
n
o
p
q
r
s
t
u
v
w
x
y
z

233

life cycle life cycles
NOUN the series of changes and developments in the life of a living thing
• *There are several stages in the life cycle of a butterfly.*

→ Have a look at the illustration

lifeguard lifeguards
NOUN a person whose job is to rescue people who are in difficulty in the sea or in a swimming pool

life jacket life jackets
NOUN a sleeveless, inflatable jacket that keeps you afloat in water

lifelike
ADJECTIVE A picture or a sculpture that is **lifelike** looks very real, almost as if it is alive.

SYNONYM: realistic

lifeline lifelines
NOUN something that helps you to survive or helps an activity to continue • *His help was a real lifeline to me after I had so many difficulties.*

lifetime lifetimes
NOUN the period of time during which you are alive

lift lifts, lifting, lifted
VERB 1 If you **lift** something, you move it to a higher position.
NOUN 2 a device that carries people or goods from one floor to another in a building

light lights, lighting, lighted or lit; lighter, lightest
NOUN 1 the brightness from the sun, moon, fire or lamps, that lets you see things

NOUN 2 a lamp or other device that gives out brightness
ADJECTIVE 3 If it is **light**, there is enough light from the sun to see things.

ANTONYM: dark

ADJECTIVE 4 A **light** colour is pale.

ANTONYM: dark

ADJECTIVE 5 A **light** object does not weigh much.

ANTONYM: heavy

VERB 6 If you **light** a fire, you make it start burning.

lighten lightens, lightening, lightened
VERB 1 When something **lightens**, it becomes brighter and less dark. • *After the storm the sky lightened.*
VERB 2 If you **lighten** a load, you make it less heavy. • *My case was too heavy, so I lightened it by taking out three books.*

lighter lighters
NOUN a device for lighting something, such as a fire or a cigarette

lighthouse lighthouses
NOUN a tower by the sea, that shines a powerful light to guide ships and warn them of danger

lighting
NOUN The **lighting** in a room or building is the way it is lit.

lightning
NOUN very bright flashes of light you see in the sky, usually during a thunderstorm. **Lightning** is caused by electrical activity in the atmosphere.

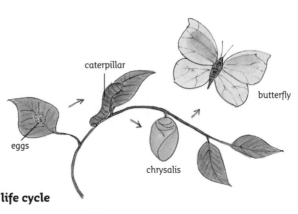

caterpillar

butterfly

eggs

chrysalis

life cycle

ght year light years
NOUN the distance that light travels in a year, which is about 6 million miles or 9.5 million kilometres

ke likes, liking, liked
VERB **1** If you **like** someone or something, you find them pleasing.
NOUN **2** a symbol on a social media website that you click to show that you like something that someone has posted
• *The video got over 200 **likes**.*
PREPOSITION **3** If one thing is **like** another, they are similar.

keable; also spelt **likable**
ADJECTIVE A **likeable** person is pleasant and friendly.

kely likelier, likeliest
ADJECTIVE If something is **likely**, it will probably happen or is probably true.

lac lilacs
NOUN **1** a small tree with sweet-smelling clusters of mauve, pink or white flowers
NOUN **2** a pale mauve colour

ly lilies
NOUN a plant with trumpet-shaped flowers of various colours

mb limbs
NOUN Your **limbs** are your arms and legs.

me limes
NOUN **1** a small, green citrus fruit, rather like a lemon
NOUN **2** a bright green colour
NOUN **3** a chemical substance used in cement or as a fertiliser

merick limericks
NOUN an amusing nonsense poem of five lines

mit limits, limiting, limited
NOUN **1** the largest or smallest amount of something that is possible or allowed
• *The speed **limit** on this road is 30 mph.*
VERB **2** If you **limit** something, you restrict it to a certain amount or number. • *The children were **limited** to two biscuits each.*

mousine limousines
NOUN a large, luxurious car, usually driven by a chauffeur

mp limps, limping, limped; **limper, limpest**
VERB **1** If you **limp**, you walk in an uneven way because you have hurt your leg or foot.
NOUN **2** an uneven way of walking • *While her leg was in plaster she walked with a **limp**.*

ADJECTIVE **3** Something that is **limp** is soft or weak.

limpet limpets
NOUN a small shellfish with a pointed shell, that attaches itself very firmly to rocks

line lines, lining, lined
NOUN **1** a long, thin mark
NOUN **2** a number of people or things that are arranged in a row
NOUN **3** a long piece of string or wire
• *a washing **line***
NOUN **4** a number of words together, for example the **lines** in a play are the words that an actor has to speak • *This is my favourite **line** in the poem.*
NOUN **5** a railway or railway track
VERB **6** If people or things **line** something, they make a border or edge along it.
• *Crowds **lined** the streets to see the Queen.*

line graph line graphs
NOUN a kind of graph where the information is shown by using straight lines to join points

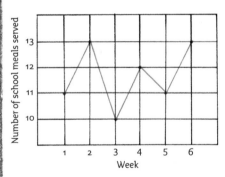

linen
NOUN **1** a type of cloth made from a plant called flax
NOUN **2** household goods made of cloth, such as sheets and tablecloths

liner liners
NOUN a large passenger ship that makes long sea journeys

linesman linesmen
NOUN an official at a sports match who watches the lines of the field or court and decides if the ball has gone outside them

a
b
c
d
e
f
g
h
i
j
k
l
m
n
o
p
q
r
s
t
u
v
w
x
y
z

235

A
B
C
D
E
F
G
H
I
J
K
L
M
N
O
P
Q
R
S
T
U
V
W
X
Y
Z

linger lingers, lingering, lingered
VERB If someone or something **lingers**, they stay for a long time. • *The smell **lingered** in the kitchen.*

linguist linguists
NOUN someone who studies languages and can speak them well

lining linings
NOUN any material that is used to line the inside of something • *There is a fleece **lining** in this jacket.*

link links, linking, linked
NOUN **1** one of the rings in a chain
NOUN **2** a relationship or connection between two things • *There is a **link** between the weather and the clothes we wear.*
NOUN **3** a physical connection between two things or places • *There is a rail **link** between the two cities.*
VERB **4** If someone or something **links** people, places, or things, they join them together. • *They want to **link** the village to the town with a better road.*

lion lions
NOUN a large member of the cat family that is found in Africa. Male **lions** have long hair on their head and neck, called a mane.

lioness lionesses
NOUN a female lion

lip lips
NOUN Your **lips** are the two outer edges of your mouth.

lipstick lipsticks
NOUN a cosmetic for colouring the lips, usually in the form of a small stick

liquid liquids
NOUN a substance such as water, which is neither a gas nor a solid and which can be poured. The particles in a **liquid** are close together but can move around. A **liquid** always takes the shape of the container it is in.

→ Have a look at the illustration for **state of matter**

liquidiser liquidisers; also spelt **liquidizer**
NOUN an electric machine used for making food into liquid • *Dad put strawberries, bananas and milk in the **liquidiser** and mixed us a delicious milkshake.*

liquorice; also spelt **licorice**
NOUN **1** a root used to flavour sweets
NOUN **2** sweets flavoured with liquorice

lisp lisps, lisping, lisped
NOUN **1** Someone who has a **lisp** pronounce the sounds *s* and *z* like *th*.
VERB **2** If someone **lisps**, they speak with a lisp.

list lists, listing, listed
NOUN **1** a set of words or items written one after the other • *a shopping **list***
VERB **2** If you **list** a number of things, you write them or say them one after another.

listen listens, listening, listened
VERB **1** If you **listen** to someone, you pay attention to what they are saying.
VERB **2** If you **listen** to something, you pay attention to its sound. • *She enjoys **listenin** to music.*

lit
VERB the past tense and past participle of **light**

literacy
NOUN the ability to read and write

literal
ADJECTIVE according to the most basic an obvious meaning of a word or text, rather than a figurative meaning

literally
ADVERB You use **literally** to emphasise that what you are saying is actually true, even though it seems unlikely. • *We **literally** almost died of thirst.*

literary
ADJECTIVE connected with or knowledgeable about literature

literate
ADJECTIVE If you are **literate**, you are able to read and write.

literature
NOUN Novels, plays and poetry are referred t as **literature**.

WORD HISTORY
from Latin *litteratura* meaning writing

litre litres
NOUN a unit for measuring liquid (l) equal to 1000 millilitres or about 1.76 pints

tter litters, littering, littered
NOUN **1** rubbish in the street and other public places
NOUN **2** baby animals born at the same time to the same mother
VERB **3** If things **litter** a place, they are scattered all over it. • *Paper **littered** the pavement.*

ttle less, lesser, least
ADJECTIVE **1** small in size or amount • *Stay a **little** longer.*

ANTONYMS: big, large

ADJECTIVE **2** not much • *I had very **little** money.*
PRONOUN **3** not much • *He ate **little** at the meal.*
NOUN **4** A **little** is a small amount or degree of something. • *He showed me a **little** of his work.*

ve lives, living, lived
VERB **1** If someone or something **lives**, they are alive.
VERB **2** If you **live** in a place, that is where your home is. • *He **lives** with his parents.*
VERB **3** The way someone **lives** is the kind of life they have. • *We **live** quite simply.*
ADJECTIVE **4** **Live** television or radio is broadcast while the event is taking place.
ADJECTIVE **5** **Live** animals or plants are alive, rather than dead or artificial.

PRONUNCIATION TIP
The verb rhymes with "give". The adjective rhymes with "five".

vely livelier, liveliest
ADJECTIVE full of energy and enthusiasm

ver livers
NOUN a large organ in your body that cleans your blood and stores substances such as vitamins and minerals

→ Have a look at the illustrations for **organ** and **stomach**

vestream livestreams, livestreaming, livestreamed
VERB If you **livestream** something as it is happening, you play it directly from the internet. • *The game will be **livestreamed** on the website.*

ving
ADJECTIVE **1** If someone or something is **living**, they are alive.
NOUN **2** Someone who works for a **living**, works to earn the money needed in order to live. • *He makes a **living** by selling cars.*

living room living rooms
NOUN a room in a house where you sit and relax, doing such things as watching television and reading

lizard lizards
NOUN a reptile with short legs and a tail

llama llamas
NOUN a South American animal that looks rather like a small camel with thick hair and no hump

load loads, loading, loaded
VERB **1** If you **load** a vehicle or container, you put things into it.
VERB **2** When you **load** a camera, you put film into it.
NOUN **3** something large or heavy that is being carried • *a tractor with a big **load** of hay*
NOUN **4** (*informal*) A **load** of something, or **loads** of something, means a lot of it. • *He's got **loads** of CDs.*

loaf loaves
NOUN a large piece of bread in a shape that can be cut into slices

loan loans, loaning, loaned
NOUN **1** a sum of money that you borrow
VERB **2** If you **loan** something to someone, you lend it to them.

loathe loathes, loathing, loathed
VERB If you **loathe** someone or something, you feel a very strong dislike for them.

lobster lobsters
NOUN an edible shellfish with two front claws and eight legs

local locals
ADJECTIVE **1** existing in or belonging to the area where you live • *the **local** newspaper*
NOUN **2** someone who lives in and comes from a particular area

locality localities
NOUN a small area of a country or a city • *Golden eagles can be seen in certain **localities** in Scotland.*

locate locates, locating, located
VERB **1** If you **locate** someone or something, you find out where they are.
VERB **2** If something is **located** in a place, it is in that place.

237

location locations
NOUN the place where something is found or where something happens • *She couldn't remember the exact location of the church.*

loch lochs
NOUN In Scottish English, a **loch** is a lake. • *They say there is a monster in Loch Ness.*

lock locks, locking, locked
VERB 1 If you **lock** something, you fasten it with a key.
VERB 2 If you **lock** something in a place, you put it there and fasten the lock.
• *They locked the money in the safe.*
NOUN 3 a device that prevents something from being opened except with a key
• *He heard a key in the lock.*

locker lockers
NOUN a small cupboard for someone's personal belongings, for example in a changing room

locket lockets
NOUN a small piece of jewellery worn on a chain around the neck, which opens so that you can put a small photograph inside

locomotive locomotives
NOUN a railway engine

locust locusts
NOUN an insect like a large grasshopper, that travels in huge swarms and eats crops

loft lofts
NOUN the space immediately under the roof of a house, often used for storing things

log logs
NOUN 1 a thick piece of wood from a branch or trunk of a tree, that has fallen or been cut off
NOUN 2 an official written account of what happens each day • *The captain wrote each day's events in the ship's log.*

logic
NOUN a way of reasoning that makes sense

logical
ADJECTIVE Something that is **logical** is sensible and reasonable. • *a logical explanation*

logically
ADVERB in a way that makes sense

logo logos
NOUN the special design that is put on all the products of an organisation

loiter loiters, loitering, loitered
VERB If you **loiter** in a place, you stand around without going very far or doing very much. • *After school they loitered round the shops.*

lollipop lollipops
NOUN a hard sweet on the end of a stick

WORD HISTORY
from Romani *lolli* meaning red and *pobbel* meaning apple

lolly lollies
NOUN 1 a lollipop
NOUN 2 a flavoured ice or ice cream on a stick

lonely lonelier, loneliest
ADJECTIVE 1 If you are **lonely**, you are unhappy because you are alone.
ADJECTIVE 2 A **lonely** place is one that very few people visit.

long longer, longest; longs, longing, longed
ADJECTIVE 1 continuing for a great amount of time • *There had been no rain for a long time.*
ADVERB 2 You use **long** to talk about amounts of time. • *How long is the film?*
ADJECTIVE 3 great in length or distance • *It's a long way home.*
ADJECTIVE 4 You use **long** to talk about the distance that something measures from one end to the other.
PHRASE 5 If something **no longer** happens, used to happen but does not happen now.
VERB 6 If you **long** to do something, you want to do it very much.

long for
VERB If you **long for** something to happen you want it to happen very much.

long division long divisions
NOUN a method of dividing one large number by another one, where you write out all the stages instead of doing them in your head or on a calculator

longitude longitudes
NOUN a position measured in degrees east or west of an imaginary line passing through Greenwich in London

→ Have a look at the illustration for **equator**

look looks, looking, looked

VERB **1** If you **look** at something, you turn your eyes towards it so that you can see it.

VERB **2** If you **look** for someone or something, you try to find them.

VERB **3** If you describe the way that something **looks**, you are describing its appearance. • *He looked a bit pale.*

NOUN **4** If you take a **look** at something, you look at it. • *Lucy took a last look in the mirror.*

SYNONYM: glance

NOUN **5** The **look** on your face is the expression on it.

look after

VERB If you **look after** someone or something, you take care of them.

look forward

VERB If you **look forward** to something, you want it to happen because you think you will enjoy it.

look out

VERB You say **look out** to warn someone of danger. • *Look out! There's a car coming.*

lookout lookouts

NOUN **1** someone who is watching for danger, or a place where someone watches for danger

PHRASE **2** If you are **on the lookout** for something, you are watching or waiting for it to happen.

loom looms, looming, loomed

NOUN **1** a machine for weaving cloth

VERB **2** If something **looms** in front of you, it suddenly appears as a tall, unclear and sometimes frightening shape. • *A monster loomed out of the darkness.*

VERB **3** If a situation or event is **looming**, it is likely to happen soon and is rather worrying. • *A storm is looming on the horizon.*

loop loops, looping, looped

NOUN **1** a curved or circular shape in something such as a piece of string or wire

VERB **2** If you **loop** rope or string around an object, you place it in a loop around the object. • *He looped the rope over the horse's neck.*

loose looser, loosest

ADJECTIVE **1** not firmly held or fixed in place • *a loose tooth*

ADJECTIVE **2** not tight • *a loose jacket*

ADVERB **3** If people or animals break **loose**, or are set **loose**, they are released after they have been held back or tied up.

PRONUNCIATION TIP
This word is pronounced **looss**.

LANGUAGE TIP
Do not confuse *loose* with *lose*.

---

loot loots, looting, looted

VERB **1** If someone **loots** shops and houses, they steal goods from them, especially during a riot or war.

NOUN **2** stolen money or goods

lopsided

ADJECTIVE Something that is **lopsided** is uneven because one side is different from the other, for example one side is heavier or larger.

lord lords

NOUN In Britain, **Lord** is a title used in front of the names of some men.

lorry lorries

NOUN a large vehicle for transporting goods by road

lose loses, losing, lost

VERB **1** If you **lose** something, you cannot find it, or you no longer have it because it has been taken from you. • *He lost his place in the team.*

VERB **2** If you **lose** a fight or an argument, you are beaten.

PRONUNCIATION TIP
This word is pronounced **looz**.

LANGUAGE TIP
Do not confuse *lose* with *loose*.

---

loss losses

NOUN The **loss** of something is the fact of having lost it or of having less of it.

lost

VERB **1** the past tense and past participle of **lose**

ADJECTIVE **2** If you are **lost**, you do not know where you are.

ADJECTIVE **3** If something is **lost**, you cannot find it.

a
b
c
d
e
f
g
h
i
j
k
l
m
n
o
p
q
r
s
t
u
v
w
x
y
z

A
B
C
D
E
F
G
H
I
J
K
L
M
N
O
P
Q
R
S
T
U
V
W
X
Y
Z

lot lots

NOUN **1** a large amount of something • *a lot of children*

NOUN **2** very much or very often • *I miss him a lot.*

NOUN **3** the whole of something • *He had a whole packet of biscuits and ate the lot.*

lotion lotions

NOUN a liquid that you put on your skin to protect or soften it • *suntan lotion*

lottery lotteries

NOUN a way of raising money by selling tickets and giving prizes to people who have winning tickets, which are selected at random

loud louder, loudest

ADJECTIVE A **loud** noise produces a lot of sound.

loudly

ADVERB in a way that produces a lot of sound

loudspeaker loudspeakers

NOUN a piece of electrical equipment that produces the sound in things such as radios, phones and CD players

lounge lounges, lounging, lounged

NOUN **1** a room in a house, hotel or airport where people can sit and relax

VERB **2** If you **lounge** around, you lean against something or lie around in a lazy way.

louse lice

NOUN a small insect that lives on people's bodies

love loves, loving, loved

VERB **1** If you **love** someone or something, you have strong feelings of affection for them.

VERB **2** If you would **love** to do something, you want very much to do it.

NOUN **3** a strong feeling of affection for someone or something

PHRASE **4** If you are **in love** with someone, you feel strongly attracted to them romantically.

lovely lovelier, loveliest

ADJECTIVE very beautiful, attractive, pleasant or enjoyable • *We had a lovely day out.*

low lower, lowest

ADJECTIVE **1** Something that is **low** is close to the ground.

ANTONYM: high

ADJECTIVE **2** below average in value or amount • *The temperature was low for the time of year*

ANTONYM: high

ADVERB **3** close to the ground • *An aeroplane flew low over the beach.*

ANTONYM: high

lower lowers, lowering, lowered

VERB **1** If you **lower** something, you move it downwards. • *She lowered the bucket into the well.*

ADJECTIVE **2** The **lower** of two things is the bottom one. • *the lower deck of the bus*

lower-case

ADJECTIVE **Lower-case** letters are small letters, not capital letters.

loyal

ADJECTIVE If you are **loyal**, you are firm in your friendship or support for someone or something.

lozenge lozenges

NOUN **1** a small sweet with medicine in it, that you can suck if you have a sore throat or a cough

NOUN **2** a diamond shape, like a rhombus

lubricant lubricants

NOUN an oily substance that you put on something such a machine so that it moves smoothly

lubricate lubricates, lubricating, lubricated

VERB If someone **lubricates** something, they put oil or grease on to it so that it moves smoothly.

WORD HISTORY
from Latin *lubricus* meaning slippery

lubrication

NOUN the process of putting oil or grease on something such as a machine so that it moves smoothly

luck

NOUN **1** something that happens by chance • *We had good luck with the weather.* • *It was bad luck that I lost the game of Monopoly.*

PHRASE **2** You say **good luck** to someone when you are wishing them success.

luckily

ADVERB You use **luckily** to say that is lucky that something happened. ● *Luckily, the cup didn't break when I dropped it.*

lucky luckier, luckiest

ADJECTIVE Someone who is **lucky** has a lot of good luck.

ANTONYM: unlucky

luggage

NOUN Your **luggage** is the bags and suitcases that you take with you when you travel.

lukewarm

ADJECTIVE slightly warm

lull lulls, lulling, lulled

NOUN **1** a pause in something, or a short time when it is quiet and calm
VERB **2** If you **lull** someone, you calm them and make them feel safe.

lullaby lullabies

NOUN a song used for sending a baby or child to sleep

lumber lumbers, lumbering, lumbered

NOUN **1** wood that has been roughly cut up
VERB **2** If you **lumber** around, you move heavily and clumsily.

luminous

ADJECTIVE Something that is **luminous** glows in the dark without being hot.

lump lumps

NOUN a solid piece of something

lunar

ADJECTIVE relating to the moon ● *The lunar module landed safely on the moon.*

WORD HISTORY
from Latin *luna* meaning moon

lunch lunches

NOUN a meal eaten in the middle of the day

lung lungs

NOUN Your **lungs** are the two organs inside your chest that you breathe with.

→ Have a look at the illustration for **organ**

lurch lurches, lurching, lurched

VERB **1** If someone or something **lurches**, they make a sudden, jerky movement.
PHRASE **2** If someone leaves you **in the lurch**, they leave you in a difficult or dangerous situation, instead of helping you.

lure lures, luring, lured

VERB If you **lure** someone or something, you tempt them into going somewhere or doing something. ● *He lured the cat back into the house with some milk.*

lurk lurks, lurking, lurked

VERB If someone **lurks** somewhere, they hide there and wait.

lush lusher, lushest

ADJECTIVE In a **lush** field or garden, the grass or plants are healthy and growing thickly.

lute lutes

NOUN an old-fashioned, stringed musical instrument that is plucked like a guitar

luxury luxuries

NOUN **1** great comfort, especially among expensive and beautiful surroundings
NOUN **2** A **luxury** is something that you would like to have but do not need, and is usually expensive.

lying

VERB the present participle of **lie**

lyrics

PLURAL NOUN The **lyrics** of a song are the words.

A
B
C
D
E
F
G
H
I
J
K
L
M
N
O
P
Q
R
S
T
U
V
W
X
Y
Z

242

Mm

m
an abbreviation for *metre*

macaroni
NOUN short, hollow tubes of pasta

WORD HISTORY
an Italian word; from Greek *makaria* meaning food made from barley

machine machines
NOUN a piece of equipment designed to do a particular job. It is usually powered by an engine or by electricity. • *a washing* **machine**

machine gun machine guns
NOUN a gun that works automatically, firing a continuous stream of bullets very quickly

machinery
NOUN machines in general • *farm* **machinery** • *factory* **machinery**

mackintosh mackintoshes
NOUN a raincoat made from waterproof cloth

mad madder, maddest
ADJECTIVE **1** Someone who is **mad** has a severe mental illness that causes them to behave in strange ways.
ADJECTIVE **2** If you describe someone as **mad**, you mean that they are very foolish.
ADJECTIVE **3** (*informal*) Someone who is **mad** is angry.
PHRASE **4** If you are **mad about** someone or something, you like them very much. • *She had always been* **mad about** *football.*

made
VERB the past tense and past participle of **make**

magazine magazines
NOUN a weekly or monthly publication containing articles and photographs

maggot maggots
NOUN the larva of some kinds of fly. **Maggots** look like small, fat worms.

magic
NOUN **1** In fairy stories, **magic** is a special power that can make impossible things happen.
NOUN **2** the art of performing tricks to entertain people

magical
ADJECTIVE **1** using a special power to make impossible things happen • *magical powe*
ADJECTIVE **2** exciting, beautiful and special • *The island is tiny but truly* **magical**.

magician magicians
NOUN **1** a person who performs tricks that seem like magic to entertain people
NOUN **2** In fairy stories, a **magician** is a ma with magic powers.

magistrate magistrates
NOUN an official who acts as a judge in a law court that deals with less serious crimes

magma
NOUN molten rock that is formed in very hot conditions inside the Earth
→ Have a look at the illustration for **volcano**

magnet magnets
NOUN a piece of iron or steel that attracts other objects made of iron or steel towards it. **Magnets** can also push away, or repel, other **magnets**.

magnetic
ADJECTIVE Something that is **magnetic** is attracted towards a magnet. Only iron, steel, nickel and cobalt are **magnetic**.

magnification
NOUN **Magnification** is the process of making something look bigger than it real is, for example by using a microscope.

magnificent
ADJECTIVE extremely beautiful or impressive

SYNONYMS: imposing, splendid

WORD HISTORY
from Latin *magnificus* meaning great in deeds

magnify magnifies, magnifying, magnified
VERB When a microscope or lens **magnifie** something, it makes it look bigger than it actually is.

magnifying glass magnifying glasses
NOUN a glass lens that magnifies things, making them appear bigger than they really are

magpie magpies
NOUN a large, black-and-white bird with a long tail

mahogany
NOUN a hard, reddish-brown wood used for making furniture

maid maids
NOUN a female servant

maiden name maiden names
NOUN the surname a woman had before she married

mail mails, mailing, mailed
NOUN 1 the letters and parcels delivered to you by the post office
NOUN 2 same as **email**
VERB 3 If you **mail** a letter, you send it by post.
VERB 4 If you **mail** someone, you send them an email.

WORD HISTORY
from Old French *male* meaning bag

maim maims, maiming, maimed
VERB To **maim** someone is to injure them very badly for life.

main mains
ADJECTIVE 1 most important or largest • My **main** interest is music.

SYNONYMS: chief, major, principal

NOUN 2 The **mains** are the large pipes or cables that carry gas, water or electricity to a building.

mainland
NOUN the main part of a country or continent, not including the islands around it

mainly
ADVERB mostly, chiefly or usually • We eat **mainly** vegetarian food.

maintain maintains, maintaining, maintained
VERB 1 If you **maintain** something, you keep it going at a particular rate or level. • You will need to **maintain** this level of fitness if you want to take part in the finals.
VERB 2 If you **maintain** a machine or a building, you keep it in good condition.
VERB 3 If you **maintain** a belief or an opinion, you have it and state it clearly.

maize
NOUN a tall plant that produces sweet corn

majestic
ADJECTIVE big, beautiful and impressive • **majestic** mountains

majesty majesties
NOUN 1 You say **His Majesty** when you are talking about a king, and **Her Majesty** when you are talking about a queen.
NOUN 2 the quality of being dignified and impressive

major majors
ADJECTIVE 1 more important or more serious than other things • She has a **major** role in the school play.

ANTONYM: minor

NOUN 2 an army officer of the rank immediately above captain

majority majorities
NOUN more than half of a group • The **majority** of the passengers became ill.

make makes, making, made
VERB 1 If you **make** something, you create or produce it. • This is the cake I **made** yesterday.
VERB 2 If you **make** someone or something do something, you force them to do it or cause it to happen. • Her mother **made** her do her homework every night.
VERB 3 If you **make** a promise to do something, you say you will definitely do it.
VERB 4 Two amounts added together **make** a sum. • 3 and 5 **make** 8.
VERB 5 If you **make** a phone call, you use a phone to speak to someone.
NOUN 6 the name of the product of a particular manufacturer • What **make** is your bicycle?

make-believe
NOUN a fantasy of pretend or imaginary things

make-up
NOUN coloured creams and powders that women and actors put on their faces

malaria
NOUN a serious tropical disease, caught from mosquitoes, that causes fever and shivering

WORD HISTORY
from Italian *mal* + *aria* meaning bad air, because people used to think that the bad air coming from the swamps around Rome caused the fever

243

A
B
C
D
E
F
G
H
I
J
K
L
M
N
O
P
Q
R
S
T
U
V
W
X
Y
Z

244

male males
NOUN **1** a person or animal belonging to the gender that cannot have babies

ANTONYM: female

ADJECTIVE **2** concerning or affecting men rather than women

ANTONYM: female

malevolent
ADJECTIVE **1** **Malevolent** people want to cause harm or do evil things.
ADJECTIVE **2** A **malevolent** act is cruel and spiteful.

PRONUNCIATION TIP
This word is pronounced ma-**lev**-oh-lent.

---

malfunction malfunctions, malfunctioning, malfunctioned
VERB If a machine **malfunctions**, it fails to work properly.

malicious
ADJECTIVE **Malicious** talk or behaviour is intended to harm someone.

mall malls
NOUN a sheltered place with cafés, shops and restaurants ● *a shopping* **mall**

mallet mallets
NOUN a wooden hammer with a square head

malnutrition
NOUN a condition resulting from not eating enough healthy food or not having enough to eat

mammal mammals
NOUN an animal that gives birth to live babies and feeds its young with milk from the mother's body. Human beings, dogs and whales are all **mammals**.

WORD HISTORY
from Latin *mamma* meaning breast

---

mammoth mammoths
ADJECTIVE **1** very large indeed
NOUN **2** a huge animal that looked like a hairy elephant with long tusks. **Mammoths** became extinct a long time ago.

man men; mans, manning, manned
NOUN **1** an adult, male human being

ANTONYM: woman

NOUN **2** Human beings, both male and female, are sometimes referred to as **man**.
● *Primitive* **man** *lived in caves.*
VERB **3** If you **man** something, you are in charge of it or you operate it. ● *Can you* **man** *the bookstall?*

manage manages, managing, managed
VERB **1** If you **manage** to do something, you succeed in doing it even if it is difficult. ● *We* **managed** *to find somewhere to sit.*
VERB **2** If someone **manages** an organisation or business, they are responsible for controlling it.

management
NOUN **1** the controlling and organising of a business
NOUN **2** the people who control an organisation

manager managers
NOUN a man or woman who is responsible for running a business or organisation

mane manes
NOUN long hair growing from the neck of a lion or a horse

manger mangers
NOUN a feeding box in a barn or stable

mangle mangles, mangling, mangled
VERB **1** If you **mangle** something, you crush or twist it out of shape.
NOUN **2** an old-fashioned piece of equipment consisting of two large rollers, for squeezing water out of wet clothes

mango mangoes or mangos
NOUN a sweet yellow fruit that grows in tropical climates

mankind
NOUN used to refer to all human beings
● *Pollution is a threat to* **mankind**.

manner manners
NOUN **1** the way you do something or behave
PLURAL NOUN **2** If you have good **manners**, you behave very politely.

manoeuvre manoeuvres, manoeuvring, manoeuvred
VERB **1** If you **manoeuvre** something into place, you move it there skilfully. ● *Mum* **manoeuvred** *the car into the small parking space.*
NOUN **2** A **manoeuvre** is a clever thing that you do or say in order to make something happen the way you want it to.

PRONUNCIATION TIP
This word is pronounced ma-**noo**-ver.

manor manors
NOUN a large country house with land, especially one that was built in the Middle Ages

mansion mansions
NOUN a very large house

manslaughter
NOUN the accidental killing of a person

mantelpiece mantelpieces
NOUN a shelf over a fireplace

mantle mantles
NOUN the part of the Earth between the crust and the core
→ Have a look at the illustration for **earth**

manual manuals
ADJECTIVE **1 Manual** work involves physical strength or skill with your hands, rather than mental skill.
ADJECTIVE **2 Manual** equipment is operated by hand rather than being automatic or operated by electricity or a motor. ● *a* **manual** *whisk*
NOUN **3** a book that tells you how to use a machine ● *an instruction* **manual**

WORD HISTORY
from Latin *manus* meaning hand

manufacture manufactures, manufacturing, manufactured
VERB **1** If someone **manufactures** goods, they make them in a factory.
NOUN **2** The **manufacture** of goods is the making of them in a factory.

manure
NOUN animal dung used to improve the soil

manuscript manuscripts
NOUN a handwritten or typed copy of a book, play or piece of music before it is printed

WORD HISTORY
from Latin *manus* meaning hand and *scribere* meaning to write

many
ADJECTIVE **1** If there are **many** people or things, there are a large number of them.
ADJECTIVE **2** You use **many** to talk about how great a number or quantity is. ● *How* **many** *tickets do you need?*
PRONOUN **3** You use **many** to talk about how great a number or quantity is. ● *He made a list of his friends. There weren't* **many**.

map maps
NOUN a detailed drawing of an area of land, showing its shape and features as it would appear if you saw it from above ● *You can see the park beside the river on this* **map**.

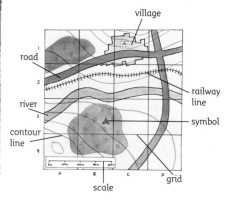

maple maples
NOUN a tree that has large leaves with five points

marathon marathons
NOUN a race in which people run 26 miles along roads ● *My dad is training for the London* **Marathon**.

WORD HISTORY
named after *Marathon*, a place from which a messenger ran more than 20 miles to Athens, bringing news of a victory in 490 BC

marble
NOUN a very hard, cold stone that is often polished to show the coloured patterns in it

a b c d e f g h i j k l m n o p q r s t u v w x y z

245

march marches, marching, marched
NOUN **1** an organised protest in which a large group of people walk somewhere together
VERB **2** When soldiers **march**, they walk with quick regular steps as a group.
NOUN **3** music with a strong beat for marching to

March
NOUN the third month of the year. **March** has 31 days.

WORD HISTORY
from Latin *Martius* month of Mars, the Roman god of war

---

mare mares
NOUN an adult female horse

margarine
NOUN a soft substance made from vegetable oil and animal fats, and used like butter

margin margins
NOUN **1** the blank space at the top and bottom and on each side of a written or printed page
NOUN **2** If you win a race or a competition by a large or small **margin**, you win it by a large or small amount.

marina marinas
NOUN a harbour for pleasure boats and yachts

marine marines
NOUN **1** a soldier who is trained for duties at sea
ADJECTIVE **2** relating to or involving the sea, and the animals and plants that live in the sea

mark marks, marking, marked
NOUN **1** a small stain or damaged area on a surface
NOUN **2** a score given to a student for homework or for an exam
NOUN **3** a written or printed symbol
VERB **4** If something **marks** a surface, it stains or damages it in some way.
VERB **5** When a teacher **marks** a student's work, they decide how good it is and give it a mark.
VERB **6** If you **mark** the opposing player in a team game such as hockey or netball, you stay close to them and prevent them from getting the ball.

market markets, marketing, marketed
NOUN **1** a place where goods are bought and sold, usually outdoors
VERB **2** If someone **markets** a product, they sell it in an organised way.

marketing
NOUN the part of a business that has to do with how goods or services are sold to customers

marmalade
NOUN a type of jam made from oranges or lemons

maroon
NOUN **1** a dark reddish-purple colour
ADJECTIVE **2** having a dark reddish-purple colour

marquee marquees
NOUN a very large tent used at a fair, a wedding or other outdoor events

---

WORD HISTORY
from French, meaning awning

---

marriage marriages
NOUN **1** the relationship between two people who are married
NOUN **2** a wedding ceremony

married
VERB **1** the past tense and past participle of **marry**
ADJECTIVE **2** If someone is **married**, they have a husband or a wife.

marrow marrows
NOUN a long, thick, green vegetable with cream-coloured flesh

marry marries, marrying, married
VERB When two people **marry**, they legally become partners in a special ceremony.

marsh marshes
NOUN an area of land that is permanently wet

marshmallow marshmallows
NOUN a soft, spongy sweet, usually pink or white

marsupial marsupials
NOUN an animal that carries its young in a pouch. Koalas, kangaroos and wallabies are **marsupials**.

WORD HISTORY
from Greek *marsupion* meaning purse

---

martial
ADJECTIVE **Martial** describes anything to do with military matters, war and soldiers.

martial arts
PLURAL NOUN The **martial arts** are techniques of self-defence, such as judo and karate, that come from the Far East.

martyr martyrs
NOUN someone who suffers or is killed for their beliefs

marvel marvels, marvelling, marvelled
VERB 1 If you **marvel** at something, you are filled with amazement and admiration for it. ● *We **marvelled** at the sight of people swimming with the dolphins.*
NOUN 2 something that fills you with surprise and admiration

marvellous
ADJECTIVE wonderful or excellent

marzipan
NOUN a paste made of almonds, sugar and egg. It is put on top of cakes or used to make small sweets.

mascot mascots
NOUN a person, animal or toy that is thought to bring good luck

masculine
ADJECTIVE typical of men, rather than women

ANTONYM: feminine

mask masks, masking, masked
NOUN 1 something you wear over your face for protection or as a disguise
VERB 2 If you **mask** something, you cover it so that it is protected or disguised.

mass masses
NOUN 1 a large amount or heap of something
NOUN 2 In science, **mass** is the amount of matter in an object. **Mass** is measured in grams (g).
NOUN 3 A **Mass** is a communion service in a Roman Catholic church.
ADJECTIVE 4 involving or affecting a large number of people

massacre massacres, massacring, massacred
NOUN 1 the killing of a very large number of people in a violent and cruel way
VERB 2 To **massacre** a group of people means to kill them in large numbers in a violent and cruel way.

massage massages, massaging, massaged
VERB 1 If you **massage** someone, you rub

parts of their body in order to help them relax or to relieve pain.
NOUN 2 treatment that involves rubbing parts of the body

massive
ADJECTIVE extremely large

SYNONYMS: huge, vast, enormous

mast masts
NOUN the tall, upright pole that supports the sails of a boat

master masters, mastering, mastered
VERB 1 If you **master** a skill, you learn how to do it well.
NOUN 2 someone who is very skilled at something ● *a **master** of disguise*
NOUN 3 a male teacher

masterpiece masterpieces
NOUN an excellent painting, novel, film or other work of art that has been made with great skill ● *The 'Mona Lisa' is considered a **masterpiece**.*

mat mats
NOUN 1 a small piece of carpet or other material that is put on floors for protection or decoration
NOUN 2 a small piece of cloth or other material that is put on a table or other surface to protect it

match matches, matching, matched
NOUN 1 an organised game of football, cricket or some other sport
NOUN 2 a small, thin wooden stick tipped with a chemical that produces a flame when you strike it against a rough surface. **Matches** are used to light things.
VERB 3 If colours **match**, they go well together. ● *My dress **matched** my shoes.*
VERB 4 If you **match** one thing with another, you find the connection between them.

mate mates, mating, mated
NOUN 1 (*informal*) Your **mates** are your friends.
NOUN 2 The first **mate** on a ship is second in importance after the captain.
VERB 3 When a pair of animals **mate**, they come together in order to breed.

material materials
NOUN 1 cloth
NOUN 2 anything from which something else can be made ● *artists' **materials***

A
B
C
D
E
F
G
H
I
J
K
L
M
N
O
P
Q
R
S
T
U
V
W
X
Y
Z

maternal
ADJECTIVE **1** used to describe things relating to a mother • *My **maternal** grandfather was Welsh.*
ADJECTIVE **2** A woman who is **maternal** has strong motherly feelings.

maternity
ADJECTIVE relating to or involving pregnant women and childbirth • *The baby was born in the **maternity** wing of the hospital.*

mathematical
ADJECTIVE involving numbers, quantities and shapes

mathematically
ADVERB in a way that involves numbers, quantities and shapes

mathematician mathematicians
NOUN someone who studies numbers, quantities and shapes

mathematics
NOUN the study of numbers, quantities and shapes

maths
NOUN an abbreviation of *mathematics*

matinee matinees
NOUN an afternoon performance at a theatre or cinema

PRONUNCIATION TIP
This word is pronounced **mat**-i-nay.

matrix matrices
NOUN In mathematics, a **matrix** is a set of numbers or letters set out in rows and columns.

PRONUNCIATION TIP
This word is pronounced **may**-trix. The plural is pronounced **may**-tri-sees.

matt
ADJECTIVE dull rather than shiny • *Mum painted the front door **matt** green.*

matter matters, mattering, mattered
NOUN **1** a task or situation that you have to attend to • *We will have to discuss the **matter** with the head teacher.*

SYNONYMS: affair, business, subject

NOUN **2** any substance • *The scientists explored how **matter** behaves at high temperatures.*
VERB **3** If something **matters**, it is important.
PHRASE **4** If you ask **What's the matter?**, you want to know what is wrong.

mattress mattresses
NOUN a large, flat, spongy pad that is put on a bed to make it comfortable to sleep on

mature matures, maturing, matured
VERB **1** When a child or other young animal **matures**, it becomes an adult.
ADJECTIVE **2** fully grown or developed

maturely
ADVERB If someone behaves **maturely**, they behave in a sensible way like you would expect an adult to behave.

maturity
NOUN **Maturity** is when a person or animal is fully grown or developed.

maul mauls, mauling, mauled
VERB If an animal **mauls** someone, they savagely attack and badly injure them.

mauve
NOUN **1** a light purple colour
ADJECTIVE **2** having a light purple colour

PRONUNCIATION TIP
This word rhymes with "stove".

maximum
ADJECTIVE **1** The **maximum** amount is the most that is possible or allowed. • *The **maximum** score for this question is five marks*

ANTONYM: minimum

NOUN **2** the most that is possible or allowed • *Pupils are allowed a **maximum** of two pounds to spend on the school trip.*

ANTONYM: minimum

may
VERB **1** If something **may** happen, it is possible that it will happen.
VERB **2** If you **may** do something, you are allowed to do it.

May
NOUN the fifth month of the year. **May** has 31 days.

WORD HISTORY
probably from the Roman goddess *Maia*

maybe
ADVERB If you think there is a possibility that something will happen, but you are not sure, you use **maybe**. • *Maybe we will be allowed to go to the cinema tonight.*

mayonnaise

NOUN a thick salad dressing made with egg yolks and oil

mayor mayors

NOUN someone who has been elected to represent the people of a town at official functions

maze mazes

NOUN a system of complicated passages which it is difficult to find your way through

me

PRONOUN A speaker or writer uses **me** to refer to himself or herself.

meadow meadows

NOUN a field of grass

meagre

ADJECTIVE very small and poor • *meagre portions*

meal meals

NOUN **1** an occasion when people eat
NOUN **2** the food people eat at meal times

mean means, meaning, meant; meaner, meanest

VERB **1** If you ask someone what something **means**, you want them to explain it to you.
VERB **2** If you **mean** to do something, you intend to do it.

SYNONYMS: aim, plan

VERB **3** If something **means** a lot to you, it is important to you.
ADJECTIVE **4** unkind
ADJECTIVE **5** Someone who is **mean** is unwilling to share with others.
NOUN **6** In mathematics, the **mean** is the average of a set of numbers.

meander meanders, meandering, meandered

VERB If a road or river **meanders**, it has a lot of bends in it.

PRONUNCIATION TIP
This word is pronounced mee-**an**-der.

WORD HISTORY
from *Maiandros*, the name of a Greek river

meaning meanings

NOUN The **meaning** of a word, expression or gesture is what it refers to or expresses.
• *Do you know the **meaning** of the proverb "more haste, less speed"?*

meanwhile

ADVERB If something happens, and **meanwhile** something else is happening, the two things are happening at the same time.

measles

NOUN an infectious illness that causes a high temperature and red spots on the skin • *an outbreak of **measles***

WORD HISTORY
from Germanic *masele* meaning spot on the skin

measure measures, measuring, measured

VERB **1** If you **measure** something, you find out the size or amount of it. • *First **measure** the length of the table.*
NOUN **2** a unit used to measure something
NOUN **3** a container or an instrument, such as a ruler or a measuring jug, that you use to measure something
NOUN **4** an action that you take to achieve something

measurement measurements

NOUN the result you obtain when you measure something

meat meats

NOUN the flesh of animals that people cook and eat • *As a vegetarian, I don't eat **meat** or fish.*

mechanic mechanics

NOUN someone whose job is to repair and maintain machines and engines

mechanical

ADJECTIVE **1** to do with machinery. Anything **mechanical** is worked by machinery.
ADJECTIVE **2** If you do something in a **mechanical** way, you do it without thinking about it.

medal medals

NOUN a small piece of decorative metal, often shaped like a large coin and attached to a ribbon, given as an award for bravery or as a prize in sport

meddle meddles, meddling, meddled

VERB If you **meddle**, you interfere and try to change things without being asked.

media

PLURAL NOUN You can refer to the television, radio and newspapers as the **media**.

LANGUAGE TIP
Media is the plural of *medium* but it is becoming more common for it to be used as a singular noun: *The media is obsessed with celebrities.*

---

median medians

NOUN In mathematics, the **median** of a set of numbers is the middle number once the numbers have been arranged in order of size. • *The median of 4, 0, 1, 2, 3 is 2, as 2 is in the middle once they are organised in order.*

medical

ADJECTIVE to do with the treatment of people who are ill

medication medications

NOUN a substance that is used to treat illness

medicine medicines

NOUN **1** a substance that you take to help cure an illness
NOUN **2** the care and treatment of people who are ill

medieval; also spelt mediaeval

ADJECTIVE relating to the period between about 1100–1500 AD, especially in Europe

mediocre

ADJECTIVE Something that is **mediocre** is of average or poor quality or standard. • *The film was mediocre.*

PRONUNCIATION TIP
This word is pronounced mee-dee-**oh**-ker.

Mediterranean

NOUN **1** the large sea between southern Europe and northern Africa
ADJECTIVE **2** relating to the Mediterranean or the countries adjoining it

medium mediums or media

ADJECTIVE **1** If something is of **medium** size, it is neither large nor small.
NOUN **2** a means of communicating or expressing something

meek meeker, meekest

ADJECTIVE A **meek** person is timid and does what other people say.

meet meets, meeting, met

VERB **1** If you **meet** someone, you make an arrangement to go to the same place at the same time as they do. • *Let's meet at my house.*

VERB **2** If you **meet** someone, you come face-to-face with them or are introduced to them for the first time. • *We met on our first day at school.*

meeting meetings

NOUN **1** an event at which people discuss things or make decisions
NOUN **2** an occasion when you meet someone by arrangement

megabyte megabytes

NOUN a unit of storage in a computer, equal to 1,048,576 bytes

melancholy

ADJECTIVE If you feel **melancholy**, you feel very sad.

melodramatic

ADJECTIVE behaving in an exaggerated, emotional way

melody melodies

NOUN a tune

WORD HISTORY
from Greek *meloidia* meaning singing

---

melon melons

NOUN a large, juicy fruit with a green or yellow skin and many seeds inside

melt melts, melting, melted

VERB When something **melts**, or when you **melt** it, it changes from a solid to a liquid because it has been heated.

---

melting point

NOUN the temperature at which a solid starts to change into a liquid

member members

NOUN one of the people or things belonging to a group

membrane membranes

NOUN a very thin skin

memoir memoirs

NOUN a book or article that you write about your own life or about the life of someone who you have known well

memorable

ADJECTIVE **Memorable** things or people are likely to be remembered because they are special or unusual.

memorial memorials

NOUN a structure built to remind people of a famous person or event • *a war memorial*

memorise memorises, memorising, memorised; also spelt **memorize**
VERB If you **memorise** something, you learn it so well that you remember it and can repeat it exactly. • *She **memorised** all the times tables from 2 to 12 in one week.*

memory memories
NOUN 1 your ability to remember things
NOUN 2 A computer's **memory** is its capacity to store information.

memory card memory cards
NOUN a small card containing computer memory that is used in digital cameras and other devices

memory stick memory sticks
NOUN a small device that connects to a computer and allows you to store and copy information

men
PLURAL NOUN the plural of **man**

menace menaces, menacing, menaced
NOUN 1 someone or something that is likely to cause harm • *That dog is a **menace**.*
VERB 2 If someone or something **menaces** you, they threaten to harm you.

menacing
ADJECTIVE threatening and making you think something bad is going to happen to you

menacingly
ADVERB in a threatening way that makes you think something bad is going to happen to you

mend mends, mending, mended
VERB If you **mend** something that is broken, you repair or fix it.

menstruate menstruates, menstruating, menstruated
VERB When a woman **menstruates**, blood comes from her womb. This normally happens once a month.

mental
ADJECTIVE relating to the mind and the process of thinking • *mental arithmetic*

mention mentions, mentioning, mentioned
VERB 1 If you **mention** something, you speak or write briefly about it.
NOUN 2 a brief comment about someone or something

menu menus
NOUN 1 a list of the food and drink you can buy in a restaurant or café
NOUN 2 a list of options shown on a computer screen, which the user must choose from

mercenary mercenaries
ADJECTIVE 1 Someone who is **mercenary** is mainly interested in getting money.
NOUN 2 a soldier who is paid to fight for a foreign country

merchandise
NOUN goods for buying and selling • *The market stalls were full of all kinds of **merchandise**.*

merchant merchants
NOUN a trader who imports and exports goods

mercury
NOUN a silver-coloured metallic element that is liquid at room temperature. **Mercury** is used in some thermometers.

mercy mercies
NOUN If you show **mercy**, you are kind and forgiving instead of punishing someone.

merge merges, merging, merged
VERB When two things **merge**, they combine or join together to make one thing. • *The two roads **merged** at the junction.*

meridian meridians
NOUN one of the lines on maps or globes, drawn from the North Pole to the South Pole, that help to describe the position of a place

merit merits, meriting, merited
NOUN 1 If something has **merit**, it is good or worthwhile.
NOUN 2 The **merits** of something are its advantages or good qualities. • *I can see now the **merits** of working hard.*
VERB 3 If something or someone **merits** a particular treatment, they deserve that treatment. • *He **merits** a place in the team.*

mermaid mermaids
NOUN a creature in stories, with a woman's body and a fish's tail instead of legs

merry merrier, merriest
ADJECTIVE happy and cheerful

mesh
NOUN threads of wire, plastic or other material twisted together like a net

A
B
C
D
E
F
G
H
I
J
K
L
M
N
O
P
Q
R
S
T
U
V
W
X
Y
Z

mess messes, messing, messed
NOUN **1** something dirty or untidy
NOUN **2** something full of problems
mess about or **mess around**
VERB If you **mess about** or **mess around**, you spend time doing silly or casual things. • Stop **messing about** and get on with your work.
mess up
VERB If you **mess up** something, you make it untidy, spoil it or do it badly. • He'd already **messed up** one piece of paper.

message messages, messaging, messaged
NOUN **1** a piece of information or a request from one person to another
VERB **2** If you **message** someone, you write to them on a social media website. • I'll **message** you with my address.

messenger messengers
NOUN someone who takes a message

messy messier, messiest
ADJECTIVE **1** dirty or untidy
ADJECTIVE **2** complicated or confused • He's got himself into a **messy** situation.

met
VERB the past tense and past participle of **meet**

metal metals
NOUN a hard substance such as iron, steel, copper or lead. **Metals** are good conductors of heat and electricity.

metallic
ADJECTIVE made of metal or like metal

metaphor metaphors
NOUN an imaginative way of describing one thing as another thing. For example, if a person is shy and timid, you could describe them as a mouse.

meteor meteors
NOUN a piece of rock or metal moving rapidly through space, that burns very briefly and brightly when it enters the Earth's atmosphere

meteorite meteorites
NOUN a piece of rock from space that has landed on Earth

meteorologist meteorologists
NOUN someone who studies the weather

meteorology
NOUN the study of the weather

meter meters
NOUN a device that measures and records something, such as a gas **meter** that records how much gas a household has used

method methods
NOUN a particular way of doing something • Use the **method** I showed you to work out the sum.

methodical
ADJECTIVE **Methodical** people do things in a careful and organised way.

metre metres
NOUN a unit of length (m) equal to 100 centimetres

metric
ADJECTIVE The **metric** system of measurement is a system that uses metres, grams and litres.

mew mews, mewing, mewed
VERB When a cat **mews**, it makes a short, high-pitched noise.

miaow miaows, miaowing, miaowed
NOUN **1** the noise a cat makes
VERB **2** When a cat **miaows**, it makes a crying sound.

mice
PLURAL NOUN the plural of **mouse**

micro-
PREFIX added to some words to mean very small. For example, a **micro**computer is a very small computer.

microbe microbes
NOUN a very small, living thing that can only be seen through a microscope. **Microbes** can feed, grow and reproduce.

microchip microchips
NOUN a small piece of silicon that has electronic circuits printed on it, and is used in computers and electronic equipment

microhabitat microhabitats
NOUN a very small habitat

micro-organism micro-organisms
NOUN a very small organism that can only be seen under a powerful microscope. Some **micro-organisms** are harmful and cause disease. Others, such as yeast, are helpful. Microbes, germs and viruses are sometimes called **micro-organisms**.

microphone microphones
NOUN a device that is used to record sounds or make them louder

microscope microscopes
NOUN a piece of equipment that magnifies very small objects so that you can study them • *When the class looked at a leaf through the **microscope**, they could see the small veins that they had not been able to see before.*

microscopic
ADJECTIVE too small to be seen without using a microscope

microwave microwaves
NOUN a type of oven that cooks food very quickly by radiation

mid-
PREFIX used to form words that refer to the middle part of a place or a period of time • *We had a break **mid**morning.*

midday
NOUN twelve o'clock in the middle of the day

middle middles
NOUN 1 The **middle** of something is the part furthest from the edges, ends or surface. • *He stood in the **middle** of the room.*
NOUN 2 The **middle** of an event is the part that comes after the first part and before the last part. • *There was an interval in the **middle** of the play.*
ADJECTIVE 3 The **middle** thing in a series is the one with an equal number of things on each side. • *M and N are the **middle** letters in the alphabet.*

Middle Ages
NOUN In European history, the **Middle Ages** were the period between about 1100 AD and 1500 AD.

midnight
NOUN twelve o'clock at night

midwife midwives
NOUN a nurse who is trained to help women during pregnancy and at the birth of their baby

might
VERB 1 You use **might** to say that something will possibly happen or is possibly true. • *I **might** not be back until tomorrow.*
NOUN 2 If you do something with all your **might**, you do it with all your strength and energy.

migraine migraines
NOUN a severe headache that makes you feel very ill

migrant migrants
NOUN 1 A **migrant** or a **migrant** worker is a person who moves from one place to another, usually to find work • ***Migrants** arrived for the fruit-picking season.*
NOUN 2 a bird, fish or animal that migrates from one part of the world to another • *The spotted flycatcher, a **migrant** from Africa, arrives in Britain in May.*

migrate migrates, migrating, migrated
VERB 1 If people **migrate**, they move from one place to another, especially to find work.
VERB 2 When birds or animals **migrate**, they move to a different place at a particular season, usually to breed or to find food.

migration
NOUN 1 **Migration** is when people move from one place to another, especially to find work.
NOUN 2 **Migration** is when birds or animals move to a different place at a particular season, usually to breed or to find food.

migratory
ADJECTIVE **Migratory** birds or animals move to a different place at a particular season, usually to breed or to find food.

mild milder, mildest
ADJECTIVE Something that is **mild** is gentle, and not very strong or severe. • ***mild** weather*

mildew
NOUN a soft, white fungus that grows on things when they are warm and damp

mile miles
NOUN a unit of distance equal to about 1.6 kilometres

WORD HISTORY
from Latin *milia passuum* meaning a thousand paces

mileage mileages
NOUN the distance you have travelled, measured in miles • *The **mileage** from home to the hotel was 120 miles.*

military
ADJECTIVE to do with the armed forces of a country

253

A
B
C
D
E
F
G
H
I
J
K
L
M
N
O
P
Q
R
S
T
U
V
W
X
Y
Z

254

milk **milks, milking, milked**
> NOUN **1** the white liquid produced by mammals to feed their young. People drink cows' and goats' **milk** and make it into butter, cheese and yogurt.
> VERB **2** When someone **milks** a cow or other animal, they get milk from it by pulling its udders.

milkman **milkmen**
> NOUN a man who delivers milk to your house

mill **mills**
> NOUN **1** a building where grain is crushed to make flour
> NOUN **2** a factory for making materials such as steel, wool or cotton • *a cotton* **mill**
> NOUN **3** a small device for grinding something. For example, a pepper **mill** grinds peppercorns.

millennium **millennia** or **millenniums**
> NOUN a period of 1000 years

milligram **milligrams**
> NOUN a unit of weight (mg). There are 1000 **milligrams** in a gram.

millilitre **millilitres**
> NOUN a unit for measuring liquid (ml). There are 1000 **millilitres** in a litre.

millimetre **millimetres**
> NOUN a unit of length (mm). There are 10 **millimetres** in a centimetre.

million **millions**
> NOUN A **million** is the number 1,000,000.

millionaire **millionaires**
> NOUN someone who has money or property worth at least a million pounds or dollars

millionth **millionths**
> NOUN **1** one of a million equal parts of something
> ADJECTIVE **2** The **millionth** item in a series is the one that you count as number million. It can be written as 1000000th.

mime **mimes, miming, mimed**
> NOUN **1** the use of movements and gestures to express something or to tell a story without using speech
> VERB **2** If you **mime** something, you describe or express it using mime.

mimic **mimics, mimicking, mimicked**
> VERB **1** If you **mimic** someone's actions or voice, you imitate them in an amusing way.
> NOUN **2** a person who can imitate other people

minaret **minarets**
> NOUN a tall, thin tower on a mosque

mince **minces, mincing, minced**
> NOUN **1** meat that has been ground into very small pieces
> VERB **2** If you **mince** meat, you grind it into very small pieces.

mincemeat
> NOUN a sweet mixture of dried fruits used, for example, in mince pies

mind **minds, minding, minded**
> NOUN **1** Your **mind** is your ability to think, together with your memory and all the thoughts you have. • *He could still see her face in his* **mind**.
> PHRASE **2** If you **change your mind**, you change a decision that you have made or an opinion that you have.
> VERB **3** If you do not **mind** what happens or what something is like, you do not have a strong preference about it. • *I don't* **mind** *where we go.*
> VERB **4** If you tell someone to **mind** something, you are warning them to be careful. • **Mind** *that plate, it's hot.*
> VERB **5** If you **mind** something for someone, you look after it for a while.

mindless
> ADJECTIVE **1** **Mindless** behaviour is stupid and destructive.
> ADJECTIVE **2** A **mindless** job or activity is so simple, or repeated so often, that you do not need to think about it at all.

> SYNONYM: repetitive

mine **mines**
> PRONOUN **1** something belonging or relating to the person who is speaking or writing • *He's a good friend of* **mine**.
> NOUN **2** a place where deep holes or tunnels are dug under the ground in order to extract minerals • *a coal* **mine**
> NOUN **3** a bomb hidden in the ground or underwater, that explodes when people or things touch it

minefield **minefields**
> NOUN an area of land or water where explosive mines have been laid

miner **miners**
> NOUN a person who works underground in mines to find and dig out coal, diamonds, gold and other minerals • *a coal* **miner**

mineral minerals
NOUN small particles that make up different rocks. For example, quartz and diamonds are **minerals**.

mineral water
NOUN water that comes from a natural spring

mingle mingles, mingling, mingled
VERB If things **mingle**, they become mixed together.

mini-
PREFIX used with another word to describe something shorter or smaller than the usual size • a **mini**skirt

miniature
ADJECTIVE a tiny copy of something much larger • I bought a **miniature** version of the Eiffel Tower as a souvenir.

minibus minibuses
NOUN a van with seats in the back, that is used as a small bus

minimum
ADJECTIVE 1 A **minimum** amount of something is the smallest amount that is possible, allowed or needed.

ANTONYM: maximum

NOUN 2 the smallest amount of something that is possible, allowed or needed

ANTONYM: maximum

minister ministers
NOUN 1 a person who is in charge of a particular government department
NOUN 2 a member of the clergy, especially in a Protestant church

WORD HISTORY
from Latin minister meaning servant

ministry ministries
NOUN a government department that deals with a particular area of work • the **Ministry** of Education

mink minks
NOUN an expensive fur used to make coats and hats

minnow minnows
NOUN a very small, freshwater fish

minor
ADJECTIVE less important or serious than other things • He had a **minor** part in the play.

ANTONYM: major

minority minorities
NOUN less than half of a group of people or things

minstrel minstrels
NOUN a singer and entertainer in medieval times

mint mints
NOUN 1 a plant with strong-smelling leaves used as flavouring in cooking
NOUN 2 a sweet flavoured with these leaves
NOUN 3 the place where the official coins of a country are made
ADJECTIVE 4 If something is in **mint** condition, it is like new.

minus
PREPOSITION 1 You use **minus** (−) to show that one number is being subtracted from another. • Ten **minus** six equals four (10 − 6 = 4).
ADJECTIVE 2 **Minus** before a number means that the number is less than zero. • There are sometimes temperatures of **minus** 65 °C (−65 °C) in the Arctic.

minute minutes
NOUN 1 a unit of time equal to sixty seconds
NOUN 2 a short period of time • See you in a **minute**.
ADJECTIVE 3 extremely small • A **minute** amount of milk is needed.

PRONUNCIATION TIP
The noun is pronounced **min**-it. The adjective is pronounced my-**nyoot**.

miracle miracles
NOUN a surprising and wonderful event, especially one believed to have been caused by God

WORD HISTORY
from Latin mirari meaning to wonder at

mirage mirages
NOUN an image that you can see in the distance in very hot weather, but that does not actually exist

PRONUNCIATION TIP
This word is pronounced mi-**rarzh**.

a
b
c
d
e
f
g
h
i
j
k
l
m
n
o
p
q
r
s
t
u
v
w
x
y
z

A
B
C
D
E
F
G
H
I
J
K
L
M
N
O
P
Q
R
S
T
U
V
W
X
Y
Z

mirror mirrors
NOUN an object made of glass in which you can see your reflection

mis-
PREFIX added to some words to mean badly or wrongly. For example, **mis**behave means to behave badly, and **mis**calculate means to calculate wrongly.

misbehave misbehaves, misbehaving, misbehaved
VERB If someone **misbehaves**, they are naughty or behave badly.

misbehaviour
NOUN naughty or bad behaviour

miscarriage miscarriages
NOUN 1 If a woman has a **miscarriage**, she gives birth to a baby too early, before it is able to survive in the outside world.
NOUN 2 A **miscarriage** of justice is a wrong decision made by a court, which results in an innocent person being punished.

miscellaneous
ADJECTIVE A **miscellaneous** group is made up of a mixture of people or things that are different from each other.

PRONUNCIATION TIP
This word is pronounced miss-uh-**lay**-nee-uss.

mischief
NOUN naughty behaviour, teasing people or playing tricks

mischievous
ADJECTIVE If you are **mischievous**, you enjoy being naughty by teasing or playing tricks on people.

miser misers
NOUN a mean person who enjoys hoarding money, but hates spending it

miserable
ADJECTIVE If you are **miserable**, you are very unhappy.

miserly
ADJECTIVE Someone who is **miserly** is mean and hates spending money.

misery miseries
NOUN great unhappiness
SYNONYM: grief

misfire misfires, misfiring, misfired
VERB If a plan **misfires**, it goes wrong.

misfit misfits
NOUN a person who cannot get on with other people or fit into a group

misfortune misfortunes
NOUN an unpleasant occurrence that is regarded as bad luck • I had the **misfortune** to fall off my bike.

mishap mishaps
NOUN an accidental or unfortunate happening that is not very serious
• Grandma had a small **mishap** when her hat blew away.

misjudge misjudges, misjudging, misjudged
VERB If you **misjudge** someone or something, you form a wrong or unfair opinion of them.

mislay mislays, mislaying, mislaid
VERB If you **mislay** something, you cannot remember where you put it.

mislead misleads, misleading, misled
VERB If you **mislead** someone, you make them believe something that is not true.

misprint misprints
NOUN a mistake such as a spelling mistake in something that has been printed

miss misses, missing, missed
VERB 1 If you **miss** someone or something, you feel sad because they are no longer with you.
VERB 2 If you **miss** a bus, plane or train, you arrive too late to catch it.
VERB 3 If you **miss** an event or activity, you fail to attend it. • I had to **miss** my piano lesson.
VERB 4 If you **miss** something that you are aiming at, you fail to hit it. • The arrow **missed** the target.
NOUN 5 **Miss** is used before the name of a girl or unmarried woman. • My teacher this year is **Miss** Weston.

missile missiles
NOUN 1 a weapon that moves long distances through the air and explodes when it reaches its target • nuclear **missiles**
NOUN 2 any object thrown to harm someone or something

missing
ADJECTIVE Something that is **missing** is lost or not in its usual place. • One of my shoes is **missing**.

mission missions
NOUN **1** a journey made by a military aeroplane or space rocket to carry out a task
NOUN **2** an important task that has to be done

missionary missionaries
NOUN a Christian who has been sent to a foreign country to work for the Church

misspell misspells, misspelling, misspelt or **misspelled**
VERB If you **misspell** a word, you spell it wrongly.

mist mists
NOUN many tiny drops of water in the air that make it hard to see clearly

mistake mistakes, mistaking, mistook, mistaken
NOUN **1** If you make a **mistake**, you do something wrong without intending to.
● *There are some spelling **mistakes** in your homework.*
VERB **2** If you **mistake** someone or something for another person or thing, you wrongly think that they are the other person or thing. ● *I **mistook** him for his brother.*

mistletoe
NOUN a plant that grows on trees and has white berries on it

mistook
VERB the past tense of **mistake**

mistreat mistreats, mistreating, mistreated
VERB If you **mistreat** a person or an animal, you treat them badly and make them suffer.

mistress mistresses
NOUN **1** a woman schoolteacher ● *There is a new French **mistress**.*
NOUN **2** a woman who is in charge of something or someone

mistrust mistrusts, mistrusting, mistrusted
VERB **1** If you **mistrust** someone, you feel that that they are not to be trusted.

ANTONYM: trust

NOUN **2** the feeling of not being able to trust someone or something

ANTONYM: trust

misunderstand misunderstands, misunderstanding, misunderstood
VERB If you **misunderstand** someone, you do not properly understand what they say or do. ● *He **misunderstood** the instructions and took the wrong turning.*

misunderstanding misunderstandings
NOUN If people have a **misunderstanding**, they have a disagreement or a slight quarrel about something.

misuse misuses, misusing, misused
NOUN **1** The **misuse** of something is the incorrect or dishonest use of it.
VERB **2** If you **misuse** something, you use it wrongly or dishonestly.

mix mixes, mixing, mixed
VERB **1** If you **mix** things, you combine them.
VERB **2** A **mixed** number is made up of a whole number and a fraction.
mix up
VERB If you **mix up** things, you get confused.

mixed up
ADJECTIVE confused ● *I got **mixed up** and went to the wrong place.*

mixture mixtures
NOUN **1** two or more things mixed together
● *They felt a **mixture** of fear and excitement as they climbed the wall.*
NOUN **2** a substance consisting of two or more other substances that have been mixed together

ml
an abbreviation for *millilitre*

mm
an abbreviation for *millimetre*

mnemonic mnemonics
NOUN a word, short poem, or sentence that can help you remember things such as spelling rules ● *Never Eat Slimy Worms is a **mnemonic** for the points of the compass.*

moan moans, moaning, moaned
VERB **1** If you **moan**, you make a low, miserable sound because you are in pain or unhappy.
VERB **2** If you **moan** about something, you complain about it.
NOUN **3** a low cry of pain or unhappiness

a
b
c
d
e
f
g
h
i
j
k
l
m
n
o
p
q
r
s
t
u
v
w
x
y
z

A
B
C
D
E
F
G
H
I
J
K
L
M
N
O
P
Q
R
S
T
U
V
W
X
Y
Z

moat moats
NOUN a wide, deep ditch around a castle, usually filled with water, to help defend the building
→ Have a look at the illustration for **castle**

mob mobs, mobbing, mobbed
NOUN **1** a large, disorganised crowd of people
VERB **2** If a group **mobs** someone, they gather closely around them in a disorderly way. • *The fans mobbed the band.*

mobile mobiles
ADJECTIVE **1** able to move or be moved easily • *He's much more mobile since getting his new wheelchair.*
NOUN **2** short for **mobile phone**
NOUN **3** an ornament made up of several parts that hang from threads and move in the breeze

mobile phone mobile phones
NOUN a small phone that you can carry around with you

mock mocks, mocking, mocked
VERB **1** If you **mock** someone, you tease them or try to make them look foolish.
SYNONYMS: laugh at, make fun of
ADJECTIVE **2** not genuine • *The ring is made of mock diamonds.*

mode modes
NOUN **1** a particular way of behaving or of doing something
NOUN **2** In mathematics, the mode is the most popular or most frequently occurring value. • *Of the following numbers – 5, 5, 6, 7, 7, 7, 8 – 7 is the mode.*

model models
NOUN **1** a smaller copy of something that shows what it looks like or how it works in real life • *a model of how the building will look*
NOUN **2** a type or version of a product • *Which model of computer did you choose?*
NOUN **3** a person who wears clothes that are being displayed to possible buyers, or who poses for a photographer or artist
ADJECTIVE **4** a smaller copy of something that shows what it looks like or how it works in real life • *Mark has a model railway in his bedroom.*
ADJECTIVE **5** A **model** student is an excellent example of a student.

modem modems
NOUN a piece of equipment that links a computer to the telephone system so that data can be sent from one computer to another

moderate moderates, moderating, moderated
ADJECTIVE **1** A **moderate** amount of something is not too much or too little of it.
ADJECTIVE **2** **Moderate** ideas and opinions are not extreme.
VERB **3** If something **moderates** or is **moderated**, it becomes less extreme. • *He should moderate his temper.*

PRONUNCIATION TIP
The adjective is pronounced **mod**-er-ut. The verb is pronounced **mod**-er-ayt.

modern
ADJECTIVE new and involving the latest ideas or equipment

WORD HISTORY
from Latin *modo* meaning just recently

modest
ADJECTIVE **1** quite small in size or amount • *He inherited a modest amount of money.*
ADJECTIVE **2** **Modest** people do not boast about how clever or how rich they are.
ANTONYM: boastful

modesty
NOUN the quality that someone has when they do not boast about how clever or how rich they are

modify modifies, modifying, modified
VERB If you **modify** something, you change it slightly to improve it. • *When he had modified his bike, it went much faster.*

module modules
NOUN **1** one of the parts which, when put together, form a whole unit or object
NOUN **2** a part of a spacecraft that can do certain things away from the main body • *the lunar module*

moist moister, moistest
ADJECTIVE slightly wet, damp

moisten moistens, moistening, moistened
VERB If you **moisten** something, you make it slightly wet.

moisture
NOUN tiny drops of water in the air or on the ground

molar molars

NOUN Your **molars** are the large teeth at the back of your mouth.

→ Have a look at the illustration for **teeth**

mole moles

NOUN **1** a small animal with black fur. **Moles** live in tunnels underground.

NOUN **2** a dark, slightly-raised spot on your skin

molecular

ADJECTIVE to do with molecules

molecule molecules

NOUN A **molecule** is made up of two or more atoms held together.

mollusc molluscs

NOUN an animal with a soft body and no backbone. Snails, slugs, clams and mussels are all **molluscs**.

molten

ADJECTIVE **Molten** rock or metal has been heated to a very high temperature and has melted to become a thick liquid. • *When the volcano erupted, **molten** lava flowed down the mountainside.*

moment moments

NOUN **1** a very short period of time • *I paused for a **moment**.*

SYNONYMS: instant, second

NOUN **2** the point at which something happens • *At that **moment**, the doorbell rang.*

PHRASE **3** If something is happening **at the moment**, it is happening now.

momentum

NOUN the ability that an object has to continue moving as a result of its mass and the speed at which it is already moving

monarchy monarchies

NOUN a system in which a queen or king reigns in a country

monastery monasteries

NOUN a place where monks live and work

WORD HISTORY
from Latin *monasterium* meaning to live alone

monastic

ADJECTIVE to do with monks or life in a monastery

Monday Mondays

NOUN the second day of the week, coming between Sunday and Tuesday

WORD HISTORY
from Old English *Monandæg* meaning moon's day

money

NOUN the coins and banknotes that you use to buy things

mongrel mongrels

NOUN a dog with parents of different breeds

monitor monitors, monitoring, monitored

VERB **1** If you **monitor** something, you regularly check its condition and progress.

NOUN **2** a machine used to check or record things

NOUN **3** the visual display unit of some computers

NOUN **4** a school pupil chosen to do special duties by the teacher

monk monks

NOUN a member of a male religious community

monkey monkeys

NOUN an agile animal that has a long tail and climbs trees

mono-

PREFIX having one of something, for example a **mono**rail is a single rail, and a sound that is **mono**tone has only one tone

monologue monologues

NOUN a long speech by one person during a play or conversation

monotonous

ADJECTIVE always the same in way that is very dull and boring • *a **monotonous** voice*

monotony

NOUN the quality that something has when it is always the same in a way that is dull and boring

monsoon monsoons

NOUN the season of very heavy rain in South-east Asia

monster monsters

NOUN **1** a large, imaginary creature that looks very frightening

NOUN **2** a cruel and frightening person

ADJECTIVE **3** extremely large • *She gave him a **monster** TV set for his birthday.*

WORD HISTORY
from Latin *monstrum* meaning omen or warning

month months
NOUN one of the twelve periods that a year is divided into

monthly
ADJECTIVE **1** happening or appearing once every month • *There is a **monthly** fee to pay for the club.*
ADVERB **2** once every month • *The magazine is published **monthly**.*

monument monuments
NOUN a large structure built to remind people of a famous person or event

WORD HISTORY
from Latin *monere* meaning to remind

moo moos, mooing, mooed
VERB **1** When cows **moo**, they make a long, deep sound.
NOUN **2** the long, deep sound that cows make

mood moods
NOUN the way you are feeling at a particular time

moodily
ADVERB in a way that shows you are annoyed or unhappy

moody moodier, moodiest
ADJECTIVE **1** **Moody** people change their mood often and very quickly, seemingly for no reason.
ADJECTIVE **2** depressed and miserable

moon moons
NOUN an object that moves round the Earth once every four weeks. You see the **moon** as a shining circle or crescent in the sky at night. Some other planets have **moons**.

moonlight
NOUN the light that comes from the moon at night

moor moors, mooring, moored
NOUN **1** a high area of open land • *The farmer had flocks of sheep grazing on the **moors**.*
VERB **2** If you **moor** a boat, you attach it to the land with a rope.

moose
NOUN a North American deer or elk, with large, flat antlers

LANGUAGE TIP
The plural of *moose* is *moose*.

mop mops, mopping, mopped
NOUN **1** a tool for washing floors. It has a string or a sponge head at the end of a long handle.
VERB **2** If you **mop** something, you wipe it or clean it up with a mop or a cloth.

mope mopes, moping, moped
VERB If you **mope**, you feel miserable and sorry for yourself • *Don't sit around and **mope** – go out and do something you enjoy.*

moral morals
PLURAL NOUN **1 Morals** are values based on beliefs that are acceptable to a particular society.
ADJECTIVE **2** relating to beliefs about what is right and wrong • ***moral** values*
NOUN **3** the lesson taught by a story, that usually tells you that good behaviour is best

morale
NOUN Your **morale** is the amount of confidence and optimism you feel.
• *The **morale** of the school was high.*

morality
NOUN **1** society's beliefs about what is good or bad behaviour
NOUN **2** The **morality** of an action or way of behaving is whether people think it is right or wrong. • *People argue about the **morality** of hunting animals.*

morally
ADVERB to do with beliefs about what is right and wrong • *Stealing is **morally** wrong.*

morbid
ADJECTIVE If you are **morbid**, you have a great interest in unpleasant things, especially death and illness.

WORD HISTORY
from Latin *morbus* meaning illness

more
ADJECTIVE **1** a greater number or extent than something else • **More** than 1500 schools took part in the event.

ANTONYMS: fewer, less

ADJECTIVE **2** an additional thing or amount of something • I would like some **more** orange juice.
PRONOUN **3** an additional thing or amount of something • We should do **more** to help people.
ADVERB **4** **More** means to a greater degree or extent. • We can talk **more** later.
ADVERB **5** You use **more** to show that something is repeated. • Repeat the exercise once **more**.
ADVERB **6** You use **more** in front of some adjectives and adverbs to form comparatives. • He did it **more** carefully the second time.

morning mornings
NOUN **1** the early part of the day, before noon
NOUN **2** the part of the day between midnight and midday

Morse code
NOUN a code for sending messages by radio signals. Each letter is represented by a series of dots (short sounds) and dashes (longer sounds).

morsel morsels
NOUN a small piece of food

mortal mortals
ADJECTIVE **1** a **mortal** wound causes death
ADJECTIVE **2** unable to live forever and certain to die
NOUN **3** an ordinary person

mortar mortars
NOUN **1** a mixture of sand, water and cement used to hold bricks firmly together
NOUN **2** a short cannon that fires missiles high into the air

mortgage mortgages
NOUN a loan that people get from a bank or building society in order to buy a house

mortuary mortuaries
NOUN a special room in a hospital where dead bodies are kept before being buried or cremated

mosaic mosaics
NOUN a design made of small, coloured stones, tiles or pieces of coloured glass set into concrete or plaster

mosque mosques
NOUN a building where Muslims go to worship

WORD HISTORY
from Arabic masjid meaning temple

mosquito mosquitoes or mosquitos
NOUN a small, flying insect that bites people and animals in order to suck their blood

moss mosses
NOUN a soft, small, green plant that grows on damp soil or stone

most
ADJECTIVE **1** **Most** of a group of things or people means nearly all of them. • **Most** people prefer sunny weather.
ADJECTIVE **2** a larger amount than anyone or anything else • She has the **most** points.
ADVERB **3** You use **most** in front of adjectives or adverbs to form superlatives. • the **most** breathtaking scenery in the world

motel motels
NOUN a hotel for people who are travelling by car, with parking spaces close to the rooms

moth moths
NOUN an insect like a butterfly that usually flies at night

mother mothers
NOUN Your **mother** is your female parent.

mother-in-law mothers-in-law
NOUN the mother of someone's husband or wife

motion motions
NOUN movement

motionless
ADJECTIVE If someone or something is **motionless**, they are not moving at all.

motivate motivates, motivating, motivated
VERB If you **motivate** someone, you make them determined to do or achieve something.

motivated
ADJECTIVE **1** determined to do or achieve something
ADJECTIVE **2** done for a particular reason • The decision was politically **motivated**.

motivation
NOUN **1** determination to do or achieve something
NOUN **2** the reason why someone does something

a
b
c
d
e
f
g
h
i
j
k
l
m
n
o
p
q
r
s
t
u
v
w
x
y
z

261

motive motives

NOUN a reason or purpose for doing something

motor motors

NOUN a part of a vehicle or machine. The **motor** uses fuel to make the vehicle or machine work

SYNONYM: engine

motorbike motorbikes

NOUN a heavy two-wheeled vehicle that is driven by an engine

motorcycle motorcycles

NOUN another word for **motorbike**

motorist motorists

NOUN a person who drives a car or rides a motorbike

motorway motorways

NOUN a wide road built for fast travel over long distances

motto mottoes or mottos

NOUN a short sentence or phrase that is a rule for good or sensible behaviour. For example, *everything in moderation.*

mould moulds, moulding, moulded

VERB 1 If you **mould** a substance, you make it into a particular shape. • *Mould the dough into balls.*
NOUN 2 a container used to make something into a particular shape • *a jelly mould*
NOUN 3 a soft, grey or green growth that forms on old food or damp walls

mouldy mouldier, mouldiest

ADJECTIVE Something that is **mouldy** is covered with mould. • *This old bread had gone mouldy.*

moult moults, moulting, moulted

VERB When an animal or bird **moults**, it loses its hair or feathers so that new ones can grow.

mound mounds

NOUN 1 a small, man-made hill
NOUN 2 a large, untidy pile

mount mounts, mounting, mounted

VERB 1 If you **mount** a horse or bicycle, you climb onto it.
VERB 2 If something **mounts**, it increases in amount. • *The contributions for the tombola were mounting.*
VERB 3 If you **mount** a picture or a photograph, you put it in a frame or an album to display it.

NOUN 4 a mountain, especially as part of the name • *Mount Everest is the highest mountain in the world.*

mountain mountains

NOUN a very high piece of land with steep sides • *Ben Nevis is the highest mountain in Scotland.*

mountaineer mountaineer

NOUN a person who climbs mountains

mourn mourns, mourning, mourned

VERB If you **mourn** for someone who has died, you feel sad and think about them a lot.

mouse mice

NOUN 1 a small, furry rodent with a long tail
NOUN 2 a computer device that you move by hand to control the position of a cursor on the screen

→ Have a look at the illustration for **computer**

moustache moustaches

NOUN the hair that grows on a man's upper lip

mouth mouths

NOUN 1 the lips of a human or animal, or the space behind them where the tongue and teeth are

→ Have a look at the illustrations for **fish** and **respiratory system**

NOUN 2 the entrance to a cave or a hole
NOUN 3 the place where a river flows into the sea

mouthful mouthfuls

NOUN the amount of food you put in your mouth • *Don't take such huge mouthfuls!*

movable

ADJECTIVE Something that is **movable** can be moved from one place to another.

move moves, moving, moved

VERB 1 When you **move** something, or when it **moves**, its position changes. • *The train began to move out of the station.*
VERB 2 If you **move** or **move house**, you go to live in a different place.
VERB 3 If something **moves** you, it causes you to feel a deep emotion. • *The film moved us to tears.*
NOUN 4 a change from one place or position to another, especially in a game • *It's your move.*

movement **movements**
NOUN **1** the action of changing position or moving from one place to another
NOUN **2** a group of people who act together to try and make something happen
• *the animal rights* **movement**
NOUN **3** one of the main parts of a piece of classical music

movie **movies**
NOUN another name for **film**

moving
ADJECTIVE Something that is **moving** makes you feel deep sadness or emotion.
• *a* **moving** *story*

mow **mows, mowing, mowed, mown**
VERB If you **mow** grass, you cut it with a lawnmower.

MP **MPs**
NOUN someone who has been elected by the people of an area to represent them in Parliament. **MP** is an abbreviation for *Member of Parliament*.

MP3 player **MP3 players**
NOUN a device that plays audio and video files, used for listening to music

Mr
NOUN **Mr** is used before a man's name when you are speaking to him or talking about him. • *My teacher is called* **Mr** *Jones.*

Mrs
NOUN **Mrs** is used before the name of a married woman when you are speaking or referring to her. • *"Good morning,* **Mrs** *Green."*

Ms
NOUN **Ms** is used before a woman's name when you are speaking or referring to her. **Ms** does not show whether the woman is married or not.

much
ADVERB **1** You use **much** to indicate the great size, extent or intensity of something.
• *He's* **much** *taller than you.*
ADVERB **2** If something does not happen **much**, it does not happen often. • *He doesn't talk* **much**.
PRONOUN **3** a large amount of something
• *There isn't* **much** *left.*
ADJECTIVE **4** You use **much** to talk about the size or amount of something. • *I've eaten too* **much** *food.*

mud
NOUN wet, sticky earth

muddle **muddles, muddling, muddled**
NOUN **1** a state of disorder or untidiness
VERB **2** If you **muddle** things, you mix them up.

WORD HISTORY
from Dutch *moddelen* meaning to make muddy

muddy
ADJECTIVE covered in or full of wet, sticky earth
• **muddy** *boots*

muesli
NOUN a mixture of cereal flakes, chopped nuts and dried fruit that you can eat with milk for breakfast

muffled
ADJECTIVE A sound that is **muffled** is low or difficult to hear.

mug **mugs, mugging, mugged**
NOUN **1** a large, deep cup
VERB **2** (*informal*) If someone **mugs** you, they attack you in the street in order to steal your money.

mule **mules**
NOUN the offspring of a female horse and a male donkey

multimedia
NOUN You use **multimedia** when you are talking about computer programs and products which involve sound, pictures, and film, as well as text.

multiple **multiples**
ADJECTIVE **1** consisting of many parts or having many uses
NOUN **2** a number that can be divided exactly by another number • *2, 4, 6, 8, 10 and 12 are all* **multiples** *of 2.*

multiplication
NOUN the process of multiplying one number by another

multiply **multiplies, multiplying, multiplied**
VERB **1** When you **multiply** one number by another, you calculate the total you would get if you added the first number to itself the number of times shown by the second number. • *Six* **multiplied** *by three is 18 ($6 \times 3 = 18$), because $6 + 6 + 6 = 18$.*
VERB **2** When something **multiplies**, it increases greatly in number or amount.

a
b
c
d
e
f
g
h
i
j
k
l
m
n
o
p
q
r
s
t
u
v
w
x
y
z

A
B
C
D
E
F
G
H
I
J
K
L
M
N
O
P
Q
R
S
T
U
V
W
X
Y
Z

264

multitude **multitudes**
NOUN (*formal*) a very large number of people or things

mum **mums**
NOUN (*informal*) mother

mumble **mumbles, mumbling, mumbled**
VERB If you **mumble**, you speak very quietly and indistinctly.

mummy **mummies**
NOUN 1 (*informal*) Your **mummy** is your mother.
NOUN 2 a dead body that was preserved long ago by being rubbed with special oils and wrapped in cloth • *Mummies have been found in tombs in Egypt.*

WORD HISTORY
(sense 2) from Persian *mum* meaning wax

mumps
NOUN a disease that causes painful swelling in the neck

munch **munches, munching, munched**
VERB If you **munch** something, you chew it steadily and thoroughly.

mural **murals**
NOUN a picture painted on a wall

murder **murders, murdering, murdered**
NOUN 1 the deliberate killing of a person
VERB 2 To **murder** someone means to kill them deliberately.

murderer **murderers**
NOUN someone who deliberately kills someone else

murk
NOUN darkness or dirt that is difficult to see through

WORD HISTORY
from Old Norse *myrkr* meaning darkness

murky **murkier, murkiest**
ADJECTIVE dark or dirty and hard to see through • *murky* water

WORD HISTORY
from Old Norse *myrkr* meaning darkness

murmur **murmurs, murmuring, murmured**
VERB 1 If you **murmur** something, you say it very quietly.
NOUN 2 something someone says that can hardly be heard • *They spoke in low murmurs.*

muscle **muscles**
NOUN Your **muscles** are the bundles of fibres connected to your bones, that enable you to move.

WORD HISTORY
from Latin *musculus* meaning little mouse, because muscles were thought to look like mice

muscular
ADJECTIVE 1 **Muscular** people have strong, well-developed muscles.
ADJECTIVE 2 involving or affecting your muscles • *muscular* pain

museum **museums**
NOUN a public building where interesting or valuable objects are kept and displayed

mushroom **mushrooms**
NOUN a fungus with a short stem and a round top. Some types of **mushroom** are edible.

music
NOUN 1 the pattern of sounds performed by people singing or playing instruments
NOUN 2 the written symbols that represent musical sounds

musical **musicals**
ADJECTIVE 1 relating to playing or studying music • *She has considerable musical talent.*
NOUN 2 a play or a film that uses songs and dance to tell the story

musician **musicians**
NOUN a person who plays a musical instrument well

Muslim **Muslims**
NOUN 1 a person who believes in the Islamic religion and lives according to its rules
ADJECTIVE 2 relating to Islam

mussel **mussels**
NOUN a small, edible shellfish with a black shell

must
VERB **1** If you tell someone that they **must** do something, you make them feel that they ought to do it. • *You **must** try this pudding – it's delicious.*
VERB **2** If something **must** happen, it is very important or necessary that it happens. • *You **must** be over 15 to see a film with a 15 certificate.*
VERB **3** If you think something is very likely, you think it **must** be so. • *You **must** be Sam's brother.*

mustard
NOUN a spicy-tasting yellow or brown paste made from seeds

mute
ADJECTIVE If you are **mute**, you do not make any sounds. • *I would have screamed, but I was **mute** with fear.*

mutilate mutilates, mutilating, mutilated
VERB **1** If you **mutilate** something, you damage or spoil it.
VERB **2** If someone is **mutilated**, they have been very badly cut and injured.

mutineer mutineers
NOUN a soldier or sailor who is part of a group of soldiers or sailors who rebel against their officers

mutiny mutinies, mutinying, mutinied
VERB **1** If a group of sailors or soldiers **mutiny**, they rebel against their officers.
NOUN **2** a rebellion against someone in authority

mutter mutters, muttering, muttered
VERB If you **mutter**, or if you **mutter** something, you speak very quietly so that it is difficult for people to hear you.

mutton
NOUN the meat of an adult sheep

mutual
ADJECTIVE **Mutual** is used to describe something that two or more people give to each other or share. • *My dad and my brother have a **mutual** love of football.*

muzzle muzzles, muzzling, muzzled
NOUN **1** the nose and mouth of an animal
NOUN **2** a cover or a strap for a dog's nose and mouth to prevent it from biting
NOUN **3** the open end of a gun where the bullets come out
VERB **4** If you **muzzle** a dog, you put a muzzle on it.

my
ADJECTIVE **My** refers to something belonging to the person who is speaking or writing. • *I ride **my** bicycle to school every day.*

myself
PRONOUN You use **myself** when you are speaking about yourself. • *I was cross with **myself** for being so mean.*

mysterious
ADJECTIVE **1** strange and puzzling • *They heard **mysterious** noises in the night.*
ADJECTIVE **2** If someone is being **mysterious**, they are being secretive about something. • *Mum is being very **mysterious** about my birthday present.*

mystery mysteries
NOUN something that is not understood or known about • *The identity of the burglar remains a **mystery**.*

mystify mystifies, mystifying, mystified
VERB If something **mystifies** you, you find it impossible to understand. • *I am **mystified** by the disappearance of my sweater.*

myth myths
NOUN a story that was made up long ago to explain natural events and people's religious beliefs

Nn

nag nags, nagging, nagged
VERB If you **nag** someone, you keep complaining to them or asking them to do something.

nail nails, nailing, nailed
NOUN **1** Your **nails** are the thin, hard areas covering the ends of your fingers and toes.
NOUN **2** a small piece of metal with a sharp point at one end, that you hammer into objects to hold them together
VERB **3** If you **nail** something somewhere, you fix it there using a nail.

naïve
ADJECTIVE If you are **naïve**, you believe that things are easier or less complicated than they really are, usually because of your lack of experience.

PRONUNCIATION TIP
This word is pronounced ny-**eeve**.

---

naked
ADJECTIVE not wearing any clothes

name names, naming, named
NOUN **1** a word that you use to identify a person, animal, place or thing
VERB **2** When you **name** someone or something, you give them a name.

nameless
ADJECTIVE not having a name or not identified
● a **nameless** terror

nanny nannies
NOUN a person whose job is to look after young children

nap naps, napping, napped
NOUN **1** a short sleep
VERB **2** When you **nap**, you have a short sleep.

napkin napkins
NOUN a small piece of cloth or paper used to wipe your hands and mouth after eating

nappy nappies
NOUN a piece of towelling or paper padding worn round a baby's bottom

narrate narrates, narrating, narrated
VERB If you **narrate** a story, you tell it.

narration
NOUN **Narration** is telling a story.

narrative narratives
NOUN a story or an account of events

narrator narrators
NOUN the person in a book or a film or in a radio or television broadcast, who tells the story or explains what is happening

narrow narrower, narrowest; narrows, narrowing, narrowed
ADJECTIVE **1** Something that is **narrow** measures a small distance from one side to the other. ● We walked down a **narrow** passageway.
VERB **2** If something **narrows**, it becomes less wide. ● The track **narrowed** ahead.

nasty nastier, nastiest
ADJECTIVE very unpleasant

SYNONYMS: unkind, rude, disgusting

nation nations
NOUN a country and all the people who live there

national
ADJECTIVE relating to a country or the whole country ● He was dressed in the **national** costume.

national anthem national anthems
NOUN the official song of a country

nationality nationalities
NOUN the fact of being a citizen of a particular nation ● I'm not sure of her **nationality**, but I think she's Canadian.

native natives
ADJECTIVE **1** Your **native** country is the country where you were born.
ADJECTIVE **2** Your **native** language is the language that you first learned to speak.
NOUN **3** A **native** of a place is someone who was born there.

Nativity
NOUN In Christianity, the **Nativity** is the birth of Christ, or the festival celebrating this.

natural

ADJECTIVE **1** normal and to be expected
• It's **natural** to want to do well.
ADJECTIVE **2** existing or happening in nature, rather than caused or made by people
• Wool is a **natural** material.

ANTONYM: artificial

ADJECTIVE **3** If you have a **natural** ability, you are born with it. • She has a **natural** flair for mathematics.

natural history

NOUN the study of animals and plants

naturally

ADVERB **1** You use **naturally** to say that something is normal and to be expected.
• **Naturally**, she was a bit nervous about her first day at a new school.
ADVERB **2** in a way that is caused by nature, rather than caused or made by people • She doesn't dye her hair. It's **naturally** red.

ANTONYM: artificially

ADVERB **3** You use **naturally** to say 'yes' or 'of course'. • "Can I come with you?" "**Naturally**".
ADVERB **4** in a relaxed way without trying too hard • Try to act **naturally**.

nature natures

NOUN **1** animals, plants and all the other things in the world that are not made by people
NOUN **2** the basic quality or character of a person or thing • They liked his warm, generous **nature**.

naughtiness

NOUN a child's bad behaviour

naughty naughtier, naughtiest

ADJECTIVE A child who is **naughty** behaves badly.

nausea

NOUN a feeling that you are going to be sick

nauseous

ADJECTIVE feeling that you are going to be sick

nautical

ADJECTIVE relating to ships or navigation

naval

ADJECTIVE relating to a navy

navel navels

NOUN the small hollow on the front of your body, just below your waist

navigate navigates, navigating, navigated

VERB When someone **navigates**, they work out the direction in which a ship, plane or car should go, using maps and sometimes instruments.

navigation

NOUN **Navigation** is the process of working out the direction in which a ship, plane or car should go, using maps and sometimes instruments.

navigator navigators

NOUN someone who works out the direction in which a ship, plane or car should go, using maps and sometimes instruments

navy navies

NOUN the part of a country's armed forces that fights at sea

near nearer, nearest; nears, nearing, neared

PREPOSITION **1** If something is **near** a place, it is a short distance from it. • They live in a cottage **near** the river.
ADVERB **2** If you come **near** a place, you come a short distance from it. • As we drew **near**, I saw that the boot lid was up.
VERB **3** When you are **nearing** a particular place or time, you are approaching it and will soon reach it. • I closed the curtains as the visitor **neared** the door.

nearby

ADJECTIVE **1** Something that is **nearby** is a short distance away. • a **nearby** street
ADVERB **2** a short distance away • He lives **nearby**.

nearly

ADVERB not completely, but almost
• I've **nearly** finished my homework.

neat neater, neatest

ADJECTIVE tidy and smart

neatly

ADVERB in a way that is tidy and smart

necessary

ADJECTIVE Something that is **necessary** is needed or must be done. • It might be **necessary** to leave quickly.

LANGUAGE TIP
Necessary has one c and two ss.

a
b
c
d
e
f
g
h
i
j
k
l
m
n
o
p
q
r
s
t
u
v
w
x
y
z

necessity necessities
> NOUN **1** the need to do something
> NOUN **2** something that is needed • *Water is a basic **necessity** of life.*

neck necks
> NOUN **1** the part of your body that joins your head to the rest of your body
> NOUN **2** the long, narrow part at one end of a bottle or guitar

necklace necklaces
> NOUN a piece of jewellery that a person wears around their neck

nectar
> NOUN a sweet liquid produced by flowers and collected by insects

nectarine nectarines
> NOUN a soft, round fruit with a smooth yellow and red skin

need needs, needing, needed
> VERB **1** If you **need** something, you cannot achieve what you want without having it or doing it. • *I **need** some help with my homework.*
> PLURAL NOUN **2** Your **needs** are the things that you need to have.

> SYNONYMS: necessities, requirements

needle needles
> NOUN **1** a small, thin piece of metal with a hole at one end and a sharp point at the other, used for sewing
> NOUN **2 Needles** are long, thin pieces of steel or plastic, used for knitting.
> NOUN **3** the sharp part of a syringe that goes into your skin when you have an injection
> NOUN **4** the thin pointer on a dial or compass that moves to show a measurement or bearing
> NOUN **5** Pine **needles** are the sharp, pointed leaves of a pine tree.

needlework
> NOUN sewing or embroidery that is done by hand

negative negatives
> ADJECTIVE **1** A **negative** answer means no.

> ANTONYM: positive

> ADJECTIVE **2** A **negative** number is less than zero.

> ANTONYM: positive

> NOUN **3** the image that is first produced when you take a photograph

neglect neglects, neglecting, neglected
> VERB **1** If you **neglect** someone or something, you do not look after them properly. • *Ben **neglected** his hamster.*
> NOUN **2** failure to look after someone or something properly • *Most of her plants died from **neglect**.*

negotiate negotiates, negotiating, negotiated
> VERB When people **negotiate**, they talk about a situation in order to reach an agreement about it.

neigh neighs, neighing, neighed
> NOUN A **neigh** is a loud, high-pitched sound made by a horse.

PRONUNCIATION TIP
This word is pronounced **nay**.

neighbour neighbours
> NOUN someone who lives next door to you or near you

neighbourhood neighbourhoods
> NOUN Your **neighbourhood** is the area where you live.

neither
> ADJECTIVE **1** You use **neither** to refer to not one or the other of two people or things. • *At first, **neither** child could speak.*
> CONJUNCTION **2** You use **neither** in front of two alternatives to mean not one and not the other. • *He spoke **neither** English nor German.*

neon
> NOUN a gas used in glass tubes to make lights and signs

nephew nephews
> NOUN Someone's **nephew** is the son of their sister or brother.

nerve nerves
> NOUN **1** long, thin fibres that send messages between your brain and other parts of your body
> NOUN **2** courage and calm in a difficult situation
> NOUN **3** (informal) rudeness or cheek • *She had the **nerve** to answer back to the head teacher.*

nervous
> ADJECTIVE easily worried and agitated

nervously
> ADVERB in a way that shows you are worried and anxious

A B C D E F G H I J K L M N O P Q R S T U V W X Y Z

nest nests
NOUN a structure that birds, insects and other animals make, in which to lay eggs or rear their young

nestle nestles, nestling, nestled
VERB If you **nestle** somewhere, you settle there comfortably, often very close to someone or something else. • *My kitten loves to **nestle** in my lap.*

PRONUNCIATION TIP
This word is pronounced ness-**sl**.

---

net nets
NOUN **1** short for **internet**
NOUN **2** material made from threads woven together with small spaces in between
NOUN **3** a piece of this material used for a particular purpose, for example a fishing **net**

netball
NOUN a game in which two teams of seven players each try to score goals by throwing a ball through a net at the top of a pole

nettle nettles
NOUN a wild plant covered with little hairs that sting

network networks
NOUN **1** a large number of lines or roads that cross each other at many points
NOUN **2** a group of computers connected to each other

neutral
ADJECTIVE **1** People who are **neutral** do not support either side in a disagreement or war.
ADJECTIVE **2** very pale or with very little colour • *The carpet was a **neutral** cream colour.*
ADJECTIVE **3** neither acid nor alkali

neutron neutrons
NOUN a particle with no electrical charge
→ Have a look at the illustration for **atom**

never
ADVERB at no time in the past, present or future • *I've **never** met such a lovely person.*

nevertheless
ADVERB in spite of what has just been said

new newer, newest
ADJECTIVE **1** recently made, created or discovered • *She's got a **new** film out.*
ADJECTIVE **2** different • *We've got a **new** maths teacher.*

news
NOUN up-to-date information about things that have happened

newsagent newsagents
NOUN a person or shop that sells newspapers and magazines

newspaper newspapers
NOUN a publication, on large sheets of folded paper, that is produced regularly and contains news and articles

newt newts
NOUN a small, amphibious creature with a moist skin, short legs and a long tail

newton newtons
NOUN a unit for measuring force (N)

WORD HISTORY
named after Sir Isaac *Newton*

New Year
NOUN the time when people celebrate the start of a year

next
ADJECTIVE **1** The **next** thing, person or event is the one that comes immediately after the present one. • *We'll catch the **next** train.*
ADJECTIVE **2** The **next** place or person is the one nearest to you. • *She lives in the **next** street.*
ADVERB **3** You use **next** to refer to an action that follows immediately after the present one. • *What shall we do **next**?*
PHRASE **4** If one thing is **next to** another, it is at the side of it. • *She sat down **next to** him.*

nib nibs
NOUN the pointed end of a pen, where the ink comes out

nibble nibbles, nibbling, nibbled
VERB **1** When you **nibble** something, you take small bites of it.
NOUN **2** a small bite of something

nice nicer, nicest
ADJECTIVE pleasant or kind

nicely
ADVERB **1** in a pleasant or kind way • *If you ask Dad **nicely**, he might take you to the zoo.*
ADVERB **2** well • *The jeans fit **nicely**.*

nickname nicknames
NOUN an informal name for someone or something

WORD HISTORY
from Middle English *an ekename* meaning an additional name

269

nicotine
NOUN an addictive substance found in tobacco

WORD HISTORY
named after Jacques *Nicot*, who first brought tobacco to France

niece nieces
NOUN Someone's **niece** is the daughter of their sister or brother. • *He bought a present for his niece.*

night nights
NOUN the time between sunset and sunrise, when it is dark

nightdress nightdresses
NOUN a loose dress that a woman or girl wears to sleep in

nightfall
NOUN the time of day when it starts to get dark • *By the time they got home it was nightfall.*

nightingale nightingales
NOUN a small, brown European bird, the male of which sings very beautifully, especially at night

nightmare nightmares
NOUN 1 a frightening dream • *She had a nightmare last night.*
NOUN 2 an unpleasant or frightening situation • *The whole journey was a nightmare.*

WORD HISTORY
from *night* + Old English *mare* meaning evil spirit

nil
NOUN zero or nothing, especially in sports scores • *Unfortunately, at half-time the score was still nil-nil.*

nimble nimbler, nimblest
ADJECTIVE able to move quickly and easily

nine
NOUN **Nine** is the number 9.

nineteen
NOUN **Nineteen** is the number 19.

nineteenth
NOUN 1 one of nineteen equal parts of something
ADJECTIVE 2 The **nineteenth** item in a series is the one that you count as number nineteen.

ninetieth
NOUN 1 one of ninety equal parts of something
NOUN 2 The **ninetieth** item in a series is the one that you count as number ninety.

ninety
NOUN **Ninety** is the number 90.

ninth ninths
NOUN 1 one of nine equal parts of something. It can be written as ⅑.
ADJECTIVE 2 The **ninth** item in a series is the one that you count as number nine. It can be written as 9th.

nip nips, nipping, nipped
VERB 1 If you **nip** someone or something, you give them a slight pinch or bite.
VERB 2 If you **nip** somewhere, you go there quickly. • *I have to nip to the shop for some milk.*
NOUN 3 A **nip** is small bite or pinch.

niqab niqabs
NOUN a veil worn by some Muslim women in public, covering all the face except the eyes

PRONUNCIATION TIP
This word is pronounced ni-**kab**.

nitrogen
NOUN a chemical element, usually found as a colourless gas. **Nitrogen** makes up about 78% of the Earth's atmosphere.

no
INTERJECTION 1 You say **no** when you do not want something or do not agree.

ANTONYM: yes

ADJECTIVE 2 none at all or not at all • *He has no excuse for his behaviour.*

noble nobler, noblest
ADJECTIVE If someone is **noble**, they are honest and brave, and deserve admiration.

nobody
PRONOUN not a single person • *For a long time nobody spoke.*

nocturnal
ADJECTIVE happening or active at night • *The hedgehog is a nocturnal animal.*

nod nods, nodding, nodded
VERB When you **nod** your head, you move it up and down, usually to say yes.

noise noises
NOUN a sound, especially one that is loud or unpleasant

noisy noisier, noisiest
ADJECTIVE making a lot of noise, or full of noise

nomad nomads
NOUN a person who travels from place to place rather than staying in just one • *The Bedouin people in Arabia are **nomads***.

WORD HISTORY
from Latin *nomas* meaning wandering shepherd

---

nominate nominates, nominating, nominated
VERB If a person **nominates** someone for a job or position, they formally suggest that they have it.

non-
PREFIX not, for example something that is **non**-existent does not exist

nonagon nonagons
NOUN a flat shape with nine straight sides

none
PRONOUN not a single thing or person, or not even a small amount of something • *They asked me for my ideas, but I had **none**.*

non-existent
ADJECTIVE If you describe something as **non-existent**, it does not exist but you think that it should • *Good shops are virtually **non-existent** in the village.*

non-fiction
NOUN writing dealing with facts and events rather than imaginative storytelling

ANTONYM: fiction

nonsense
NOUN foolish or meaningless words or behaviour

nonsmoking
ADJECTIVE A **nonsmoking** area is a place where smoking is forbidden.

nonstop
ADJECTIVE continuing without any pauses or breaks

SYNONYM: continuous

noodle noodles
NOUN a kind of pasta shaped into long, thin pieces

noon
NOUN midday

no one; also spelt **no-one**
PRONOUN not a single person • ***No one*** *goes to that play park any more.*

SYNONYM: nobody

noose nooses
NOUN a loop at the end of a piece of rope, with a knot that tightens when the rope is pulled

nor
CONJUNCTION used after *neither*, or to add emphasis • ***Neither*** *you **nor** I know the answer.* • *I couldn't afford to go to the fair, and **nor** could my friends.*

normal
ADJECTIVE usual and ordinary

north
NOUN one of the four main points of the compass. If you face the point where the sun rises, **north** is on your left. The abbreviation for **north** is N.

→ Have a look at the illustration for **compass point**

north-east
NOUN a point halfway between north and east. The abbreviation for **north-east** is NE.

→ Have a look at the illustration for **compass point**

northern
ADJECTIVE in or from the north • *The mountains of **northern** Spain are very beautiful.*

north-west
NOUN a point halfway between north and west. The abbreviation for **north-west** is NW.

→ Have a look at the illustration for **compass point**

nose noses
NOUN the part of your face above your mouth, that you use for smelling and breathing

→ Have a look at the illustration for **respiratory system**

nostalgia
NOUN a feeling of affection for the past, and sadness that things have changed

nostalgic
ADJECTIVE feeling affectionate about the past, and sad that things have changed

a
b
c
d
e
f
g
h
i
j
k
l
m
n
o
p
q
r
s
t
u
v
w
x
y
z

271

nostril nostrils
NOUN Your **nostrils** are the two openings in your nose that you breathe through.

nosy nosier, nosiest; also spelt nosey
ADJECTIVE **Nosy** people always want to know about other people's business, and like to interfere where they are not wanted.

not
ADVERB used to make a sentence mean the opposite • I am **not** very happy.

note notes
NOUN 1 a short letter
NOUN 2 You take **notes** to help you remember what has been said.
NOUN 3 In music, a **note** is a musical sound of a particular pitch, or a written symbol that represents this sound.
NOUN 4 a piece of paper money • a ten-pound **note**

notebook notebooks
NOUN a small book for writing notes in

nothing
PRONOUN not a single thing, or not a single part of something

notice notices, noticing, noticed
VERB 1 If you **notice** something, you become aware of it. • She **noticed** a bird sitting on the fence.
NOUN 2 a written announcement
PHRASE 3 If you **take notice of** something, you pay attention to it.

noticeable
ADJECTIVE obvious and easy to see

notification notifications
NOUN 1 an official statement telling someone about something
NOUN 2 a sound or symbol on your phone or computer telling you that someone has sent you a message or posted something on a social media website • When he switched on his phone, he had six new **notifications**.

notify notifies, notifying, notified
VERB If you **notify** someone of something, you officially inform them of it. • You must **notify** us of any change of address.

notorious
ADJECTIVE well known for something bad • a **notorious** criminal

nought noughts
NOUN the number 0, zero

noun nouns
NOUN a word that refers to a person, thing or idea. Examples of **nouns** are table, happiness and John.

nourish nourishes, nourishing, nourished
VERB If you **nourish** people or animals, you give them plenty of food.

nourishing
ADJECTIVE If food is **nourishing**, it is good for you and makes you strong and healthy.

nourishment
NOUN the food that your body needs to grow and stay healthy, including vitamins and minerals • "Eat your vegetables, they're full of **nourishment**."

novel novels
NOUN 1 a book that tells a long story about imaginary people and events
ADJECTIVE 2 new and interesting • This whole trip has been a **novel** experience.

novelty novelties
NOUN 1 the quality of being new and interesting
NOUN 2 something new and interesting
NOUN 3 a small object sold as a gift or souvenir

November
NOUN the eleventh month of the year. **November** has 30 days.

WORD HISTORY
from Latin November meaning the ninth month

novice novices
NOUN someone who is not yet experienced at something • Most of the group are **novices** at horse riding.

now
ADVERB 1 at the present time or moment
CONJUNCTION 2 as a result or consequence of a particular fact • Your writing will improve **now** you have a new pen.

nowhere
ADVERB not anywhere • There was **nowhere** to hide.

nozzle nozzles
NOUN a spout fitted onto the end of a pipe or hose to control the flow of liquid or gas

nuclear

ADJECTIVE relating to the energy produced when atoms are split • *We live near a* **nuclear** *power station.*

nucleus nuclei

NOUN **1** the central part of an atom or a cell

→ Have a look at the illustration for **atom**

NOUN **2** the important or central part of something • *We still have the* **nucleus** *of the team.*

PRONUNCIATION TIP
The singular is pronounced **nyoo**-clee-us. The plural is pronounced **nyoo**-clee-eye.

nude nudes

ADJECTIVE **1** If someone is **nude**, they are naked.
NOUN **2** A **nude** is a picture or statue of a naked person.

nudge nudges, nudging, nudged

VERB **1** If you **nudge** someone, you push them gently with your elbow to get their attention or to make them move.
NOUN **2** a gentle push with your elbow

nugget nuggets

NOUN a small rough lump of something, especially gold

nuisance nuisances

NOUN someone or something that is annoying or causing problems

numb

ADJECTIVE unable to feel anything • *I was so cold my hands and feet felt* **numb**.

WORD HISTORY
from Middle English *nomen* meaning paralysed

number numbers, numbering, numbered

NOUN **1** a word or symbol used for counting or calculating
NOUN **2** the series of numbers that you dial when you phone someone
VERB **3** If you **number** something, you give it a number, usually in a sequence. • *Please* **number** *each page you write on.*

number bond number bonds

NOUN any pair of numbers that add together to make up another number

numeracy

NOUN the ability to do arithmetic

numeral numerals

NOUN a symbol that is used to represent a number

numerator numerators

NOUN the top number of a fraction. It tells you the number of pieces or parts you are dealing with.

numerical

ADJECTIVE expressed in numbers or relating to numbers • *Please put these pages in* **numerical** *order.*

numerous

ADJECTIVE Things that are **numerous** exist or happen in large numbers. • *There are* **numerous** *things to do in a large city.*

nun nuns

NOUN a woman who has taken religious vows and is a member of a religious community

nurse nurses, nursing, nursed

NOUN **1** a person whose job is to look after people who are ill
VERB **2** If you **nurse** someone, you look after them when they are ill. • *I helped dad to* **nurse** *mum when she had flu.*

nursery nurseries

NOUN **1** a place where young children are looked after when their parents are working
NOUN **2** a place where plants are grown and sold

nursery rhyme nursery rhymes

NOUN a short poem or song for young children, such as *Little Miss Muffet* and *Jack and Jill*

nursery school nursery schools

NOUN a school for children aged three to five years old

nut nuts

NOUN **1** a fruit with a hard shell that grows on certain trees and bushes
NOUN **2** a piece of metal with a hole in the middle that a bolt screws into

nutrient nutrients

NOUN one of the substances that help plants and animals to grow • *Very heavy rainfall washes valuable* **nutrients** *from the soil.*

nutrition

NOUN the food that you eat that helps you to grow and keeps you healthy • *Good* **nutrition** *is vital for healthy development.*

a
b
c
d
e
f
g
h
i
j
k
l
m
n
o
p
q
r
s
t
u
v
w
x
y
z

273

nutritious
ADJECTIVE If food is **nutritious** it helps you to grow and remain healthy. • *Spinach is a very* **nutritious** *vegetable.*

nylon
NOUN a type of strong, artificial fibre used for making, for example, clothes, ropes and brushes • *The rock climbers used brightly coloured ropes made of* **nylon** *to abseil down the rock face.*

oak oaks
NOUN a large tree that produces acorns. The **oak** has a hard wood that is often used to make furniture.

oar oars
NOUN a pole with a flat end used to row a boat through water

oasis oases
NOUN a small area in a desert where water and plants are found

oath oaths
NOUN a formal promise, especially a promise to tell the truth in a court of law

oats
PLURAL NOUN a type of grain

obedience
NOUN **Obedience** is when you do what someone tells you to do.

ANTONYM: disobedience

obedient
ADJECTIVE If you are **obedient**, you do as you are told.

ANTONYM: disobedient

obey obeys, obeying, obeyed
VERB If you **obey** a person or an order, you do what you are told to do.

obituary obituaries
NOUN a piece of writing about the life and achievements of someone who has just died

object objects, objecting, objected
NOUN **1** anything solid that you can touch or see, and that is not alive • *This painting is a* **object** *of beauty.*
NOUN **2** an aim or purpose • *The* **object** *of the marathon is to raise money.*
VERB **3** If you **object** to something, you dislike it, disagree with it or disapprove of it

PRONUNCIATION TIP
The noun is pronounced **ob**-jekt. The verb is pronounced ob-**jekt**.

A B C D E F G H I J K L M N O P Q R S T U V W X Y Z

objection objections

NOUN If you have an **objection** to something, you dislike it or disagree with it.

oblige obliges, obliging, obliged

VERB **1** If you are **obliged** to do something, you have to do it.

VERB **2** If you **oblige** someone, you help them. • *He **obliged** us by showing the way.*

VERB **3** If you are **obliged** to someone, you are grateful to them. • *I would be much **obliged** if you could show me where this street is.*

obliging

ADJECTIVE willing to help someone

oblique

ADJECTIVE An **oblique** line slopes at an angle.

oblong oblongs

NOUN **1** a four-sided plane shape with four right angles, similar to a square but with two sides longer than the other two

ADJECTIVE **2** shaped like an oblong

obnoxious

ADJECTIVE extremely unpleasant

SYNONYMS: hateful, odious

oboe oboes

NOUN a woodwind instrument that makes a high-pitched sound

WORD HISTORY

from French *haut bois* meaning literally high wood, a reference to the instrument's pitch

oboist oboists

NOUN someone who plays the oboe

obscene

ADJECTIVE very rude and likely to upset people

obscure obscures, obscuring, obscured

ADJECTIVE **1** Something **obscure** is difficult to see or to understand.

ANTONYMS: obvious, clear

VERB **2** If something **obscures** something else, it makes it difficult to see or understand. • *The moon **obscured** the sun during the eclipse.*

observant

ADJECTIVE An **observant** person notices things that are not usually noticed.

observation observations

NOUN the act of watching something closely • *You will need to make careful **observations** of the experiment before you do the writing.*

WORD HISTORY

from Latin *observare* meaning to watch

observe observes, observing, observed

VERB If you **observe** someone or something, you watch them carefully.

obsessed

ADJECTIVE If you are **obsessed** with someone or something, you cannot stop thinking about them.

obsession obsessions

NOUN If someone has an **obsession** about something or someone, they cannot stop thinking about them.

obsessive

ADJECTIVE unable to stop thinking about someone or something

obsolete

ADJECTIVE out of date and no longer used

obstacle obstacles

NOUN something that is in your way and makes it difficult for you to do something

obstinate

ADJECTIVE Someone who is **obstinate** is stubborn and unwilling to change their mind.

obstruct obstructs, obstructing, obstructed

VERB If something **obstructs** a road or path, it blocks it.

obtain obtains, obtaining, obtained

VERB If you **obtain** something, you get it.

obtuse

ADJECTIVE In mathematics, an **obtuse** angle is an angle between 90° and 180°.

a
b
c
d
e
f
g
h
i
j
k
l
m
n
o
p
q
r
s
t
u
v
w
x
y
z

275

obvious

ADJECTIVE easy to see or understand • *It was **obvious** that he didn't know the answer.*

obviously

ADVERB You use **obviously** to show that something is easy to see or understand. • ***Obviously**, you need to do your homework or you'll get into trouble.*

occasion occasions

NOUN a time when something happens • *I met her on several **occasions**.*

LANGUAGE TIP
There are two *c*s but only one *s* in *occasion*.

---

occasional

ADJECTIVE happening sometimes, but not often • *We go for an **occasional** walk in the woods.*

occasionally

ADVERB sometimes, rather than always or never • *He misbehaves **occasionally**.*

occupant occupants

NOUN the people who live or work in a building

occupation occupations

NOUN a job or profession

occupy occupies, occupying, occupied

VERB 1 The people who **occupy** a building are the people who live or work there.
VERB 2 If something **occupies** you, you spend your time doing it or thinking about it.

occur occurs, occurring, occurred

VERB If something **occurs**, it happens.

occur to

VERB If something **occurs to** you, you suddenly think of it or realise it.

occurrence occurrences

NOUN something that happens • *Accidents in the factory were a frequent **occurrence**.*

ocean oceans

NOUN one of the five very large areas of sea in the world

o'clock

ADVERB You use **o'clock** after the number of the hour to say what the time is. • *We have to be at school by eight **o'clock**.*

octagon octagons

NOUN a flat shape with eight straight sides

octagonal

ADJECTIVE having eight straight sides

octahedron octahedrons

NOUN a solid figure with eight identical flat surfaces

octave octaves

NOUN the difference in pitch between the first note and the eighth note of a musical scale

October

NOUN the tenth month of the year. **October** has 31 days.

WORD HISTORY
from Latin *October* meaning the eighth month, as it was the eighth month in the Roman calendar

---

octopus octopuses

NOUN a sea creature with eight long tentacles that it uses to catch food

odd odder, oddest

ADJECTIVE 1 strange or unusual
ADJECTIVE 2 **Odd** things do not match each other. • *She always ended up with **odd** socks.*
ADJECTIVE 3 **Odd** numbers cannot be divided exactly by two. 3 and 7 are examples of **odd** numbers.

ANTONYM: even

odour odours

NOUN (*formal*) a strong smell

oesophagus oesophagi

NOUN the passage between the mouth and the stomach

of

PREPOSITION 1 consisting of or containing • *a cup **of** tea*
PREPOSITION 2 used when talking about things that are characteristic of something • *a woman **of** great importance*
PREPOSITION 3 belonging to or connected with • *a friend **of** Eve*

off

PREPOSITION **1** away from or out of a place
• *They got **off** the bus.*
PREPOSITION **2** used to show separation or distance from a place • *There are several islands **off** the coast of Britain.*
ADVERB **3** used to show movement away from or out of a place • *At the next station, the man got **off**.*
ADVERB **4** not at school or work • *He took a day **off**.*
ADVERB **5** not switched on • *The television was **off**.*
ADJECTIVE **6** cancelled or postponed • *The match is **off**.*
ADJECTIVE **7** Food that is **off** is no longer fresh enough to eat, usually tastes unpleasant, and may make you ill.

LANGUAGE TIP
Do not use *of* after *off*. It is correct to say *I got off the bus*, not *I got off of the bus*.

offence offences

NOUN **1** a crime • *Burglary is a serious **offence**.*
PHRASE **2** If you **cause offence**, you embarrass or upset someone.
PHRASE **3** If you **take offence**, you feel that someone has been rude or hurtful to you.

offend offends, offending, offended

VERB **1** If you **offend** someone, you upset them.
VERB **2** If someone **offends**, they break the law.

offensive

ADJECTIVE If something is **offensive**, it is rude and upsetting.

offer offers, offering, offered

VERB **1** If you **offer** something to someone, you ask them if they would like it, or say that you are willing to do it. • *I **offered** to wash the car.*
NOUN **2** something that someone says they will give you or do for you

office offices

NOUN **1** a room where people work at desks
NOUN **2** a place where people can go for information, tickets or other services

officer officers

NOUN a person with a position of authority in the armed forces, the police or a government organisation

official

ADJECTIVE approved by the government or by someone in authority

offline

ADJECTIVE **1** If a computer is **offline**, it is not connected to the internet.
ADVERB **2** If you do something **offline**, you do it while not connected to the internet.

offspring

NOUN (*formal*) You can refer to a person's children or to an animal's young as their **offspring**.

often

ADVERB happening many times or a lot of the time • *He **often** goes swimming on Sunday.*

ogre ogres

NOUN a cruel, frightening giant in fairy stories

oil oils, oiling, oiled

NOUN **1** a thick, sticky liquid found underground that is used for fuel, lubrication and for making plastics and chemicals
NOUN **2** a thick, greasy liquid made from plants or animal fat • *cooking **oil***
VERB **3** If you **oil** something, you put oil in it or on it to make it work better. • *This squeaky hinge needs to be **oiled**.*

oily oilier, oiliest

ADJECTIVE Something that is **oily** is covered with or contains oil.

ointment ointments

NOUN a smooth, thick substance that you put on sore skin to heal it

OK; also spelt okay

ADJECTIVE all right; fine • *She slipped on the ice but she was **OK**.*

old older, oldest

ADJECTIVE **1** having lived or existed for a long time
ADJECTIVE **2** **Old** is used to give the age of someone or something. • *The baby is six months **old**.*
ADJECTIVE **3** You can use **old** to talk about something that is no longer used or has been replaced by something else. • *I bumped into my teacher from my **old** primary school.*

a
b
c
d
e
f
g
h
i
j
k
l
m
n
o
p
q
r
s
t
u
v
w
x
y
z

A
B
C
D
E
F
G
H
I
J
K
L
M
N
O
P
Q
R
S
T
U
V
W
X
Y
Z

old-fashioned

ADJECTIVE **1** Something **old-fashioned** is out of date and no longer fashionable.

ANTONYM: fashionable

ADJECTIVE **2** If someone is **old-fashioned**, they believe in the values and standards of the past.

olive olives

NOUN **1** a small green or black fruit containing a stone. **Olives** are usually pickled and eaten as a snack, or crushed to produce oil for cooking.
NOUN **2** a dark yellowish-green colour
ADJECTIVE **3** having a dark yellowish-green colour

Olympic Games

NOUN (trademark) a series of international sporting contests held in a different country every four years

---

WORD HISTORY

The word *Olympic* comes from *Olympia* in Greece, where games were held in ancient times

---

omelette omelettes

NOUN a dish made by beating eggs together and cooking them in a flat pan

omit omits, omitting, omitted

VERB If you **omit** something, you do not include it. ● *She **omitted** to mention that her mother could not come.*

omni-

PREFIX added to some words to mean all or everywhere, for example **omni**potent means all-powerful, and **omni**present means present everywhere

omnibus omnibuses

NOUN **1** a book containing a collection of stories or articles by the same author or about the same subject
ADJECTIVE **2** An **omnibus** edition of a radio or television series contains two or more episodes that were originally shown separately.

omnivore omnivores

NOUN an animal that eats all kinds of food, including meat and plants

omnivorous

ADJECTIVE An **omnivorous** animal eats all kinds of food, including meat and plants.

on

PREPOSITION **1** touching something or attached to it ● *We sat **on** the seat.*
PREPOSITION **2** If you are **on** a bus, a plane or a train, you are inside it.
PREPOSITION **3** If something happens **on** a particular day, that is when it happens.
PREPOSITION **4** If something is done **on** an instrument or a machine, it is done using it.
PREPOSITION **5** A book or a talk **on** a particular subject is about that subject.
ADVERB **6** If someone has a piece of clothing **on**, they are wearing it.
ADVERB **7** If your turn a machine or a switch **on**, you make it work. ● *"Please would you switch the radio **on**?"*

once

ADVERB **1** If something happens **once**, it happens one time only. ● *I met her **once**, at a party.*
ADVERB **2** If something was **once** true, it was true in the past, but is no longer true. ● *That ground was **once** covered by trees.*
CONJUNCTION **3** If something happens **once** another thing has happened, it happens immediately afterwards. ● *I'll do my homework **once** I've finished my tea.*
PHRASE **4** If you do something **at once**, you do it immediately. ● *We must go home **at once**.*
PHRASE **5** If several things happen **at once**, they all happen at the same time. ● *He tried to hold three glasses **at once**.*

one

NOUN **1 One** is the number 1.
ADJECTIVE **2** When you refer to **one** person or **one** thing, you mean a single person or thing. ● *We have **one** main holiday a year.*
PRONOUN **3 One** refers to a particular person or thing. ● *This book was the best **one** she had read for ages.*

onion onions

NOUN a small, round vegetable with a very strong taste

online

ADJECTIVE **1** If a computer is **online**, it is connected to the internet.
ADVERB **2** If you do something **online**, you do it while connected to the internet.

only

ADVERB **1** You use **only** to show the one thing or person involved. • **Only** one girl was able to complete the race.
ADVERB **2** You use **only** to make a condition that must happen before something else can happen. • You will be allowed in **only** if you have a ticket.
ADVERB **3** You use **only** to emphasise that something is unimportant or small. • He's **only** very young.
ADJECTIVE **4** If you talk about the **only** thing or person, you mean that there are no others. For example, if you are an **only** child, you have no brothers or sisters.
CONJUNCTION **5** You can use **only** to mean but or except. • He was very much like you, **only** with blond hair.

onomatopoeia

NOUN the use of words that sound like the thing that they represent. Hiss and buzz are examples of **onomatopoeia**

PRONUNCIATION TIP
This word is pronounced on-uh-mat-uh-**pee**-a.

onto; also spelt on to

PREPOSITION If you put something **onto** an object, you put it on it. • He threw the pillow **onto** the bed.

ooze oozes, oozing, oozed

VERB When a thick liquid **oozes**, it flows slowly. • The cold mud **oozed** over her toes.

WORD HISTORY
from Old English wos meaning juice

opaque

ADJECTIVE If something is **opaque**, it does not let light through, so you cannot see through it. • **opaque** glass windows
ANTONYM: clear

open opens, opening, opened

ADJECTIVE **1** Something that is **open** is not closed or fastened, allowing things to pass through. • A light breeze came through the **open** window.
ADJECTIVE **2** not enclosed or covered • At last we were out in the **open** countryside.
VERB **3** When you **open** something, or when it **opens**, it is moved so that it is no longer closed. • She **opened** the box of chocolates.
VERB **4** When a shop or office **opens**, people are allowed to go in to do business.
VERB **5** If you **open** a book, you turn back the cover so that you can read it.
VERB **6** If something **opens**, it starts or begins.
ADJECTIVE **7** Someone who is **open** is honest and not secretive.

opening openings

NOUN **1** a hole or gap • There was a small **opening** in the fence.
ADJECTIVE **2** coming first • He sang the **opening** song in the concert.
NOUN **3** the first part of a book or film • I love the **opening** of that book.

openly

ADVERB in a way that is honest and does not hide your feelings or any facts

opera operas

NOUN a play in which the words are sung rather than spoken

operate operates, operating, operated

VERB **1** When you **operate** a machine, you make it work. • I know how to **operate** the computer.
VERB **2** When surgeons **operate**, they cut open a person's body to remove or repair a damaged part.

operation operations

NOUN **1** a form of medical treatment in which a surgeon cuts open a patient's body to remove or repair a damaged part
NOUN **2** a complex, planned event • Moving house is going to be quite a difficult **operation**.

opinion opinions

NOUN a belief or view

opponent opponents

NOUN someone who is against you in an argument or a contest

opportunity opportunities

NOUN a chance to do something

oppose opposes, opposing, opposed

VERB If you **oppose** something or someone, you disagree with them and are against them.

opposing

ADJECTIVE **Opposing** means opposite or very different. • We managed to be friends even though we had **opposing** points of view.

A
B
C
D
E
F
G
H
I
J
K
L
M
N
O
P
Q
R
S
T
U
V
W
X
Y
Z

opposite **opposites**

PREPOSITION **1** If one thing is **opposite** another, it is facing it. • *Our house is* **opposite** *the park.*
NOUN **2** If people or things are **opposites**, they are completely different from each other.

opposition

NOUN **1** If there is **opposition** to something, there is resistance to it and people oppose it. • *There is a lot of* **opposition** *to the building of a new road.*
NOUN **2** In a games or sports event, the **opposition** is the person or team that you are competing against.

opt **opts, opting, opted**

VERB **1** If you **opt** for something, you choose to do it. • *I* **opted** *to go to the Gym Club.*
VERB **2** If you **opt** out of something, you choose not to do it or be involved with it. • *I* **opted** *out of football practice.*

optical

ADJECTIVE concerned with vision, light or images

optician **opticians**

NOUN someone who tests people's eyesight, and makes and sells glasses and contact lenses

optimism

NOUN a hopeful feeling that everything will turn out well in the future

ANTONYM: pessimism

optimist **optimists**

NOUN An **optimist** is a person who is always hopeful that everything will turn out well in the future.

ANTONYM: pessimist

optimistic

ADJECTIVE believing that everything will turn out well in the future

ANTONYM: pessimistic

option **options**

NOUN a choice between two or more things

optional

ADJECTIVE If something is **optional**, you can choose whether to do it or not. • *Tennis is* **optional** *at our school.*

ANTONYM: compulsory

or

CONJUNCTION used to link two alternatives or choices • *You need to decide whether to stay* **or** *leave.*

oral

ADJECTIVE **1** spoken rather than written • *Tomorrow we have our French* **oral** *examination.*
ADJECTIVE **2** to do with your mouth or using your mouth • **Oral** *hygiene is vital for healthy teeth.*

orange **oranges**

NOUN **1** a round citrus fruit that is juicy and sweet and has a thick reddish-yellow skin
NOUN **2** a reddish-yellow colour
ADJECTIVE **3** having a reddish-yellow colour

WORD HISTORY
from Sanskrit *naranga* meaning orange

orang-utan **orang-utans**; also spelt **orang-utang**

NOUN a large ape with reddish-brown hair

orbit **orbits, orbiting, orbited**

NOUN **1** the curved path followed by an object going round a planet or the sun
VERB **2** If something **orbits** a planet or the sun, it goes round and round it. • *Our moon* **orbits** *the Earth.*

orchard **orchards**

NOUN a piece of land where fruit trees are grown

orchestra **orchestras**

NOUN a large group of musicians who play musical instruments together

orchid **orchids**

NOUN a type of plant with beautiful and unusual flowers

ordeal **ordeals**

NOUN a very difficult and unpleasant experience

order **orders, ordering, ordered**

NOUN **1** a command given by someone in authority
NOUN **2** If things are arranged or done in a particular **order**, they are arranged or done in that sequence. • *alphabetical* **order**
VERB **3** If you **order** someone to do something, you tell them firmly to do it.
VERB **4** When you **order** something, you ask for it to be brought or sent to you.

ordinal

ADJECTIVE An **ordinal** number a word like "first" and "tenth" that tells you where a particular thing occurs in order.

ordinary

ADJECTIVE not special or different in any way

ore ores

NOUN rock or earth from which metal can be obtained

organ organs

NOUN **1** Your **organs** are parts of your body that have a particular purpose, for example your lungs are the **organs** with which you breathe.

NOUN **2** a large musical instrument with a keyboard and windpipes through which air is forced to produce a sound

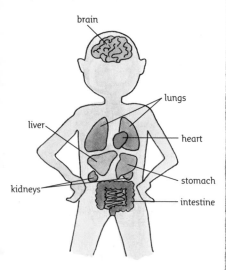

brain
lungs
liver
heart
kidneys
stomach
intestine

organic

ADJECTIVE **1 Organic** food is produced without the use of artificial fertilisers or pesticides.

ADJECTIVE **2** produced or found in living things

organisation organisations; also spelt organization

NOUN **1** any business or group of people working together for a purpose

NOUN **2** the act of planning and arranging something

organise organises, organising, organised; also spelt organize

VERB If you **organise** something, you plan and arrange it.

organism organisms

NOUN any living animal or plant

oriental

ADJECTIVE Something that is **oriental** comes from the Far East, which includes countries such as India, China and Japan. • *I like oriental food.*

orienteering

NOUN a sport in which people find their way from one place to another in the countryside, using a map and compass

origin origins

NOUN the beginning or cause of something
• *The origins of man have been written about in many books.*

original originals

ADJECTIVE **1** the first or earliest • *The original owner of this house made lots of alterations.*

ADJECTIVE **2** imaginative and clever • *His paintings are highly original.*

NOUN **3** a work of art or a document that is the one that was produced first, and is not a copy

originally

ADVERB in the beginning or at first • *The house was originally a school.*

ornament ornaments

NOUN a small, attractive object that you display in your home or that you wear in order to look attractive

ornithologist ornithologists

NOUN someone who studies birds

ornithology

NOUN the study of birds

orphan orphans

NOUN a child whose parents are dead

orphanage orphanages

NOUN a place where orphans are looked after

ostrich ostriches

NOUN the largest bird in the world. **Ostriches** can run fast but cannot fly.

other others

PRONOUN **1** The **other** can mean the second of two things. • *One of the rooms is empty, but the other is not.*

ADJECTIVE **2 Other** people or things are different from those already mentioned.

ADJECTIVE **3** The **other** day means a few days ago.

a
b
c
d
e
f
g
h
i
j
k
l
m
n
o
p
q
r
s
t
u
v
w
x
y
z

281

otherwise
ADVERB **1** or else
ADVERB **2** apart from the thing mentioned
• *The food was good, but **otherwise** the party was awful.*

otter otters
NOUN a small, furry animal with a long tail, that lives near water. **Otters** swim well and eat fish.

ought
VERB **1** If you say that someone **ought** to do something, you mean they should do it.
VERB **2** If you say that something **ought** to be the case, you mean that you expect it to be the case. • *He **ought** to be here by now.*

ounce ounces
NOUN a unit of weight equal to one-sixteenth of a pound or about 28.35 grams

our
ADJECTIVE belonging to us • *Our cat is black.*

ours
PRONOUN belonging to us • *That cat is **ours**.*

ourselves
PRONOUN **Ourselves** is used when talking about a group of people that includes the speaker or writer. • *We didn't hurt **ourselves** too badly.*

out
ADVERB **1** towards the outside of a place or thing • *Take the ice cream **out** of the freezer.*
ADVERB **2** not at home • *I came to your door yesterday, but you were **out**.*

outbreak outbreaks
NOUN If there is an **outbreak** of something unpleasant, such as war, it suddenly occurs. • *The **outbreak** of the disease made many people unwell.*

outburst outbursts
NOUN a sudden strong expression of emotion, especially anger or violent action • *He apologised for his angry **outburst**.*

outcome outcomes
NOUN a result

outdoor
ADJECTIVE happening or used outside

outdoors
ADVERB If something happens **outdoors**, it takes place outside in the open air.

outer
ADJECTIVE The **outer** parts of something are the parts furthest from the centre.
• *the **outer** doors*

outer space
NOUN everything beyond the Earth's atmosphere

outfit outfits
NOUN a set of clothes • *I bought a new **outfit** for the party.*

outgoing
ADJECTIVE Someone who is **outgoing** is friendly and not shy. • *She is always fun to be with as she has such an **outgoing** personality.*

outgrow outgrows, outgrowing, outgrew, outgrown
VERB **1** If you **outgrow** a piece of clothing, you grow too big to wear it. • *I've already **outgrown** my best jeans.*
VERB **2** If you **outgrow** a way of behaving, you stop behaving that way because you are older and more mature.

outing outings
NOUN a trip made for pleasure

outlaw outlaws, outlawing, outlawed
VERB **1** If someone **outlaws** something, they ban it.
NOUN **2** In the past, an **outlaw** was a criminal.

outlet outlets
NOUN **1** a hole or pipe through which water or air can flow away
NOUN **2** a shop that sells goods made by a particular manufacturer

outline outlines, outlining, outlined
NOUN **1** The **outline** of something is its shape.
VERB **2** If you **outline** a plan or idea, you give brief details of it.

outlook outlooks
NOUN **1** Your **outlook** is your general attitude towards life. • *His **outlook** on life is always positive.*
NOUN **2** The **outlook** of a situation is the way it is likely to develop. • *The **outlook** for the weather over the next few days is not very good.*

outnumber outnumbers, outnumbering, outnumbered
VERB If there is more of one group than of another, the first group **outnumbers** the second. • *Boys **outnumber** girls in our class.*

A B C D E F G H I J K L M N O P Q R S T U V W X Y Z

outpatient outpatients
NOUN someone who receives treatment in hospital without staying overnight

output outputs
NOUN **1** the amount of something produced by a person or organisation
NOUN **2** The **output** of a computer is the information that it produces.

outrage outrages, outraging, outraged
VERB **1** If something **outrages** you, it angers and shocks you.
NOUN **2** a feeling of anger and shock
NOUN **3** something very shocking or violent

outrageous
ADJECTIVE making you feel angry and shocked

outright
ADJECTIVE **1** total and complete • *She made an* **outright** *refusal to come with us.*
ADVERB **2** completely, totally • *Smoking in the building has been banned* **outright**.

outside
PREPOSITION **1** not inside • *The teacher found him* **outside** *the classroom.*
ADJECTIVE **2** describes something that is not inside a building • *The* **outside** *wall is painted white.*
ADVERB **3** out of a building • *She went* **outside** *to look for Sam.*
NOUN **4** The **outside** of something is the part that surrounds or encloses the rest of it. • *We wandered around the* **outside** *of the house.*

ANTONYM: inside

NOUN **5** not included in something • *The building will be closed* **outside** *school hours.*

LANGUAGE TIP
Do not use *of* after *outside* when it is a preposition. It is correct to say *I met her outside the school*, not *I met her outside of the school.*

outskirts
PLURAL NOUN the parts around the edge of a city or town • *Our home is on the* **outskirts** *of a large town.*

outspoken
ADJECTIVE **Outspoken** people give their opinions openly, even if they shock other people.

outstanding
ADJECTIVE extremely good

outwit outwits, outwitting, outwitted
VERB If you **outwit** someone, you use your intelligence or a clever trick to defeat them or get the better of them.

oval ovals
NOUN **1** a shape similar to a circle, but wider in one direction than the other
ADJECTIVE **2** shaped like an oval

WORD HISTORY
from Latin *ovalis* meaning egg-shaped

oven ovens
NOUN the part of a cooker that you use for baking or roasting food

over overs
PREPOSITION **1** directly above something or covering it • *She hung the picture* **over** *the fireplace.* • *He put his hands* **over** *his eyes.*
PREPOSITION **2** A view **over** an area is a view across it. • *I love the view* **over** *the lake to the mountains.*
PREPOSITION **3** If something happens **over** a period of time, it happens during that period. • *I went to New Zealand* **over** *Christmas.*
ADVERB **4** If an amount of something is left **over**, that amount remains.
ADVERB **5** If you lean **over**, you bend your body in a particular direction. • *He leant* **over** *to open the door of the car.*
ADVERB **6** If something rolls or turns **over**, it moves so that its other side is facing upwards.
ADJECTIVE **7** Something that is **over** is completely finished.
NOUN **8** In cricket, an **over** is a series of six balls bowled by one bowler.

over-
PREFIX too much, or to too great an extent. For example, if fruit is **over**ripe, it is too ripe, and if someone **over**eats, they eat too much.

a
b
c
d
e
f
g
h
i
j
k
l
m
o
p
q
r
s
t
u
v
w
x
y
z

A
B
C
D
E
F
G
H
I
J
K
L
M
N
O
P
Q
R
S
T
U
V
W
X
Y
Z

overall

ADVERB **1** taking into account all the parts or aspects of something • *Overall, the project has been a success.*

ADJECTIVE **2** describing something that takes into account all the parts or aspects of something • the **overall** cost of the school's new computers

overalls

PLURAL NOUN a piece of clothing that you wear to protect your other clothes when you are working

overboard

ADVERB If you fall **overboard**, you fall over the side of a ship into the water.

overcast

ADJECTIVE When the sky is **overcast**, it is covered by thick cloud.

overcoat overcoats

NOUN a thick, warm coat

overcome overcomes, overcoming, overcame, overcome

VERB **1** If you **overcome** a problem or a feeling, you manage to deal with it or control it.

VERB **2** If you are **overcome**, you are affected by strong emotions. • *They were **overcome** with happiness.*

VERB **3** If you are **overcome** by fumes, gas or smoke, for example, you are made unconscious by them.

overcrowded

ADJECTIVE If a place is **overcrowded**, there are too many things or people in it.

overdue

ADJECTIVE If someone or something is **overdue**, they are late. • *The train is now **overdue**.*

overflow overflows, overflowing, overflowed

VERB If a liquid **overflows**, it spills over the edge of its container. If a river **overflows**, it flows over its banks.

overgrown

ADJECTIVE If a place is **overgrown**, it is thickly covered with plants and weeds.

overhaul overhauls, overhauling, overhauled

VERB **1** If you **overhaul** something, you examine and check it carefully, and repair any faults.

NOUN **2** An **overhaul** is a careful and detailed examination of something in order to repair its faults.

overhead

ADVERB **1** above your head, or in the sky • *Seagulls flew **overhead**.* • *The **overhead** wires were being repaired.*

ADJECTIVE **2** describing something that is above your head • *The **overhead** wires were being repaired.*

overhear overhears, overhearing, overheard

VERB If you **overhear** someone's conversation, you hear what they are saying to someone else.

overlap overlaps, overlapping, overlapped

VERB If one thing **overlaps** another, it covers part of the other thing.

overload overloads, overloading, overloaded

VERB If you **overload** someone or something, you give them too much to do or to carry.

overlook overlooks, overlooking, overlooked

VERB **1** If a building or window **overlooks** a place, it has a view of it from above.

VERB **2** If you **overlook** something, you ignore it or do not notice it.

overnight

ADJECTIVE **1** during the night • *We took an **overnight** flight.*

ADVERB **2** describing something that happens during the night • *We flew **overnight** to Canada.*

ADVERB **3** sudden or suddenly • *He seemed to become such a good player **overnight**.*

overseas

ADJECTIVE **1** describing things or people that are in or that come from foreign countries • *We have some **overseas** students visiting the school.*

ADVERB **2** abroad • *My brother is going **overseas** for a year.*

oversleep oversleeps, oversleeping, overslept

VERB If you **oversleep**, you sleep on past the time you intended to wake up.

overtake overtakes, overtaking, overtook, overtaken

VERB If you **overtake** someone or something, you pass them because you are moving faster than they are.

overtime
NOUN time that someone works in addition to their normal working hours

overture **overtures**
NOUN the opening piece of music at a concert, show or ballet

overweight
ADJECTIVE People or animals that are **overweight** are too heavy for their size.

overwhelm **overwhelms, overwhelming, overwhelmed**
VERB 1 If something **overwhelms** you, it affects you very strongly.
VERB 2 If one group of people **overwhelms** another, they completely defeat them.
VERB 3 If you **overwhelm** someone with something, you load them with too much of it. • He was **overwhelmed** with work.

owe **owes, owing, owed**
VERB 1 If you **owe** someone money, they have lent it to you and you have not yet paid it back.
VERB 2 If you **owe** a quality or skill to someone, you only have it because of them. • He **owes** his success as a tennis player to his coach.

owl **owls**
NOUN a bird of prey that hunts at night. **Owls** have large eyes and short, hooked beaks.

own **owns, owning, owned**
ADJECTIVE 1 If something is your **own**, it belongs to you or is associated with you. • She now has her **own** bedroom.
PRONOUN 2 If something is your **own**, it belongs to you or is associated with you. • His desk is a few centimetres from my **own**.
VERB 3 If you **own** something, it belongs to you.
PHRASE 4 **On your own** means alone.

owner **owners**
NOUN the person to whom something belongs

ox **oxen**
NOUN **Oxen** are cattle used for carrying or pulling things.

oxygen
NOUN a colourless gas that makes up about 21% of the Earth's atmosphere. All animals and plants need **oxygen** to live, and fires need it to burn.

oyster **oysters**
NOUN a large, flat shellfish. Some **oysters** can be eaten, and others produce pearls.

oz
an abbreviation for *ounce*

ozone
NOUN a form of oxygen that is poisonous and has a strong smell

WORD HISTORY
from Greek *ozein* meaning smell

ozone layer
NOUN a layer of the Earth's atmosphere that protects living things from the harmful radiation of the sun
→ Have a look at the illustration for **greenhouse effect**

a
b
c
d
e
f
g
h
i
j
k
l
m
n
o
p
q
r
s
t
u
v
w
x
y
z

P p

pace paces, pacing, paced
NOUN **1** the distance you move when you take one step
NOUN **2** Your **pace** is the speed at which you are walking or running.
VERB **3** If you **pace**, you walk up and down, usually because you are anxious or impatient.

Pacific
NOUN the ocean separating North and South America from Asia and Australia

pacifism
NOUN the belief that all violence and war is wrong

pacifist pacifists
NOUN someone who is opposed to all violence and war

pacify pacifies, pacifying, pacified
VERB If you **pacify** someone who is angry, you calm them.

pack packs, packing, packed
VERB **1** If you **pack** things, you put them neatly into a container, bag or box.
NOUN **2** a complete set of playing cards
NOUN **3** a group of wolves or dogs

package packages
NOUN a small parcel

packaging
NOUN the wrapping or container in which an item is sold or sent • *Make sure you recycle all of the* ***packaging***.

packet packets
NOUN a small box or bag in which something is sold

pact pacts
NOUN a formal agreement or treaty

pad pads
NOUN **1** a set of sheets of paper glued together at one end
NOUN **2** a thick, soft piece of material
NOUN **3** one of the soft parts under an animal's paws

paddle paddles, paddling, paddled
NOUN **1** a short pole with a broad blade at one or both ends, used to move a small boat or a canoe
VERB **2** If someone **paddles** a boat, they move it using a paddle.
VERB **3** If you **paddle**, you walk in shallow water with bare feet.

paddock paddocks
NOUN a small field where horses are kept

padlock padlocks, padlocking, padlocked
NOUN **1** a special kind of metal lock used to fasten two things together
VERB **2** If you **padlock** something, you lock it with a padlock.

pagan pagans
NOUN **1** someone who does not believe in any of the main religions of the world
ADJECTIVE **2** involving beliefs and worship outside the main religions of the world
• ***pagan*** *myths and cults*

page pages
NOUN **1** one side of a sheet of paper in a book or magazine • *Turn to* ***page*** *four.*
NOUN **2** a single sheet of paper

pagoda pagodas
NOUN a tall, elaborately decorated Buddhist or Hindu temple

paid
VERB past tense and past participle of **pay**

pail pails
NOUN a bucket

pain pains
NOUN **1** a feeling of discomfort and hurt in your body, caused by an illness or injury
PHRASE **2** If you are **in pain** you are hurting.

WORD HISTORY
from Latin *poena* meaning punishment

painful
ADJECTIVE causing emotional or physical pain

painkiller painkillers
NOUN a drug that reduces or stops pain

painless
ADJECTIVE Something that is **painless** causes no pain.

paint paints, painting, painted
NOUN **1** a coloured liquid used to decorate buildings and make pictures
VERB **2** If you **paint** a picture of something, you make a picture of it using paint.
VERB **3** If you **paint** something such as a wall, you cover it with paint.

painting paintings
NOUN **1** a picture that someone has created using paints
NOUN **2** the activity of painting pictures

pair pairs
NOUN **1** two things of the same type that are meant to be used together • a **pair** of socks
NOUN **2** objects that have two main parts of the same size and shape • a **pair** of scissors

LANGUAGE TIP
Do not confuse pair with pear.

pal pals
NOUN (*informal*) a friend

WORD HISTORY
from the Romani for brother

palace palaces
NOUN a large, grand house, especially the home of a king or queen

palaeontology
NOUN the scientific study of fossils

pale paler, palest
ADJECTIVE not strong or bright in colour

palette palettes
NOUN a board on which an artist mixes colours

palindrome palindromes
NOUN a word or a phrase that is the same whether you read it backwards or forwards, for example "refer"

palm palms
NOUN **1** a tropical tree with no branches and broad, long leaves at the top of its trunk. **Palm** trees often produce fruit, such as coconuts or dates.
NOUN **2** the flat area on the inside of your hand

pamper pampers, pampering, pampered
VERB If you **pamper** someone, you give them a lot of kindness and comfort.

pamphlet pamphlets
NOUN a very thin book in paper covers, giving information about something

pan pans
NOUN a round metal container with a long handle, used for cooking things

pancake pancakes
NOUN a thin, flat piece of fried batter that can be served with savoury or sweet fillings

panda pandas
NOUN a large animal, rather like a bear, that lives in China. A giant **panda** has black fur with large patches of white.

pane panes
NOUN a sheet of glass in a window or door

panel panels
NOUN **1** a group of people who are chosen to discuss or decide something
NOUN **2** a flat piece of wood, metal or other material that is part of a larger object, such as a door or a wall

panic panics, panicking, panicked
NOUN **1** a sudden strong feeling of fear or anxiety
VERB **2** If you **panic**, you become so afraid or anxious that you cannot act sensibly.

panorama panoramas
NOUN an extensive view over a wide area of land

panoramic
ADJECTIVE giving a view over a wide area of land • The restaurant had **panoramic** views.

pansy pansies
NOUN a small brightly coloured garden flower with large round petals

pant pants, panting, panted
VERB If you **pant**, you take short, quick breaths through your mouth.

panther panthers
NOUN a large wild animal belonging to the cat family, especially the black leopard

pantomime pantomimes
NOUN a funny musical play, usually based on a fairy story and performed at Christmas

pants
PLURAL NOUN **1** underpants or knickers
PLURAL NOUN **2** another word for **trousers**

a
b
c
d
e
f
g
h
i
j
k
l
m
n
o
p
q
r
s
t
u
v
w
x
y
z

287

A
B
C
D
E
F
G
H
I
J
K
L
M
N
O
P
Q
R
S
T
U
V
W
X
Y
Z

paper papers

NOUN **1** a material that you write on or wrap things with

NOUN **2** a newspaper

WORD HISTORY
from *papyrus*, the plant from which paper was made in ancient Egypt, Greece and Rome

paperback paperbacks

NOUN a book with a thin cardboard cover

papier-mâché

NOUN a mixture of mashed wet paper and glue that can be moulded into shapes, then dried and decorated to make bowls, ornaments and other objects

PRONUNCIATION TIP
This word is pronounced pap-yey **mash**-ay.

WORD HISTORY
from French, meaning chewed paper

parable parables

NOUN a short story that makes a moral or religious point

parachute parachutes

NOUN a large umbrella-like piece of fabric attached by lines to a person or package so that it can fall safely to the ground from an aircraft

parade parades, parading, paraded

NOUN **1** a line of people or vehicles moving together through a public place in order to celebrate something

VERB **2** When people **parade**, they walk together in a group, usually in front of spectators.

VERB **3** When soldiers **parade**, they gather together for inspection.

paradise

NOUN **1** According to some religions, **paradise** is a wonderful place where good people go when they die.

NOUN **2** Somewhere very beautiful and wonderful in real life can be called **paradise**. • *Some of the beaches we went to on holiday were* ***paradise***.

paraffin

NOUN a strong-smelling liquid used as a fuel

paragraph paragraphs

NOUN a section of a piece of writing. **Paragraphs** begin on a new line.

parallel

ADJECTIVE If two lines or objects are **parallel**, they are the same distance apart along the whole of their length.

parallelogram parallelograms

NOUN a four-sided shape, each side of which is parallel to the opposite side

paralyse paralyses, paralysing, paralysed

VERB If something such as an accident **paralyses** you, it makes you unable to move part of your body.

paralysed

ADJECTIVE If a part of your body is **paralysed**, you cannot move it. • *Since the accident my uncle has been* ***paralysed*** *from the waist down.*

paralysis

NOUN **Paralysis** is when you cannot move part of your body, for example because of an accident.

paramedic paramedics

NOUN a person who does some types of medical work, for example for the ambulance service

parasite parasites

NOUN a small animal or plant that lives on or inside a larger animal or plant

WORD HISTORY
from Greek *parasitos* meaning someone who eats at someone else's table

parasitic

ADJECTIVE A **parasitic** animal or plant lives on or inside a larger animal or plant.

paratroops or paratroopers

PLURAL NOUN soldiers trained to be dropped from aircraft by parachute

parcel parcels

NOUN something wrapped up in paper

parched

ADJECTIVE **1** very dry and in need of water
• *The earth was* ***parched*** *during the drought.*
ADJECTIVE **2** very thirsty • *I was* ***parched*** *after the race.*

pardon pardons, pardoning, pardoned

PHRASE **1** You say **pardon** or **I beg your pardon** when you want someone to repeat something they have said.

VERB **2** If you **pardon** someone, you forgive or excuse them for something they have done wrong.

parent parents
NOUN Your **parents** are your father and mother.

parenthesis parentheses
NOUN **Parentheses** are brackets that you put around words or numbers to indicate that they are separate or less important.

parish parishes
NOUN an area with its own church and priest or vicar

park parks, parking, parked
VERB 1 When someone **parks** a vehicle, they drive it into a position where it can be left.
NOUN 2 a public area with grass and trees

parliament parliaments
NOUN the group of people who make or change the laws of a country

parole
NOUN When prisoners are given **parole**, they are released early on condition that they behave well.

parrot parrots
NOUN a brightly coloured tropical bird with a curved beak

parsley
NOUN a herb with curly leaves used for flavouring in cooking

parsnip parsnips
NOUN a long, pointed, cream-coloured root vegetable

part parts, parting, parted
NOUN 1 a piece of something, and not all of it
NOUN 2 If you have a **part** in a play, you have a role in it.
VERB 3 If you **part** people or things, you separate them.

partial
ADJECTIVE 1 not complete or whole
PHRASE 2 If you are **partial to** someone or something, you like them.

participate participates, participating, participated
VERB If you **participate** in an activity, you take part in it or join in with other people.

participle participles
NOUN a word that is formed from a verb and used as part of the verb or as an adjective. For example, *eating* is the present **participle** of *eat*, and *loaded* is the past **participle** of *load*.

particle particles
NOUN 1 a very small piece of something
• There were **particles** of dust floating in the air.
NOUN 2 a piece of a substance that is even smaller than an atom, for example a proton or an electron

particular
ADJECTIVE 1 to do with only one person or thing • That **particular** recipe is very easy to make.
ADJECTIVE 2 If you are **particular**, you are fussy and pay attention to detail.

particularly
ADVERB You say **particularly** to show that something applies more to one thing, person or situation than to others. • A good diet is **particularly** important for pregnant women.

partition partitions
NOUN a screen separating one part of a room or vehicle from another

partly
ADVERB to some extent, but not completely
• It's **partly** my fault.

partner partners
NOUN 1 Someone's **partner** is the person they are married to or living with.
NOUN 2 one of two people who do something together, such as dancing or running a business

part of speech parts of speech
NOUN one of the groups that words are divided into in grammar, such as a noun or an adjective

partridge partridges
NOUN a brown game bird with a round body and a short tail

part-time
ADJECTIVE If you have a **part-time** job, you work for only a part of each normal working day or week.

party parties
NOUN 1 a social occasion when people meet to enjoy themselves, often in order to celebrate something
NOUN 2 a group of people who are doing something together • A **party** of school children visited the museum.

a
b
c
d
e
f
g
h
i
j
k
l
m
n
o
p
q
r
s
t
u
v
w
x
y
z

289

pass passes, passing, passed
VERB **1** If you **pass** someone or something, you go past them without stopping.
VERB **2** If you **pass** something to someone, you give it to them.
VERB **3** If you **pass** an examination, you are successful in it.

passage passages
NOUN **1** a long, narrow corridor or space that connects two places • *There was a **passage** from the front garden through to the back garden.*
NOUN **2** a section of a book or piece of music

passenger passengers
NOUN a person travelling in a vehicle, aircraft or ship

passion passions
NOUN a very strong feeling

passive
ADJECTIVE **1** Someone who is **passive** does not take action or react strongly to things.
NOUN **2** In grammar, the **passive**, or **passive** voice, is the form of the verb in which the person or thing to which an action is being done is the subject of the sentence. For example, the sentence *The burglar was seen by the police* is in the **passive**. For the active, or active voice, the subject of the sentence is the person or thing doing the activity: *The police saw the burglar.*

ANTONYM: active

Passover
NOUN an eight-day Jewish festival held in spring

passport passports
NOUN an official document showing your identity and nationality, that you need to show when you enter or leave a country

password passwords
NOUN **1** a secret word known to only a few people. It allows people on the same side to recognise a friend.
NOUN **2** a word you need to know to get into some computer files

past
NOUN **1** the period of time before the present
ADJECTIVE **2** **Past** events are ones that happened or existed before the present.
PREPOSITION **3** You use **past** to tell the time when it is thirty minutes or less after a particular hour. • *It's ten **past** eleven.*
PREPOSITION **4** If you go **past** something, you move towards it and continue until you are

on the other side. • *She walked right **past** Anita.*
ADVERB **5** Something that goes **past** moves towards you and continues until you are on the other side. • *An ambulance drove **past**.*
PREPOSITION **6** Something that is **past** a place is situated on the other side of it. • *The farm is just **past** the next village.*

pasta
NOUN a dried mixture of flour, eggs and water, formed into different shapes

WORD HISTORY
an Italian word meaning flour mixture

paste pastes, pasting, pasted
NOUN **1** a soft, sticky mixture that can be spread easily
VERB **2** If you **paste** something somewhere, you stick it there with glue.

pasteurised; also spelt **pasteurized**
ADJECTIVE **Pasteurised** milk has been heated by a special process to kill bacteria.

WORD HISTORY
after the French chemist Louis *Pasteur* who invented the process

pastime pastimes
NOUN something that you enjoy doing in your spare time

pastry pastries
NOUN **1** a mixture of flour, fat and water that is used for making pies
NOUN **2** a small cake • *There is a selection of **pastries** for tea.*

pasture pastures
NOUN an area of grass where cows, horses and sheep can graze

pasty pasties; pastier, pastiest
NOUN **1** a small pie containing meat and vegetables
ADJECTIVE **2** Someone who is **pasty** looks pale and unhealthy.

PRONUNCIATION TIP
The noun rhymes with "nasty". The adjective rhymes with "tasty".

pat pats, patting, patted
VERB If you **pat** someone or something, you tap them lightly with an open hand.

patch patches, patching, patched
NOUN **1** a piece of material used to cover a hole in something ● *She put a **patch** over the hole in her jeans.*
NOUN **2** an area of a surface that is different in appearance from the rest ● *We want to grow vegetables on that **patch** of ground.*
VERB **3** If you **patch** something that has a hole in it, you mend it by fixing something over the hole.

patchy patchier, patchiest
ADJECTIVE uneven in quantity, quality or both ● *We drove through **patchy** fog.*

pâté pâtés
NOUN a paste made from meat, fish or vegetables, and spread on toast or biscuits

PRONUNCIATION TIP
This word is pronounced pa-**tay**.

WORD HISTORY
from the French word for paste

patent patents
NOUN the official right given to someone to make something they have invented. It stops others from copying it.

paternal
ADJECTIVE relating to or like a father

WORD HISTORY
from Latin *pater* meaning father

path paths
NOUN **1** a strip of ground for people to walk or ride along
NOUN **2** the direction in which something travels ● *The trail of smoke showed the **path** of the plane.*

pathetic
ADJECTIVE **1** If something is **pathetic**, it makes you feel pity.
ADJECTIVE **2** very poor or unsuccessful ● *He made a **pathetic** attempt to swim.*

WORD HISTORY
from Greek *pathetikos* meaning sensitive

patience
NOUN the ability to stay calm in a difficult or irritating situation

patient patients
ADJECTIVE **1** If you are **patient**, you stay calm in a difficult or irritating situation.

NOUN **2** a person receiving treatment from a doctor

patiently
ADVERB calmly even though you are in a difficult or annoying situation

patio patios
NOUN a paved area close to a house

patriot patriots
NOUN someone who loves their own country and is very loyal to it

patriotic
ADJECTIVE showing that you love your country and are very loyal to it

patriotism
NOUN behaviour or beliefs that show you love your country and are very loyal to it

patrol patrols, patrolling, patrolled
VERB **1** When soldiers, police or guards **patrol** an area, they walk or drive around it to make sure there is no trouble.
NOUN **2** a group of people patrolling an area

patter patters, pattering, pattered
VERB **1** If something **patters** on a surface, it makes quick, light, tapping sounds. ● *The rain **pattered** against the window.*
NOUN **2** a series of light, tapping sounds ● *We could hear the **patter** of light rain.*

pattern patterns
NOUN **1** a design of shapes repeated at regular intervals
NOUN **2** a drawing that can be copied to make something else, such as clothes

pause pauses, pausing, paused
VERB **1** If you **pause**, you stop speaking or doing something for a short time.
NOUN **2** a period when something stops for a short time before continuing

pavement pavements
NOUN a raised pathway with a hard surface along the side of a road

WORD HISTORY
from Latin *pavimentum* meaning hard floor

pavilion pavilions
NOUN a building at a sports ground, especially a cricket pitch, where players can change

paw paws
NOUN the foot of an animal that has claws and pads

A
B
C
D
E
F
G
H
I
J
K
L
M
N
O
P
Q
R
S
T
U
V
W
X
Y
Z

pawn pawns, pawning, pawned
VERB **1** If you **pawn** something, you leave it with someone called a pawnbroker who lends you money. When you repay the money, the pawnbroker will give back the item you **pawned**.
NOUN **2** the smallest and least valuable piece in the game of chess

pay pays, paying, paid
VERB **1** If you **pay** someone, you give them money in exchange for something.
PHRASE **2** If you **pay attention**, you listen carefully to what is being said.

payment payments
NOUN If you make a **payment** for something, you give someone money in exchange for goods or a service.

PC PCs
NOUN **1** the abbreviation of *personal computer*
NOUN **2** In Britain, **PC** is also the abbreviation of *police constable*.

PE
NOUN an abbreviation of *physical education*, which is the sports that you do at school

pea peas
NOUN a small, round green seed that is eaten as a vegetable

peace
NOUN **1** a state of undisturbed calm and quiet
NOUN **2** If a country is at **peace**, it is not at war.

LANGUAGE TIP
Do not confuse *peace* with *piece*.

---

peaceful
ADJECTIVE quiet and calm

peach peaches
NOUN a soft, round fruit with yellow flesh and a yellow and red skin

peacock peacocks
NOUN a large male bird with very long green and blue tail feathers that it can spread out in a fan. The female is called a peahen.

peak peaks
NOUN **1** the highest point of a mountain
→ Have a look at the illustration for **glacier**
NOUN **2** The **peak** of an activity or process is the point at which it is strongest or most successful.
NOUN **3** the part of a cap that sticks out over your eyes

peal peals
NOUN the loud musical sound made by bells ringing one after another

peanut peanuts
NOUN a small nut that grows under the ground

pear pears
NOUN a green or yellow fruit that is narrow at the top and wider at the bottom

---

LANGUAGE TIP
Do not confuse *pear* with *pair*.

---

pearl pearls
NOUN a hard, round, creamy-white ball used in jewellery. **Pearls** grow inside the shell of an oyster.

peasant peasants
NOUN a person who works on the land, earning little money

peat
NOUN dark-brown decaying plant material found in cool, wet regions. Dried **peat** can be used as fuel or fertiliser.

pebble pebbles
NOUN a smooth, round stone often found on the beach

peck pecks, pecking, pecked
VERB If a bird **pecks** something, it bites at it quickly with its beak. ● *The birds **pecked** at the seeds on the ground.*

peculiar
ADJECTIVE strange and unusual ● *She thought the food tasted **peculiar**.*

peculiarity
NOUN the quality that something or someone has when they are strange and unusual

peculiarly
ADVERB in a way that is strange and unusual ● *She thought the food tasted **peculiar**.*

pedal pedals, pedalling, pedalled
VERB **1** When you **pedal** a bicycle, you push the pedals around with your feet to make it move.
NOUN **2** a control lever that you press with your foot to make a machine or vehicle wor
→ Have a look at the illustration for **bicycl**

pedestrian pedestrians
NOUN someone who is walking ● *Only **pedestrians** are allowed down this street.*

pedigree pedigrees
ADJECTIVE **1** A **pedigree** animal is bred from a single breed and its ancestors are known and recorded.
NOUN **2** a list of a person's or an animal's ancestors

peek peeks, peeking, peeked
VERB **1** If you **peek** at something, you have a quick look at it.
NOUN **2** a quick look at something

peel peels, peeling, peeled
NOUN **1** the skin of a fruit or vegetable
VERB **2** When you **peel** fruit or vegetables, you remove the skin.
VERB **3** If a layer of something **peels**, it comes off a surface. • *Paint was **peeling** off the walls.*

peep peeps, peeping, peeped
VERB **1** If you **peep** at something, you have a quick, secretive look at it, or you look at it through a small opening.
NOUN **2** a quick look at something

peer peers, peering, peered
VERB **1** If you **peer** at something, you look at it very hard. • *He **peered** into the dark room.*
NOUN **2** Your **peers** are your equals in age, interests and background.

peg pegs
NOUN **1** a plastic or wooden clip for attaching clothes to a washing line
NOUN **2** a hook where you can hang things

pelican pelicans
NOUN a large water bird with a pouch beneath its beak in which it stores fish

pellet pellets
NOUN a small ball of food, paper, lead or other material

pelt pelts, pelting, pelted
NOUN **1** the skin and fur of an animal, especially when it is used for making clothes
VERB **2** If you **pelt** someone with something, you throw it at them very hard.
VERB **3** If rain **pelts** down, it rains very hard.

pelvis pelvises
NOUN the group of bones near the bottom of your spine to which your legs are attached

→ Have a look at the illustration for **skeleton**

pen pens
NOUN **1** an instrument with a pointed end used for writing with ink
NOUN **2** a small, fenced area where farm animals are kept • *a sheep **pen***

penalty penalties
NOUN **1** a punishment
NOUN **2** In sport, a **penalty** is an advantage or point given to one team when their opponents break the rules.

pence
NOUN a plural form of **penny**

pencil pencils
NOUN a small stick of wood with a type of soft mineral called graphite in the centre, used for drawing or writing

WORD HISTORY
from Latin *pencillus* meaning painter's brush

pendant pendants
NOUN a piece of jewellery attached to a chain and worn round the neck

penetrate penetrates, penetrating, penetrated
VERB If someone or something **penetrates** an object or area, they succeed in getting into or through it. • *Eventually they **penetrated** the forest and found the cabin.*

pen friend pen friends
NOUN someone living in a different place or country whom you write to regularly, although you may never have met each other

penguin penguins
NOUN a black and white bird with webbed feet and small wings like flippers. **Penguins** are found mainly in the Antarctic.

penicillin
NOUN a powerful antibiotic obtained from fungus and used to treat infections

peninsula peninsulas
NOUN an area of land almost surrounded by water

WORD HISTORY
from Latin *paene* + *insula* meaning almost an island

penis penises
NOUN A man's **penis** is the part of the body he uses when urinating.

penknife penknives
NOUN a small folding knife

a
b
c
d
e
f
g
h
i
j
k
l
m
n
o
p
q
r
s
t
u
v
w
x
y
z

293

A
B
C
D
E
F
G
H
I
J
K
L
M
N
O
P
Q
R
S
T
U
V
W
X
Y
Z

penny pennies or **pence**
NOUN a unit of currency in Britain and some other countries. In Britain, there are 100 **pence** in a pound.

pension pensions
NOUN a regular sum of money paid to a retired or widowed person or to someone with a disability

pentagon pentagons
NOUN a flat shape with five straight sides

pentagonal
ADJECTIVE having five straight sides

pentathlon pentathlons
NOUN a sports contest in which athletes compete in five different events

WORD HISTORY
from Greek *pente* meaning five and *athlon* meaning contest

people
PLURAL NOUN human beings – men, women and children

pepper peppers
NOUN **1** a hot-tasting powdered spice used for flavouring in cooking
NOUN **2** a hollow green, red or yellow vegetable, with sweet-flavoured flesh

peppermint peppermints
NOUN **1** a plant with a strong taste. It is used for making sweets and in medicine.
NOUN **2** a sweet flavoured with peppermint

per
PREPOSITION **Per** means *for each* and is used when speaking about prices, measurements, rates and ratios
● *60 kilometres* **per** *hour* ● *three times* **per** *year* ● *90p* **per** *kilo*

perceive perceives, perceiving, perceived
VERB If you **perceive** something, you see, notice or understand it.

per cent
PHRASE You use **per cent** to show amounts out of a hundred. The symbol for per cent is %. ● *She got 98* **per cent** *(98%) for her maths test.*

WORD HISTORY
from Latin *per* meaning each and *centum* meaning hundred

percentage percentages
NOUN an amount or rate expressed as a number of hundredths

perceptive
ADJECTIVE Someone who is **perceptive** notices and understands things more quickly than other people.

SYNONYMS: observant, sharp

perch perches, perching, perched
VERB **1** If you **perch** on something, you sit on the edge of it.
VERB **2** When a bird **perches** on something, it stands on it.
NOUN **3** a short rod for a bird to stand on
NOUN **4** an edible freshwater fish

percussion
ADJECTIVE **Percussion** instruments are musical instruments that you hit or shake to produce sounds, such as drums and tambourines

percussionist percussionists
NOUN someone who plays musical instruments that you hit or shake, such as drums and tambourines

perennial
ADJECTIVE occurring or lasting for many years

perfect perfects, perfecting, perfected
ADJECTIVE **1** Something that is **perfect** is as good as it possibly can be.
VERB **2** If you **perfect** something, you make it as good as it possibly can be.

PRONUNCIATION TIP
The adjective is pronounced **pur**-fikt. The verb is pronounced pur-**fekt**.

perform performs, performing, performed
VERB **1** If you **perform** a play or piece of music, you do a show of it in front of an audience.
VERB **2** If you **perform** a task or action, you do it.

performance performances
NOUN an entertainment provided for an audience ● *The orchestra gave an excellent performance.*

performer performers
NOUN someone who does something in front of an audience, such as acting, dancing or playing a piece of music

perfume perfumes
NOUN 1 a pleasant-smelling liquid that people put on their skin
NOUN 2 a pleasant smell ● *These roses have a lovely perfume.*

perhaps
ADVERB You use **perhaps** when you are not sure if something is true or possible. ● *Perhaps we could see you tomorrow?*

peril perils
NOUN (*formal*) great danger

perilous
ADJECTIVE (*formal*) very dangerous

perimeter perimeters
NOUN 1 the distance all the way round the edge of an area
NOUN 2 the edge or boundary of something

period periods
NOUN 1 a particular length of time ● *We will be away for a period of a few months.*
NOUN 2 A woman's **period** is the monthly bleeding from her womb.
NOUN 3 In American English, a **period** is a full stop.

periodical periodicals
NOUN a magazine that is published regularly

periodic table
NOUN a table showing the chemical elements arranged in a particular order

periscope periscopes
NOUN a tube with mirrors placed in it so that you can see things that are otherwise out of sight. **Periscopes** are used for seeing out of submarines.

perish perishes, perishing, perished
VERB 1 If fruit, rubber or fabric **perishes**, it rots.
VERB 2 (*formal*) If someone or something **perishes**, they die or are destroyed.

perishable
ADJECTIVE If food or a material is **perishable**, it can rot.

perm perms
NOUN If someone has a **perm**, their hair is curled and treated with chemicals to keep the curls for several months.

permanent
ADJECTIVE lasting forever or present all the time

permission
NOUN If you have **permission** to do something, you are allowed to do it.

permit permits, permitting, permitted
VERB 1 If someone or something **permits** you to do something, they allow it or make it possible. ● *We permit children to ride bicycles to school.*

SYNONYM: give permission

NOUN 2 an official document that says that you are allowed to do something

PRONUNCIATION TIP
The verb is pronounced pur-**mit**. The noun is pronounced **pur**-mit.

perpendicular
ADJECTIVE A line that is **perpendicular** to another one meets it at a right angle (90°).

perpetual
ADJECTIVE never ending

perplexed
ADJECTIVE If you are **perplexed**, you are puzzled and do not know what to do.

SYNONYM: confused

persecute persecutes, persecuting, persecuted
VERB If someone **persecutes** another person, they continually treat them with cruelty and unfairness, often because of their religious beliefs.

persecution
NOUN **Persecution** is when someone continually treats another person in a cruel and unfair way, especially because of their religious beliefs.

persecutor persecutors
NOUN someone who continually treats another person in a cruel and unfair way, especially because of their religious beliefs

perseverance
NOUN the quality someone has when they keep trying to do something and do not give up

a
b
c
d
e
f
g
h
i
j
k
l
m
n
o
p
q
r
s
t
u
v
w
x
y
z

295

persevere perseveres, persevering, persevered
VERB If you **persevere**, you keep trying to do something and do not give up.

persist persists, persisting, persisted
VERB 1 If something **persists**, it continues and will not stop. • The rain **persisted** all day.
VERB 2 If you **persist** in doing something, you continue with it in spite of difficulties or opposition.

person people or **persons**
NOUN 1 a man, woman or child

SYNONYMS: human being, individual

NOUN 2 In grammar, the first **person** is the speaker (I), the second **person** is the person being spoken to (you), and the third **person** is anyone else being referred to (he, she, they).
PHRASE 3 If you do something **in person**, you do it yourself rather than letting someone else do it for you.

WORD HISTORY
from Latin persona meaning actor's mask

LANGUAGE TIP
The usual plural of person is people. Persons is much less common, and is used only in formal English.

personal
ADJECTIVE 1 belonging or relating to a particular person

SYNONYMS: individual, own

ADJECTIVE 2 **Personal** matters are personal things that you may not wish to discuss with other people. • I cannot tell you for **personal** reasons.

personality personalities
NOUN Your **personality** is your character and nature. • She's got a very lively **personality**.

personally
ADVERB 1 in person • He came to school to thank us **personally** for the money we raised for the charity.
ADVERB 2 You use **personally** to express your own opinion of something. • **Personally**, I don't mind where we go.

personnel
PLURAL NOUN the people who work for an organisation

perspective perspectives
NOUN 1 the impression of distance and depth in a picture or a drawing
NOUN 2 a particular way of thinking about something or looking at something • What is your **perspective** on discipline?

perspiration
NOUN sweat or the process of sweating

perspire perspires, perspiring, perspired
VERB When people **perspire**, they sweat.

persuade persuades, persuading, persuaded
VERB If you **persuade** someone to do something, or **persuade** them that something is true, you make them do it or believe it by giving them good reasons.

persuasion
NOUN the process of trying to make someone do something or believe something by giving them good reasons

persuasive
ADJECTIVE able to make someone do something or believe something by using good reasons • a **persuasive** argument

pessimism
NOUN the feeling that bad things will always happen

pessimist pessimists
NOUN If you are a **pessimist**, you think that bad things will always happen.

ANTONYM: optimist

pessimistic
ADJECTIVE believing that bad things will always happen

ANTONYM: optimistic

pest pests
NOUN 1 an insect or other small animal that damages plants or food supplies
NOUN 2 someone who keeps bothering or annoying you

pester pesters, pestering, pestered
VERB If you **pester** someone, you keep bothering them or asking them to do something.

pesticide pesticides
NOUN a chemical sprayed onto plants to kill insects and grubs

pet pets
NOUN **1** a tame animal kept at home
NOUN **2** a person who is treated as a favourite

petal petals
NOUN one of the coloured outer parts of a flower that attract insects. Some **petals** are perfumed.
→ Have a look at the illustration for **flower**

petition petitions
NOUN a written document, signed by a lot of people, requesting official action be taken on something

petrified
ADJECTIVE If you are **petrified**, you are very frightened.
SYNONYM: terrified

petrol
NOUN a liquid that is used as a fuel for motor vehicles

petty pettier, pettiest
ADJECTIVE trivial and unimportant • We should not argue over **petty** things.

pew pews
NOUN a long wooden seat with a back, that people sit on in church

pH
NOUN The **pH** of a solution or of the soil is a measurement of how acid or alkaline it is. Substances with a **pH** above 7 are alkaline and substances with a **pH** below 7 are acid.

phantom phantoms
NOUN **1** a ghost
ADJECTIVE **2** imagined or unreal

pharmacy pharmacies
NOUN a shop where medicines are sold

phase phases
NOUN a particular stage in the development of something

pheasant pheasants
NOUN a large, long-tailed game bird

phenomenal
ADJECTIVE unusually great or good • The show was a **phenomenal** success.

phenomenally
ADVERB in a way that is unusually good

phenomenon phenomena
NOUN something that happens or exists, especially something extraordinary or remarkable • The eclipse was a fascinating **phenomenon**.

philosophy philosophies
NOUN **1** the study or creation of ideas about humans, their relationship to the universe and beliefs
NOUN **2** a set of beliefs a person has

phobia phobias
NOUN a deep fear or dislike of something

phobic
ADJECTIVE having a deep fear or dislike of something • I'm **phobic** about spiders.

phoenix phoenixes
NOUN an imaginary bird that, according to myth, sets fire to itself every five hundred years, and rises from the ashes

PRONUNCIATION TIP
This word is pronounced **fee**-niks.

phone phones, phoning, phoned
NOUN **1** a piece of electrical or electronic equipment for talking directly to someone who is in a different place
VERB **2** If you **phone** someone, you speak to them using a phone.

WORD HISTORY
short for *telephone*

phonetics
NOUN the study of the sounds made in speech

phoney phonier, phoniest; also spelt **phony**
ADJECTIVE false, not genuine, and meant to trick • He had a **phoney** passport.
ANTONYM: genuine

photo photos
NOUN an abbreviation of **photograph**

photocopier photocopiers
NOUN a machine that makes instant copies of documents

photocopy photocopies, photocopying, photocopied
VERB **1** If you **photocopy** a document, you make a copy of it using a photocopier.
NOUN **2** a copy of a document made using a photocopier

photograph **photographs,**
photographing, photographed
NOUN **1** a picture taken with a camera and
then printed on special paper • *She took lots
of photographs of her friends.*
VERB **2** If you **photograph** someone or
something, you use a camera to take a
picture of them.

photographer **photographers**
NOUN someone whose job is to take
photographs

photography
NOUN the job or hobby of taking photographs

photosynthesis
NOUN the process by which green plants
make their own food from carbon dioxide
and water in the presence of sunlight

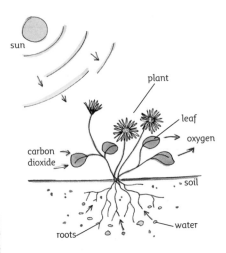

sun
plant
leaf
oxygen
carbon dioxide
soil
water
roots

phrase **phrases**
NOUN a short group of words or musical notes

physical
ADJECTIVE concerning the body rather than
the mind

WORD HISTORY
from Greek *phusis* meaning nature

physical education
NOUN physical exercise and sports that you
do at school

physics
NOUN the scientific study of the forces and
properties of matter, such as heat, light,
sound and electricity

pi
NOUN a number, approximately 3.142,
which is equal to the circumference a
circle divided by its diameter and usually
represented by the Greek letter π

pianist **pianists**
NOUN someone who plays the piano

piano **pianos**
NOUN a large musical instrument with a row
of black and white keys. When the keys are
pressed, little hammers hit wires to produce
different notes.

piccolo **piccolos**
NOUN a high-pitched wind instrument like a
small flute

pick **picks, picking, picked**
VERB **1** If you **pick** someone or something,
you choose them. • *I picked Hannah for my
partner.*
VERB **2** If you **pick** a flower or a fruit, you
break it off from where it is growing.
VERB **3** If someone **picks** a lock, they open it
with a piece of wire instead of a key.

pick on
VERB If you **pick on** someone, you treat
them unkindly and unfairly.

pick up
VERB **1** If you **pick up** someone or
something, you lift them.
VERB **2** If you **pick up** someone or
something from a place, you collect them
from there. • *What time will you pick
me up?*

picket **pickets, picketing, picketed**
VERB **1** When a group of people **picket** a
place of work during a strike, they stand
outside and try to persuade other workers
not to go in to work.
NOUN **2** a group of people who picket a place

pickle **pickles**
NOUN **Pickles** are vegetables or fruit
preserved in vinegar or salt water.

pickpocket **pickpockets**

NOUN a thief who steals things from pockets or bags

picnic **picnics, picnicking, picnicked**

NOUN **1** a meal eaten out of doors

NOUN **2** to have a picnic

pictogram **pictograms**

NOUN a type of graph that uses small pictures to show information

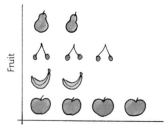

Number of students who prefer it

pictorial

ADJECTIVE relating to or using pictures ● *The book is a **pictorial** history of air travel.*

picture **pictures**

NOUN a drawing, painting, photograph or television image of someone or something

picturesque

ADJECTIVE A place that is **picturesque** is very attractive and unspoiled.

WORD HISTORY

from Italian *pittoresco* meaning in the style of a painter

pie **pies**

NOUN a dish of meat, vegetables or fruit covered with pastry

piece **pieces**

NOUN **1** a portion or part of something ● *a cake divided into six **pieces***

NOUN **2** an individual thing of a particular kind ● *This is a good **piece** of work.*

NOUN **3** a coin ● *a 50 pence **piece***

LANGUAGE TIP

Do not confuse *piece* with *peace*.

pie chart **pie charts**

NOUN a circular diagram that is divided into segments to show how a quantity or an amount of something is shared

Favourite sports

☐ Football ■ Cricket

☐ Athletics ☐ Tennis

pier **piers**

NOUN a large structure at the seaside, with a platform built from the shore out into the sea, that people can walk along

pierce **pierces, piercing, pierced**

VERB If a sharp object **pierces** something, it goes through it, making a hole.

piercing

ADJECTIVE **1** a **piercing** sound is high pitched and sharp, and it hurts your ears

SYNONYM: shrill

ADJECTIVE **2** Someone with **piercing** eyes seems to stare at you intensely.

pig **pigs**

NOUN a farm animal with pink or black skin, a curly tail and a snout, that is kept for its meat. Pork, ham and bacon all come from **pigs**.

pigeon **pigeons**

NOUN a grey bird with a small head and large chest, often found in towns and cities

piglet **piglets**

NOUN a young pig

pigsty **pigsties**

NOUN **1** a small shelter with an enclosed area where pigs are kept

NOUN **2** If you say a place is like a **pigsty**, you mean that it is very dirty and untidy.

a
b
c
d
e
f
g
h
i
j
k
l
m
n
o
p
q
r
s
t
u
v
w
x
y
z

A
B
C
D
E
F
G
H
I
J
K
L
M
N
O
P
Q
R
S
T
U
V
W
X
Y
Z

pigtail pigtails
NOUN a plait of hair ● *She wore her hair in* **pigtails***.*

pike pikes
NOUN **1** a large freshwater fish with strong, sharp teeth
NOUN **2** a weapon used in medieval times. A **pike** was a long pole with a spike on the end.

pile piles, piling, piled
NOUN **1** a quantity of things lying on top of one another
VERB **2** If you **pile** things somewhere, you put them on top of one another.

pilgrim pilgrims
NOUN a person who goes on a journey to a holy place for religious reasons

pilgrimage pilgrimages
NOUN a journey to a holy place for religious reasons

pill pills
NOUN a small, round tablet of medicine that you swallow

pillar pillars
NOUN a tall, solid structure like a large post, often made of stone and usually supporting part of a building

pillow pillows
NOUN a large cushion that you rest your head on when you are in bed

pilot pilots
NOUN **1** a person who is trained to fly an aircraft
NOUN **2** the person who guides a ship into port

pimple pimples
NOUN a small spot on the skin

pin pins, pinning, pinned
NOUN **1** a thin, pointed piece of metal, used to fasten things like paper or cloth together
VERB **2** If you **pin** something, you attach it with a pin.

pincers
PLURAL NOUN **1** The **pincers** of a crab or a lobster are its large front claws.
PLURAL NOUN **2** a tool consisting of two pieces of metal hinged in the middle, used for gripping and pulling things

pinch pinches, pinching, pinched
VERB **1** If you **pinch** something, you squeeze it between your thumb and first finger.
VERB **2** (*informal*) If someone **pinches** something, they steal it.
NOUN **3** A **pinch** of something is the amount that you can hold between your thumb and first finger. ● *Add a* **pinch** *of salt to the soup.*

pine pines, pining, pined
NOUN **1** an evergreen tree with very thin leaves called needles
VERB **2** If you **pine** for something or someone, you feel sad because they are not there.

pineapple pineapples
NOUN a large, oval tropical fruit with sweet, yellow flesh and thick, woody skin

pink pinker, pinkest
ADJECTIVE pale reddish-white

pint pints
NOUN a unit of measurement for liquids equal to about 0.568 litres

pioneer pioneers
NOUN one of the first people to go to a place or to do something new

pip pips
NOUN **1** the hard seeds in a fruit
NOUN **2** a short, high-pitched sound

pipe pipes, piping, piped
NOUN **1** a long, hollow tube through which liquid or gas can flow
NOUN **2** an object that is used for smoking tobacco, consisting of a small hollow bowl attached to a thin tube
NOUN **3** a tube-shaped musical instrument
VERB **4** If liquid or gas is **piped** somewhere, it is transferred there through a pipe.

pipeline pipelines
NOUN **1** a large underground pipe that carries oil or gas over a long distance
PHRASE **2** If something is **in the pipeline**, it is already planned or has begun.

pirate pirates
NOUN a sailor who attacks and robs other ships

pistol pistols
NOUN a small gun held in the hand

pit pits
NOUN **1** a large hole in the ground
NOUN **2** a coal mine

pitch pitches, pitching, pitched
NOUN **1** an area of ground marked out for playing a game such as football or cricket
NOUN **2** The **pitch** of a sound is how high or low it is.
NOUN **3** a black substance painted onto roofs and boat bottoms to make them waterproof
VERB **4** If you **pitch** something somewhere, you throw it there with a lot of force.
VERB **5** If you **pitch** a tent, you put it up.

pitcher pitchers
NOUN a large jug

pitchfork pitchforks
NOUN a long-handled fork with two large prongs, used for lifting and moving hay

pitfall pitfalls
NOUN one of the difficulties or dangers of a situation

pitta pittas
NOUN a flat disc of bread with a hollow inside, that can be filled with food

---
WORD HISTORY
from Greek, meaning a cake

---

pity pities, pitying, pitied
VERB **1** If you **pity** someone, you feel sorry for them.
NOUN **2** a feeling of sadness and concern for someone
NOUN **3** If you say that something is a **pity**, you mean it is disappointing. • *It's a pity we couldn't play tennis.*

pivot pivots, pivoting, pivoted
VERB **1** If something **pivots**, it balances or turns on a central point.
NOUN **2** the central point on which something balances or turns

pivotal
ADJECTIVE very important and affecting how something develops

pizza pizzas
NOUN a flat piece of dough usually covered with cheese, tomato and other savoury food and baked in an oven

---
WORD HISTORY
an Italian word

---

placard placards
NOUN a large notice carried at a demonstration or displayed in a public place • *The man carried a placard advertising the furniture sale.*

place places, placing, placed
NOUN **1** a particular point, position, building or area • *They found a good place to camp.*
NOUN **2** a particular position in a race, competition, or series • *Last year she finished in third place.*
NOUN **3** If you have a **place** in a team or on a course, you are allowed to join the team or course. • *I eventually got a place at the new school.*
VERB **4** If you **place** something somewhere, you put it there. • *She placed her hand gently on my shoulder.*
PHRASE **5** When something **takes place**, it happens. • *The competition will take place next month.*

placid
ADJECTIVE calm and not easily excited or upset

SYNONYMS: even-tempered, unexcitable

plague plagues, plaguing, plagued
NOUN **1** a very infectious disease that kills large numbers of people
NOUN **2** A **plague** of unpleasant things is a large number of them occurring at the same time.
VERB **3** If you **plague** someone, you keep pestering them.
VERB **4** If problems **plague** you, they keep causing you trouble.

PRONUNCIATION TIP
This word is pronounced **playg**.

---

plaice
NOUN an edible European flat fish

LANGUAGE TIP
The plural of *plaice* is *plaice*.

---

plaid plaids
NOUN woven material with a tartan design

PRONUNCIATION TIP
This word is pronounced **plad**.

---

plain plainer, plainest; plains
ADJECTIVE **1** very simple in style, with no pattern or decoration
ADJECTIVE **2** obvious or easy to understand
NOUN **3** a large, flat area of land with very few trees

a
b
c
d
e
f
g
h
i
j
k
l
m
n
o
p
q
r
s
t
u
v
w
x
y
z

A
B
C
D
E
F
G
H
I
J
K
L
M
N
O
P
Q
R
S
T
U
V
W
X
Y
Z

plait plaits, plaiting, plaited

VERB **1** If you **plait** hair or rope, you twist three lengths together in turn to make one thick length.
NOUN **2** a length of hair that has been plaited

PRONUNCIATION TIP
This word is pronounced **plat**.

---

plan plans, planning, planned

NOUN **1** a method of achieving something that has been worked out beforehand
VERB **2** If you **plan** something, you decide in detail what you are going to do.
VERB **3** If you **plan** to do something, you intend to do it.

plane planes

NOUN **1** an abbreviation of *aeroplane*
NOUN **2** a tool for smoothing wood
ADJECTIVE **3** A **plane** shape has a flat, level surface. A **plane** mirror is flat and not curved.

planet planets

NOUN a large sphere in space that orbits a sun. The Earth and Mars are both **planets** that revolve around our sun.

plank planks

NOUN a long rectangular piece of wood

plankton

NOUN a layer of tiny plants and animals that live just below the surface of a sea or lake

plant plants, planting, planted

NOUN **1** a living thing that grows in the earth and has a stem, leaves and roots.

→ Have a look at the illustration for **photosynthesis**

VERB **2** If you **plant** things such as flowers or trees, you put them in the ground so that they will grow.

plantation plantations

NOUN **1** a large area of land where crops such as tea, cotton or sugar are grown
NOUN **2** a large number of trees planted together

plaque plaques

NOUN **1** a flat piece of metal or porcelain, fixed to a wall, with an inscription on it in memory of a famous person or event
NOUN **2** a substance that forms around your teeth. It is made up of bacteria, saliva and food.

PRONUNCIATION TIP
This word is pronounced **plak**.

---

plaster plasters

NOUN **1** a paste made of sand, lime and water, that is used to form a smooth surface for inside walls and ceilings
NOUN **2** a strip of sticky material with a small pad, used for covering cuts on your body
● *The bleeding stopped once I had put a plaster on.*
NOUN **3 Plaster** of Paris is a white powder mixed with water, that becomes hard when it dries. It is used for making moulds and for holding broken bones in place while they heal.

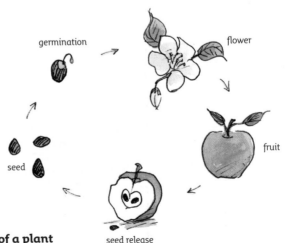

germination

flower

fruit

seed

seed release

life cycle of a plant

plasterer plasterers
NOUN someone whose job is to cover the walls and ceiling of a room with a paste made of sand, lime and water to form a smooth surface for painting

plastic plastics
NOUN **1** a light synthetic material made from oil by a chemical process. **Plastics** can be moulded into different shapes for many different uses.
ADJECTIVE **2** made of plastic

Plasticine
NOUN (trademark) a soft, coloured material like clay, used for making models

plate plates
NOUN **1** a flat dish used to hold food
NOUN **2** a flat piece of hard material such as glass or metal

plateau plateaus or **plateaux**
NOUN a large area of high and fairly flat land

WORD HISTORY
from Old French *platel* meaning a flat piece of metal

---

platform platforms
NOUN **1** a raised structure on which someone or something can stand
NOUN **2** the raised area in a railway station where passengers get on and off trains

platinum
NOUN a valuable silver-coloured metal

platypus platypuses
NOUN an Australian mammal that lives in rivers. It has brown fur, webbed feet and a beak like a duck.

WORD HISTORY
from Greek *platus* meaning flat and *pous* meaning foot

---

play plays, playing, played
VERB **1** When children **play**, they take part in games or use toys for fun.
VERB **2** When you **play** a sport or game, you take part in it.
VERB **3** If an actor **plays** a character in a play or film, they perform that role.
VERB **4** If you **play** a musical instrument, you produce music from it.
NOUN **5 Play** is the activity of playing a game or sport.
NOUN **6** a story acted out in the theatre, on the radio or on television

player players
NOUN **1** someone who takes part in a sport or game • football **players**
NOUN **2** someone who plays a musical instrument • a violin **player**

playground playgrounds
NOUN a special area for children to play in

playgroup playgroups
NOUN an informal group of very young children who play together, supervised by adults

playtime playtimes
NOUN the time in a school day when children go out to play

playwright playwrights
NOUN a person who writes plays

plea pleas
NOUN **1** If you make a **plea**, you make an urgent request or an appeal for something.
NOUN **2** In a law court, a **plea** is someone's statement that they are guilty or not guilty.

plead pleads, pleading, pleaded
VERB **1** If you **plead** with someone, you beg them for something. • She came to **plead** for help.
VERB **2** In a law court, when a person **pleads** guilty or not guilty, they state that they are guilty or not guilty.

pleasant
ADJECTIVE nice, pleasing, enjoyable or attractive in some way

please pleases, pleasing, pleased
1 You say **please** when you are asking someone politely to do something.
• Can you help me, **please**?
VERB **2** If something **pleases** you, it makes you feel happy and satisfied.

pleasure pleasures
NOUN a feeling of happiness, satisfaction or enjoyment

pleat pleats
NOUN a permanent fold in fabric, made by folding one part over another

pledge pledges, pledging, pledged
NOUN **1** a solemn promise
VERB **2** If you **pledge** something, you promise that you will do it or give it.

plenty
NOUN If you have **plenty** of something, you have more than enough for your needs.
• We've got **plenty** of time.

a
b
c
d
e
f
g
h
i
j
k
l
m
n
o
p
q
r
s
t
u
v
w
x
y
z

A
B
C
D
E
F
G
H
I
J
K
L
M
N
O
P
Q
R
S
T
U
V
W
X
Y
Z

pliable

ADJECTIVE If something is **pliable**, you can bend it without breaking it. • *This **pliable** material will be easier to work with.*

SYNONYM: flexible

pliers

PLURAL NOUN a small tool with metal jaws for gripping small objects such as nails and bending wire

plight plights

NOUN a difficult or dangerous situation • *the **plight** of the homeless*

plod plods, plodding, plodded

VERB If you **plod**, you walk slowly and heavily. • *We **plodded** home through the mud.*

plop plops, plopping, plopped

NOUN **1** a gentle sound of something lightweight dropping into a liquid
VERB **2** If something **plops** into a liquid, it drops into it with a gentle sound.

plot plots, plotting, plotted

NOUN **1** a secret plan made by a group of people
NOUN **2** The **plot** of a film, novel or play is the story.
VERB **3** If people **plot** to do something, they plan it secretly.

plough ploughs, ploughing, ploughed

NOUN **1** a large farming tool that is pulled across a field to turn the soil over before planting seeds
VERB **2** When farmers **plough** land, they use a plough to turn over the soil.

pluck plucks, plucking, plucked

VERB **1** If you **pluck** a fruit or flower, you remove it with a sharp pull.
VERB **2** If you **pluck** a dead bird, such as a chicken or a turkey, you pull the feathers off it before cooking it.
VERB **3** When you **pluck** a stringed instrument, you pull the strings and let them go.

plug plugs, plugging, plugged

NOUN **1** a device that connects a piece of electrical equipment to an electric socket
NOUN **2** a thick circular piece of rubber or plastic that you use to block the hole in a sink or bath

plug in

VERB If you **plug in** a piece of electrical equipment, you push its plug into an electric socket.

plum plums

NOUN a small fruit with a smooth red or yellow skin and a stone in the middle

plumage

NOUN a bird's feathers

plumber plumbers

NOUN a person who connects and repairs water pipes

plump plumper, plumpest

ADJECTIVE rounded, or slightly fat

plunge plunges, plunging, plunged

VERB If you **plunge** somewhere, especially into water, you fall or rush there.

SYNONYMS: dive, drop, fall

plural plurals

NOUN the form of a word that is used when referring to more than one person or thing • *The usual **plural** of person is people.*

ANTONYM: singular

plus

PREPOSITION **1** You use **plus** to show that one number is being added to another. • *Two **plus** two equals four.*
PREPOSITION **2** You can use **plus** when you mention an additional item. • *She gave us our coats, **plus** a blanket.*

plywood

NOUN wooden board made from several thin sheets of wood glued together under pressure

p.m.

used to show times between 12 noon and 12 midnight • *I go to bed at 8 **p.m.** on schooldays and 9 **p.m.** at weekends.*

WORD HISTORY
from Latin *post meridiem* meaning after noon

PM PMs

NOUN **1** an abbreviation for *prime minister*
NOUN **2** an abbreviation for *private message*

pneumatic

ADJECTIVE operated by or filled with compressed air • *a **pneumatic** drill*

pneumonia

NOUN a serious disease that affects a person's lungs and makes breathing difficult

poach poaches, poaching, poached
VERB **1** If someone **poaches** animals, they hunt them illegally on someone else's land.
VERB **2** When you **poach** food, especially fish, or an egg taken out of its shell, you cook it gently in hot liquid.

poacher poachers
NOUN someone who illegally hunts animals on someone else's land

pocket pockets
NOUN a small pouch for keeping things in, that forms part of a piece of clothing

pocket money
NOUN an amount of money given regularly to children by their parents

pod pods
NOUN a long, narrow seed container that grows on plants such as peas or beans

podcast podcasts
NOUN a file similar to a radio broadcast that can be downloaded for listening to on a computer or MP3 player

poem poems
NOUN a piece of writing, usually arranged in short rhythmic lines, with words chosen for their sound or impact

poet poets
NOUN a person who writes poems

poetry
NOUN poems, considered a form of literature

point points, pointing, pointed
VERB **1** If you **point** at or to something, you hold out your finger towards it to show where it is.
NOUN **2** the thin, sharp end of something such as a needle or knife
NOUN **3** a particular place or time • *At some point during the night, the storm began.*
NOUN **4** a single mark in a competition • *They won by 21 points to 18.*
NOUN **5** the purpose or the most important part of something • *What do you think is the point of this exercise?*
NOUN **6** an opinion or fact expressed by someone • *That's a very good point.*
NOUN **7** In mathematics, the decimal **point** in a number is marked by a dot, as in 5.2.
NOUN **8** one of the 32 marks on the circumference of a compass to show direction

pointed
ADJECTIVE A **pointed** object has a thin, sharp end.

pointless
ADJECTIVE Something that is **pointless** has no purpose.

point of view points of view
NOUN Your **point of view** is your opinion about something or your attitude towards it.

poised
ADJECTIVE If you are **poised** to do something, you are ready to do it at any moment.

poison poisons, poisoning, poisoned
NOUN **1** a substance that harms or kills you if you swallow it or absorb it
VERB **2** To **poison** someone means to harm them by giving them poison.

poke pokes, poking, poked
VERB If you **poke** someone or something, you give them a push with your finger or a sharp object.
poke out
VERB If something **pokes out** from behind or from underneath another thing, it shows. • *The label poked out from the back of his anorak.*

polar
ADJECTIVE relating to the area around the North Pole or the South Pole • *the polar regions*

polar bear polar bears
NOUN a large white bear that lives in the area around the North Pole

pole poles
NOUN **1** a long, slender, rounded piece of wood or metal
NOUN **2** The Earth has two **poles** at the opposite ends of its imaginary axis, called the North Pole and the South Pole.

→ Have a look at the illustration for **equator**

NOUN **3** either of the opposite ends of a magnet or electric cell

pole vault
NOUN an athletics event in which contestants jump over a high bar using a long, flexible pole to lift themselves into the air

police
PLURAL NOUN the official organisation responsible for making sure that people obey the law

police officer police officers
NOUN a member of the police force

a
b
c
d
e
f
g
h
i
j
k
l
m
n
o
p
q
r
s
t
u
v
w
x
y
z

A
B
C
D
E
F
G
H
I
J
K
L
M
N
O
P
Q
R
S
T
U
V
W
X
Y
Z

policy policies

NOUN a set of plans and ideas, especially in politics or business • *What is their* **policy** *on education?*

polish polishes, polishing, polished

NOUN **1** a substance that you put on an object to clean it and make it shine

VERB **2** If you **polish** something, you put polish on it or rub it with a cloth to make it shine.

polite

ADJECTIVE Someone who is **polite** has good manners and is not rude to other people.

SYNONYM: courteous

political

ADJECTIVE to do with politics and politicians

politician politicians

NOUN a person who is involved in the government of a country

politics

NOUN the activity of governing a country

poll polls

NOUN a survey in which people are asked their opinions about something

pollen

NOUN a fine yellow or orange powder produced by the male part of a flowering plant

→ Have a look at the illustration for **flower**

pollinate pollinates, pollinating, pollinated

VERB A plant is **pollinated** when pollen from the male part of another plant lands on its female part. This leads to fertilisation and the formation of seeds.

pollination

NOUN the process by which plants are fertilised with pollen

pollute pollutes, polluting, polluted

VERB If water, air or land is **polluted**, it is dirty and dangerous to use or live in.

pollution

NOUN dirty or dangerous substances that pollute the water, air or land • *Recycling helps to control environmental* **pollution**.

polo

NOUN a game played between two teams of players on horseback. The players use wooden hammers with long handles to hit a ball.

poltergeist poltergeists

NOUN a noisy, mischievous ghost that moves or throws things around in a house

poly-

PREFIX added to some words to mean many, for example **poly**gons and **poly**hedrons are many-sided shapes

polyester

NOUN a man-made fibre, especially used to make clothes

polygon polygons

NOUN any two-dimensional shape whose sides are all straight

polyhedron polyhedra

NOUN a solid shape with many faces

polystyrene

NOUN a very light plastic, especially used as insulating material or to make containers

polythene

NOUN a type of plastic that is used to make thin sheets or bags

pomposity

NOUN the quality someone has when they think they are important and they show this by behaving in a way that is too serious and formal

pompous

ADJECTIVE Someone who is **pompous** thinks they are very important and behaves in a way that is too serious and formal.

pond ponds

NOUN a small area of water enclosed by land

ponder ponders, pondering, pondered

VERB If you **ponder**, you think carefully and seriously about something.

pony ponies

NOUN a small horse

ponytail ponytails

NOUN a hairstyle in which long hair is scooped up and tied at the back of the head so that it hangs down like a tail

pool pools

NOUN **1** a small area of still water, such as a pond or a puddle

NOUN **2** an abbreviation of *swimming pool*

poor poorer, poorest
ADJECTIVE **1** having very little money
ADJECTIVE **2** of a low quality or standard

poorly
ADJECTIVE **1** If you are **poorly**, you feel ill.
ADVERB **2** If something is done **poorly**, it is not done well.

pop pops, popping, popped
NOUN **1** modern music, played and enjoyed especially by young people
NOUN **2** a short, sharp, explosive sound
NOUN **3** a fizzy, non-alcoholic drink
VERB **4** If you **pop** somewhere, you go there quickly for a short while. • *I will* **pop** *in to see you before tea.*

popcorn
NOUN a snack food made from grains of maize that are heated until they puff up and burst

Pope Popes
NOUN the head of the Roman Catholic Church

poplar poplars
NOUN a type of tall, narrow tree

poppadom poppadoms
NOUN thin, round, crisp bread, fried or roasted and served with Indian food

WORD HISTORY
from Tamil *pappadam* meaning lentil cake

poppy poppies
NOUN a plant with a large red flower on a hairy stem, that often grows in cornfields and meadows

popular
ADJECTIVE liked or approved of by a lot of people

populated
ADJECTIVE If a place is **populated**, people or animals live there.

population populations
NOUN **1** the people who live in a place
NOUN **2** the number of people living in a place

porch porches
NOUN a covered area at the entrance to a building

porcupine porcupines
NOUN a large rodent with long spines covering its body

WORD HISTORY
from Old French *porc d'espins* meaning pig with spines

pore pores, poring, pored
NOUN **1** The **pores** in your skin or on the surface of a plant are very small holes that allow moisture to pass through.
VERB **2** If you **pore** over a piece of writing or a diagram, you study it carefully.

pork
NOUN meat from a pig

porous
ADJECTIVE If something is **porous**, it lets water through.

porpoise porpoises
NOUN a sea mammal related to the dolphin

WORD HISTORY
from Latin *porcus* meaning pig and *piscis* meaning fish

porridge
NOUN a thick, sticky food made from oats cooked in water or milk

port ports
NOUN **1** a town or area that has a harbour or docks
NOUN **2** a place on a computer where you can attach another piece of equipment
→ Have a look at the illustration for **computer**
ADJECTIVE **3** The **port** side of a ship is the left side when you are facing the front.

portable
ADJECTIVE designed to be easily carried
• *a* **portable** *tripod*

portcullis portcullises
NOUN a strong gate above an entrance to a castle, that could be lowered to keep out enemies
→ Have a look at the illustration for **castle**

porter porters
NOUN **1** a person employed to carry luggage and other goods at a railway station or in a hotel
NOUN **2** a person employed to move patients from place to place in a hospital

a b c d e f g h i j k l m n o p q r s t u v w x y z

307

porthole portholes
NOUN a small window in the side of a ship or aircraft
→ Have a look at the illustration for **ship**

portion portions
NOUN **1** a part of something
SYNONYMS: bit, piece
NOUN **2** an amount of food sufficient for one person

portrait portraits
NOUN a picture or photograph of someone, often of only their head and shoulders

pose poses, posing, posed
NOUN **1** a way of standing, sitting or lying for a photograph to be taken, or a drawing or painting to be made of you • *Try to hold this* **pose** *while the others draw it.*
VERB **2** If you **pose** for a photograph or painting, you stay in a particular position so that someone can photograph or paint you.
VERB **3** If you **pose** as someone or something, you pretend to be someone or something you are not.
VERB **4** If something **poses** a problem or danger, it causes it. • *This polluted water could* **pose** *a threat to their health.*

position positions, positioning, positioned
NOUN **1** When someone or something is in a particular **position**, they are sitting or lying in that way. • *I raised myself to a sitting* **position**.
NOUN **2** The **position** that you are in is the situation that you are in. • *Your request puts me in a difficult* **position**.
PHRASE **3** If you are **in position** at the beginning of a race, you are ready to start.
VERB **4** If you **position** something, you put it in place.

positive
ADJECTIVE **1** If something is **positive**, it is certain.
ADJECTIVE **2** If someone is **positive**, they are confident and hopeful.
ADJECTIVE **3** A **positive** number is greater than zero.
ANTONYM: negative

possess possesses, possessing, possessed
VERB If you **possess** something, you own it.

possession possessions
NOUN a thing that you own, or that you have with you

possessive
ADJECTIVE **1** A **possessive** person wants to keep things for themselves.
NOUN **2** In grammar, the **possessive** is the form of a noun or pronoun used to show possession, for example, *my, his, theirs, Harry's*.

possibility possibilities
NOUN something that might happen

possible
ADJECTIVE If something is **possible**, it can be done or can happen.

possibly
ADVERB used to say that something may be true or may happen but you are not certain

possum possums
NOUN a nocturnal marsupial with thick fur and a long tail that lives in trees

post posts, posting, posted
NOUN **1** the system by which letters and parcels are collected and delivered
NOUN **2** letters and parcels that are delivered to you
NOUN **3** a piece of information, message or picture that you put on a website for other people to see
NOUN **4** an upright pole fixed into the ground
VERB **5** If you **post** a letter, you send it to someone through the post.
VERB **6** If you **post** a piece of information, message or picture on a website, you put it there so that other people can see it. • *She* **posted** *the cat picture on Facebook to get more likes.*

postage
NOUN the money that you pay to send letters and parcels by post • *You will need to send extra money for* **postage** *and packing.*

post box post boxes
NOUN a box into which you put letters that are to be sent by post

postcard postcards
NOUN a card, often with a picture on one side, that you write on and send to someone without an envelope

postcode postcodes
NOUN a short sequence of letters and numbers at the end of an address

poster posters
NOUN a large notice, picture or advertisement that you stick on a wall

postman postmen
NOUN a man who collects and delivers parcels and letters

post office post offices
NOUN a building where you can buy stamps and post letters and parcels

postpone postpones, postponing, postponed
VERB If you **postpone** an event, you arrange for it to take place at a later time than was originally planned.

postwoman postwomen
NOUN a woman who collects and delivers parcels and letters

potato potatoes
NOUN a round, white root vegetable that has a brown or red skin and grows beneath the ground

potential
ADJECTIVE 1 capable of happening or of becoming a particular kind of person or thing • He's a **potential** world champion.
NOUN 2 If someone or something has **potential**, they are capable of being successful or useful in the future.

pothole potholes
NOUN 1 a hole in the surface of a road caused by bad weather or traffic
NOUN 2 a deep, natural hole in the ground that often leads to an underground cavern

potion potions
NOUN a drink containing medicine, poison or supposed magical powers

WORD HISTORY
from Latin *potio* meaning a drink

potter potters, pottering, pottered
NOUN 1 a person who makes pottery
VERB 2 If you **potter** about, you pass the time doing pleasant, unimportant things.

pottery
NOUN 1 pots, dishes and other items made from clay and fired in a kiln
NOUN 2 the craft of making pottery

pouch pouches
NOUN 1 a small, soft container with a fold-over top, like a bag or a pocket
NOUN 2 a pocket of skin in which marsupials carry their young

poultry
NOUN chicken, turkeys and other birds that are kept for their meat or eggs

pounce pounces, pouncing, pounced
VERB If a person or other animal **pounces** on something, they jump on it suddenly.

pound pounds, pounding, pounded
NOUN 1 the main unit of currency in Britain
NOUN 2 a unit of weight equal to 16 ounces, or about 0.454 kilograms
VERB 3 If you **pound** something, or **pound** on it, you hit it repeatedly or crush it.
VERB 4 If your heart **pounds**, it beats very fast and strongly.
VERB 5 If you **pound** somewhere, you run there with loud, heavy footsteps.

pour pours, pouring, poured
VERB 1 If you **pour** liquid out of a container, you tip the container until the liquid flows out.
VERB 2 If something **pours** somewhere, it flows there quickly and in large quantities.
VERB 3 If it is **pouring** with rain, it is raining very heavily.

pout pouts, pouting, pouted
VERB If you **pout**, you stick out your lips, or your bottom lip, because you are cross or annoyed.

poverty
NOUN the state of being very poor

powder powders
NOUN many tiny particles of a solid, dry substance, such as flour

power powers
NOUN 1 control over people and events
NOUN 2 physical strength
NOUN 3 the rate at which energy is changed from one form to another, such as electrical energy changed into light or heat

powerful
ADJECTIVE **Powerful** people or organisations have a great deal of power or influence.

powerless
ADJECTIVE If you are **powerless**, you are unable to control or influence events.

power station power stations
NOUN a building where electricity is produced

a
b
c
d
e
f
g
h
i
j
k
l
m
n
o
p
q
r
s
t
u
v
w
x
y
z

309

practical

ADJECTIVE **1** Someone who is **practical** is efficient and sensible, and good at getting things done.

ADJECTIVE **2** Something that is **practical** is sensible and useful.

ADJECTIVE **3** involving real situations and doing things, rather than ideas or theories ● *We will do some **practical** experiments in Science today.*

WORD HISTORY
from Greek *praktikos* meaning concerned with action

practical joke practical jokes

NOUN a trick you play on someone

practice practices

NOUN **1** regular training or exercise that you do to improve your skill at something

NOUN **2** A doctor's or lawyer's **practice** is their business.

LANGUAGE TIP
The noun *practice* ends in *ce*.

practise practises, practising, practised

VERB **1** If you **practise** something, you do it regularly in order to do it better. ● *She **practises** every day on the piano.*

VERB **2** When people **practise** a religion, custom or craft, they regularly take part in the activities associated with it. ● *a custom still **practised** in some areas*

VERB **3** If you **practise** medicine or law, you work as a doctor or lawyer.

LANGUAGE TIP
The verb *practise* ends in *se*.

prairie prairies

NOUN a large area of flat, grassy land in North America

praise praises, praising, praised

VERB **1** If you **praise** someone or something, you say good things about them, or tell them they have done well.

NOUN **2** what you say or write when you praise someone or something

pram prams

NOUN a small carriage, like a baby's cot on wheels, for pushing a baby around in

prank pranks

NOUN a childish trick

prawn prawns

NOUN a small, edible shellfish with a long tail

pray prays, praying, prayed

VERB When someone **prays**, they speak to God, to give thanks or to ask for help.

prayer prayers

NOUN the activity of praying or the words said when someone prays

pre-

PREFIX added to some words to mean before a particular time or event, for example **pre**school, **pre**war, **pre**history

preach preaches, preaching, preached

VERB When someone **preaches**, they give a short talk on a religious or moral subject.

preacher preachers

NOUN someone who gives a talk about a religious subject in a church or other religious place

precarious

ADJECTIVE **1** Someone or something in a **precarious** position is not very safe or secure, and they may fall or fail at any time. ● *Her position was **precarious** because she needed only one point to win.*

ADJECTIVE **2** Something that is **precarious** is likely to fall because it is not well balanced or secured.

precaution precautions

NOUN an action that is intended to prevent something unwanted or unpleasant from happening

precede precedes, preceding, preceded

VERB **1** If one event **precedes** another, it happens before it. ● *A short film **preceded** the talk about elephants.*

VERB **2** If you **precede** someone, you go in front of them.

precinct precincts

NOUN a pedestrian shopping area

precious

ADJECTIVE Something that is **precious** is valuable or important and should be looked after or used carefully.

WORD HISTORY
from Latin *pretiosus* meaning valuable

precipice precipices

NOUN a very steep rock face or cliff

precipitation
NOUN rain, snow, sleet or hail
➔ Have a look at the illustration for **water cycle**

precise
ADJECTIVE very accurate • *We will never know the **precise** details of what happened.*

SYNONYM: exact

predator **predators**
NOUN an animal that kills and eats other animals

predatory
ADJECTIVE A **predatory** animal kills and eats other animals.

predecessor **predecessors**
NOUN Someone's **predecessor** is the person who used to do their job before them.

predicament **predicaments**
NOUN a difficult or awkward situation

predict **predicts, predicting, predicted**
VERB If you **predict** something, you say what you think will happen in the future.

preen **preens, preening, preened**
VERB When a bird **preens**, it cleans and tidies its feathers using its beak.

preface **prefaces**
NOUN an introduction at the beginning of a book, explaining what it is about or why it was written

prefect **prefects**
NOUN a pupil who has special duties at a school

WORD HISTORY
from Latin *praefectus* meaning someone put in charge

prefer **prefers, preferring, preferred**
VERB If you **prefer** one thing to another, you like it better than the other thing.

preferable
ADJECTIVE Something that is **preferable** to something else, is more suitable or you like it better than the other thing. • *We thought that going to the cinema was **preferable** to watching TV.*

prefix **prefixes**
NOUN a letter or group of letters added to the beginning of a word to make a new word, for example *dis-*, *pre-* and *un-*

pregnant
ADJECTIVE A woman or other female animal who is **pregnant** has a baby developing in their womb.

prehistoric
ADJECTIVE existing at a time in the past before anything was written down

prejudice **prejudices**
NOUN an unreasonable and unfair dislike of or preference for a particular person or thing

prejudiced
ADJECTIVE having an unreasonable and unfair dislike of someone or something

preliminary
ADJECTIVE **Preliminary** activities take place before something starts and in preparation for it. • *They lost in the **preliminary** rounds of the competition.*

prelude **preludes**
NOUN **1** something that happens before an event and prepares you for it
NOUN **2** a short piece of music

premature
ADJECTIVE happening too early, or earlier than expected • *The **premature** baby had to spend time in hospital to gain weight.*

premier **premiers**
NOUN **1** The leader of a government is sometimes referred to as the **premier**.
NOUN **2** In Australia, the leader of a State government is called the **Premier**.
ADJECTIVE **3** considered to be the best or most important • *the **premier** department store*

PRONUNCIATION TIP
This word is pronounced **prem**-mee-uh.

WORD HISTORY
from Latin *primarius* meaning principal

premiere **premieres**
NOUN the first public performance of a new play or film • *The **premiere** of the new film is in London next week.*

PRONUNCIATION TIP
This word is pronounced **prem**-mee-er.

WORD HISTORY
from French *premier* meaning first

311

premises
PLURAL NOUN buildings and land belonging to an organisation

premium premiums
NOUN 1 an extra sum of money that has to be paid for something
NOUN 2 money paid regularly to an insurance company

premonition premonitions
NOUN a feeling that something unpleasant is going to happen

preoccupied
ADJECTIVE If you are **preoccupied**, you are deep in thought or totally involved with something, and you do not notice anything else. ● *It is difficult to talk to him as he seems so **preoccupied**.*

preparation preparations
NOUN 1 **Preparation** is the act of getting things ready.
NOUN 2 **Preparations** are all the things you do and the arrangements you make before an event can happen. ● *We started making **preparations** for the party by buying some decorations.*

prepare prepares, preparing, prepared
VERB If you **prepare** something, or **prepare** for something, you get it ready or get ready for it.

preposition prepositions
NOUN a word that is used before a noun or pronoun to show how it is connected to other words. For example, in the sentence *I put the book on the table*, the word *on* is the **preposition**.

prescribe prescribes, prescribing, prescribed
VERB If a doctor **prescribes** a medicine for a patient, he or she tells the patient what medicine they need and gives them a prescription.

prescription prescriptions
NOUN a written instruction from a doctor to a chemist, to provide a person with a particular medicine

presence
NOUN the **presence** of a person in a place is the fact that they are there

present presents, presenting, presented
ADJECTIVE 1 If someone is **present** at a place or an event, they are there.
ADJECTIVE 2 happening now

SYNONYMS: contemporary, current

ANTONYM: absent

NOUN 3 the period of time that is taking place now
NOUN 4 something that you give to someone for them to keep, especially on their birthday or at Christmas, or on some other special occasion

SYNONYM: gift

VERB 5 If you **present** someone with something, or if you **present** it to them, you formally give it to them.

PRONUNCIATION TIP
Meanings 1, 2, 3 and 4 are pronounced **prez**-ent. Meaning 5 is pronounced pri-**zent**.

presentation presentations
NOUN 1 a talk or a lecture showing or describing something
NOUN 2 a ceremony where awards or prizes are given
NOUN 3 The **presentation** of something is the way it looks. ● *My teacher was pleased with the **presentation** of my project.*

presently
ADVERB If something will happen **presently**, it will happen soon. ● *I'll finish the job **presently**.*

preservative preservatives
NOUN a substance or a chemical that stops things such as food from going bad

preserve preserves, preserving, preserved
VERB If you **preserve** something, you make sure that it stays as it is and does not change or end.

president presidents
NOUN The **president** of a country that has no king or queen is the leader of the country. ● *the **President** of the United States*

press presses, pressing, pressed
VERB 1 If you **press** something, you push it or hold it firmly against something else.
VERB 2 If you **press** clothes, you iron them.
VERB 3 If you **press** someone to do something, you try to make them do it.
NOUN 4 a machine for printing
NOUN 5 The **press** is a term used for all the newspapers and the journalists who work for them.

pressure pressures
NOUN **1** the amount of force that is pushing on a particular area
NOUN **2** If there is **pressure** on you to do something, someone is trying to persuade or force you to do it.
NOUN **3** If someone does something because of peer **pressure**, they do it because other people in their social group do it.

presume presumes, presuming, presumed
VERB If you **presume** something, you think that it is probably true without knowing for certain.

SYNONYMS: believe, suppose

presumption presumptions
NOUN something that you think is probably true without knowing for certain

pretend pretends, pretending, pretended
VERB If you **pretend** that something is the case, you try to make people believe that it is true when it is not.

pretty prettier, prettiest
ADJECTIVE **1** attractive and pleasant
ADVERB **2** (*informal*) quite or rather ● He spoke **pretty** good English.

prevent prevents, preventing, prevented
VERB If you **prevent** something, you stop it happening.

preview previews
NOUN **1** a showing of something like a film, play or exhibition before it is shown to the general public
NOUN **2** a version of a computer document or page that is shown before it is produced in its final form

previous
ADJECTIVE A **previous** time or thing is one that occurred before the present one.
● I'm happier in this class than I was in the **previous** one.

previously
ADVERB before now

prey preys, preying, preyed
NOUN **1** an animal that is hunted and eaten by another animal
VERB **2** An animal that **preys** on another animal lives by hunting and eating it.

price prices
NOUN the amount of money that you pay to buy something ● The **price** of bread has increased significantly.

priceless
ADJECTIVE Something that is **priceless** is so valuable that it is difficult to work out how much it is worth.

prick pricks, pricking, pricked
VERB If you **prick** something, you stick a sharp object into it.

prickle prickles, prickling, prickled
NOUN **1** a small sharp point or thorn growing on a plant
VERB **2** If your skin **prickles**, it feels as if a lot of sharp points are being stuck into it.

prickly pricklier, prickliest
ADJECTIVE **1** A **prickly** plant has small sharp points or thorns on it.
ADJECTIVE **2** If your skin feels **prickly**, it feels as if a lot of sharp points are being stuck into it.

pride prides
NOUN **1** a feeling of satisfaction and pleasure you have when you, or people close to you, have done something well
NOUN **2** a feeling of dignity and self-respect
NOUN **3** a group of lions that live together

priest priests
NOUN **1** a member of the clergy in some Christian Churches
NOUN **2** someone who performs religious ceremonies in non-Christian religions

prim primmer, primmest
ADJECTIVE Someone who is **prim** always behaves very correctly and is easily shocked by anything rude.

primary
ADJECTIVE extremely important or most important

primary colour primary colours
NOUN The **primary colours** are red, yellow and blue. From these all the other colours can be made.

primary school primary schools
NOUN a school for children between the ages of 5 and 11

a
b
c
d
e
f
g
h
i
j
k
l
m
n
o
p
q
r
s
t
u
v
w
x
y
z

313

A
B
C
D
E
F
G
H
I
J
K
L
M
N
O
P
Q
R
S
T
U
V
W
X
Y
Z

prime

ADJECTIVE **1** main or most important
ADJECTIVE **2** of the best quality
ADJECTIVE **3** A **prime** number is a whole number which can only be divided by itself and 1 without leaving a remainder.

WORD HISTORY
from Latin *primus* meaning first

prime minister **prime ministers**

NOUN the leader of the government

primitive

ADJECTIVE **1** connected with a society in which people live very simply
ADJECTIVE **2** very simple, basic or old-fashioned • *Their accommodation was **primitive**, but they still enjoyed their trip.*

primrose **primroses**

NOUN a small plant that has pale yellow flowers in spring

WORD HISTORY
from Latin *prima rosa* meaning first rose

prince **princes**

NOUN a male member of a royal family, especially the son of a king or queen

princess **princesses**

NOUN a female member of a royal family, especially the daughter of a king or queen, or the wife of a prince

principal **principals**

ADJECTIVE **1** main or most important • *He had the **principal** role in the play.*
NOUN **2** the person in charge of a school or college

LANGUAGE TIP
Do not confuse *principal* with *principle*.

principle **principles**

NOUN **1** a general rule or law about how something works
NOUN **2** a belief that you have about the way you should behave • *I try to help others as a matter of **principle**.*

LANGUAGE TIP
Do not confuse *principle* with *principal*.

print **prints, printing, printed**

VERB **1** When words or pictures are **printed**, they are put onto paper in large numbers by a printing machine, for example to make books or newspapers.
VERB **2** If you **print** your name, or some other writing, you write letters that are not joined up.
NOUN **3** The letters and numbers on the pages of a book or newspaper are referred to as the **print**. • *The columns of tiny **print** were difficult to read.*

printer **printers**

NOUN **1** a person who prints books and newspapers
NOUN **2** a machine that prints the data from a computer onto paper

print-out **print-outs**

NOUN a printed copy of information from a computer

priority **priorities**

NOUN something that needs to be dealt with first because it is more urgent or important than other things • *He needed to make his homework a **priority**.*

prism **prisms**

NOUN **1** In mathematics, a **prism** is any three-dimensional shape that has the same size and shape of face at each end. A **prism** is the same size and shape along its length.
NOUN **2** a solid piece of clear glass or plastic with flat sides, that can be used to separate light passing through it into the colours of the rainbow

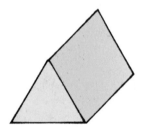

prison **prisons**

NOUN a building where people who have broken the law are locked up as a punishment

prisoner **prisoners**

NOUN someone who is kept in prison or held in captivity

privacy

NOUN If you have **privacy**, you have somewhere private where you can be alone without being disturbed.

private privates

ADJECTIVE **1** for the use of only one person or group of people, rather than for the general public • The hotel had a **private** beach.

ADJECTIVE **2** meant to be kept secret

NOUN **3** a soldier of the lowest rank

private message private messages

NOUN a message sent to someone privately on a social media website

privilege privileges

NOUN a special right or advantage that is given to a person or group

prize prizes

NOUN a reward given to the winner of a competition or game

pro-

PREFIX supporting or being in favour of • a **pro**-animal rights march

ANTONYM: anti-

probability

NOUN the measure of how likely an event is

probable

ADJECTIVE likely to happen or likely to be true

probably

ADVERB likely but not certainly • I am **probably** having a party for my birthday.

probation

NOUN **1** a period of time during which a person convicted of a crime is supervised by a social worker called a **probation** officer, instead of being sent to prison

NOUN **2** a period of time when someone is tried out to see if they are suitable for a particular job

probe probes, probing, probed

VERB **1** If you **probe**, you investigate something, often by asking a lot of questions to discover the facts about it.

VERB **2** If you **probe** something, you gently push a long, thin instrument into it, usually to find something.

NOUN **3** a long, thin instrument used to look closely at something

WORD HISTORY

from Latin probare meaning to test

problem problems

NOUN **1** an unsatisfactory situation that causes difficulties

SYNONYMS: difficulty, predicament

NOUN **2** a puzzle or question that you solve using logical thought or mathematics

procedure procedures

NOUN a way of doing something, especially the correct or usual way • The entire **procedure** takes about 15 minutes.

proceed proceeds, proceeding, proceeded

VERB **1** If you **proceed** to do something, you do it after doing something else. • He then **proceeded** to tell us the story.

VERB **2** If you **proceed**, you move in a particular direction. • We **proceeded** along the corridor.

PLURAL NOUN **3** The **proceeds** of an event are the money that is obtained from it. • The **proceeds** from the concert will go towards famine relief.

PRONUNCIATION TIP

Meanings 1 and 2 are pronounced pro-**seed**. Meaning 3 is pronounced **pro**-seedz.

WORD HISTORY

from Latin pro + cedere meaning to go onward

process processes, processing, processed

NOUN **1** a series of actions or events that have a particular result

PHRASE **2** If you are **in the process** of doing something, you have started doing it but have not yet finished.

VERB **3** You **process** something when you put it through a series of actions in order to have a particular result. For example, you **process** milk to pasteurise it.

procession processions

NOUN a group of people or vehicles moving together in a line, often as part of a ceremony • There was a **procession** of musicians along the high street on Sunday.

proclaim proclaims, proclaiming, proclaimed

VERB If someone **proclaims** something, they announce it or make it known publicly.

proclamation proclamations

NOUN an important announcement that someone makes publicly

a
b
c
d
e
f
g
h
i
j
k
l
m
n
o
p
q
r
s
t
u
v
w
x
y
z

315

A
B
C
D
E
F
G
H
I
J
K
L
M
N
O
P
Q
R
S
T
U
V
W
X
Y
Z

prod prods, prodding, prodded
VERB If you **prod** something or somebody, you give them a poke with your finger.

produce produces, producing, produced
VERB 1 If someone or something **produces** something, they make it or cause it to happen.
VERB 2 If you **produce** something from somewhere, you bring it out so that it can be seen. • The magician **produced** a rabbit out of the hat.
VERB 3 If you **produce** a film, play or other form of entertainment, you are in charge of organising it.
NOUN 4 food that is grown to be sold

PRONUNCIATION TIP
The verb is pronounced pro-**dewss**. The noun is pronounced **prod**-yooss.

producer producers
NOUN The **producer** of a record, film, play or programme is the person in charge of making it or putting it on. • a television **producer**

product products
NOUN 1 something that is made or produced to be sold
NOUN 2 The **product** is the answer to a multiplication sum. • The **product** of 4 and 6 is 24.

production productions
NOUN 1 the process of manufacturing or growing something in large quantities
NOUN 2 a version of something such as a play or a film

profession professions
NOUN a job for which you need special training and education • the medical **profession** • the teaching **profession**

professional professionals
ADJECTIVE 1 **Professional** is used to describe activities that are done to earn money rather than as a hobby. • He earns a lot of money as a **professional** footballer.
ADJECTIVE 2 You can use **professional** to describe work that is of a very high standard.
NOUN 3 someone who does a particular type of work to earn money

professor professors
NOUN the most senior teacher in a department of a British university, or a teacher at an American college or university

proficient
ADJECTIVE If you are **proficient** at something, you can do it well. • I am pleased to see how **proficient** you are in reading.

profile profiles
NOUN 1 the outline of a face seen from the side
NOUN 2 Your **profile** on a social media website is where you post your name, picture and other personal information.

WORD HISTORY
from Italian profilare meaning to sketch lightly

profit profits, profiting, profited
NOUN 1 an amount of money that you gain when you are paid more for something than it cost to buy or make
VERB 2 If you **profit** from something, you gain or benefit from it. • I think you will **profit** from some extra lessons.

profound
ADJECTIVE 1 very deep or intense • discoveries that have a **profound** effect on life today
ADJECTIVE 2 showing or needing deep thought or understanding • He asked a **profound** question for someone of his age.

program programs, programming, programmed
NOUN 1 a set of instructions that a computer follows in order to perform particular tasks
VERB 2 When someone **programs** a computer, they prepare a program and put it into the computer.

programme programmes
NOUN 1 something that is broadcast on television or radio
NOUN 2 a planned series of events
NOUN 3 a booklet giving information about a play, concert or show

progress progresses, progressing, progressed
NOUN 1 the process of gradually improving or getting near to achieving something
VERB 2 If you **progress**, you become more advanced or skilful at something.
VERB 3 to continue or move forward • As the trip **progressed**, I began to feel sick.

PRONUNCIATION TIP
The noun is pronounced **proh**-gress. The verb is pronounced pro-**gress**.

prohibit prohibits, prohibiting, prohibited

VERB If someone **prohibits** something, they forbid it or make it illegal. • *Visitors are* **prohibited** *from smoking.*

project projects, projecting, projected

NOUN **1** a carefully planned task that requires a lot of time or effort

VERB **2** If you **project** an image onto a screen, you make it appear there using a projector.

VERB **3** If something **projects**, it sticks out.

PRONUNCIATION TIP

The noun is pronounced **proj**-ekt. The verb is pronounced pro-**jekt**.

projector projectors

NOUN a piece of equipment that produces a large image on a screen by shining light through a photographic slide or film strip

prologue prologues

NOUN a short piece of writing at the beginning of a book, or a speech that introduces a play

prolong prolongs, prolonging, prolonged

VERB If you **prolong** something, you make it last longer. • *We* **prolonged** *the holiday.*

promenade promenades

NOUN a path or road by the sea for walking along

PRONUNCIATION TIP

This word is pronounced prom-un-**ahd**.

prominent

ADJECTIVE **1** A **prominent** person is important or well known.

ADJECTIVE **2** very noticeable • *The church is a* **prominent** *landmark.*

WORD HISTORY

from Latin *prominere* meaning to stick out

promise promises, promising, promised

VERB **1** If you **promise** to do something, you say that you will definitely do it.

NOUN **2** a statement made by someone that they will definitely do something

NOUN **3** Someone or something that shows **promise** seems likely to be successful in the future.

promising

ADJECTIVE likely to be successful or good

promote promotes, promoting, promoted

VERB **1** If someone **promotes** something, they try to make it happen, or become more popular or successful.

VERB **2** If someone is **promoted**, they are given a more important job at work.

prompt prompts, prompting, prompted

VERB **1** If something or someone **prompts** you to do something, they encourage you or make you decide to do it.

VERB **2** If you **prompt** an actor, you remind them of their lines in a play if they forget them.

ADJECTIVE **3** A **prompt** action is done immediately, without any delay.

prone

ADJECTIVE **1** If you are **prone** to something, you have a tendency to be affected by it or to do it. • *I am* **prone** *to catching colds in the winter.*

ADJECTIVE **2** If you are **prone**, you are lying flat and face downwards.

prong prongs

NOUN The **prongs** of a fork are the long pointed parts.

pronoun pronouns

NOUN a word that is used to replace a noun. **Pronouns** are used instead of naming a person or a thing. *He, she* and *them* are all examples of **pronouns**.

pronounce pronounces, pronouncing, pronounced

VERB **1** When you **pronounce** a word, you say it.

VERB **2** When someone **pronounces** something, they state or announce it formally.

pronunciation pronunciations

NOUN the way a word is usually said

proof

NOUN If you have **proof** of something, you have evidence which shows that it is true or exists.

SYNONYM: confirmation

prop props, propping, propped

VERB **1** If you **prop** an object somewhere, you lean it against something for support.

NOUN **2** an object, such as a piece of wood or metal, used to support something

NOUN **3** an object or piece of furniture used on stage in the theatre, or on a film set

a
b
c
d
e
f
g
h
i
j
k
l
m
n
o
p
q
r
s
t
u
v
w
x
y
z

317

A
B
C
D
E
F
G
H
I
J
K
L
M
N
O
P
Q
R
S
T
U
V
W
X
Y
Z

propaganda
NOUN information, sometimes untrue and often exaggerated, that is used by political groups to influence people

propel propels, propelling, propelled
VERB To **propel** something is to push it forward.

propeller propellers
NOUN a device on a boat or aircraft with rotating blades, that makes the boat or aircraft move

→ Have a look at the illustration for **aeroplane**

proper
ADJECTIVE **1** If you do something in the **proper** way, you do it correctly.
ADJECTIVE **2** In mathematics, a **proper fraction** is a fraction where the denominator is bigger than the numerator.

properly
ADVERB If something is done **properly**, it is done correctly and to the right standard.

proper noun proper nouns
NOUN A proper noun is the name of a person, place or institution, and usually starts with a capital letter. For example, *Mary*, *London* and the *Statue of Liberty* are all **proper nouns**.

property properties
NOUN **1** A person's **property** is something, or all the things, that belong to them.
NOUN **2** A **property** is a building and the land around it.
NOUN **3** a characteristic that something has
• *A **property** of mint is its strong smell.*

WORD HISTORY
from Latin *proprietas* meaning something personal

prophet prophets
NOUN a person who predicts what will happen in the future

proportion proportions
NOUN **1** part of an amount or group
NOUN **2** The **proportion** of one amount to another is its size in relation to the whole amount, usually expressed as a fraction or percentage. • *The **proportion** of boys in the school is 58%.*

propose proposes, proposing, proposed
VERB **1** If you **propose** a plan or idea, you suggest it.
VERB **2** If you **propose** to someone, you ask them to marry you.

proprietor proprietors
NOUN the owner of a shop or business

prose
NOUN ordinary written language, rather than poetry

prosecute prosecutes, prosecuting, prosecuted
VERB If someone is **prosecuted**, they are charged with a crime and put on trial.

prospect prospects, prospecting, prospected
NOUN **1** something that may happen in the future
NOUN **2** Your **prospects** are your chances of being successful in the future. • *If she works hard at school, her **prospects** are good.*
VERB **3** When people **prospect** for gold, oil or other minerals, they search for them.

prosper prospers, prospering, prospered
VERB When people or businesses **prosper**, they are successful and make money.

prosperity
NOUN **Prosperity** is when people or businesses are successful and make money.

prosperous
ADJECTIVE successful and rich

protect protects, protecting, protected
VERB If you **protect** someone or something, you prevent them from being harmed.

protein proteins
NOUN a substance that is found in meat, eggs and milk. It is needed by your body to make you grow and keep you healthy.

protest protests, protesting, protested
VERB **1** If you **protest**, you say or do something to show that you strongly disapprove of something.
NOUN **2** a demonstration or statement to show that you strongly disapprove of something

PRONUNCIATION TIP
The verb is pronounced pro-**test**. The noun is pronounced **pro**-test.

Protestant Protestants
NOUN someone who belongs to the branch of the Christian Church that separated from the Catholic Church in the sixteenth century

proton protons
NOUN a particle with a positive electrical charge
→ Have a look at the illustration for **atom**

prototype prototypes
NOUN a new type of machine or device which is still to be made in large numbers and sold

protractor protractors
NOUN a flat, semicircular instrument used for measuring angles

protrude protrudes, protruding, protruded
VERB (formal) If something **protrudes** from a surface or edge, it sticks out. • The handle of his racket **protruded** from his sports bag.

protrusion protrusions
NOUN (formal) something that sticks out from something else

proud prouder, proudest
ADJECTIVE 1 If you are **proud** of something, you feel satisfaction and pleasure because of something you own or have achieved.
ADJECTIVE 2 Someone who is **proud** has a lot of dignity and self-respect.

prove proves, proving, proved or proven
VERB If you **prove** that something is true, you show by means of argument or evidence that it is definitely true.

SYNONYMS: confirm, verify

proverb proverbs
NOUN a short, well-known saying that gives advice or makes a comment about life. For example, A stitch in time saves nine.

proverbial
ADJECTIVE well-known because of being part of a saying • Looking for his tooth in the long grass was like looking for the **proverbial** needle in a haystack.

provide provides, providing, provided
VERB If you **provide** something for someone, you give it to them or make it available to them.

province provinces
NOUN one of the areas into which some large countries are divided • Each **province** has its own administration.

provision provisions
NOUN the act of supplying or making something available to people

provisional
ADJECTIVE A **provisional** arrangement is one that has been agreed on for the time being, but has not yet been made definite.

provisions
PLURAL NOUN supplies of food and drink

provocation
NOUN **Provocation** is when you deliberately try to make someone angry.

provoke provokes, provoking, provoked
VERB 1 If you **provoke** someone, you deliberately try to make them angry.
VERB 2 If something **provokes** a reaction or feeling, it causes it.

prow prows
NOUN the front part of a boat or ship

prowl prowls, prowling, prowled
VERB If a person or animal **prowls** around, they move around quietly and secretly, as if hunting.

proximity
NOUN (formal) nearness to someone or something • I lost my bag in the **proximity** of the swimming pool.

prune prunes, pruning, pruned
NOUN 1 a dried plum
VERB 2 When someone **prunes** a tree or shrub, they cut back some of the branches to make it grow well.

pry pries, prying, pried
VERB If someone **pries**, they try to find out about something secret or private.

PS
PS is written at the end of a letter to give an extra message. It is an abbreviation of postscript.

WORD HISTORY
from Latin postscribere meaning to write (scribere) after (post)

psalm psalms
NOUN one of the 150 songs, poems and prayers that form the Book of **Psalms** in the Bible

WORD HISTORY
from Greek psalmos meaning song accompanied on the harp

a
b
c
d
e
f
g
h
i
j
k
l
m
n
o
p
q
r
s
t
u
v
w
x
y
z

319

A
B
C
D
E
F
G
H
I
J
K
L
M
N
O
P
Q
R
S
T
U
V
W
X
Y
Z

pseudonym **pseudonyms**
NOUN a false name an author uses rather than using their real name

psychiatric
ADJECTIVE to do with the study and treatment of mental illness • a **psychiatric** hospital

psychiatrist
NOUN a doctor who treats mental illness

PRONUNCIATION TIP
This word is pronounced sy-**ky**-a-trist.

psychiatry
NOUN the branch of medicine concerned with mental illness

PRONUNCIATION TIP
This word is pronounced sy-**ky**-a-tree.

WORD HISTORY
from Greek *psukhe* meaning mind and *iatros* meaning healer

psychic
ADJECTIVE having unusual mental powers, such as the ability to read people's minds or predict the future

psychology
NOUN the scientific study of the mind and of the reasons for people's behaviour

PTO
an abbreviation of *please turn over*. **PTO** is written at the bottom of a page to show that there is more writing on the other side.

pub **pubs**
NOUN a place where people go to buy and drink alcoholic and other drinks, and to talk to their friends. **Pub** is an abbreviation of *public house*.

puberty
NOUN the stage when a person's body changes from that of a child into that of an adult

public
NOUN 1 You can refer to people in general as the **public**. • *The castle is open to the public on Sundays.*
ADJECTIVE 2 relating to people in general • **public** opinion
ADJECTIVE 3 provided for everyone to use • *We try to use public transport whenever possible.*

publication **publications**
NOUN 1 The **publication** of a book is the act of printing it and making it available.
NOUN 2 a book, newspaper or magazine

publicity
NOUN information or advertisements about an item or event to attract attention to it

public school **public schools**
NOUN 1 In England and Wales, a **public school** is a private secondary school that charges fees.
NOUN 2 In Scotland and America, a **public school** is a state school.

publish **publishes, publishing, published**
VERB 1 When a company **publishes** a book, newspaper or magazine, they print copies of it and distribute it.
VERB 2 When a newspaper or magazine **publishes** an article or photograph, they print it.

publisher **publishers**
NOUN a person or company that publishes books, newspapers or magazines

pudding **puddings**
NOUN 1 a cooked sweet food, often made with flour and eggs, and usually served hot
NOUN 2 You can refer to the sweet course of a meal as the **pudding**.

puddle **puddles**
NOUN a small shallow pool of rain water or other liquid

puff **puffs, puffing, puffed**
VERB 1 If you are **puffing**, you are breathing loudly and quickly with your mouth open.
VERB 2 If something **puffs out** or **puffs up**, it swells and becomes larger and rounder.
NOUN 3 a small blast of air, smoke or steam

pull **pulls, pulling, pulled**
VERB 1 If you **pull** something, you get hold of it and move it towards you with force.
VERB 2 If a vehicle or an animal **pulls** something, they move it along behind them.
VERB 3 When you **pull** the curtains, you move them across a window.
VERB 4 If you **pull** a muscle, you damage it temporarily by stretching it too much.
pull down
VERB If someone **pulls down** a building, they demolish it.
pull out
VERB If you **pull out** of an activity, you decide not to do it.

pulley pulleys
NOUN a piece of machinery with a wheel and chain or rope over it, used for lifting heavy things

pullover pullovers
NOUN a knitted piece of clothing, put on over your head, that covers the top part of your body

pulpit pulpits
NOUN the small raised platform in a church or cathedral where a member of the clergy stands to preach

pulse pulses
NOUN the regular beating of your heart as it pumps blood through your body. You can feel your **pulse** at your wrists and some other places on your body. Your **pulse** rate is a measure of how fast your heart is beating.

pump pumps, pumping, pumped
NOUN **1** a machine that is used to force a liquid or gas to move in a particular direction
VERB **2** If someone or something **pumps** a liquid or gas somewhere, they force it to flow in that direction, using a pump.

pumpkin pumpkins
NOUN a very large, round, orange vegetable

pun puns
NOUN a clever and amusing use of words so that what you say has two different meanings

punch punches, punching, punched
VERB **1** If you **punch** someone or something, you hit them hard with your fist.
NOUN **2** a hard hit with the fist

punchline punchlines
NOUN The **punchline** of a joke or a story is the last part, that makes it funny.

punctual
ADJECTIVE arriving at the correct time
SYNONYMS: on time, prompt

punctuality
NOUN arrival at the correct time

punctuation
NOUN the marks in writing that make it easier to understand, such as full stops, question marks and commas

puncture punctures
NOUN a small hole in a car or bicycle tyre, made by a sharp object

pungency
NOUN the quality something has when it has a strong, unpleasant smell or taste

pungent
ADJECTIVE having a strong, unpleasant smell or taste

punish punishes, punishing, punished
VERB To **punish** someone means to make them suffer for doing wrong.

punishment punishments
NOUN something unpleasant that is done to someone because they have done something wrong

puny punier, puniest
ADJECTIVE very small and weak

pupa pupae
NOUN an insect at the stage of development between a larva and a fully grown adult
SYNONYM: chrysalis

pupil pupils
NOUN **1** The **pupils** at a school are the children who attend it.
NOUN **2** Your **pupils** are the small, round, black holes in the centre of your eyes.
→ Have a look at the illustration for **eye**

puppet puppets
NOUN a doll that can be moved by pulling strings or by putting your hand inside its body

puppy puppies
NOUN a young dog

purchase purchases, purchasing, purchased
VERB **1** When you **purchase** something, you buy it.
NOUN **2** something that you have bought

pure purer, purest
ADJECTIVE **1** Something that is **pure** is not mixed with anything else.
ADJECTIVE **2** clean and free from harmful substances

purification
NOUN the process of removing dirty or harmful substances from something

purify purifies, purifying, purified
VERB If someone **purifies** something, they remove all dirty or harmful substances from it.

purple
NOUN **1** a reddish-blue colour
ADJECTIVE **2** having a reddish-blue colour

purpose purposes
NOUN **1** the reason for something
NOUN **2** the thing that you want to achieve
PHRASE **3** If you do something **on purpose**, you do it deliberately.

purr purrs, purring, purred
VERB When a cat **purrs**, it makes a low vibrating sound because it is contented.

purse purses
NOUN **1** a container, usually made of leather, plastic or fabric and like a very small bag, for carrying money and credit cards
NOUN **2** In American English, a **purse** is a handbag.

pursue pursues, pursuing, pursued
VERB **1** If you **pursue** someone, you follow them in order to catch them.
VERB **2** If you **pursue** an activity or plan, you try to achieve it.

pus
NOUN a thick yellowish liquid that forms in an infected wound or a boil

push pushes, pushing, pushed
VERB If you **push** someone or something, you use force to move them away from you.

pushchair pushchairs
NOUN a small folding chair on wheels in which a baby or a toddler can be pushed along

put puts, putting, put
VERB **1** If you **put** something somewhere, you move it into that position.
VERB **2** If you **put** an idea in a particular way, you express it.
put off
VERB If you **put off** doing something, you delay it.
put out
VERB If you **put out** the light, you switch it off.
put up
VERB If you **put up** with something, you let it happen without complaining.

putt putts
NOUN In golf, a **putt** is a gentle stroke made when the ball is near the hole.

putty
NOUN a paste used to fix panes of glass into window frames

puzzle puzzles, puzzling, puzzled
VERB **1** If something **puzzles** you, it confuses you and you do not understand it.
NOUN **2** a game or question that requires a lot of thought to complete or solve

PVC
NOUN a plastic material used for making various things, including clothing, drainpipes and tiles. **PVC** is an abbreviation of *polyvinyl chloride*.

pyjamas
PLURAL NOUN loose trousers and a loose jacket that you wear in bed

WORD HISTORY
from Persian *pay jama* meaning leg clothing

pylon pylons
NOUN a tall metal structure that carries overhead electricity cables

pyramid pyramids
NOUN **1** a three-dimensional shape with a flat base and flat triangular sides sloping upwards to a point
NOUN **2** an ancient stone structure in this shape, built over the tombs of Egyptian kings and queens

python pythons
NOUN a large snake that kills other animals by squeezing them with its body

WORD HISTORY
from Greek *Puthon,* a huge mythical serpent

Qq

quack quacks, quacking, quacked
VERB **1** When a duck **quacks**, it makes a loud harsh sound.
NOUN **2** A **quack** is the sound made by a duck.

quadrangle quadrangles
NOUN **1** a courtyard with buildings all round it
NOUN **2** In geometry, a **quadrangle** is a four-sided shape.

quadrant quadrants
NOUN a quarter of a circle

quadrilateral quadrilaterals
NOUN a plane shape with four straight sides

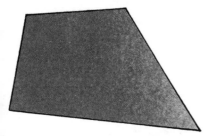

quadruple quadruples, quadrupling, quadrupled
VERB If you **quadruple** something, or if it **quadruples**, it becomes four times greater in number or size.

quadruplet quadruplets
NOUN one of four children born at the same time to the same mother

quail quails
NOUN a type of small game bird with a round body and a short tail

quaint quainter, quaintest
ADJECTIVE If something is **quaint**, it is attractive and charming in an old-fashioned or unusual way. ● *The quaint little village was filled with thatched cottages.*

quake quakes, quaking, quaked
VERB **1** If you **quake**, you tremble because you are very frightened.
VERB **2** If the ground **quakes**, it moves, usually because of an earthquake.
NOUN **3** an abbreviation of *earthquake*

Quaker Quakers
NOUN a member of a Christian group called the Society of Friends, that gathers together for peaceful thought and prayer

qualification qualifications
NOUN Your **qualifications** are your skills and achievements. You gain **qualifications** by passing tests and examinations.

qualify qualifies, qualifying, qualified
VERB If you **qualify**, you pass examinations and gain qualifications, often for a particular job. ● *After many years of study and training, she qualified as a doctor.*

quality qualities
NOUN **1** The **quality** of something is how good it is.
NOUN **2** You can describe a particular characteristic of a person or thing as a **quality**. ● *His paintings have a childlike quality.*

quantity quantities
NOUN an amount that you can measure or count

quarantine
NOUN a period of time that a person or animal has to spend apart from others to prevent the possible spread of disease

PRONUNCIATION TIP
This word is pronounced **kwo**-ran-teen.

WORD HISTORY
from Italian *quarantina* meaning forty days

quarrel quarrels, quarrelling, quarrelled
NOUN **1** an angry argument
VERB **2** If people **quarrel**, they have an angry argument.

quarry quarries
NOUN a place where stone is removed from the ground by digging or blasting

a b c d e f g h i j k l m n o p q r s t u v w x y z

quart quarts
NOUN a unit of liquid volume equal to two pints or about 1.136 litres

---

PRONUNCIATION TIP
This word is pronounced **kwort**.

---

quarter quarters
NOUN **1** one of four equal parts of something. It can be written as ¼.
NOUN **2** When you are telling the time, **quarter** means fifteen minutes before or after the hour. • *The programme starts at a **quarter** to six, and finishes at a **quarter** past.*
NOUN **3** an American or Canadian coin worth 25 cents, which is a **quarter** of a dollar

quartet quartets
NOUN **1** a group of four musicians who sing or play together
NOUN **2** a piece of music written for four instruments or singers

quartz
NOUN a type of hard, shiny crystal used in making very accurate watches and clocks

quay quays
NOUN a place where boats are tied up and loaded or unloaded

queasy queasier, queasiest
ADJECTIVE If you feel **queasy**, you feel slightly sick.

queen queens
NOUN a female monarch or a woman married to a king

queer queerer, queerest
ADJECTIVE very strange

quench quenches, quenching, quenched
VERB If you **quench** your thirst, you have a drink so that you are no longer thirsty.

query queries
NOUN a question • *I cannot answer your **query**.*

quest quests
NOUN a long search for something

question questions, questioning, questioned
NOUN **1** a sentence that asks for information
VERB **2** If you **question** someone, you ask them questions.
PHRASE **3** If something is **out of the question**, it is impossible and not worth considering.

question mark question marks
NOUN a punctuation mark (?) used at the end of a question

questionnaire questionnaires
NOUN a list of questions that people fill in as part of a survey

queue queues, queuing or queueing, queued
NOUN **1** a line of people or vehicles that are waiting for something
VERB **2** When people **queue**, or **queue up**, they stand in a line waiting for something.

LANGUAGE TIP
Queuing and *queueing* are both correct spellings.

---

quibble quibbles, quibbling, quibbled
VERB If you **quibble** about something, you argue about something that is not very important.

quiche quiches
NOUN a tart with a savoury filling made of eggs

PRONUNCIATION TIP
This word is pronounced **keesh**.

---

quick quicker, quickest
ADJECTIVE If you are **quick**, you move or do things with great speed.

quicksand quicksands
NOUN an area of deep, wet sand that you sink into if you walk on it

quid
NOUN (*informal*) In British English, a **quid** is a pound in money.

quiet quieter, quietest
ADJECTIVE **1** If someone or something is **quiet**, they are not making much noise, or they are not making any noise at all.
ADJECTIVE **2** A **quiet** place, time or situation is calm and peaceful.
NOUN **3** silence

quill quills
NOUN **1** a pen made from a feather
NOUN **2** A bird's **quills** are the large feathers on its wings and tail.
NOUN **3** A porcupine's **quills** are its spines.

quilt quilts
NOUN a thick, soft, warm cover for a bed, usually padded

quit quits, quitting, quit
VERB If you **quit** something, you leave it or stop doing it.

quite
ADVERB fairly but not very ● She's **quite** old, but not as old as my grandma.

quiver quivers, quivering, quivered
VERB 1 If something **quivers**, it trembles.
● The leaves on the trees **quivered** in the breeze.
NOUN 2 a container for carrying arrows

quiz quizzes
NOUN a game in which someone tests your knowledge by asking you questions

quota quotas
NOUN a number or quantity of something that is allowed by the rules ● We have already had our **quota** of class outings for this term.

WORD HISTORY
from Latin quot meaning how many

quotation quotations
NOUN a small part of a piece of writing taken from a book or speech

quotation marks
PLURAL NOUN the punctuation marks (" " ' ') that show where written speech or quotations begin and end

quote quotes, quoting, quoted
VERB If you **quote** something that someone has written or said, you repeat their words.

quotient quotients
NOUN the number of times one number can be divided into another. For example, in 42 ÷ 6 = 7, 7 is the **quotient**.

Qur'an
NOUN another spelling of **Koran**

rabbi rabbis
NOUN a Jewish religious leader

rabbit rabbits
NOUN a small furry rodent with long ears

rabies
NOUN a disease that causes humans and some other animals, especially dogs, to go mad and die

race races, racing, raced
NOUN 1 a competition to see who is fastest at something
NOUN 2 a large group of people who look alike in some way. Different **races** have, for example, different skin colour or differently shaped eyes.
VERB 3 If you **race**, you take part in a race.
● She has **raced** against some of the best in the world.
VERB 4 If you **race** somewhere, you go there as quickly as possible. ● He **raced** after the others.

racehorse racehorses
NOUN a horse that is trained to run fast for races

racial
ADJECTIVE to do with the different races that people belong to

racism
NOUN 1 hostility shown by one race of people to another
NOUN 2 believing that one race of people is better than all others

racist racists
NOUN 1 someone who does not like people who belong to a different race from them, and treats them unfairly
ADJECTIVE 2 not liking people, or treating them unfairly because they belong to a different race from you

rack racks
NOUN a piece of equipment for holding things or hanging things on

a
b
c
d
e
f
g
h
i
j
k
l
m
n
o
p
q
r
s
t
u
v
w
x
y
z

325

racket rackets

NOUN **1** a bat with an oval frame and strings across and down it, used in games like tennis

NOUN **2** If someone is making a **racket**, they are making a lot of noise.

radar

NOUN a way of discovering the position or speed of objects, such as ships or aircraft, by using radio signals

WORD HISTORY
an abbreviation for *radio detecting and ranging*

radiant

ADJECTIVE **1** shining or sparkling

ADJECTIVE **2** Someone who is **radiant** looks beautiful because they are so happy.

radiate radiates, radiating, radiated

VERB **1** Things that **radiate** from something come out in lines from a central point, like the spokes of a wheel or the sun's rays.

VERB **2** When a fire or a light **radiates** heat or light, it gives them out.

radiation

NOUN **1** very small particles given out by radioactive substances

NOUN **2** the heat and light energy given out from a source such as the sun

radiator radiators

NOUN **1** a hollow metal device filled with hot water for heating a room

NOUN **2** the part of a car that is filled with water to cool the engine

radio radios

NOUN **1** a system of sending sound over a distance by transmitting electrical signals

NOUN **2** the broadcasting of programmes for the public to listen to by radio

NOUN **3** a piece of equipment for listening to radio programmes • *They are in daily* **radio** *contact with the expedition.*

NOUN **4** a piece of equipment for sending and receiving **radio** messages • *A police officer raised the alarm on his* **radio**.

radioactive

ADJECTIVE **Radioactive** substances give out energy in the form of powerful and harmful rays.

radish radishes

NOUN a small salad vegetable with a red skin and white flesh, and with a hot taste

radius radii

NOUN **1** a straight line going from the centre of a circle to the outside edge

NOUN **2** the length of a straight line going from the centre of a circle to the outside edge

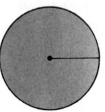

raffle raffles, raffling, raffled

NOUN **1** a competition in which people buy numbered tickets and win a prize if their ticket is chosen

VERB **2** If you **raffle** something, you give it as a prize in a raffle.

raft rafts

NOUN a floating platform made from long pieces of wood tied together

rafter rafters

NOUN the sloping pieces of wood that support a roof

rag rags

NOUN **1** a piece of old cloth used to wipe or clean things

NOUN **2** If someone is dressed in **rags**, they are wearing very old, torn clothes.

rage rages, raging, raged

NOUN **1** strong, uncontrollable anger

SYNONYMS: anger, fury, wrath

VERB **2** If something such as a storm or battle **rages**, it continues with great force or violence.

ragged

ADJECTIVE torn or frayed, with rough edges

raid raids, raiding, raided

VERB **1** When people **raid** a place, they enter it by force in order to attack it or to look for something or someone.

NOUN **2** a sudden, surprise attack

rail rails

NOUN **1** a fixed bar that you can hang things on

NOUN **2** one of the heavy metal bars that trains run along

railings

PLURAL NOUN a series of metal bars that make up a fence

railway railways
NOUN a route along which trains travel on metal tracks
→ Have a look at the illustration for **map**

rain rains, raining, rained
NOUN **1** water falling from the clouds in small drops
VERB **2** When it **rains**, small drops of water fall from clouds in the sky.

LANGUAGE TIP
Do not confuse *rain* with *rein* or *reign*.

---

rainbow rainbows
NOUN an arch of different colours that sometimes appears in the sky after it has been raining

raincoat raincoats
NOUN a waterproof coat

rainfall
NOUN the amount of rain that falls in one place during a particular period of time

rainforest rainforests
NOUN a dense forest of tall trees that grows in a tropical area where there is a lot of rain
→ Have a look at the illustration

raise raises, raising, raised
VERB **1** If you **raise** something, you make it higher. ● *He **raised** his hand.*
VERB **2** If you **raise** your voice, you speak more loudly.

VERB **3** If you **raise** money for something, you get people to give money towards it.

raisin raisins
NOUN a dried grape

rake rakes
NOUN a garden tool with a row of metal teeth and a long handle, for collecting together dead leaves or cut grass

rally rallies
NOUN **1** a competition in which vehicles race along public roads
NOUN **2** a large public meeting
NOUN **3** In tennis or squash, a **rally** is a continuous series of shots exchanged by the players.

ram rams, ramming, rammed
VERB **1** If you **ram** something somewhere, you push it there firmly. ● *She **rammed** her purse into her bag as she ran for the bus.*
VERB **2** If one vehicle **rams** another, it crashes into it.
NOUN **3** an adult male sheep

Ramadan
NOUN the ninth month of the Muslim year, during which Muslims eat and drink nothing during daylight

---

WORD HISTORY
from Arabic *Ramadan* meaning be hot, as the fasting takes place during a hot month

---

a
b
c
d
e
f
g
h
i
j
k
l
m
n
o
p
q
r
s
t
u
v
w
x
y
z

emergent layer

canopy

understorey

forest floor

rainforest

A
B
C
D
E
F
G
H
I
J
K
L
M
N
O
P
Q
R
S
T
U
V
W
X
Y
Z

ramble rambles, rambling, rambled
NOUN **1** a long walk in the countryside
VERB **2** to go for a ramble
VERB **3** If you **ramble**, you talk in a confused way.

rambler ramblers
NOUN someone who goes for a long walk in the countryside

ramp ramps
NOUN a sloping surface linking two places that are at different levels

rampage rampages, rampaging, rampaged
VERB If you **rampage**, you rush about wildly, causing damage.

rampart ramparts
NOUN an earth bank, often with a wall on top, built to protect a castle or city

→ Have a look at the illustration for **castle**

ramshackle
ADJECTIVE A **ramshackle** building is in very poor condition.

ran
VERB the past tense of **run**

ranch ranches
NOUN a large farm where cattle or horses are reared, especially in the USA

random
ADJECTIVE **1** Something that is done in a **random** way is done by chance or without a definite plan. • We picked a **random** sample of twenty pupils.

SYNONYMS: chance, haphazard

NOUN **2** Something that is done at **random** is done by chance or without a definite plan. • We got ten replies and we picked one at **random**.

rang
VERB the past tense of **ring**

range ranges, ranging, ranged
NOUN **1** a selection or choice of different things of the same kind • This top is available in a wide **range** of colours.
NOUN **2** a set of values on a scale
NOUN **3** the maximum distance over which something can reach things or detect things
NOUN **4** a long line of hills or mountains
VERB **5** When a set of things **ranges** between two points, they vary within these points on a scale.

ranger rangers
NOUN someone whose job is to look after a forest or park

rank ranks
NOUN **1** a position or grade that someone holds in an organisation
NOUN **2** a row of people or things • We went to the taxi **rank** outside the station to catch a taxi home.

ransack ransacks, ransacking, ransacked
VERB If you **ransack** a place, you disturb everything in order to search for or steal something, and leave it in a mess.

ransom ransoms
NOUN money that is demanded by kidnappers to free someone they have taken prisoner

rap raps, rapping, rapped
NOUN **1** a quick knock on something • There was a sharp **rap** on the door.
NOUN **2** a type of music in which the words are spoken in a rapid, rhythmic way
VERB **3** If you **rap** something, or **rap** on it, you hit it quickly several times.

rapid
ADJECTIVE happening or moving very quickly

rapier rapiers
NOUN a long thin sword with a sharp point

rare rarer, rarest
ADJECTIVE **1** Something that is **rare** is not common or does not often happen.
ADJECTIVE **2** Meat that is **rare** is cooked very lightly.

rascal rascals
NOUN someone who does naughty or mischievous things

rash rashes
NOUN **1** an area of red spots that appear on your skin when you are ill or have an allergy
ADJECTIVE **2** If you are **rash**, you do something without thinking properly about it.

rasher rashers
NOUN a thin slice of bacon

raspberry raspberries
NOUN a small soft red fruit that grows on a bush

rat rats
NOUN a rodent with a long tail, that looks like a large mouse

rate rates
NOUN how quickly or slowly, or how often something happens

rather
ADVERB **1** fairly, or to a certain extent • *rather large*
ADVERB **2** If you would **rather** do one thing than another, you would prefer to do it. • *I don't want to go out. I'd **rather** stay here.*

ratio ratios
NOUN The **ratio** between two things shows how many times one is bigger than another. A **ratio** is used to compare two or more quantities, for example, if a class has 15 boys and 10 girls, the **ratio** of boys to girls is 15 to 10.

ration rations, rationing, rationed
NOUN **1** the amount of something you are allowed to have
VERB **2** When something is **rationed**, you are only allowed a limited amount of it because there is a shortage.

rational
ADJECTIVE well thought out, sensible and reasonable • *It was a **rational** decision.*
ANTONYM: irrational

rationing
NOUN a system in which people are only allowed a limited amount of something because there is not enough of it, for example during a war

rattle rattles, rattling, rattled
VERB When something **rattles**, or when you **rattle** it, it makes short, regular knocking sounds, for example because it is shaking.

rattlesnake rattlesnakes
NOUN a poisonous American snake that can rattle its tail

rave raves, raving, raved
VERB **1** If someone **raves**, they talk in an excited and uncontrolled way.
VERB **2** (*informal*) If you **rave** about something, you talk about it very enthusiastically.
NOUN **3** (*informal*) a large dance event with electronic music

raven ravens
NOUN **1** a large black bird with a deep, harsh call
ADJECTIVE **2** **Raven** hair is black and shiny.

ravenous
ADJECTIVE very hungry

ravine ravines
NOUN a deep, narrow valley with steep sides

ravioli
NOUN an Italian dish made of small squares of pasta filled with meat or vegetable paste and served with sauce

raw
ADJECTIVE **1** **Raw** food is uncooked.
ADJECTIVE **2** If part of your body is **raw**, the skin has been rubbed or scraped away.
ADJECTIVE **3** A **raw** substance is in its natural state before being processed.

raw material raw materials
NOUN natural substances used to make things

ray rays
NOUN a beam of light • *the sun's **rays***
→ Have a look at the illustration for **greenhouse effect**

razor razors
NOUN an instrument that people use for shaving

re-
PREFIX used to form words that show something is being done again. For example, if you **re**use something you use it again, if you read something again you **re**read it, and if you marry for a second time you **re**marry.

reach reaches, reaching, reached
VERB **1** When you **reach** a place, you arrive there.
VERB **2** When you **reach** for something, you stretch out your arm to touch or get hold of it. • *I can't **reach** that shelf.*

react reacts, reacting, reacted
VERB **1** When you **react** to something, you behave in a particular way because of it.
VERB **2** When two chemicals **react**, they combine to form another substance.

reaction reactions
NOUN **1** Your **reaction** to something is what you say, do or feel because of it.
NOUN **2** the process in which two chemicals combine to form another substance

reactor reactors
NOUN a device used to produce nuclear energy

a
b
c
d
e
f
g
h
i
j
k
l
m
n
o
p
q
r
s
t
u
v
w
x
y
z

329

A
B
C
D
E
F
G
H
I
J
K
L
M
N
O
P
Q
R
S
T
U
V
W
X
Y
Z

read reads, reading, read

VERB When you **read** something that is written, you look at it and understand or say aloud the words that are there.

reader readers

NOUN The **readers** of a newspaper or magazine are the people who read it regularly.

readily

ADVERB **1** willingly or eagerly ● They **readily** tidied their bedrooms.
ADVERB **2** easily or quickly ● Help was **readily** available.

reading readings

NOUN **1** the act of reading books, newspapers or magazines
NOUN **2** The **reading** on a meter, gauge or other measuring instrument is the amount it shows.

ready

ADJECTIVE If someone or something is **ready**, they are prepared for doing something.
● Your glasses will be **ready** in a fortnight.

real

ADJECTIVE **1** actually true and not imagined

ANTONYM: imaginary

ADJECTIVE **2** genuine and not artificial

realise realises, realising, realised; also spelt realize

VERB If you **realise** something, you become aware of it or understand it.

realistic

ADJECTIVE **1** A **realistic** painting, story or film shows things in a way that is like real life.
ADJECTIVE **2** If you are **realistic** about a situation, you recognise and accept that it is true.

reality

NOUN **1** what is real, and not imagined or invented

SYNONYMS: fact, truth

NOUN **2** If something has become a **reality**, it has happened. ● Her dream of being a dancer had become a **reality**.

really

ADVERB **1** You use **really** to emphasise a point. ● It is a **really** good film.
ADVERB **2** You use **really** when you are talking about the true facts about something. ● What was **really** going on?

reap reaps, reaping, reaped

VERB When someone **reaps** a crop, such as corn, they cut and gather it.

reappear reappears, reappearing, reappeared

VERB When people or things **reappear**, they can be seen again after they have been out of sight.

rear rears, rearing, reared

NOUN **1** The **rear** of something is the part at the back.
VERB **2** To **rear** children or other young animals means to bring them up until they are able to look after themselves.
VERB **3** When a horse **rears**, it raises the front part of its body, so that its front legs are in the air.

rearrange rearranges, rearranging, rearranged

VERB If you **rearrange** something, you organise it or arrange it in a different way.

reason reasons, reasoning, reasoned

NOUN **1** the fact that explains why something happens
VERB **2** to think in a logical way and draw conclusions
VERB **3** If you **reason** with someone, you discuss something with them in a sensible way.

reasonable

ADJECTIVE **1** fair and sensible
ADJECTIVE **2** A **reasonable** amount is a fairly large amount.

reassure reassures, reassuring, reassured

VERB If you **reassure** someone, you say or do things to calm their fears or stop them from worrying.

rebel rebels, rebelling, rebelled

NOUN **1** someone who does not agree with rules, and behaves differently from other people
NOUN **2** one of a group of people who are fighting against their own country's army in order to change how it is ruled
VERB **3** When someone **rebels**, they refuse to obey rules, and they behave differently from other people.

PRONUNCIATION TIP
The noun is pronounced **reb**-el. The verb is pronounced rib-**el**.

rebellion rebellions
NOUN an organised act of resistance by a group of people to authority

rebellious
ADJECTIVE Someone who is **rebellious** breaks rules and refuses to obey orders.

rebound rebounds, rebounding, rebounded
VERB If something **rebounds**, it bounces back after hitting something.

rebuild rebuilds, rebuilding, rebuilt
VERB When something is **rebuilt**, it is built again after being damaged or destroyed.

rebuke rebukes, rebuking, rebuked
VERB If you **rebuke** someone, you tell them off for something wrong that they have done.

recall recalls, recalling, recalled
VERB When you **recall** something, you remember it.

recede recedes, receding, receded
VERB 1 When something **recedes**, it moves away into the distance. ● *We watched the tide receding.*
VERB 2 When a man's hair **recedes**, he starts to go bald from the front of his head.

receipt receipts
NOUN a piece of paper given to you as proof that you have paid for something or delivered something

receive receives, receiving, received
VERB When you **receive** something, you get it after someone has given or sent it to you.

receiver receivers
NOUN the part of a telephone connected to a landline that you hold near to your ear and your mouth

recent
ADJECTIVE A **recent** event is something that happened a short time ago.

reception receptions
NOUN 1 the place near the entrance of a hotel or office where appointments and enquiries are dealt with
NOUN 2 a formal party

receptionist receptionists
NOUN In a hotel or office, the **receptionist** is the person who receives and welcomes visitors as they arrive, answers the phone and arranges appointments.

recipe recipes
NOUN a list of ingredients and instructions for cooking or preparing a particular dish ● *My grandma gave me her recipe for Yorkshire pudding.*

recital recitals
NOUN a performance of poetry or music, usually by one person

recitation
NOUN When someone does a **recitation**, they say something such as a poem aloud.

recite recites, reciting, recited
VERB If you **recite** something such as a poem, you say it aloud.

reckless
ADJECTIVE If you are **reckless**, you do not care about any danger or damage you cause.

reckon reckons, reckoning, reckoned
VERB 1 If you **reckon** an amount, you calculate it.
VERB 2 If you **reckon** something is true, you think it is true.

reclaim reclaims, reclaiming, reclaimed
VERB 1 When you **reclaim** something, you fetch it after losing it or leaving it somewhere.
VERB 2 If land is **reclaimed**, it is made useable again, for example by draining water from it.

recline reclines, reclining, reclined
VERB to lean or lie back ● *We reclined on deckchairs in the sun.*

recognise recognises, recognising, recognised; also spelt **recognize**
VERB When you **recognise** someone or something, you realise you know who or what they are.

recoil recoils, recoiling, recoiled
VERB If you **recoil**, you suddenly back away from something, usually because it shocks or horrifies you. ● *I recoiled from the huge spider.*

recollect recollects, recollecting, recollected
VERB If you **recollect** something, you remember it.

recollection recollections
NOUN If you have a **recollection** of something, you remember it. ● *I have no recollection of seeing him that night.*

a
b
c
d
e
f
g
h
i
j
k
l
m
n
o
p
q
r
s
t
u
v
w
x
y
z

recommend recommends, recommending, recommended
VERB If you **recommend** something to someone, you suggest that they try it because you think it is good.

reconcile reconciles, reconciling, reconciled
VERB When people are **reconciled**, they become friendly again after a quarrel.

reconciliation
NOUN **Reconciliation** is when people become friendly again after they have been arguing.

reconstruct reconstructs, reconstructing, reconstructed
VERB To **reconstruct** something that has been damaged means to build it again.

record records, recording, recorded
NOUN **1** a written account of something
NOUN **2** a round, flat piece of plastic on which music has been recorded
NOUN **3** an achievement that is the best of its type ● *He holds the world **record** for the high jump.*
VERB **4** If you **record** information, you write it down so that it can be referred to later.
VERB **5** If you **record** sounds and pictures, you copy them onto a tape or disc, or onto your phone or computer, so that they can be listened to or watched again.

PRONUNCIATION TIP
The noun is pronounced **rek**-ord. The verb is pronounced ri-**kord**.

recorder recorders
NOUN **1** a small woodwind instrument
NOUN **2** a machine for copying sounds and pictures, such as a tape **recorder** or a video **recorder**

recount recounts, recounting, recounted
VERB **1** If you **recount** a story, you tell it.
VERB **2** If you **recount** something such as votes, you count them for a second time.

PRONUNCIATION TIP
Meaning 1 is pronounced ri-**count**.
Meaning 2 is pronounced **ree**-count.

recover recovers, recovering, recovered
VERB **1** When you **recover**, you get better after being ill.
VERB **2** If you **recover** something that has been lost or stolen, you get it back.

recreation recreations
NOUN the things you do for enjoyment in your spare time

recruit recruits, recruiting, recruited
VERB **1** If you **recruit** people, you persuade them to join a group or help with something.
NOUN **2** someone who has joined the army or some other organisation

rectangle rectangles NOUN a four-sided plane shape with four right angles

rectangular
ADJECTIVE shaped like a rectangle

recuperate recuperates, recuperating, recuperated
VERB When you **recuperate**, you gradually recover after being ill or injured.

recur recurs, recurring, recurred
VERB If something **recurs**, it happens again.

recycle recycles, recycling, recycled
VERB When you **recycle** something, you use it again for a different purpose.

red redder, reddest; reds
NOUN **1** the colour of blood or of a ripe tomato
ADJECTIVE **2** having the colour of blood or of a ripe tomato
ADJECTIVE **3** **Red** hair is between orange and brown in colour.

redden reddens, reddening, reddened
VERB If something **reddens**, it becomes red.
● *His face **reddened** with embarrassment.*

red-handed
ADJECTIVE If you catch someone **red-handed**, you catch them while they are doing something wrong.

redraft redrafts, redrafting, redrafted
VERB If you **redraft** a piece of writing, you rewrite it to improve or change it.

reduce reduces, reducing, reduced
VERB If you **reduce** something, you make it smaller in size or amount.

SYNONYMS: cut, decrease

reduction reductions
NOUN If there is a **reduction** in something, it becomes smaller or less. ● *There are great reductions in prices during the sales.*

redundant
ADJECTIVE **1** When people are made **redundant**, they lose their jobs because there is no more work for them.
ADJECTIVE **2** If something becomes **redundant**, it is no longer needed or useful.

reed reeds
NOUN **1** a hollow-stemmed plant that grows in shallow water or on wet ground
NOUN **2** a thin piece of cane or metal inside some wind instruments, that vibrates and makes a sound when air is blown over it

reef reefs
NOUN a long line of rocks or coral close to the surface of the sea

reek reeks, reeking, reeked
VERB **1** If something **reeks**, it has a strong, unpleasant smell.
NOUN **2** a strong, unpleasant smell

reel reels, reeling, reeled
NOUN **1** a cylindrical object around which you wrap something such as a fishing line, a film or thread
NOUN **2** a fast Scottish dance
VERB **3** If you **reel**, you stagger and look as if you will fall.

refer refers, referring, referred
VERB **1** If you **refer** to someone or something, you mention them when you are speaking or writing.
VERB **2** If you **refer** to a book or other source of information, you look at it in order to find something out.
VERB **3** If someone **refers** a problem or a question to someone else, they pass it on to them to deal with.

referee referees
NOUN the official who controls a sports match and makes sure that the rules are not broken

reference references
NOUN **1** a mention of someone or something in a speech or a piece of writing
NOUN **2** a document written by someone who knows you, that describes your character and abilities, usually when you are applying for a job

reference book reference books
NOUN a book that you use to get information

referendum referendums or referenda
NOUN a vote in which all the people of voting age in a country are asked to say if they agree with a particular government policy or not

refill refills, refilling, refilled
VERB **1** If you **refill** something, you fill it again.
NOUN **2** a container of something to replace something that is used up ● *I need a refill for my pen.*

refine refines, refining, refined
VERB If substances such as oil or sugar are **refined**, all the impurities are taken out of them.

refined
ADJECTIVE Someone who is **refined** is very polite and well mannered.

refinery refineries
NOUN a factory where sugar or oil are refined

reflect reflects, reflecting, reflected
VERB **1** When rays of heat or light **reflect** off something, they bounce back from it.
VERB **2** When something smooth and shiny, such as a mirror, **reflects** something, it shows an image of it.
VERB **3** When you **reflect** on something, you think about it carefully.

reflection reflections
NOUN the image you see when you look in a mirror or in very clear, still water ● *I looked closely at my reflection in the mirror.*

reflective
ADJECTIVE If a surface or material is **reflective**, it bounces back rays of light or heat.

reflex reflexes
NOUN **1** a sudden uncontrollable movement that you make when a particular nerve is pressed or hit
NOUN **2** If you have good **reflexes**, you respond very quickly when something unexpected happens.

a
b
c
d
e
f
g
h
i
j
k
l
m
n
o
p
q
r
s
t
u
v
w
x
y
z

333

NOUN **3** In mathematics, a **reflex** angle is an angle between 180° and 360°.

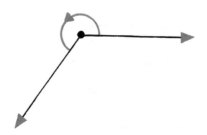

reform reforms, reforming, reformed
VERB **1** When organisations or laws are **reformed**, changes are made to them to improve them.
VERB **2** When people **reform**, they stop doing bad things such as committing crimes.

refrain refrains, refraining, refrained
VERB **1** (*formal*) If you **refrain** from doing something, you do not do it.
NOUN **2** a short, simple part of a song that is repeated

SYNONYM: chorus

refresh refreshes, refreshing, refreshed
VERB If something **refreshes** you, it makes you feel less tired or less thirsty.

refreshing
ADJECTIVE If something is **refreshing**, it makes you cool or less tired after you have been hot or busy. • *We went for a refreshing swim after walking along the beach.*

refreshments
PLURAL NOUN drinks and snacks

refrigerator refrigerators
NOUN an electrically cooled container for putting food in to keep it fresh

refuel refuels, refuelling, refuelled
VERB When an aircraft or vehicle is **refuelled**, it is filled with more fuel.

refuge refuges
NOUN a place where you go for safety and protection

SYNONYMS: haven, sanctuary, shelter

WORD HISTORY
from Latin *refugere* meaning to flee

refugee refugees
NOUN a person who has been forced to leave their country and live elsewhere, for example because of war, famine or persecution

refund refunds, refunding, refunded
NOUN **1** a sum of money that is paid back to you, for example because you have returned goods to a shop
VERB **2** If someone **refunds** your money, they pay it back to you.

refuse refuses, refusing, refused
VERB **1** If you **refuse** something, you say no to it, or decide firmly that you will not do it or do not accept it.
NOUN **2** rubbish or waste

PRONUNCIATION TIP
The verb is pronounced ri-**fyooz**. The noun is pronounced **ref**-yooss.

regal
ADJECTIVE very grand and suitable for a king or queen

regard regards, regarding, regarded
VERB **1** To **regard** someone or something in a certain way is to think of them in that way. • *We regarded him as a friend.*
VERB **2** to look closely at someone or something
NOUN **3** If you have a high **regard** for someone, you have a very good opinion of them.

regarding
PREPOSITION on the subject of • *"I will now answer any questions regarding your homework," said the teacher.*

regardless
ADVERB If you do something **regardless** of something else or what may happen as a result, you do it anyway. • *The society helps anyone regardless of their age.*

regards
PLURAL NOUN kind wishes or friendly feelings for someone, usually sent in a message • *Give him my regards when you see him.*

regatta regattas
NOUN a race meeting for sailing or rowing boats

reggae
NOUN a type of music with a strong beat, originally from the West Indies

regiment regiments
NOUN a large group of soldiers commanded by a colonel

A B C D E F G H I J K L M N O P Q R S T U V W X Y Z

region regions
NOUN a large area of a country or of the world

register registers, registering, registered
NOUN **1** an official list that is used to keep a record of things that happen or people who attend an event
VERB **2** When something is **registered**, it is recorded on an official list.

regret regrets, regretting, regretted
VERB **1** If you **regret** something, you wish that it had not happened or you had not done it.
VERB **2** You can use **regret** to say you are sorry about something. ● *We regret any inconvenience caused to passengers by the delay.*

regretful
ADJECTIVE If you are **regretful**, you are sorry or sad about something.

regular
ADJECTIVE **1** **Regular** events happen at equal or frequent intervals.
ADJECTIVE **2** If you are a **regular** visitor somewhere, you go there often.

regulate regulates, regulating, regulated
VERB If someone or something **regulates** something, they control it. ● *My grandad takes tablets to regulate his blood pressure.*

regulation regulations
NOUN an official rule

rehearsal rehearsals
NOUN a practice of a performance in preparation for the actual event

rehearse rehearses, rehearsing, rehearsed
VERB When people **rehearse** a performance, they practise it in preparation for the actual event.

reign reigns, reigning, reigned
VERB **1** When a king or queen **reigns**, he or she is the leader of the country.
NOUN **2** The **reign** of a king or queen is the period when they reign.

LANGUAGE TIP
Do not confuse *reign* with *rain* or *rein*.

rein reins
NOUN one of the thin leather straps that you hold when you are riding a horse

LANGUAGE TIP
Do not confuse *rein* with *rain* or *reign*.

reindeer
NOUN a deer with large antlers, that lives in northern regions of the world

reinforce reinforces, reinforcing, reinforced
VERB If you **reinforce** something, you strengthen it.

reject rejects, rejecting, rejected
VERB If you **reject** something, you throw it away or refuse to accept it.

rejoice rejoices, rejoicing, rejoiced
VERB If you **rejoice**, you celebrate because you are very pleased about something.

relate relates, relating, related
VERB **1** If one thing **relates** to another, it is concerned or connected with it in some way, or can be compared with it.
VERB **2** If you **relate** a story, you tell it.

related
ADJECTIVE If people, animals or plants are **related**, they belong to the same family groups or species.

relation relations
NOUN **1** one of the people who are related to you, such as aunts, uncles and grandparents
NOUN **2** the way that one thing is connected or compared with another

relationship relationships
NOUN **1** The **relationship** between two people or groups is the way they feel and behave towards each other.
NOUN **2** a close friendship, especially one involving romantic feelings

relative relatives
ADJECTIVE **1** compared with other things or people of the same kind
NOUN **2** a member of your family

relax relaxes, relaxing, relaxed
VERB **1** When you **relax**, or when something **relaxes** you, you become calm and less worried or tense. ● *Massage is used to relax muscles.*
VERB **2** If you **relax**, you stop work and rest or enjoy your free time.

SYNONYMS: take it easy, unwind

A
B
C
D
E
F
G
H
I
J
K
L
M
N
O
P
Q
R
S
T
U
V
W
X
Y
Z

relay relays, relaying, relayed
VERB **1** If you **relay** something, such as a message, you pass it from one person to the next.
NOUN **2** a race between teams, in which each team member runs one part of the race

release releases, releasing, released
VERB If you **release** someone or something, you set them free or unfasten them.

relent relents, relenting, relented
VERB If someone **relents**, they give in and allow something that they refused to allow before.
• Dad **relented** and allowed us to stay up late.

relevant
ADJECTIVE connected with what is being discussed or dealt with

reliable
ADJECTIVE **Reliable** people and things can be trusted and depended upon.

relic relics
NOUN **1** an object or custom that has survived from an earlier time
NOUN **2** an object regarded as holy because it is thought to be connected with a saint

relief
NOUN If you feel **relief**, you feel glad because something unpleasant is over or has been avoided.

relieve relieves, relieving, relieved
VERB If something **relieves** an unpleasant feeling, it makes it less unpleasant.

relieved
ADJECTIVE If you are **relieved**, you are thankful that something worrying or unpleasant has stopped. • I was **relieved** when the exams were over.

religion religions
NOUN **1** belief in a god or gods
NOUN **2** a particular set of religious beliefs
• the Christian **religion**

religious
ADJECTIVE to do with religion

relish relishes, relishing, relished
VERB **1** If you **relish** something, you enjoy it very much. • He **relished** the thought of chocolate cake for tea.
NOUN **2** enjoyment • "I'm allowed to stay up as long as like," she said with **relish**.
NOUN **3** a savoury pickle

reluctant
ADJECTIVE If you are **reluctant** to do something, you do not want to do it.

rely relies, relying, relied
VERB If you **rely** on someone or something, you trust and depend on them. • I **relied** on my friends to help me.

remain remains, remaining, remained
VERB **1** If you **remain** in a particular place, you stay there.
PLURAL NOUN **2** The **remains** of something are the parts that are left after most of it has been destroyed or used.

remainder
NOUN **1** the part of something that is left
NOUN **2** In arithmetic, the **remainder** is the amount left over when one number cannot be divided exactly by another.

remark remarks, remarking, remarked
VERB **1** If you **remark** on something, you mention it or comment on it.
NOUN **2** a comment you make or something you say

remarkable
ADJECTIVE impressive and noticeable
• Her tennis skills were **remarkable**.

remedy remedies, remedying, remedied
NOUN **1** a cure for something
NOUN **2** a way of dealing with a problem
VERB **3** If you **remedy** a problem, you put it right.

remember remembers, remembering, remembered
VERB **1** If you **remember** someone or something from the past, you still have an idea of them and you are able to think about them.
VERB **2** If you **remember** to do something, you do it when you intended to.
VERB **3** If you **remember** something, it suddenly comes into your mind again.

remind reminds, reminding, reminded
VERB **1** If someone **reminds** you of something, they help you remember it.
VERB **2** If someone or something **reminds** you of another person or thing, they are similar to the other person or thing and make you think of them.

remnant remnants
NOUN a small part of something that is left after the rest has been used or destroyed

remorse
NOUN (formal) a strong feeling of guilt and regret

remote remoter, remotest
ADJECTIVE **1** far away from where most people live
ADJECTIVE **2** far away in time

remote control
NOUN **1** a system of controlling a machine or vehicle from a distance, using radio or electronic signals
NOUN **2** a hand-held device for controlling a machine or vehicle from a distance
● a TV **remote control**

removal removals
NOUN **1** the act of taking something away
● The house felt very bare after the **removal** of the furniture.
ADJECTIVE **2** A **removal** company moves furniture from one building to another.

remove removes, removing, removed
VERB If you **remove** something, you take it away.

rendezvous
NOUN a meeting or meeting place

PRONUNCIATION TIP
This word is pronounced **ron**-day-voo.

WORD HISTORY
a French word, meaning present yourselves!

renew renews, renewing, renewed
VERB **1** If you **renew** something such as a piece of equipment, you replace it or parts of it with a new one or new parts.
VERB **2** If you **renew** an activity or relationship, you begin it again.

renewable
ADJECTIVE **1** able to be renewed ● a good source of **renewable** energy
NOUN **2** a renewable form of energy, such as wind power or solar power ● Our energy mix needs more **renewables**.

renovate renovates, renovating, renovated
VERB If you **renovate** something old, you repair it and restore it to good condition.

renovation
NOUN the process of repairing something old and restoring it to good condition

renowned
ADJECTIVE well known, especially for something good ● She's **renowned** for her kindness and compassion.

rent rents, renting, rented
VERB **1** If you **rent** something, you pay the owner a regular sum of money to use it.
NOUN **2** the amount of money you pay regularly to use something that belongs to someone else

rental rentals
NOUN **1** the amount paid as rent
ADJECTIVE **2** to do with rent ● a small **rental** car

repair repairs, repairing, repaired
NOUN **1** something that you do to mend something that is damaged
VERB **2** If you **repair** something that is damaged, you mend it.

repay repays, repaying, repaid
VERB **1** When you **repay** money, you give it back to the person who lent it to you.
VERB **2** If you **repay** a favour, you do something to help the person who helped you.

repeat repeats, repeating, repeated
VERB **1** If you **repeat** something, you say, write or do it again. ● Please can you **repeat** the question?
NOUN **2** something that is done again or happens again

repeatedly
ADVERB again and again, several times
● He knocked **repeatedly** on the door, but nobody answered.

repel repels, repelling, repelled
VERB **1** If something **repels** you, it disgusts you.
VERB **2** If someone **repels** an attack, they defend themselves successfully against it.
VERB **3** If someone or something **repels** something, they push it away. ● True magnets can **repel** other magnets.

repetition
NOUN If there is a **repetition** of something, it happens again or is repeated.

repetitive
ADJECTIVE Something that is **repetitive** is repeated over and over again, and can be extremely boring. ● Fruit picking is a **repetitive** job.

a
b
c
d
e
f
g
h
i
j
k
l
m
n
o
p
q
r
s
t
u
v
w
x
y
z

replace replaces, replacing, replaced
VERB **1** If you **replace** something, you put it back.

VERB **2** If you **replace** something old, broken or missing, you put another one or a new one in its place. • Ben **replaced** Tina in the team.

replay replays, replaying, replayed
VERB **1** If you **replay** a tape or a film, you play it again.
NOUN **2** a sports match that is played for a second time

replica replicas
NOUN an accurate copy of something

reply replies, replying, replied
VERB **1** If you **reply** to something, you say or write something as an answer to it.
NOUN **2** what you say or write when you answer someone

report reports, reporting, reported
VERB **1** If you **report** that something has happened, you inform someone about it.
NOUN **2** an account of an event or situation

reporter reporters
NOUN someone who writes news articles or broadcasts news reports

represent represents, representing, represented
VERB If someone **represents** you, they act on your behalf.

representative representatives
NOUN a person who acts on behalf of another person or group of people

reprieve reprieves
NOUN a cancellation or postponement of a punishment, especially the death penalty

reprimand reprimands, reprimanding, reprimanded
VERB If you **reprimand** someone, you officially tell them that they should not have done something.

reproach reproaches, reproaching, reproached
VERB **1** If you **reproach** someone, you blame them for something, or criticise them.
NOUN **2** the act of reproaching someone

reproduce reproduces, reproducing, reproduced
VERB **1** If you **reproduce** something, you make a copy of it.
VERB **2** When living things **reproduce**, they produce more of their own kind. • Rats **reproduce** up to five times every year.

reproduction
NOUN the process by which each living thing produces young

reptile reptiles
NOUN an animal such as a snake, turtle or lizard that has scales on its skin, lays eggs and is cold-blooded

WORD HISTORY
from Latin reptilis meaning creeping

republic republics
NOUN a country that has a president rather than a king or queen

repulsion
NOUN the force pushing two magnets away from each other

repulsive
ADJECTIVE horrible and disgusting

reputation reputations
NOUN the opinion that people have of someone or something

request requests, requesting, requested
VERB **1** If you **request** something, you ask for it politely or formally.
NOUN **2** If you make a **request** for something, you ask for it.

require requires, requiring, required
VERB **1** If you **require** something, you need it.
VERB **2** If you are **required** to do something, you have to do it. • You are **required** to report to the office at 9 a.m.

requirement requirements
NOUN something you must have or must do

rescue rescues, rescuing, rescued
VERB **1** If you **rescue** someone, you save them from a dangerous or unpleasant situation.
NOUN **2** an attempt to save someone from a dangerous or unpleasant situation

research researches, researching, researched
NOUN **1** detailed study to discover facts about something
VERB **2** If you **research** something, you study it carefully to discover facts about it.

resemble resembles, resembling, resembled
VERB If one thing or person **resembles** another, they are similar to each other.

resent resents, resenting, resented
VERB If you **resent** something, you feel bitter and angry about it.

reserve reserves, reserving, reserved
VERB 1 If you **reserve** something, you ask for it to be kept aside or ordered for you, or you keep it for a particular purpose. ● We have **reserved** this table for someone else.
NOUN 2 an area of land where animals, birds or plants are officially protected and can safely breed
NOUN 3 If you are a **reserve** in a team, you play if one of the other team members cannot.

reserved
ADJECTIVE 1 kept for someone ● All of these tables are **reserved**.
ADJECTIVE 2 People who are **reserved** are quiet and shy.

reservoir reservoirs
NOUN a lake, often artificial, used for storing water before it is supplied to people

PRONUNCIATION TIP
This word is pronounced **rez**-uh-vwar.

residence residences
NOUN (formal) Your **residence** is your home.

resident residents
NOUN A **resident** of a house or area is someone who lives there.

resign resigns, resigning, resigned
VERB 1 If you **resign** from your job, you give it up.
VERB 2 If you **resign** yourself to an unpleasant situation, you accept it because you know it cannot be changed.

resignation resignations
NOUN 1 If you hand in your **resignation**, you tell the company you work for that you have decided to leave your job.
NOUN 2 the feeling you have when you accept an unpleasant situation because you know it cannot be changed

resist resists, resisting, resisted
VERB 1 If you **resist** something, you refuse to accept it and try to stop it happening.
VERB 2 If you **resist** an attack, you fight back.

resistance
NOUN 1 fighting or taking action against something or someone ● Her body's **resistance** to disease helped her to get well.
NOUN 2 Wind or air **resistance** is a force which slows down a moving object or vehicle. ● The design of the bicycle has reduced the effects of wind **resistance**.

resolute
ADJECTIVE If you are **resolute**, you are determined not to change your mind.

resolution resolutions
NOUN 1 determination
NOUN 2 If you make a **resolution**, you promise yourself that you will do something.
NOUN 3 a decision made at a meeting
● The **resolution** to improve the play area was agreed.

resolve resolves, resolving, resolved
VERB 1 If you **resolve** a problem, you find a way of sorting it out.
VERB 2 If you **resolve** to do something, you make up your mind firmly to do it.
NOUN 3 determination to do something

resort resorts, resorting, resorted
NOUN 1 a place where a lot of people spend their holidays, especially by the sea
VERB 2 If you **resort** to doing something, you do it because everything else has failed and you have no alternative.
PHRASE 3 If you do something **as a last resort**, you do it because you can find no other way of solving a problem.

resource resources
NOUN 1 The **resources** of a country, organisation or person are the materials, money or skills they have and can use.
NOUN 2 Natural **resources** are all the land, forests, energy sources and minerals existing naturally in a place that can be used by people.

resourceful
ADJECTIVE A **resourceful** person is good at solving problems and finding ways to do things.

respect respects, respecting, respected
VERB 1 If you **respect** someone, you admire and like them.
VERB 2 If you **respect** someone's feelings or wishes, you treat them with consideration.
NOUN 3 a feeling of admiration for someone's good qualities or achievements
NOUN 4 consideration for other people

respectable
ADJECTIVE Someone who is **respectable** behaves in a way that is approved of in the society where they live.

respiration

NOUN breathing • *His **respiration** was affected by his cold.*

respiratory system respiratory systems

NOUN Your **respiratory system** is the system in your body that is to do with your breathing.

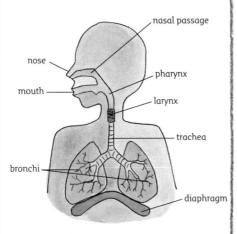

nasal passage

nose

pharynx

mouth

larynx

trachea

bronchi

diaphragm

respond responds, responding, responded

VERB If you **respond** to someone or something, you react to them by doing or saying something.

response responses

NOUN a reply or a reaction to something

responsibility responsibilities

NOUN **1** If you have **responsibility** for someone or something, you are in charge of them. • *He has **responsibility** for organizing the school fair.*
NOUN **2** If you accept **responsibility** for something bad that has happened, you say that it is your fault. • *No one admitted **responsibility** for breaking the window*
NOUN **3** something that you have to do as part of your job

responsible

ADJECTIVE **1** If you are **responsible** for something, you are in charge of it and must take the blame if it goes wrong. • *If we get a pet, you will be **responsible** for looking after it.*
ADJECTIVE **2** A **responsible** person is sensible, trustworthy and reliable.

ADJECTIVE **3** If you are **responsible** for something, you are the cause of it.
• *She was **responsible** for the accident.*

rest rests, resting, rested

VERB **1** If you **rest**, you take a break from what you are doing and relax for a while.
VERB **2** If you **rest** something against something else, you lean it there.
NOUN **3** The **rest** of something is all the parts that are left or have not been mentioned.
NOUN **4** If you have a **rest**, you do not do anything active for a while.
NOUN **5** an object that supports something else, such as a headrest or a footrest

restaurant restaurants

NOUN a place where you can buy and eat a meal • *an Italian **restaurant***

restless

ADJECTIVE If you are **restless**, you find it hard to stay still or relaxed because you are bored or impatient.

restore restores, restoring, restored

VERB If you **restore** something, you get it back to its original state.

restrain restrains, restraining, restrained

VERB If you **restrain** someone or something, you hold them back or stop them from doing what they want to.

restrict restricts, restricting, restricted

VERB To **restrict** someone or something means to set limits on them. • *The police **restricted** parking outside the school.*

result results, resulting, resulted

NOUN **1** The **result** of an action or situation is what happens because of it.
NOUN **2** The **result** of a contest, calculation or exam is the final score, figure or mark at the end of it.
VERB **3** If something **results** from a particular event, it is caused by that event.

resume resumes, resuming, resumed

VERB If you **resume** something, you start doing it again after a break. • *After dinner, Dad **resumed** his work on the car.*

retail

NOUN the activity of selling goods to the public, for example, in a shop

ANTONYM: wholesale

retailer retailers

NOUN a business or person that sells things to people

retain retains, retaining, retained
VERB If you **retain** something, you keep it.

retaliate retaliates, retaliating, retaliated
VERB If you **retaliate**, you do something to harm or upset someone because they have harmed or upset you.

retire retires, retiring, retired
VERB 1 When older people **retire**, they leave their job and stop working.
VERB 2 If you **retire** from a race, you withdraw from it.

retort retorts, retorting, retorted
VERB 1 If you **retort**, you reply angrily.
NOUN 2 a short, angry reply

retrace retraces, retracing, retraced
VERB If you **retrace** your steps, you go back exactly the same way you came.

retreat retreats, retreating, retreated
VERB If you **retreat** from someone or something unpleasant or dangerous, you move away from them.

retrieve retrieves, retrieving, retrieved
VERB If you **retrieve** something, you get it back or find it again.

return returns, returning, returned
VERB 1 If you **return** to a place, you go back there.
VERB 2 If you **return** something to someone, you give it back to them.
NOUN 3 the act of giving or putting something back
NOUN 4 a ticket for a journey to a place and back again

reunion reunions
NOUN a meeting or a party at which people who have not seen each other for a long time get together

reunite reunites, reuniting, reunited
VERB to bring people together again

rev revs, revving, revved
VERB 1 When someone **revs** an engine, they press the accelerator to increase its speed.
NOUN 2 The speed of an engine is measured in **revs**, which is an abbreviation of *revolutions per minute*.

reveal reveals, revealing, revealed
VERB 1 If you **reveal** something, you tell people about it.
VERB 2 If you **reveal** something that has been hidden, you uncover it.

revenge
NOUN the act of hurting someone who has hurt you

revenue revenues
NOUN money that a government, company or organisation receives

Reverend
NOUN a title used before the name of a member of the clergy

reverse reverses, reversing, reversed
VERB 1 If you **reverse** the order of things, you arrange them in the opposite order.
VERB 2 When someone **reverses** a car, they drive it backwards.

reversible
ADJECTIVE **Reversible** clothing can be worn with either side on the outside.

review reviews, reviewing, reviewed
NOUN 1 an article in a magazine or newspaper, or a talk on television or radio, giving an opinion of a new book, play or film
VERB 2 When someone **reviews** a book, play or film, they write an account or have a discussion expressing their opinion of it.

revise revises, revising, revised
VERB If you **revise** for an exam, you go over your work to make sure you know it properly.

revive revives, reviving, revived
VERB When you **revive** someone who has fainted, they become conscious again.

revolt revolts, revolting, revolted
NOUN 1 a violent uprising or rebellion against authority
VERB 2 When people **revolt**, they rebel against the system that governs them.
VERB 3 If something **revolts** you, it disgusts you.

revolting
ADJECTIVE horrible and disgusting

revolution revolutions
NOUN a violent attempt by a large number of people to change the way their country is run

revolutionise revolutionises, revolutionising, revolutionised; also spelt **revolutionize**
VERB If something is **revolutionised**, it is changed completely, usually for the better. ● *Science and technology have **revolutionised** the way we live.*

revolve **revolves, revolving, revolved**
VERB When something **revolves**, it turns in a circle around a central point.

revolver **revolvers**
NOUN a small gun held in the hand

reward **rewards, rewarding, rewarded**
NOUN **1** something you are given because you have done something good
VERB **2** If you **reward** someone, you give them a reward.

rewarding
ADJECTIVE Something that is **rewarding** gives you a lot of satisfaction. • *Nursing is a **rewarding** job.*

rewind **rewinds, rewinding, rewound**
VERB If you **rewind** a cassette or video tape, you wind it back to the beginning.

rewrite **rewrites, rewriting, rewrote, rewritten**
VERB If you **rewrite** something you have written, you write it again to make changes to it and improve it.

SYNONYM: redraft

rhetorical
ADJECTIVE A question that is **rhetorical** is asked in order to make a statement, rather than to get an answer. For example, *What's the world coming to?*

rheumatism
NOUN an illness that makes your joints and muscles stiff and painful

rhinoceros **rhinoceroses**
NOUN a large African or Asian mammal with one or two horns on its nose

WORD HISTORY
from Greek *rhin* meaning of the nose and *keras* meaning horn

rhombus **rhombuses** or **rhombi**
NOUN a plane shape like a diamond, with four equal sides and no right angles

rhubarb
NOUN a plant with long red stems that can be cooked with sugar and eaten

rhyme **rhymes, rhyming, rhymed**
VERB **1** If one word **rhymes** with another, both words have a very similar sound in their final syllable. For example, *Sally* rhymes with *valley*.
NOUN **2** a word that rhymes with another • *He couldn't find a **rhyme** for "orange".*

LANGUAGE TIP
There is an *h* before the *y* in *rhyme* and *rhythm*.

rhythm **rhythms**
NOUN a regular series of sounds, movements or actions • *The poem was easy to learn because it had a strong **rhythm**.*

rib **ribs**
NOUN Your **ribs** are the curved bones that go from your spine to your chest.

→ Have a look at the illustration for **skeleton**

ribbon **ribbons**
NOUN a long, narrow piece of cloth used as a fastening or decoration

rice
NOUN white or brown grains taken from a cereal plant and used for food

rich **richer, richest; riches**
ADJECTIVE **1** Someone who is **rich** has a lot of money or possessions.
ADJECTIVE **2** Something that is **rich** in something contains a large amount of it.
• *Fruit is **rich** in vitamins.*
ADJECTIVE **3 Rich** food contains a large amount of fat, oil or sugar.
PLURAL NOUN **4 Riches** are valuable possessions or large amounts of money.

rickshaw **rickshaws**
NOUN a two-wheeled, hand-pulled cart used in Asia for carrying passengers

ricochet **ricochets, ricocheting** or **ricochetting, ricocheted** or **ricochetted**
VERB When an object **ricochets**, it hits a surface and then bounces away from it.

PRONUNCIATION TIP
This word is pronounced **rik**-oh-shay.

rid

PHRASE When you **get rid of** something you do not want, you throw it away.

riddle **riddles**

NOUN an amusing or puzzling question, sometimes in rhyme, to which you must find an answer

ride **rides, riding, rode, ridden**

VERB **1** When you **ride** a horse or a bicycle, you sit on it and control it as it moves along.

VERB **2** When you **ride** in a car, you travel in it.

NOUN **3** a journey on a horse or bicycle or in a vehicle

ridge **ridges**

NOUN a long, narrow piece of high land

ridicule **ridicules, ridiculing, ridiculed**

VERB **1** If you **ridicule** someone, you make fun of them in an unkind way.

NOUN **2** unkind laughter or teasing

ridiculous

ADJECTIVE very foolish

rifle **rifles**

NOUN a gun with a long barrel

rig **rigs, rigging, rigged**

NOUN **1** a large structure used for taking oil or gas from the ground or the sea bed • *an oil rig*

VERB **2** When someone **rigs** a boat, they fit it with ropes and sails.

right **rights**

NOUN **1** correct behaviour • *At least he knew right from wrong.*

ANTONYM: wrong

NOUN **2** If you have a **right** to do something, you are allowed to do it.

NOUN **3** one of two opposite directions, sides or positions. If you are facing north and you turn to the **right**, you will be facing east.

ANTONYM: left

ADJECTIVE **4** If something is **right**, it is correct. • *Jack was right about the result of the match.* • *Is my answer right?*

ANTONYM: wrong

ADJECTIVE **5** on the **right** of something • *He held out his right arm.*

ANTONYM: left

ADVERB **6** on or towards the **right** of something • *Turn right at the corner.*

ANTONYM: left

right angle **right angles**

NOUN an angle of 90°

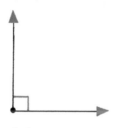

right-angled

ADJECTIVE A **right-angled** triangle has a right angle as one of its angles.

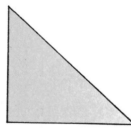

rigid

ADJECTIVE A **rigid** object is stiff and does not bend easily.

rim **rims**

NOUN the outer edge of something such as a bowl or wheel

→ Have a look at the illustration for **bicycle**

rind **rinds**

NOUN the skin on bacon, cheese and some fruits

ring **rings, ringing, rang, rung**

VERB **1** If you **ring** someone, you phone them.

VERB **2** When a phone or bell **rings**, it makes a clear, loud sound. • *The school bell rings at nine o'clock.*

NOUN **3** a small circle of metal that you wear on your finger

a
b
c
d
e
f
g
h
i
j
k
l
m
n
o
p
q
r
s
t
u
v
w
x
y
z

343

ringleader ringleaders

NOUN the leader of a group, who leads the others into mischief or crime

rink rinks

NOUN a large indoor area for ice skating or roller skating

rinse rinses, rinsing, rinsed

VERB When you **rinse** something, you wash it in clean water, without soap.

riot riots, rioting, rioted

NOUN **1** When there is a **riot**, a crowd of people behave violently in a public place.
VERB **2** When people **riot**, they behave violently in a public place.

rip rips, ripping, ripped

VERB If you **rip** something, you tear it.

ripe riper, ripest

ADJECTIVE **Ripe** fruit or grain is fully developed and ready to be eaten.

ripple ripples, rippling, rippled

NOUN **1** a little wave on the surface of calm water
NOUN **2** If there is a **ripple** of laughter or applause, people laugh or clap their hands gently for a short time.
VERB **3** When the surface of water **ripples**, little waves appear on it.

rise rises, rising, rose, risen

VERB **1** If something **rises**, it moves upwards.
• *Wilson watched the smoke **rise** from the fire.*
VERB **2** When the sun or moon **rises**, it appears from below the horizon.
NOUN **3** When something goes up, it is called a **rise**, for example a **rise** in the land or a **rise** in prices.
VERB **4** When you **rise**, you get out of bed.
VERB **5** If something such as a sound, or the level of a liquid or prices **rise**, they become higher.

risk risks, risking, risked

NOUN **1** If there is a **risk** of something unpleasant, it might happen.
NOUN **2** Someone or something that is a **risk** is likely to cause harm or have bad results.
VERB **3** If you **risk** something, you do something knowing that an unpleasant thing might happen as a result. • *If he doesn't play, he **risks** losing his place in the team.*

ritual rituals

NOUN **1** a traditional ceremony
ADJECTIVE **2 Ritual** activities happen as part of a tradition or ritual.

rival rivals

NOUN Someone's **rival** is the person they are competing with.

river rivers

NOUN a large, continuous stretch of fresh water flowing in a channel across land, to a larger **river**, a lake or the sea

→ Have a look at the illustration for **map**

road roads

NOUN a long stretch of hard ground built between two places so that people can travel along it easily

→ Have a look at the illustration for **map**

roam roams, roaming, roamed

VERB If you **roam** around, you wander around without any particular reason.

roar roars, roaring, roared

VERB **1** If something **roars**, it makes a very loud noise.
NOUN **2** a very loud noise

roast roasts, roasting, roasted

VERB **1** When you **roast** meat or other food, you cook it in an oven or over a fire.
ADJECTIVE **2 Roast** meat or vegetables have been roasted.

rob robs, robbing, robbed

VERB If someone **robs** a person or place, they steal money or property from them.

robe robes

NOUN a long, loose piece of clothing that covers the body

robin robins

NOUN a small bird with a red breast

robot robots

NOUN a machine that moves and does things automatically

WORD HISTORY
from Czech *robota* meaning work

rock rocks, rocking, rocked

NOUN **1 Rock** is made up of small pieces of one or more minerals. The Earth's surface is made up of **rock**.
NOUN **2** A **rock** is a piece of rock.
NOUN **3** music with a strong beat, usually involving electric guitars and drums
NOUN **4** a hard sweet, usually brightly coloured and shaped like a long stick

VERB **5** When something **rocks**, or when you **rock** it, it moves regularly backwards and forwards or from side to side.

rocket rockets
NOUN **1** a space vehicle, usually shaped like a long pointed tube
NOUN **2** an explosive missile

rod rods
NOUN a long, thin pole or bar

rode
VERB the past tense of **ride**

rodent rodents
NOUN a small mammal with sharp front teeth that it uses for gnawing. Rabbits and mice are **rodents**.

WORD HISTORY
from Latin *rodere* meaning to gnaw

---

rogue rogues
NOUN a dishonest or mischievous person

role roles
NOUN An actor's **role** is the character that he or she plays in a play or film.

roll rolls, rolling, rolled
VERB **1** If something **rolls**, or if you **roll** it, it moves along a surface, turning over many times.
VERB **2** If you **roll** something, or **roll it up**, you wrap it around itself so that it has a rounded shape.
NOUN **3** A **roll** of paper or cloth is a long piece of it that has been rolled into a tube.
NOUN **4** a small, circular loaf of bread

roller coaster roller coasters
NOUN a pleasure ride at a fun fair, consisting of a small railway that goes up and down steep slopes and around bends

roller skate roller skates
NOUN **Roller skates** are shoes or boots with small wheels underneath.

ROM
NOUN a computer storage device that holds information that cannot be changed by the programmer. **ROM** is an abbreviation for *read only memory*.

Roman Catholic Roman Catholics
NOUN someone who belongs to the branch of the Christian Church that has the Pope in Rome as its leader

romance romances
NOUN **1** a love story
NOUN **2** If two people have a **romance**, they have a romantic relationship.

Romani; also spelt Romany
NOUN the language of the Gypsies

Roman numerals
PLURAL NOUN numbers written in the form of letters and used by ancient Romans. For example, I = 1, V = 5, X = 10, L = 50, C = 100, D = 500, M = 1000.

romantic
ADJECTIVE **1** to do with romance and love
ADJECTIVE **2** A **romantic** person is rather emotional and not very realistic about life and love.

roof roofs
NOUN the covering on top of a building or vehicle

rook rooks
NOUN **1** a large black bird
NOUN **2** a chess piece that can move any number of squares in a straight but not diagonal line. It is also called a castle.

room rooms
NOUN **1** a separate section in a building, divided from other **rooms** by walls
NOUN **2** If there is **room** for something, there is enough space for it.

roost roosts, roosting, roosted
NOUN **1** a place where birds rest or build their nests
VERB **2** When birds **roost**, they settle somewhere for the night.

root roots
NOUN **Roots** are the parts of a plant that usually grow underground. They anchor the plant and carry water from the soil.

→ Have a look at the illustrations for **flower** and **photosynthesis**

root word root words
NOUN a word that you can add a prefix or a suffix to in order to make other words. For example, in the words *unclear*, *clearly* and *cleared*, the **root word** is *clear*.

rope ropes, roping, roped
NOUN **1** a thick, strong cord made by twisting together several thinner cords
VERB **2** If you **rope** one thing to another, you tie them together with rope.

a
b
c
d
e
f
g
h
i
j
k
l
m
n
o
p
q
r
s
t
u
v
w
x
y
z

345

rosary rosaries
> NOUN a string of beads that Catholics use for counting prayers

rose roses
> NOUN **1** a flower that has a pleasant smell and grows on a bush with thorns
> VERB **2** the past tense of **rise**

rosette rosettes
> NOUN a large circular badge of coloured ribbons worn as a prize in a competition or to support a political party

Rosh Hashanah; also spelt **Rosh Hashana**
> NOUN the festival celebrating the Jewish New Year

rosy rosier, rosiest
> ADJECTIVE **1** reddish-pink ● *Our cheeks were* **rosy** *after our walk on the windy beach.*
> ADJECTIVE **2** hopeful and positive ● *He always has a* **rosy** *outlook on life.*

rot rots, rotting, rotted
> VERB When food, wood or other substances **rot**, or when something **rots** them, they decay and fall apart.

> SYNONYM: decompose

rotary
> ADJECTIVE moving or able to move in a circular direction around a fixed point

rotate rotates, rotating, rotated
> VERB When something **rotates**, it turns with a circular movement, like a wheel.

rotation rotations
> NOUN **1** a complete circular movement ● *the* **rotation** *of a wheel* ● *the* **rotation** *of the Earth*
> NOUN **2** A shape that has **rotation** symmetry looks exactly the same when it is turned in a circular movement.
> PHRASE **3** If you do things **in rotation**, you do them one after the other, and when you finish you start all over again.

rotor rotors
> NOUN **1** the part of a machine that turns
> NOUN **2** The **rotors**, or **rotor** blades, of a helicopter are the four long, flat pieces of metal on top of it, that rotate and lift it off the ground.

rotten
> ADJECTIVE **1** Something that is **rotten** has decayed.
> ADJECTIVE **2** (*informal*) bad, unpleasant or unfair ● *I think it's a* **rotten** *idea.*

rough rougher, roughest
> ADJECTIVE **1** uneven and not smooth ● *His hands were hard and* **rough**.

> ANTONYM: smooth

> ADJECTIVE **2** using too much force ● *Don't be so* **rough** *with that toy or you'll break it.*

> ANTONYM: gentle

> ADJECTIVE **3** approximate ● *At a* **rough** *guess, it is five o'clock.*

> ANTONYMS: exact, precise

roughly
> ADVERB **1** almost or approximately ● *There are* **roughly** *100 marbles in that box.*
> ADVERB **2** If you treat someone or something **roughly**, you treat them clumsily or violently.

round rounder, roundest; rounds
> ADJECTIVE **1** Something **round** is shaped like a ball or a circle.
> PREPOSITION **2** If something is **round** something else, it surrounds it.
> PREPOSITION **3** If you go **round** something, you go to the other side of it. ● *Suddenly a car came* **round** *the corner.*
> ADVERB **4** If something goes **round**, it moves in a circle. ● *The sails of the windmill went* **round**.
> ADVERB **5** If you turn or look **round**, you turn or look in a different direction.
> ADVERB **6** If you move things **round**, you move them so that they are in different places.
> ADVERB **7** If you go **round** to someone's house, you visit them.
> NOUN **8** one of a series of events, especially in a competition
> NOUN **9** a series of calls or deliveries ● *Our house is the last one on the milkman's* **round**.
> NOUN **10** a whole slice of bread, or a sandwich made of two slices
> NOUN **11** a type of song in which people sing the same words but start at different times

roundabout roundabouts
> NOUN **1** a meeting point of several roads with a circle in the centre that vehicles have to travel around
> NOUN **2** a circular platform that goes round and that children can ride on in a playground
> NOUN **3** a large, circular platform with horses or cars on it, for children to ride on as it goes round and round

> SYNONYM: merry-go-round

rounded
> ADJECTIVE curved in shape

rounders
NOUN a team game in which players hit a ball with a bat and run round a circuit

rouse rouses, rousing, roused
VERB **1** If you **rouse** someone, you wake them up.
VERB **2** If you **rouse** yourself, you make yourself get up and do something.
ADJECTIVE **3** Something that is **rousing**, such as a game, speech or song, makes you feel excited and emotional.

rousing
ADJECTIVE Something that is **rousing**, such as a game, speech or song, makes you feel excited and emotional.

route routes
NOUN a way from one place to another • *the most direct **route** to the town centre*

routine routines
ADJECTIVE **1** **Routine** activities are done regularly.
NOUN **2** the usual way or order in which you do things

row rows, rowing, rowed
VERB **1** When you **row** a boat, you use oars to make it move through the water.
NOUN **2** several objects or people in a line
NOUN **3** an argument
NOUN **4** a lot of noise

PRONUNCIATION TIP
Meanings 1 and 2 rhyme with "snow".
Meanings 3 and 4 rhyme with "cow".

---

rowdily
ADVERB in a noisy and rough way

rowdy rowdier, rowdiest
ADJECTIVE noisy and rough

royal
ADJECTIVE belonging to or involving a queen, a king, or a member of their family

RSVP
RSVP written at the end of a letter or an invitation means please reply.

WORD HISTORY
an abbreviation for the French expression *Répondez s'il vous plaît* meaning please reply

---

rub rubs, rubbing, rubbed
VERB If you **rub** something, you move your hand, or a cloth, very firmly backwards and forwards over it.

rubber rubbers
NOUN **1** a strong, elastic substance used for making tyres, boots and other products
NOUN **2** a small piece of rubber or plastic that you use to remove mistakes when writing or drawing with a pencil

rubbish
NOUN **1** unwanted things or waste material

SYNONYMS: garbage, refuse, trash

NOUN **2** something foolish
NOUN **3** something of very poor quality

rubble
NOUN bits of old brick and stone

ruby rubies
NOUN a type of red jewel

rucksack rucksacks
NOUN a bag with shoulder straps for carrying things on your back

rudder rudders
NOUN a piece of wood or metal at the back of a boat or plane that is moved to make the boat or plane turn

→ Have a look at the illustrations for **aeroplane** and **ship**

rude ruder, rudest
ADJECTIVE **1** not polite
ADJECTIVE **2** embarrassing or offensive because of reference to body parts or bodily functions

ruff ruffs
NOUN a stiff circular collar with many pleats in it, popular in the 16th century.

ruffle ruffles, ruffling, ruffled
VERB **1** If you **ruffle** someone's hair, you move your hand quickly backwards and forwards over their head.
VERB **2** If something **ruffles** you, it makes you annoyed or upset.
NOUN **3** **Ruffles** are small folds made in a piece of material for decoration.

rug rugs
NOUN **1** a small thick carpet
NOUN **2** a warm covering for your knees or for sitting on outdoors

rugby
NOUN a game played by two teams, who try to kick or throw an oval ball past a line at their opponents' end of the pitch

---

WORD HISTORY
named after *Rugby* School where it was first played

---

a
b
c
d
e
f
g
h
i
j
k
l
m
n
o
p
q
r
s
t
u
v
w
x
y
z

A
B
C
D
E
F
G
H
I
J
K
L
M
N
O
P
Q
R
S
T
U
V
W
X
Y
Z

rugged
ADJECTIVE **1** Somewhere **rugged** is rocky, wild and unsheltered.
ADJECTIVE **2** Someone **rugged** is strong and tough.

ruin ruins, ruining, ruined
VERB **1** If you **ruin** something, you destroy or spoil it completely.
NOUN **2** the part that is left after something has been severely damaged

rule rules, ruling, ruled
NOUN **1 Rules** are instructions that tell you what you must do.
VERB **2** When someone **rules** a country or a group of people, they govern it and are in charge of its affairs.

ruler rulers
NOUN **1** a person who rules a country
NOUN **2** a long, flat object with straight edges, marked with a scale, used for measuring things or drawing straight lines

rum rums
NOUN a strong alcoholic drink made from sugar cane juice

rumble rumbles, rumbling, rumbles
VERB **1** If something **rumbles**, it makes a continuous low sound. • *My stomach is rumbling because I am hungry.*
NOUN **2** a continuous deep sound • *There was a rumble of thunder.*

rumour rumours
NOUN a piece of information or a story that people are talking about, but which may not be true

run runs, running, ran
VERB **1** When you **run**, you move quickly, with both feet leaving the ground at each stride.
VERB **2** If you **run** water, you turn on the tap to let the water flow out.
VERB **3** If your nose is **running**, a lot of liquid is coming out of it.
VERB **4** If you **run** an activity or a place such as a school or shop, you are in charge of it.
VERB **5** If you **run away** from a place, you leave it suddenly and secretly.

run out
VERB If you **run out** of something, you have no more left.

rung rungs
NOUN one of the bars that form the steps of a ladder

runner runners
NOUN **1** a person who runs as a sport, especially in competitions
NOUN **2** a person who takes messages or runs errands
NOUN **3** A **runner** on a plant such as a strawberry is a long shoot from which a new plant develops.

runny runnier, runniest
ADJECTIVE flowing or moving like liquid

runway runways
NOUN a long strip of ground used by aeroplanes for taking off and landing

rural
ADJECTIVE to do with the countryside

rush rushes, rushing, rushed
VERB **1** If you **rush** somewhere, or if you are **rushed** there, you go there quickly.
VERB **2** If you **rush** something, or if you are **rushed** into something, you do it too quickly.
NOUN **3** a type of plant that grows in or beside fresh water, such as rivers, ponds and lakes

rust rusts, rusting, rusted
NOUN **1** a reddish-brown substance that forms on metal when it is exposed to water and the oxygen in the air
VERB **2** When metal **rusts**, it corrodes and a reddish-brown substance is formed. **Rusting** occurs when iron or steel is exposed to water and the oxygen in the air.

rustle rustles, rustling, rustled
VERB If something **rustles**, it makes a soft, crisp sound as it moves, like the sound of dry leaves moving.

rusty rustier, rustiest
ADJECTIVE **1** covered with rust • *The old bicycle was rusty.*
ADJECTIVE **2** not as good as it once was because of lack of practice • *Dad's maths is a bit rusty.*

rut ruts
NOUN a deep, narrow groove in the ground made by the wheels of a vehicle

ruthless
ADJECTIVE very harsh or cruel, and without any pity

rye
NOUN a cereal crop that produces light-brown grain used to make flour

Ss

Sabbath Sabbaths

NOUN the day of the week that some religious groups, such as Jews and Christians, use for rest and prayer

WORD HISTORY
from Hebrew *shabbath* meaning to rest

sabotage sabotages, sabotaging, sabotaged

NOUN **1** the deliberate damaging of machinery and equipment such as railway lines
VERB **2** If something is **sabotaged**, it is deliberately damaged.

saboteur saboteurs

NOUN someone who deliberately damages machinery and equipment such as railway lines

sabre sabres

NOUN **1** a heavy curved sword
NOUN **2** a light sword used in fencing

sachet sachets

NOUN a small packet containing something like sugar or shampoo

sack sacks

NOUN **1** a large bag made of rough material, for carrying such things as potatoes and grain • a **sack** of potatoes
PHRASE **2** (*informal*) If someone **gets the sack**, they are dismissed from their job by their employer.

sacred

ADJECTIVE holy, or connected with religion or religious ceremonies

sacrifice sacrifices, sacrificing, sacrificed

VERB If you **sacrifice** something valuable or important, you give it up.

sad sadder, saddest

ADJECTIVE If you are **sad**, you feel unhappy.

ANTONYM: happy

sadden saddens, saddening, saddened

VERB If something **saddens** you, it makes you feel sad.

saddening

ADJECTIVE making you feel sad

saddle saddles, saddling, saddled

NOUN **1** a leather seat strapped to an animal's back, for the rider to sit on
NOUN **2** the seat on a bicycle
VERB **3** If you **saddle** a horse, you put a saddle on it.

safari safaris

NOUN an expedition for hunting or observing wild animals ·

WORD HISTORY
from Swahili *safari* meaning journey

safari park safari parks

NOUN a large park where wild animals such as lions, giraffes and elephants are free to roam

safe safer, safest; safes

ADJECTIVE **1** If you are **safe**, you are not in any danger. • *I feel very **safe** when I am inside the school.*
ADJECTIVE **2** Something that is **safe** does not cause harm or danger. • *We must try to make our roads **safer**.*
NOUN **3** a strong metal box with special locks, in which you can keep valuable things

safeguard safeguards, safeguarding, safeguarded

VERB **1** If you **safeguard** something, you protect it.
NOUN **2** a law or a rule to help protect people or things from harm

safety

NOUN protection, being safe • *child **safety*** • *Everyone believes that we should have **safety** in our homes.*

saga sagas

NOUN a very long story, usually telling of many different adventures

said

VERB the past tense and past participle of **say**

A
B
C
D
E
F
G
H
I
J
K
L
M
N
O
P
Q
R
S
T
U
V
W
X
Y
Z

sail sails, sailing, sailed
VERB **1** When a ship **sails**, it moves across water.
VERB **2** If you **sail** somewhere, you go there by ship.
NOUN **3** one of the large pieces of material attached to a ship's mast. The wind blows against the **sail** and moves the ship.
NOUN **4** The arm of a windmill is called a **sail**.

sailor sailors
NOUN **1** a member of a ship's crew
NOUN **2** someone who sails

saint saints
NOUN a person who is given a special honour by a Christian Church, after they have died, because they lived a very holy life

sake sakes
PHRASE If you do something for someone's **sake**, you do it to help or please them.

salad salads
NOUN a mixture of foods eaten cold or warm, and often raw

salami
NOUN a kind of spicy sausage

WORD HISTORY
Italian plural of *salame*, from *salare* meaning to salt

salary salaries
NOUN a payment made each month to an employee

sale sales
NOUN **1** The **sale** of goods is the selling of them.
NOUN **2** an occasion when a shop sells things at reduced prices

saliva
NOUN the watery liquid in your mouth that softens food, which helps you chew and digest it

salmon
NOUN a large, edible, silver-coloured fish with pink flesh

LANGUAGE TIP
The plural of *salmon* is *salmon*.

salt
NOUN a white substance used to flavour and preserve food

salute salutes, saluting, saluted
NOUN **1** a formal sign of respect. Soldiers give a **salute** by raising their right hand to their forehead.
VERB **2** If you **salute** someone, you give them a salute.

salvage salvages, salvaging, salvaged
VERB If you **salvage** things, you save them from, for example, a wrecked ship or a destroyed building.

same
ADJECTIVE **1** If two things are the **same**, they are like one another.
ADJECTIVE **2** just one thing and not two different ones ● *They were born in the **same** town.*

sample samples, sampling, sampled
NOUN **1** a small amount of something that you can try or test, for example for quality or to find out more about it
VERB **2** If you **sample** something, you try it.
● *I **sampled** his cooking.*

sanctuary sanctuaries
NOUN **1** a place where you are safe from harm or danger
NOUN **2** a place where wildlife is protected

sand sands
NOUN a substance consisting of tiny pieces of stone. Beaches are made of **sand**.

sandal sandals
NOUN **Sandals** are light shoes with straps, worn in warm weather.

sandwich sandwiches
NOUN two slices of bread with a filling between them

WORD HISTORY
named after the 4th Earl of Sandwich in the 18th century, who used to ask for beef served between two slices of bread when playing card games, so that he wouldn't get grease from his hands on the cards

sandy sandier, sandiest
ADJECTIVE **1** A **sandy** area is covered with sand. ● *We walked until we got to a long* **sandy** *beach.*
ADJECTIVE **2 Sandy** hair is a light orange-brown colour.

sane saner, sanest
ADJECTIVE If someone is **sane**, they have a healthy mind.

sang
VERB the past tense of **sing**

sanity
NOUN A person's **sanity** is the health of their mind.

sank
VERB the past tense of **sink**

sap saps, sapping, sapped
NOUN **1** the juice found in the stems of plants
VERB **2** If something such as an illness **saps** your energy or your strength, it gradually weakens you.

sapling saplings
NOUN a young tree

sapphire sapphires
NOUN a blue precious stone

sarcastic
ADJECTIVE If someone is **sarcastic**, they say the opposite of what they really mean in order to mock or insult someone.

sardine sardines
NOUN a small edible sea fish

sari saris
NOUN a piece of clothing consisting of a long piece of material folded around the body, worn especially by Indian women

WORD HISTORY
a Hindi word

sash sashes
NOUN a long piece of cloth worn round the waist or over one shoulder

sat
VERB the past tense and past participle of **sit**

satchel satchels
NOUN a leather or cloth bag with a long strap, especially used for carrying books to and from school

satellite satellites
NOUN **1** a spacecraft sent into space to orbit the Earth, to collect information, or as part of a communications system
NOUN **2** a natural object in space that moves round another, larger object, such as a planet or star

satellite dish satellite dishes
NOUN a dish-shaped aerial that receives television signals sent by satellite

satellite television
NOUN television programmes received by signals from artificial satellites

satin satins
NOUN a kind of smooth, shiny fabric often made from silk

satisfactorily
ADVERB in an acceptable or adequate way

satisfactory
ADJECTIVE acceptable or adequate

satisfy satisfies, satisfying, satisfied
VERB If you **satisfy** someone, you do something or give them something to make them pleased or contented.

saturated
ADJECTIVE soaking wet

Saturday Saturdays
NOUN the seventh day of the week, coming between Friday and Sunday

sauce sauces
NOUN a liquid eaten with food to add flavour ● *It's pasta with tomato* **sauce** *for dinner.*

saucepan saucepans
NOUN a deep metal pan with a handle and a lid used for cooking

a
b
c
d
e
f
g
h
i
j
k
l
m
n
o
p
q
r
s
t
u
v
w
x
y
z

351

saucer saucers
NOUN a small curved plate for a cup to stand on

sauna saunas
NOUN If you have a **sauna**, you go into a very hot room in order to sweat, then have a cold bath or shower.

PRONUNCIATION TIP
This word is pronounced **saw**-nah.

WORD HISTORY
a Finnish word

saunter saunters, sauntering, sauntered
VERB If you **saunter** somewhere, you walk there slowly and casually.

sausage sausages
NOUN a mixture of minced meat and herbs formed into a tubular shape and served cooked

savage savages, savaging, savaged
ADJECTIVE 1 cruel and violent

SYNONYMS: brutal, vicious

VERB 2 If an animal **savages** you, it attacks you and bites you.

savannah savannahs
NOUN a grassy plain with few trees in a hot country

save saves, saving, saved
VERB 1 If you **save** someone, you rescue them or help to keep them safe.
VERB 2 If you **save** something, you keep it so that you can use it later.
VERB 3 If you **save** time, money or effort, you stop it from being wasted.

savings
PLURAL NOUN Your **savings** are money you have saved.

saviour saviours
NOUN 1 a person who saves others from danger or loss
PROPER NOUN 2 In Christianity, the **Saviour** is Jesus Christ.

savoury
ADJECTIVE salty or spicy • *Salt and vinegar crisps are my favourite* **savoury** *snack.*

saw saws, sawing, sawed, sawn
NOUN 1 a tool that has a blade with sharp teeth along one edge for cutting wood

VERB 2 If you **saw** something, you cut it with a saw.
VERB 3 the past tense of **see**

sawdust
NOUN the fine powder produced when you saw wood

saxophone saxophones
NOUN a curved metal wind instrument often played in jazz bands

WORD HISTORY
named after Adolphe *Sax* (1814–1894), who invented the instrument

say says, saying, said
VERB If you **say** something, you speak words.

saying sayings
NOUN a well-known sentence or phrase that tells you something about life

scab scabs
NOUN a hard, dry covering that forms over a wound while it is healing

scaffolding
NOUN a framework of poles and boards that is used by workmen to stand on while they are working on the outside of a building

scald scalds, scalding, scalded
VERB 1 If you **scald** yourself, you burn yourself with very hot liquid or steam.
NOUN 2 a burn caused by very hot liquid or steam

scale scales
NOUN 1 the size or extent of something • *The* **scale** *of the building was enormous.*
NOUN 2 a set of marks or numbers used for measuring something
NOUN 3 The **scale** of something like a map, a plan or a model shows the relationship between the measurements represented and those in the real world. For example, a **scale** of 1:10 tells you that one centimetre on a model represents 10 centimetres in real life.
→ Have a look at the illustration for **map**
NOUN 4 one of the small, hard pieces of skin covering the body of a fish or a reptile
→ Have a look at the illustration for **fish**
NOUN 5 a series of musical notes going upwards or downwards in a particular order
PLURAL NOUN 6 **Scales** are a piece of equipment used for weighing things or people.

scalene

ADJECTIVE A **scalene** triangle has sides of different lengths.

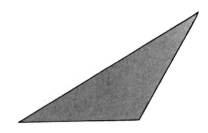

scalp **scalps**

NOUN the skin under the hair on your head

scamper **scampers, scampering, scampered**

VERB If you **scamper**, you run quickly and lightly.

scampi

PLURAL NOUN large prawns, often eaten fried in breadcrumbs

scan **scans, scanning, scanned**

VERB **1** If you **scan** something, you look at every part of it carefully.
VERB **2** If you **scan** a piece of writing, you look at it quickly but not in detail.
VERB **3** If a machine **scans** something, it examines it with a beam of light or X-rays.
NOUN **4** an examination of part of the body with X-ray or laser equipment

scandal **scandals**

NOUN **1** a situation or event that people think is shocking and immoral
NOUN **2** gossip about bad things that can ruin a person's reputation

scanner **scanners**

NOUN a machine that is used to examine, identify or record things by using a beam of light or an X-ray

scapegoat **scapegoats**

NOUN If someone is made a **scapegoat**, they are blamed for something, although it may not be their fault.

scar **scars, scarring, scarred**

NOUN **1** a mark left on your skin after a wound has healed • *She had a scar over her eye.*
VERB **2** If an injury **scars** you, it leaves a mark on your skin for ever.

scarce **scarcer, scarcest**

ADJECTIVE If something is **scarce**, there is not very much of it.

scare **scares, scaring, scared**

VERB **1** If something **scares** you, it frightens you.
NOUN **2** something that gives you a fright

scarecrow **scarecrows**

NOUN an object shaped like a person and put in a field to scare birds away from the crops

scarf **scarfs** or **scarves**

NOUN a piece of cloth worn round your neck or head to keep you warm

scarlet

NOUN **1** a bright red colour
ADJECTIVE **2** having a bright red colour

scary **scarier, scariest**

ADJECTIVE *(informal)* frightening • *The film was so scary I hid behind the sofa.*

scatter **scatters, scattering, scattered**

VERB **1** When you **scatter** things, you throw or drop them so they spread over a large area.
VERB **2** If a group of people or animals **scatter**, they suddenly move off in different directions.

scavenge **scavenges, scavenging, scavenged**

VERB If a human or other animal **scavenges** for things, they search for them among waste and rubbish.

scavenger **scavengers**

NOUN a person or animal that searches for things among waste and rubbish

scenario **scenarios**

NOUN **1** the way in which a situation might develop in the future • *That is the worst possible scenario!*
NOUN **2** a piece of writing that gives an outline of the story in a film

scene **scenes**

NOUN part of a play or film in which a series of events happen in one place

scenery

NOUN **1** In the countryside, you can refer to everything you see as the **scenery**.
NOUN **2** In a theatre, the **scenery** is the painted cloth on the stage that makes it seem like a particular place.

a
b
c
d
e
f
g
h
i
j
k
l
m
n
o
p
q
r
s
t
u
v
w
x
y
z

A
B
C
D
E
F
G
H
I
J
K
L
M
N
O
P
Q
R
S
T
U
V
W
X
Y
Z

scent scents
NOUN a smell, especially a pleasant one

sceptic sceptics
NOUN someone who does not believe things easily

PRONUNCIATION TIP
This word is pronounced **skep**-tik.

schedule schedules
NOUN a list of events or things you have to do, and the times at which each thing should be done or will happen

scheme schemes, scheming, schemed
NOUN **1** a plan or arrangement
VERB **2** When people **scheme**, they make secret plans.

scholar scholars
NOUN **1** a person who studies an academic subject and knows a lot about it
NOUN **2** In South African English, a **scholar** is a school pupil.

scholarship scholarships
NOUN If you win a **scholarship** to a school or university, your studies are paid for by the school or university, or by some other organisation.

school schools
NOUN a place where children are educated

science sciences
NOUN the study of living things, materials and physical processes such as forces, electricity, sound and light

science fiction
NOUN stories about travelling through space, and imaginary events happening in the future or in other worlds

scientist scientists
NOUN someone who studies science or is an expert in science

scissors
PLURAL NOUN a cutting tool with two sharp blades

scold scolds, scolding, scolded
VERB If you **scold** someone, you tell them off.

scone scones
NOUN a small cake made from flour and fat, and usually eaten with cream and jam

scoop scoops, scooping, scooped
VERB **1** If you **scoop** something up, you pick it up using a spoon or the palm of your hand.
NOUN **2** an object like a large spoon that is used for picking up food such as ice cream

scooter scooters
NOUN **1** a small, light motorcycle
NOUN **2** a simple cycle that a child rides, with two wheels and a narrow platform for standing on while pushing the ground with one foot

scope
NOUN **1** the opportunity or freedom to do something
NOUN **2** the extent of something • *That subject is beyond the* **scope** *of this lesson.*

scorch scorches, scorching, scorched
VERB If you **scorch** something, you burn it slightly.

score scores, scoring, scored
VERB **1** If you **score** in a game, you get a goal, a run or a point.
NOUN **2** the number of goals, runs or points obtained by the two opponents in a game
NOUN **3** the written version of a piece of music which shows the parts for each musician

scornful
ADJECTIVE If you are **scornful** of something or someone, you think very little of them and show very little respect for them.

scorpion scorpions
NOUN an animal that looks like a small lobster. It has a long tail with a poisonous sting on the end.

scour scours, scouring, scoured
VERB **1** If you **scour** a place, you look all over it in order to find something.
VERB **2** If you **scour** something like a pan, you clean it by rubbing it hard with something rough.

scout scouts, scouting, scouted
NOUN **1** A **Scout** is a boy who is a member of the **Scout** Association, an organisation for boys that aims to develop character and responsibility.
NOUN **2** someone who is sent on ahead to get information about something
VERB **3** If you **scout** around for something, you look around for it.

scowl scowls, scowling, scowled
VERB **1** If you **scowl**, you frown because you are angry.
NOUN **2** an angry expression

scrabble scrabbles, scrabbling, scrabbled
VERB If you **scrabble** at something, you scrape at it with your hands.

scramble scrambles, scrambling, scrambled
VERB **1** If you **scramble** over something, you climb over it using your hands to help you.
VERB **2** When you **scramble** eggs, you mix them up and cook them in a pan.
NOUN **3** a motorcycle race over rough ground

scrap scraps, scrapping, scrapped
NOUN **1** a very small piece of something
NOUN **2** unwanted or waste material
NOUN **3** (*informal*) If you get into a **scrap**, you get into a fight.
VERB **4** If you **scrap** something, you get rid of it.

scrapbook scrapbooks
NOUN a book with blank pages that you can fill with photographs or cuttings that interest you

scrape scrapes, scraping, scraped
VERB **1** If you **scrape** something off a surface, you remove it by pulling a rough or sharp object over it.
VERB **2** If you **scrape** past something, you pass very close to it.

scratch scratches, scratching, scratched
VERB **1** If you **scratch** something, you make a small cut or mark on it with something sharp.
VERB **2** If you **scratch**, you rub your skin with your nails because it is itching.
NOUN **3** a small cut or mark on the surface of something

scrawl scrawls, scrawling, scrawled
VERB **1** If you **scrawl** something, you write it in a careless and untidy way.
NOUN **2** careless and untidy writing

scream screams, screaming, screamed
VERB **1** If you **scream**, you shout or cry in a loud, high-pitched voice.
NOUN **2** a loud, high-pitched cry

screech screeches, screeching, screeched
VERB **1** If a person, animal or machine **screeches**, they make an unpleasant, high-pitched noise.
NOUN **2** an unpleasant high-pitched noise

screen screens, screening, screened
NOUN **1** a vertical surface on which a picture can be shown, such as a phone, computer or television **screen**
→ Have a look at the illustration for **computer**
NOUN **2** a panel used to separate different parts of a room, or to protect or hide something
VERB **3** If a doctor **screens** you for a disease, they test to see if you have it.

screenplay screenplays
NOUN the script of a film

screw screws, screwing, screwed
NOUN **1** a small, sharp piece of metal with a spiral groove cut into it, used for fixing things together or for fixing something to a wall using a twisting action
VERB **2** If you **screw** something onto something else, you fix it there by twisting it round and round, or by using a screw. • *He **screwed** the top on the ink bottle.*
screw up
VERB If you **screw up** paper or cloth, you twist it or squeeze it into a tight ball.

screwdriver screwdrivers
NOUN a tool for putting in or taking out screws

scribble scribbles, scribbling, scribbled
VERB **1** If you **scribble** something, you write it quickly and untidily.
VERB **2** To **scribble** also means to make meaningless marks. • *When Caroline was three she **scribbled** on a wall.*

script scripts
NOUN the written version of a play or film

scripture scriptures
NOUN sacred writings, especially the Bible

scroll scrolls, scrolling, scrolled
NOUN **1** a long roll of paper or parchment with writing on it
VERB **2** When you **scroll** text on a computer screen, you move it up or down to see the text that is not visible on the screen.

scrounge scrounges, scrounging, scrounged
VERB (*informal*) If you **scrounge** something, you get it by asking for it rather than by earning or buying it.

scrub scrubs, scrubbing, scrubbed
VERB **1** If you **scrub** something, you clean it by rubbing it very hard, especially with a brush and water.
NOUN **2** ground covered with bushes and small trees

scruffy scruffier, scruffiest
ADJECTIVE untidy

scrum scrums
NOUN When rugby players form a **scrum**, they form a group and push against each other with their heads down in an attempt to get the ball.

scuba diving
NOUN the sport of swimming underwater with special breathing equipment

WORD HISTORY
an abbreviation for *self-contained underwater breathing apparatus*

scuffle scuffles, scuffling, scuffled
VERB **1** When people **scuffle**, they have a short, rough fight.
NOUN **2** a short, rough fight

sculptor sculptors
NOUN someone who makes sculptures

sculpture sculptures
NOUN a work of art made by shaping or carving stone, clay or wood

scum
NOUN a layer of dirty froth on the surface of a liquid

scurry scurries, scurrying, scurried
VERB If you **scurry**, you run with quick, short steps.

scuttle scuttles, scuttling, scuttled
VERB **1** If a person or an animal **scuttles**, they run with short, quick steps.
VERB **2** To **scuttle** a ship means to sink it deliberately by making holes in the bottom.
NOUN **3** a container for coal

scythe scythes
NOUN a tool with a long handle and a curved blade used for cutting grass or grain

sea seas
NOUN one of the areas of salty water that cover much of the Earth's surface • *They swam in the warm **sea**.*

seafood
PLURAL NOUN fish or shellfish from the sea eaten as food

seagull seagulls
NOUN a common white, grey and black bird that lives near the sea

seahorse seahorses
NOUN a small fish that swims upright, with a head that looks rather like a horse's head

seal seals, sealing, sealed
NOUN **1** a fish-eating mammal with flippers, that lives partly on land and partly in the sea
NOUN **2** something fixed over the opening of a container that prevents anything getting in or out, and which must be broken before the container can be opened
VERB **3** If you **seal** an envelope, you stick down the flap.

seam seams
NOUN **1** a line of stitches joining two pieces of cloth
NOUN **2** a long, narrow layer of coal beneath the ground

search searches, searching, searched
VERB **1** If you **search** for something, you look for it very thoroughly. • *I spent an hour searching for my glasses.*
VERB **2** If a person is **searched**, their body and clothing are examined to see if they are hiding anything.
NOUN **3** an attempt to find something • *I found my purse after a long **search**.*

search engine search engines
NOUN a service on the internet which lets you search for information

searchlight searchlights
NOUN a light with a powerful beam that can be turned in different directions

seashore
NOUN the land along the edge of the sea

seasick
ADJECTIVE feeling sick because of the movement of a boat

seaside
NOUN a place by the sea, especially where people go on holiday

season seasons, seasoning, seasoned
NOUN **1** one of the periods into which a year is divided and which have their own typical weather conditions. The **seasons** are spring, summer, autumn and winter.
VERB **2** If you **season** food, you add salt, pepper, herbs or spices to it.

seasoning seasonings
NOUN something with a strong taste, like salt, pepper or spices, used to add flavour to food

seat seats
NOUN something you can sit on

seat belt seat belts
NOUN a strap that you put around your body for safety when you are travelling in a car, coach or aircraft

seaweed
NOUN plants that grow in the sea

secluded
ADJECTIVE quiet and hidden from view ● *We found a lovely **secluded** beach.*

second seconds
ADJECTIVE **1** The **second** item in a series is the one that you count as number two. It can be written as 2ⁿᵈ.
NOUN **2** one of the sixty parts that a minute is divided into

secondary
ADJECTIVE **1** Something **secondary** is less important than something else.
ADJECTIVE **2 Secondary** education is education for pupils between the ages of 11 and 18.

secondary school secondary schools
NOUN a school for pupils aged between 11 and 18

second-hand
ADJECTIVE Something that is **second-hand** has already been owned by someone else.

second person
NOUN In grammar, you use the **second person** *you* when you speak or write to someone directly, for example, *you said, you are.*

secret secrets
ADJECTIVE **1** Something that is **secret** is known to only a small number of people and hidden from everyone else. ● *a **secret** meeting*
NOUN **2** something known to only a small number of people and hidden from everyone else

secretary secretaries
NOUN a person employed by an organisation to keep records, write letters and do office work

secretive
ADJECTIVE **Secretive** people tend to hide their feelings and intentions, and like to keep things secret.

sect sects
NOUN a group of people who have special or unusual religious beliefs

section sections
NOUN one of the parts that something is divided into

secure secures, securing, secured
VERB **1** If you **secure** something, you make it safe or fix it firmly.
ADJECTIVE **2** If something is **secure**, it is safe from harm.

security
NOUN all the things you do to make sure that you and your property are safe

sedimentary
ADJECTIVE formed from fragments of many layers of shell or rock

see sees, seeing, saw, seen
VERB **1** If you **see** something, you look at it or notice it with your eyes.
VERB **2** If you **see** something, you understand it or realise what it means. ● *I **see** what you mean.*
VERB **3** If you **see** that something happens, you make sure that it is done.

seed seeds
NOUN the part of a plant that can grow into a new plant of the same type
→ Have a look at the illustration for **plant**

seek seeks, seeking, sought
VERB (*formal*) If you **seek** something, you try to find it.

seem seems, seeming, seemed
VERB If something **seems** to be the case, it appears to be the case, or you think it is the case.

seen
VERB the past participle of **see**

seep seeps, seeping, seeped
VERB If a liquid or gas **seeps**, it flows very slowly.

a b c d e f g h i j k l m n o p q r s t u v w x y z

357

A
B
C
D
E
F
G
H
I
J
K
L
M
N
O
P
Q
R
S
T
U
V
W
X
Y
Z

seesaw seesaws
NOUN a long plank supported in the middle, so that one person can sit on either end and each can move up and down

seethe seethes, seething, seethed
VERB **1** When a liquid **seethes**, it boils or bubbles.
ADJECTIVE **2** If you are **seething**, you are very angry.

segment segments
NOUN **1** one part of something
NOUN **2** The **segments** of an orange or grapefruit are the sections you can divide it into.

segregate segregates, segregating, segregated
VERB To **segregate** two groups of people means to keep them apart from each other.

seize seizes, seizing, seized
VERB If you **seize** something, you grab it firmly.

seldom
ADVERB not very often ● They **seldom** watch television.

select selects, selecting, selected
VERB If you **select** something, you choose it.

self selves
NOUN your own personality or nature that makes you different from anyone else

self-conscious
ADJECTIVE Someone who is **self-conscious** is easily embarrassed, and worried about what other people think of them. ● She was **self-conscious** when the teacher asked her to read her poem.

self-defence
NOUN the use of special physical techniques to protect yourself when someone attacks you

selfie selfies
NOUN (informal) a photograph taken by pointing a camera at yourself

selfish
ADJECTIVE caring only about yourself, and not about other people

self-service
ADJECTIVE A **self-service** shop or restaurant is one where you serve yourself.

sell sells, selling, sold
VERB If you **sell** something, you let someone have it in return for money.

Sellotape
NOUN (trademark) a transparent sticky tape

semaphore
NOUN a system of signalling by holding flags out with your arms in different positions to show letters of the alphabet

semi-
PREFIX You add **semi-** to the beginning of a word to mean half or partly. For example, a **semi**circle is half of a circle.

semicircle semicircles
NOUN a half of a circle, or something with this shape

semicircular
ADJECTIVE having the shape of a half circle

semicolon semicolons
NOUN the punctuation mark (;) is used to separate different parts of a sentence or to show a pause

semidetached
ADJECTIVE A **semidetached** house is joined to another house on one side.

semifinal semifinals
NOUN one of the two matches or races in a competition that are held to decide who will compete in the final

send sends, sending, sent
VERB **1** When you **send** something to someone, you arrange for it to be delivered to them.
VERB **2** If a person **sends** someone somewhere, they tell them to go there.

senile
ADJECTIVE If old people become **senile**, they become confused and cannot look after themselves.

senior seniors

ADJECTIVE **1** A **senior** official or employee has one of the highest and most important jobs in an organisation.

NOUN **2** If you are someone's **senior**, you are older than they are, or in a more important position.

senior citizen senior citizens

NOUN an elderly person, especially one receiving a pension

sensation sensations

NOUN **1** a feeling that you have

NOUN **2** If something causes a **sensation**, it causes great interest and excitement.

sensational

ADJECTIVE **1** (*informal*) extremely good
• *The concert was **sensational**.*

ADJECTIVE **2** causing great excitement or interest

sense senses

NOUN **1** the physical abilities of sight, hearing, smell, touch and taste • *I have a good **sense** of smell.*

NOUN **2** a feeling • *a **sense** of guilt*

NOUN **3** the ability to think and behave sensibly

PHRASE **4** If something **makes sense**, you can understand it or it seems sensible.

senseless

ADJECTIVE **1** Something **senseless** has no reason to it. • *The violence of the hooligans was **senseless**.*

ADJECTIVE **2** If someone is **senseless**, they are unconscious.

sensible

ADJECTIVE showing good sense and judgment

sensitive

ADJECTIVE **1** If you are **sensitive**, you understand other people's feelings.

SYNONYM: perceptive

ADJECTIVE **2** If you are **sensitive** about something, you are easily worried or upset about it.

SYNONYM: touchy

ADJECTIVE **3** easily affected or harmed by something • *My skin is **sensitive** to the sun.*

sent

VERB the past tense and past participle of **send**

sentence sentences, sentencing, sentenced

NOUN **1** a group of words that make a statement, question or command. When written down, a **sentence** begins with a capital letter and ends with a full stop.

NOUN **2** In a law court, a **sentence** is a punishment given to someone who has been found guilty.

VERB **3** When a guilty person is **sentenced**, they are told officially what their punishment will be.

sentimental

ADJECTIVE **1** having an exaggerated feeling of tenderness or sadness

ADJECTIVE **2** having something to do with a person's feelings

sentry sentries

NOUN a soldier who keeps watch and guards a camp or building

separate separates, separating, separated

ADJECTIVE **1** If something is **separate** from something else, the two things are not connected.

VERB **2** If you **separate** people or things, you cause them to be apart from each other.

VERB **3** If people or things **separate**, they move away from each other.

LANGUAGE TIP

There are two *a*s in *separate*.

September

NOUN the ninth month of the year. **September** has 30 days.

WORD HISTORY

from the Latin word *septem* meaning seven, because it was the seventh month of the Roman calendar

---

septic

ADJECTIVE If a wound becomes **septic**, it becomes infected by harmful bacteria.

sequel sequels

NOUN A **sequel** to a book or film is another book or film that continues the story.

sequence sequences

NOUN **1** a number of events coming one after the other

NOUN **2** the order in which things are arranged or happen • *Put the pictures in **sequence** to tell the story.*

a
b
c
d
e
f
g
h
i
j
k
l
m
n
o
p
q
r
s
t
u
v
w
x
y
z

A
B
C
D
E
F
G
H
I
J
K
L
M
N
O
P
Q
R
S
T
U
V
W
X
Y
Z

serene
ADJECTIVE peaceful and calm

sergeant sergeants
NOUN a rank in the police force, the army or the air force

serial serials
NOUN a story that is broadcast or published in a number of parts over a period of time

series
NOUN **1** a number of things coming one after the other
NOUN **2** A radio or television **series** is a set of programmes with the same title.
NOUN **3** A **series** circuit is an electric circuit in which the current passes through each element in order.

serious
ADJECTIVE **1** A **serious** problem or situation is very bad and worrying.
ADJECTIVE **2** **Serious** matters are important and should be thought about carefully.
ADJECTIVE **3** If you are **serious** about something, you really mean it.
ADJECTIVE **4** People who are **serious** are thoughtful, quiet and do not laugh much.

sermon sermons
NOUN a talk on a religious or moral subject given as part of a church service

serpent serpents
NOUN (*literary*) a snake

servant servants
NOUN someone who is employed to work in another person's house

serve serves, serving, served
VERB **1** If you **serve** food or drink to people, you give it to them.
VERB **2** When someone **serves** customers in a shop, bar or restaurant, they help them and supply them with what they want.
● *The shop was very busy so we had to wait for the assistant to serve us.*
VERB **3** In some games, such as tennis, when you **serve** you start the game by hitting the ball to your opponent.

server servers
NOUN part of a computer network which does a particular task, for example storing information, for all or part of the network

service services
NOUN **1** a system organised to provide something for the public ● *The bus service from our village into town is very good.*
NOUN **2** Motorway **services** consist of a petrol station, toilets, a shop and a restaurant.
NOUN **3** If your car has a **service**, it is checked over and repaired if it is broken or damaged.
NOUN **4** a religious ceremony

session sessions
NOUN the period during which an activity takes place

set sets, setting, set
VERB **1** When something such as jelly or concrete **sets**, it changes from a liquid into a solid.
NOUN **2** a group of things that go together
NOUN **3** In mathematics, a **set** is a collection of numbers that are treated as a group.
NOUN **4** In tennis, a **set** is a group of six or more games.
VERB **5** If you **set** your watch or clock, you adjust it for a particular time.
ADJECTIVE **6** If you do something at a **set** time, it is fixed at that time and does not change.

settee settees
NOUN a long comfortable seat for two or three people to sit on
SYNONYM: sofa

setting settings
NOUN The **setting** of something like a play or a story is its surroundings, and where it happens.

settle settles, settling, settled
VERB **1** If you **settle** something, you decide on it or sort it out. ● *Let's settle this argument as quickly as possible.*
VERB **2** If you **settle** in a place, you make it your home.
VERB **3** If you **settle**, or **settle** down, you relax and make yourself comfortable.
VERB **4** If snow or dust **settles**, it sinks slowly down and comes to rest.

settlement settlements
NOUN a place where people have settled and made their homes

seven
NOUN **Seven** is the number 7.

seventeen
NOUN **Seventeen** is the number 17.

seventeenth **seventeenths**
NOUN **1** one of seventeen equal parts of something
ADJECTIVE **2** The **seventeenth** item in a series is the one that you count as number seventeen.

seventh **sevenths**
NOUN **1** one of seven equal parts of something. It can be written as ⅟₇.
ADJECTIVE **2** The **seventh** item in a series is the one that you count as number seven. It can be written as 7ᵗʰ.

seventieth **seventieths**
NOUN **1** one of seventy equal parts of something
ADJECTIVE **2** The **seventieth** item in a series is the one that you count as number seventy.

seventy
NOUN **Seventy** is the number 70.

sever **severs, severing, severed**
VERB If you **sever** something, you cut it off or cut right through it.

PRONUNCIATION TIP
This word rhymes with "never".
---

several
ADJECTIVE used to refer to a small number of people or things • There were **several** blue boxes on the table.

severe
ADJECTIVE **1** extremely bad or serious
ADJECTIVE **2** strict or harsh

PRONUNCIATION TIP
This word is pronounced with suh-**veer**.
---

sew **sews, sewing, sewed, sewn**
VERB When you **sew** something, you use a needle and thread to make or mend it.

sewage
NOUN dirty water and waste that is carried away in drains from buildings

sewer **sewers**
NOUN a series of pipes and drains that carries away dirty water and waste from buildings

sex **sexes**
NOUN **1** one of the two groups, male and female, into which animals, including humans, are divided
NOUN **2** the physical activity by which people and animals produce young

sexism
NOUN the belief that one gender is less intelligent or less able than the other, or in some way not as good as the other

sexist **sexists**
ADJECTIVE **1** believing that one gender is less intelligent or less good at doing something than the other
NOUN **2** someone who believes that one gender is less intelligent or less good at doing something than the other

shabby **shabbier, shabbiest**
ADJECTIVE Something or someone who is **shabby** looks old and ragged.

shack **shacks**
NOUN a small, roughly built hut

shade **shades, shading, shaded**
NOUN **1** an area of darkness and coolness that sunshine does not reach
NOUN **2** the different forms of a colour. For example, olive green is a **shade** of green.
NOUN **3** an object that decreases or shuts out light, such as a lampshade
VERB **4** If you **shade** a person or a thing, you protect them from the sun's heat or light.

shadow **shadows, shadowing, shadowed**
NOUN **1** the dark shape formed when an opaque object stops light from reaching a surface
VERB **2** When you **shadow** someone, you follow them and watch them closely.

shady **shadier, shadiest**
ADJECTIVE A **shady** place is sheltered from the sunlight by trees or buildings.

shaft **shafts**
NOUN **1** A **shaft** in a mine or for a lift is a passage that goes straight down.
NOUN **2** a beam of light
NOUN **3** In a machine, the **shaft** is a rod that turns in order to transmit power or movement.

shaggy **shaggier, shaggiest**
ADJECTIVE covered with thick, long, untidy hair

shake **shakes, shaking, shook, shaken**
VERB **1** If you **shake** something, you move it quickly from side to side or up and down.
VERB **2** If something **shakes**, it moves from side to side or up and down with small, quick movements.
VERB **3** When you **shake** your head, you move it from side to side in order to say no.

NOUN **4** If you give something a **shake**, you shake it.

PHRASE **5** When you **shake hands** with someone, you grasp their hand in yours as a way of greeting them.

shaky shakier, shakiest
ADJECTIVE rather weak, shaking and unsteady • *The foal got up on **shaky** legs.*

shall should
VERB used with *I* and *we* to refer to the future • *I **shall** go shopping tomorrow.* • *I **should** wait till next week to open my birthday present.*

shallow shallower, shallowest
ADJECTIVE not deep • *The water here is quite **shallow**.*

shame
NOUN **1** the feeling of guilt or embarrassment you get when you know you have done something wrong or foolish
NOUN **2** If you say something is a **shame**, you mean you are sorry about it. • *It's a **shame** you can't come round to tea.*

shampoo shampoos
NOUN a soapy liquid used for washing your hair

WORD HISTORY
from the Hindi word *champna* meaning press or massage

shamrock shamrocks
NOUN a plant with three round leaves on each stem, which is the national emblem of Ireland

WORD HISTORY
from Irish Gaelic *seamrog* meaning little clover

shanty shanties
NOUN **1** a small, rough hut
NOUN **2** A sea **shanty** is a song sailors used to sing.

shape shapes
NOUN **1** The **shape** of something is the form or pattern of its outline, for example whether it is round or square. • *The chocolates came in a box in the **shape** of a heart.*
NOUN **2** something with a definite form, for example a circle or square

share shares, sharing, shared
VERB **1** If two people **share** something, they both use it, do it, or have it. • *We **shared** a bar of chocolate.*
NOUN **2** A **share** of something is a portion of it. • *I want a fair **share** of the cake.*
share out
VERB If you **share out** something, you give it out equally among a group of people. • *They **shared out** the food between them.*

shark sharks
NOUN a large, powerful fish, usually with two fins on its back and rows of sharp teeth

sharp sharper, sharpest
ADJECTIVE **1** A **sharp** object has an edge or point that is good for cutting or piercing things.
ADJECTIVE **2** A **sharp** change is sudden and noticeable. • *There was a **sharp** rise in temperature after the sun came up.*
ADJECTIVE **3** A **sharp** taste is sour.
ADJECTIVE **4** Someone who is **sharp** can pick up ideas very quickly.
ADJECTIVE **5** A **sharp** pain is strong and sudden.

sharpen sharpens, sharpening, sharpened
VERB If you **sharpen** an object such as a knife, you make its edge or point sharper.

shatter shatters, shattering, shattered
VERB If something **shatters**, it breaks into a lot of small pieces. • *The glass **shattered** when it hit the floor.*

shave shaves, shaving, shaved
VERB When someone **shaves**, they remove hair with a razor from part of their body.

shavings
PLURAL NOUN small, fine pieces of wood that have been cut off a larger piece

shawl shawls
NOUN a large piece of cloth worn round a woman's head or shoulders, or used to wrap a baby in

she
PRONOUN **She** is used to refer to a woman or girl who has already been mentioned.

sheaf sheaves
NOUN **1** a bundle of papers
NOUN **2** a bundle of ripe corn

shear shears, shearing, sheared, shorn
VERB When someone **shears** a sheep, they cut the wool off it.

A B C D E F G H I J K L M N O P Q R S T U V W X Y Z

shears
PLURAL NOUN **Shears** are a tool like a large pair of scissors, used especially for cutting hedges.

sheath sheaths
NOUN a cover for the blade of a knife or a sword

she'd
a contraction of *she had* or *she would*

shed sheds, shedding, shed
NOUN **1** a small building used for storing things, especially in a garden
VERB **2** When an animal **sheds** hair or skin, some of it comes off.
VERB **3** If you **shed** tears, you cry.

sheen
NOUN a gentle shine on the surface of something

sheep
NOUN a mammal kept on farms for its meat and wool

LANGUAGE TIP
The plural of *sheep* is *sheep*.

---

sheepdog sheepdogs
NOUN a breed of dog often used for controlling sheep

sheepish
ADJECTIVE If you look **sheepish**, you look shy or embarrassed.

sheer sheerer, sheerest
ADJECTIVE **1** A **sheer** cliff or drop is vertical.
ADJECTIVE **2** complete and total • *sheer exhaustion*
ADJECTIVE **3** **Sheer** fabrics are very light and delicate.

sheet sheets
NOUN **1** a large rectangular piece of cloth used to cover a bed
NOUN **2** a rectangular piece of paper

sheikh sheikhs
NOUN an Arab chief or ruler

PRONUNCIATION TIP
This word rhymes with "make".

WORD HISTORY
from Arabic *shaykh* meaning old man

---

shelf shelves
NOUN a flat piece of wood, metal or glass fixed to a wall or a cabinet or cupboard and used for putting things on

she'll
a contraction of *she will* or *she shall*

shell shells
NOUN **1** the hard covering of an egg or nut
NOUN **2** the hard, protective covering on the back of a tortoise, snail or crab

shellfish shellfish or shellfishes
NOUN a small sea creature with a shell

shelter shelters, sheltering, sheltered
NOUN **1** a small building made to protect people from bad weather or danger • *We waited in the bus shelter.*
NOUN **2** If a place gives **shelter**, it protects you from bad weather or danger.
VERB **3** If you **shelter** in a place, you stay there and are safe and protected.
VERB **4** To **shelter** someone or something means to protect them from bad weather or danger.

shepherd shepherds
NOUN a person who looks after sheep

sheriff sheriffs
NOUN **1** in America, a person elected to enforce the law in a county
NOUN **2** in Scotland, the senior judge of a county or district
NOUN **3** in Australia, an officer of the Supreme Court who does certain paperwork

sherry sherries
NOUN a kind of strong wine

she's
a contraction of *she is* or *she has*

shield shields, shielding, shielded
NOUN **1** a large piece of a strong material like metal or plastic that soldiers or police officers carry to protect themselves
VERB **2** If you **shield** someone or something, you protect them from something. • *He **shielded** his eyes from the sun with his hand.*

shift shifts, shifting, shifted
VERB **1** If you **shift** something, you move it.
VERB **2** If something **shifts**, it moves.
NOUN **3** a set period during which people work • *the night shift*

shilling shillings
NOUN a coin that was once used in Britain, Australia and New Zealand. There were 20 **shillings** in a pound.

a
b
c
d
e
f
g
h
i
j
k
l
m
n
o
p
q
r
s
t
u
v
w
x
y
z

363

A B C D E F G H I J K L M N O P Q R S T U V W X Y Z

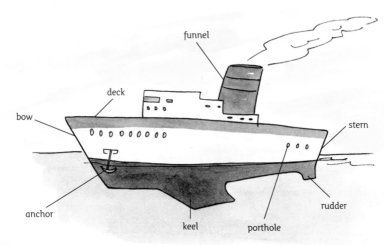

funnel

deck

bow

stern

anchor

keel

porthole

rudder

ship

shimmer shimmers, shimmering, shimmered
VERB **1** If something **shimmers**, it shines with a faint, flickering light.
NOUN **2** a faint, flickering light

shin shins
NOUN the front part of your leg between your knee and your ankle

shine shines, shining, shone or shined
VERB **1** When something **shines**, it is bright because it gives out or reflects light.
VERB **2** If you **shine** a torch or lamp somewhere, you point it there so that it becomes light.
VERB **3** If you **shine** your shoes, you polish them.

shingle
NOUN small pebbles on the seashore

shingles
PLURAL NOUN a disease that causes a painful red rash, especially around the waist

shiny shinier, shiniest
ADJECTIVE **Shiny** things are bright and look as if they have been polished.

ship ships, shipping, shipped
NOUN **1** a large boat that carries passengers or cargo

VERB **2** If people or things are **shipped** somewhere, they are transported there by ship.

→ Have a look at the illustration

shipwreck shipwrecks; shipwrecked
NOUN **1** When there is a **shipwreck**, a ship is destroyed in a storm or an accident at sea.
NOUN **2** the remains of a ship that has been damaged or sunk
ADJECTIVE **3** If someone is **shipwrecked**, they survive a shipwreck and manage to reach land.

shipyard shipyards
NOUN a place where ships are built and repaired

shirk shirks, shirking, shirked
VERB If you **shirk** a task, you try to avoid doing it.

shirt shirts
NOUN a piece of clothing with a collar, sleeves and buttons down the front, worn on the upper part of the body

shiver shivers, shivering, shivered
VERB When you **shiver**, you tremble slightly because you are cold or scared.

shoal shoals
NOUN a large group of fish swimming together

shock shocks, shocking, shocked
NOUN **1** a sudden upsetting experience
VERB **2** If something **shocks** you, it upsets you because it is unpleasant and unexpected.

shocking
ADJECTIVE **1** Something that shocks people is **shocking**.
ADJECTIVE **2** (*informal*) very bad • *The weather has been **shocking**.*

shoddy shoddier, shoddiest
ADJECTIVE badly made or done

shoe shoes
NOUN a strong covering for each of your feet. **Shoes** cover most of your foot, but not your ankle.

shoelace shoelaces
NOUN a cord for fastening a shoe

shone
VERB the past tense and past participle of **shine**

shook
VERB the past tense of **shake**

shoot shoots, shooting, shot
VERB **1** If someone **shoots** a person or an animal, they injure or kill them by firing a gun at them.
VERB **2** When a film is **shot**, it is filmed.

shooting star shooting stars
NOUN a meteor

shop shops, shopping, shopped
NOUN **1** a place where things are sold
NOUN **2** a place where a particular type of work is done • *a bicycle repair **shop***
VERB **3** When you **shop**, you go to the shops to buy things.

shopkeeper shopkeepers
NOUN someone who owns or manages a small shop

shopping
NOUN Your **shopping** is the goods you have bought in a shop.

shore shores
NOUN the land along the edge of a sea, lake or wide river

short shorter, shortest
ADJECTIVE **1** not lasting very long
ADJECTIVE **2** small in length, distance or height
ADJECTIVE **3** If you are **short** of something, you do not have enough of it.

ADJECTIVE **4** If a name is **short** for another name, it is a quick way of saying it. • *her friend Kes (**short** for Kesewa)*

shortage shortages
NOUN If there is a **shortage** of something, there is not enough of it.

shortcut shortcuts
NOUN **1** a quicker way of getting somewhere than the usual route
NOUN **2** a quicker way of doing something than the usual way

shorten shortens, shortening, shortened
VERB If you **shorten** something, you make it shorter.

ANTONYM: lengthen

shorthand
NOUN a way of writing in which signs represent words or syllables. It is used to write down quickly what someone is saying.

shortly
ADVERB soon • *I'll be there **shortly**.*

shorts
PLURAL NOUN trousers with legs that stop at or above the knee

short-sighted
ADJECTIVE If you are **short-sighted**, you cannot see things clearly when they are far away.

shot shots
VERB **1** the past tense of **shoot**
NOUN **2** the act of firing a gun
NOUN **3** In football, golf, tennis and other ball games, a **shot** is the act of kicking or hitting the ball.
NOUN **4** a photograph or short film sequence

should
VERB **1** You use **should** to say that something ought to happen. • *Kylie **should** have done better.*
VERB **2** You also use **should** to say that you expect something to happen. • *We **should** have heard by now.*
VERB **3** **Should** is used in questions where you are asking someone for advice about what to do. • ***Should** we tell her about it?*

shoulder shoulders
NOUN Your **shoulders** are the parts of your body between your neck and the tops of your arms.

a
b
c
d
e
f
g
h
i
j
k
l
m
n
o
p
q
r
s
t
u
v
w
x
y
z

A
B
C
D
E
F
G
H
I
J
K
L
M
N
O
P
Q
R
S
T
U
V
W
X
Y
Z

shouldn't
VERB a contraction of *should not*

shout shouts, shouting, shouted
NOUN **1** a loud call or cry
VERB **2** If you **shout** something, you say it very loudly.

shove shoves, shoving, shoved
VERB **1** If you **shove** someone or something, you push them roughly.
NOUN **2** a rough push

shovel shovels, shovelling, shovelled
NOUN **1** a tool like a spade, with the sides curved up, used for moving earth or snow
VERB **2** If you **shovel** earth or snow, you move it with a shovel.

show shows, showing, showed, shown
VERB **1** If you **show** someone something, you let them see it.
VERB **2** If you **show** someone how to do something, you demonstrate it to them.
• *Jake **showed** me how to make a chocolate cake.*
VERB **3** If something **shows**, you can see it.
VERB **4** If you **show** someone to a room or seat, you lead them there.
NOUN **5** a form of entertainment at the theatre or on television • *My favourite talk **show** is on TV tonight.*
NOUN **6** a display or exhibition • *a flower **show***

show off
VERB (*informal*) If someone is **showing off**, they are trying to impress people.

shower showers, showering, showered
NOUN **1** a device that sprays you with water so that you can wash yourself
NOUN **2** If you have a **shower**, you wash yourself by standing under a **shower**.
NOUN **3** a short period of rain
VERB **4** If you are **showered** with a lot of things, they fall on you like rain.

showroom showrooms
NOUN a shop where goods such as cars or electrical items are displayed for customers to look at

shrank
VERB the past tense of **shrink**

shrapnel
NOUN small pieces of metal scattered from an exploding shell

WORD HISTORY
named after General Henry *Shrapnel* (1761–1842), who invented it

shred shreds, shredding, shredded
VERB **1** If you **shred** something, you cut or tear it into very small pieces.
NOUN **2** a small, narrow piece of paper or material

shrew shrews
NOUN a small mouse-like mammal with a long pointed nose

shrewd shrewder, shrewdest
ADJECTIVE Someone who is **shrewd** makes good judgments and uses their common sense.

shriek shrieks, shrieking, shrieked
NOUN **1** a high-pitched cry or scream
VERB **2** If you **shriek**, you make a high-pitched cry or scream.

shrill shriller, shrillest
ADJECTIVE A **shrill** sound is unpleasantly high-pitched and piercing.

shrimp shrimps
NOUN a small edible shellfish with a long tail and many legs

shrine shrines
NOUN a place of worship connected with a sacred person or object

shrink shrinks, shrinking, shrank, shrunk
VERB If something **shrinks**, it becomes smaller.

shrinkage
NOUN the amount by which something shrinks

shrivel shrivels, shrivelling, shrivelled
VERB When something **shrivels**, it becomes dry and withered.

shrub shrubs
NOUN a bushy plant with woody stems

shrug shrugs, shrugging, shrugged
VERB If you **shrug** your shoulders, you raise them slightly as a sign that you do not know or do not care about something.

shrunk
VERB the past participle of **shrink**

shudder shudders, shuddering, shuddered

VERB **1** If you **shudder**, you tremble with fear or horror.

VERB **2** If a machine or vehicle **shudders**, it shakes violently.

NOUN **3** a shiver of fear or horror

shuffle shuffles, shuffling, shuffled

VERB **1** If you **shuffle**, you walk without lifting your feet off the ground properly, so that they drag.

VERB **2** If you **shuffle** a pack of cards, you mix them up before you begin a game.

shut shuts, shutting, shut

VERB **1** If you **shut** something, you close it.

ADJECTIVE **2** If something is **shut**, it is closed.

shutter shutters

NOUN **1** a screen that can be closed over a window

NOUN **2** the device in a camera that opens and closes to let light onto the film

shuttle shuttles

ADJECTIVE **1** A **shuttle** service is an air, bus or train service that makes frequent journeys between two places.

NOUN **2** a type of American spacecraft

shuttlecock shuttlecocks

NOUN the feathered object that players hit over the net in the game of badminton

shy shyer, shyest

ADJECTIVE A **shy** person is quiet and uncomfortable in the company of other people.

sibling siblings

NOUN (*formal*) Your **siblings** are your brothers and sisters.

WORD HISTORY
from Old English *sibling* meaning relative

---

sick sicker, sickest

ADJECTIVE **1** If you are **sick**, you are ill.

ADJECTIVE **2** If you feel **sick**, you feel as if you are going to vomit.

ADJECTIVE **3** If you are **sick**, you vomit.

sickness sicknesses

NOUN an illness or disease

side sides, siding, sided

NOUN **1** a position to the left or right of something • *There were trees on both **sides** of the road.*

NOUN **2** The **sides** of something are its outside surfaces, or edges, that are not at the top, bottom, front or back. • *There is a label on the **side** of the box.*

NOUN **3** The **sides** of an area, surface or object are its different surfaces or edges. • *Write on one **side** of the paper.*

NOUN **4** Your **sides** are the parts of your body from your armpits down to your hips.

NOUN **5** The two **sides** in a war, argument or relationship are the two people or groups involved. • *Whose **side** are you on?*

ADJECTIVE **6** situated on a side of a building or vehicle • *the **side** door*

VERB **7** If you side with someone, you support them in a quarrel or an argument.

sideways

ADVERB moving or facing towards one side
• *I took a step **sideways**.*

siding sidings

NOUN a short railway track beside the main tracks, where engines and carriages are left when not in use

siege sieges

NOUN a military operation in which an army surrounds a place to stop food or help from reaching the people inside

sieve sieves, sieving, sieved

NOUN **1** a tool made of mesh, used for sifting or straining things

VERB **2** If you **sieve** a powder or liquid, you pass it through a sieve to get rid of lumps and make it smooth.

sift sifts, sifting, sifted

VERB If you **sift** a powdery substance like flour or sugar, you pass it through a sieve to remove lumps.

sigh sighs, sighing, sighed

VERB When you **sigh**, you let out a deep breath, usually because you are tired, sad or relieved.

sight sights

NOUN **1** being able to see

NOUN **2** something you see • *The sunset was a beautiful **sight**.*

PLURAL NOUN **3** **Sights** are interesting places that tourists visit.

sightseeing

NOUN visiting the interesting places that tourists usually visit

a
b
c
d
e
f
g
h
i
j
k
l
m
n
o
p
q
r
s
t
u
v
w
x
y
z

A
B
C
D
E
F
G
H
I
J
K
L
M
N
O
P
Q
R
S
T
U
V
W
X
Y
Z

sign signs, signing, signed

NOUN **1** a mark or symbol that always has a particular meaning, for example in mathematics or music • *a plus **sign***

NOUN **2** a board or notice with words, a picture or a symbol on it, giving information or a warning • *a stop **sign***

VERB **3** If you **sign** a document, you write your name on it by hand, in the way you usually write it.

signal signals

NOUN **1** a gesture, sound or action that is meant to give a message to someone

NOUN **2** A railway **signal** is a piece of equipment beside the track that tells train drivers whether or not to stop.

signature signatures

NOUN If you write your **signature**, you write your name by hand in the way you usually write it.

significant

ADJECTIVE **1** A **significant** amount is large enough to be noticed and to matter. • *A **significant** number of people can't read.*

ADJECTIVE **2** Something that is **significant** is important and means something.

sign language

NOUN a way of communicating using your hands, used especially by deaf people

signpost signposts

NOUN a road sign with information on it, such as the name of a town and how far away it is

Sikh Sikhs

NOUN a person who believes in Sikhism, an Indian religion that separated from Hinduism in the 16th century and which teaches that there is only one God

silence

NOUN When there is **silence**, there is no sound.

SYNONYM: quietness

silent

ADJECTIVE **1** If you are **silent**, you are not saying anything.

ADJECTIVE **2** When something is **silent**, it makes no noise.

silhouette silhouettes

NOUN the dark outline of a shape against a light background

silicon

NOUN an element found in sand, clay and stone. It is used to make glass and parts of computers.

silk silks

NOUN fine, soft cloth made from threads produced from silkworm cocoons

sill sills

NOUN a strip of stone, wood or metal underneath a window or a door

silly sillier, silliest

ADJECTIVE foolish or childish

silver

NOUN a valuable greyish-white metal used for making jewellery and ornaments

similar

ADJECTIVE If one thing is **similar** to another, they are quite like each other.

simile similes

NOUN an expression in which a person or thing is described as being similar to someone or something else. An example of a **simile** is *she runs like a deer* and *he's as white as a sheet.*

simmer simmers, simmering, simmered

VERB When food **simmers**, it cooks gently, just below boiling point.

simple simpler, simplest

ADJECTIVE **1** Something that is **simple** is easy to understand or do.

ADJECTIVE **2** plain in style

simplify simplifies, simplifying, simplified

VERB If you **simplify** something, you make it simple or easy to understand.

simply

ADVERB in a simple way

simultaneous

ADJECTIVE Things that are **simultaneous** happen at the same time.

sin sins, sinning, sinned

NOUN **1** wicked behaviour, particularly if it breaks a religious or moral law

VERB **2** To **sin** means to do something wicked.

since

PREPOSITION **1** from a particular time until now • *I've been waiting **since** half past three.*

ADVERB **2** from a particular time until now • *They met at school and have been friends ever **since**.*

CONJUNCTION **3** because • *I had a drink, **since** I was feeling thirsty.*

sincere
ADJECTIVE If you are **sincere**, you are genuine and truly mean what you say.

sincerely
ADVERB used to show that you genuinely mean or feel something • *"Well done!" he said* **sincerely***.*

sing sings, singing, sang, sung
VERB 1 When you **sing**, you make musical sounds with your voice, usually with words that fit a tune.
VERB 2 When birds or insects **sing**, they make pleasant and tuneful sounds.

singe singes, singeing, singed
VERB If you **singe** something, you burn it slightly so that it goes brown but does not catch fire.

single singles
ADJECTIVE 1 only one and not more • *A* **single** *copy of the book was on sale in the shop.*
ADJECTIVE 2 People who are **single** are not married.
ADJECTIVE 3 A **single** bed or bedroom is for one person.
NOUN 4 A **single**, or a **single** ticket, is a ticket for a journey to a place but not back again.
NOUN 5 a recording of one or two short pieces of music

singular
NOUN In grammar, the **singular** is the form of a word that means just one person or thing.
ANTONYM: plural

sinister
ADJECTIVE Something or someone **sinister** seems harmful or evil.

WORD HISTORY
from Latin *sinister* meaning left-hand side, because the left side was considered unlucky

sink sinks, sinking, sank, sunk
NOUN 1 a fixed basin with taps supplying water, usually in a kitchen or bathroom
VERB 2 If something **sinks**, it moves downwards, especially through water.

sip sips, sipping, sipped
VERB If you **sip** a drink, you take small mouthfuls.

sir
NOUN 1 *(formal)* a polite way to address a man
NOUN 2 **Sir** is the title of a knight or baronet.

siren sirens
NOUN a warning device, for example on an ambulance, that makes a loud, wailing noise • *The fire engines switched on their* **sirens** *as they raced to the fire.*

sister sisters
NOUN Your **sister** is a girl or woman who has the same parents as you.

sister-in-law sisters-in-law
NOUN Someone's **sister-in-law** is the sister of their husband or wife, or the wife of one of their siblings.

sit sits, sitting, sat
VERB When you **sit**, you rest your bottom on something such as a chair or the floor. • *We* **sat** *on the bench at the bus stop.*

site sites
NOUN 1 a piece of ground where something happens or will happen • *the* **site** *for the fairground*
NOUN 2 a place on the internet where you can find out about a particular subject or person

sitting room sitting rooms
NOUN a room with comfortable chairs for relaxing in

situated
ADJECTIVE in a particular place • *The cottage was* **situated** *on the edge of a forest.*

situation situations
NOUN 1 what is happening in a particular place at a particular time
NOUN 2 The **situation** of a town or a building is its surroundings and its position.

six
NOUN **Six** is the number 6.

sixteen
NOUN **Sixteen** is the number 16.

sixteenth sixteenths
NOUN 1 one of sixteen equal parts of something
ADJECTIVE 2 The **sixteenth** item in a series is the one that you count as number sixteen.

369

A
B
C
D
E
F
G
H
I
J
K
L
M
N
O
P
Q
R
S
T
U
V
W
X
Y
Z

sixth sixths

NOUN **1** one of six equal parts of something. It can be written as ⅙.
ADJECTIVE **2** The **sixth** item in a series is the one that you count as number six. It can be written as 6th.

sixtieth sixtieths

NOUN **1** one of sixty equal parts of something
ADJECTIVE **2** The **sixtieth** item in a series is the one that you count as number sixty.

sixty

NOUN **Sixty** is the number 60.

size sizes

NOUN **1** The **size** of something is how big it is.
NOUN **2** a standard measurement for clothes, shoes and other objects

sizzle sizzles, sizzling, sizzled

VERB If something **sizzles**, it makes a hissing sound. • *The sausages **sizzled** in the frying pan.*

skate skates, skating, skated

NOUN **1** **Skates** are ice **skates** or roller **skates**.
VERB **2** If you **skate**, you move about wearing skates.

skateboard skateboards

NOUN a narrow board on wheels, that you stand on and ride for fun

skateboarding

NOUN the activity of standing and riding on a skateboard

skeleton skeletons

NOUN the framework of bones in your body
→ Have a look at the illustration

sketch sketches, sketching, sketched

NOUN **1** a quick, rough drawing
VERB **2** If you **sketch** something, you draw it quickly and roughly.

sketchy sketchier, sketchiest

ADJECTIVE If something is **sketchy**, it has little detail. • *The map showing how to get to the new house was **sketchy**.*

ski skis, skiing, skied

NOUN **1** **Skis** are long pieces of wood, metal or plastic that you fasten to special boots so you can move easily on snow.
VERB **2** When you **ski**, you move on snow wearing skis, especially as a sport.

WORD HISTORY
from Old Norse *skith* meaning snowshoes

skid skids, skidding, skidded

VERB **1** If someone or something **skids**, they slide accidentally.
NOUN **2** a skidding movement

skilful

ADJECTIVE having a lot of skill

skilfully

ADVERB in a way that shows you have a lot of skill

skill skills

NOUN **1** the knowledge and ability that enable you to do something well
NOUN **2** a type of work or technique that needs special training and knowledge
• *I would like to learn some new **skills**.*

skim skims, skimming, skimmed

VERB **1** If you **skim** something from the surface of a liquid, you remove it.
VERB **2** If something **skims** a surface, it moves lightly, smoothly and quickly over it.
• *seagulls **skimming** the waves*

skin skins

NOUN **1** the natural covering of a person or animal
NOUN **2** the outer covering a fruit or vegetable

skinny skinnier, skinniest

ADJECTIVE thin

skip skips, skipping, skipped

VERB **1** When you **skip**, you jump lightly from one foot to the other, often over a rope.
VERB **2** If you **skip** something, you miss it out.
• *Amy **skipped** the part with the long words.*

skipper skippers

NOUN (*informal*) the captain of a ship or boat

skirt skirts

NOUN a piece of clothing that fastens at a woman's or girl's waist and hangs down over her legs

skittle skittles

NOUN **1** a wooden or plastic object, shaped like a bottle, that people try to knock down with a ball
NOUN **2** **Skittles** is a game in which players roll a ball and try to knock down objects called skittles.

SKELETON

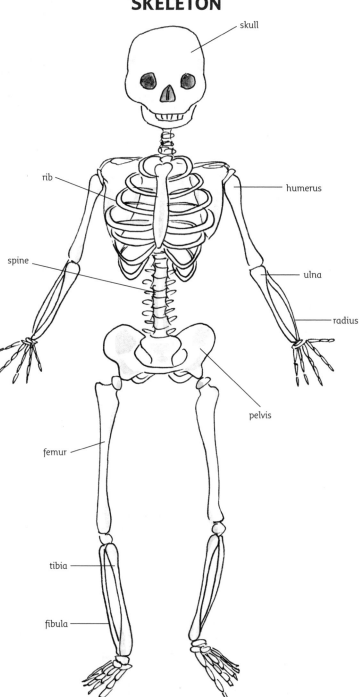

skull

rib

humerus

spine

ulna

radius

pelvis

femur

tibia

fibula

A
B
C
D
E
F
G
H
I
J
K
L
M
N
O
P
Q
R
S
T
U
V
W
X
Y
Z

skull skulls
NOUN the bony part of your head that surrounds your brain
→ Have a look at the illustration for **skeleton**

skunk skunks
NOUN a small black and white animal from North America that gives off an unpleasant smell if it is frightened

sky skies
NOUN the space around the Earth that you can see when you look upwards

Skype Skypes, Skyping, Skyped
VERB If you **Skype** someone, you call them over the internet, usually with a video connection. • *I Skyped Emma while she was in America.*

skyscraper skyscrapers
NOUN a very tall building

slab slabs
NOUN a thick, flat piece of something, such as stone

slack slacker, slackest
ADJECTIVE Something that is **slack** is loose and not firmly stretched or pulled tight.

slam slams, slamming, slammed
VERB If you **slam** something, such as a door, or if it **slams**, it shuts with a loud bang.

slang
NOUN very informal words and expressions

slant slants, slanting, slanted
VERB 1 If something **slants**, it slopes.
NOUN 2 a slope or a leaning position

slap slaps, slapping, slapped
VERB 1 If you **slap** someone, you hit them with the palm of your hand.
NOUN 2 If you give someone a **slap**, you slap them.

slash slashes, slashing, slashed
VERB 1 If someone **slashes** something, they make a long, deep cut in it.
NOUN 2 a long, deep cut

slate slates
NOUN 1 a dark grey rock that splits easily into thin layers
NOUN 2 **Slates** are small, flat pieces of slate used for covering roofs.

slaughter slaughters, slaughtering, slaughtered
VERB 1 To **slaughter** farm animals means to kill them for meat.

VERB 2 To **slaughter** animals or people means to kill a large number of them unjustly or cruelly.
NOUN 3 the killing of many people or animals

slave slaves, slaving, slaved
NOUN 1 someone who is owned by another person and must work for them
VERB 2 If you **slave** over something, you work very hard at it.

slay slays, slaying, slew, slain
VERB (*literary*) To **slay** someone means to kill them.

sledge sledges
NOUN a vehicle on runners used for travelling over snow

sledgehammer sledgehammers
NOUN a large, heavy hammer

sleek sleeker, sleekest
ADJECTIVE If something such as hair is **sleek**, it is smooth and shiny.

sleep sleeps, sleeping, slept
VERB When you **sleep**, you close your eyes and your whole body rests.

sleepily
ADJECTIVE in a way that shows you are tired and feel like sleeping

sleepless
ADJECTIVE unable to sleep or without sleep • *I had a sleepless night last night.*

sleepy sleepier, sleepiest
ADJECTIVE tired and feeling like sleeping

sleet
NOUN a mixture of rain and snow

sleeve sleeves
NOUN The **sleeves** of a piece of clothing are the parts that cover your arms. • *a shirt with long sleeves*

sleigh sleighs
NOUN a sledge pulled by animals

slender
ADJECTIVE slim

slept
VERB the past tense and past participle of **sleep**

slice slices, slicing, sliced
NOUN 1 A **slice** of cake, bread or other food is a piece of it cut from a larger piece.
VERB 2 If you **slice** food, you cut it into thin pieces.

VERB **3** To **slice** through something means to cut or move through it quickly, like a knife. • *The ship **sliced** through the water.*

slick slicker, slickest; slicks
ADJECTIVE **1** A **slick** action is done quickly and smoothly.
NOUN **2** An oil **slick** is a layer of oil floating on the surface of the sea or a lake.

slide slides, sliding, slid
VERB When something **slides**, it moves smoothly over or against something else. • *She **slid** the door open.*

slight slighter, slightest
ADJECTIVE **1** small in amount • *a **slight** dent in the car*
ADJECTIVE **2** A **slight** person has a slim, small body.

slim slimmer, slimmest
ADJECTIVE **1** A **slim** person is thin.
ADJECTIVE **2** A **slim** object is fairly thin. • *a **slim** book*
ADJECTIVE **3** If there is only a **slim** chance that something will happen, there is only a small chance that it will happen.

slime
NOUN an unpleasant, thick, slippery substance

sling slings, slinging, slung
VERB **1** (*informal*) If you **sling** something somewhere, you throw it there.
VERB **2** If you **sling** a rope between two points, you attach it so that it hangs loosely between them.
NOUN **3** a piece of cloth tied round a person's neck to support a broken or injured arm

slip slips, slipping, slipped
VERB **1** If you **slip**, you accidentally lose your balance.
VERB **2** If you **slip** somewhere, you go there quickly and quietly.
NOUN **3** a small mistake
NOUN **4** a small piece of paper

slipper slippers
NOUN **Slippers** are loose, soft shoes that you wear indoors.

slippery
ADJECTIVE smooth, wet or greasy, and difficult to hold or walk on

slit slits
NOUN a long cut or narrow opening

slither slithers, slithering, slithered
VERB To **slither** somewhere means to move there by sliding along the ground in an uneven way. • *The snake **slithered** away.*

sliver slivers
NOUN a small, thin piece of something

slog slogs, slogging, slogged
VERB **1** If you **slog** at something, you work hard at it.
NOUN **2** a piece of hard work or effort

slogan slogans
NOUN a short, easily-remembered phrase used in advertising or by a political party

SYNONYMS: catch phrase, motto

WORD HISTORY
from Scottish Gaelic *sluagh-ghairm* meaning war cry

slope slopes, sloping, sloped
NOUN **1** a flat surface that is at an angle, so that one end is higher than the other
VERB **2** If a surface **slopes**, it is at an angle.

sloppily
ADVERB carelessly or badly

sloppy sloppier, sloppiest
ADJECTIVE **1** liquid and spilling easily
ADJECTIVE **2** careless or badly done
ADJECTIVE **3** sentimental

slot slots
NOUN a narrow opening in a machine or container for pushing something into

sloth sloths
NOUN a South and Central American animal that moves very slowly and hangs upside down from the branches of trees

slouch slouches, slouching, slouched
VERB If you **slouch**, you stand or sit with your shoulders and head drooping forwards.

slow slower, slowest; slows, slowing, slowed
ADJECTIVE **1** moving, happening or doing something with very little speed
ADJECTIVE **2** If a clock or watch is **slow**, it shows a time earlier than the correct one.
VERB **3** If something **slows**, or you **slow** it, it moves or happens more slowly.
slow down
VERB If something **slows down** or something **slows** it **down**, it moves or happens more slowly.

373

slug slugs
NOUN a small, slow-moving animal with a slimy body, like a snail without an outer shell

sluggish
ADJECTIVE moving slowly and without much energy

slum slums
NOUN a poor, run-down area of a city or town

slumber slumbers, slumbering, slumbered
NOUN **1** (*literary*) sleep
VERB **2** (*literary*) When you **slumber**, you sleep.

slump slumps, slumping, slumped
VERB If you **slump** somewhere, you fall or sit down heavily.

slush
NOUN melting snow

sly slyer or **slier, slyest** or **sliest**
ADJECTIVE **1** A **sly** person is cunning and good at deceiving people.
ADJECTIVE **2** A **sly** expression or remark shows that you know something other people do not know.

smack smacks, smacking, smacked
VERB **1** If you **smack** someone, you hit them with your open hand.
NOUN **2** If you give someone a **smack**, you smack them.

small smaller, smallest
ADJECTIVE not large in size, number or amount

smart smarter, smartest
ADJECTIVE **1** A **smart** person is clean and neatly dressed.
ADJECTIVE **2** clever • *That's a **smart** idea.*

smartphone smartphones
NOUN a mobile phone that can send emails and access the internet

smash smashes, smashing, smashed
VERB **1** If you **smash** something, you break it into a lot of pieces by hitting it or dropping it.
VERB **2** If someone or something **smashes** through something, such as a fence, they go through it by breaking it.
VERB **3** To **smash** against something means to hit it with great force. • *A huge wave **smashed** against the boat.*

smear smears, smearing, smeared
NOUN **1** a dirty, greasy mark on a surface
VERB **2** If something **smears** something else, it leaves a dirty or greasy mark by rubbing against it.

smell smells, smelling, smelled or **smelt**
VERB **1** When you **smell** something, you notice it with your nose.
VERB **2** If something **smells**, it gives out an odour that people notice.
NOUN **3** Your sense of **smell** is your ability to smell things.
NOUN **4** an odour or scent, especially an unpleasant one

LANGUAGE TIP
You can write either *smelled* or *smelt* as the past form of *smell*.

smile smiles, smiling, smiled
VERB When you **smile**, you are happy. Your lips curve upwards at the edges and open a little.

smirk smirks, smirking, smirked
VERB When you **smirk**, you smile in a sneering, unpleasant way.

smog
NOUN a mixture of smoke and fog that occurs in some industrial cities

WORD HISTORY
from a combination of *smoke* and *fog*

smoke smokes, smoking, smoked
NOUN **1** a mixture of gases and small bits of solid material sent into the air when something burns
→ Have a look at the illustration for **volcano**
VERB **2** If something is **smoking**, smoke is coming from it.
VERB **3** When someone **smokes** a cigarette, cigar or pipe, they suck smoke from it into their mouth and blow it out again.

smooth smoother, smoothest; smooths, smoothing, smoothed
ADJECTIVE **1** A **smooth** surface has no roughness and no holes in it.
ANTONYM: rough
ADJECTIVE **2** A **smooth** liquid or mixture has no lumps in it.
VERB **3** If you **smooth** something, you move your hands over it to make it smooth and flat.

smoothie smoothies
NOUN a thick drink made mainly from crushed fruit • *a strawberry and banana* **smoothie**

smother smothers, smothering, smothered
VERB 1 If you **smother** a fire, you cover it with something to put it out.
VERB 2 To **smother** a person means to cover their face with something so that they cannot breathe.

smoulder smoulders, smouldering, smouldered
VERB When something **smoulders**, it burns slowly, producing smoke but no flames.

smudge smudges, smudging, smudged
NOUN 1 a dirty or blurred mark or a smear on something
VERB 2 If you **smudge** something, you make it dirty or messy by touching it or rubbing it. • *Be careful you don't* **smudge** *the ink!*

smug smugger, smuggest
ADJECTIVE Someone who is **smug** is very pleased with how good or clever they are, and is self-satisfied in an unpleasant way.

smuggle smuggles, smuggling, smuggled
VERB To **smuggle** goods means to take them in or out of a country secretly and against the law.

snack snacks
NOUN 1 a small, quick meal
NOUN 2 something eaten between meals

snag snags, snagging, snagged
NOUN 1 a small problem • *We seem to have hit a* **snag**.
VERB 2 If you **snag** your clothes, you catch them on something sharp.

snail snails
NOUN a small, slow-moving animal with a long, shiny body and a shell on its back

snake snakes
NOUN a long, thin reptile with scales and no legs

snap snaps, snapping, snapped
VERB 1 If something **snaps**, it breaks suddenly with a sharp noise.
VERB 2 If an animal **snaps** at you, it shuts its jaws together quickly as if it is going to bite you.
NOUN 3 an informal photograph

snare snares, snaring, snared
NOUN 1 a trap for catching birds or small animals
VERB 2 To **snare** an animal or bird means to catch it using a snare.

snarl snarls, snarling, snarled
VERB 1 When an animal **snarls**, it bares its teeth and makes a fierce, growling noise.
VERB 2 If you **snarl**, you say something in a fierce, angry way.
NOUN 3 the noise an animal makes when it snarls

snatch snatches, snatching, snatched
VERB 1 If you **snatch** something, you reach out for it quickly and grab it.
NOUN 2 A **snatch** of conversation or song is a very small piece of it.

sneak sneaks, sneaking, sneaked
VERB If you **sneak** somewhere, you go there quietly, trying not to be seen or heard.

sneaky sneakier, sneakiest
ADJECTIVE dishonest or deceitful

sneer sneers, sneering, sneered
VERB If you **sneer** at someone or something, you show by what you say that you think they are stupid or inferior.

sneeze sneezes, sneezing, sneezed
VERB 1 When you **sneeze**, you suddenly take a breath and blow it noisily down your nose, because there is a tickle in your nose or you have a cold.
NOUN 2 the action or sound of sneezing

sniff sniffs, sniffing, sniffed
VERB When you **sniff**, you breathe in air through your nose hard enough to make a sound.

snigger sniggers, sniggering, sniggered
VERB If you **snigger**, you laugh quietly and disrespectfully.

snip snips, snipping, snipped
VERB If you **snip** something, you make small, quick cuts in it or through it.

sniper snipers
NOUN a person who shoots at people from a hiding place

snivel snivels, snivelling, snivelled
VERB When someone **snivels**, they cry and sniff in an irritating way.

a b c d e f g h i j k l m n o p q r s t u v w x y z

375

A
B
C
D
E
F
G
H
I
J
K
L
M
N
O
P
Q
R
S
T
U
V
W
X
Y
Z

snob snobs

NOUN **1** someone who admires people considered to be socially superior and looks down on people considered to be socially inferior

NOUN **2** someone who believes that they are better than other people

snobbery

NOUN behaviour or an attitude that shows you think you are better than other people and have a higher social class than they do

snooker

NOUN a game played on a large table covered with smooth, green cloth. Players score points by hitting differently coloured balls into pockets using a long stick called a cue.

snoop snoops, snooping, snooped

VERB (*informal*) If you **snoop**, you secretly look round a place to find out things.

snooze snoozes, snoozing, snoozed

VERB **1** (*informal*) If you **snooze**, you sleep lightly for a short time, especially during the day.

NOUN **2** (*informal*) a short, light sleep

snore snores, snoring, snored

VERB When a sleeping person **snores**, they make a loud noise each time they breathe.

snorkel snorkels, snorkelling, snorkelled

NOUN **1** a tube you can breathe through when you are swimming just under the surface of the sea

VERB **2** If you **snorkel**, you swim underwater using a snorkel.

snorkelling

NOUN the activity of swimming just under the surface of water, using a tube you can breathe through

snout snouts

NOUN An animal's **snout** is its nose.

snow snows, snowing, snowed

NOUN **1** soft, white flakes of ice that fall from the sky in cold weather

VERB **2** When it **snows**, snow falls from the sky.

snowball snowballs

NOUN a ball of snow for throwing

snowboard snowboards

NOUN a board you stand on to slide across snow

snowboarding

NOUN the activity of standing on a board to slide across snow

snowflake snowflakes

NOUN a flake of snow

snowman snowmen

NOUN a pile of snow shaped like a person

snowstorm snowstorms

NOUN a storm with snow falling

snub snubs, snubbing, snubbed

VERB **1** If you **snub** someone, you behave rudely towards them, especially by making an insulting remark or ignoring them.

ADJECTIVE **2** A **snub** nose is short and turned-up.

snug

ADJECTIVE **1** A **snug** place is warm and comfortable.

ADJECTIVE **2** If you are **snug**, you are warm and comfortable.

ADJECTIVE **3** If something is a **snug** fit, it fits very closely.

snuggle snuggles, snuggling, snuggled

VERB If you **snuggle** somewhere, you cuddle up more closely to something or someone.

so

ADVERB **1** also ● *She laughed, and* **so** *did the teacher.*

ADVERB **2** very ● *You are* **so** *funny.*

CONJUNCTION **3** therefore, for that reason ● *I was cold,* **so** *I put on a coat.*

soak soaks, soaking, soaked

VERB **1** If you **soak** something, or leave it to **soak**, you put it in a liquid and leave it there for some time.

VERB **2** When a liquid **soaks** something, it makes it very wet.

VERB **3** When something **soaks** up a liquid, the liquid is drawn up into it. ● *The cloth* **soaked** *up the spilt milk.*

soap soaps

NOUN a substance used with water for washing yourself ● *a bar of* **soap**

soap opera soap operas

NOUN a popular television drama serial about people's daily lives

---

WORD HISTORY

so called because soap manufacturers were often sponsors of these

---

soar soars, soaring, soared
VERB If something **soars** into the air, it rises high into it.

sob sobs, sobbing, sobbed
VERB When someone **sobs**, they cry noisily, gulping in short breaths.

sober soberer, soberest
ADJECTIVE **1** not drunk
ADJECTIVE **2** serious and thoughtful

soccer
NOUN a game played by two teams of eleven players kicking a ball in an attempt to score goals

sociable
ADJECTIVE **Sociable** people are friendly and enjoy talking to other people.

SYNONYM: friendly

social
ADJECTIVE **1** to do with society or life within a society • *women from similar* **social** *backgrounds*
ADJECTIVE **2** to do with leisure activities that involve meeting other people • *We should organise more* **social** *events.*

social media
NOUN You can refer to websites and computer programs that you use to communicate with other people as **social media**.

social networking site social networking sites
NOUN a website that lets people connect, chat and share pictures and videos

society societies
NOUN **1** the community of people in a particular country or region
NOUN **2** an organisation for people who have the same interests

sock socks
NOUN a piece of clothing that covers your foot and ankle

socket sockets
NOUN **1** a place on a wall or on a piece of electrical equipment into which you can put a plug or bulb
NOUN **2** any hollow part of something, or an opening into which another part fits
• *eye* **sockets**

sofa sofas
NOUN a long comfortable seat, with a back and arms, for two or more people

WORD HISTORY
from Arabic *suffah* meaning an upholstered raised platform

soft softer, softest
ADJECTIVE **1** not hard, stiff or firm • *a* **soft** *towel*
ADJECTIVE **2** very gentle • *a* **soft** *breeze*

soften softens, softening, softened
VERB When you **soften** something, you make it softer.

software
NOUN computer programs

soggy soggier, soggiest
ADJECTIVE unpleasantly wet

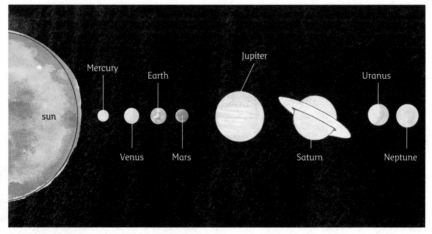

solar system

a
b
c
d
e
f
g
h
i
j
k
l
m
n
o
p
q
r
s
t
u
v
w
x
y
z

A
B
C
D
E
F
G
H
I
J
K
L
M
N
O
P
Q
R
S
T
U
V
W
X
Y
Z

soil **soils, soiling, soiled**

NOUN **1** the top layer of the land surface of the earth, in which plants can grow

→ Have a look at the illustration for **photosynthesis**

VERB **2** If you **soil** something, you make it dirty.

solar

ADJECTIVE to do with the sun • **solar** energy

solar system

NOUN the sun and all the planets, comets and asteroids that orbit round it

→ Have a look at the illustration

sold

VERB the past tense and past participle of **sell**

soldier **soldiers**

NOUN a person in an army

sole **soles**

NOUN The **sole** of your foot or shoe is the underneath part.

solemn

ADJECTIVE serious rather than cheerful

solicitor **solicitors**

NOUN a lawyer who gives legal advice and prepares legal documents and cases

solid **solids**

NOUN **1** a substance that is not a liquid or gas. The particles in a **solid** are close together and cannot move around.

→ Have a look at the illustration for **state of matter**

NOUN **2** an object that is hard or firm
ADJECTIVE **3** You say that something is **solid** when it does not have any space in it.
• a **solid** steel bar
ADJECTIVE **4** A **solid** shape is a three-dimensional shape such as a cylinder.

solidify **solidifies, solidifying, solidified**

VERB If something **solidifies**, it changes from a liquid into a solid.

solitary

ADJECTIVE alone

solo **solos**

NOUN **1** a piece of music played or sung by one person alone
ADJECTIVE **2** A **solo** performance or activity is done by one person alone.
ADVERB **3** alone • to sail **solo** around the world

solstice **solstices**

NOUN one of two times in the year when the sun is at its furthest point south or north of the equator

solubility

NOUN the ability of a substance to dissolve

soluble

ADJECTIVE able to be dissolved in a liquid
• **soluble** aspirin

solution **solutions**

NOUN **1** a way of dealing with a problem or difficult situation
NOUN **2** the answer to a riddle or a puzzle
NOUN **3** a liquid in which a solid substance has been dissolved

solve **solves, solving, solved**

VERB If you **solve** a problem or a question, you find a solution or answer to it.

SYNONYM: work out

sombre

ADJECTIVE **1** **Sombre** colours are dark and dull.
ADJECTIVE **2** A **sombre** person is serious, sad or gloomy.

some

ADJECTIVE **1** You use **some** to refer to a quantity or number when you are not stating the exact quantity or number.
• There's **some** money on the table.
PRONOUN **2** You use **some** to refer to a quantity or number when you are not stating the exact quantity or number.
• When the berries were ripe, we picked **some**.

somebody

PRONOUN some person

somehow

ADVERB **1** You use **somehow** to say that you do not know how something was done or will be done. • You'll find a way of doing it **somehow**.
ADVERB **2** You use **somehow** to say that you do not know the reason for something.
• **Somehow** it didn't feel quite right.

someone

PRONOUN You use **someone** to refer to a person without saying exactly who you mean. • I need **someone** to help me.

somersault somersaults, somersaulting, somersaulted

NOUN **1** a forwards or backwards roll in which the head is placed on the ground and the body is brought over it
VERB **2** If you **somersault**, you perform a somersault.

something

PRONOUN You use **something** to refer to anything that is not a person, without saying exactly what it is. ● *There was **something** wrong.*

sometimes

ADVERB occasionally, rather than always or never

somewhere

ADVERB **1 Somewhere** is used to refer to a place without stating exactly where it is. ● *a flat **somewhere** in the city*
ADVERB **2 Somewhere** is used when giving an approximate amount, number or time. ● *It was **somewhere** between four and five o'clock.*

son sons

NOUN a person's male child

song songs

NOUN **1** a piece of music with words that are sung to the music
NOUN **2** singing ● *I was woken by the bird **song** early in the morning.*

sonnet sonnets

NOUN a poem with 14 lines that rhyme according to fixed patterns

soon sooner, soonest

ADVERB If something is going to happen **soon**, it will happen in a very short time.

soot

NOUN black powder that rises in the smoke from a fire

soothe soothes, soothing, soothed

VERB **1** If you **soothe** someone who is angry or upset, you make them calmer.
VERB **2** Something that **soothes** pain makes the pain less severe.

sooty

ADJECTIVE covered in a black powder that has come from the smoke from a fire

sophisticated

ADJECTIVE **1** A **sophisticated** person is experienced in social situations and able to talk easily about anything.

SYNONYMS: cultured, urbane

ADJECTIVE **2** Something **sophisticated** is made using advanced and complicated methods, or is able to do advanced and complicated things. ● *a **sophisticated** new telescope*

SYNONYM: highly developed

sorcerer sorcerers

NOUN someone in stories who performs magic by using the power of evil spirits

sore sorer, sorest; sores

ADJECTIVE **1** If part of your body is **sore**, it causes you pain and is uncomfortable. ● *I have a cough and a **sore** throat.*

SYNONYMS: painful, sensitive, tender

NOUN **2** a painful place where your skin has become infected

sorrow sorrows

NOUN deep sadness or regret

sorry sorrier, sorriest

ADJECTIVE If you are **sorry** about something, you feel sadness, regret or sympathy because of it.

sort sorts, sorting, sorted

NOUN **1** Different **sorts** of something are different types of it.

SYNONYM: kind

VERB **2** If you **sort** things, you arrange them into different groups.
sort out
VERB If you **sort out** a problem or misunderstanding, you find a solution to it.

SOS

NOUN a signal appealing urgently for help from someone whose life is in danger. **SOS** stands for Save Our Souls.

sought

VERB the past tense and past participle of **seek**

soul souls

NOUN the spiritual part of a person that some people think continues after the body is dead

A
B
C
D
E
F
G
H
I
J
K
L
M
N
O
P
Q
R
S
T
U
V
W
X
Y
Z

sound sounds, sounding, sounded
NOUN **1 Sound** is everything that can be heard.
NOUN **2** something particular that you hear
• the **sound** of a door opening
VERB **3** If something **sounds**, or if you **sound** it, it makes a noise. • He **sounded** his horn to warn them.

sound effect sound effects
NOUN **Sound effects** are added to films or plays to make them sound more life-like.

soundproof soundproofs, soundproofing, soundproofed
ADJECTIVE **1** If a room is **soundproof**, sound cannot get into it or out of it.
VERB **2** To **soundproof** something means to make it soundproof.

soup soups
NOUN liquid food made by boiling meat, fish or vegetables in water

sour
ADJECTIVE **1** If something is **sour**, it has a sharp, acid taste like lemons or vinegar.
ADJECTIVE **2** If milk is **sour**, it is no longer fresh.

source sources
NOUN The **source** of something is the person, place or thing that it originally comes from. • the **source** of the river

south
NOUN one of the four main points of the compass. If you face the point where the sun rises, **south** is on your right. The abbreviation for **south** is S.

→ Have a look at the illustration for **compass point**

south-east
NOUN a point halfway between south and east. The abbreviation for **south-east** is SE.

→ Have a look at the illustration for **compass point**

southern
ADJECTIVE in or from the south

south-west
NOUN a point halfway between south and west. The abbreviation for **south-west** is SW.

→ Have a look at the illustration for **compass point**

souvenir souvenirs
NOUN something you keep to remind you of a holiday, place or event

sovereign sovereigns
NOUN **1** a king, queen or royal ruler of a country
NOUN **2** In the past, a **sovereign** was a British gold coin worth one pound.

sow sows, sowing, sowed, sown
NOUN **1** a female pig
VERB **2** If you **sow** seeds, you put them in the ground so they can grow.

PRONUNCIATION TIP
The noun ryhmes with "cow". The verb rhymes with "go".

---

soya
NOUN a protein derived from **soya** beans. **Soya** beans are used to make **soya** flour, margarine, oil and milk.

space spaces
NOUN **1** the area that is empty or available in a place, building or container
NOUN **2** the area beyond the Earth's atmosphere surrounding the stars and planets
NOUN **3** a gap between two things

spacecraft spacecraft
NOUN a vehicle for travelling in outer space

spaceship spaceships
NOUN a spacecraft

spacesuit spacesuits
NOUN protective clothing that astronauts wear in outer space

spacious
ADJECTIVE having or providing a lot of space

spade spades
NOUN **1** a tool with a flat metal blade and a long handle used for digging
NOUN **2 Spades** is one of the four suits in a pack of playing cards. It is marked by a black symbol in the shape of a heart-shaped leaf with a stem.

spaghetti
NOUN long, thin pieces of pasta

WORD HISTORY
the plural of the Italian word *spaghetto* meaning string

---

span spans, spanning, spanned
NOUN **1** a period of time • *looking back over a **span** of 40 years*
NOUN **2** the total length of something from one end to the other • *Seagulls have a large wing **span**.*
NOUN **3** Your **span** is the distance from the top of your thumb to the top of your little finger when your hand is stretched.
VERB **4** If something **spans** a particular length of time, a distance or a gap, it stretches across it. • *The bridge **spanned** the width of the river.*

spaniel spaniels
NOUN a breed of dog with long ears and silky fur

spank spanks, spanking, spanked
VERB If a child is **spanked**, it is punished by being slapped, usually on the leg or bottom.

spanner spanners
NOUN a tool with a specially shaped end that fits round a nut to turn it

spare spares, sparing, spared
ADJECTIVE **1** extra, or kept to be used when it is needed • *There is a **spare** tyre in the boot of the car.*
VERB **2** If you **spare** something for a particular purpose, you make it available. • *Can you **spare** the time to help me later?*
VERB **3** If someone is **spared** an unpleasant experience, they are prevented from suffering it.

spark sparks
NOUN a tiny, bright piece of burning material thrown up by a fire

sparkle sparkles, sparkling, sparkled
VERB If something **sparkles**, it shines with a lot of small, bright points of light.

SYNONYMS: glitter, twinkle

sparrow sparrows
NOUN a common, small bird with brown and grey feathers

sparse sparser, sparsest
ADJECTIVE small in number or amount and spread out over an area

spatter spatters, spattering, spattered
VERB If something **spatters** a surface, it covers it with small drops of liquid.

spawn spawns, spawning, spawned
NOUN **1** a jelly-like substance containing the eggs of fish or amphibians
VERB **2** When fish or amphibians **spawn**, they lay their eggs.

speak speaks, speaking, spoke, spoken
VERB **1** When you **speak**, you use your voice to say words.

SYNONYMS: say, talk, utter

VERB **2** If you **speak** a foreign language, you know it and can use it.

speaker speakers
NOUN **1** a person who is speaking or making a speech
NOUN **2** the part of a radio or stereo system from which the sound comes

spear spears, spearing, speared
NOUN **1** a weapon consisting of a long pole with a sharp point
VERB **2** To **spear** something means to pierce it with a spear or other pointed object.

special
ADJECTIVE Someone or something **special** is different from other people or things, often in a way that makes it more important or better than others.

specialist specialists
NOUN an expert in a particular subject

species
NOUN a group of plants or animals that have the same main features and are able to breed with each other

LANGUAGE TIP
The plural of *species* is *species*.

specimen specimens
NOUN an example or small amount of something that gives an idea of what the whole is like • *a **specimen** of your writing*

speck specks
NOUN **1** a very small stain
NOUN **2** a very small amount of something

speckled
ADJECTIVE Something that is **speckled** is covered in small marks or spots.

spectacle spectacles
NOUN **1** a grand and impressive event or performance
PLURAL NOUN **2** Someone's **spectacles** are their glasses.

a b c d e f g h i j k l m n o p q r s t u v w x y z

spectacular
ADJECTIVE very impressive or dramatic

spectator spectators
NOUN a person who watches an event or a show

spectrum spectra or spectrums
NOUN the range of different colours produced when light passes through a prism or a drop of water. A rainbow shows the colours in a **spectrum**.

speech speeches
NOUN **1** the ability to speak or the act of speaking
NOUN **2** a formal talk given to an audience
NOUN **3** In grammar, direct **speech** is speech which is reported by using the exact words that the speaker used. Indirect or reported **speech** tells you what someone said, but does not use the person's actual words.

speech bubble speech bubbles
NOUN a line around words, used in comic strips or cartoons to show what characters are saying

speechless
ADJECTIVE unable to speak

speech marks
PLURAL NOUN punctuation marks (" " ' ') used in written texts to show when someone is speaking

speed speeds, speeding, sped or speeded
NOUN **1** the rate at which something moves or happens
NOUN **2** very fast movement or travel
VERB **3** If you **speed** somewhere, you move or travel there quickly.
VERB **4** Someone who is **speeding** is driving a vehicle faster than the legal speed limit.

speedboat speedboats
NOUN a fast motorboat

speedometer speedometers
NOUN the instrument in a vehicle which shows how fast the vehicle is moving

→ Have a look at the illustration for **car**

spell spells, spelling, spelt or spelled
VERB **1** When you **spell** a word, you name or write its letters in order.
NOUN **2** a short period of something • We expect a **spell** of good weather.
NOUN **3** words or rhymes used to perform magic

LANGUAGE TIP
You can write either *spelt* or *spelled* as the past form of *spell*.

spellbound
ADJECTIVE If you are **spellbound**, you are so fascinated by something that you cannot think of anything else.

spellcheck spellchecks, spellchecking, spellchecked
VERB If you **spellcheck** a document, you run a program over it to find any words that have not been spelt correctly.

spelling spellings
NOUN the correct order of letters in a word

spend spends, spending, spent
VERB **1** When you **spend** money, you buy things with it. • By lunchtime, I had **spent** all my money.
VERB **2** If you **spend** time or energy, you use it. • She **spends** hours working in the garden.

sphere spheres
NOUN a perfectly round object, such as a ball

spherical
ADJECTIVE shaped like a sphere

sphinx sphinxes
NOUN In mythology, the **sphinx** was a monster with a person's head and a lion's body.

spice spices
NOUN a substance obtained from a plant, often in the form of a powder or a seed, and added to food to give it flavour

spicy spicier, spiciest
ADJECTIVE strongly flavoured with spices

spider spiders

NOUN a small animal with eight legs. Some **spiders** spin webs to catch insects for food, others hunt.

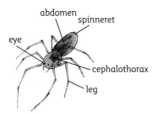

abdomen
spinneret
eye
cephalothorax
leg

spike spikes

NOUN something long and sharply pointed. Runners often have **spikes** on the soles of their shoes to stop them slipping.

spill spills, spilling, spilled or spilt

VERB If you **spill** something, or if it **spills**, it accidentally falls or runs out of a container.

LANGUAGE TIP

You can write either *spilled* or *spilt* as the past form of *spill*.

spin spins, spinning, spun

VERB **1** If someone or something **spins**, it turns quickly around a central point.
• *The Earth **spins** on its own axis.*
NOUN **2** a rapid turn around a central point

spinach

NOUN a vegetable with large green leaves

spine spines

NOUN **1** the row of bones down the middle of your back

→ Have a look at the illustration for **skeleton**

SYNONYM: backbone

NOUN **2** a spike on a plant or an animal
• *Porcupines are covered in **spines**.*
NOUN **3** the part of a book where the pages are joined together

spiral spirals

NOUN **1** a continuous curve that winds round and round, with each curve moving further out or further up
ADJECTIVE **2** in the shape of a spiral

spire spires

NOUN the pointed structure on top of a steeple

spirit spirits

NOUN **1** the part of you that is not physical and that is connected with the way you are
NOUN **2** a ghost or supernatural being
NOUN **3** liveliness, energy and self-confidence

spiritual

ADJECTIVE **1** to do with people's thoughts and beliefs, rather than their bodies and physical surroundings
ADJECTIVE **2** to do with people's religious beliefs

spit spits, spitting, spat

VERB **1** If you **spit**, you forcefully send saliva out of your mouth.
NOUN **2** saliva
NOUN **3** a long piece of metal or wood that you push through meat so that it can be hung over a fire to cook
NOUN **4** a long, flat, narrow piece of land sticking out into the sea

spite

NOUN **1** the desire to deliberately hurt or upset somebody
PHRASE **2** **In spite of** is used to begin a statement that makes the rest of what you are saying seem surprising. • *In spite of the rain, they watched the fireworks outside.*

spiteful

ADJECTIVE A **spiteful** person does or says nasty things to people to hurt them.

spitefully

ADVERB in a nasty way that is intended to hurt or upset someone

splash splashes, splashing, splashed

VERB **1** If you **splash** around in water, you make the water fly around in a noisy way.
NOUN **2** the sound made when something hits or falls into water

splendid

ADJECTIVE very good or very impressive

splint splints

NOUN a straight piece of metal or wood that is tied to a broken arm or leg to stop it moving

splinter splinters, splintering, splintered

NOUN **1** a thin, sharp piece of wood or glass that has broken off a larger piece
VERB **2** If something **splinters**, it breaks into thin, sharp pieces.

split splits, splitting, split

VERB If something **splits**, or if you **split** it, it divides into two or more parts.

a
b
c
d
e
f
g
h
i
j
k
l
m
n
o
p
q
r
s
t
u
v
w
x
y
z

383

split second split seconds
NOUN an extremely short period of time

splutter splutters, spluttering, spluttered
VERB 1 If you **splutter**, you speak in a confused way because you are embarrassed or angry.
VERB 2 If someone or something **splutters**, they make a series of short, coughing, spitting noises.

spoil spoils, spoiling, spoiled or spoilt
VERB 1 To **spoil** something means to damage it or stop it being successful or satisfactory. • My holiday was **spoiled** by rain.
VERB 2 To **spoil** children means to give them everything they want, making them selfish.

LANGUAGE TIP
You can write either spoiled or spoilt as the past form of spoil.

---

spoilsport spoilsports
NOUN someone who spoils other people's fun

spoke spokes
NOUN 1 The **spokes** of a wheel are the bars that connect the hub to the rim.
→ Have a look at the illustration for **bicycle**
VERB 2 the past tense of **speak**

spoken
VERB the past participle of **speak**

sponge sponges
NOUN 1 a soft, natural or man-made material with lots of small holes, used for washing yourself
NOUN 2 an animal found in the sea that has a body made up of many cells
NOUN 3 a soft, light cake or pudding

spongy spongier, spongiest
ADJECTIVE soft and full of small holes

sponsor sponsors, sponsoring, sponsored
VERB 1 If an organisation **sponsors** something, such as an event or someone's training, it gives money to pay for it.
VERB 2 If you **sponsor** someone who is doing something for charity, you agree to give them a sum of money for the charity if they manage to do it.
NOUN 3 a person or organization that sponsors something or someone

spontaneous
ADJECTIVE not planned or arranged

spontaneously
ADVERB in a way that is not planned or arranged

spooky spookier, spookiest
ADJECTIVE frightening and creepy

spoon spoons
NOUN an object shaped like a small shallow bowl with a long handle, used for eating, stirring and serving food

spore spores
NOUN **Spores** are cells produced by some plants and bacteria which can develop into new plants or bacteria.

sport sports
NOUN games and other enjoyable activities that need physical effort and skill

spot spots, spotting, spotted
NOUN 1 a small, round, coloured area on a surface
NOUN 2 a pimple on a person's skin
NOUN 3 a small amount of something
NOUN 4 a particular place
VERB 5 If you **spot** something, you suddenly see it.
PHRASE 6 If you do something **on the spot**, you do it immediately.

spotless
ADJECTIVE perfectly clean

spotlight spotlights
NOUN a powerful light that can be directed to light up a small area • stage **spotlights**

spotty spottier, spottiest
ADJECTIVE marked with spots

spouse spouses
NOUN Someone's **spouse** is the person they are married to.

spout spouts, spouting, spouted
VERB 1 When liquid or flame **spouts** out of something, it shoots out in a long stream.
NOUN 2 a tube or opening from which liquid can pour
VERB 3 When someone **spouts** what they have learned, they say it in a boring way.

sprain sprains, spraining, sprained
VERB 1 If you **sprain** a joint, you accidentally damage it by twisting it violently.
NOUN 2 the injury caused by spraining a joint

sprang
VERB the past tense of **spring**

sprawl sprawls, sprawling, sprawled
VERB **1** If you **sprawl** somewhere, you sit or lie there with your legs and arms spread out. • *She sprawled on the bed reading her book.*
VERB **2** A place that **sprawls** is spread out over a large area.

spray sprays, spraying, sprayed
NOUN **1** many small drops of liquid splashed or forced into the air
NOUN **2** a liquid kept under pressure in a container
VERB **3** If you **spray** a liquid over something, you cover it with drops of the liquid. • *We sprayed the dry lawn with water from the hose pipe.*

spread spreads, spreading, spread
VERB **1** If you **spread** a substance on a surface, you put a thin layer of it on the surface. • *Spread the butter on the bread before you make the sandwich.*
VERB **2** If you **spread** something out, you open it out or arrange it so that it can be seen or used easily. • *He spread the map out on his knees.*
VERB **3** If something **spreads**, it gradually reaches more people. • *The news spread quickly.*

spreadsheet spreadsheets
NOUN a computer program that is used for displaying and dealing with numbers

sprightly sprightlier, sprightliest
ADJECTIVE lively and active

spring springs, springing, sprang, sprung
NOUN **1** the season between winter and summer, when most plants start to grow
NOUN **2** a coil of wire that returns to its original shape after being pressed or pulled
NOUN **3** a place where water naturally comes up through the ground
VERB **4** If you **spring**, you jump upwards or forwards.

springboard springboards
NOUN a springy board on which a gymnast or diver jumps to gain height

springbok springboks
NOUN a small South African antelope that moves in leaps

sprinkle sprinkles, sprinkling, sprinkled
VERB If you **sprinkle** a liquid or powder over something, you scatter it over it.

sprint sprints, sprinting, sprinted
NOUN **1** a short, fast race
VERB **2** If you **sprint**, you run fast over a short distance.

sprout sprouts, sprouting, sprouted
VERB **1** When something **sprouts**, it starts to grow.
VERB **2** If things **sprout** up, they appear very quickly.
NOUN **3** an abbreviation of *Brussels sprout*

sprung
VERB the past participle of **spring**

spun
VERB the past tense and past participle of **spin**

spur spurs, spurring, spurred
VERB **1** If you **spur** someone on, you encourage them.
NOUN **2** a sharp device worn on the heel of a rider's boot to urge the horse to go faster

spurt spurts, spurting, spurted
NOUN **1** a jet of liquid or flame
NOUN **2** a sudden increase in speed
VERB **3** If a liquid **spurts**, it gushes in a sudden stream. • *Water spurted out of the hose.*

spy spies, spying, spied
NOUN **1** a person sent to find out secret information about a country or organisation
VERB **2** Someone who **spies** tries to find out secret information about another country or organisation.
VERB **3** If you **spy** on someone, you watch them secretly.

squabble squabbles, squabbling, squabbled
VERB **1** When people **squabble**, they quarrel about something unimportant.
NOUN **2** a quarrel

squad squads
NOUN a small group of people chosen to do a particular activity

squadron squadrons
NOUN a section of one of the armed forces, especially the air force

WORD HISTORY
from Italian *squadrone* meaning soldiers drawn up in a square formation

squalid
ADJECTIVE dirty, untidy and in bad condition

A
B
C
D
E
F
G
H
I
J
K
L
M
N
O
P
Q
R
S
T
U
V
W
X
Y
Z

squander squanders, squandering, squandered
VERB If you **squander** money or resources, you waste them.

square squares
NOUN **1** a plane shape with four equal sides and four right angles
NOUN **2** In a town or city, a **square** is a flat, open area with buildings or streets around the edge.
ADJECTIVE **3** shaped like a **square**
ADJECTIVE **4 Square** is used after units of length when you are giving the length of each side of something that is square in shape. • *two pieces of wood 4 inches* **square**
ADJECTIVE **5** A **square** number is a number like 4, 16 or 25 which is the prodcut of a number multiplied by itself. The **square** root of a number like 16 is the number which is multiplied by itself, in this case 4.

WORD HISTORY
from Latin *quadra* meaning square

---

squash squashes, squashing, squashed
VERB If you **squash** something, you press it so that it becomes flat or loses its shape.

squat squats, squatting, squatted, squatter, squattest
VERB **1** If you **squat** down, you crouch, balancing on your feet with your legs bent.
VERB **2** A person who **squats** in an unused building lives there without permission and without paying.
ADJECTIVE **3** short and thick

squawk squawks, squawking, squawked
VERB **1** When a bird **squawks**, it makes a loud, harsh noise.
NOUN **2** a loud, harsh noise made by a bird

squeak squeaks, squeaking, squeaked
VERB **1** If something or someone **squeaks**, they make a short, high-pitched sound.
NOUN **2** a short, high-pitched sound

squeal squeals, squealing, squealed
VERB **1** When things or people **squeal**, they make long, high-pitched sounds.
NOUN **2** a long, high-pitched sound

squeamish
ADJECTIVE easily upset by unpleasant sights or situations

squeeze squeezes, squeezing, squeezed
VERB **1** When you **squeeze** something, you press it firmly from two sides.
VERB **2** If you **squeeze** somewhere, you force yourself into a small space or through a gap.
VERB **3** If you **squeeze** something somewhere, you force it into a small space.

squelch squelches, squelching, squelched
VERB If something **squelches**, it makes a wet, sucking sound.

squid squids
NOUN an animal that lives in the sea, with a long, soft body and ten limbs

squiggle squiggles
NOUN a wiggly line

squint squints, squinting, squinted
VERB **1** If you **squint**, you screw up your eyes to look at something.
NOUN **2** If someone has a **squint**, their eyes look in different directions from each other.

squirm squirms, squirming, squirmed
VERB If you **squirm**, you wriggle and twist your body about, usually because you are nervous or embarrassed.

squirrel squirrels
NOUN a small, furry rodent with a long, bushy tail

squirt squirts, squirting, squirted
VERB **1** If a liquid **squirts**, or you **squirt** it, it comes out of a narrow opening in a thin, fast stream.
NOUN **2** a thin, fast stream of liquid

stab stabs, stabbing, stabbed
VERB To **stab** someone means to wound them by pushing a knife into their body.

stable stables
NOUN **1** a building in which horses are kept
ADJECTIVE **2** Something that is **stable** cannot be moved or shaken.
ADJECTIVE **3** If someone is **stable**, they are level-headed and dependable.

stack stacks, stacking, stacked
NOUN **1** a pile of things, one on top of the other
VERB **2** If you **stack** items, you pile them up neatly.

stadium stadiums
NOUN a sports ground with rows of seats around it for spectators

staff staffs
NOUN the people who work for an organisation

stag stags
NOUN an adult male deer

stage stages, staging, staged
NOUN **1** In a theatre, the **stage** is the raised platform where the actors or entertainers perform.
VERB **2** If someone **stages** a play or event, they organise it or present it.

stagger staggers, staggering, staggered
VERB **1** If you **stagger**, you walk unsteadily, for example because you are ill.
VERB **2** If something **staggers** you, it amazes you.
VERB **3** If events are **staggered**, they are arranged so that they do not all happen at the same time.

stagnant
ADJECTIVE **Stagnant** water is still rather than flowing, and is often smelly and dirty.

stain stains
NOUN a mark on something that is difficult or impossible to clean off

stair stairs
NOUN one of a set of steps, usually inside a building going from one floor to another
• He walked slowly up the **stairs**.

staircase staircases
NOUN a set of stairs

stake stakes, staking, staked
PHRASE **1** If something is **at stake**, it might be lost or damaged if something else is not successful. • The cup was **at stake** if he missed the goal.
VERB **2** If you say you would **stake** your money, life or reputation on the result of something, you mean you would risk it.

stalactite stalactites
NOUN a stony spike hanging down like an icicle from the ceiling of a cave

stalactite

stalagmite

stalagmite stalagmites
NOUN a pointed piece of rock standing on the floor of a cave

stale staler, stalest
ADJECTIVE **Stale** food or air is no longer fresh.

SYNONYMS: fusty, musty, old

stalk stalks, stalking, stalked
NOUN **1** The **stalk** of a flower or leaf is its stem.
VERB **2** To **stalk** a person or an animal means to follow them quietly in order to catch, kill or observe them. • The cat is **stalking** the bird in the garden.

stall stalls, stalling, stalled
NOUN **1** a large table displaying goods for sale or information
PLURAL NOUN **2** In a theatre, the **stalls** are the seats at the lowest level, in front of the stage.
VERB **3** When a vehicle **stalls**, the engine suddenly stops.

stallion stallions
NOUN an adult male horse that can be used for breeding

stamen stamens
NOUN the part of a flower that produces pollen

→ Have a look at the illustration for **flower**

stamina
NOUN the physical or mental energy needed to do something for a very long time
• Running a marathon takes determination and **stamina**.

a
b
c
d
e
f
g
h
i
j
k
l
m
n
o
p
q
r
s
t
u
v
w
x
y
z

387

stammer stammers, stammering, stammered
VERB **1** When someone **stammers**, they speak with difficulty, repeating words and sounds and hesitating.
NOUN **2** Someone who has a **stammer** tends to stammer when they speak.

stamp stamps, stamping, stamped
NOUN **1** a small piece of paper that you stick on a letter or parcel before posting it, to prove that you have paid the postage
VERB **2** To **stamp** a piece of paper means to make a mark on it using a small block with a pattern cut into it. • He **stamped** her passport.
VERB **3** If you **stamp**, you lift your foot and put it down hard on the ground.

stamp out
VERB To **stamp out** something means to put an end to it. • We must try to **stamp out** this kind of behaviour.

stampede stampedes, stampeding, stampeded
VERB **1** When a group of animals **stampede**, they rush forward in a wild, uncontrolled way.
NOUN **2** a group of animals stampeding

stand stands, standing, stood
VERB **1** If you are **standing**, you are upright with your weight on your feet.
VERB **2** If something **stands** somewhere, that is where it is. • The house **stands** on top of a hill.
VERB **3** If you cannot **stand** someone or something, you do not like them at all.
VERB **4** If you **stand** in an election, you are a candidate.
NOUN **5** A **stand** at a sports ground is a building where people can watch what is happening.

stand up
VERB When you **stand up**, you get into a standing position.

standard standards
NOUN **1** how good something is
NOUN **2** an officially agreed level against which things can be measured or judged

standstill
NOUN a complete stop

stank
VERB the past tense of **stink**

stanza stanzas
NOUN a verse of a poem

staple staples, stapling, stapled
NOUN **1** a small piece of wire that holds sheets of paper firmly together. You insert it with a device called a stapler.
VERB **2** If you **staple** sheets of paper, you fasten them together with staples.

star stars
NOUN **1** a large ball of burning gases in space that appears as a point of light in the sky at night. Our sun is a **star**.
NOUN **2** a shape with several points, usually five or six, sticking out in a regular pattern
NOUN **3** a famous actor, sports player or musician

starboard
ADJECTIVE The **starboard** side of a ship is the right-hand side when you are facing the front.

starch starches
NOUN **1** a substance found in foods such as bread, rice, pasta and potatoes that gives you energy
NOUN **2** a substance used for stiffening fabric

stare stares, staring, stared
VERB **1** If you **stare** at something, you look at it for a long time.
NOUN **2** a long, fixed look at something

starfish starfishes or starfish
NOUN a star-shaped animal found in the sea that has five pointed limbs

starling starlings
NOUN a common European bird with shiny dark feathers

start starts, starting, started
VERB **1** If you **start** something, you begin it.
NOUN **2** The **start** of something is the point or time at which it begins.

startle startles, startling, startled
VERB If something sudden and unexpected **startles** you, it surprises you and gives you a slight fright.

starve starves, starving, starved
VERB If people are **starving**, they are suffering from a serious lack of food and are likely to die.

state states, stating, stated

NOUN **1** The **state** of something or someone is their condition, or how they are.

NOUN **2** Some countries are divided into regions called **states** that make some of their own laws.

NOUN **3** You can call the government and the officials of a country the **state**. • *Carmen received a pension from the* **state**.

VERB **4** If you **state** something, you say it or write it clearly, especially in a formal way. • *Please* **state** *your name and address.*

statement statements

NOUN something you say or write that gives information in a formal way

state of matter states of matter

NOUN one of the forms of matter, for example solid, liquid or gas

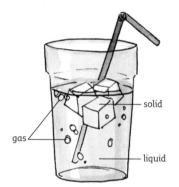

gas

solid

liquid

static

ADJECTIVE **1** never moving or changing • *The temperature is fairly* **static**.

NOUN **2** an electrical charge caused by friction

station stations

NOUN **1** a building where trains or buses stop to let passengers on and off

NOUN **2** A building that is used by people such as the police and fire brigade. • *police* **station**

stationary

ADJECTIVE not moving • *a* **stationary** *car*

SYNONYM: motionless

stationery

NOUN paper, pens and other writing equipment

statistics

PLURAL NOUN facts worked out by looking at information that is given in numbers • *They gathered* **statistics** *about journeys to school.*

statue statues

NOUN a sculpture, often of a person

stay stays, staying, stayed

VERB **1** If you **stay** in one place, you do not move away from it.

VERB **2** If you **stay** with a friend, you spend time with them as a visitor.

steady steadier, steadiest

ADJECTIVE firm and not moving about • *She made sure the ladder was* **steady** *before she climbed up it.*

SYNONYMS: firm, secure, stable

steak steaks

NOUN a large, good-quality piece of beef or fish

steal steals, stealing, stole, stolen

VERB If someone **steals** something, they take it without permission and without meaning to return it.

steam

NOUN the hot vapour formed when water boils • *The* **steam** *rose into the air.*

steam-engine steam-engines

NOUN any engine that is powered by steam

steel

NOUN a very strong metal made mainly from iron

steel band steel bands

NOUN a group of people who play music on special metal drums

steep steeper, steepest

ADJECTIVE A **steep** slope rises sharply and is difficult to go up.

steeple steeples

NOUN a tall, pointed structure above a church roof

steer steers, steering, steered

VERB When someone **steers** a vehicle or boat, they control it so that it goes in the direction they want.

steering wheel steering wheels

NOUN the wheel inside a car or other vehicle which the driver holds when he or she is driving

→ Have a look at the illustration for **car**

a
b
c
d
e
f
g
h
i
j
k
l
m
n
o
p
q
r
s
t
u
v
w
x
y
z

stem stems

NOUN the thin, usually upright, part of a plant that grows above the ground and on which the leaves and flowers grow

→ Have a look at the illustration for **flower**

stencil stencils, stencilling, stencilled

NOUN **1** a thin sheet of card, metal or plastic with a pattern cut out of it. The pattern can be copied onto another surface by painting over the **stencil**.

VERB **2** If you **stencil** a design onto a surface, you create it using a stencil.

step steps, stepping, stepped

NOUN **1** the movement of lifting your foot and putting it down again when you are walking, running or dancing

NOUN **2** one of the places at different levels that you put your feet on when you go up and down a ladder or stairs

VERB **3** If you **step** in a particular direction, you take a step there.

stepbrother stepbrothers

NOUN the son of someone's stepmother or stepfather

stepchild stepchildren

NOUN a stepdaughter or stepson

stepdaughter stepdaughters

NOUN someone's daughter by their wife's or husband's previous marriage

stepfather stepfathers

NOUN a man who is married to your mother but who is not your natural father

stepmother stepmothers

NOUN a woman who is married to your father but who is not your natural mother

stepsister stepsisters

NOUN the daughter of someone's stepmother or stepfather

stepson stepsons

NOUN someone's son by their wife's or husband's previous marriage

stereo stereos

NOUN a piece of equipment that reproduces sound from records, tapes or CDs, directing the sound through two speakers

stereotype stereotypes

NOUN a simplified way people think of a particular type of person or thing ● *the* **stereotype** *of the polite, industrious Japanese*

sterile

ADJECTIVE **1** clean and free from germs

ADJECTIVE **2** unable to have children or reproduce

sterility

NOUN **1** the quality that something has when it is clean and free from germs

NOUN **2 Sterility** is when someone is unable to have children or reproduce.

sterling

NOUN the money system of Great Britain

stern sterner, sternest

ADJECTIVE **1** very serious and strict

NOUN **2** the back part of a ship

→ Have a look at the illustration for **ship**

stethoscope stethoscopes

NOUN a device used by doctors to listen to a patient's heart and breathing, made of earpieces connected to a hollow tube and a small disc

stew stews, stewing, stewed

NOUN **1** a dish of small pieces of savoury food cooked together slowly in a liquid

VERB **2** If you **stew** meat, vegetables or fruit, you cook them slowly in a liquid.

WORD HISTORY

from Middle English *stuen* meaning to take a very hot bath

steward stewards

NOUN **1** a person who works on a ship or plane looking after passengers and serving meals

NOUN **2** a person who helps to direct the public at events such as a race or a concert

stick sticks, sticking, stuck

NOUN **1** a long, thin piece of wood

VERB **2** If you **stick** a long or pointed object into something, you push it in.

VERB **3** If you **stick** one thing to another, you attach it with glue or tape.

VERB **4** If something **sticks**, it becomes fixed or jammed.

stick out

VERB If something **sticks out**, it projects from something else.

stick up for

VERB (*informal*) If you **stick up for** someone or something, you support or defend them.

sticker stickers

NOUN a label with words or pictures on it for sticking on something

sticky stickier, stickiest
ADJECTIVE If something is **sticky**, it is covered with a substance that can stick to other things.

stiff stiffer, stiffest
ADJECTIVE **1** Something that is **stiff** is firm and not easily bent. • *a stiff piece of card*
ADJECTIVE **2** If you feel **stiff**, your muscles or joints ache when you move.
ADJECTIVE **3 Stiff** behaviour is formal, and not friendly or relaxed.
ADJECTIVE **4** difficult or severe • *It was a stiff competition.*

stifle stifles, stifling, stifled
VERB **1** If you feel **stifled**, you feel you cannot breathe properly.
VERB **2** If you **stifle** something, you stop it happening. • *She stifled a yawn.*
ADJECTIVE **3 Stifling** heat is very hot and makes it difficult to breathe. • *The atmosphere in the greenhouse was stifling.*

stigma stigmas
NOUN the top of the centre part of a flower which takes in pollen

→ Have a look at the illustration for **flower**

stile stiles
NOUN a step built in a hedge or wall so that people can climb over or through it

still stiller, stillest
ADVERB **1** You say **still** when something is the same as it was before. • *I've still got a headache.*
ADVERB **2** even then • *I've worked all day and there's still more to do.*
ADJECTIVE **3** If someone or something is **still**, they stay in the same position without moving.
ADJECTIVE **4** When the air is **still**, there is no wind.
ADJECTIVE **5** A **still** drink is not fizzy.

stilts
PLURAL NOUN **1** long poles on which people balance or walk
PLURAL NOUN **2** long poles on which houses are sometimes built

stimulate stimulates, stimulating, stimulated
VERB **1** To **stimulate** something means to encourage it to begin or develop. • *to stimulate interest*

SYNONYM: inspire

VERB **2** If something **stimulates** you, it interests and excites you.

SYNONYM: inspire

sting stings, stinging, stung
VERB **1** If an animal or plant **stings** you, it pricks your skin and hurts.
VERB **2** If a part of your body **stings**, you feel a sharp, tingling pain there.

stink stinks, stinking, stank, stunk
VERB **1** Something that **stinks** smells very unpleasant.
NOUN **2** a very unpleasant smell

stir stirs, stirring, stirred
VERB **1** When you **stir** a liquid, you move it around using a spoon or a stick.
VERB **2** If someone **stirs**, they move slightly, or start to move after sleeping or being still. • *It was very noisy but the baby didn't stir.*

stirrup stirrups
NOUN one of the two metal loops hanging by leather straps from a horse's saddle, that you put your feet in when riding

stitch stitches, stitching, stitched
VERB **1** When you **stitch** pieces of material together, you use a needle and thread to sew them together.
NOUN **2** one of the pieces of thread that can be seen where material has been sewn
NOUN **3** one of the pieces of thread that can be seen where skin has been sewn together to heal a wound • *He had eleven stitches in his lip.*
NOUN **4** a sharp pain you feel in your side after running

stoat stoats
NOUN a small wild mammal with a long body, brown fur and a black-tipped tail

stock stocks
NOUN **1** the total amount of goods a shop has for sale
NOUN **2** If you have a **stock** of things, you have a supply ready for use.

stocking stockings
NOUN one of a pair of long pieces of fine, stretchy fabric that cover a woman's leg and foot

stole stoles
VERB **1** the past tense of **steal**
NOUN **2** a shawl to cover a woman's shoulders

stolen
VERB the past participle of **steal**

a
b
c
d
e
f
g
h
i
j
k
l
m
n
o
p
q
r
s
t
u
v
w
x
y
z

stomach stomachs

NOUN **1** the organ inside your body where food is digested

→ Have a look at the illustration for **organ**

NOUN **2** the front part of your body below your waist

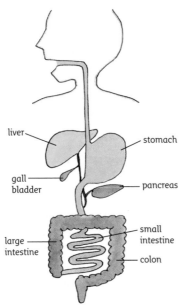

liver

stomach

gall bladder

pancreas

large intestine

small intestine

colon

stone stones

NOUN **1** the hard solid substance found in the ground and used for building

NOUN **2** a small piece of rock

NOUN **3** a unit of weight equal to 14 pounds or about 6·35 kilograms

stony stonier, stoniest

ADJECTIVE **Stony** ground has many stones in it.

stood

VERB the past tense and past participle of **stand**

stool stools

NOUN a seat with legs but no back or arms

stoop stoops, stooping, stooped

VERB **1** If you **stoop**, you bend your body forwards.

VERB **2** If you would not **stoop** to something, you would not disgrace yourself by doing it.

stop stops, stopping, stopped

VERB **1** If you **stop** doing something, you no longer do it.

VERB **2** If an activity **stops**, it comes to an end.

VERB **3** If you **stop** something, you prevent it from happening or continuing.

VERB **4** If people or things that are moving **stop**, they no longer move.

NOUN **5** a place where a bus, train or other vehicle stops to let passengers on and off

stopwatch stopwatches

NOUN a watch that can be started and stopped, that is used to time things such as races

storage

NOUN **1** the keeping of something somewhere until it is needed

NOUN **2** the process of storing data in a computer

store stores, storing, stored

NOUN **1** a shop

NOUN **2** a supply of something that is kept until it is needed

NOUN **3** a place where things are kept while they are not used

VERB **4** When you **store** something somewhere you keep it there until it is needed.

storey storeys

NOUN one of the floors or levels of a building

stork storks

NOUN a very large white and black bird with long red legs and a long bill. **Storks** live mainly near water in Eastern Europe and Africa.

storm storms, storming, stormed

NOUN **1** a period of bad weather, when there is heavy rain, a strong wind and often thunder and lightning

VERB **2** If soldiers **storm** a defended place, they make a surprise attack on it.

NOUN **3** If there is a **storm** of protest, many people complain loudly.

story stories

NOUN a telling of events, real or imaginary, spoken or written

stout stouter, stoutest

ADJECTIVE **1** rather fat

ADJECTIVE **2** thick, strong and sturdy

● *stout walking shoes*

stove stoves

NOUN a piece of equipment for heating a room or for cooking ● *She warmed the milk on the stove.*

straddle straddles, straddling, straddle

VERB If you **straddle** something, you stand or sit with your legs either side of it.

straight **straighter, straightest**
ADJECTIVE **1** continuing in the same direction without curving or bending • a **straight** road
ADJECTIVE **2** A **straight** angle is an angle of 180°.
ADJECTIVE **3** honest and direct • a **straight** answer
ADVERB **4** immediately and directly • We will go **straight** to school.
ADVERB **5** If you stand up **straight**, you stand upright.

straighten **straightens, straightening, straightened**
VERB If you **straighten** something, you make it straight.

straightforward
ADJECTIVE **1** easy to understand
ADJECTIVE **2** honest and truthful

strain **strains, straining, strained**
ADJECTIVE **1** If you feel **strained**, you feel tense and anxious.
NOUN **2** If a **strain** is put on something, it is affected by a strong force that may damage it.
VERB **3** If you **strain** a muscle, you use it too much and injure it so that it is painful.
VERB **4** If you **strain** food or a mixture, you separate the solid parts from the liquid parts, for example by putting it through a sieve.

strait **straits**
NOUN a narrow strip of sea between two pieces of land, that connects two larger areas of sea

stranded
ADJECTIVE If someone or something is **stranded**, they are stuck somewhere and cannot leave. • **stranded** on the rocks

strange **stranger, strangest**
ADJECTIVE **1** unusual or unexpected • a **strange** dream
ADJECTIVE **2** not known, seen or experienced before • She was all alone in a **strange** country.

stranger **strangers**
NOUN someone you have never met before

strangle **strangles, strangling, strangled**
VERB To **strangle** someone means to kill them by squeezing their throat to stop them breathing.

strap **straps**
NOUN a narrow piece of leather or cloth, used to fasten or hold things together

strategy **strategies**
NOUN a plan for achieving something

stratosphere
NOUN the layer of the Earth's atmosphere which lies between 10 and 50 kilometres above the Earth

straw **straws**
NOUN **1** a hollow tube of paper or plastic that you use to suck a drink into your mouth
NOUN **2** the dry, yellowish stalks of some crops

strawberry **strawberries**
NOUN a small red fruit with tiny seeds in its skin

stray **strays, straying, strayed**
VERB **1** When people or animals **stray**, they wander away from where they should be.
VERB **2** If your thoughts **stray**, you stop concentrating.
ADJECTIVE **3** A **stray** dog or cat is one that has wandered away from where it lives.
NOUN **4** a stray dog or cat

streak **streaks**
NOUN a long, narrow mark or stain

stream **streams, streaming, streamed**
NOUN **1** a small river
NOUN **2** You can refer to a steady flow of something as a **stream**. • a constant **stream** of children
VERB **3** If something **streams**, it flows fast, without stopping. • Rain **streamed** down the windscreen.

streamer **streamers**
NOUN a long piece of paper or ribbon used as a decoration

street **streets**
NOUN a road in a town or village, usually with buildings along it

strength
NOUN how strong or powerful someone or something is

SYNONYMS: might, force, power

strenuous
ADJECTIVE involving a lot of effort or energy

stress **stresses, stressing, stressed**
NOUN **1** worry and nervous tension

SYNONYMS: anxiety, pressure, strain

VERB **2** If you **stress** a point, you emphasise it and draw attention to how important it is.

a
b
c
d
e
f
g
h
i
j
k
l
m
n
o
p
q
r
s
t
u
v
w
x
y
z

393

stretch stretches, stretching, stretched

VERB **1** If you **stretch** something soft or elastic, you pull it to make it longer or bigger.

VERB **2** Something that **stretches** over an area covers the whole of that area. • *Forests stretched the length of the valley.*

VERB **3** When you **stretch**, you move part of your body as far away from you as you can.

NOUN **4** an area of something • *This is a quiet stretch of beach.*

stretcher stretchers

NOUN a long piece of material with a pole along each side, used to carry an injured person

strict stricter, strictest

ADJECTIVE **1** Someone who is **strict** controls other people very firmly.

ADJECTIVE **2** exact or complete • *We were given strict instructions.*

stride strides, striding, strode, stridden

VERB **1** If you **stride** along, you walk quickly with long steps.

NOUN **2** a long step

strike strikes, striking, struck

VERB **1** If you **strike** something, you hit it with a lot of force.

VERB **2** If workers **strike**, they refuse to work because they want better working conditions or more money.

VERB **3** If you **strike** a match, you make a flame by rubbing it against something rough.

striking

ADJECTIVE very noticeable because of being unusual or attractive

string strings

NOUN **1** thin rope made of twisted threads

NOUN **2** a row or series of similar things • *a string of islands*

strip strips, stripping, stripped

NOUN **1** a long, narrow piece of something

VERB **2** If you **strip**, you take off all your clothes.

stripe stripes

NOUN a long, thin line of colour

strode

VERB the past tense of **stride**

stroke strokes, stroking, stroked

VERB **1** If you **stroke** something, you move your hand smoothly and gently over it.

NOUN **2** The **strokes** of a brush or pen are the movements that you make with it.

NOUN **3** If someone has a **stroke**, a blood vessel in the brain bursts or gets blocked, possibly causing death or paralysis.

NOUN **4** a style of swimming • *My best stroke is the front crawl.*

stroll strolls, strolling, strolled

VERB **1** If you **stroll** along, you walk slowly in a relaxed way.

SYNONYMS: amble, saunter

NOUN **2** a slow, pleasurable walk

SYNONYMS: amble, saunter

strong stronger, strongest

ADJECTIVE **1** Someone who is **strong** has a lot of physical power.

ADJECTIVE **2** You also say that someone is **strong** when they are confident and have courage.

ADJECTIVE **3** **Strong** objects are able to withstand rough treatment, and are not easily damaged.

ADJECTIVE **4** great or intense • *a strong wind*

struck

VERB the past tense and past participle of **strike**

structure structures

NOUN **1** The **structure** of something is the way it is made, built or organised.

NOUN **2** something that has been built or put together

struggle struggles, struggling, struggled

VERB **1** If you **struggle** to do something difficult, you try hard to do it.

VERB **2** When people **struggle**, they twist and move violently to get free of something or someone.

NOUN **3** Something that is a **struggle** is difficult to achieve and takes a lot of effort.

stubble

NOUN **1** the short stalks remaining in the ground after a crop is harvested

NOUN **2** If a man has **stubble** on his face, he has very short hair growing there because he has not shaved recently.

stubborn

ADJECTIVE Someone who is **stubborn** is determined not to change the way they think or how they do things.

SYNONYM: obstinate

stuck

ADJECTIVE **1** If something or someone is **stuck**, they cannot be moved.

ADJECTIVE **2** If you are **stuck**, you cannot go on with your work because you are finding it too difficult.

VERB **3** the past tense and past participle of **stick**

stud studs

NOUN **1** a small piece of metal, or other material, fixed into something • *Rachel wore gold studs in her ears.*

NOUN **2** A male horse or other animal that is kept for **stud** is kept for breeding purposes.

NOUN **3** a place where horses are kept and bred

student students

NOUN a person studying at a university, college or school

studio studios

NOUN **1** a room where an artist works

NOUN **2** a room containing special equipment where records, films, or radio or television programmes are made

studious

ADJECTIVE Someone who is **studious** studies hard or is fond of studying.

study studies, studying, studied

VERB **1** If you **study** a particular subject, you spend time learning about it.

VERB **2** If you **study** something, you look at it carefully.

NOUN **3** a room for studying or working in

stuff stuffs, stuffing, stuffed

NOUN **1** You can refer to a substance or a group of things as **stuff**. • *She spread out her stuff on top of the table.*

VERB **2** If you **stuff** something somewhere, you push it there quickly and carelessly.

VERB **3** If you **stuff** something, you fill it with something else. • *Mum stuffed the turkey.*

stuffy stuffier, stuffiest

ADJECTIVE **1** If it is **stuffy** in a room, there is not enough fresh air.

ADJECTIVE **2** boring and old-fashioned

stumble stumbles, stumbling, stumbled

VERB **1** If you **stumble** while you are walking or running, you trip and nearly fall.

VERB **2** If you **stumble** when you are speaking, you hesitate or make mistakes.

stump stumps, stumping, stumped

NOUN **1** a small part of something that is left when the rest has gone • *a tree stump*

NOUN **2** In cricket, the **stumps** are the three upright wooden sticks that support the bails, forming the wicket.

VERB **3** If a question or problem **stumps** you, you cannot think of an answer or solution.

stun stuns, stunning, stunned

VERB **1** If you are **stunned**, or something **stuns** you, you are very shocked by it.

VERB **2** If something **stuns** a person or an animal, it knocks them unconscious.

stung

VERB the past tense and past participle of **sting**

stunk

VERB the past participle of **stink**

stunt stunts

NOUN an unusual or dangerous and exciting thing that someone does to get publicity or as part of a performance

stupid stupider, stupidest

ADJECTIVE If you are **stupid**, you are not sensible and do not make wise decisions.

sturdy sturdier, sturdiest

ADJECTIVE strong, firm and well built

stutter stutters, stuttering, stuttered

NOUN **1** Someone who has a **stutter** finds it difficult to speak smoothly and often repeats the beginning of words.

VERB **2** When someone **stutters**, they hesitate or repeat sounds when speaking.

sty sties

NOUN a hut with a yard where pigs are kept on a farm

style styles

NOUN **1** how something is done, made, said or written • *The food was cooked in Cantonese style.*

NOUN **2** A person or place that has **style** is smart, elegant and fashionable.

sub-

PREFIX You add **sub-**to the beginning of a word to mean below or beneath. For example, something that is **sub**standard is below the required standard, and a **sub**heading comes somewhere below a main heading.

subheading subheadings

NOUN a title to a part of a larger section of a book. A chapter may have several sections in it, each with a **subheading**.

a
b
c
d
e
f
g
h
i
j
k
l
m
n
o
p
q
r
s
t
u
v
w
x
y
z

395

subject subjects, subjecting, subjected

NOUN **1** The **subject** of a book, programme or conversation is the thing or person it is about. • *Horses are the **subject** of this book.*

NOUN **2** something that you learn about • *Maths is my favourite **subject**.*

NOUN **3** The **subjects** of a country are the people who live there.

NOUN **4** In grammar, the **subject** is the word or words representing the person or thing doing the action. For example, in the sentence *My cat keeps catching birds*, *my cat* is the **subject**.

VERB **5** If you **subject** someone to something, you make them experience it.

PRONUNCIATION TIP

The noun is pronomced **sub**-jekt. The verb is pronounced sub-**jekt**.

submarine submarines

NOUN a type of ship that can travel beneath the surface of the sea

submerge submerges, submerging, submerged

VERB To **submerge** means to go beneath the surface of a liquid, or to push something beneath the surface of a liquid.

submit submits, submitting, submitted

VERB **1** If you **submit** to something or someone, you give in to them.

VERB **2** If you **submit** something like a report or an essay, you hand it in.

subscribe subscribes, subscribing, subscribed

VERB If you **subscribe** to something, you regularly pay a sum of money to be a member of something or to receive a magazine.

subside subsides, subsiding, subsided

VERB **1** If something **subsides**, it sinks.

VERB **2** To **subside** is to become quiet or back to normal after a fuss.

substance substances

NOUN anything that is a solid, a powder, a liquid or a paste

SYNONYM: material

substantial

ADJECTIVE **1** very large in degree or amount

ADJECTIVE **2** large and strongly built

substitute substitutes, substituting, substituted

VERB **1** If you **substitute** one thing for another, you use it instead of the other thing.

NOUN **2** If one thing is a **substitute** for another, it is used instead of it or put in its place.

SYNONYMS: alternative, replacement

subtitle subtitles

NOUN A film or television programme with **subtitles** has the speech, or a translation of it, printed at the bottom of the screen.

subtle subtler, subtlest

ADJECTIVE very fine, delicate or small in degree

subtract subtracts, subtracting, subtracted

VERB If you **subtract** one number from another, you take away the first number from the second.

subtraction

NOUN the process of taking one number away from another

suburban

ADJECTIVE to do with the outskirts of a town or city

subway subways

NOUN **1** a footpath that goes underneath a road

NOUN **2** an underground railway

succeed succeeds, succeeding, succeeded

VERB **1** If you **succeed**, you manage to do what you are trying to do.

ANTONYM: fail

VERB **2** If one person **succeeds** another, they come after them and take their place.

success successes

NOUN the achievement of something you have been trying to do

successful

ADJECTIVE having success

succession successions

NOUN **1** a number of things happening one after the other

NOUN **2** When someone becomes the next person to have an important position, you can call this event their **succession**.

such

ADVERB **1** You can use **such** to emphasise something. • *He's **such** a nice boy.*

ADJECTIVE **2** the same kind or similar • *I have never seen **such** flowers.*

PHRASE **3** You can use **such as** to introduce examples of something. • *There were trees **such as** oak, ash and elm.*

suck **sucks, sucking, sucked**
VERB If you **suck** something, you hold it in your mouth and pull at it with your cheeks and tongue, usually to get liquid out of it.

sudden
ADJECTIVE happening quickly and unexpectedly • *We heard a **sudden** cry.*

sue **sues, suing, sued**
VERB To **sue** someone means to start a legal case against them, usually to claim money from them.

suede
NOUN a thin, soft leather with a velvety surface

suffer **suffers, suffering, suffered**
VERB If you **suffer**, you feel pain or sadness.

sufficient
ADJECTIVE If an amount is **sufficient**, there is enough of it available.

suffix **suffixes**
NOUN a group of letters that is added to the end of a word to form a new word, for example *-ness* or *-ship*, which would make *good* into *goodness* and *friend* into *friendship*

suffocate **suffocates, suffocating, suffocated**
VERB If someone **suffocates**, they die because they have no air to breathe.

sugar
NOUN a sweet substance obtained from some plants and used to sweeten food and drinks

suggest **suggests, suggesting, suggested**
VERB When you **suggest** something, you offer it as an idea.

suicide
NOUN People who commit **suicide** deliberately kill themselves.

suit **suits, suiting, suited**
NOUN 1 a matching jacket and trousers or skirt
VERB 2 If an arrangement **suits** you, it is convenient and suitable for you.
VERB 3 If a piece of clothing or a colour **suits** you, you look good when you are wearing it.
NOUN 4 A **suit** in a pack of cards is one of the sets of diamonds, clubs, hearts or spades.

suitable
ADJECTIVE right or acceptable for a certain person, occasion, time or place • *Many roads are not **suitable** for cycling.*

suitcase **suitcases**
NOUN a case in which you carry your belongings when you are travelling

suite **suites**
NOUN 1 a set of rooms in a hotel
NOUN 2 a set of matching furniture or bathroom fittings

sulk **sulks, sulking, sulked**
VERB If you **sulk**, you show your annoyance by being silent and moody.

sullen
ADJECTIVE behaving in a bad-tempered and disagreeably silent way

sulphur
NOUN a yellow chemical used in industry and medicine. **Sulphur** burns with a very unpleasant smell.

sultana **sultanas**
NOUN a dried, seedless grape

sum **sums**
NOUN 1 an amount of money
NOUN 2 the total of numbers added together

summarise **summarises, summarising, summarised**; also spelt **summarize**
VERB If you **summarise** something, you give a short account of its main points.

summary **summaries**
NOUN a short account of the main points of something said or written

summer **summers**
NOUN the warmest season of the year, between spring and autumn

summit **summits**
NOUN the top of a mountain • *The view from the **summit** was spectacular.*

summon **summons, summoning, summoned**
VERB If someone **summons** you, they order you to go to them.

sun
NOUN 1 the star in our solar system around which the Earth and other planets travel, and that gives us heat and light

→ Have a look at the illustration for **solar system**

NOUN 2 the heat and light from the sun

→ Have a look at the illustrations at **greenhouse effect** and **photosynthesis**

a
b
c
d
e
f
g
h
i
j
k
l
m
n
o
p
q
r
s
t
u
v
w
x
y
z

397

A
B
C
D
E
F
G
H
I
J
K
L
M
N
O
P
Q
R
S
T
U
V
W
X
Y
Z

sunbathe sunbathes, sunbathing, sunbathed
VERB When you **sunbathe**, you sit in the sun to get brown.

sunburn
NOUN sore red skin due to being in the sun for too long

Sunday Sundays
NOUN the first day of the week, coming before Monday

sunflower sunflowers
NOUN a tall flower with a very large, round yellow head

sung
VERB the past participle of **sing**

sunglasses
PLURAL NOUN dark glasses worn to protect your eyes from the sun

sunk
VERB the past participle of **sink**

sunlight
NOUN the light from the sun

sunny sunnier, sunniest
ADJECTIVE having lots of sunshine

sunrise sunrises
NOUN the time in the day when the sun first appears

sunset sunsets
NOUN the time when the sun goes down

sunshine
NOUN warmth and light that come from the sun

super
ADJECTIVE excellent, very good

superb
ADJECTIVE very good indeed

superficial
ADJECTIVE only on the surface

superior
ADJECTIVE **1** better or of higher quality than other similar things
ADJECTIVE **2** in a more important position than another person

superlative superlatives
ADJECTIVE **1** of the highest quality, the best
NOUN **2** the form of an adverb or adjective that expresses *most*. For example, the **superlative** of *hot* is *hottest*, and the **superlative** of *easy* is *easiest*.

supermarket supermarkets
NOUN a very large self-service shop that sells food and household goods

supernatural
ADJECTIVE Something that is **supernatural**, such as ghosts or witchcraft, cannot be explained by natural, scientific laws.

supersonic
ADJECTIVE faster than the speed of sound

WORD HISTORY
from Latin *super* + *sonus* meaning above sound

superstar superstars
NOUN a very famous entertainer or sportsperson

superstitious
ADJECTIVE People who are **superstitious** believe in things like magic and powers that bring good or bad luck.

supervise supervises, supervising, supervised
VERB If you **supervise** someone, you check what they are doing to make sure that they do it correctly.

supper suppers
NOUN a meal eaten in the evening or a snack eaten before you go to bed

supple
ADJECTIVE able to bend and move easily
• *Gymnasts are usually very supple.*

supplement supplements, supplementing, supplemented
VERB **1** To **supplement** something means to add something to it to improve it. • *Many villagers supplemented their food supply by fishing for salmon.*
NOUN **2** something that is added to something else to improve it

supply supplies, supplying, supplied
VERB **1** If you **supply** someone with something, you provide them with it.
PLURAL NOUN **2 Supplies** are food and equipment for a special purpose. • *His medical supplies were running low.*

support supports, supporting, supported
VERB **1** If something **supports** an object, it is underneath it and holding it up.
VERB **2** If you **support** a sports team, you are a fan.
VERB **3** If you **support** someone, you give them money, help or encouragement.
NOUN **4** If you give **support** to someone, you are kind, encouraging and helpful to them.
NOUN **5** something that supports an object

suppose supposes, supposing, supposed
VERB If you **suppose** that something is so, you think that it is likely.

suppress suppresses, suppressing, suppressed
VERB If an army or government **suppresses** something, it stops people doing it.

supreme
ADJECTIVE greatest, best or most important

sure surer, surest
ADJECTIVE 1 If you are **sure** about something, you know you are right.
ADJECTIVE 2 If something is **sure** to happen, it will definitely happen.

surf surfs, surfing, surfed
NOUN 1 the white foam that forms on the top of waves when they break near the shore
VERB 2 When you **surf**, you ride towards the shore on top of a wave, on a special board called a surfboard.
VERB 3 When you **surf** the internet, you go from website to website reading the information.

surface surfaces
NOUN the top or outside area of something • The wind ruffled the **surface** of the lake.

surge surges, surging, surged
NOUN 1 a sudden great increase in the amount of something • After the rain there was a **surge** of water down the river.
VERB 2 If someone or something **surges**, they move suddenly and powerfully. • The crowd **surged** forward.

surgeon surgeons
NOUN a doctor who performs operations

surgery surgeries
NOUN 1 medical treatment in which part of the patient's body is cut open • He had to have **surgery** to repair his knee.
NOUN 2 a room where doctors or dentists see their patients

surname surnames
NOUN your last name. Members of the same family usually have the same **surname**.

surplus surpluses
NOUN If there is a **surplus** of something, there is more of it than is needed.

surprise surprises, surprising, surprised
NOUN 1 an unexpected event
NOUN 2 the feeling caused when something unexpected happens

VERB 3 If something **surprises** you, it gives you a feeling of surprise.

surrender surrenders, surrendering, surrendered
VERB If someone **surrenders**, they admit that they are defeated.

surround surrounds, surrounding, surrounded
VERB To **surround** someone or something means to be situated all around them. • The house is **surrounded** by a high fence.

surroundings
PLURAL NOUN the things and conditions around a person or place

survey surveys, surveying, surveyed
VERB 1 If you **survey** something, you look carefully at the whole of it. • They stood back and **surveyed** the scene.
VERB 2 to make a detailed inspection of something
NOUN 3 A **survey** of something, such as people's habits, is a detailed examination of it, often in a report.

PRONUNCIATION TIP
The verb is pronounced sur-**vey**. The noun is pronounced **sur**-vey.

survival
NOUN managing to go on living or existing in spite of danger or difficulties

survive survives, surviving, survived
VERB To **survive** means to continue to live or exist in spite of danger or difficulties.

suspect suspects, suspecting, suspected
VERB 1 If you **suspect** something, you think that it might be true.
VERB 2 If you **suspect** someone of doing something wrong, you think that they have done it.
NOUN 3 someone who is thought to be guilty of a crime

PRONUNCIATION TIP
The verb is pronounced sus-**spekt**. The noun is pronounced **suss**-pekt.

suspend suspends, suspending, suspended
VERB 1 to hang something up
VERB 2 to delay something for a time

suspense
NOUN the feeling of excitement or fear when you are waiting for something to happen

a
b
c
d
e
f
g
h
i
j
k
l
m
n
o
p
q
r
s
t
u
v
w
x
y
z

399

suspicion suspicions
NOUN the feeling of not trusting someone or that something is wrong

suspicious
ADJECTIVE **1** If you are **suspicious** of someone, you do not trust them.
ADJECTIVE **2** If something is **suspicious**, it causes suspicion.

swallow swallows, swallowing, swallowed
VERB If you **swallow** something, you make it go down your throat and into your stomach.

swam
VERB the past tense of **swim**

swamp swamps, swamping, swamped
NOUN **1** an area of permanently wet land
VERB **2** If something is **swamped**, it is covered or filled with water.
VERB **3** If you are **swamped** by things, you have more than you can manage.

swan swans
NOUN a large, usually white, bird with a long neck that lives on rivers or lakes

swap swaps, swapping, swapped
VERB If you **swap** one thing for another, you replace the first thing with the second.

SYNONYM: exchange

PRONUNCIATION TIP
This word rhymes with "stop".

swarm swarms, swarming, swarmed
NOUN **1** a large group of insects flying together
VERB **2** When bees or other insects **swarm**, they fly together in a large group.
VERB **3** If a place is **swarming** with people, it is crowded with people.

swat swats, swatting, swatted
VERB If you **swat** an insect, you hit it quickly to kill it.

sway sways, swaying, swayed
VERB If something or someone **sways**, they lean or swing slowly from side to side.

swear swears, swearing, swore, sworn
VERB **1** If you **swear**, you use very rude words.
VERB **2** If you **swear** to do something, you promise that you will do it.

sweat sweats, sweating, sweated
NOUN **1** the salty liquid that comes through your skin when you are hot or afraid
VERB **2** When you **sweat**, sweat comes through your skin.

sweater sweaters
NOUN a knitted piece of clothing covering your upper body and arms

sweatshirt sweatshirts
NOUN a piece of clothing made of thick cotton, covering your upper body and arms

swede swedes
NOUN a large round root vegetable with yellow flesh and a brownish-purple skin

sweep sweeps, sweeping, swept
VERB **1** If you **sweep** the floor, you use a brush to gather up dust or rubbish from it.
VERB **2** If you **sweep** things off a surface, you push them all off with a quick, smooth movement.
VERB **3** If something **sweeps** from one place to another, it moves there very quickly.
● The boat **swept** down the river with the outgoing tide.

sweet sweeter, sweetest; sweets
ADJECTIVE **1** tasting of sugar or honey
ADJECTIVE **2** A **sweet** sound is gentle and tuneful.
ADJECTIVE **3** attractive and delightful
● He's such a **sweet** little baby.
NOUN **4** small pieces of sweet food, such as toffees, chocolates and mints
NOUN **5** something sweet that you eat at the end of a meal

SYNONYM: dessert

sweet corn
NOUN a long stalk covered with juicy yellow seeds that can be eaten as a vegetable

sweetheart sweethearts
NOUN You can call someone you are very fond of **sweetheart**.

swell swells, swelling, swelled, swollen
VERB If something **swells**, it becomes larger and rounder.

sweltering
ADJECTIVE If the weather is **sweltering**, it is very hot.

swept
VERB the past tense and past participle of **sweep**

swerve swerves, swerving, swerved
VERB If someone or something **swerves**, they suddenly change direction to avoid colliding with something.

swift swifter, swiftest; swifts
ADJECTIVE **1** happening or moving very quickly
NOUN **2** a bird with narrow crescent-shaped wings

A B C D E F G H I J K L M N O P Q R S T U V W X Y Z

swim swims, swimming, swam, swum
VERB When you **swim**, you move through water by making movements with your arms and legs.

swimming
NOUN the act of moving through water using your arms and legs

swimming costume swimming costumes
NOUN a garment you wear while swimming

swimming pool swimming pools
NOUN an area of water made for swimming, usually a large hole that has been tiled and filled with water

swimsuit swimsuits
NOUN a one-piece swimming costume

swindle swindles, swindling, swindled
VERB 1 If someone **swindles** someone else, they trick them to obtain money or property.
NOUN 2 a trick in which someone is cheated out of money or property

swine swine
NOUN (old-fashioned) a pig

LANGUAGE TIP
The plural of *swine* is *swine*.

swing swings, swinging, swung
VERB 1 If something **swings**, or if you **swing** it, it moves repeatedly from side to side or backwards and forwards from a fixed point.
NOUN 2 a seat hanging from a frame or a branch, that moves backwards and forwards when you sit on it

swipe swipes, swiping, swiped
VERB 1 If you **swipe** at something, you try to hit it with a curved swinging movement.
VERB 2 If a credit card is **swiped**, it is put though an electronic machine to read it when paying.
VERB 3 If you **swipe**, you move your finger across the screen of a phone or computer.
• Simply **swipe** up to video.
VERB 4 (informal) If someone **swipes** something, they steal it.

switch switches, switching, switched
NOUN 1 a device used to control an electrical device or machine. When the **switch** is on, or closed, it completes the circuit and electricity can flow.
NOUN 2 a change
VERB 3 To **switch** to a different task or topic means to change to it.

switch off
VERB If you **switch off** a light or a machine, you stop it working by pressing a switch.

switch on
VERB If you **switch on** a light or a machine, you start it working by pressing a switch.

switchboard switchboards
NOUN a panel with switches on for connecting telephone lines

swivel swivels, swivelling, swivelled
VERB 1 to turn round on a central point
ADJECTIVE 2 A **swivel** chair or lamp is made so that you can move the main part of it while the base remains in a fixed position.

swollen
ADJECTIVE 1 Something that is **swollen** has swelled up.

SYNONYMS: enlarged, puffed up

VERB 2 the past participle of **swell**

swoop swoops, swooping, swooped
VERB To **swoop** is to move downwards through the air in a fast curving movement.

swop swops, swopping, swopped
VERB to swap

sword swords
NOUN a weapon consisting of a very long blade with a short handle

swum
VERB the past participle of **swim**

swung
VERB the past tense and past participle of **swing**

sycamore sycamores
NOUN a tree that has large leaves with five points, and winged seed cases

syllable syllables
NOUN a part of a word that contains a single vowel sound and is said as one unit • "Book" has one **syllable** and "reading" has two.

syllabus syllabuses or syllabi
NOUN the subjects that are studied for a particular course or examination

symbol symbols
NOUN a shape, design or idea that is used to represent something • Apple blossom is a Chinese **symbol** of peace and beauty.

→ Have a look at the illustration for **map**

symmetrical

ADJECTIVE **Symmetrical** objects can be divided in half so that both halves match, with one half like a reflection of the other.

symmetry

NOUN If something has **symmetry**, it is the same in both halves. The line drawn through something so that both sides of the line look exactly the same is called a line of **symmetry**.

sympathetic

ADJECTIVE feeling sympathy or understanding for someone

sympathy

NOUN an understanding of people's feelings and opinions, especially someone who is in difficulties

SYNONYM: compassion

symphony symphonies

NOUN a piece of music for an orchestra, usually in four parts called movements

symptom symptoms

NOUN something wrong with your body that is a sign of illness

synagogue synagogues

NOUN a building where Jewish people meet for worship and religious instruction

synonym synonyms

NOUN two words that have the same or a very similar meaning • *Speak is a synonym for talk.*

synthetic

ADJECTIVE made from artificial substances rather than natural ones

syringe syringes

NOUN a hollow tube with a plunger, used for drawing up or pushing out liquids. Doctors and vets use them to give injections.

syrup syrups

NOUN a thick, sweet liquid made by boiling sugar with water

WORD HISTORY
from Arabic *sharab* meaning drink

---

system systems

NOUN an organised way of doing or arranging something according to a fixed plan or set of rules

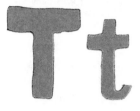

tab tabs

NOUN a small extra piece that is attached to something and sticks out, for example a sticky marker that you put in a book to mark your place

table tables

NOUN **1** a piece of furniture with a flat top supported by one or more legs
NOUN **2** a set of facts or figures arranged in rows or columns

tablecloth tablecloths

NOUN a cloth used to cover a table and to keep it clean

tablespoon tablespoons

NOUN **1** a large spoon used for serving food
NOUN **2** the amount that a **tablespoon** contains • *For this recipe you need two **tablespoons** of caster sugar.*

tablet tablets

NOUN **1** medicine in a small, solid lump that you swallow

SYNONYM: pill

NOUN **2** a flat piece of stone with words carved on it
NOUN **3** a small mobile personal computer with a screen that you tap or swipe

table tennis

NOUN a game for two or four people who use bats to hit a small ball over a net across the middle of the table

tabloid tabloids

NOUN a newspaper with small pages, short news stories, and lots of photographs

tachometer tachometers

NOUN the instrument in a vehicle which shows the speed of the engine

→ Have a look at the illustration for **car**

tack tacks, tacking, tacked
NOUN **1** a short nail with a flat top
NOUN **2** If you change **tack**, you find a different way of doing something.
VERB **3** If you **tack** something to a surface, you fix it there with a tack.
VERB **4** If you **tack** in a boat, you sail in a zigzag course to catch the wind.
VERB **5** If you **tack** a piece of fabric, you sew it with long, loose stitches.
NOUN **6** equipment for horses, such as bridles, saddles and harnesses

tackle tackles, tackling, tackled
VERB **1** If you **tackle** a difficult task, you start dealing with it.
VERB **2** If you **tackle** someone in a game such as hockey or soccer, you try to get the ball away from them.
NOUN **3** an attempt to get the ball away from your opponent in certain sports

tact
NOUN the ability to deal with people without upsetting or offending them

tactful
ADJECTIVE able to deal with people without upsetting or offending them

tactfully
ADVERB in a way that shows you are trying not to upset or offend someone

tactic tactics
NOUN one of the methods you use in order to achieve what you want

tactless
ADJECTIVE unable to deal with people without upsetting or offending them

tadpole tadpoles
NOUN a young frog or toad. **Tadpoles** are black with round heads and long tails, and live in water.

→ Have a look at the illustration for **frog**

WORD HISTORY
Middle English *tadde* meaning toad and *pol* meaning head

tag tags, tagging, tagged
NOUN **1** a small label made of cloth
NOUN **2** a game in which one person chases the other people who are playing
VERB **3** If you **tag along** behind someone, you follow and try to keep up.

tail tails
NOUN **1** The **tail** of an animal or bird is the part extending beyond the end of its body. For example, a fox has a bushy **tail**.

→ Have a look at the illustrations for **bird** and **fish**

NOUN **2** the end part of something

→ Have a look at the illustration for **aeroplane**

NOUN **3** When you toss a coin, the side called **tails** is the one that does not have a person's head on it.

LANGUAGE TIP
Do not confuse *tail* with *tale*.

tailor tailors
NOUN a person who makes, alters and repairs clothes, especially for men

take takes, taking, took, taken
VERB **1** If you **take** someone or something to a place, you get them there. ● She **took** the cat to the vet.
VERB **2** **Take** is used to show what activity is being done. ● Sam **took** a shower.
VERB **3** If you **take** a pill or some medicine, you swallow it.
VERB **4** When you **take** one number from another, you subtract it.
VERB **5** If you **take** a photograph, you use a camera to produce it.
take after
VERB If you **take after** a member of your family, you are like them in some way.
take away
VERB If you **take** one number **away** from another, you make one number smaller by the value of the other number. ● Seven **take away** two is five (7 − 2 = 5).
take off
VERB When a plane **takes off**, it goes into the air.

takeaway takeaways
NOUN **1** a shop or restaurant that sells hot, cooked food to be taken away and eaten elsewhere
NOUN **2** a hot cooked meal bought from a takeaway restaurant

talcum powder
NOUN a soft, perfumed powder to put on the skin to dry it

403

A
B
C
D
E
F
G
H
I
J
K
L
M
N
O
P
Q
R
S
T
U
V
W
X
Y
Z

tale **tales**
NOUN a story

LANGUAGE TIP
Do not confuse *tale* with *tail*.

talent **talents**
NOUN the ability to do something very well

talk **talks, talking, talked**
VERB **1** When you **talk**, you say things to someone.
NOUN **2** a conversation or discussion
NOUN **3** an informal speech about something

talkative
ADJECTIVE If you are **talkative**, you talk a lot.
SYNONYM: chatty

tall **taller, tallest**
ADJECTIVE **1** If you are **tall**, you are more than the average height.
ADJECTIVE **2** having a particular height
• *How **tall** are you?*

tally **tallies**
NOUN an informal record that you keep as you count objects

Talmud
NOUN a collection of books of the ancient Jewish ceremonies and laws

talon **talons**
NOUN a sharp, hooked claw, especially of a bird of prey

tambourine **tambourines**
NOUN a percussion instrument made of a skin stretched tightly over a circular frame. It has small round pieces of metal around the edge that jangle when the **tambourine** is beaten or shaken.

WORD HISTORY
from Old French *tambourin* meaning little drum

tame **tamer, tamest; tames, taming, tamed**
ADJECTIVE **1** A **tame** animal is not afraid of people.
VERB **2** If you **tame** a wild animal, you train it not to be afraid of humans.

tamper **tampers, tampering, tampered**
VERB If you **tamper** with something, you interfere with it.

tan **tans, tanning, tanned**
NOUN **1** a suntan
NOUN **2** a yellowish-brown colour
VERB **3** If your skin **tans**, it goes brown in the sun.
VERB **4** When an animal's skin is **tanned**, it is turned into leather by treating it with chemicals.

tang **tangs**
NOUN a strong flavour or smell

tangerine **tangerines**
NOUN **1** a type of small sweet orange that is easy to peel
NOUN **2** a reddish-orange colour
ADJECTIVE **3** having a reddish-orange colour

tangle **tangles, tangling, tangled**
NOUN **1** a mass of things, such as hairs or fibres, that are twisted together and difficult to separate
VERB **2** If you **tangle** something, you twist it into knots.

tank **tanks**
NOUN **1** a large container for storing liquid or gas
NOUN **2** an armoured military vehicle that moves on tracks and has guns or rockets

tanker **tankers**
NOUN a ship or lorry designed to carry large quantities of gas or liquid

tantrum **tantrums**
NOUN a noisy and sometimes violent outburst of bad temper, especially by a child

tap **taps, tapping, tapped**
NOUN **1** a device for controlling the flow of gas or liquid from a pipe
VERB **2** If you **tap** something, you hit it lightly and quickly.
NOUN **3** a light hit, or its sound

tape **tapes, taping, taped**
NOUN **1** a long plastic ribbon covered with a magnetic substance and used to record sounds, pictures and computer information
NOUN **2** a cassette with magnetic **tape** wound round it • *video **tape***
NOUN **3** a strip of sticky plastic used for sticking things together
VERB **4** If you **tape** sounds or television pictures, you record them using a tape recorder or a video recorder.

tape measure **tape measures**
NOUN a long, narrow tape marked with centimetres or inches, and used for measuring

taper **tapers, tapering, tapered**
VERB Something that **tapers** becomes thinner towards one end.

tape recorder **tape recorders**
NOUN a machine that records sounds onto a special magnetic tape that can be played back later

tapestry **tapestries**
NOUN a piece of heavy cloth with designs embroidered on it

→ Have a look at the illustration

WORD HISTORY
from Old French *tapisserie* meaning carpeting

---

tar
NOUN a thick, black, sticky substance that is used in making roads

tarantula **tarantulas**
NOUN a large, hairy, poisonous spider

target **targets**
NOUN something you aim at when firing a weapon

tarmac
NOUN a mixture of tar and crushed stones, used for making road surfaces

---

WORD HISTORY
short for *tarmacadam*, from the name of John *McAdam*, the Scottish engineer who invented it

---

tarnish **tarnishes, tarnishing, tarnished**
VERB If metal **tarnishes**, it becomes stained and loses its shine.

tarpaulin **tarpaulins**
NOUN a sheet of heavy waterproof material used as a protective covering

tart **tarts**
NOUN **1** a pastry case, usually filled with something sweet such as fruit or jam
ADJECTIVE **2** Something **tart** has a sharp or sour taste.

tartan **tartans**
NOUN a coloured, woollen fabric from Scotland, with a special pattern of checks and stripes, depending on which clan it belongs to

a
b
c
d
e
f
g
h
i
j
k
l
m
n
o
p
q
r
s
t
u
v
w
x
y
z

tapestry

405

A
B
C
D
E
F
G
H
I
J
K
L
M
N
O
P
Q
R
S
T
U
V
W
X
Y
Z

task tasks
NOUN any piece of work that has to be done
SYNONYMS: chore, duty, job

tassel tassels
NOUN a tuft of loose threads tied by a knot and used for decoration

taste tastes, tasting, tasted
NOUN **1** Your sense of **taste** is your ability to recognise the flavour of things in your mouth.
NOUN **2** The **taste** of something is its flavour.
NOUN **3** your own particular choice of things such as clothes, music and food • *Jenny and I have the same taste in music.*
VERB **4** When you can **taste** something in your mouth, you know what its flavour is like.
VERB **5** If food or drink **tastes** of something, it has that flavour.

tasty tastier, tastiest
ADJECTIVE Something that is **tasty** has a pleasant flavour.

tattered
ADJECTIVE ragged and torn

tattoo tattoos, tattooing, tattooed
VERB **1** If someone is **tattooed**, they have a design drawn on their skin by pricking little holes and filling them with coloured dye.
NOUN **2** a picture or design tattooed on someone's body

taught
VERB the past tense and past participle of **teach**

taunt taunts, taunting, taunted
VERB If you **taunt** someone, you tease them about their weaknesses or failures in order to make them angry or upset.

taut
ADJECTIVE Something that is **taut** is stretched very tight.

tawny
ADJECTIVE brownish-yellow

tax taxes, taxing, taxed
NOUN **1** an amount of money that people have to pay to the government so that it can provide public services such as health care and education
VERB **2** If a sum of money is **taxed**, a certain amount of it is paid to the government.
VERB **3** If something **taxes** you, it exhausts you and drains your energy.

taxi taxis
NOUN a car with a driver that you hire, usually for a short journey

tea teas
NOUN **1** the dried leaves of a shrub found in Asia
NOUN **2** a drink made by soaking the leaves of the tea plant in hot water
NOUN **3** a meal taken in the late afternoon or early evening

tea bag tea bags
NOUN a small paper packet with tea leaves in it, that you use to make a drink of tea

teach teaches, teaching, taught
VERB If someone **teaches** you something, they help you learn about it or show you how to do it.
SYNONYMS: educate, instruct, train

teacher teachers
NOUN someone who teaches at a school or college

teak
NOUN a hard wood that comes from a large Asian tree

team teams
NOUN a group of people who play together against another group in a sport or game

team-mate team-mate
NOUN In a game or sport, your **team-mates** are the other members of your team.

teapot teapots
NOUN a container in which tea is made. It has a handle, a spout and a lid.

tear tears, tearing, tore, torn
NOUN **1** a drop of liquid that comes out of your eyes when you cry
NOUN **2** a hole or rip that has been made in something • *There was a tear in the curtain.*
VERB **3** If you **tear** something, you damage it by pulling so that a hole or rip appears in it.

PRONUNCIATION TIP
Meaning I rhymes with "fear". Meanings 2 and 3 rhyme with "hair".

tearful
ADJECTIVE If you are **tearful**, you cry easily or you are crying.

tease teases, teasing, teased
VERB If someone **teases** you, they deliberately make fun of you or embarrass you.

teaspoon teaspoons
NOUN **1** a small spoon used for stirring drinks
NOUN **2** the amount that a **teaspoon** holds
• *I have two **teaspoons** of sugar in my coffee.*

teat teats
NOUN **1** a nipple on a female animal
NOUN **2** a piece of rubber or plastic that is shaped like a nipple and fitted to a baby's feeding bottle

technical
ADJECTIVE If something is **technical**, it is to do with machines, the way things work, and materials used in industry, transport and communications.

technique techniques
NOUN a particular way of doing something

PRONUNCIATION TIP
This word is pronounced tek-**neek**.

---

technology
NOUN practical things that have come about because of a greater understanding of science • *New **technology** has helped us develop faster computers.*

teddy bear teddy bears
NOUN a soft, furry toy bear

tedious
ADJECTIVE boring and lasting for a long time

teenager teenagers
NOUN a person aged between 13 and 19 years old

teeth
PLURAL NOUN the plural of **tooth**

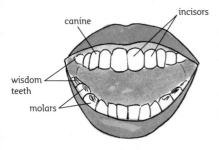

incisors
canine
wisdom teeth
molars

tele-
PREFIX You add **tele-**to the beginning of a word to mean at or over a distance.
• ***tele**phone*

WORD HISTORY
from the Greek *tele* meaning far

---

telecommunications
NOUN the science and activity of sending signals and messages over long distances, for example by radio and telephone

telegram telegrams
NOUN a message that is sent electronically and then printed and delivered to someone's home • *He received many letters and **telegrams** of congratulations when he won the race.*

telegraph
NOUN a system of sending messages over long distances using electrical or radio signals

telephone telephones, telephoning, telephoned
NOUN **1** a piece of electrical or electronic equipment for talking directly to someone who is in a different place
VERB **2** If you **telephone** someone, you speak to them using a telephone.

telescope telescopes
NOUN a long instrument, shaped like a tube, that contains lenses. When you look through it with one eye, distant objects appear larger and nearer.

televise televises, televising, televised
VERB If an event is **televised**, it is filmed and shown on television.

television televisions
NOUN a piece of electronic equipment that receives pictures and sounds transmitted over a distance

tell tells, telling, told
VERB **1** If you **tell** someone something, you let them know about it.
VERB **2** If you **tell** someone to do something, you order them to do it.

telly tellies
NOUN an abbreviation of *television*

temper
NOUN **1** Your **temper** is the mood you are in and the way you are feeling, whether you are irritable and angry or calm and peaceful. • *I started the day in a bad **temper**.*
PHRASE **2** If you **lose your temper**, you become very angry.

temperamental
ADJECTIVE Someone who is **temperamental** changes their mood often and suddenly.

a
b
c
d
e
f
g
h
i
j
k
l
m
n
o
p
q
r
s
t
u
v
w
x
y
z

407

A
B
C
D
E
F
G
H
I
J
K
L
M
N
O
P
Q
R
S
T
U
V
W
X
Y
Z

temperature **temperatures**
NOUN **1** how hot or cold something is ● *There was a sudden drop in* **temperature** *once the sun had gone down.*
NOUN **2** Your **temperature** is the temperature of your body. The normal body **temperature** for humans is 37°C. ● *His* **temperature** *continued to rise.*

temple **temples**
NOUN **1** a building used for the worship of a god in various religions
NOUN **2** the part on either side of your head between your forehead and your ear

tempo **tempos** or **tempi**
NOUN The **tempo** of a piece of music is its speed.

temporary
ADJECTIVE lasting for only a short time

tempt **tempts, tempting, tempted**
VERB **1** If you **tempt** someone, you try to persuade them to do something by offering them something they want.
ADJECTIVE **2** If something is **tempting**, it is attractive and difficult to resist.

ten
NOUN **Ten** is the number 10.

tenancy **tenancies**
NOUN the period of time that someone pays rent to live in a house or to use land or buildings

tenant **tenants**
NOUN someone who pays rent for the place they live in, or for land or buildings that they use

tend **tends , tending, tended**
VERB **1** If something **tends** to happen, it usually happens.
VERB **2** If you **tend** something or someone, you look after them. ● *Bob* **tended** *the plants.*

tendency **tendencies**
NOUN the way a person or a thing is likely to behave or has a habit of behaving ● *She has a* **tendency** *to write messily.*

tender **tenderer, tenderest**
ADJECTIVE **1** Someone who is **tender** is gentle and caring.

SYNONYMS: affectionate, gentle, loving

ADJECTIVE **2 Tender** food is easy to cut and chew.

ANTONYM: tough

ADJECTIVE **3** If a part of your body is **tender**, it is painful and sore.

tendon **tendons**
NOUN **Tendons** are like strong cords. They hold your muscles and bones together.

tennis
NOUN a game played by two or four players on a rectangular court. The players hit a ball over a central net.

tense **tenser, tensest; tenses, tensing, tensed**
ADJECTIVE **1** If you are **tense**, you feel worried and unable to relax.
NOUN **2** The **tense** of a verb shows whether it is in the past, present or future.
VERB **3** If you **tense** your muscles, you tighten them up.

tension **tensions**
NOUN the feeling of nervousness or worry that you have when something dangerous or important is happening

tent **tents**
NOUN a shelter made of fabric held up by poles and pinned down at the bottom with pegs and ropes

tentacle **tentacles**
NOUN the long, bending parts of an animal, such as an octopus, that it uses to feel and hold things

tenth **tenths**
NOUN **1** one of ten equal parts of something. It can be written as 1/10.
ADJECTIVE **2** The **tenth** item in a series is the one that you count as number ten. It can be written as 10th.

tepid
ADJECTIVE **Tepid** liquid is only slightly warm.

term **terms**
NOUN **1** one of the periods of time that each year is divided into at a school or college
NOUN **2 Terms** are words that relate to a particular subject, for example, medical **terms**, legal **terms** and scientific **terms**.
NOUN **3 Terms** are the conditions of an agreement. ● *He made a list of* **terms** *for doing the job.*
NOUN **4** If you are on good **terms** with someone, you get on well with them.

terminal **terminals**

NOUN **1** a place where vehicles, passengers or goods begin or end a journey

NOUN **2** a keyboard and screen connected to a main computer

ADJECTIVE **3** A **terminal** illness or disease cannot be cured and gradually causes death.

WORD HISTORY
from Latin *terminus* meaning end

terminate **terminates, terminating, terminated**

VERB When you **terminate** something, or it **terminates**, it stops or ends.

terrace **terraces**

NOUN **1** a row of houses joined together
NOUN **2** a flat area of stone next to a building, where people can sit

terrapin **terrapins**

NOUN a small North American freshwater turtle

WORD HISTORY
an American Indian word

terrible

ADJECTIVE **1** serious and unpleasant ● *He had a* **terrible** *illness.*
ADJECTIVE **2** very bad or of poor quality ● *That is a* **terrible** *haircut.*

terrier **terriers**

NOUN a breed of small dog

WORD HISTORY
from Old French *chien terrier* meaning earth dog, because they were originally bred to hunt animals living in holes in the ground, such as rabbits and badgers

terrific

ADJECTIVE **1** very pleasing or impressive ● *That was a* **terrific** *film.*
ADJECTIVE **2** very great or strong ● *There is a* **terrific** *wind blowing down on the beach.*

terrify **terrifies, terrifying, terrified**

VERB If something **terrifies** you, it makes you feel extremely frightened.

territory **territories**

NOUN The **territory** of a country is the land that it controls.

terror **terrors**

NOUN great fear or panic

terrorism

NOUN the use of violence for political purposes

test **tests, testing, tested**

VERB **1** When you **test** something, you try it to find out what it is, what condition it is in, or how well it works.
VERB **2** To **test** someone means to ask them questions to find out how much they know.
NOUN **3** a set of questions or tasks given to someone to find out what they know or can do

test tube **test tubes**

NOUN a small cylindrical glass container that is used in chemical experiments

tetanus

NOUN a painful infectious disease caused by germs getting into wounds

tether **tethers, tethering, tethered**

VERB **1** If you **tether** an animal, you tie it to something such as a post.
NOUN **2** a rope for tying an animal to something such as a post

tetrahedron **tetrahedrons** or **tetrahedra**

NOUN a solid shape with four triangular faces

text **texts, texting, texted**

NOUN **1** the written part of a book, rather than the pictures or the index
NOUN **2** short for **text message**
VERB **3** If you **text** someone, you send them a text message.

a
b
c
d
e
f
g
h
i
j
k
l
m
n
o
p
q
r
s
t
u
v
w
x
y
z

A
B
C
D
E
F
G
H
I
J
K
L
M
N
O
P
Q
R
S
T
U
V
W
X
Y
Z

textbook **textbooks**

NOUN a book about a particular subject for students to use

textile **textiles**

NOUN a woven cloth or fabric

text message **text messages**

NOUN a written message sent using a mobile phone

texture **textures**

NOUN the way something feels when you touch it • *Silk has a very smooth, soft **texture**.*

than

PREPOSITION **1** You use **than** when you compare one thing with another. • *She is bigger **than** her sister.*
CONJUNCTION **2** You use **than** when you compare one thing with another.
• *He should have helped her more **than** he did.*

thank **thanks, thanking, thanked**

VERB When you **thank** someone, you show that you are pleased or grateful for something that they have done for you.

thank you

INTERJECTION You say **thank you** to show that you are grateful to someone for something.

that **those**

ADJECTIVE **1 That** is used when you are talking about someone or something that is a distance away from you. • *Look at that **tree** over there.*
PRONOUN **2 That** is used when you are referring to someone or something you have already mentioned. • ***That** is the film I want to see.*
CONJUNCTION **3 That** is used to introduce a fact, a statement or a result. • *His writing was so bad **that** nobody could read it.*

thaw **thaws, thawing, thawed**

VERB **1** When snow or ice **thaws**, it melts.
VERB **2** When you **thaw** frozen food, or when it **thaws**, it defrosts.

the

ADJECTIVE called the definite article. You use **the** in front of a noun when you are referring to something in particular.
• *That's **the** chair I bought yesterday.*

theatre **theatres**

NOUN **1** a building where plays and other shows are performed on a stage
NOUN **2** a room in a hospital where operations are carried out

theatrical

ADJECTIVE involving or performed in the theatre

theft **thefts**

NOUN the crime of stealing

SYNONYM: robbery

their

ADJECTIVE **Their** refers to something belonging to people or things, other than yourself or the person you are talking to, that have already been mentioned. • *The children had been playing football, and **their** shirts were dirty.*

LANGUAGE TIP
Do not confuse *their* with *there* or *they're*.

theirs

PRONOUN **Theirs** refers to something belonging to people or things, other than yourself or the person you are talking to, that have already been mentioned. • *The children said that the ball that came over the wall was **theirs**.*

them

PRONOUN **Them** refers to things or people, other than yourself or the person you are talking to, that have already been mentioned. • *She took her gloves off and put **them** in a drawer.*

theme **themes**

NOUN a main idea in a piece of writing, painting, film or music • *The main **theme** of the book is growing up.*

themselves

PRONOUN **Themselves** is used when people, other than yourself or the person you are talking to, do an action and are affected by it. • *They enjoyed **themselves** at the fair.*

then

ADVERB after that; next • *He put on his shoes and **then** went for a walk.*

theology

NOUN the study of religion and God

theory **theories**

NOUN an idea or set of ideas that is meant to explain something

therapist **therapists**

NOUN someone whose job is to give a specific treatment for a mental or physical illness

therapy
NOUN the treatment of a mental or physical illness

there
ADVERB in that place or to that place • *He's sitting over **there**.* • *We decided to go **there** after school.*

LANGUAGE TIP
Do not confuse *there* with *their* or *they're*.

therefore
ADVERB as a result • *I worked hard and **therefore** I won a prize.*

thermal
ADJECTIVE **1** to do with or caused by heat
ADJECTIVE **2 Thermal** clothing is specially designed to keep you warm in cold weather.

thermometer thermometers
NOUN an instrument for measuring the temperature of a room or a person's body

Thermos
NOUN (trademark) a container used to keep drinks hot or cold

thermostat thermostats
NOUN a device used to control temperature, for example on a central heating system

thesaurus thesauruses
NOUN a reference book in which words with similar meanings are grouped together

these
ADJECTIVE **1 These** means the ones here, not a different ones. • ***These** bananas look good.*
PRONOUN **2 These** means the ones here, not a different ones. • *Have you seen **these**?*

they
PRONOUN **They** refers to people or things that have already been mentioned.
• *I saw Tom and Ben. **They** were looking in a shop window.*

they'd
a contraction of *they had* or *they would*

they'll
a contraction of *they will* or *they shall*

they're
a contraction of *they are*

LANGUAGE TIP
Do not confuse *they're* with *their* or *there*.

they've
a contraction of *they have*

thick thicker, thickest
ADJECTIVE **1** Something **thick** has a large distance between its two sides. • *I'd like a **thick** slice of bread and butter.*

ANTONYM: thin

ADJECTIVE **2** If you want to know how **thick** something is, you want to know the measurement between its two sides.
• *How **thick** is this wall?*

ANTONYM: thin

ADJECTIVE **3** close together and in a large number • *She has **thick**, dark hair.*
ADJECTIVE **4 Thick** liquids contain little water and do not flow easily. • *The **thick** soup was very filling.*

ANTONYM: thin

thicken thickens, thickening, thickened
VERB If you **thicken** something, or if it **thickens**, it becomes thicker. • *Stir the custard in the pan until it **thickens**.*

thickness thicknesses
NOUN how thick something is

thief thieves
NOUN a person who steals

thigh thighs
NOUN the top part of your leg, between your knee and your hip

thimble thimbles
NOUN a small metal or plastic cap that you put on the end of your finger to protect it from the needle when you are sewing

thin thinner, thinnest
ADJECTIVE **1** Something that is **thin** is much narrower than it is long.

ANTONYM: thick

ADJECTIVE **2** A **thin** person or animal has very little fat on their body.
ADJECTIVE **3 Thin** liquids contain a lot of water and flow easily.

ANTONYM: thick

thing things
NOUN an object rather than a plant, animal or person

a
b
c
d
e
f
g
h
i
j
k
l
m
n
o
p
q
r
s
t
u
v
w
x
y
z

think thinks, thinking, thought

VERB **1** When you **think** about ideas or problems, you use your mind to sort them out.

VERB **2** If you **think** something, you believe it is true. • *I **think** she's got a bike for her birthday.*

VERB **3** If you **think** of something, you remember it or it comes into your mind.

VERB **4** If you are **thinking** of doing something, you might do it.

third thirds

NOUN **1** one of three equal parts of something. It can be written as ⅓.

ADJECTIVE **2** The **third** item in a series is the one that you count as number three. It can be written as 3ʳᵈ.

third person

NOUN In grammar, the **third person** is *he*, *she*, *it* or *they*.

thirst

NOUN If you have a **thirst**, you feel the need to drink something.

thirstily

ADVERB in a way that shows you are thirsty

thirsty thirstier, thirstiest

ADJECTIVE If you are **thirsty**, you feel as if you need to drink something.

thirteen

NOUN **Thirteen** is the number 13.

thirteenth thirteenths

NOUN **1** one of thirteen equal parts of something.

ADJECTIVE **2** The **thirteenth** item in a series is the one that you count as number thirteen.

thirtieth thirtieths

NOUN **1** one of thirty equal parts of something.

ADJECTIVE **2** The **thirtieth** item in a series is the one that you count as number thirty.

thirty

NOUN **Thirty** is the number 30.

this those

ADJECTIVE **1** **This** means the one here, not a different one. • *This food looks nice.*

PRONOUN **2** **This** means the one here, not a different one. • *Have you seen this?*

thistle thistles

NOUN a wild plant with prickly-edged leaves and purple flowers

thorn thorns

NOUN one of many sharp points growing on the stems of some plants. For example, brambles have many **thorns**.

thorough

ADJECTIVE done very carefully and completely

thoroughly

ADVERB **1** very carefully so that you do not miss anything • *He washed his hands **thoroughly**.*

ADVERB **2** completely • *She was **thoroughly** ashamed of what she'd done.*

those

PRONOUN **1** **Those** is used when you are referring to people or things you have already mentioned. • *Those are the shoes I was talking about.*

ADJECTIVE **2** **Those** is used when you are talking about people or things that are a distance away from you. • *Look at those trees over there.*

though

CONJUNCTION **1** despite the fact that • *She felt better, **though** her cough was still bad.*

CONJUNCTION **2** You can use **though** to mean if. • *Try to look as **though** you're working.*

PRONUNCIATION TIP
This word rhymes with "show".

thought thoughts

VERB **1** the past tense and past participle of **think**

NOUN **2** the activity of thinking • *She was lost in **thought**.*

thoughtful

ADJECTIVE **1** If you are **thoughtful**, you are quiet and serious.

ADJECTIVE **2** A **thoughtful** person thinks of what other people need and what they would like.

thoughtfully

ADVERB **1** in a way that shows you are thinking about something

ADVERB **2** in a kind way that shows you are thinking of what other people need and would like

thoughtless

ADJECTIVE A **thoughtless** person does not care or think about other people's needs.

thousand thousands

NOUN A **thousand** is the number 1000.

thousandth thousandths

NOUN **1** one of a thousand equal parts of something. It can be written as ¹⁄₁₀₀₀.
ADJECTIVE **2** The **thousandth** item in a series is the one that you count as number one thousand. It can be written as 1000ᵗʰ.

thrash thrashes, thrashing, thrashed

VERB **1** To **thrash** someone is to beat them by hitting them with something like a stick or a whip.
VERB **2** If you **thrash** someone in a contest or fight, you defeat them completely.
VERB **3** If you **thrash**, or **thrash** about, you move about wildly and violently.

thread threads

NOUN **1** a long, fine piece of cotton, silk, nylon or wool
NOUN **2** a number of messages on the internet from different people about one particular subject • *I saw the post but didn't read the **thread** below it.*

threadbare

ADJECTIVE Fabric or clothes that are **threadbare** are old and worn thin.

threat threats

NOUN **1** a warning that someone will harm you if you do not do what they want
NOUN **2** a danger or something that might cause harm

threaten threatens, threatening, threatened

VERB If you **threaten** someone, you tell them that you intend to harm them in some way.

three

NOUN **Three** is the number 3.

three-dimensional

ADJECTIVE A **three-dimensional** object or shape is not flat, but has height or depth as well as length and width.

threw

VERB the past tense of **throw**

thrill thrills, thrilling, thrilled

NOUN **1** a sudden feeling of great excitement, pleasure or fear
VERB **2** If something **thrills** you, it gives you a feeling of great pleasure and excitement.

thrilled

ADJECTIVE extremely pleased and excited

thriller thrillers

NOUN a book, film or play that tells an exciting story about dangerous or mysterious events

thrilling

ADJECTIVE exciting and very interesting

thrive thrives, thriving, throve or thrived

VERB to grow strongly and healthily, or to prosper

throat throats

NOUN **1** the back of your mouth and the top part of the tubes inside your neck that lead to your stomach and lungs
NOUN **2** the front part of a human or other animal's neck

→ Have a look at the illustration for **bird**

throb throbs, throbbing, throbbed

VERB If something **throbs**, it beats or vibrates with a strong, regular rhythm. • *My finger **throbbed** after I trapped it in the door.*

throne thrones

NOUN a ceremonial chair used by a king or queen on important official occasions

throng throngs, thronging, thronged

NOUN **1** a large crowd of people • *There was a **throng** of fans waiting at the stage door.*
VERB **2** If people **throng** somewhere, or **throng** a place, they go there in great numbers. • *Hundreds of royal admirers **thronged** to see the procession.*

throttle throttles, throttling, throttled

VERB If a person **throttles** someone, they kill or injure them by squeezing their throat.

SYNONYM: strangle

through

PREPOSITION If you move **through** something, you go from one side of it to the other. • *We followed the path **through** the woods.*

throughout

PREPOSITION **1** all the way through • *It rained heavily **throughout** the game.*
ADVERB **2** all the way through • *The house is painted white **throughout**.*

throw throws, throwing, threw, thrown

VERB When you **throw** something you let it go with a quick movement of your arm, so that it moves through the air.

SYNONYMS: chuck, fling, toss

throw away

VERB If you **throw away** something that you do not want, you get rid of it, usually by putting it in the rubbish bin.

thrush thrushes

NOUN a small brown songbird

a
b
c
d
e
f
g
h
i
j
k
l
m
n
o
p
q
r
s
t
u
v
w
x
y
z

413

thrust thrusts, thrusting, thrust
VERB If you **thrust** something somewhere, you move or push it there quickly and with a lot of force.

thud thuds, thudding, thudded
VERB **1** to fall heavily
NOUN **2** the dull sound of something heavy falling

thug thugs
NOUN a very rough and violent person

WORD HISTORY
from Hindi *thag* meaning thief

---

thumb thumbs
NOUN the short, thick, jointed part on the side of your hand, similar to a finger but lower down

thump thumps, thumping, thumped
VERB **1** If you **thump** someone or something, you hit them hard with your fist.
VERB **2** When your heart **thumps**, it beats strongly and quickly.
NOUN **3** a hard hit
NOUN **4** a fairly loud, dull sound

thunder
NOUN the loud, rumbling noise that you hear from the sky during some storms, often after a flash of lightning

thunderstorm thunderstorms
NOUN a storm with thunder and lightning

Thursday
NOUN the fifth day of the week, coming between Wednesday and Friday

---

WORD HISTORY
from Old English *Thursdæg* meaning Thor's day; Thor was the Norse god of thunder

---

tick ticks, ticking, ticked
NOUN **1** a written mark to show that something is correct
VERB **2** If you **tick** something written on a piece of paper, you put a tick next to it.
VERB **3** When a clock **ticks**, it makes a regular clicking noise as it works.

ticket tickets
NOUN a piece of paper or card which shows that you have paid for a journey or have paid to go into a place • *Don't lose your bus ticket.*

tickle tickles, tickling, tickled
VERB When you **tickle** someone, you move your fingers lightly over their body in order to make them laugh.

tidal wave tidal waves
NOUN a very large wave, often caused by an earthquake, that flows onto the land and destroys things

tide tides
NOUN the regular change in the level of the sea on the shore

tidy tidier, tidiest; tidies, tidying, tidied
ADJECTIVE **1** Something that is **tidy** is neat and arranged in an orderly way.
ADJECTIVE **2** Someone who is **tidy** always keeps their things neat.
VERB **3** If you **tidy** a place, you make it neat by putting things in their proper place.

tie ties, tying, tied
VERB **1** If you **tie** one thing to another, you fasten it using cord of some kind.
VERB **2** If you **tie** a piece of cord or cloth, you fasten the ends together in a knot or bow.
NOUN **3** a long, narrow piece of cloth worn around the neck under a shirt collar, and tied in a knot at the front

tiger tigers
NOUN a large wild cat that has an orange-coloured coat with black stripes

tight tighter, tightest
ADJECTIVE **1** If clothes are **tight**, they fit you very closely.
ADVERB **2** If you hold **tight**, you hold on very firmly.

tighten tightens, tightening, tightened
VERB **1** If you **tighten** something like a rope or a chain, you pull it until it is straight and firmly stretched.
VERB **2** If you **tighten** something like a screw or a knot, you fasten or fix it more firmly.

tightrope tightropes
NOUN a tightly-stretched rope on which an acrobat balances and performs tricks

tights
PLURAL NOUN a piece of clothing made of thin, stretchy material that fits closely round a person's hips, legs and feet

tile tiles, tiling, tiled
NOUN **1** a flat, rectangular piece of something, such as slate, carpet or baked clay, that is used to cover surfaces
VERB **2** If you **tile** a surface, you fix tiles to it.

A
B
C
D
E
F
G
H
I
J
K
L
M
N
O
P
Q
R
S
T
U
V
W
X
Y
Z

till tills, tilling, tilled
NOUN **1** a drawer or box in a shop where money is kept, usually in a cash register
PREPOSITION **2** up to a certain time • *You can stay up **till** nine o'clock.*
CONJUNCTION **3** If something does not happen **till** a particular time, it does not happen before that time and only starts happening at that time. • *You can't go out to play **till** you've finished your homework.*
VERB **4** If someone **tills** the soil, they plough it.

tiller tillers
NOUN a handle fixed to the top of the rudder on a boat. It turns the rudder and steers the boat.

tilt tilts, tilting, tilted
VERB If you **tilt** an object, you move it so that one end or side is higher than the other.

timber timbers
NOUN **1** wood that has been cut and prepared ready for building and making furniture
NOUN **2** The **timbers** of a ship or house are the large pieces of wood that have been used to build it.

time times, timing, timed
NOUN **1** what we measure in minutes, hours, days, weeks and years
NOUN **2** a particular point in the day • *What **time** is it?*
NOUN **3** a particular period in history
VERB **4** If you **time** something like a race, you measure how long it takes.

times
PLURAL NOUN multiplied by • *Two **times** three is six (2 × 3 = 6).*

timetable timetables
NOUN **1** a plan of the times when particular activities or jobs should be done
NOUN **2** a list of the times when particular trains, boats, buses or aircraft arrive and depart

timid
ADJECTIVE If you are **timid**, you are shy and lacking in confidence.
ANTONYM: bold

tin tins
NOUN **1** a soft, silvery-white metal
NOUN **2** a metal container that is filled with food and then sealed in order to keep the food fresh
NOUN **3** a small metal container that may have a lid

tingle tingles, tingling, tingled
VERB When a part of your body **tingles**, you feel a slight prickling sensation there.

tinkle tinkles, tinkling, tinkled
VERB Something that **tinkles** makes a light, ringing sound.

tinsel
NOUN long threads with strips of shiny paper attached, used as a decoration at Christmas

tint tints
NOUN a shade of a particular colour, particularly a pale one

tiny tinier, tiniest
ADJECTIVE extremely small

tip tips, tipping, tipped
NOUN **1** the point or the very end of something
NOUN **2** a small gift of money given to someone like a waiter, who has done a service for you
NOUN **3** a place where rubbish is left
NOUN **4** a piece of useful information or advice
VERB **5** If you **tip** something, you tilt or overturn it. • *When he jumped up, he **tipped** the chair over.*
VERB **6** If you **tip** something somewhere, you pour it quickly and carelessly, or you empty it from a container. • *When they had finished the washing up, they **tipped** the water out of the bowl.*

tiptoe tiptoes, tiptoeing, tiptoed
VERB If you **tiptoe** somewhere, you walk there very quietly on your toes.

tire tires, tiring, tired
VERB **1** If something **tires** you, it makes you use a lot of energy so that you want to rest or sleep afterwards.
VERB **2** If you **tire** of something, you become bored with it.

tired
ADJECTIVE **1** feeling as if you want to rest or sleep
ADJECTIVE **2** If you are **tired** of something, you are bored with it. • *I'm **tired** of watching television. Can we do something else?*

tiredness
NOUN the feeling you have when you want to rest or sleep

tissue tissues
NOUN a small piece of soft paper that you use as a handkerchief

415

A
B
C
D
E
F
G
H
I
J
K
L
M
N
O
P
Q
R
S
T
U
V
W
X
Y
Z

title titles
NOUN the name of something such as a book, play, film or piece of music

to
PREPOSITION **1** towards
PREPOSITION **2** used to compare units • *There are 100 centimetres to a metre.*
PREPOSITION **3** compared with or rather than • *I prefer fruit to chocolate.*
PREPOSITION **4** used to indicate the limit of something • *I am allowed to spend up to an hour watching television each night.*
ADVERB **5** if you push something like a door **to**, you close it but do not shut it completely

LANGUAGE TIP
Do not confuse *to* with *too* or *two*.

toad toads
NOUN an animal similar to a frog, but with drier skin and living more on land and less in the water

toadstool toadstools
NOUN a type of fungus similar to a mushroom and often poisonous

toast toasts, toasting, toasted
NOUN **1** slices of bread made brown and crisp by cooking them at a high temperature
VERB **2** If you **toast** bread, you cook it at a high temperature so that it becomes brown and crisp.

toaster toasters
NOUN an electrical device for toasting bread

tobacco
NOUN the dried leaves of a plant called **tobacco**. People smoke it in pipes, cigarettes and cigars.

toboggan toboggans, tobogganing, tobogganed
NOUN **1** a flat seat with two wooden or metal runners, used for sliding over the snow

SYNONYM: sledge

VERB **2** If you **toboggan**, you use a toboggan to slide over the snow.

SYNONYM: sledge

today
NOUN **1** the day that is happening now
ADVERB **2** on the day that is happening now • *How are you feeling today?*

toddler toddlers
NOUN a small child who has just learned to walk

toe toes
NOUN **1** one of the five movable parts at the end of your foot
NOUN **2** the part of a shoe or sock that covers the end of your foot

toffee toffees
NOUN a sticky, chewy sweet made by boiling sugar and butter together with water

toga togas
NOUN a long, loose robe worn in ancient Rome

together
ADVERB **1** If people do something **together**, they do it with each other.
ADVERB **2** If two things happen **together**, they happen at the same time.
ADVERB **3** If things are joined, mixed or fixed **together**, they are put with each other.

toil toils, toiling, toiled
VERB **1** If you **toil**, you work very hard.
NOUN **2** very hard work

toilet toilets
NOUN **1** a large bowl, connected to the drains, which you use to get rid of waste from your body

SYNONYM: lavatory

NOUN **2** a small room containing a toilet

SYNONYM: lavatory

token tokens
NOUN **1** a piece of paper or card that is worth a particular amount of money and can be exchanged for goods • *I got a book token for my birthday.*
NOUN **2** a flat round piece of metal or plastic that can sometimes be used instead of money • *Some of the phones only take tokens.*
NOUN **3** a sign or symbol of something • *We bought her some flowers as a token of our thanks.*

told
VERB the past tense and past participle of **tell**

tolerate tolerates, tolerating, tolerated
VERB If you **tolerate** something, you put up with it even though you do not like it.

tomato **tomatoes**
NOUN a small, round, red fruit used as a vegetable and eaten cooked or raw

tomb **tombs**
NOUN a large grave where one or more people are buried

tomorrow
NOUN **1** the day after today
ADVERB **2** on the day after today • *I'm staying home* **tonight**.

LANGUAGE TIP
Tomorrow has one *m* and two *r*s.

ton **tons**
NOUN a unit of weight equal to 2240 pounds or about 1016 kilograms

tone **tones**
NOUN **1** a particular quality that a sound has • *the clear* **tone** *of the bell*
NOUN **2** a shade of a colour

tongs
PLURAL NOUN two long, narrow pieces of metal joined together at one end. You press the pieces together to pick up objects.

tongue **tongues**
NOUN the soft part in your mouth that you can move and use for tasting, licking and speaking

tongue twister **tongue twisters**
NOUN a sentence or a rhyme that is very difficult to say

tonight
NOUN **1** the evening or night that will come at the end of today
ADVERB **2** on the evening or night that will come at the end of today • *What will we learn* **tomorrow**?

tonne **tonnes**
NOUN a unit of weight equal to 1000 kilograms

tonsil **tonsils**
NOUN one of the two small, soft lumps at the back of your throat

tonsillitis
NOUN a painful swelling of your tonsils caused by an infection

too
ADVERB **1** also or as well • *She was there* **too**.
ADVERB **2** **Too** shows that there is more of something than you want. • *I've had* **too** *much to eat.*

LANGUAGE TIP
Do not confuse *too* with *to* or *two*.

took
VERB the past tense of **take**

tool **tools**
NOUN any hand-held piece of equipment that you use to help you do a particular kind of work

tooth **teeth**
NOUN one of the hard, white bony parts in your mouth that you use for biting and chewing food

toothache
NOUN a pain in one of your teeth

toothbrush **toothbrushes**
NOUN a brush for cleaning your teeth

toothpaste
NOUN the substance that you use with a toothbrush to clean your teeth

top **tops**
NOUN **1** the highest point of something • *There was snow on the mountain* **top**.
NOUN **2** the upper side of something • *There was a vase of flowers on the table* **top**.
NOUN **3** a piece of clothing that you wear on the top half of your body
NOUN **4** a toy that can be made to spin
ADJECTIVE **5** The **top** thing of a series of things is the highest one. • *the* **top** *floor of the building*

topic **topics**
NOUN a particular subject that you write about or discuss

topical
ADJECTIVE to do with things that are happening now

Torah
NOUN Jewish law and teaching

torch **torches**
NOUN a small electric light carried in the hand and powered by batteries

WORD HISTORY
from Old French *torche* meaning handful of twisted straw, which was set on fire and held up to provide light

tore
VERB the past tense of **tear**

A
B
C
D
E
F
G
H
I
J
K
L
M
N
O
P
Q
R
S
T
U
V
W
X
Y
Z

torment torments, tormenting, tormented
> NOUN **1** great pain or unhappiness
> VERB **2** If something **torments** you, it causes you great unhappiness.
> VERB **3** If someone **torments** you, they keep deliberately annoying you.

torn
> VERB the past participle of **tear**

tornado tornadoes or tornados
> NOUN a violent storm with strong circular winds around a funnel-shaped cloud

torpedo torpedoes, torpedoing, torpedoed
> NOUN **1** a tube-shaped bomb that travels underwater and explodes when it hits a target
> VERB **2** If a ship is **torpedoed**, it is hit, and usually sunk, by a torpedo.

torrent torrents
> NOUN a very strong stream or fall of water
> • The rain fell in a **torrent**.

torrential
> ADJECTIVE **Torrential** rain pours down very fast and in great quantities.

tortoise tortoises
> NOUN a slow-moving reptile with a hard shell over its body into which it can pull its head and legs for protection

torture tortures, torturing, tortured
> VERB If someone **tortures** another person, they deliberately cause them great pain, usually as a punishment or to get information from them.

toss tosses, tossing, tossed
> VERB **1** If you **toss** something somewhere, you throw it there lightly and carelessly.
> VERB **2** If you **toss** a coin, you decide something by throwing a coin into the air and guessing which side will face upwards when it lands.

total totals, totalling, totalled
> NOUN **1** the number you get when you add several numbers together
> VERB **2** If you **total** amounts, you add them together to find the total.
> ADJECTIVE **3** complete

toucan toucans
> NOUN a large tropical bird with a large, colourful beak

touch touches, touching, touched
> VERB **1** If you **touch** something, you put your fingers or hand on it.
> VERB **2** When two things **touch**, they come into contact.
> VERB **3** If something **touches** you, it affects your emotions. • The sad story **touched** us all
> NOUN **4** Your sense of **touch** is your ability to feel things by touching them.

touchdown touchdowns
> NOUN the landing of an aircraft or spacecraft

touchy touchier, touchiest
> ADJECTIVE sensitive and easily offended

tough tougher, toughest
> ADJECTIVE **1** A **tough** person is strong and able to put up with things that are difficult.
> ADJECTIVE **2** Something that is **tough** is strong and difficult to break or damage.
> ADJECTIVE **3** **Tough** food is difficult to cut and chew.

> ANTONYM: tender

tour tours, touring, toured
> NOUN **1** a long journey during which you visit several places
> NOUN **2** a short trip round a place such as a city or a famous building
> VERB **3** If you **tour** a place, you go on a journey or a trip round it.

tourist tourists
> NOUN someone who is travelling on holiday

tournament tournaments
> NOUN a competition in which many players or teams compete in a series of games or contests

tow tows, towing, towed
> VERB **1** If a vehicle **tows** another vehicle, it pulls it along behind it.
> NOUN **2** To give a vehicle a **tow** is to pull it along behind.

towards
> PREPOSITION If you go **towards** something, you move in its direction.

owel towels
NOUN a piece of thick, soft cloth that you use to dry yourself with

ower towers
NOUN a tall, narrow building, sometimes attached to a larger building such as a castle or church

→ Have a look at the illustrations for **castle** and **turbine**

own towns
NOUN a place with many streets and buildings where people live and work

oxic
ADJECTIVE poisonous

oy toys
NOUN something to play with

race traces, tracing, traced
VERB 1 If you **trace** something like a drawing, you copy it by drawing on thin paper over the top, which you can see through.
VERB 2 If you **trace** something, you find it after looking for it. • Scientists **traced** the origin of the disease.
NOUN 3 a tiny amount of something or a small mark

rack tracks, tracking, tracked
NOUN 1 a narrow road or path
NOUN 2 a strip of ground with rails on it that a train travels along
NOUN 3 a piece of ground, shaped like a ring, that horses, cars or athletes race around
VERB 4 If you **track** someone or something, you follow them by following the marks they leave as they pass.

rackpad trackpads
NOUN a flat smooth area on the keyboard of some computers that you slide your finger over in order to move the cursor

→ Have a look at the illustration for **computer**

racksuit tracksuits
NOUN a loose, warm suit of trousers and a top, worn for outdoor sports

ractor tractors
NOUN a vehicle with large rear wheels, that is used on farms for pulling machinery and other heavy loads

trade trades
NOUN the activity of buying, selling or exchanging goods or services between people or countries
SYNONYM: business

trademark trademarks
NOUN a name or symbol that a manufacturer always uses on its products. **Trademarks** are usually protected by law so that no one else can use them.

trade union trade unions
NOUN an organisation of workers that tries to improve the pay and conditions of its members

tradition traditions
NOUN a custom or belief that has existed for a long time and been passed down through the generations without changing

WORD HISTORY
from Latin *traditio* meaning a handing down

traditional
ADJECTIVE 1 passed down from one generation to the next
ADJECTIVE 2 having existed or gone on for a long time

traffic
NOUN all the vehicles, ships, aircraft or people moving along a route at a particular time

traffic lights
PLURAL NOUN a set of lights used to control traffic at road junctions

traffic warden traffic wardens
NOUN an official whose job is to make sure that vehicles are not parked in the wrong place or for longer than is allowed

tragedy tragedies
NOUN 1 a very sad or disastrous event or situation, especially one in which people are killed
NOUN 2 a serious story or play that usually ends with the death of the main character

tragic
ADJECTIVE very sad and distressing, usually involving death, destruction or disaster

trail trails
NOUN 1 a rough path across open country or through forests
NOUN 2 a series of marks or other signs left by someone or something as they move along • He left a **trail** of mud behind him.

trailer trailers
NOUN **1** a small vehicle that can be loaded with things and pulled behind a car or lorry
NOUN **2** a series of short pieces taken from a film or television programme in order to advertise it

train trains, training, trained
NOUN **1** a number of carriages or trucks that are pulled by a railway engine along railway lines
VERB **2** If you **train**, you learn how to do a particular job.
VERB **3** If you **train**, or someone **trains** you, for a sports match or a race, you prepare for it by doing exercises.

trainers
PLURAL NOUN special shoes worn for running and other sports

traitor traitors
NOUN someone who betrays their country or the group that they belong to

tram trams
NOUN a passenger vehicle that runs on rails along the street and is powered by electricity from an overhead wire

tramp tramps, tramping, tramped
NOUN **1** a person who has no home, no job, and very little money
NOUN **2** a long country walk
VERB **3** If you **tramp** from one place to another, you walk with slow, heavy footsteps.

trample tramples, trampling, trampled
VERB If you **trample** on something, you tread heavily on it so that it is damaged.

trampoline trampolines
NOUN a piece of gymnastic equipment made of a large piece of strong cloth held tight by springs in a frame, on which a gymnast bounces

trance trances
NOUN If someone is in a **trance**, they seem to be asleep, but they can still see, hear, answer questions and obey orders.

trans-
PREFIX You add **trans-** to a word to mean across, through or beyond. For example, **trans**atlantic means across or beyond the Atlantic Ocean.

transaction transactions
NOUN a business deal that involves buying and selling something

transatlantic
ADJECTIVE used to describe something that crosses the Atlantic Ocean or is on the other side of it

transfer transfers, transferring, transferred
VERB **1** If you **transfer** something from one place to another, you move it there.
NOUN **2** a piece of paper with a design or drawing on one side that can be ironed or pressed onto another surface, such as cloth, paper or china

transform transforms, transforming, transformed
VERB If you **transform** something, or it **transforms**, it changes completely.

transfusion transfusions
NOUN a process in which blood donated by a healthy person is injected into the body of another person who needs it because they are badly injured or ill

transistor transistors
NOUN **1** a small electrical device in something such as a television or radio, which is used to control electric currents
NOUN **2** a small portable radio

translate translates, translating, translated
VERB If you **translate** something that someone has said or written, you say it or write it in a different language.

translucent
ADJECTIVE If something is **translucent**, it allows the light to shine through and appears to glow.

transmit transmits, transmitting, transmitted
VERB **1** When a message or an electronic signal is **transmitted**, it is sent by radio waves.
VERB **2** If you **transmit** something, you send it to a different place.
VERB **3** If you **transmit** a disease, you pass it on to other people.

transmitter transmitters
NOUN a device for sending radio messages

transparency
NOUN the quality that an object or substance has when you can see through it

transparent

ADJECTIVE If an object or substance is **transparent**, you can see through it.

SYNONYMS: clear, see-through

transpiration

NOUN the evaporation of water from a plant's leaves, stem or flowers

→ Have a look at the illustration for **water cycle**

transplant transplants, transplanting, transplanted

VERB **1** To **transplant** something living, like a plant or an organ, means to remove it from one place and put it in another.

NOUN **2** an operation where an organ, such as a heart or a kidney, is taken from one person and put into another

transport transports, transporting, transported

VERB **1** If you **transport** someone or something, you take them from one place to another.

NOUN **2** the name for vehicles you travel in
● *Cars and planes are forms of* **transport**.

trap traps, trapping, trapped

NOUN **1** a piece of equipment or a hole that is dug to catch animals

NOUN **2** a plan to trick, capture or cheat a person

VERB **3** If you **trap** animals, you catch them using a trap.

VERB **4** If you **trap** someone, you trick, capture or cheat them.

trapeze trapezes

NOUN a bar hanging from two ropes on which acrobats and gymnasts swing and perform skilful movements

trapezium trapeziums

NOUN a plane shape with two parallel sides of different lengths

trash

NOUN rubbish

traumatic

ADJECTIVE A **traumatic** experience is very upsetting and causes great stress.

travel travels, travelling, travelled

VERB **1** If you **travel**, you go from one place to another.

NOUN **2** the journeys that people make

trawler trawlers

NOUN a fishing boat that pulls a wide net behind it to catch fish

tray trays

NOUN a flat piece of wood, metal or plastic used for carrying things on

treacherous

ADJECTIVE **1** disloyal and untrustworthy

ADJECTIVE **2** dangerous or unreliable

treacle

NOUN a thick, sweet syrup used to make cakes and toffee

tread treads, treading, trod, trodden

VERB **1** If you **tread** on something, you walk on it or step on it.

NOUN **2** The **tread** of a tyre or shoe is the pattern of ridges on it that stops it slipping.

NOUN **3** the part of a staircase or ladder that you put your foot on

treason

NOUN the crime of betraying your country, for example by helping its enemies

treasure treasures, treasuring, treasured

NOUN **1** a collection of gold, silver, jewels or other precious objects, especially one that has been hidden

NOUN **2** a valuable object, such as a work of art

VERB **3** If you **treasure** something, you look after it carefully because it is important to you. ● *She* **treasured** *the shells she had collected on her holiday.*

treasury treasuries

NOUN **1** a place where treasure is stored

NOUN **2** The **Treasury** is the government department that looks after a country's finances.

treat treats, treating, treated

NOUN **1** If you give someone a **treat**, you buy or arrange something special for them that they will enjoy.

VERB **2** When a doctor **treats** a patient or an illness, he or she gives them medical care and attention.

VERB **3** If you **treat** someone or something in a particular way, you behave that way towards them.

treaty treaties

NOUN a written agreement between countries, in which they agree to do something or to help each other

a
b
c
d
e
f
g
h
i
j
k
l
m
n
o
p
q
r
s
t
u
v
w
x
y
z

421

treble trebles, trebling, trebled
VERB **1** If something **trebles**, or is **trebled**, it becomes three times greater in number or amount.
NOUN **2 Treble** the amount of something is three times the amount.

tree trees
NOUN a large plant with a hard trunk, branches and leaves

trek treks, trekking, trekked
VERB **1** If you **trek** somewhere, you go on a long and difficult journey to get there.
NOUN **2** a long and difficult journey, especially one made on foot

WORD HISTORY
an Afrikaans word

tremble trembles, trembling, trembled
VERB If you **tremble**, you shake slightly, usually because you are frightened or cold.

tremendous
ADJECTIVE **1** large or impressive • *It was a **tremendous** performance.*
ADJECTIVE **2** (*informal*) very good or pleasing • *The game was **tremendous** fun.*

tremor tremors
NOUN **1** a small earthquake
NOUN **2** a slight, uncontrollable shaking movement

trench trenches
NOUN a long narrow channel or ditch dug into the ground

trend trends, trending, trended
NOUN **1** a general direction in which something is moving
NOUN **2** a fashion
VERB **3** If you say a topic or name is **trending** on social media, you mean that a lot of people are discussing it.

trendy trendier, trendiest
ADJECTIVE (*informal*) fashionable

trespass trespasses, trespassing, trespassed
VERB If you **trespass** on someone's land or property, you go onto it without their permission.

trial trials
NOUN **1** a legal process in which a court listens to evidence to decide whether a person is innocent or guilty of a crime
NOUN **2** a type of experiment in which someone or something is tested to see how well they perform

triangle triangles
NOUN **1** a plane shape with three straight sides
NOUN **2** a percussion instrument consisting of a thin steel bar bent in the shape of a triangle. It produces a note when struck with a small metal rod.

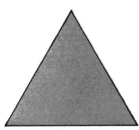

triangular
ADJECTIVE shaped like a triangle

tribal
ADJECTIVE to do with a tribe

tribe tribes
NOUN a group of people of the same race, who have the same customs, religion, beliefs, language or land

tributary tributaries
NOUN a stream or river that flows into a larger river

tribute tributes
NOUN something said or done to show admiration and respect for someone

trick tricks, tricking, tricked
VERB **1** If someone **tricks** you, they deceive you.
NOUN **2** an action done to deceive someone
NOUN **3** a clever or skilful action that is done in order to entertain people • *a card **trick***

trickle trickles, trickling, trickled
VERB When a liquid **trickles**, it flows slowly in a thin stream.

tricky trickier, trickiest
ADJECTIVE difficult to do or deal with

tricycle tricycles
NOUN a vehicle similar to a bicycle but with three wheels, two at the back and one at the front

tried
VERB the past tense and past participle of **try**

trifle **trifles**
NOUN **1** a cold pudding made of layers of sponge cake, fruit, jelly and custard
NOUN **2** something unimportant or of little value

trigger **triggers**
NOUN the small lever on a gun that is pulled in order to fire it

trillion **trillions**
NOUN A **trillion** is one million million, which is written as 1,000,000,000,000.

trim **trims, trimming, trimmed;**
trimmer, trimmest
VERB **1** If you **trim** something, you cut small amounts off it to make it more tidy.
ADJECTIVE **2** neat and tidy
NOUN **3** If something is given a **trim**, it is cut a little.
NOUN **4** a decoration along the edges of something • *a coat with a velvet* **trim**

trinket **trinkets**
NOUN a cheap ornament or piece of jewellery

trio **trios**
NOUN **1** a group of three musicians who sing or play together
NOUN **2** a piece of music written for three instruments or singers

trip **trips, tripping, tripped**
NOUN **1** a journey made to a place
VERB **2** If you **trip**, or **trip over**, you catch your foot on something and fall over.
VERB **3** If you **trip** someone, or **trip** them up, you make them fall over by making them catch their foot on something.

triple **triples, tripling, tripled**
ADJECTIVE **1** made of three things or three parts
VERB **2** If you **triple** something, or if it **triples**, it becomes three times greater in number or size.

triplet **triplets**
NOUN one of three children born at the same time to the same mother

tripod **tripods**
NOUN a stand with three legs used to support something like a camera or telescope

triumph **triumphs, triumphing,**
triumphed
NOUN **1** a great success or achievement
NOUN **2** a feeling of great satisfaction when you win or achieve something

VERB **3** If you **triumph**, you win a victory or succeed in overcoming something.

triumphant
ADJECTIVE If you are **triumphant**, you feel very happy because you have won a victory or achieved something.

trivial
ADJECTIVE unimportant

trod
VERB the past tense of **tread**

trodden
VERB the past participle of **tread**

troll **trolls**
NOUN an imaginary creature in Scandinavian mythology, that is either a dwarf or a giant and lives in caves or mountains

trolley **trolleys**
NOUN **1** a basket or cart on wheels, in which you can carry your shopping or luggage
NOUN **2** a small table on wheels, used to serve food and drink

trombone **trombones**
NOUN a brass wind instrument with a U-shaped tube that you slide to produce different notes

troop **troops, trooping, trooped**
PLURAL NOUN **1** **Troops** are soldiers.
NOUN **2** A **troop** of people or animals is a group of them.
VERB **3** If people **troop** somewhere, they go there in a group.

trophy **trophies**
NOUN a cup or shield given as a prize to the winner of a competition

tropic **tropics**
NOUN The **tropics** are the hottest regions of the world, that lie on either side of the equator.

→ Have a look at the illustration for **equator**

tropical
ADJECTIVE belonging to or typical of the tropics

trot **trots, trotting, trotted**
VERB **1** When a horse **trots**, it runs with short steps, lifting its feet quite high off the ground.
VERB **2** If you **trot**, you run slowly with small steps.

trouble troubles, troubling, troubled
NOUN **1** a difficulty or problem

SYNONYM: worry

PHRASE **2** If you are **in trouble**, someone is angry with you because of something you have done wrong.
VERB **3** If something **troubles** you, it worries or bothers you.
VERB **4** If you **trouble** someone, you worry or bother them.

trough troughs
NOUN a long, narrow container from which animals drink or feed

trousers
PLURAL NOUN a piece of clothing for the lower half of your body, from the waist down, covering each leg separately

trout
NOUN a type of edible freshwater fish

LANGUAGE TIP
The plural of *trout* can be either *trout* or *trouts*, but *trout* is more common.

trowel trowels
NOUN **1** a garden tool like a small spade, used for planting or weeding
NOUN **2** a small, flat spade used by builders for spreading cement and mortar

truant truants
NOUN a child who stays away from school without permission

truce truces
NOUN an agreement between two people or groups to stop fighting for a short time

truck trucks
NOUN a large motor vehicle used for carrying heavy loads

trudge trudges, trudging, trudged
VERB **1** If you **trudge**, you walk with slow, heavy steps.
NOUN **2** a slow, tiring walk

true truer, truest
ADJECTIVE **1** A **true** story or statement is based on facts and is not invented.

SYNONYMS: accurate, correct, factual

PHRASE **2** If something **comes true**, it actually happens. • *I hope your wish comes true.*

trumpet trumpets
NOUN a wind instrument made of a narrow brass tube that widens at the end into a bell-like shape

truncheon truncheons
NOUN a short, thick stick that police officers carry as a weapon

trunk trunks
NOUN **1** the main stem of a tree from which the branches and roots grow
NOUN **2** the long, flexible nose of an elephant
NOUN **3** a large, strong case or box with a hinged lid, used for storing things
NOUN **4** In American English, the **trunk** of a car is the boot, a covered space at the back or front that is used for luggage.
NOUN **5** the main part of your body, excluding your arms, legs and head
PLURAL NOUN **6** A man's **trunks** are his bathing pants or shorts.

trust trusts, trusting, trusted
VERB **1** If you **trust** someone, you believe that they are honest and reliable, and will treat you fairly.
VERB **2** If you **trust** someone to do something, you believe they will do it.
NOUN **3** the feeling that someone can be trusted
NOUN **4** the responsibility you have to people who trust you

trustworthy
ADJECTIVE A **trustworthy** person is responsible and reliable, and you know that they will do what they say they will do.

truth truths
NOUN the facts about something, rather than things that are imagined or invented

truthful
ADJECTIVE A **truthful** person is honest and tells the truth.

try tries, trying, tried
VERB **1** If you **try** to do something, you make an effort to do it.
VERB **2** If you **try** something, you use it, taste it or experiment with it to see how good or suitable it is.
VERB **3** When a court **tries** a person, they listen to evidence to decide if that person is guilty of a crime.
VERB **4** A person who **tries** your patience is extremely irritating and difficult.
NOUN **5** an attempt to do something

tsunami

NOUN **6** A **try** in rugby is when a player scores by carrying the ball over the opponents' goal line and putting it on the ground.

try on
VERB If you **try on** a piece of clothing, you wear it to see if it fits you or if it looks nice.

T-shirt T-shirts; also spelt **tee shirt**
NOUN a simple short-sleeved cotton shirt with no collar

tsunami tsunamis
NOUN a very large wave, often caused by an earthquake, that flows onto the land and destroys things

tub tubs
NOUN a wide, circular container

tuba tubas
NOUN a large brass musical instrument that can produce very low notes

tube tubes
NOUN a hollow cylinder made of metal, plastic, rubber or other material

tuck tucks, tucking, tucked
VERB **1** If you **tuck** a piece of fabric into or under something, you push the loose ends inside or under it to make it tidy.
VERB **2** If you **tuck** into a meal, you eat eagerly and with pleasure.
VERB **3** If you **tuck** someone up in bed, you put the bedclothes snugly round them.

Tuesday
NOUN the third day of the week, coming between Monday and Wednesday

WORD HISTORY
an Anglo-Saxon name honouring the god of war called *Tiw*, said *tue*

tuft tufts
NOUN A **tuft** of something, such as hair or grass, is a bunch of it growing closely together.

tug tugs, tugging, tugged
VERB **1** If you **tug** something, you give it a quick, hard pull.
NOUN **2** a small, powerful boat that tows large ships

tulip tulips
NOUN a brightly coloured spring flower

WORD HISTORY
from Turkish *tulbend* meaning turban, because of the flower's shape

tumble tumbles, tumbling, tumbled
VERB If you **tumble**, you fall with a rolling or bouncing movement.

tumbler tumblers
NOUN a drinking glass with no handle or stem

tumour tumours
NOUN an abnormal growth in the body

tuna
NOUN a large, edible fish that lives in warm seas

LANGUAGE TIP
The plural of *tuna* can be either *tuna* or *tunas*, but *tuna* is more common.

a b c d e f g h i j k l m n o p q r s t u v w x y z

425

tune tunes
NOUN a series of musical notes arranged in a particular way

tunnel tunnels
NOUN a long underground passage
• a railway **tunnel**

turban turbans
NOUN a long piece of cloth worn wound round the head, especially by a Hindu, Muslim or Sikh man

turbine turbines
NOUN a machine or engine powered by a stream of air, gas, water or steam

---

WORD HISTORY
from Latin *turbo* meaning whirlwind

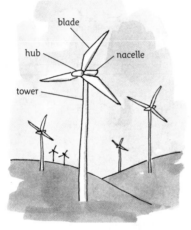

blade
hub
nacelle
tower

turf
NOUN short, thick, even grass and the layer of soil beneath it

turkey turkeys
NOUN a large bird kept for its meat

turn turns, turning, turned
VERB **1** When you **turn**, you move so that you are facing or going in a different direction.
VERB **2** When you **turn** something, or when it **turns**, it moves so that it faces in a different direction or is in a different position. • *She* **turned** *the key in the lock.*
VERB **3** When something **turns**, or **turns into** something else, it becomes something different, or has a different appearance or quality. • *The leaves* **turned** *brown in autumn.*

NOUN **4** If it is your **turn** to do something, you do it next.
VERB **5** If you **turn down** something, you refuse it. • *I was not hungry, so I* **turned down** *the chips.*
VERB **6** If you **turn up** the television, for example, you increase the volume.
VERB **7** If someone **turns up**, they arrive.

turnip turnips
NOUN a round root vegetable with a white or yellow skin

turquoise
NOUN **1** light bluish-green
NOUN **2** A light bluish-green stone used in jewellery.

turret turrets
NOUN a small, narrow tower on top of a larger tower or other building, such as a castle

→ Have a look at the illustration for **castle**

turtle turtles
NOUN a large reptile with flippers for swimming and a thick shell covering its body. It lays its eggs on land but lives the rest of its life in the sea.

tusk tusks
NOUN one of the pair of long, curving, pointed teeth of an elephant, wild boar or walrus

tutor tutors
NOUN a private teacher or a teacher at a college or university

TV
NOUN an abbreviation of *television*

tweed tweeds
NOUN a thick woollen cloth. Someone wearing **tweeds** is wearing a **tweed** suit.

tweet tweets, tweeting, tweeted
NOUN **1** a short, high-pitched sound made by a small bird
NOUN **2** a short message on the Twitter website
VERB **3** If you **tweet**, or **tweet** something, you put a short message on the Twitter website.

tweezers
PLURAL NOUN a small tool with two arms that can be closed together to grip something. **Tweezers** are used for pulling out hairs or picking up small objects.

A B C D E F G H I J K L M N O P Q R S T U V W X Y Z

twelfth twelfths
NOUN **1** one of twelve equal parts of something. It can be written as ½.
ADJECTIVE **2** The **twelfth** item in a series is the one that you count as number twelve. It can be written as 12th.

twelve
NOUN **Twelve** is the number 12.

twentieth twentieths
NOUN **1** one of twenty parts of something. It can be written as ½₀.
ADJECTIVE **2** The **twentieth** item in a series is the one that you count as number twenty. It can be written as 20th.

twenty
NOUN **Twenty** is the number 20.

twice
ADVERB two times

twiddle twiddles, twiddling, twiddled
VERB If you **twiddle** something, you turn it quickly round and round or over and over.

twig twigs
NOUN a small branch on a tree or bush

twilight
NOUN the time after sunset when it is just getting dark

twin twins
NOUN If two people are **twins**, they have the same mother and were born on the same day.

twinkle twinkles, twinkling, twinkled
VERB Something that **twinkles** shines with little flashes of light.
SYNONYMS: glitter, sparkle

twirl twirls, twirling, twirled
VERB If you **twirl** something, you make it spin round quickly.

twist twists, twisting, twisted
VERB **1** When you **twist** something, you turn the two ends in opposite directions.
VERB **2** If you **twist** part of your body, you injure it by turning it too sharply or in an odd direction.

two
NOUN **Two** is the number 2.

LANGUAGE TIP
Do not confuse *two* with *to* or *too*.

two-dimensional
ADJECTIVE A **two-dimensional** object or shape is flat.

tying
VERB the present participle of **tie**

type types, typing, typed
NOUN **1** If something is the same **type** as something else, they belong to the same group and have many things in common.
SYNONYMS: kind, sort
VERB **2** If you **type** something, you use a typewriter or computer to write it.

typewriter typewriters
NOUN a machine with keys that are pressed to write numbers and letters on a page

typhoon typhoons
NOUN a very violent tropical storm

WORD HISTORY
from Chinese *tai fung* meaning great wind

typical
ADJECTIVE Something that is **typical** of a person or animal is usual and what is to be expected of them.

tyrannosaurus tyrannosauruses
NOUN a very large meat-eating dinosaur that walked upright on its back legs

tyrant tyrants
NOUN a person who treats the people they have power over with cruelty

tyre tyres
NOUN a thick ring of rubber fitted round each wheel of a vehicle and filled with air
→ Have a look at the illustrations for **bicycle** and **car**

a b c d e f g h i j k l m n o p q r s t u v w x y z

427

U u

udder **udders**
NOUN the bag-like part of a cow, goat or ewe from which milk comes

UFO **UFOs**
NOUN an abbreviation of *unidentified flying object*. **UFOs** are objects seen in the skies, which some people believe come from other planets because they cannot be identified.

ugly **uglier, ugliest**
ADJECTIVE very unattractive or unpleasant

ulcer **ulcers**
NOUN a sore area on the skin or inside the body, that can take a long time to heal

ultimate
ADJECTIVE **1** final
NOUN **2** the best example of something

ultraviolet light
NOUN **Ultraviolet light** is not visible to the human eye. It is a form of radiation that causes your skin to tan in sunlight.

umbrella **umbrellas**
NOUN a folding frame covered in fabric and attached to a long stick, which you can open over you to protect you from the rain

umpire **umpires, umpiring, umpired**
NOUN **1** The **umpire** in a cricket or tennis match is the person who makes sure that the game is played fairly and the rules are not broken.
VERB **2** If a person **umpires** a game, they are the umpire.

un-
PREFIX You add **un-** to the beginning of a word to mean not. For example, **un**common means not common, and **un**likely means not likely.

unable
ADJECTIVE If you are **unable** to do something, you cannot do it.
ANTONYM: able

unanimous
ADJECTIVE A **unanimous** decision or vote has the agreement of everyone involved.

unaware
ADJECTIVE not aware

unbearable
ADJECTIVE Something **unbearable** is so painful or upsetting that you feel that you cannot bear or endure it.

unbelievable
ADJECTIVE **1** very surprising or wonderful
ADJECTIVE **2** so unlikely that it is hard to believe

uncanny
ADJECTIVE strange and mysterious

uncertain
ADJECTIVE If you are **uncertain** about something, you are not sure about it.
SYNONYM: doubtful

uncertainty
NOUN the feeling you have when you are not sure about something
SYNONYM: doubt

uncle **uncles**
NOUN Your **uncle** is the brother of your mother or father, or the husband of your aunt.

WORD HISTORY
from Latin *avunculus* meaning mother's brother

uncomfortable
ADJECTIVE **1** If you are **uncomfortable**, your body is not relaxed or comfortable.
ADJECTIVE **2** If something like a chair or a piece of clothing is **uncomfortable**, it is not comfortable to sit in or to wear.
ADJECTIVE **3** If you feel **uncomfortable** in a situation, you feel worried or nervous.

uncommon
ADJECTIVE not common

unconscious
ADJECTIVE If someone is **unconscious**, they are unable to see, feel or hear anything that is going on. This is usually because they have fainted or been badly injured.

uncover uncovers, uncovering, uncovered
VERB **1** to take the cover off something
VERB **2** to find out a secret or discover something

under
PREPOSITION **1** below or beneath
PREPOSITION **2** less than • *children under the age of 14*
PREPOSITION **3** controlled or ruled by • *The soldiers were under his command.*
PREPOSITION **4** If something like a building is **under** construction, or **under** repair, it is in the process of being built or repaired.

under-
PREFIX You add **under-** at the beginning of a word to mean beneath or below. For example, if you **under**estimate an amount, you estimate it below what it really is.

undercarriage undercarriages
NOUN the part of an aircraft, including the wheels, that supports the aircraft when it is on the ground
→ Have a look at the illustration for **aeroplane**

underestimate underestimates, underestimating, underestimated
VERB **1** If you **underestimate** someone, you do not realise how much they can do.
VERB **2** If you **underestimate** something, you do not realise how big it is or how long it will take.

undergo undergoes, undergoing, underwent, undergone
VERB If you **undergo** something, you experience it or are subjected to it. • *She underwent an operation to remove her tonsils.*

underground
ADJECTIVE **1** below the surface of the ground
NOUN **2** a railway system in which trains travel in tunnels below the ground

undergrowth
NOUN small plants growing under trees

underline underlines, underlining, underlined
VERB If you **underline** a word or sentence, you draw a line under it.

undermine undermines, undermining, undermined
VERB **1** If you **undermine** a person's efforts or plans, you weaken them.
VERB **2** To **undermine** something is to make a hollow or tunnel beneath it. When the sea **undermines** a cliff, for example, it gradually wears away the base and weakens it.

underneath
PREPOSITION below or beneath • *He wore a white shirt underneath a blue sweater.*

underpants
PLURAL NOUN a piece of men's underwear worn under trousers

underpass underpasses
NOUN a place where one road or path goes under another

underprivileged
ADJECTIVE **Underprivileged** people have less money and fewer opportunities than other people.

understand understands, understanding, understood
VERB **1** If you **understand** what someone says, or what you read, you know what it means.
VERB **2** If you **understand** how something works, you know how it works.
VERB **3** If you **understand** someone, you know them well and think you know why they behave the way they do.

understudy understudies
NOUN someone who has learnt the lines of a part in a play, and plays the part when the main actor or actress cannot perform

undertake undertakes, undertaking, undertook, undertaken
VERB If you **undertake** to do something, you agree to do it.

undertaker undertakers
NOUN someone whose job is to prepare bodies for burial and arrange funerals

underwater
ADVERB **1** below the surface of the water • *Submarines can travel fast underwater.*
ADJECTIVE **2** happening or used below the surface of the water • *The divers used underwater cameras.*

underwear
NOUN Your **underwear** is the clothing you wear next to your skin under your other clothes.

undo undoes, undoing, undid, undone
VERB **1** If you **undo** something like a knot, you loosen or unfasten it.
VERB **2** If you **undo** something that has been done, you reverse or remove the effects of it.

A
B
C
D
E
F
G
H
I
J
K
L
M
N
O
P
Q
R
S
T
U
V
W
X
Y
Z

undress **undresses, undressing, undressed**
VERB If you **undress**, you take your clothes off.

unearth **unearths, unearthing, unearthed**
VERB If you **unearth** something, you dig it up or discover it.

uneasy **uneasier, uneasiest**
ADJECTIVE anxious or worried

unemployed
ADJECTIVE An **unemployed** person has no job.

uneven
ADJECTIVE An **uneven** surface is not level or smooth.

unexpected
ADJECTIVE Something **unexpected** is surprising because it was not thought likely to happen.

unfair
ADJECTIVE Something **unfair** does not seem right, reasonable or fair.

unfold **unfolds, unfolding, unfolded**
VERB **1** If you **unfold** something that is folded, such as a map, you open it out.
VERB **2** When a story **unfolds**, it gradually becomes clear.

unfollow **unfollows, unfollowing, unfollowed**
VERB If you **unfollow** someone on a social media website, you choose to stop looking at the messages and pictures that they post.

unfortunate
ADJECTIVE unlucky

unfriend **unfriends, unfriending, unfriended**
VERB If you **unfriend** someone, you stop being their friend on a social media website.

unfriendly
ADJECTIVE not friendly

ungrateful
ADJECTIVE not grateful

unhappy **unhappier, unhappiest**
ADJECTIVE sad, not happy

unhealthy
ADJECTIVE not healthy

unicorn **unicorns**
NOUN an imaginary animal that looks like a white horse with a straight horn growing from its forehead

WORD HISTORY
from Latin *unicornis* meaning having one horn

uniform **uniforms**
NOUN a special set of clothes worn by people at work or school

WORD HISTORY
from Latin *uniformis* meaning of one kind

unify **unifies, unifying, unified**
VERB If several things, especially countries, are **unified**, they join together to make one.

uninhabited
ADJECTIVE An **uninhabited** place is a place where nobody lives.

uninterested
ADJECTIVE not interested ● *I am totally **uninterested** in football.*

union **unions**
NOUN an organisation of workers that aims to improve the working conditions, pay and benefits of its members

unique
ADJECTIVE Something that is **unique** is the only one of its kind.

WORD HISTORY
from Latin *unicus* meaning one and only

unisex
ADJECTIVE designed to suit either men or women

unison
NOUN If a group of people does something in **unison**, they all do it together at the same time.

WORD HISTORY
from Latin *unisonus* meaning making the same musical sound

unit **units**
NOUN **1** one single, complete thing
NOUN **2** a term used to describe a fixed quantity or measurement ● *A centimetre is a **unit** of length.*

unite **unites, uniting, united**
VERB If a number of people **unite**, they join together and act as a group.

universal
ADJECTIVE concerning or relating to everyone and everything

universe universes
NOUN everything that exists, including the whole of space, all the stars and the planets

WORD HISTORY
from Latin *universum* meaning whole world

university universities
NOUN a place where students study for degrees • *My brother goes to **university** later this year.*

unkempt
ADJECTIVE untidy and not looked after properly

WORD HISTORY
from Old English *uncembed* meaning not combed

unjust
ADJECTIVE not fair • *The group campaigns against **unjust** laws.*

unkind
ADJECTIVE rather cruel, not kind

unknown
ADJECTIVE If someone or something is **unknown**, people do not know about them or have not heard of them.

unleaded
ADJECTIVE **Unleaded** petrol does not contain any lead, and is less harmful to the atmosphere than petrol that does contain lead.

unless
CONJUNCTION You use **unless** to introduce the only circumstances in which something may or may not happen or is not true. • *The team will play tomorrow **unless** it is raining.* • *I won't go **unless** you ask me.*

unlike
ADJECTIVE **1** If one thing is **unlike** another, the two things are different.
PREPOSITION **2** not like • *Unlike me, she hates chocolate.*

unlikely unlikelier, unlikeliest
ADJECTIVE not likely to happen or be true

unload unloads, unloading, unloaded
VERB to take things out of or off a container, a vehicle or a trailer

unlock unlocks, unlocking, unlocked
VERB When you **unlock** something, you open it by turning a key in the lock.

unlucky unluckier, unluckiest
ADJECTIVE If you are **unlucky**, you are unfortunate and have bad luck.

ANTONYMS: fortunate, lucky

unnatural
ADJECTIVE not natural or normal

unnecessary
ADJECTIVE not necessary

unoccupied
ADJECTIVE A house that is **unoccupied** has no one living in it.

unpack unpacks, unpacking, unpacked
VERB When you **unpack**, you take everything out of a suitcase, bag or box.

unpleasant
ADJECTIVE **1** Something **unpleasant** is not enjoyable and may make you uncomfortable or upset.
ADJECTIVE **2** An **unpleasant** person is unfriendly or rude.

unplug unplugs, unplugging, unplugged
VERB If you **unplug** something, you take the plug out of the socket to disconnect it from the electricity supply.

unpopular
ADJECTIVE not liked very much

unravel unravels, unravelling, unravelled
VERB **1** If you **unravel** threads that are knitted or tangled, you undo or untangle them.
VERB **2** If you **unravel** a mystery, you solve it.

unreal
ADJECTIVE existing only in the imagination, not real

unreasonable
ADJECTIVE not reasonable or fair

unroll unrolls, unrolling, unrolled
VERB If you **unroll** something that has been rolled up, you open it and make it flat.

unruly
ADJECTIVE badly behaved and difficult to control

unsafe
ADJECTIVE not safe

a b c d e f g h i j k l m n o p q r s t u v w x y z

431

unscrew unscrews, unscrewing, unscrewed
VERB If you **unscrew** something, you remove it by turning it or by removing the screws that are holding it.

unselfish
ADJECTIVE An **unselfish** person is not selfish and is concerned about other people's needs.

unsteady
ADJECTIVE If you are **unsteady**, you are not steady and have difficulty balancing.

unsuccessful
ADJECTIVE If you are **unsuccessful**, you do not manage to succeed in what you are trying to do.

unsuitable
ADJECTIVE Things that are **unsuitable** are not right or suitable for a particular purpose.

untidy untidier, untidiest
ADJECTIVE not tidy

untie unties, untying, untied
VERB If you **untie** something that has been tied, you unfasten or undo it.

until
PREPOSITION **1** If something happens **until** a particular time, it happens before that time and stops at that time. ● *The shops stay open **until** eight o'clock on Thursdays.*
PREPOSITION **2** If something does not happen **until** a particular time, it does not happen before that time and only starts happening at that time. ● *It didn't rain **until** the middle of the afternoon.*
CONJUNCTION **3** If something does not happen **until** a particular time, it does not happen before that time and only starts happening at that time. ● *You can't go out on your bike **until** you've finished cleaning your room.*

untrue
ADJECTIVE not true

unusual
ADJECTIVE Something that is **unusual** is not usual and does not happen very often.

unwell
ADJECTIVE If you are **unwell**, you are ill.

unwilling
ADJECTIVE If you are **unwilling** to do something, you do not want to do it.

unwillingly
ADVERB in a way that shows you do not want to do something

unwind unwinds, unwinding, unwound
VERB **1** If you **unwind** something that was wound into a ball or around something else, you undo it.
VERB **2** If you **unwind** after working hard, you relax.

unwrap unwraps, unwrapping, unwrapped
VERB If you **unwrap** something, you take off the paper or other wrapping that is around it.

up
PREPOSITION **1** towards or in a higher place ● *They went **up** the stairs to bed.*
ADVERB **2** towards or in a higher place ● *Keep your head **up**.*
ADVERB **3** If an amount of something goes **up**, it increases.
PREPOSITION **4** If you go **up** the road, you go along it.
ADJECTIVE **5** If you are **up**, you are not in bed.

upbringing
NOUN the way you have been brought up, and how your parents have taught you to behave

upheaval upheavals
NOUN a sudden big change that causes a lot of disturbance

uphill
ADVERB If you go **uphill**, you go up a hill or a slope.

upholstery
NOUN the soft covering on chairs and sofas that makes them comfortable

upload uploads, uploading, uploaded
VERB When you **upload** a computer file or program, you put it onto a computer or the internet.

upon
PREPOSITION on or on top of

upper
ADJECTIVE The **upper** of two things is the top or higher one. ● *the **upper** deck of the bus*

upper-case
ADJECTIVE Upper-case letters are written as capitals. For example, A, H, L and P are all **upper-case** letters.

upright
ADJECTIVE **1** Something or someone that is **upright**, is standing up straight or vertically, rather than bending or lying down.
ADJECTIVE **2** An **upright** person is decent and honest.

uproar

NOUN a lot of shouting and noise, often because people are angry

SYNONYMS: commotion, pandemonium

WORD HISTORY
from Dutch *oproer* meaning revolt

upset upsets, upsetting, upset

ADJECTIVE **1** unhappy and disappointed
VERB **2** If something **upsets** you, it makes you feel worried or unhappy.
VERB **3** If you **upset** something, you knock it over or spill it accidentally.
NOUN **4** A stomach **upset** is a slight stomach illness.

upside down

ADJECTIVE **1** the wrong way up ● *She was **upside down** on the climbing frame.*
ADJECTIVE **2** If a place is **upside down**, it is very untidy.

upstairs

ADVERB **1** If you go **upstairs**, you go up to a higher floor.
ADJECTIVE **2** on a lower floor

upthrust

NOUN **Upthrust** is the force that pushes an object up and makes it seem to lose weight in a liquid or gas.

up-to-date

ADJECTIVE If something is **up-to-date**, it is modern or is the newest thing of its kind.

upwards

ADVERB going towards a higher place

uranium

NOUN a radioactive metallic element used to make nuclear energy and weapons

urban

ADJECTIVE to do with towns or cities rather than the country

WORD HISTORY
from Latin *urbs* meaning city

urge urges, urging, urged

NOUN **1** If you have an **urge** to do something, you very much want to do it.
VERB **2** If you **urge** someone to do something, you try to persuade and encourage them to do it.

urgent

ADJECTIVE If something is **urgent**, it needs to be dealt with immediately.

urine

NOUN the waste liquid that you get rid of from your body when you go to the toilet

URL URLs

NOUN A website's **URL** is its address on the internet. **URL** is an abbreviation for *uniform resource locator*.

us

PRONOUN A speaker or writer uses **us** to mean himself or herself and one or more other people.

USB USBs

NOUN a place on a computer where you can attach another piece of equipment, for example a printer or a memory stick

→ Have a look at the illustration for **computer**

use uses, using, used

VERB **1** If you **use** something, you do something with it that helps you to do a job or sort out a problem.
NOUN **2** the purpose or value of something, and the way it is used

PRONUNCIATION TIP
The verb is pronounced **yooz**. The noun is pronounced **yooss**.

used

VERB **1** If something **used to** happen, it happened before but does not happen now. ● *We **used to** fish in this stream.*
ADJECTIVE **2** If you are **used to** something, you are familiar with it and have often experienced it.
VERB **3** the past tense and past participle of **use**
ADJECTIVE **4** A **used** item has already belonged to someone else.

PRONUNCIATION TIP
Meanings 1 and 2 are pronounced **yoosst**. Meanings 3 and 4 are pronounced **yoozd**.

useful

ADJECTIVE If something is **useful**, you can use it to help you in some way.

useless

ADJECTIVE Something that is **useless** is no good for anything.

a b c d e f g h i j k l m n o p q r s t u v w x y z

433

A
B
C
D
E
F
G
H
I
J
K
L
M
N
O
P
Q
R
S
T
U
V
W
X
Y
Z

user-friendly
ADJECTIVE If something is **user-friendly**, it is easy to understand and use. ● *the most **user-friendly** camera available*

usher ushers
NOUN a person who shows people where to sit at the theatre or cinema

usual
ADJECTIVE **1** Something **usual** is expected and happens often.
PHRASE **2** If something happens **as usual**, it happens as you would expect, and is not surprising because it often happens that way.

utensil utensils
NOUN a tool ● *A whisk is a kitchen **utensil**.*

utility utilities
NOUN a service that is useful for everyone, such as water and gas supplies

utter utters, uttering, uttered
VERB **1** When you **utter** sounds, you make or say them.
ADJECTIVE **2** complete or total ● *This is **utter** nonsense.*

Vv

vacant
ADJECTIVE If something is **vacant**, it is not being used or no one is in it. ● *I couldn't find a **vacant** seat on the train.*

vacation vacations
NOUN a holiday

vaccinate vaccinates, vaccinating, vaccinated
VERB If someone **vaccinates** you, they give you an injection to protect you against a disease.

PRONUNCIATION TIP
This word is pronounced **vak**-si-nayt.

---

vacuum vacuums, vacuuming, vacuumed
NOUN **1** a completely empty space containing no matter, solid, liquid or gas
VERB **2** If you **vacuum** something, you clean it using a vacuum cleaner.

WORD HISTORY
from Latin *vacuum* meaning empty space

---

vacuum cleaner vacuum cleaners
NOUN an electrical device that sucks up dust and dirt from the floor

vagina vaginas
NOUN A woman's **vagina** is the passage that leads from the outside of her body to her womb.

vague vaguer, vaguest
ADJECTIVE not clear, definite or certain
● *They could see the **vague** outline of the mountains in the distance.*

SYNONYM: unclear

PRONUNCIATION TIP
This word is pronounced **vayg**.

---

vaguely
ADVERB in a way that is not clear, definite or certain

vain vainer, vainest

ADJECTIVE **1** A **vain** person is too proud of their looks, intelligence or other good qualities.
ADJECTIVE **2** A **vain** attempt to do something is an unsuccessful attempt.

valentine valentines

NOUN **1** someone you love and send a card to on Saint **Valentine's** Day, February 14th
NOUN **2** a card you send to someone you love on Saint **Valentine's** Day

WORD HISTORY
Saint *Valentine* was a third-century martyr

valiant

ADJECTIVE brave and courageous

valid

ADJECTIVE A **valid** ticket or document is legal and accepted by people in authority.

valley valleys

NOUN a long stretch of land between hills, often with a river flowing through it

valuable

ADJECTIVE of great worth or very important ● *The diamond ring was very **valuable**.*

value values, valuing, valued

NOUN **1** the importance or usefulness of something
NOUN **2** the amount of money that something is worth
VERB **3** If you **value** something, you think it is important and valuable.

valve valves

NOUN **1** a device attached to a pipe or tube that controls the flow of gas or liquid
NOUN **2** a small flap in your heart or in a vein that controls the flow and direction of blood

vampire vampires

NOUN In horror stories, **vampires** come out of graves at night and suck people's blood.

van vans

NOUN a vehicle for carrying goods

vandal vandals

NOUN someone who deliberately damages or destroys things, particularly public property

vandalise vandalises, vandalising, vandalised; also spelt vandalize

VERB to deliberately damage or destroy things, particularly public property

vandalism

NOUN damage that someone deliberately causes to public or private property

vanilla

NOUN a flavouring used in food such as ice cream. It comes from the pod of a tropical plant.

vanish vanishes, vanishing, vanished

VERB If something **vanishes**, it disappears or does not exist any more.

vapour

NOUN a mass of tiny drops of water or other liquids in the air, which looks like mist

WORD HISTORY
from Latin *vapor* meaning steam

variable variables

NOUN a symbol such as *x* which can stand for any one of a set of values

variety varieties

NOUN a number of different kinds of similar things ● *There was a **variety** of food from different countries on the menu.*

SYNONYMS: assortment, range

various

ADJECTIVE of several different types ● *trees of **various** sorts*

SYNONYMS: different, miscellaneous

varnish varnishes, varnishing, varnished

NOUN **1** a liquid which, when painted onto a surface such as wood, gives it a hard, clear, shiny finish
VERB **2** If you **varnish** something, you paint it with varnish.

vary varies, varying, varied

VERB If something **varies**, it changes and is not always the same.

vase vases

NOUN a jar or other container for putting cut flowers in

vast

ADJECTIVE extremely large

vat vats

NOUN a large container used for storing liquids

a
b
c
d
e
f
g
h
i
j
k
l
m
n
o
p
q
r
s
t
u
v
w
x
y
z

435

A
B
C
D
E
F
G
H
I
J
K
L
M
N
O
P
Q
R
S
T
U
V
W
X
Y
Z

VAT
NOUN an abbreviation of *value-added tax*, which is a tax you pay on things you buy

vault vaults, vaulting, vaulted
NOUN **1** a strong secure room where valuables are stored, often underneath a building, or where people are buried underneath a church
NOUN **2** an arched roof, often found in churches
VERB **3** If you **vault** over something, you jump over it using your hands or a pole to help.

VDU
NOUN an abbreviation of *visual display unit*, which is a monitor screen for computers

veal
NOUN the meat from a calf

Veda
NOUN the collection of ancient sacred writings of the Hindu religion

vegetable vegetables
NOUN **Vegetables** are plants or parts of plants that can be eaten. Peas, carrots, cabbage and potatoes are **vegetables**.

vegetarian vegetarians
NOUN a person who does not eat meat, poultry or fish

vegetation
NOUN the plants growing in a particular area

vehicle vehicles
NOUN a machine, often with an engine, such as a car, bus or lorry, used for moving people or goods from one place to another

veil veils
NOUN a piece of thin, soft cloth that women sometimes wear over their heads and faces

vein veins
NOUN Your **veins** are the tubes in your body through which your blood flows to your heart.

velvet
NOUN a very soft material that has a thick layer of short threads on one side

venison
NOUN the meat from a deer

Venn diagram Venn diagrams
NOUN a diagram using circles to show how sets of things relate to each other. **Venn diagrams** are used in mathematics.

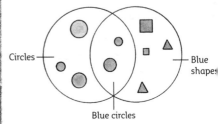

Circles — Blue shapes

Blue circles

venom
NOUN the poison of a snake, scorpion or spider

WORD HISTORY
from Latin *venenum* meaning love potion or poison

venomous
ADJECTIVE A **venomous** snake, scorpion or spider is poisonous.

vent vents
NOUN an opening in something, especially to let out smoke or gas
→ Have a look at the illustration for **volcano**

ventilate ventilates, ventilating, ventilated
VERB If you **ventilate** a place, you allow fresh air to move freely through it.

venture ventures, venturing, ventured
NOUN **1** something new that you do which involves some sort of risk
VERB **2** If you **venture** somewhere that might be dangerous, you go there.

veranda verandas; also spelt verandah
NOUN a platform with a roof that is fixed to the outside wall of a house at ground level. It is often made of wood.

verb verbs
NOUN In grammar, a **verb** is a word that expresses actions and states, for example *be*, *become*, *take* and *run*.

verbal
ADJECTIVE spoken rather than written

verdict verdicts
NOUN In a law court, a **verdict** is the decision reached by the judge or jury about whether a prisoner is guilty or not guilty.

verge verges
NOUN the narrow strip of grassy ground at the side of a road • We walked along the **verge**.

verify verifies, verifying, verified
VERB If you **verify** something, you check that it is true or correct.

verruca verrucas
NOUN a small, hard, infectious growth that you can get on the sole of your foot

versatile
ADJECTIVE If someone or something is **versatile**, they have many different skills or uses.

versatility
NOUN the quality that someone or something has when they have many different skills or uses

verse verses
NOUN 1 another word for **poetry**
NOUN 2 one part of a poem, song or chapter of the Bible

version versions
NOUN A **version** of something is a form of it that is different in some way from earlier or later forms.

versus
PREPOSITION **Versus** means against, and is used to show that two people or teams are competing against each other.

vertebra vertebrae
NOUN one of the bones that make up your backbone

vertebrate vertebrates
NOUN an animal with a backbone

vertex vertices
NOUN the highest point of a hill, or a corner of a two-dimensional or three-dimensional shape

vertical
ADJECTIVE Something that is **vertical** is in an upright position or points straight up.

very
ADVERB **Very** is used before words to emphasise them. • I had a **very** bad dream.

SYNONYMS: extremely, greatly, really

vessel vessels
NOUN 1 a ship or large boat
NOUN 2 a container for liquids
NOUN 3 one of the tubes in an animal or a plant that carries blood or other liquid around the body

vest vests
NOUN a piece of underwear worn on the top half of the body for warmth

WORD HISTORY
from Latin vestis meaning clothing

vet vets
NOUN a doctor for animals. **Vet** is an abbreviation of veterinary surgeon.

veteran veterans
NOUN 1 a person with a lot of experience of something, or who has been involved in something for a long time
NOUN 2 someone who has served in the armed forces, particularly during a war • My uncle is a Gulf War **veteran**.

via
PREPOSITION If you go to one place **via** another, you travel through that other place to get to your destination.

WORD HISTORY
from Latin via meaning way or road

viaduct viaducts
NOUN a high bridge that carries a road or railway across a valley

vibrate vibrates, vibrating, vibrated
VERB If something **vibrates**, it moves a tiny amount backwards and forwards very quickly.

vibration vibrations
NOUN tiny, very fast backward and forward movements • Crayfish can detect weak **vibrations** in the water.

vicar vicars
NOUN a priest in the Church of England

vice vices
NOUN a bad habit, such as being greedy or smoking

vice versa
ADVERB the other way around

vicinity vicinities
NOUN an area round something • She was seen in the **vicinity** of the school.

vicious
ADJECTIVE cruel and violent

victim victims
NOUN someone who has been harmed or injured by someone or something

437

A
B
C
D
E
F
G
H
I
J
K
L
M
N
O
P
Q
R
S
T
U
V
W
X
Y
Z

438

victor **victors**
> NOUN the winner of a contest or battle

victory **victories**
> NOUN a success in a battle or competition

> SYNONYMS: conquest, triumph, win

video **videos, videoing, videoed**
> NOUN **1** a sound and picture recording that can be played back on a television set
> NOUN **2** the recording and showing of films and events using a **video** recorder, tape and a television set
> NOUN **3** a video recorder ● *Set the **video** to record a programme at eight o'clock.*
> VERB **4** If you **video** something, you record it on video tape to watch later.

WORD HISTORY
from Latin *videre* meaning to see
---

video game **video games**
> NOUN a game that can be played by using an electronic control to move symbols on a screen

view **views**
> NOUN **1** everything you can see from a particular place
> NOUN **2** If something you post on a website has a certain number of **views**, then people have looked at it that number of times.
> NOUN **3** Your **view** is your opinion.

viewer **viewers**
> NOUN one of the people who watch something, especially a television programme

viewpoint **viewpoints**
> NOUN Your **viewpoint** is your attitude towards something.

vigilance
> NOUN **Vigilance** is watching carefully what is happening so that you will notice any danger or trouble.

vigilant
> ADJECTIVE careful and alert to danger or trouble

vigilantly
> ADVERB in a careful way so that you notice any danger or trouble

vigorous
> ADJECTIVE energetic or enthusiastic

villa **villas**
> NOUN a house, especially a pleasant holiday home in a country with a warm climate

village **villages**
> NOUN a collection of houses and other buildings in the countryside

> → Have a look at the illustration for **map**

WORD HISTORY
from Old French *ville* meaning farm
---

villain **villains**
> NOUN someone who harms others or breaks the law

> SYNONYMS: criminal, rogue

vine **vines**
> NOUN a climbing plant, especially one that produces grapes

vinegar
> NOUN a sharp-tasting liquid made from sour wine and used for flavouring food

---
WORD HISTORY
from French *vin aigre* meaning sour wine
---

vineyard **vineyards**
> NOUN an area of land where grapes are grown for making wine

vintage
> ADJECTIVE **1** A **vintage** wine is a good quality wine made in a particular year.
> ADJECTIVE **2** A **vintage** car is one made between 1918 and 1930.

vinyl
> NOUN a strong plastic used to make things such as furniture and floor coverings

viola **violas**
> NOUN a musical instrument like a violin, but larger and with a lower pitch

violence
> NOUN **1** behaviour that is intended to hurt or kill
> NOUN **2** force that does harm or damage ● *The **violence** of the storm surprised everyone.*

violent
> ADJECTIVE **1** behaving in a way that is intende to hurt or kill someone
> ADJECTIVE **2** having a lot of force that causes damage ● *a **violent** storm*

violet violets
NOUN **1** a plant with dark purple flowers
NOUN **2** a bluish-purple colour
ADJECTIVE **3** having a bluish-purple colour

violin violins
NOUN a musical instrument with four strings that is held under the chin and played with a bow

VIP
NOUN an abbreviation of *very important person*
• The **VIPs** had the best seats at the concert.

viper vipers
NOUN a type of poisonous snake

viral
ADJECTIVE **1** A **viral** infection or disease is caused by a virus.
PHRASE **2** If a film clip, story, picture or message **goes viral**, it spreads quickly because people share it on social media and send it to each other.

virtual
ADJECTIVE almost exactly the same as the real thing, especially when created by a computer

virtual reality
NOUN an environment or image that has been created by a computer and looks real to the person using it

virtue virtues
NOUN **1** moral goodness
NOUN **2** a good quality in someone's character

virus viruses
NOUN **1** a tiny organism that can cause disease
NOUN **2** A disease caused by a virus can be called a **virus**.
NOUN **3** a program that damages the information stored in a computer system

visible
ADJECTIVE able to be seen

vision visions
NOUN **1** the ability to see
NOUN **2** a picture of something in your mind or imagination

visit visits, visiting, visited
VERB **1** If you **visit** someone, you go to see them and spend time with them.
VERB **2** If you **visit** a place, you go to see it.
NOUN **3** a trip to see a person or place

visor visors
NOUN **1** a transparent, movable shield attached to a helmet, which can be pulled down to protect the eyes or face
NOUN **2** a shade to protect your eyes from the sun

visual
ADJECTIVE to do with sight and seeing

vital
ADJECTIVE necessary or very important
SYNONYM: essential

vitality
NOUN People who have **vitality** are energetic and lively.

vitamin vitamins
NOUN one of a group of substances you need to have in your diet in order to stay healthy. For example, **vitamin** C is found in oranges.

vivid
ADJECTIVE very bright in colour or clear in detail

vivisection
NOUN the use of living animals for medical research

vixen vixens
NOUN a female fox

vlog vlogs
NOUN a set of videos, often about a particular subject, that someone posts on the internet
• She has her own beauty **vlog**.

vlogger vloggers
NOUN someone who regularly posts a vlog

vocabulary vocabularies
NOUN **1** the total number of words someone knows in a particular language
NOUN **2** all the words in a language

vocal
ADJECTIVE to do with or involving the use of the human voice

vocation vocations
NOUN **1** If you have a **vocation**, you want very much to do a particular job, especially one that involves helping other people.
NOUN **2** a profession or career

voice voices
NOUN Your **voice** is what you hear when you speak or sing.

a
b
c
d
e
f
g
h
i
j
k
l
m
n
o
p
q
r
s
t
u
v
w
x
y
z

439

A
B
C
D
E
F
G
H
I
J
K
L
M
N
O
P
Q
R
S
T
U
V
W
X
Y
Z

volcano

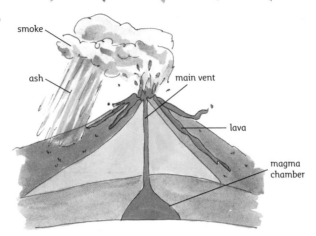

smoke

ash

main vent

lava

magma
chamber

void **voids**
NOUN a very large empty space or deep hole

volcano **volcanoes**
NOUN a mountain with an opening at the top called a crater, from which lava, gas and ash sometimes erupt

→ Have a look at the illustration

WORD HISTORY
named after *Vulcan*, the Roman god of fire

vole **voles**
NOUN a small mammal like a mouse with a short tail, which lives in fields and near rivers

volley **volleys**
NOUN **1** A **volley** of shots or missiles is a lot of them fired or thrown at the same time.
NOUN **2** In tennis, a **volley** is a stroke in which the player hits the ball before it bounces.

volleyball
NOUN a game in which two teams hit a ball back and forth over a high net with their hands. The ball is not allowed to bounce on the ground.

volt **volts**
NOUN the unit used to measure the voltage of a battery

WORD HISTORY
named after Alessandro *Volta* who invented the electric battery

voltage **voltages**
NOUN the measure of how much electrical current a battery can push through an electric circuit

volume **volumes**
NOUN **1** the amount of space something contains or occupies
NOUN **2** The **volume** of a radio, TV or record player is how loud it is.
NOUN **3** a book, or one of a series of books

voluntarily
ADVERB If you do something **voluntarily** you do it because you want to do it, not because you are paid or told to do it.

voluntary
ADJECTIVE Something **voluntary** is done because you want to do it, not because you are paid or told to do it.

volunteer **volunteers, volunteering, volunteered**
NOUN **1** someone who does work that they are not paid for
VERB **2** If you **volunteer** to do something, you offer to do it without expecting any reward.

vomit **vomits, vomiting, vomited**
VERB If you **vomit**, food and drink comes back up from your stomach and out through your mouth.

vote **votes, voting, voted**
NOUN **1** Someone's **vote** is their choice in an election, or at a meeting where decisions are taken.
VERB **2** When people **vote**, they show their choice or opinion, usually by writing on a piece of paper or by raising their hand.

voucher **vouchers**
NOUN a piece of paper that can be used instead of money to pay for something

vow vows, vowing, vowed
VERB **1** If you **vow** to do something, you make a promise to do it.
NOUN **2** a promise

vowel vowels
NOUN **1** a sound made without your tongue touching the roof of your mouth or your teeth
NOUN **2** In the English language the letters a, e, i, o and u are **vowels**.

voyage voyages
NOUN a long journey on a ship or in a spacecraft

vulgar
ADJECTIVE rude or offensive

vulnerable
ADJECTIVE without protection and easily hurt or damaged

SYNONYM: defenceless

vulture vultures
NOUN a large bird that lives in hot countries and eats the flesh of dead animals

waddle waddles, waddling, waddled
VERB to walk with short, quick steps, swaying slightly from side to side ● *A duck **waddled** past.*

wade wades, wading, waded
VERB If you **wade**, you walk through water or mud.

wafer wafers
NOUN a thin, crisp biscuit, often eaten with ice cream

waffle waffles, waffling, waffled
VERB **1** When someone **waffles**, they talk or write a lot without being clear or without saying anything of importance.
NOUN **2** a thick, crisp pancake with squares marked on it, often eaten with syrup poured over it

wag wags, wagging, wagged
VERB **1** When a dog **wags** its tail, it shakes it repeatedly from side to side.
VERB **2** If you **wag** your finger, you move it repeatedly up and down.

wage wages
NOUN the regular payment made to someone each week for the work they do

wagon wagons; also spelt **waggon**
NOUN a strong four-wheeled cart for carrying heavy loads. **Wagons** are usually pulled by horses or tractors.

wail wails, wailing, wailed
VERB If a person or an animal **wails**, they cry or moan loudly.

waist waists
NOUN the middle part of your body where it narrows slightly above your hips

waistcoat waistcoats
NOUN a sleeveless piece of clothing, usually worn over a shirt and under a jacket

a
b
c
d
e
f
g
h
i
j
k
l
m
n
o
p
q
r
s
t
u
v
w
x
y
z

441

A
B
C
D
E
F
G
H
I
J
K
L
M
N
O
P
Q
R
S
T
U
V
W
X
Y
Z

wait waits, waiting, waited

VERB **1** If you **wait**, you spend time in a place or a situation, usually doing little or nothing, before something happens.

VERB **2** to serve people food and drinks as a waiter or waitress

NOUN **3** A **wait** is a period of time before something happens.

waiter waiters

NOUN a man who works in a restaurant, serving people with food and drink

waitress waitresses

NOUN a woman who works in a restaurant, serving people with food and drink

wake wakes, waking, woke, woken

VERB When you **wake**, or when something **wakes** you, you become conscious again after being asleep.

walk walks, walking, walked

VERB **1** When you **walk**, you move along by putting one foot in front of the other on the ground.

NOUN **2** If you go for a **walk**, you go from one place to another on foot.

wall walls

NOUN **1** a narrow structure of brick or stone built round a garden or building

NOUN **2** one of the four sides of a room

wallaby wallabies

NOUN a marsupial that looks like a small kangaroo

WORD HISTORY

from *wolaba*, an Australian Aboriginal word

---

wallet wallets

NOUN a small, flat, folding case made of leather or plastic, used for holding paper money and sometimes credit cards

wallpaper wallpapers

NOUN thick coloured or patterned paper that comes in rolls, for pasting onto the walls of rooms to decorate them

walnut walnuts

NOUN **1** a nut that you can eat. It has a wrinkled shape and a hard, round, light-brown shell.

NOUN **2** the tree on which walnuts grow. The wood from these trees is often used for making expensive furniture.

walrus walruses

NOUN an animal that lives in the sea. It looks like a large seal with a tough skin, coarse whiskers and two tusks.

waltz waltzes, waltzing, waltzed

NOUN **1** a dance that has a rhythm of three beats to the bar

VERB **2** If you **waltz** with someone, you dance a waltz with them.

wand wands

NOUN a long, thin rod used by magicians when they perform magic tricks, and by fairies in stories

wander wanders, wandering, wandered

VERB If you **wander** in a place, you walk around in a casual way.

want wants, wanting, wanted

VERB **1** If you **want** something, you feel that you would like to have it or do it.

VERB **2** to need something

wanted

ADJECTIVE being looked for, especially by the police as a suspected criminal

war wars

NOUN a period of fighting between countries or states, when weapons are used and many people may be killed

ward wards

NOUN **1** a long room with beds in for patients in a hospital

NOUN **2** a child who is looked after by a guardian rather than their parents

warden wardens

NOUN **1** a person in charge of a place like a park or a block of flats, or an institution like a prison or a hostel

NOUN **2** an official who makes sure that certain laws or rules are obeyed

wardrobe wardrobes

NOUN a tall cupboard in which you can hang your clothes

WORD HISTORY

from Old French *warder* meaning to guard robes and *robes* meaning clothing

---

warehouse warehouses

NOUN a large building where goods are stored

warm warmer, warmest; warms, warming, warmed
ADJECTIVE **1** Something that is **warm** has some heat, but not enough to be hot.
ADJECTIVE **2 Warm** clothes or blankets are made of material that protects you from the cold.
VERB **3** If you **warm** something, you heat it up gently so that it stops being cold.

warm-blooded
ADJECTIVE A **warm-blooded** animal has quite a high body temperature which does not change according to the surrounding temperature.

warn warns, warning, warned
VERB If you **warn** someone, you tell them that they may be in danger or in trouble.

warning warnings
NOUN something said or written to warn someone of a possible danger or problem

warp warps, warping, warped
VERB If something **warps**, or is **warped**, it becomes bent and twisted, usually because of heat or dampness.

warrant warrants
NOUN a special document that gives someone permission to do something • *The police had a **warrant** to search the house for evidence.*

warren warrens
NOUN an area of ground where there are many rabbit burrows

warrior warriors
NOUN a fighting man or soldier

wart warts
NOUN a small, hard growth on the skin

wary warier, wariest
ADJECTIVE If you are **wary** of something or someone, you are not sure about them, so you are cautious.

was
VERB a past tense of **be**

wash washes, washing, washed
VERB **1** If you **wash** something, you clean it with water and soap.
VERB **2** If you **wash**, you clean yourself using soap and water.
wash up
VERB If you **wash up**, you wash the dishes, pans and cutlery used in preparing and eating a meal.

washable
ADJECTIVE able to be washed without being damaged

washing
NOUN clothes that need to be washed or that have been washed

washing machine washing machines
NOUN a machine for washing clothes

washing-up
NOUN the task of washing plates, cutlery and pots after a meal

wasp wasps
NOUN a flying insect with yellow and black stripes across its body, which can sting

waste wastes, wasting, wasted
VERB **1** If you **waste** time, money or energy, you use too much of it on something that is not important or that you do not need.
NOUN **2** using more money or some other resource than you need to
NOUN **3** rubbish or other material that is no longer wanted, or that is left over

watch watches, watching, watched
NOUN **1** a small clock, usually worn on a strap on a person's wrist
VERB **2** If you **watch** something, you look at it for some time and pay attention to what is happening.
watch out
VERB **1** If you **watch out** for something or someone, you keep alert to see if they are near you.
VERB **2** If you tell someone to **watch out**, you are warning them to be careful.

water waters, watering, watered
NOUN **1** a clear, colourless, tasteless liquid that falls from clouds as rain

→ Have a look at the illustration for **photosynthesis**

VERB **2** If you **water** a plant, you pour water into the soil around it.
VERB **3** If your eyes or mouth **water**, they produce tears or saliva. • *My mouth started **watering** when I smelled Mum's baking.*

watercolour watercolours
NOUN **1** a type of paint that is mixed with water and used for painting pictures
NOUN **2** a picture that has been painted using watercolours

a
b
c
d
e
f
g
h
i
j
k
l
m
n
o
p
q
r
s
t
u
v
w
x
y
z

443

A
B
C
D
E
F
G
H
I
J
K
L
M
N
O
P
Q
R
S
T
U
V
W
X
Y
Z

water cycle

NOUN the continuous circulation of water throughout the Earth through evaporation, condensation, precipitation and transpiration

→ Have a look at the illustration

waterfall **waterfalls**

NOUN water from a stream or river as it flows over rocks or the edge of a steep cliff and falls to the ground below

waterlogged

ADJECTIVE Something that is **waterlogged** is so wet that it cannot soak up any more water.

watermark **watermarks**

NOUN **1** a mark showing the level of water
NOUN **2** a faint design in some types of paper which you can see if you hold it up to the light

waterproof

ADJECTIVE Something that is **waterproof** does not let water pass through it. • *We put on our **waterproof** jackets as it was raining.*

watertight

ADJECTIVE Something that is **watertight** does not allow water to pass in or out.

waterworks

NOUN the place where the public supply of water is stored and cleaned, and from where it is supplied to our homes

watt **watts**

NOUN a unit of measurement of electrical power

PRONUNCIATION TIP
This word is pronounced **wot**.

WORD HISTORY
Named after James *Watt* (1736–1819) who invented the steam engine

wave **waves, waving, waved**

VERB **1** If you **wave** your hand, you move it from side to side, usually to say hello or goodbye.
VERB **2** If you **wave** something, you hold it up and move it from side to side. • *People in the crowd were **waving** flags.*
NOUN **3** a ridge of water on the surface of the sea caused by wind or by tides
NOUN **4** the form in which some types of energy, such as heat, light or sound, travel

wax **waxes**

NOUN **1** a solid, slightly shiny substance made of fat or oil, that melts easily and is used to make candles and polish
NOUN **2** the sticky yellow substance in your ears

way **ways**

NOUN **1** The **way** of doing something is how you do it.
NOUN **2** The **way** to a place is how you get there.

WC **WCs**

NOUN an abbreviation of *water closet*. It is used on plans and signs to show where the toilet is located.

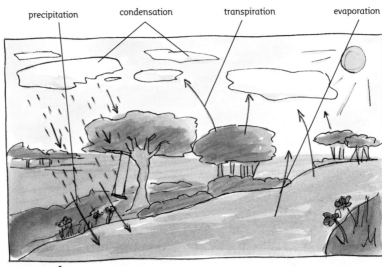

precipitation   condensation   transpiration   evaporation

water cycle

we

PRONOUN **We** refers to the person writing or talking and one or more other people.

weak weaker, weakest

ADJECTIVE If someone is **weak**, they do not have much strength or energy.

wealth

NOUN a large amount of money or property that someone owns

wealthy wealthier, wealthiest

ADJECTIVE Someone who is **wealthy** has a lot of money.

weapon weapons

NOUN an object used to hurt or kill people in a fight or war

wear wears, wearing, wore, worn

VERB When you **wear** something, such as clothes, make-up or jewellery, you have them on your body or face.

wear out

VERB When something **wears out**, or when you **wear** it **out**, it is used so much that it becomes thin, weak and no longer usable.

wearily

ADVERB in a way that shows you are very tired

weariness

NOUN the feeling you have when you are very tired

weary wearier, weariest

ADJECTIVE If you are **weary**, you are very tired.

weasel weasels

NOUN a small wild mammal with a long, thin body and short legs

weather

NOUN the conditions of sunshine, rain, wind or snow at a particular time in a particular place

weave weaves, weaving, wove, woven

VERB **1** If you **weave** something like cloth or a basket, you make it by crossing threads or grasses over and under each other. Cloth is often **woven** using a machine called a loom.

VERB **2** If you **weave** your way, you move from side to side past people and other obstacles.

web webs

NOUN a fine net of threads that a spider makes from a sticky substance that it produces in its body

Web

NOUN short for **World Wide Web**

webbed

ADJECTIVE **Webbed** feet have skin joining the toes together, like ducks' feet.

webcam webcams

NOUN a camera that sends pictures over the internet

a b c d e f g h i j k l m n o p q r s t u v w x y z

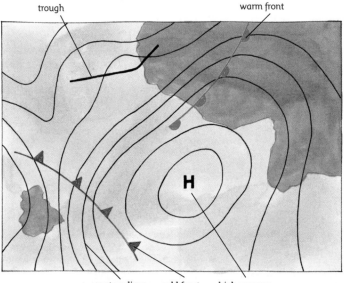

trough — warm front — contour lines — cold front — high pressure

weather map

445

website websites
NOUN a place on the internet where you can find out about a particular subject or person

we'd
a contraction of *we had* or *we would*

wedding weddings
NOUN a marriage ceremony

wedge wedges, wedging, wedged
VERB **1** If you **wedge** something somewhere, you make it stay there by holding it tightly, or by fixing something next to it to stop it from moving.
NOUN **2** a piece of something such as wood, metal or rubber with one thin edge and one thick edge, used to hold something still • *I put a **wedge** under the door to keep it open.*
NOUN **3** a piece of something that has a thick triangular shape • *I cut a **wedge** of cheese.*

Wednesday
NOUN the fourth day of the week, coming between Tuesday and Thursday

WORD HISTORY
Wednesday was the day the Anglo-Saxons honoured their god *Odin* or *Woden*

weed weeds, weeding, weeded
NOUN **1** a wild plant growing somewhere it is not wanted
VERB **2** If you **weed** an area of ground, you remove the weeds from it.

week weeks
NOUN **1** a period of seven days, especially one beginning on a Sunday and ending on a Saturday
NOUN **2** the part of a week that does not include Saturday and Sunday

weekday weekdays
NOUN any day except Saturday and Sunday

weekend weekends
NOUN Saturday and Sunday.

weekly
ADJECTIVE **1** happening or appearing once every week • *We do the **weekly** shopping every Thursday.*
ADVERB **2** once every week • *The bins are emptied **weekly**.*

weep weeps, weeping, wept
VERB If someone **weeps**, they cry.

weigh weighs, weighing, weighed
VERB **1** If something **weighs** a particular amount, that is how heavy it is.

VERB **2** If you **weigh** something, you find out how heavy it is by using scales.

weight weights
NOUN the heaviness of something

weightless
ADJECTIVE A person or object is **weightless** when they are in space and, because the Earth's gravity does not affect them, they float around.

weir weirs
NOUN a low dam built across a river to raise the water level, control the flow of water, or change the direction of the water

WORD HISTORY
from Old English *wer* meaning river-dam or enclosure for fish

weird weirder, weirdest
ADJECTIVE strange or odd

welcome welcomes, welcoming, welcomed
VERB **1** If you **welcome** a visitor, you greet them in a friendly way when they arrive.
GREETING **2** **Welcome** can be said as a greeting to a visitor who has just arrived.
ADJECTIVE **3** If someone is **welcome** at a place, they will be accepted there in a friendly way.

WORD HISTORY
from Old English *wilcuma* meaning welcome guest

weld welds, welding, welded
VERB If you **weld** two pieces of metal together, you join them by heating their edges and pressing them together.

welfare
NOUN The **welfare** of a person or group is their health, comfort and happiness.

welfare state
NOUN a system in which the government uses money from taxes to provide health care and education, and to give benefits to certain people

we'll
a contraction of *we will* or *we shall*

well better, best; wells
ADJECTIVE **1** If you are **well**, you are healthy.
ADVERB **2** If you do something **well**, you do it to a high standard.
NOUN **3** a hole in the ground with water or oil at the bottom

wellington wellingtons
NOUN a long waterproof rubber boot. The word 'welly' is often used for short.

WORD HISTORY
named after the Duke of *Wellington*

---

went
VERB the past tense of **go**

wept
VERB the past tense and past participle of **weep**

we're
a contraction of *we are*

were
VERB a past tense of **be**

west
NOUN one of the four main points of the compass. The sun sets in the **west**. The abbreviation for **west** is W.
→ Have a look at the illustration for **compass point**

western westerns
ADJECTIVE 1 in or from the west
NOUN 2 a film or book about the west of America in the nineteenth and early twentieth centuries

wet wetter, wettest; wets, wetting, wet or wetted
ADJECTIVE 1 covered or soaked with water or other liquid
ADJECTIVE 2 **Wet** weather is rainy. • *It's so wet today.*
VERB 3 If you **wet** something, you make it wet.

we've
a contraction of *we have*

whale whales
NOUN a very large sea mammal that breathes out water through a hole on the top of its head

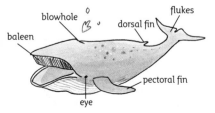
blowhole   flukes
baleen   dorsal fin
pectoral fin
eye

wharf wharves or wharfs
NOUN a platform beside a river or the sea, where ships load and unload

what
ADJECTIVE 1 **What** is used in questions.
• *What time is it?*
ADJECTIVE 2 You use **what** to emphasise a comment. • *What excellent work!*
PHRASE 3 You use **what about** to show that you are making a suggestion or a question.
• *What about the homework from last night?*
PRONOUN 4 refers to information about something • *I really have no idea what you mean.*

whatever
PRONOUN 1 anything or everything of a particular type
CONJUNCTION 2 You use **whatever** to mean no matter what. • *I will go whatever happens.*

wheat
NOUN a cereal plant grown for its grain that is used to make flour

wheel wheels, wheeling, wheeled
NOUN 1 a circular object that turns on a rod attached to its centre. **Wheels** are fixed underneath vehicles so that they can move along.
→ Have a look at the illustrations for **bicycle** and **car**
VERB 2 If you **wheel** something somewhere, you push it along on wheels.

wheelbarrow wheelbarrows
NOUN a small cart with a single wheel at the front, pushed along by two handles at the back. It is used by people such as gardeners and builders.

wheelchair wheelchairs
NOUN a chair with large wheels, for use by people who find walking difficult or impossible

wheeze wheezes, wheezing, wheezed
VERB If someone **wheezes**, they breathe with difficulty, making a whistling sound.

when
ADVERB 1 You use **when** to ask at what time something will happen or how long ago it has happened. • *When shall I see you?*
CONJUNCTION 2 You use **when** to refer to a certain time. • *I had fun when I was on holiday.*

a
b
c
d
e
f
g
h
i
j
k
l
m
n
o
p
q
r
s
t
u
v
w
x
y
z

whenever
CONJUNCTION at any time, or every time that something happens • *I go to the park* **whenever** *I can.*

where
ADVERB **1** You use **where** to ask which place something is in, is from, or is going to. • **Where** *are we?*
CONJUNCTION **2** You use **where** to refer to a place in which something or someone is. • *You do not know* **where** *we live.*

wherever
CONJUNCTION in, at or to any place or situation • *Alex heard the same thing* **wherever** *he went.*

whether
CONJUNCTION You use **whether** when you are talking about two or more things to choose from. • *I don't know* **whether** *that's true or false.*

which
ADJECTIVE **1** You use **which** to talk or ask about alternatives. • **Which** *girl is your sister?*
PRONOUN **2 Which** shows the thing you are talking about or gives more detail about it. • *The book* **which** *is on the table is mine.*

whichever
PRONOUN You use **whichever** when talking about different possibilities. • *You can have cake or chocolate,* **whichever** *you prefer.*

whiff whiffs
NOUN a slight smell of something • *I caught a* **whiff** *of her perfume as she passed.*

while
CONJUNCTION **1** If something happens **while** something else is happening, the two things happen at the same time. • *Mum went to the café* **while** *I had my lesson.*
CONJUNCTION **2 While** can be used to mean but or although. • *I like dogs,* **while** *my brother prefers cats.*
NOUN **3** a period of time • *a little* **while** *earlier*

whim whims
NOUN a sudden wish or desire

> SYNONYM: impulse

whimper whimpers, whimpering, whimpered
VERB When children or animals **whimper**, they make soft, low, unhappy sounds.

whine whines, whining, whined
VERB **1** If a person or an animal **whines**, they make a long, high-pitched noise, especially one that sounds sad or unpleasant.
VERB **2** If someone **whines** about something, they complain about it in an annoying way.

whip whips, whipping, whipped
NOUN **1** a long, thin piece of leather or rope attached to a handle
VERB **2** To **whip** a person or animal means to hit them with a whip.

whirl whirls, whirling, whirled
VERB When something **whirls**, or when you **whirl** it round, it turns or spins round very fast.

whirlpool whirlpools
NOUN a small area in a river or the sea where the water is moving quickly round and round in a circle so that objects floating near it are pulled into its centre

whirlwind whirlwinds
NOUN a tall column of air that spins round and round very fast

whirr whirrs, whirring, whirred
VERB When something like a machine **whirrs**, it makes a continuous buzzing sound.

whisk whisks, whisking, whisked
VERB **1** If you **whisk** eggs or cream, you stir air into them quickly.
VERB **2** If you **whisk** something somewhere, you move it there quickly.
NOUN **3** a kitchen utensil for whisking things

whisker whiskers
NOUN **1** The **whiskers** of an animal such as a cat are the long, stiff hairs near its mouth.
NOUN **2** You can refer to the hair on a man's face, especially on his cheeks, as his **whiskers**.

whisky whiskies
NOUN a strong alcoholic drink made from grain such as barley

whisper whispers, whispering, whispered
VERB When you **whisper**, you talk very quietly and softly.

whistle whistles, whistling, whistled
VERB **1** When you **whistle**, you make a high-pitched sound by forcing your breath out between your lips. • *He* **whistled** *a tune.*
VERB **2** If something **whistles**, it makes a loud, high sound. • *The kettle* **whistled**.

NOUN **3** a small metal tube that you blow into to produce a whistling sound

white *whiter, whitest; whites*
NOUN **1** the lightest possible colour, like milk or fresh snow
NOUN **2** The **white** of an egg is the clear liquid around the yolk.
ADJECTIVE **3** having the lightest possible colour
ADJECTIVE **4 White** coffee contains milk or cream.

whiteboard *whiteboards*
NOUN **1** a shiny white board that you can write on and then wipe clean
NOUN **2** a large screen that shows computer images which can be moved or altered by a pen, a finger or a stylus • *The teacher wrote the answer on the **whiteboard**.*

who
PRONOUN **1** You use **who** when you are asking about someone's identity. • *Who are you?*
PRONOUN **2** You use **who** to refer to the person you are talking about. • *I know you are the one **who** was in trouble yesterday.*

whoever
PRONOUN **Whoever** means the person who. • *Whoever wants to can go on the excursion.*

whole *wholes*
NOUN **1** The **whole** of something is all of it. • *We were abroad the **whole** of the summer.*
ADJECTIVE **2** all of something • *He ate the **whole** cake.*
ADJECTIVE **3** A **whole** number an exact number such as 1, 7, and 24, rather than a number with fractions or decimals.
ADVERB **4** in one piece • *He swallowed the sweet **whole**.*

wholemeal
ADJECTIVE **Wholemeal** flour is made from the whole grain of the wheat plant, including the husk.

wholesale
ADVERB **1** If a shopkeeper buys his or her goods **wholesale**, he or she buys large amounts of them cheaply before selling them on to his or her customers.

ANTONYM: retail

ADJECTIVE **2** You can use **wholesale** to describe something unpleasant that is done to a large extent. • *the **wholesale** destruction of villages*

wholesome
ADJECTIVE healthy or good for you

who's
a contraction of *who is* or *who has*

LANGUAGE TIP
Do not confuse *who's* with *whose*.

whose
PRONOUN **1** You use **whose** to ask who something belongs to. • *Whose shoe is this?*
PRONOUN **2 Whose** gives information about something belonging to the person or things just mentioned. • *She is the pupil **whose** poem won the prize.*

LANGUAGE TIP
Do not confuse *whose* with *who's*.

why
PRONOUN **1** You use **why** when you are asking about the reason for something. • *Why did you do that?*
ADVERB **2** You use **why** when you are talking about the reason for something. • *I wondered **why** he did that.*

wick *wicks*
NOUN the cord that burns in the middle of a candle

wicked
ADJECTIVE **1** very bad

SYNONYMS: evil, sinful

ADJECTIVE **2** mischievous in an amusing or attractive way

WORD HISTORY
from Old English *wicca* meaning witch

wicker
NOUN things made of reed or cane woven together, such as baskets or furniture

wicket *wickets*
NOUN **1** one of the two sets of stumps and bails at which the bowler aims the ball in cricket
NOUN **2** The grass between the **wickets** in cricket is also called the **wicket**.

wide *wider, widest*
ADJECTIVE **1** measuring a large distance from one side to the other
ADJECTIVE **2** measuring a certain amount from one side to the other • *The pool is 10 metres wide.*
ADJECTIVE **3** If there is a **wide** variety, range or selection of something, there are many different kinds of it.

ADVERB **4** If you open or spread something **wide**, you open it as far as you can. ● *Open your mouth **wide**.*

widow widows
NOUN a woman whose spouse has died

widower widowers
NOUN a man whose spouse has died

width widths
NOUN The **width** of something is how wide it is from one side to the other.

wife wives
NOUN Someone's **wife** is the woman they are married to.

Wi-Fi
NOUN a system of accessing the internet from machines such as laptop computers that are not physically connected to a network

wig wigs
NOUN a covering of artificial hair worn over someone's own hair to change their appearance or to hide their baldness

WORD HISTORY
short for *periwig*, from Italian *perrucca* meaning wig

wiggle wiggles, wiggling, wiggled
VERB If you **wiggle** something, you move it up and down or from side to side with small, jerky movements.

wiggly
ADJECTIVE A **wiggly** line has lots of curves in it.

wigwam wigwams
NOUN a kind of tent used by Native Americans

WORD HISTORY
from American Indian *wikwam* meaning their house

wiki wikis
NOUN a website that allows anyone visiting it to change or add to the material in it

wild wilder, wildest; wilds
ADJECTIVE **1 Wild** animals and plants live and grow in natural surroundings and are not looked after by people.
ADJECTIVE **2 Wild** land is natural and not used for farming.
ADJECTIVE **3 Wild** behaviour is excited and uncontrolled.
NOUN **4** a free and natural state of living ● *There are very few tigers left in the **wild**.*

wilderness wildernesses
NOUN an area of natural land that is not cultivated

wildlife
NOUN wild animals and plants

wilful
ADJECTIVE **1** Someone who is **wilful** is determined to get their own way.

SYNONYMS: headstrong, stubborn

ADJECTIVE **2** Something that is **wilful** is done or said deliberately. ● ***wilful** damage*

wilfully
ADVERB **1** in a way that shows you are determined to get your own way
ADVERB **2** deliberately ● *The child had been **wilfully** neglected.*

will wills
VERB **1** You use **will** to form the future tense. ● *I **will** do the washing up after dinner.*
NOUN **2** the determination to do something
NOUN **3** a legal document in which people say what they want to happen to their money and property when they die
NOUN **4** what you choose or want to do ● *Don't make them do it against their **will**.*

willing
ADJECTIVE If you are **willing**, you are glad and ready to do what is wanted or needed.

willow willows
NOUN a tree with long, thin branches and narrow leaves that often grows near water

wilt wilts, wilting, wilted
VERB If a plant **wilts**, it droops because it needs more water or is dying.

wily wilier, wiliest
ADJECTIVE clever and cunning

wimp wimps
NOUN (*informal*) someone who is feeble and timid

win wins, winning, won
VERB **1** If you **win** a fight, game or argument, you defeat your opponent.
VERB **2** If you **win** a prize, you receive it as a reward for succeeding in something.

winch winches, winching, winched
NOUN **1** a machine used to lift or pull heavy objects. It consists of a cylinder or wheel around which a rope or cable is wound.
VERB **2** If you **winch** an object or person somewhere, you lift, lower or pull them using a winch.

wind winds, winding, wound

VERB **1** If a road or river **winds**, it is not straight, but twists and turns.

VERB **2** When you **wind** something round something else, you wrap it round it several times.

VERB **3** When you **wind** a clock or machine, or **wind** it up, you turn a key or handle several times to make it work.

NOUN **4** a current of air that moves across the land and sea

ADJECTIVE **5** A **wind** instrument is a musical instrument that you play by blowing into it.

PRONUNCIATION TIP

Meanings 1, 2 and 3 rhyme with "mind".
Meanings 4 and 5 rhyme with "tinned".

---

wind farm wind farms

NOUN a place where wind turbines are used to convert the power of the wind into electricity

windmill windmills

NOUN a machine in a special building, for generating electricity, grinding grain or pumping water. It is powered by long arms called sails that are turned by the wind.

window windows

NOUN a space in a wall or roof or in the side of a vehicle, usually with glass in it so that light can pass through and people can see in or out

windpipe windpipes

NOUN the tube through which air travels in and out of your lungs when you breathe

windscreen windscreens

NOUN the glass at the front of a vehicle through which the driver looks

→ Have a look at the illustration for **car**

windsurfer windsurfers

NOUN someone who does the sport of moving over the surface of the sea or a lake on a board with a sail fixed to it

windsurfing

NOUN the sport of moving over the surface of the sea or a lake on a board with a sail fixed to it

windy windier, windiest

ADJECTIVE If it is **windy**, there is a lot of wind.

wine wines

NOUN an alcoholic drink usually made from grapes

wing wings

NOUN **1** A bird's or insect's **wings** are the parts of its body that it uses for flying.

→ Have a look at the illustrations for **bird** and **insect**

NOUN **2** An aeroplane's **wings** are the long, flat parts on each side that support it while it is in the air.

→ Have a look at the illustration for **aeroplane**

NOUN **3** A **wing** of a building is a part of it which sticks out from the main part.

• The party was held in the east **wing** of the palace.

NOUN **4** The **wings** of a car are the parts around the wheels.

→ Have a look at the illustration for **car**

NOUN **5** In a game such as football or hockey, the **left wing** and the **right wing** are the areas on the far left and the far right of the pitch.

wink winks, winking, winked

VERB When you **wink**, you close and open one eye very quickly, often to show that something is a joke or a secret.

winner winners

NOUN someone who wins something

winter winters

NOUN the coldest season of the year, between autumn and spring

wipe wipes, wiping, wiped

VERB If you **wipe** something, you rub its surface lightly with a cloth or your hand to clear off dirt or liquid.

wire wires, wiring, wired

NOUN **1** long, thin, bendy metal that can be used to make or fasten things, or to conduct an electric current

VERB **2** If someone **wires** something, or **wires** it up, they connect it so that electricity can pass through it.

wireless wirelesses

ADJECTIVE **1** If a computer network is **wireless**, it is connected by radio signals rather than cables.

NOUN **2** an old-fashioned word for **radio**

wisdom

NOUN a person's ability to use the things they have done and learned to give good advice or make good decisions

a
b
c
d
e
f
g
h
i
j
k
l
m
n
o
p
q
r
s
t
u
v
w
x
y
z

451

wisdom tooth **wisdom teeth**

NOUN Your **wisdom teeth** are large teeth at the back of your mouth that grow in when you are an adult.

→ Have a look at the illustration for **teeth**

wise **wiser, wisest**

ADJECTIVE Someone who is **wise** can use their experience and knowledge to make sensible decisions and judgements.

wish **wishes, wishing, wished**

NOUN 1 something that you want very much

NOUN 2 the act of wishing for something

VERB 3 If you **wish** something for someone, you hope that they will have it. • I **wished** her good luck in her exams.

VERB 4 If you **wish** to do something, you want to do it.

VERB 5 If you **wish** something was true, you would like it to be, but know it is not very likely.

wisp **wisps**

NOUN A **wisp** of something such as smoke or hair is a small, thin, streak or bunch of it. • A **wisp** of hair fell over her eyes.

wispy **wispier, wispiest**

ADJECTIVE forming long thin pieces or lines • **wispy** hair

wit **wits**

NOUN the ability to use words or ideas in an amusing and clever way

witch **witches**

NOUN a woman who claims to have magic powers and to be able to use them for good or evil. **Witches** are often characters in fairy stories.

WORD HISTORY
from Old English *wicca* meaning witch

witchcraft

NOUN the skill or art of using magic powers, especially evil ones

with

PREPOSITION If you are **with** someone, you are in their company. • We went **with** Mum to the shops.

withdraw **withdraws, withdrawing, withdrew, withdrawn**

VERB 1 If you **withdraw** something, you take it out. • He **withdrew** the money from his bank.

VERB 2 If you **withdraw** from something,

you do not continue with it. • She **withdrew** from the race because of injury.

wither **withers, withering, withered**

VERB If a plant **withers**, it wilts or shrivels up and dies.

within

PREPOSITION 1 inside, not going outside certain limits • Stay **within** the school grounds.

PREPOSITION 2 before a period of time has passed • Bring back the book **within** three weeks.

without

PREPOSITION 1 not having, not feeling or not showing something • They went out **without** coats as it was a warm, dry day.

PREPOSITION 2 If you do something **without** someone else, they are not with you when you do it. • He went **without** me.

witness **witnesses**

NOUN 1 someone who has seen an event, such as an accident, and can describe what happened

NOUN 2 someone who appears in a court of law to say what they know about a crime or other event

witty **wittier, wittiest**

ADJECTIVE amusing in a clever way

wizard **wizards**

NOUN a man in a fairy story who has magic powers

wobble **wobbles, wobbling, wobbled**

VERB If something **wobbles**, it shakes or moves from side to side because it is loose or unsteady.

wok **woks**

NOUN a large bowl-shaped pan used for Chinese cooking

woke

VERB the past tense of **wake**

woken

VERB the past participle of **wake**

wolf **wolves; wolfs, wolfing, wolfed**

NOUN 1 a wild animal related to the dog. **Wolves** hunt in packs and kill other animals for food.

VERB 2 (informal) If you **wolf** food, or **wolf** down, you eat it up quickly and greedily.

woman women
NOUN an adult female human being

ANTONYM: man

womb wombs
NOUN A woman's **womb** is the part inside her body where her unborn baby grows.

women
PLURAL NOUN the plural of **woman**

won
VERB the past tense and past participle of **win**

wonder wonders, wondering, wondered
VERB 1 If you **wonder** about something, you think about it and try to guess or understand more about it.
VERB 2 If you **wonder** at something, you are amazed by it.
NOUN 3 a feeling of amazement and admiration

wonderful
ADJECTIVE marvellous or impressive

won't
VERB a contraction of *will not*

wood woods
NOUN 1 the substance that forms the trunks and branches of trees
NOUN 2 a large area of trees growing near each other

wooden
ADJECTIVE Something **wooden** is made of wood.

woodland woodlands
NOUN land that is mostly covered with trees

woodlouse woodlice
NOUN a small animal with seven pairs of legs, that lives in damp soil and rotten wood

woodpecker woodpeckers
NOUN a climbing bird with a long, sharp beak that it uses to drill holes in trees to find the insects that live in the bark

woodwind
ADJECTIVE **Woodwind** instruments are musical instruments such as flutes, oboes, clarinets and bassoons, made of wood or metal. They are played by being blown into.

woodwork
NOUN 1 the activity of making things out of wood
NOUN 2 the parts of a building that are made of wood

woof woofs
NOUN the sound a dog makes

wool wools
NOUN 1 the hair that grows on sheep and some other animals
NOUN 2 thread or cloth made from the wool of animals, and used to make clothes, blankets and carpets

woollen
ADJECTIVE made of wool

woolly
ADJECTIVE made of wool, or looking like wool

word words
NOUN 1 a single unit of language in speech or writing which has a meaning. *Bird*, *hot* and *sing* are all **words**.
PLURAL NOUN 2 The **words** of a play or song are the words you say or sing.
NOUN 3 If you give someone your **word** about something, you promise to do it.
NOUN 4 If you ask for a **word** with someone, you want to say something briefly to them.

wore
VERB the past tense of **wear**

work works, working, worked
VERB 1 People who **work** have a job that they are paid to do.
VERB 2 When you **work**, you spend time and energy doing something useful.
VERB 3 If something **works**, it does what it is supposed to do.
PHRASE 4 If something **works its way** into a certain position, it moves itself there gradually.

work out
VERB If you **work out** an answer to a problem, you solve it.

workout workouts
NOUN a session of exercise or training for the body

workshop workshops
NOUN a room or building that has tools or machinery in it that are used for making or repairing things

world worlds
NOUN 1 the planet we live on
NOUN 2 A person's **world** is the life they lead and the people they know.
NOUN 3 a particular field of activity ● *He is a top player in the rugby world.*
PHRASE 4 If you **think the world** of someone, you like or admire them very much.

a
b
c
d
e
f
g
h
i
j
k
l
m
n
o
p
q
r
s
t
u
v
w
x
y
z

453

World Wide Web

NOUN The **World Wide Web** is a system of linked documents accessed via the internet.

worm worms

NOUN a small, thin animal without bones or legs, especially an earthworm

worn

VERB **1** the past participle of **wear**

ADJECTIVE **2** looking old or exhausted

worry worries, worrying, worried

VERB **1** If you **worry**, you feel anxious about a problem or about something that might happen.

NOUN **2** a problem, or something that makes you worry

worse

ADJECTIVE **1** less good. The comparative form of *bad*. • *The team's results are* **worse** *this year than they were last year.*

ANTONYM: better

ADVERB **2** less food or well. The comparative form of *bad* or *badly*. • *I feel* **worse** *than I did yesterday.*

ANTONYM: better

worship worships, worshipping, worshipped

VERB If you **worship** a god, you show your love and respect by praying or singing hymns.

worst

ADJECTIVE **1** the least good. The superlative form of *bad*. • *It was the* **worst** *meal I have ever eaten.*

ANTONYM: best

ADVERB **2** the least good or the least well. The superlative form of *bad* or *badly*. • *Rural areas were* **worst** *affected by the fires.*

ANTONYM: best

worth

ADJECTIVE **1** If something is **worth** a sum of money, it has that value.

ADJECTIVE **2** If something is **worth** doing, it deserves to be done.

worthless

ADJECTIVE Something that is **worthless** has no use or no value.

worthwhile

ADJECTIVE If something is **worthwhile**, it is important enough to spend time or effort doing it.

would

VERB **1** the past tense of **will**

VERB **2** You use **would** to talk about something that was in the future the last time you were talking about it. • *We were sure it* **would** *be a success.*

VERB **3** You use **would** in polite questions. • **Would** *you like some lunch?*

wouldn't

VERB a contraction of *would not*

wound wounds, wounding, wounded

VERB **1** the past tense and past participle of **wind**

NOUN **2** an injury to part of a person's or an animal's body, especially a cut

VERB **3** If someone or something **wounds** a person or an animal, they injure them, especially with a cut.

PRONUNCIATION TIP
Meanings 1 and 2 rhyme with "sound". Meaning 3 is pronounced **woond**.

wove

VERB the past tense of **weave**

woven

VERB the past participle of **weave**

wrap wraps, wrapping, wrapped

VERB If you **wrap** something, you fold cloth or paper around it.

wrapping wrappings

NOUN material used to wrap something, such as a present

wrath

NOUN great anger

wreath wreaths

NOUN an arrangement of flowers and leaves, often in the shape of a circle, which is put on a grave to remember someone who has died

wreck wrecks, wrecking, wrecked

VERB **1** To **wreck** something means to break it, destroy it or spoil it completely.

NOUN **2** a vehicle or ship that has been badly damaged, usually in an accident

wreckage

NOUN the parts of a vehicle or ship that are left after it has been badly damaged, usually in an accident • *Divers found the* **wreckage** *of the ship on the seabed.*

wren wrens

NOUN a small, brown songbird

wrench wrenches, wrenching, wrenched
VERB **1** If you **wrench** something, you give it a sudden and violent twist or pull.
VERB **2** If you **wrench** a limb or a joint, you twist and injure it.
NOUN **3** a wrenching movement
NOUN **4** a tool for gripping or tightening nuts and bolts

wrestle wrestles, wrestling, wrestled
VERB If you **wrestle** someone, or **wrestle** with them, you fight them by holding or throwing them, but not hitting them.

wrestler wrestlers
NOUN someone who takes part in a sport in which you fight someone by holding them or throwing them but not hitting them

wretched
ADJECTIVE very unhappy or unfortunate

wriggle wriggles, wriggling, wriggled
VERB **1** If a person or an animal **wriggles**, they twist and turn their body in a lively and excited way.
VERB **2** If you **wriggle** out of doing something that you do not want to do, you manage to avoid doing it.

wring wrings, wringing, wrung
VERB When you **wring** a wet cloth, or **wring** it out, you squeeze the water out of it by twisting it.

wrinkle wrinkles, wrinkling, wrinkled
NOUN **1** a soft fold or crease in something, especially a person's skin as they grow older
VERB **2** If something **wrinkles**, folds or creases develop in it.

wrinkled
ADJECTIVE Something that is **wrinkled** has wrinkles in it.

wrist wrists
NOUN the part of your body between your hand and your arm, which bends when you move your hand

wristwatch wristwatches
NOUN a watch you wear on your wrist

write writes, writing, wrote, written
VERB **1** When you **write**, you use a pencil, pen or keyboard to form letters, words or numbers on a surface. ● *I have **written** my name in the front of my book.*

VERB **2** If you **write** something such as a poem, a book or a piece of music, you think of the words or notes for yourself.
VERB **3** When you **write** to someone, you send them a letter.

writer writers
NOUN **1** a person who writes books, stories or articles as a job
NOUN **2** The **writer** of something is the person who wrote it.

writhe writhes, writhing, writhed
VERB If you **writhe**, you twist and turn your body, often because you are in pain.

writing writings
NOUN **1** something that has been written or printed
NOUN **2** Your **writing** is the way you write with a pen or pencil.

written
VERB the past participle of **write**

wrong
ADJECTIVE **1** If there is something **wrong** with an object, it is not working properly or has a fault. ● *There must be something **wrong** with the car as it will not start.*
ADJECTIVE **2** If something is **wrong**, it is not correct or truthful.

ANTONYM: right

ADJECTIVE **3** An action that is **wrong** is bad or against the law.

wrote
VERB the past tense of **write**

wrung
VERB the past tense and past participle of **wring**

Xmas
NOUN (*informal*) Christmas

X-ray X-rays, X-raying, X-rayed
NOUN **1** a type of radiation that can pass through some solid materials. **X-rays** are used by doctors to examine the bones or organs inside a person's body.

NOUN **2** a picture made by sending X-rays through someone's body in order to examine the inside of it

VERB **3** If someone **X-rays** something, they make a picture of the inside of it by passing X-rays through it.

xylophone xylophones
NOUN a musical instrument made of a row of wooden bars of different lengths. It is played by hitting the bars with special hammers.

PRONUNCIATION TIP
This word is pronounced **ziy**-lu-fohn.

yacht yachts
NOUN a boat with sails or an engine, used for racing or for pleasure trips

yak yaks
NOUN a type of long-haired ox with long horns, found mainly in the mountains of Tibet

yam yams
NOUN a root vegetable that grows in tropical regions

yard yards
NOUN **1** a unit of length equal to 36 inches or about 91·4 centimetres

NOUN **2** a paved space with walls around it, next to a building

NOUN **3** a place where certain types of work are carried out, such as a ship**yard** or a builder's **yard**

yarn yarns
NOUN **1** thread used for knitting or making cloth

NOUN **2** (*informal*) a story that someone tells, often with invented details to make it more interesting or exciting

yawn yawns, yawning, yawned
VERB When you **yawn**, you open your mouth wide and take in more air than usual, often when you are tired or bored.

year years
NOUN **1** a period of twelve months or 365 days (366 days in a leap year), usually measured from the first of January to the thirty-first of December. It takes a **year** for the Earth to orbit the sun.

NOUN **2** the part of a year during which something happens or is organised ● *the school year*

yeast
NOUN a type of fungus used in baking and in making beer

yell yells, yelling, yelled
VERB **1** If you **yell**, you shout loudly, usually because you are angry, excited or in pain.
NOUN **2** a loud shout

yellow yellower, yellowest
NOUN **1** the colour of buttercups, egg yolks or lemons
ADJECTIVE **2** having the colour of buttercups, egg yolks or lemons

yelp yelps, yelping, yelped
VERB **1** When people or animals **yelp**, they give a sudden cry.
NOUN **2** a sudden cry

yes
INTERJECTION You say **yes** to agree with someone, to say that something is true or to accept something.

ANTONYM: no

yesterday
NOUN **1** the day before today
ADVERB **2** on the day before today ● *She left* ***yesterday***.

yet
ADVERB **1** If something has not happened **yet**, you expect it to happen in the future.
ADVERB **2** If something should not be done **yet**, it should be done later. ● *Don't switch it off* ***yet***.
CONJUNCTION **3** You use **yet** to introduce something that is rather surprising. ● *He doesn't like maths,* ***yet*** *he always does well.*

yew yews
NOUN an evergreen tree with bright red berries

yodel yodels, yodelling, yodelled
VERB When someone **yodels**, they sing normal notes with high quick notes in between. You can hear this style of singing in the Swiss and Austrian Alps.

yoga
NOUN a Hindu form of exercise that develops the body and the mind, making you relaxed and fit

yogurt yogurts; also spelt yoghurt
NOUN a slightly sour, thick, liquid food made from milk that has had bacteria added to it

yoke yokes
NOUN a wooden bar laid across the necks of animals such as oxen to hold them together when they pull a plough or a cart

yolk yolks
NOUN the yellow part in the middle of an egg

Yom Kippur
NOUN an annual Jewish religious holiday, which is a day of fasting and prayers. It is also called the Day of Atonement.

WORD HISTORY
from Hebrew *yom* meaning day and *kippur* meaning atonement

you
PRONOUN **You** refers to the person or people you are talking or writing to.

you'd
a contraction of *you had* or *you would*

you'll
a contraction of *you will* or *you shall*

young younger, youngest
ADJECTIVE **1** A **young** person, animal or plant has not lived very long and is not yet mature.
PLURAL NOUN **2** The **young** of an animal are its babies.

your
ADJECTIVE belonging to you

you're
a contraction of *you are*

yours
PRONOUN belonging to you

yourself yourselves
PRONOUN you and only you ● *Have you hurt* ***yourself***?

youth youths
NOUN **1** Someone's **youth** is the time of their life before they are a fully mature adult.
NOUN **2** a boy or young man
NOUN **3** young people in general

you've
a contraction of *you have*

yo-yo yo-yos
NOUN a round wooden or plastic toy attached to a string. You play by making the **yo-yo** move up and down the string.

a
b
c
d
e
f
g
h
i
j
k
l
m
n
o
p
q
r
s
t
u
v
w
x
y
z

Zz

zany **zanier, zaniest**
ADJECTIVE odd in a funny way

WORD HISTORY
from Italian *zanni* meaning clown

zap **zaps, zapping, zapped**
VERB (*informal*) If you **zap** someone or something in a computer game, you get rid of them.

zeal
NOUN eagerness and enthusiasm

zebra **zebras**
NOUN a type of African wild horse with black and white stripes

zebra crossing **zebra crossings**
NOUN part of a road marked with broad black and white stripes, where pedestrians can cross

zero
NOUN nought. The sign for zero is 0.

zest
NOUN **1** a feeling of great enjoyment and enthusiasm
NOUN **2** The **zest** of a citrus fruit such as an orange or lemon is the outside of the peel, used to flavour food and drinks.

zestful
ADJECTIVE exciting and lively

zestfully
ADVERB in an exciting and lively way

zigzag **zigzags, zigzagging, zigzagged**
NOUN **1** a line that has a series of sharp, angular bends to the right and left
VERB **2** If you **zigzag**, you move forward in a series of sharp turns to the left and right.

zinc
NOUN a bluish-white metal used to coat other metals to stop them rusting

zip **zips, zipping, zipped**
NOUN **1** a fastener used on clothes and bags, with two rows of metal or plastic interlocking teeth that separate or fasten together as you pull a small tag along them
VERB **2** When you **zip** something, or **zip** it up, you fasten it using a zip.

zodiac
NOUN a diagram used by astrologers to represent the movement of the stars. It is divided into 12 sections, each with a special name and symbol. • *Capricorn, Gemini, Taurus and Pisces are all signs of the* **zodiac**.

WORD HISTORY
from the Greek *zoidiakos kuklos* meaning "circle of signs"

zone **zones**
NOUN an area of land or sea that is considered different from the areas around it, or is separated from the areas around it in some way

zoo **zoos**
NOUN a place where live animals are kept so that people can look at them

zoologist **zoologists**
NOUN someone who studies animals

zoology
NOUN the scientific study of animals

zoom lens **zoom lenses**
NOUN A **zoom lens** on a camera helps the photographer to take close-up pictures from far away.

zucchini
PLURAL NOUN small vegetable marrows with dark green skin. They are also called courgettes.

WORD HISTORY
from Italian plural of *zucchino* meaning gourd

Word Wizard

Word classes

Nouns

A **noun** is a word that is used for talking about a person or thing. **Nouns** are sometimes called "naming words" because they are often the names of people, places, things and ideas, for example:

> **mum** *noun*
> **park** *noun*
> **bird** *noun*
> **happiness** *noun*

Nouns are very often found after the words *a* and *the* or words like *our*, *my* or *his*.

We watched a <u>cartoon</u> on the <u>laptop</u>.
My <u>brother</u> is playing in the <u>park</u>.
What a great <u>idea</u>!

Proper nouns are the names of people, places, days and months, and always start with a capital letter.

> **Emma** *noun*
> **London** *noun*
> **Friday** *noun*
> **June** *noun*

<u>John</u> lives in <u>Glasgow</u>.
He went home on <u>Friday</u>.

When a **noun** is used with another word or words, this can be called a **noun phrase**.

She was wearing <u>a beautiful red dress</u>.
<u>All the children</u> were sleeping.

Adjectives

An **adjective** is a word that tells you more about a person or thing. **Adjectives** are often called "describing words" because they describe what something looks, feels or smells like, for example:

> **big** *adjective*
> **soft** *adjective*
> **nice** *adjective*

Adjectives are very often found before a noun, or after the verb *to be*.

She lives in a <u>big</u> house.
The caterpillar is <u>long and green</u>.

When you want to talk about something that is more than something else, you can use an **adjective** in the comparative (**-er**) or superlative (**-est**) forms.

> **bigger, biggest**
> **soft, softer**
> **nicer, nicest**

I have the <u>nicest</u> sister in the world!
Yesterday was the <u>wettest</u> day of the year.

Verbs

A **verb** is a word that you use for saying what someone or something does. **Verbs** are often called "doing words" because they talk about an action that someone or something is doing, for example:

> **eat** *verb*
> **cry** *verb*
> **talk** *verb*

Verbs are often found after nouns, or words like *she, they* or *it*.

The dog <u>barks</u> at the cat.
She <u>eats</u> sandwiches for lunch.

When you want to talk about something that you are doing right now (in the present), you use the **present tense** of the verb.

The children <u>talk</u> to each other.
She <u>does</u> her homework before dinner.

When you want to talk about something that you did earlier (in the past), you use the **past tense** of the verb.

Anna <u>cried</u> when she fell off her bike.
We <u>went</u> on holiday to Spain.

You can make the **past tense** of many verbs by adding *d* or *ed* to the end of the verb, for example:

> *walk* → *walked*
> *dance* → *danced*

Sometimes you need to add another letter before the *ed* ending in the **past tense**, for example:

> *stop* → *stopped*
> *hug* → *hugged*

Some verbs have a completely different way of making the **past tense**, for example:

> *go* → *went*
> *do* → *done*
> *sing* → *sang*

The **subjunctive** is a form of the verb which is sometimes used in formal speech and writing. The most frequent usage is in the phrase *"If I were..."*, for example:

If I <u>were</u> you, I'd tell her how you feel.
What would you do if you <u>were</u> in my position?

A **modal verb** is used to change the meaning of other verbs, especially when you want to talk about how certain something is, or your duty to do something, for example:

It looks like it <u>might</u> rain today.
You <u>should</u> help your little brother.

The main **modal verbs** are *will, would, can, could, may, might, shall, should, must* and *ought*.

She <u>could</u> play the piano really well.

Adverbs

An **adverb** is a word that tells you more about how someone does something, for example:

> **happily** *adverb*
> **slowly** *adverb*
> **well** *adverb*

Adverbs are very often found after verbs, or sometimes before adjectives.

He walked <u>slowly</u> into the house.
The game was <u>really</u> exciting!

If a word or phrase is used in the same way as an adverb to talk about how or when something is done, it is called an **adverbial**, for example:

The bus leaves <u>in five minutes</u>.

Pronouns

A **pronoun** is a word you use instead of a noun to refer to someone or something, for example:

> **I** *pronoun*
> **you** *pronoun*
> **our** *pronoun*
> **them** *pronoun*

Are <u>you</u> going to school tomorrow?
This is <u>our</u> first time in London.

A **possessive pronoun** is a pronoun that you use instead of a noun and shows that something belongs to someone, for example:

Those pens are <u>mine</u>.

A **relative pronoun** is one of the words *that, who* or *which* that you use to introduce information about the person or thing being talked about, for example:

Is there a bus <u>that</u> goes into town?

Prepositions

A **preposition** is a word that links a noun, pronoun or noun phrase to some other word in the sentence, for example:

> **with** *preposition*
> **for** *preposition*
> **since** *preposition*

Come <u>with</u> me.
I haven't seen my cat <u>since</u> this morning.

Prepositions are very often found before a word ending in *ing*.

Use this towel <u>for</u> drying your hands.

Conjunctions

A **conjunction** is a word that links two words or phrases or two parts of a sentence, for example:

> **and** *conjunction*
> **but** *conjunction*
> **because** *conjunction*

It's raining <u>and</u> it's very cold.
I left <u>because</u> I was bored.

Determiners

A **determiner** is a specific word you use before a noun and/or an adjective, for example:

> **a** *determiner*
> **the** *determiner*
> **some** *determiner*
> **my** *determiner*

I had <u>an</u> apple in my lunch box.
Tomorrow we are getting <u>our</u> new car.

Plurals

A **singular** word is the word we use when there is only one of something, for example:

a dog the house one child

She saw a <u>dog</u> in the park.

A **plural** word is the word we use when there is more than one of something, for example:

the dogs two houses some children

The <u>children</u> played in the garden.

A **plural** is often made by adding s to a singular word, for example:

> singular **duck**
> plural **ducks**

Shall we feed the <u>ducks</u>?

Some **plurals** are made by adding es to the end of the singular word so that the plural is easier to say. Words which end in ch, sh, ss, x and z add es, for example:

> singular **brush** singular **fox**
> plural **brushes** plural **foxes**

He uses different <u>brushes</u> when he's painting.

Sometimes **plurals** are made by taking away the y at the end of the singular word and adding ies, for example:

> singular **pony**
> plural **ponies**

The <u>ponies</u> were rolling around in the mud.

Be careful: words ending in ay and ey just add s in the plural, for example:

> singular **day** singular **key**
> plural **days** plural **keys**

It's three <u>days</u> until I go to Spain.

Some words have **plurals** which look very different to the singular form, for example:

> singular **child** singular **mouse**
> plural **children** plural **mice**

How many <u>children</u> are in the class?

Grammar and punctuation

Grammar is the way that words can be put together to make sentences. **Punctuation** is used in writing to make sense of the words that have been written. You use **punctuation** to show sentences, questions, speech and exclamations, and to help with spelling.

Grammar terms

active
An **active** verb follows the usual pattern of subject – verb – object
The school <u>arranged</u> a visit to the museum.

ambiguity
If there is some **ambiguity** in a sentence, it means that there is more than one possible meaning.
I saw a man on a hill with a telescope.

antonym
Two words are **antonyms** if their meanings are opposites.

clause
A **clause** is a special type of phrase with a verb.

cohesion
A piece of writing has **cohesion** if it is clear how the meanings of its parts fit together.

command
A **command** is a sentence where someone is told to do something.
A **command** starts with a capital letter and ends with an exclamation mark.
Shut the door!

consonant
A **consonant** is any of the letters that are not vowels (*a, e, i, o* or *u*).

direct speech
Direct speech is speech which shows the exact words that the speaker used, for example:
"Would you like to go to the cinema?" she asked.

exclamation
An **exclamation** is a sentence that shows a strong feeling.
An **exclamation** starts with a capital letter and ends with an exclamation mark.
What a lovely day it is!

letter　A **letter** is a single shape that people use in writing. Words are made when you put **letters** together in a special way.
d+o+g → dog

main clause　A **main clause** is a clause that can stand on its own.
Emma likes cats.

object　The **object** of a verb is usually the noun, noun phrase or pronoun that describes who or what is having something done to it by the verb. It normally comes after the verb.
Our class made <u>puppets</u> yesterday.

passive　The **passive** is a form of the verb that is used when the subject of the verb is the person or thing affected by the action.
A visit to the museum <u>was arranged</u> by the school.

question　A **question** is a sentence when someone asks about something. A **question** starts with a capital letter and ends with a question mark.
Where are you going?

relative clause　A **relative clause** is a kind of subordinate clause that gives you more information about a noun using *who* or *that*.
There's the boy <u>who lives near to the school</u>.

sentence　A **sentence** is a group of words that are connected to each other. **Sentences** can be short, or very long. A **sentence** starts with a capital letter and ends with a full stop.
I like cats.
The girl, who had been playing in the garden, decided she was going to the park after tea.

statement　A **statement** is the same as a **sentence**.

subject　The **subject** of a verb is usually the noun, noun phrase or pronoun that tells you who or what is doing the verb. It normally comes before the verb in the sentence, or after the verb in a question.
<u>The children</u> went to the park.
What are <u>you</u> doing?

subordinate clause　A **subordinate clause** is a clause in a sentence which adds to the information given in the main clause. It cannot usually stand alone as a sentence.
They went out to play <u>as soon as the rain stopped</u>.

syllable	A **syllable** is one of the "beats" that a word is broken up into: *cat* has one syllable; *parrot* has two syllables; *hippopotamus* has five syllables.
synonym	Two words are **synonyms** if they have the same meaning, or similar meanings.
vowel	A **vowel** is one of the letters *a, e, i, o* or *u*.
word	A **word** is a collection of letters that are put together to make a meaning. **Words** are usually separated from each other by spaces. *The bird sat on the branch.*
word family	The words in a **word family** are usually related to each other by their structure, grammar and meaning.

Punctuation marks

. You put a **full stop** at the end of a sentence.
This is a sentence.

? You put a **question mark** at the end of a question.
Can you come to my party?

, You use a **comma** to separate parts of a sentence or items on a list.
She brought sandwiches, crisps, apples and juice to the picnic.

! You use an **exclamation mark** at the end of a sentence to show a strong feeling, or when a command has been given.
Wow, look how fast he's going!

' An **apostrophe** is used in contractions, and also to show belonging.
I don't know where my brother's toy is.

- A **colon** is used before a list and to introduce a reason or explanation.
She used three main colours: green, blue and pink.

- A **semi-colon** is used to separate longer items in a list or to show a contrast between two parts of a sentence.
Jack loves football; his brother hates it.

" " **Speech marks** (also called **inverted commas**) show where speech begins and ends.
"I like your hair," she said.

( ) **Brackets** are used to separate off extra information in a sentence – the sentence still makes sense without the information in the brackets.
Bring some snacks (like chocolate and popcorn) to the sleepover.

... **Ellipsis** is used to show that some words are missing, to show a pause when someone is speaking, or to create a dramatic ending to a piece of writing.
Well... I'm not really sure.
Two red eyes appeared in the cave...

- A **hyphen** is used to join two words together to make one word. There is no space on either side of a hyphen.
We took our luggage to the check-in desk.

- A **dash** is a short line that is longer than a hyphen and has a space on each side of it. It is used to show a break in a sentence or in the same way that brackets are used.
Don't leave your plate there – put it in the dishwasher!

- **Bullet points** are used to show a list of important items for discussion or action in a document.
You will need to bring:
  - *pyjamas*
  - *toiletries*
  - *towel*

Prefixes and suffixes

Prefixes

A **prefix** is a letter or group of letters that are added to the beginning of a word to make a new word:

anti- *meaning* opposite of, against   **anti**clockwise

e- *meaning* electronic   **e**mail

ex- *meaning* former   **ex**-husband

mini- *meaning* smaller   **mini**bus

non- *meaning* not   **non**-fiction

semi- *meaning* half   **semi**circle

under- *meaning* below   **under**ground

There are some common prefixes that are added to words to give them the opposite meaning.

dis- agree ⟶ **dis**agree   **im-** possible ⟶ **im**possible

il- legal ⟶ **il**legal   **un-** happy ⟶ **un**happy

Suffixes

A **suffix** is a letter or group of letters that are added to the end of a word to make a new word.

Some suffixes can change nouns into other nouns:

-ship friend ⟶ friend**ship**   champion ⟶ champion**ship**

Some suffixes can change adjectives into adverbs:

-ly slow ⟶ slow**ly**   happy ⟶ happi**ly**

Some suffixes can change verbs or adjectives into nouns:

-ment enjoy ⟶ enjoy**ment**   argue ⟶ argu**ment**

-ness sad ⟶ sad**ness**   happy ⟶ happi**ness**

Some suffixes can change nouns or verbs into adjectives:

-ful care ⟶ care**ful**   wish ⟶ wish**ful**

-less hope ⟶ hope**less**   help ⟶ help**less**

Contractions and compounds

Contractions

A **contraction** is a short way of writing two words together. We often use **contractions** when we speak, for example, _Don't play on the grass!_ There are some rules for writing these short forms.

When the two words are written together, an apostrophe (') takes the place of the missing letter or letters.

I have → I've		you have → you've		we have → we've
I am → I'm		you are → you're		we are → we're
I will → I'll		you will → you'll		we will → we'll
it is → it's		he is → he's		they have → they've

Many contractions are formed with the word _not_, for example:

do not → don't	could not → couldn't	has not → hasn't
did not → didn't	would not → wouldn't	was not → wasn't
will not → won't	should not → shouldn't	were not → weren't

Be careful with these ones! Although they sound like _could of, would of_ and _should of_, they are actually **contractions** of _could have, would have_ and _should have_.

could have → could've   would have → would've   should have → should've

Compounds

Many words are formed by joining two words together to make a new word. These are called **compounds**. There are no missing letters, so an apostrophe is not needed.

white + board	→	whiteboard
butter + fly	→	butterfly
class + room	→	classroom
play + ground	→	playground
black + bird	→	blackbird
super + man	→	superman
straw + berry	→	strawberry
foot + ball	→	football

Spelling: confusable words

Some words sound similar, or even the same, but are spelt in different ways and mean different things. Learn confusable words like these, and you won't make mistakes!

accept	Please **accept** my apology.	**loose**	His front tooth is **loose**.
except	Mum works every day **except** Tuesday.	**lose**	Be careful not to **lose** your pocket money.
affect	Tiredness **affects** your concentration.	**of**	What are you scared **of**?
effect	The medicine had an instant **effect**.	**off**	They got **off** the bus.
aloud	I read my story **aloud** in class.	**passed**	We **passed** through a couple of pretty villages.
allowed	I'm **allowed** to play after I've finished my homework.	**past**	I heard my big brother tiptoe **past** my room.
board	A notice had been pinned on the **board**.	**their**	It's not **their** fault.
bored	I get **bored** playing the same computer games.	**they're**	**They're** not to blame.
		there	She is sitting over **there**.
desert	The programme was about the Gobi **Desert**.	**to**	I'm going **to** write a story.
dessert	Would you like ice cream or fruit for **dessert**?	**too**	I've had **too** much to eat.
		two	**Two** plus **two** equals four.
its	The bird flew out of **its** cage.	**wander**	They **wandered** through the town.
it's	**It's** rude to stare.	**wonder**	I **wondered** where my friends had got to.
lead	He snapped the **lead** of the pencil.	**who's**	**Who's** coming out to play?
led	The delicious smell of bread **led** us to the bakery.	**whose**	**Whose** pencil is this?
		where	**Where** do you live?
leant	He **leant** against the tree.	**wear**	We have to **wear** school uniform.
lent	She **lent** me her bike.	**were**	**Were** you at the show?
		your	I like **your** drawing.
		you're	**You're** getting on my nerves!

Spelling: tricky words

The words on this list are tricky, and may not be spelt the way you would expect. Learn all of them to be a top speller!

achieve	desperate	interfere	rhythm
attached	determined	language	sacrifice
amateur	develop	leisure	secretary
ancient	dictionary	lightning	shoulder
available	disastrous	mischievous	signature
average	environment	muscle	sincerely
awkward	equip	neighbour	soldier
bargain	equipment	nuisance	stomach
bruise	existence	parliament	symbol
category	explanation	persuade	system
cemetery	familiar	physical	temperature
competition	foreign	prejudice	thorough
conscience	forty	privilege	twelfth
conscious	frequently	pronunciation	variety
controversy	government	queue	vegetable
convenience	guarantee	recognise	vehicle
criticise	hindrance	relevant	yacht
curiosity	identity	restaurant	
definite	individual	rhyme	

In some tricky words, you must remember the double letters and where they are:

accommodate	communicate	excellent	occur
accompany	community	harass	opportunity
according	correspond	immediately	profession
aggressive	embarrass	interrupt	programme
apparent	equipped	marvellous	recommend
appreciate	especially	necessary	suggest
committee	exaggerate	occupy	tomorrow

And remember the days of the week and months of the year!

Monday	January	July
Tuesday	February	August
Wednesday	March	September
Thursday	April	October
Friday	May	November
Saturday	June	December
Sunday		

Spelling: other tips

Silly sentences

Sometimes thinking of a silly phrase or sentence can help you remember how to spell tricky words or parts of words, for example:

because = Big Elephants Can Always Understand Small Elephants

beautiful = Big Elephants Are Useful

If you think of the initial letters of each word in the phrase above, you will remember the order the vowels come in at the start of the word *beautiful*.

Look, say, cover, write, check!

- **Look** at the word carefully in the dictionary.
- **Say** the word out loud to yourself, listening to how it sounds.
- **Cover** the word and try to remember what it looks like.
- **Write** the word on a piece of paper.
- **Check** the word in the dictionary to see if you got it right.

If you haven't got the word right, go through the five steps again until you can spell it correctly!

Sound it out

A good way to remember the spelling of some words is to sound out their different parts, for example:

answer	**cupboard**	**Wednesday**
Say "ans-wer"	Say "cup-board"	Say "Wed-nes-day"

Words within words

Look for complete words inside the word you are trying to remember, for example:

iron in *environment*   *here* in *there*
get in *vegetable*   *ear* in *hear*
rat in *separate*

See the shape

It can help to remember the shape of some words, for example:

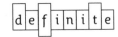